THIS DAY IN NORTH CAROLINA HISTORY

THIS DAY IN NORTH CAROLINA HISTORY

Ansley Herring Wegner with Jeff Miles

ISBN 978-0-86526-472-4

Front Cover: Pocket watch from the RMS *Lusitania*. RMS *Lusitania* was a British ocean liner that a German submarine sank in World War I, causing a major diplomatic uproar. The sinking caused a storm of protest in the United States because 128 American citizens were among the dead. The sinking helped shift public opinion in the United States against Germany, and was a factor in the United States declaration of war. The watch appears courtesy of Liberty Hall Restoration, Kenansville.

Watch Photo Credit: North Carolina Museum of History

Background Image Credit: iStock

Distributed by the University of North Carolina Press, Inc.
www.uncpress.org

PREFACE

History happens every day, as this book illustrates. Drawing its inspiration from the markers that the Office of Archives and History has erected across the state since 1935, and expanding a bit upon those markers' few terse words, this work takes a new accounting of North Carolina history, matching people, places, and events with days of the year. The result is a headlong plunge into a remarkable variety of topics. The reader might start with his or her birthday, mindful that there are three hundred and sixty-five other days to explore. Yes, we include February 29, Leap Day. Check out the story of the thirteen-overtime basketball game in Harnett County.

While governors, rebellions, battles, and political initiatives find their place here, it's the offbeat that likely will attract more interest. Brevard's "Great Ostrich Race" of 1935. The "blood shower" in Chatham County in 1884. North Carolina's ties to the Donner Party, the John Birch Society, John Brown's raid, Custer's Last Stand, and the fall of Saigon. Unusual characters like con man Gaston Means and socialite Mary Van Landingham. A look back at streakers. Disasters like hurricanes, doomed ships, and train wrecks. The mystery of the Dare Stones.

Landmark events covered include sit-ins, the day we almost lost Wayne County in a nuclear accident, the signing of the Halifax Resolves, and the opening of the Land of Oz. We include the Wright Brothers but also the Man Will Never Fly Society. Set the table and array the drinks (or take-out boxes): Bojangles, Biscuitville, Hardees, Lance crackers, Mt. Olive pickles, and Lay's potato chips. Cheerwine and Pepsi, surely, but also moonshine produced by the likes of Percy Flowers, Popcorn Sutton, and Amos Owens, the "Cherry Bounce King."

For some, pop culture topics will have special appeal. The night Elvis Presley upstaged Faron Young in Raleigh. The Love Valley Festival in Iredell County. Chart toppers like "Girl Watcher" and "Disco Duck." Fred Kirby and "Atomic Power." Little Eva and "The Loco-Motion." Ben E. King and "Stand by Me." The premier of *Bull Durham*. Entertainers with Tar Heel roots like Randolph Scott, Pam Grier, Soupy Sales, Moms Mabley, Link Wray, Root Boy Slim, and, of course, Andy Griffith. Others who retired to the state like wrestler Andre the Giant and Kate Smith of "God Bless America" fame.

All part of life's rich pageant in the Old North State.

Kevin Cherry
Deputy Secretary
North Carolina Department of Natural and Cultural Resources

INTRODUCTION

This Day in North Carolina History began as a blog, in cooperation with the North Carolina News Network, with the first essays published online and read on the radio in October 2012. Month by month, the authors prepared a list of topics and solicited contributors to write roughly two-hundred word essays, enough to fill a few minutes of airtime.

North Carolina foodstuffs were perennial favorites, as were murders, train wrecks, and oddities. Readers take great pride in the people, inventions, and products born in the Tar Heel State. Some of the most popular blog posts were about Bojangles, the Jeffrey McDonald murder case, Tom Dula (Tom Dooley), the man with the world's longest beard, the Wreck of the Old 97, and the original Siamese Twins, Eng and Chang Bunker.

The blog ran fresh for four years, so each day has the potential for four essays about things that happened that day. Some days had very popular topics that we were encouraged to run again, such as Babe Ruth's first home run, the beginning of the Trail of Tears, and the skirmish at the House in the Horseshoe. For other days it was difficult to find interesting subjects to explore, so some essays present a North Carolina angle to a national story, such as William Polk at the winter encampment at Valley Forge or finding Abraham Lincoln in a photograph taken at the Gettysburg Address. A few bountiful days have five topics—rare days for which we had more than we needed or days when we had a date correction after publishing the blog.

The authors are grateful to Kelly Agan, Jessica Bandel, Debbi Blake, RoAnn Bishop, Mike Coffey, Sarah Downing, Andrew Duppstadt, Michael Hill, Marty Matthews, Chris Meekins, Joe Newberry, Karen Nilsen, Ardath Weaver, and all the other volunteers and staff members of the North Carolina Department of Natural and Cultural Resources who contributed thoughtful pieces to the project. Interns Majonica Haithcox and Marilyn McHugh assisted in locating images for the book during the summer of 2017. Kim Andersen, Michael Ausbon, Eric Blevins, Chandrea Burch, Ian Dunn, Bill Garrett, Keith Longiotti, Dale Sauter, Jason Tomberlin, and Mathew Waehner were particularly helpful in plumbing their collections and providing photographs. Thanks to Sheilah Barrett Carroll who designed the book and Mac McGee who proofread and indexed it.

The authors appreciate the support and partnership of Bruce Ferrell at the North Carolina News Network and Jennifer Babich at Spectrum News for making the project accessible to nearly all North Carolinians via radio and television.

The authors also especially wish to thank Secretary Linda Carlisle, Kevin Cherry, Cary Cox, Secretary Susi Hamilton, Michael Hill, Secretary Susan Kluttz, and Jennifer Woodward for their tireless support of this project throughout its incarnations.

Ansley Herring Wegner
Jeff Miles

1864 Parker Robbins, U.S. Colored Troops Officer, Lawmaker, and Inventor

On January 1, 1864, Parker Robbins of Bertie County, a free person of color of mixed African and Native American descent, enlisted in the Second United States Colored Cavalry Regiment at Fort Monroe, Virginia.

Federal military authorities in eastern North Carolina began actively recruiting and enlisting African Americans for the United States Colored Troops in 1863, eventually establishing one artillery and three infantry regiments. Those wishing to join a mounted unit had to travel to Virginia to join. Robbins and his younger brother both did just that.

With few exceptions blacks were not allowed to hold commissioned ranks as officers, and the highest rank available was that of sergeant major. Robbins was promoted from private to sergeant major 10 days after his enlistment. He saw combat in southeastern Virginia and northeastern North Carolina. After the war he returned to Bertie County, where he was chosen as a delegate to the 1868 constitutional convention and served two terms as a state representative.

Robbins then moved to Duplin County. He went on to own a steamboat, sawmill, and cotton gin and to secure several patents. He received a pension for his service and was active in local Union veterans' affairs until his death in 1917.

1942 Duke Hosted Rose Bowl Game in Durham, 1942

On January 1, 1942, the Rose Bowl was played in Durham—the only time the game has not been played in Pasadena, California. With America having then joined World War II, there was concern about holding the match or, indeed, any large public gathering on the west coast for fear of attack. The Duke University Blue Devils, the Oregon State University Beavers, and all of their fans potentially would be in great danger.

Shortly before the Tournament of Roses Committee would have officially called the game off, Duke football coach Wallace Wade offered to host the game at Duke. The city of Durham and Duke University had only about two weeks to prepare for the festivities. During that time they managed to increase the capacity of the stadium from 34,000 to 56,000 seats by borrowing bleachers from the neighboring University of North Carolina and N.C. State. The tickets sold out in three days. The face value of tickets for bleacher seats was $4.40, though scalpers offered tickets for as much as $25.

Duke was the clear favorite to win the hastily relocated bowl game. Wade had led the Blue Devils to an unbeaten and untied season in 1941. The game, however, became a major upset when Oregon State won 20 to 16.

1996 Gubernatorial Veto Instituted, 1996

On January 1, 1996, North Carolina became the last state to grant its governor the veto power. The state's voters ratified that change the previous November when they overwhelming approved a constitutional amendment on the statewide ballot.

North Carolina had historically opted for a weaker role for its governors, partially as a reaction to the harsh treatment the state suffered under British royal governors during the colonial era. The governor wasn't even popularly elected until 1835. Before then governors were elected by the state legislature.

Though a contentious issue in 1995, governors have chosen to exercise the power only fifty-three times. The first use didn't come until 2002, when Governor Mike Easley sent a bill appointing people to various boards and commissions back to the legislature.

Local bills, amendments to the state and federal constitutions, and several other types of legislation cannot be vetoed by the governor. A three-fifths majority of the legislature can override any veto action.

Duke vs. Oregon State at the Rose Bowl game played in Durham. Photograph courtesy of the *News and Observer*.

1926 At the Corner of Cucumber and Vine

On January 2, 1926, the Mt. Olive Pickle Company was formally incorporated by local business people in Wayne County. The effort to start the company arose within the community, and the original group of thirteen local shareholders invested $19,500 to establish a local business to pack and sell pickles.

The shareholders purchased an acre of land for $1,000, constructed a 3,600-square-foot building and hired a factory superintendent and a sales representative. The salesman, Shickrey Baddour, a Lebanese immigrant, had conceived the idea for the factory when he saw cucumbers rotting in area fields. Within just a few weeks the number of shareholders grew to twenty-one from the original thirteen.

Mt. Olive Pickle Company started an employee profit-sharing program in 1943 and was one of the first companies in the country to do so. Records from the early days indicate that most of the work at the plant was done by hand. Since then it has grown into an innovative and modern facility distributing the country's bestselling brand of pickles. Today, the factory complex still includes that original acre and is located at the corner of Cucumber and Vine Streets in Mt. Olive.

1975 First Woman Takes Oath as Chief Justice of N.C. Supreme Court

On January 2, 1975, Susie Sharp took the oath of office as Chief Justice of the Supreme Court of North Carolina.

Governor Kerr Scott had appointed her a Superior Court judge 26 years earlier in 1949, making her the first female judge in state history. As she rode the circuit, she encountered the usual challenges but some unexpected ones too. In Morganton the judge's bathroom had only a sink and a urinal. In another instance an attorney in one of her trials began his summation, "Gentlemen of the jury, the presence of sweet womanhood in this courtroom today rarefies the atmosphere."

Governor Terry Sanford appointed her to the state's high bench in 1962, and she was elected by the people that fall. Twelve years later she received 74% of the vote to become the first woman in the nation popularly elected Chief Justice. The petite jurist, who served until 1979, was a native of Rocky Mount but lived most of her life in Reidsville. She was progressive, an advocate for judicial reform and for humane prison conditions, but also deeply conservative, an outspoken opponent of the Equal Rights Amendment. *Time* magazine named Sharp one of twelve "Women of the Year" in 1975.

JAN 2

1787 "Old Bill" Williams and the Old West

On January 3, 1787, frontiersman William Sherley Williams was born in what's now Polk County.

Williams moved to the frontier town of St. Louis with his family in the 1790s and began his career as an itinerant Baptist preacher at age 17. Several years later he radically changed the course of his life to become an explorer, trapper, scout, and guide. "Old Bill," as he as commonly known, began his life as an adventurer by living among the Osage Indians for more than two decades, adopting their language and customs, marrying a member of the tribe, and learning to be a master fur trapper.

During the War of 1812 Williams served as an official interpreter for the U.S. government and, after the war's conclusion, helped broker a treaty between the Osage and the federal government. Williams is perhaps best known for scouting and surveying the nation's far western frontier and Santa Fe Trail and for his role in the ill-fated Fremont expedition. Williams was blamed for the tragedy that the ended expedition, when 11 men died in a mountain snowstorm from exposure and starvation.

In 1849 Williams was killed by Ute warriors while trying to recover some of the equipment lost on the expedition. In addition to his talents as a trader, negotiator, and scout, the larger-than-life Williams became known for his fearlessness, fighting, and drinking. The Arizona town of Williams and Bill Williams Mountain were named for "Old Bill."

Old Bill Williams historical marker

1837 Cherokee Chief and Solidifier Nimrod Jarrett Smith

On January 3, 1837, Nimrod Jarrett Smith was born near what is now Murphy at the height of the Cherokee removal. He was raised in the Cherokee communities of Valley Town and Cheowa but was also well acquainted with William Holland Thomas and the Oconaluftee Cherokees. During the Civil War he enlisted with Thomas's Sixty-Ninth N.C. Volunteer Infantry, also known as "Thomas's Legion," and rose to the rank of First Sergeant of Company B.

Smith was deeply involved in post-Civil War Cherokee politics. During this pivotal time the North Carolina Cherokees sought to solidify not only their land holdings but also their very existence in the state. At a Grand Council held at what is now Robbinsville, in 1868, the body politic of the Eastern Band of Cherokee Indians was created.

In 1880 Smith was elected the third Principal Chief of the EBCI. He centralized Cherokee politics around his farm in modern-day Cherokee. During his tenure Smith developed an education system in cooperation with Quakers, who constructed an industrial school and common school. Smith's most important effort, though, was gaining official state recognition of the Eastern Band of Cherokee Indians in 1889. He served as Principal Chief until 1891.

1893 Origins of BB&T in Wilson

On January 3, 1893, Alpheus Branch, founder of the bank now known as BB&T, died at age 50.

The son of a successful Halifax County planter, Branch was a Confederate veteran and merchant who moved to Wilson in 1865. His first enterprise was a mercantile business. He entered banking in 1872, when he founded Branch and Hadley Bank in Wilson with his friend Thomas Jefferson Hadley. The pair were interested in starting a bank so that local people could have a trustworthy local financial intuition, and, as such, the small private firm mostly supported businesses and farmers in the young town.

In 1887 Branch purchased Hadley's share of the business and changed the name to Branch and Company, Bankers. Two years later, Branch, Hadley, and a few other Wilson men secured a charter for a state bank and initially called it Wilson Banking and Trust Company.

Just before Branch's death the charter was amended to The Branch Banking Company. Branch's private bank was incorporated into the rest of the business in 1900, and the name was changed in 1912 to Branch Banking and Trust Company to reflect its distinctive trust department.

Alpheus Branch portrait

1659 The Durants of Durants Neck

1856 Origins of Maco Light Legend Date to 1856

1969 Modern-Day Conjoined Twins in Charlotte

JAN 4

On January 4, 1659, George and Ann Marwood Durant, pioneer settlers of the Albemarle region of Carolina, were married.

By 1665 they were living on the peninsula now known as Durant's Neck in modern Perquimans County. George was instrumental in establishing local government in an area overlooked and under-appreciated by the Lords Proprietors; he even traveled to London to represent the interests of the colonists of the area. After not getting redress for his concerns he was one of the chief leaders of the uprising known as Culpeper's Rebellion in 1677.

Two years after he rebelled against the proprietors in London, Durant was one of the most influential politicians in the region due largely to his success in protecting the interests of the Albemarle region and Carolina more broadly. In 1679 he was appointed speaker of North Carolina's first legislative assembly and also served as attorney general under Thomas Harvey. Durant died in 1693 or 1694, according to his will, which his wife administered.

In her husband's frequent absence Ann Durant ran their plantation, often providing accommodations at their house for officials attending meetings of the Assembly and Council. In 1673 she became the first woman to act in the capacity of an attorney in Carolina. On at least 20 other occasions she appeared before colonial courts on behalf of herself, her husband, and others.

On January 4, 1856, a train accident on the Wilmington and Manchester Railroad occurred near Wilmington, giving rise to an enduring North Carolina legend.

In the neighborhood of Hood's Creek, about 8 miles outside of Wilmington, the locomotive on the night mail train was using steam faster than new water could be pumped into the boiler. The mechanical pump only worked when the wheels were turning, so the crew uncoupled the engine and ran it ahead to pump water without the heavy train attached. Upon returning to their train, they couldn't see it in the dark and collided with the first car, throwing Conductor Charles Baldwin from an open door. Baldwin received severe head injuries during the accident and died three days later. He is buried in Oakdale Cemetery.

The legend of the Maco Light, which grew from the accident, recounts the tale of "Joe" Baldwin, a train conductor who was decapitated in a collision. A mysterious light seen frequently along the railroad tracks at the small crossroads was reputed to be Joe Baldwin swinging a lantern as he searched for his head. The light could be seen from a distance but disappeared as one approached it. The railroad tracks were removed in 1977, and the light has not been seen since.

On January 4, 1969, conjoined twins Daisy and Violet Hilton were found dead in their home in Charlotte. The 60-year old women most likely died of complications of the Hong Kong flu.

Born in Brighton, England in 1908, the twins were unofficially adopted by their biological mother's midwife, Mary Hilton, when the mother rejected the children. From the time they were infants they were exhibited by Hilton and her daughter. Soon Hilton's son-in-law, Myer Myers, became their agent and exhibited them in the United States. They were kept in insolation when not being exhibited on midways across the country.

By 1931 the sisters had enough and sued for independence and damages. They won a settlement of one hundred thousand dollars, a fraction of what they had earned. They performed in vaudeville productions and in 1932 appeared in the film *Freaks*. They published their autobiography, *The Lives and Loves of the Hilton Sisters*, in 1942. After World War II the popularity of sideshows diminished, and they toured drive-in theaters in support of the film *Chained for Life*, in which they acted in 1950. Their manager abandoned them in Charlotte, where they settled and worked as produce clerks in a local grocery store.

Mid-nineteenth century locomotive departs from Hamlet Station.

A *Washington Post* caption: Fred Sandberg, district police fingerprint expert, tells Daisy and Violet Hilton (*right*), "Siamese Twins," apart by their fingerprints in 1926.

1878 Justice and Law Teacher Richmond Pearson

On January 5, 1878, North Carolina Supreme Court Justice and law instructor Richmond Mumford Pearson died in Winston.

Born in what's now Davie County in 1805, Pearson began his law practice in Salisbury in 1826. After representing Rowan County in the House of Commons, he became a Superior Court judge in 1836.

That same year Pearson established a law school in Mocksville. It later moved to Pearson's estate in what is now Yadkin County. The school's students included several future governors, politicians, and influential attorneys. In 1848 Pearson was elected to the state Supreme Court by the General Assembly. He became the state's Chief Justice in 1859.

During the Civil War, Pearson was responsible for several controversial decisions granting the rights of habeas corpus to those seeking exemption from the Confederate draft and limiting the use of the North Carolina Militia and Home Guard in enforcing Confederate conscription laws.

Following the war Pearson continued to serve as chief justice, surviving impeachment attempts. He also continued to operate his law school until his death. Pearson lay in state in the State Capitol rotunda until January 9, when his remains were laid to rest in Raleigh's Oakwood Cemetery.

1891 Governor Daniel Fowle Settles In

On January 5, 1891, Gov. Daniel G. Fowle, two years into his term, moved into the state's new Executive Mansion before construction was completely finished.

Nine years earlier, Gov. Thomas Jarvis appealed to the General Assembly for a suitable Governor's Mansion on Raleigh's Burke Square, insisting that it was inappropriate for the governor to live in a hotel. While he had no expectation that he would live in it, Jarvis hoped that his successor might be provided with a comfortable home suitable to the office. The legislature was persuaded and authorized the construction of a new governor's residence.

Work on the building was performed almost entirely with inmate labor, and building materials from within the state were used whenever possible. The bricks were made from Wake County clay, the sandstone trim came from Anson County, and the marble steps came from Cherokee County.

A magnificent example of the Queen Anne Cottage style of Victorian architecture, the mansion is noted for its turrets, porches, multicolored slate roof, and elaborate woodwork. The building was once described by Pres. Franklin D. Roosevelt as "the most beautiful governor's residence interior in America."

Fowle enjoyed the new governor's residence for only three months before his death in April 1891. The Executive Mansion has been occupied by 29 governors' families.

1921 "Brother Exum" Takes Her Seat, 1921

On January 5, 1921, Lillian Exum Clement took her seat in the North Carolina House of Representatives, becoming the first woman in the South to hold legislative office. Nominated as a Democratic candidate two months before the Nineteenth Amendment granted her and other women the right to vote, she beat two male opponents in the primary by an astounding margin of 10,368 to 41.

Clement was born in Black Mountain in 1886, and she worked in the Buncombe County sheriff's office while studying law at night. In 1916 she passed the bar exam and the next year opened her own practice. An active legislator, she introduced seventeen bills. She sponsored a bill to have the state assume control of a home for unwed mothers, garnering widespread opposition (she was pelted with eggs and vegetables while speaking on the bill's behalf in Asheville). Clement did not seek reelection but was appointed director of the State Hospital at Morganton. At age thirty-one she died of pneumonia and was buried in Riverside Cemetery.

In 1997 an organization to promote and support Democratic women running for public office in North Carolina was established. It took the name Lillian's List, in honor of Clement.

Lillian E. C. Stafford

JAN 5

JAN 6

1870 Central Prison Opens in Raleigh

On January 6, 1870, Central Prison opened in Raleigh. The first three prisoners—one man and two women—had been convicted of robbery in Johnston County. Prior to the prison's opening North Carolina did not have a central, state-operated prison and instead relied on the counties to manage inmates. Central Prison's construction was proposed as early as 1846 but did not begin until the adoption of the North Carolina Constitution of 1868 as part of Reconstruction.

A committee appointed by the General Assembly originally chose a tract in Chatham County for the prison, but the legislature selected a site near downtown Raleigh instead. Prisoners were housed in temporary structures until the first permanent building was completed in 1884.

Though inmates accounted for most of the labor used to build the 1884 structure, some outside help was brought in, perhaps most notably stone carver W.O. Wolfe, the father of novelist Thomas Wolfe. The prison complex underwent extensive renovations in the 1940s, 1960s, and 1970s, and rebuilding in the 1980s. Today it is the intake site for all male felons over age twenty-two with sentences longer than twenty years.

1889 Pioneering Black Physician, James F. Shober of Wilmington

On January 6, 1889, James Francis Shober, the first black physician with a medical degree to set up practice in North Carolina, died.

The son of an 18-year-old slave, Shober was born in the Moravian community of Salem in 1853. Circumstantial evidence suggests that his father was Francis Edwin Shober, an attorney and congressman.

Educated first at Lincoln University in Pennsylvania, the younger Shober completed medical studies at Howard University in 1878. After graduation he returned to his native state and began practicing medicine in his home in Wilmington, then the state's largest city. As the only black doctor in a city of more than 10,000, he was quite busy.

Shober was active in his church and in the Old North State Medical Society, an association of African American physicians still in existence today. His life was tragically short; he died in 1889 at age thirty-six.

1924 Banjo Master and Innovator Earl Scruggs

On January 6, 1924, Earl Eugene Scruggs was born near Shelby. The renowned bluegrass musician elevated the banjo from a rhythm instrument to a lead instrument through his distinctive three-finger picking style, now named for him.

Scruggs formed the Foggy Mountain Boys with Lester Flatt in 1948. The group soon gained success, playing radio stations across the South and recording for Mercury and Columbia Records. In 1962 "The Beverly Hillbillies" debuted on television with Flatt and Scruggs performing the theme song, "The Ballad of Jed Clampett." The single version of that song quickly rose to number one on the country charts, and Flatt and Scruggs made a number of appearances on the popular sitcom.

The Foggy Mountain Boys became the first country act to have their own syndicated television series; "Flatt and Scruggs Grand Ole Opry Show" ran from 1955 until the duo broke up in 1969. Scruggs then formed the Earl Scruggs Revue with his three sons.

In addition to inspiring a generation of banjo players, Scruggs received a number of honors, including two Grammy Awards. He was also inducted into the Country Music Hall of Fame and the International Bluegrass Music Hall of Fame. Scruggs recorded and performed until his death in 2012

1965 Federal Investment, 1965, Boosted RTP

On January 6, 1965, Governor Terry Sanford announced that the U.S. Department of Health, Education and Welfare (HEW) would invest $70 million in the Research Triangle Park (RTP) by locating its National Environmental Health Sciences Center there. That investment proved pivotal in the growth of the park.

The idea for RTP can be traced back to the early 1950s, when some of North Carolina's progressive leaders began to call for a shift in economic development strategy as traditional industries like textiles, tobacco, and furniture declined.

A committee, predecessor to what's now the Research Triangle Foundation, was formed in September 1956 to shepherd the project through its early years, and by 1959 Wachovia Chairman Archie Davis had raised enough money to purchase land between Raleigh and Durham for the creation of RTP.

The nonprofit contract research organization Research Triangle International and the U.S. Forest Service were among the park's first tenants, but the announcement by HEW helped ensure the park's success. IBM announced it would move to RTP three months later, and several large pharmaceutical, information technology, biotechnology, and environmental sciences companies and organizations soon followed.

Today RTP is home to nearly 200 companies and organizations, which employ tens of thousands of workers across 7,000 acres.

Central Prison, Cell block B, 1910s (*background photo*).

1839 Public Schools Prospered under Calvin Wiley

On January 7, 1839, the legislature passed an act to establish North Carolina's common school system. The law authorized counties to hold elections in which voters would approve or reject new taxes for public schools.

As a result of the law, voters in 61 of the 68 counties that then existed in the state chose to support school taxes in the elections later that year. The remaining seven counties soon followed course, and by 1846 every county had at least one public school. Initially, counties received only enough money to pay a teacher for two or three months of the year, and students of all ages were taught in a single class.

There was little regulation in the state's schools until the election of Calvin Wiley as the state's first superintendent of public schools in 1853. Wiley had a deep interest in public education, even going so far as to publish the state's first standard textbook at his own expense. Within seven years Wiley and his staff elevated North Carolina's educational system to probably the best in the South.

During his tenure as superintendent, Wiley and his staff were able to raise North Carolina's educational system to what many considered to be the most efficient in the South within a relatively short amount of time. Several elementary, middle and high schools around the state are named in his honor.

1839 Nineteenth Century Silver Mining in Davidson County

On January 7, 1839, the first silver mine in the United States opened at Silver Hill, near Lexington in Davidson County.

Silver was first discovered on the site in 1838. Prospector Roswell A. King purchased the land and along with John W. Thomas was issued a charter by the General Assembly in 1839. The site became known as the Washington Mine.

Loss of silver and lead in the refining process caused financial troubles for the Washington Mining Company. Experiments in refining failed to improve the situation, and in 1852 the mine closed. In 1854 the operation reopened as the Silver Hill Mine under the management of a New York entity, the Zinc and Silver Mining Company. The company owned the town that grew up around the mine, and the original workers were poor whites, who were paid wages less rent and other costs. By the late 1850s white workers were increasingly replaced by rented slave labor.

During the Civil War the mine produced lead for the Confederate war effort. The Zinc and Silver Mining Company resumed operations after the conflict, but the company ceased operations in 1882 due to continuing refining problems and legal difficulties over the title.

Attempts to revive it in later years were unsuccessful.

1931 Gertrude McKee, Groundbreaking Lawmaker

On January 7, 1931, Gertrude McKee became the first female member of the North Carolina Senate.

Among the most prominent North Carolinians of her day, McKee brought to the legislature a wealth of experience in public affairs. Born and raised in Dillsboro, she was the daughter of the town's founder.

McKee's first involvement in politics came in 1928 when she worked on Zeb Weaver's campaign for Congress. After being elected to the state Senate seat from the 32nd District in 1930 and taking her seat in 1931, she jokingly referred to her forty-nine male colleagues as her children. As chair of the public welfare committee, she took a special interest in child labor laws and old age assistance.

Voters returned her to the Senate four times, and there was even talk of her becoming North Carolina's first female governor. McKee died in 1948, three weeks after being elected to a fourth Senate term.

Gertrude McKee portrait.

JAN 7

JAN 8

1926 Slapstick Comic, TV Pioneer Soupy Sales

On January 8, 1926, children's television show host Soupy Sales, noted for taking pies in the face, was born Milton Supman in Franklinton. His father, Irving, immigrated to America from Hungary in 1894. Irving Supman, a Jewish merchant, operated a dry goods store in small-town North Carolina. His son, the funnyman, later quipped that his father supplied all the sheet needs of the local Ku Klux Klan.

The Supman family eventually relocated to Huntington, W. Va., where Milton graduated from Marshall University. After a military stint in the South Pacific, Supman took a new name upon entering show business. Soupy came from a family nickname, "Soup Man, and Sales" from a famous vaudeville performer of the time.

Sales first became successful in Detroit and Los Angeles. In 1964 his show moved to New York and was picked up by ABC. The broad slapstick humor involved live performers and puppets, notably White Fang and Black Tooth. The show also appealed to adults, featuring stars of the day like Frank Sinatra, who asked to be plastered with a cream pie. Later in life Sales was a regular on game shows such as "Hollywood Squares" and "Match Game." He died in 2009.

1975 "Carbine" Williams, Inventor and Inmate

On January 8, 1975, Cumberland County native David M. "Carbine" Williams, designer of the .30 caliber M-1 carbine, died. More than eight million Allied soldiers carried the M-1, a light, semiautomatic rifle, in World War II. General Douglas MacArthur described the weapon as "one of the strongest contributing factors to our victory in the Pacific." J. Edgar Hoover and others had similar praise for "Carbine" Williams.

In 1921 law enforcement officers raided one of Williams's illegal distilleries, and in the ensuing gunfight Deputy Al Pate was shot to death. Williams denied firing the fatal shot but pleaded guilty to second degree murder and was sentenced to thirty years. As a "trusty" in the blacksmith shop at Caledonia prison, Williams began innovating with scraps. His designs drew the attention of Colt Firearms, whose representatives visited him in prison.

Governor Angus McLean commuted Williams' sentence, and in 1929 he was released. In 1940 working with a team at Winchester, Williams created the .30 caliber M-1 carbine. A colorful character with his long sideburns, Stetson hat, and cigar, Williams became wealthy and patented over fifty inventions. In 1971 Carbine Williams gave his workshop and its contents to the North Carolina Museum of History.

David Marshall "Carbine" Williams outside his shop in Godwin, N.C., c.1970.

1779 James Hogun, Brigadier General in Revolutionary War

On January 9, 1779, James Hogun of Halifax County was chosen as a brigadier general for the North Carolina Continental Line (North Carolina units within the Continental Army). Hogun, a native of Ireland, settled near Hobgood around 1751. He was appointed the first major of the Halifax militia in 1776. Later that year he was promoted to colonel of the Seventh North Carolina Continental Regiment. He led the Seventh to serve under George Washington at the Battles of Brandywine and Georgetown in 1777.

When the Continental Congress called for the creation of four new North Carolina regiments, Hogun returned home to recruit men. By August 1778 the first new brigade was full, and Hogun marched the men to meet Washington in New York. Within a few months the Continental Congress appointed Hogun a brigadier general.

In November 1779 General Hogun marched his brigade to South Carolina to defend Charles Town. He was captured when Major General Benjamin Lincoln surrendered on May 12, 1780. As a prisoner of war at Haddrel's Point on Sullivan's Island, Hogun declined parole and chose to endure the same hardships as the men of his brigade. His health failed, and he died there on January 4, 1781.

1878 Tabitha Holton, a First for Tar Heel Courtrooms

On January 9, 1878, Tabitha Holton became the first woman licensed to practice law in North Carolina. Born in 1854 near Jamestown, she had three brothers, all of whom were attorneys. She is said to have gained her training in the law from having tutored her siblings.

In January 1878 Holton traveled to Raleigh with her brother Samuel to take the bar examination administered by the state Supreme Court. The court questioned whether it could admit a woman, but a family friend, Albion Tourgée, stepped up to say it could. He relished the chance to argue Holton's case against an old nemesis, former state Supreme Court Justice and UNC professor William H. Battle. Battle made the argument that a southern lady should not be "permitted to sully her sweetness by breathing the pestiferous air of the courtroom."

Tourgée carried the day, and Holton was permitted to take the exam, which she passed. She and her brother Samuel opened a practice across from the courthouse in Dobson. They advertised their services as attorneys-at-law in a local newspaper in 1881, but county court records include only a single instance where Tabitha appeared in court. She died in 1886 at age thirty-two.

1859 Albemarle and Chesapeake Canal, Vestige of the Age of Steam

On January 9, 1859, the Albemarle and Chesapeake Canal opened, connecting Albemarle Sound and Chesapeake Bay and providing a vital economic link between North Carolina and Virginia.

The canal was first proposed by William Byrd II in 1728, but engineering complications held up the project. The full canal was seventy-five miles long, but only fourteen of those cut through land. Of those fourteen miles only five are in North Carolina, essentially bisecting Currituck County at Coinjock. The rest of the canal followed natural channels and dredged rivers.

Construction was authorized by bills introduced in both the North Carolina and Virginia legislatures in 1854. Bonds to pay for the project, totaling just over $1 million dollars, were sold in the two states.

Though the nearby Dismal Swamp Canal had been dug by hand 50 years earlier, newly invented steam dredges were used to cut through massive stumps, roots, and buried logs on the Albemarle and Chesapeake project.

During the Civil War the canal was the site of partisan action, with ships sunk at the mouths to block entry. After the war commercial use increased, especially by steamship lines.

The canal's operation was taken over by the federal government in 1913. Today the canal is still in use, mostly by recreational watercraft, as part of the Intracoastal Waterway.

1951 Thomasville Chair, Fit for Paul Bunyan

On January 9, 1951, the cornerstone of the "World's Largest Chair" was laid in downtown Thomasville. The purpose of the chair was to recognize the significant role that Thomasville, then home to Thomasville Furniture, and the entire foothills region played in the furniture industry.

The big chair actually wasn't Thomasville's first. That monument was built in September 1922, at sixteen feet, six inches tall, and was fabricated by Thomasville Furniture Company from the materials it took to make 100 normal chairs.

A victim to the elements, the wooden structure was scrapped in 1936, and it wasn't until the formation of a local chamber of commerce in 1948 that interest in recreating the roadside landmark was revived. A team of designers drew up plans, and the decision was made to build this giant chair out of concrete and steel.

A Winston-Salem company fashioned a steel skeleton, which was covered with a wire mesh outlining the design and topped with a half-inch layer mixture of cement and granite. That in turn was painted to make the chair look like furniture. The sculpture took six months to complete and today stands proudly at thirty feet tall.

Tugboats on the Albemarle and Chesapeake Canal, circa 1930–1938.

1881 Progressive Farmer Editor Clarence Poe Born

1924 Jazz Drummer Max Roach, N.C. Native

1934 Bromine Extraction at Kure Beach

1936 John Penn's Second Distinction

JAN 10

On January 10, 1881, Clarence Poe, social and agricultural reformer, was born. During his more than 50 years at *The Progressive Farmer*, Poe became one of the most influential opinion-molders in the modern South. Born in Chatham County and never educated beyond grade school, Poe was eventually the recipient of five honorary doctorates.

At age sixteen Polk became a writer and office boy for the Raleigh-based magazine founded by L. L. Polk. Two years later he became the editor, and in 1903 he purchased the publication for $7,500 and became its publisher. During the next several decades the journal became the preeminent agricultural publication in the South.

Through his speeches, books, and editorials, Poe promoted numerous Progressive initiatives such as "two-armed farming," the idea that farmers should diversify into both crops and livestock. Poe crusaded for better rural education and cooperative marketing.

Although he was urged to run for governor in 1940, Poe never sought political office. He never learned to drive and rode a horse three miles into work every working day. Although he officially retired in 1954, he continued to contribute to and serve as editor-in-chief of *The Progressive Farmer* until his death in 1964.

On January 10, 1924, popular jazz drummer Max Roach was born in Pasquotank County. Shortly after moving to New York City with his family in 1928, Roach began to study piano with his aunt. He showed an early aptitude for music and played in jazz bands throughout high school.

Roach began filling in for the drummer in Coleman Hawkins's band in 1943, and in 1944 he cut his first record with a group that included Dizzy Gillespie. From there he had a career marked by collaboration with the jazz and bebop greats of his day, including Miles Davis, Charles Mingus, Charlie Parker, Thelonious Monk, and others. Later in his career Roach wrote music for the civil rights movement, taught percussion at the University of Massachusetts at Amherst, and composed pieces for the theater.

Among Roach's many accolades were designation as a Jazz Master by the National Endowment for the Arts, receipt of a MacArthur Foundation Genius Grant, and membership in the N.C. Music Hall of Fame.

On January 10, 1934, the Dow Chemical Company and the Ethyl Corporation began extracting bromine from sea water on a neck of land near Wilmington. Bromine was used in photography and chemical warfare, but its primary use was in Ethyl, an anti-knock compound in gasoline.

Before 1934 bromine had been extracted aboard ships at sea, but increased demand for the product meant a land-based production facility was needed. Dow and Ethyl purchased ninety acres at Kure Beach. The site proved ideal, as it had a natural basin for a holding reservoir, which was formed by a Carolina bay and an abandoned berm trench thrown up as part of the Cape Fear defense system in 1865.

The plant, erected at a cost of $3 million, proved to be a boon to the local economy during the Depression. At peak production, it extracted 15,000 pounds of bromine per day, treating 2,000 gallons of water in order to yield a single pound of the substance.

Production ceased in 1946 when another plant opened in Texas. Parts of the plant in North Carolina were used for other industrial purposes, and the concrete bases of the Kure Beach facility's towers have defied destruction to this day.

On January 10, 1936, the first state highway historical marker was dedicated and placed in the small Granville County town of Stovall to commemorate the life of John Penn, an early political leader and signer of the Declaration of Independence.

Though not authorized until 1935, the highway marker program has its roots in the 1903 legislation creating the North Carolina Historical Commission, which noted the lack of markers "commemorating the services of eminent sons of the state, or marking the sites of historic events."

Christopher Crittenden, longtime secretary of the commission, spearheaded the effort to found the program. Modeled after a similar program Virginia started in 1926, the State Highway Historical Marker Program was officially created after the General Assembly appropriated $5,000 and established an advisory committee for the purpose of placing markers in January 1935.

Crittenden gathered suggestions for markers from citizens around the state, and the committee, made up of college professors who were experts in North Carolina history, selected Penn for the first marker.

The program continues today as a joint effort of the state departments of Natural and Cultural Resources and of Transportation. Since 1935 around 1,600 state highway historical markers have been erected. At least one stands in every county.

Photo of first marker dedication.

1740 Thomas Robeson, Patriot Leader at Moore's Creek Bridge

On January 11, 1740, Revolutionary War colonel and state legislator Thomas Robeson was born in Bladen County.

Robeson first entered politics as a member of the Third Provincial Congress, held at Hillsborough in August 1775. During that session he was appointed colonel of the Bladen militia. He served in the Fourth Provincial Congress at Halifax the following year and was a member of the first General Assembly at New Bern in 1777.

Leading the Bladen militia was not an easy task. A large number of loyal Scots had settled in the Sandhills region, meaning that Tories, those loyal to the British crown, greatly outnumbered Patriots. In 1775 Robeson and his men joined forces with local Patriots, known as Whigs, and defeated General Donald McDonald and his Scottish Loyalist militia at the Battle of Moore's Creek Bridge. When the Tories regained ground in the region in 1781, Robeson led between 60 and 70 men against several hundred British at Elizabethtown.

After the Revolution Robeson served in the state legislature. He died in May 1785 and is buried near Tar Heel in Bladen County. In 1787 Robeson County was formed out of western Bladen County and named in his honor.

1909 Tab Smith and the Birth of Rhythm and Blues

On January 11, 1909, alto saxophonist Talmage "Tab" Smith was born in Kinston.

Smith's first professional musical endeavor came in 1929, when he formed the Carolina Stompers, and he soon achieved national acclaim as part of bands fronted by Count Basie and Lucky Millinder. Through the 1940s he recorded with some of the finest performers, including Billie Holiday, Earl Hines, and Coleman Hawkins. His peers on the alto sax included Johnny Hodges of the Duke Ellington Band and Earl Bostic.

With the evolution of musical tastes, Smith gravitated toward rhythm and blues in the 1950s, recording primarily on United Records. His version of the Tony Bennett hit "Because of You" was a chart topper in 1951. Most of Smith's numbers were short and were favorites on jukeboxes. He recorded a sax version of "Try a Little Tenderness," later covered by Otis Redding, and toured with the Five Royales, based in Winston-Salem, in the mid-1950s.

1961 Charlotte Hawkins Brown, Founder of Palmer Institute, Died

On January 11, 1961, noted African American educator and founder of the Palmer Memorial Institute Charlotte Hawkins Brown died. Born in Henderson, Brown moved to Cambridge, Massachusetts with her family when she was young and was educated there. In 1901, at age eighteen, she was persuaded by the American Missionary Association to return to North Carolina to assist in its effort to educate southern blacks.

Brown established the Palmer Memorial Institute in Sedalia, naming it for Alice Freeman Palmer, former president of Wellesley College, who was a friend and benefactor. The school, which opened in 1902, first operated out of an old blacksmith shop but eventually grew to house hundreds of students in more than a dozen buildings. Palmer became known as an elite black preparatory school, hosting students from all over the country and world.

During her tenure at Palmer, Brown actively toured, speaking on behalf of women's suffrage and racial equality. She devoted her life to the improvement of the African American community's social standing and was active in the National Council of Negro Women, an organization founded in 1935 by celebrated educator Mary McLeod Bethune. As president of the North Carolina State Federation of Negro Women's Clubs, Brown directed African American women's formal civic experiences for more than twenty years.

Tab Smith, circa1946 and 1948.

1896 Campus Hijinks at Davidson Involved X-rays, 1896

JAN 12

On January 12, 1896, three students at Davidson College experimented with x-rays, just six days after the Associated Press announced that German physicist Wilhelm Roentgen had discovered a new form of radiation. While experimenting with cathode rays, Roentgen found that mysterious "x"-rays passed through a variety of objects. He put his hand in front of the rays and saw the silhouette of his bones. At the time many physics labs had equipment to duplicate the x-ray. Henry Louis Smith, a physics professor and future president at Davidson, was the first professional in North Carolina to work with x-rays.

It was actually a group of Smith's students who appear to have been the first people in the state to perform x-ray experiments. Three juniors professed to having bribed a janitor to let them into the building housing the physics equipment only six days after Roentgen's announcement reached America. The students placed objects on photographic paper to take "roentgenograms" (photographs) of an eggshell with a button in it, a rubber-covered magnifying glass, a cadaver's finger, pins, cartridges, and paperclips. Years passed before the students' escapade was made public. The original x-ray images are now housed in the Davidson College Archives.

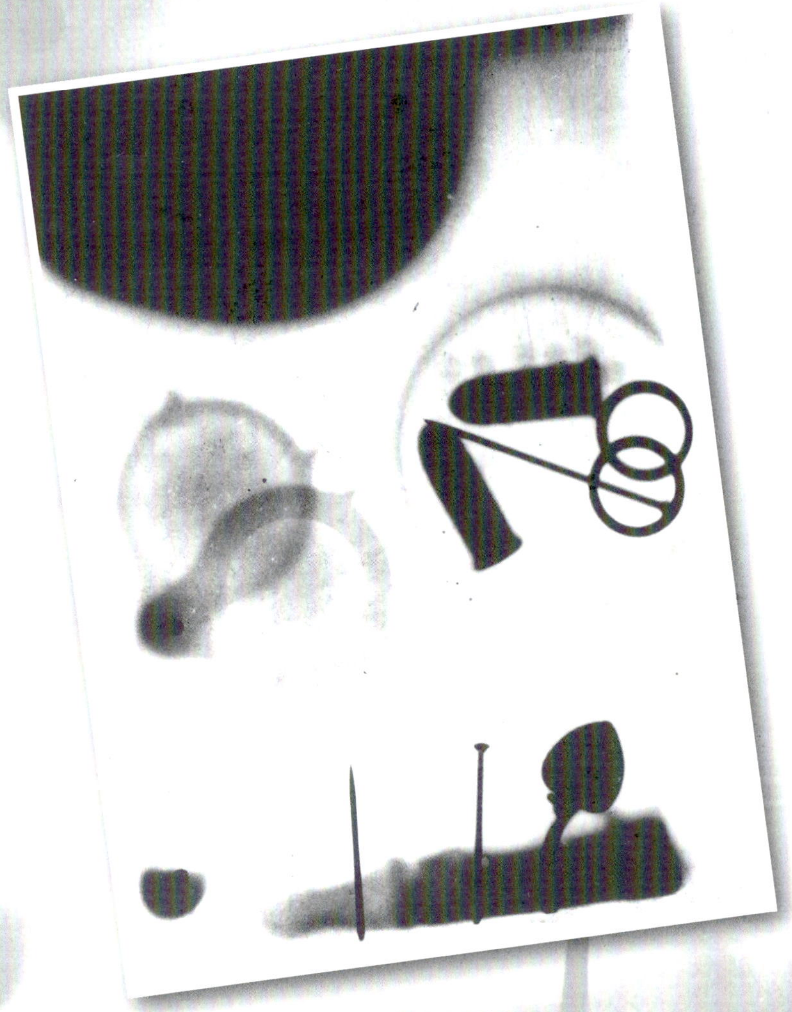

The first X-ray taken at Davidson College by students Eben Hardin, Pender Porter, and Osmond L. Barringer, 1896.

1909 Juvenile Offenders Remanded to Concord, 1909

On January 12, 1909, Stonewall Jackson Training School, a state correctional facility for juvenile male offenders, opened near Concord. The effort to establish the facility was led by James P. Cook, editor of a Concord newspaper. Cook witnessed the prosecution of a 13-year-old boy who received a three-and-a-half year sentence to serve on a chain gang for petty theft in 1890. Convinced that such a system was unjust, Cook devoted the next 17 years of his life to campaigning for a better alternative.

Success came only after a party of Confederate veterans sponsored the bill that supported the school's construction. Supporters suggested naming the institution after Confederate icon Thomas J. "Stonewall" Jackson, and the General Assembly agreed.

Male offenders under age eighteen were remanded to Stonewall Jackson Training School in lieu of prison time. At its peak the school's population reached nearly 500 students, and, while at the school, the young men lived in a series of dormitory style buildings and received an academic education, while also learning a trade.

Students worked in industries including shoemaking, printing, barbering, textiles, and machining. Many of the young men worked on the school's farm, learning modern agricultural techniques and maintaining the fields and cattle herds that supported the school.

JAN 13

1825 Birthday of State's Oldest Newspaper

On January 13, 1825, the first issue of the *Fayetteville Observer*, the state's oldest newspaper still in print, was published by Edward Jones Hale. The issue announced the visit of the Marquis de Lafayette to the nation's capital. The newspaper actually dates back to 1816, when it was launched as a four-page weekly paper called the *Carolina Observer* under different ownership.

Hale was a strong political force and his influential paper had the largest circulation in the state by 1850. When General William T. Sherman entered Fayetteville in 1865, he ordered that the offices of the *Observer*, one of the principal Confederate newspapers, be burned. Hale had removed his important files prior to the fire and, when contacted about the destruction later, claimed that Sherman and his men "could not have paid him a higher compliment."

The *Fayetteville Observer* became a daily paper in 1896. It was operated by the Hale family until 1919. After a few other ownership changes, the paper was purchased by a New York businessman, who formed the Fayetteville Publishing Company. Charles Robert Wilson became the publisher of the paper in its new and modern quarters in 1924.

1868 St. Augustine's: Freedmen's School to University

On January 13, 1868, classes began at Raleigh's Saint Augustine's University.

Episcopal Bishop Thomas Atkinson pressed for the creation of the school, originally called St. Augustine's Normal School and Collegiate Institute, to educate teachers to serve African American children across the state and nation. Atkinson said that such a school would be indispensable to the church in its mission to assist the nation's newly freed African American population.

Brinton Smith, who had come to North Carolina from New Jersey in 1866 to aid African Americans, was hired as the school's first principal. Many of the school's first students were former slaves.

The national Episcopal church began to officially support St. Augustine's in 1907, and the school began offering junior college classes in the early 1920s. In 1928 the college gained four-year college status, conferring its first bachelor's degrees in 1932. St. Augustine's was the first historically black college to develop on-campus commercial radio and television stations.

It became a university in 2012 and, despite persistent financial difficulties, has remained vibrant, offering more than thirty areas of study to just under 2,000 students from around the country and the world.

1962 Mary Martin Sloop and Education in Avery County

On January 13, 1962, Mary Martin Sloop, founder of Crossnore School in Avery County, died at age eighty-eight. Sloop was raised at Davidson College, where her father was a professor of geology and chemistry, and went to Philadelphia to study medicine after being rejected by schools in North Carolina. She married surgeon Eustace Sloop in 1908, and they determined to seek their fortune in the North Carolina mountains.

Settling into a joint practice first at Plumtree and soon after at Crossnore, they attended to the medical and educational needs of the community. Sloop founded Crossnore School because of the deficiencies of the public school system. As local schools improved, Crossnore's mission changed to serve orphans and children from broken homes. She worked to reduce through education the problems of child brides and illegal liquor. In 1928 she helped organize the Southern Highlands Handicrafts Guild.

The Weaving Room at Crossnore played an important role in the revival of Appalachian handicrafts. Of students' craft work, Dr. Sloop said, "It is their character building qualities which concern us most at the school."

Campus of St. Augustine's University, ca. 1900.

JAN 14

1771 Freemasonry Grand Master, Joseph Montfort

On January 14, 1771, Joseph Montfort was appointed Grand Master of the Freemasons of America by the Duke of Beaufort, Grand Master of England.

Montford was born in England in 1724, and little is known about his early life. After settling in Halifax sometime in the middle of the eighteenth century, he quickly became active in civic affairs, representing Halifax in the colonial assembly from 1766 to 1774 and eventually serving as a treasurer of the colony.

One of the wealthiest North Carolinians of the time, Montfort owned more than 30,000 acres of land scattered in large tracts across the state. Active in the freemasonry movement before the official formation of the Grand Lodge of North Carolina in 1787, Montford established early masonic lodges across the state.

Montfort died in 1776 and is buried near the Masonic Lodge in Halifax, one of the state's first.

1834 William Polk, Last of N.C.'s Revolutionary Officers

On January 14, 1834, William Polk, the last surviving field officer of the North Carolina Continental Line (North Carolina units within the Continental Army), died in Raleigh. Polk served during the Revolutionary War with distinction, seeing action at Germantown, Brandywine, Eutaw Springs, and Cowan's Ford. After the Battle of Guilford Courthouse, he was promoted from major to lieutenant colonel and became known as "Colonel Polk."

Shortly before the turn of the century Polk moved from his native Mecklenburg County to Raleigh, where he lived the rest of his life and played a prominent role in state and local affairs. His first public role was as a member of the Council of State in 1806. With the establishment of the State Bank in 1810, Polk was elected its first president, serving in that position for 19 years.

In 1821 he spoke at the dedication of the Canova statue at the State Capitol. Four years later he welcomed Lafayette, with whom he had fought at Brandywine, to Raleigh and breakfasted with him at his North Street home. He was among the incorporators of the "Experimental Railroad" built in 1833 for the new Capitol. Polk was also an early member of the board of trustees of the University of North Carolina, serving in that capacity for forty-two years.

1868 Black Delegates Had Voice at 1868 Convention

On January 14, 1868, a North Carolina constitutional convention, now known as the "Convention of 1868," opened in Raleigh.

The convention was required by an act of Congress that ordered North Carolina to create a new state constitution. The General Assembly decided to hold a referendum in November 1867 to choose delegates to a constitutional convention to be held in early 1868.

Many former Confederate leaders had not yet taken an Oath of Allegiance to the United States and were not eligible to vote or serve. Chosen for the convention were 107 Republicans and 13 Democrats. The members of the first "Black Caucus" were all Republicans.

The participants in the Black Caucus were not legislators, exactly. But they came together at the State Capitol in January 1868 to take part in a very important process—to expand freedom for all.

The members of this first Black Caucus were James Walker Hood, Parker Robbins, Henry Cherry, Bryant Lee, Wilson Carey, Clinton Pierson, John H. Williamson, Cuffie Mayo, Henry Eppes, W.T.J Hayes, John Hyman, Abraham Galloway, and James H. Harris.

Joseph Montfort's grave in front of the Masonic Lodge he founded, Halifax County, 1938.

JAN 15

1771 The Original Queen's College in Charlotte

On January 15, 1771, the legislature passed an act to establish Queen's College in Charlotte. The act stressed the urgent need for educational opportunities in what was at the time the "backcountry." Creating the school, though, which was to be established under the auspices of the Presbyterian Church, was in conflict with royal authority and the Church of England.

Gov. William Tryon believed that the school's charter would show his appreciation to the Presbyterians, who aided him in the ongoing conflict with the Regulators. The British government determined that it would not be appropriate for the crown to approve a Scots-Irish institution that could perpetuate anti-royalist views in the colony, and the charter was revoked.

The trustees continued to apply for a charter and operated the school under the name of Queen's Museum. During the Revolution school trustees sympathized with the colonial cause, and many future leaders, including William R. Davie and Andrew Jackson, were educated there. When independence was declared, the school became known as Liberty Hall Academy. It relocated to Salisbury in 1784.

The institution that we know today as Queens University of Charlotte was founded by Presbyterians in 1857.

1865 The Fall of Fort Fisher

On January 15, 1865, Fort Fisher, nicknamed "Gibraltar of the South," fell to Union troops.

Built on a peninsula known as Federal Point at the mouth of the Cape Fear River, 18 miles south of Wilmington, Fort Fisher was the largest earthen fortification in the Confederacy. It guarded the port of Wilmington and, in that capacity, was the most powerful seacoast fort in the South. Fort Fisher became the last remaining lifeline in the closing months of the Civil War, allowing blockade runners to take advantage of the Cape Fear River to route supplies to troops inland.

On December 23 and 24, 1864, the Union Navy bombarded the fort. At the same time the fort's forces were reinforced with about 600 more men from Wilmington, increasing the number to around 2,000. The Union Navy attacked again on January 13, 1865. After two days Union forces led by Gen. Alfred Terry overwhelmed the Confederate defenders led by Maj. Gen. W.H.C. Whiting and Col. William Lamb and captured Fort Fisher.

Its fall robbed Robert E. Lee's army of its last connection to the outside and served as the beginning of the Wilmington Campaign, which resulted in the fall of Fort Anderson and the occupation of Wilmington.

The Union attack on the fort, featured in the 2012 film *Lincoln*, was the largest amphibious attack by American forces until World War II. Fort Fisher is now one of North Carolina's state historic sites.

1948 Powerful Editor Josephus Daniels

On January 15, 1948, Josephus Daniels, newspaper editor and former Secretary of the Navy, died in Raleigh. While at school in Wilson, Daniels developed a love of journalism and became editor of the *Wilson Advance*. He later bought the newspaper, and over the next few years purchased several other papers with various partners.

Daniels remained a loyal Democrat throughout his career. In 1892 he was appointed to a post in the Department of the Interior. He held the position for two years before returning to North Carolina, having just recently purchased Raleigh's *News and Observer* at public auction.

Because of his staunch support of the Democratic Party in the early 1900s, Daniels became close friends with President Woodrow Wilson. He served as Wilson's publicity chief during the 1912 campaign and was appointed Secretary of the Navy, a post he held through both of Wilson's terms. In 1921 Daniels returned to Raleigh and his beloved newspaper.

Franklin D. Roosevelt appointed Daniels ambassador to Mexico in 1934, a post he held for 7 years. Late in life Daniels wrote a series of memoirs. Daniels remained active until his death from pneumonia. He was buried in Oakwood Cemetery in Raleigh.

1974 Harold Cooley, Powerful Agriculture Committee Chair

On January 15, 1974, congressman and agricultural advocate Harold Cooley died from the effects of emphysema. As longtime chairman of the U.S. House of Representatives Agriculture Committee, Cooley, a native of Nash County, was a powerful spokesman for farmers from the New Deal to the Great Society.

Democrat Cooley, by virtue of a special election in July 1934, filled the House seat in the Fourth District vacated by the death of Edward Pou. He went on to serve 17 terms in the U.S. House. His length of service as Agriculture Committee chairman (from 1949 to 1952 and from 1955 to 1967, interrupted by the Eight-Third Congress when Republicans held the majority) has not been exceeded.

Cooley joined the Agriculture Committee during the height of the New Deal and was a driving force in the development of Roosevelt's agricultural program. He backed several reforms including those that provided for allotments, price supports, rural electrification, and soil conservation. Cooley also sought to reach the world market with agricultural products, stating that "bread and butter rather than bullets and bayonets are the most powerful weapons in our arsenal."

Cooley returned to his home in Nashville after losing his reelection campaign in 1966.

BOMBARDMENT OF FORT FISHER N.C.

by the Squadron of Rear Admiral D.D. Porter U.S.N.

BY A. HOEN & CO. BALTIMORE.

JAN 16

1831 "Giant" Peter Francisco

On January 16, 1831, Peter Francisco, the "Virginia Giant," died in Richmond, Virginia. Francisco was noted for his many feats of bravery during the American Revolution, especially during North Carolina's Battle of Guilford Courthouse in March 1781.

Not much is known of Francisco's origins, except that he arrived in Virginia in 1765, possibly from Portugal. He grew to nearly six feet, eight inches in height and weighed nearly 260 pounds. He enlisted in the Tenth Virginia Continentals at the beginning of the American Revolution and saw much heavy fighting during his four-year term.

Upon his discharge Francisco quickly re-enlisted and continued to serve in the American army in South Carolina. He was cited for saving a cannon at the Battle of Camden in August 1780 and, while serving with Colonel William Washington's dragoons at Guilford Courthouse, was described as killing 11 British soldiers in succession with his broadsword. When one British soldier pinned Francisco's leg to his horse with a bayonet, he killed the soldier with a stroke from his sword. Despite his wounds Francisco continued to fight till the end of the engagement.

After the war Francisco lived in Richmond. He later became famous for saving a number of people from a burning theater.

1944 Award-Winning Musician Ronnie Milsap

On January 16, 1944, award-winning country musician Ronnie Milsap was born in Robbinsville with congenital glaucoma. He lost his eyesight early in life and spent 12 years learning to play the violin and piano at the school for the blind in the Raleigh.

Though he loved music, he received a scholarship and pursued a career as a lawyer. At a chance encounter in 1965, Ray Charles heard Milsap play the piano and encouraged him to follow his heart. Milsap formed his own band.

After his 1969 hit "Never Had It So Good," Milsap moved to Memphis to advance his career. He would go on to become one of country music's biggest stars, winning eight CMAs, four ACM Awards, and six Grammy Awards. He has also had a total of forty number-one hits and has sold more than 35 million albums.

1975 Asheville's "Old Kentucky Home," Now State-Owned

On January 16, 1975, the state of North Carolina obtained Thomas Wolfe's "Old Kentucky Home" from the city of Asheville. That boardinghouse at 48 Spruce Street was the setting for Wolfe's first novel, *Look Homeward, Angel*. He renamed it "Dixieland" and incorporated his own experiences among the boarders into the novel.

The property dates at least to 1883, when Asheville banker Erwin Sluder built a smaller residence on the site. Between 1885 and 1889 Alice Johnston Reynolds, who had purchased the property from Sluder, made a massive addition to Sluder's original structure and began operating the building as a boardinghouse in 1890.

A subsequent owner, Rev. Thomas M. Myers, named it the "Old Kentucky Home" in honor of his home state. Julia E. Wolfe, Thomas's mother, bought the house for $6,500 in August 1906 and used it as a source of income to reinvest in real estate. Her husband W. O. Wolfe disliked boardinghouses and, although he went for meals and visits, rarely stayed the night. The Wolfes maintained two residences, with all the children except Tom living with their father. As the youngest child, he stayed with his mother at the boardinghouse.

Old Kentucky Home (later Wolfe Memorial) in 1908. Identified (*left to right*): W.O. Wolfe sitting in a chair on the lawn, Ben Wolfe sitting on the porch steps at left, Mrs. W.O. (Julia) Wolfe sitting in a chair on the porch, Mabel Wolfe sitting on the ground, and Thomas Wolfe sitting on the wall by the sidewalk.

1865 Massive Explosions Rock Fort Caswell, 1865

On January 17, 1865, Fort Caswell was abandoned as Confederates retreating from Fort Fisher detonated Caswell's powder magazines. The explosion destroyed the entire southeast face of the fort and damaged the western face.

A soldier quoted in the *Daily North Carolinian* stated, "We were aroused from our slumbers at 2 o'clock yesterday morning by an explosion, which shook our office to its foundation. We have ascertained since that it was Fort Caswell, blown up by our troops after its evacuation."

Another witness recorded from his position at what's now Southport, "As I looked, a vivid flash of light shot through the darkness and traveled with lightning rapidity, toward the fort, and then, as if a mighty volcano had sprung its blazing contents from the sea into the sky, a great light flashed up from Caswell, accompanied by a roar and a jar that smashed the glass in our house like a wave of an earthquake."

The 1865 explosion ended the most active period of Fort Caswell's military history, although it was occupied by troops in both the Spanish-American War and World War I. Today the property is a retreat and conference center for the Baptist State Convention. Remnants of the fort remain on the site.

1874 Twins from Siam, World Sensation, Died in Surry County

On January 17, 1874, Chang and Eng Bunker, the original Siamese twins, died.

The Bunkers were born in Thailand (then Siam) in 1811 and amassed a fortune for themselves on the circus and exhibition circuit before retiring to North Carolina in 1839. They first lived in Wilkes County, where they married sisters Sarah and Adelaide Yates. With growing families, the brothers purchased land in Surry County and built large homes a little over a mile apart. For the rest of their lives they spent three nights at one house, then three nights at the other. Eng and Sarah Bunker eventually had eleven children, while Chang and Adelaide had ten.

After devastating financial losses during the Civil War, the twins returned briefly to the circus. They traveled to Europe, where between shows they searched in vain for a doctor to separate them. In January 1874 Chang contracted bronchitis and died in his sleep. Eng awakened and, horrified by the sight of his dead twin, quickly fell into paralysis. A doctor was summoned but did not arrive until after Eng had died. The two were buried in a common grave at the White Plains Baptist Church cemetery in Surry County.

1863 Madison County Atrocity a Measure of the War's Extremes

On January 18, 1863, a Civil War-era tragedy that has come to be known as the Shelton Laurel Massacre took place. The incident grew out of a series of raids on the town of Marshall by Unionists claiming that Confederate authorities had denied them provisions.

Under the command of Confederate Brig. Gen. Harry Heth, Lt. Col. James A. Keith and his men went into the Shelton Laurel area and marched three boys, ages thirteen to seventeen, and ten men, twenty to fifty-six, out from their homes and into the woods. The group, suspected of being Unionists, was ordered to kneel. Hesitating on the first command to shoot the thirteen, the troops complied with the second. In addition, "several women were severely whipped and ropes were tied around their necks." No one was prosecuted as a result of the incident.

Within days of the killings, Gov. Zebulon B. Vance wrote that the affair was "shocking and outrageous in the extreme." A writer in 1955 observed that "nowhere is there a microcosm more chill and revealing than this episode of war at its heart and core."

In 1968 William and Bud Shelton placed new granite stones at the graves of family members slain in 1863. Six of the thirteen youths and men killed were members of the Shelton family.

1942 Oil Transport Torpedoed by German U-boat, 1942

On January 18, 1942, the Standard Oil tanker *Allan Jackson* was torpedoed by a German submarine seventy miles off the coast of Cape Hatteras.

The vessel, transporting oil from Colombia to New York, was struck by two torpedoes. The second blast split the ship in two, spilling 7.5 million gallons of oil. Of the thirty-five crew members, twenty-two perished. The survivors told harrowing tales of clinging to scattered pieces of wreckage and trying to avoid the burning oil.

During World War II German U-boats were a very real threat to vessels along the eastern coast of North America. Survivors from one merchant vessel said that enemy submarines were "almost as thick as catfish" in the waters where they were attacked. In 1941 and 1942 about one hundred ships were sunk at Diamond Shoals, off the coast of the Outer Banks, in what became known as the "Battle of Torpedo Junction."

Coast Guard patrol planes, the Civil Air Patrol, antisubmarine vessels, and underwater mine fields eventually brought an end to the menacing U-boat presence in North Carolina's waters.

1958 Lumbees Rally, Klansmen Scurry, in Robeson County

On January 18, 1958, the Ku Klux Klan rallied in a field outside of Maxton in Robeson County to "put the Indians in their place, to end race mixing."

A generator powered the public address system and the single light bulb that illuminated the speaker's immediate area. With only that dim light the Klansmen, numbering fewer than one hundred, could not see the hundreds of Lumbee, some armed, surrounding them. The two groups clashed and struggled over the light bulb until a gunshot shattered it. More gunshots rang out in the darkness as the Lumbee routed the Klansmen from the field, ending the night's event. Police arrested the Klan leader, James "Catfish" Cole, for inciting a riot. He was convicted and served a year in prison.

The incident garnered national attention in contemporary news outlets, including a three-page spread in *Life* magazine. Several images captured the unfolding events and the aftermath, including a triumphant Simeon Oxendine wrapped in the captured KKK banner. Oxendine was a prominent Lumbee community leader and a World War II veteran who flew more than thirty bombing missions.

In 1967 folklorist Malvina Reynolds paid homage to the confrontation in her song "Battle of Maxton Field."

JAN 18

"Battle of Hayes Pond." Robeson County Lumbee Indians and others in the crowd involving weapons, 1958.

1942 German U-boat Attacks Three Vessels Off N.C. Coast

On January 19, 1942, a German U-boat, designated *U-123*, attacked three ships north of Cape Hatteras. The U-boat was part of what was called the "Second Happy Time" campaign during which Axis submarines attacked merchant vessels along the Atlantic coast.

In the early morning hours the American passenger-freighter *City of Atlanta* was sunk and survivors were left floating in the icy water; only three, all crewmen, lived. Just before dawn the *U-123* slipped into a group of Allied ships and attacked. The American tanker *Malay* was damaged and disabled by gunfire from the *U-123's* deck guns. The U-boat then torpedoed a nearby Latvian freighter, killing two of her thirty-two crewmen and leaving her sinking. The *U-123* returned to finish off the wounded *Malay*, hitting her with its last torpedo, then headed east for home. The Norwegian tanker *Kosmos II* tried unsuccessfully to ram the fleeing U-boat as it escaped.

The tanker *Malay*, although damaged by cannon fire and the torpedo, survived the attack with the loss of only four of her thirty-four crewmen. The Latvian freighter was abandoned by her crew and floated northward for several days before finally sinking somewhere off Oregon Inlet.

1955 Department Store Magnate, Paul H. Rose

On January 19, 1955, Paul Howard Rose, founder of the chain of Rose's discount department stores, died at age seventy-three.

Born in 1881 in Seaboard, Rose discovered his knack for merchandising early on. At age twelve he set up a wooden packing crate outside his hometown pharmacy and sold bundles of wood, his mother's homemade cookies, and other items. After attending business school in Virginia, Rose opened a store in Littleton. At times his capital was so limited he used empty shoeboxes to help fill the shelves. For a time Rose worked as a traveling salesman, using that experience to educate himself about competitive pricing strategies.

Rose partnered with two businessmen, purchased stock in United 5 & 10 Cent Stores, and opened retail outlets in Henderson and Charlotte. The venture failed, but in 1915 Rose borrowed $500, bought a shop in Henderson and opened the first Rose's. A novelty at the time, Rose innovatively removed merchandise from behind counters (where it had to be retrieved by stock clerks) to shelves that shoppers could peruse at their own pace. The entrepreneur eventually operated 280 Rose's stores in eleven southeastern states.

Postcard showing Main Street in Oxford, and featuring Rose's 5–10–25 cent store, between 1915 and 1930.

1779 Old Bute County, One for the History Books

On January 20, 1779, the North Carolina General Assembly abolished Bute County less than 15 years after establishing it the northeastern county in June 1764 and naming it in honor of John Stuart, Third Earl of Bute.

A Scottish nobleman, Bute was the tutor of Great Britain's Prince George. After the prince became King George III in 1760, Bute served as the king's advisor and eventually became prime minister.

Carved from eastern Granville County, Bute County provided the residents of the area better access to local government. In 1766 the legislature expanded the county by annexing part of northwestern Northampton County.

By the late 1760s, though, the Earl of Bute had become very unpopular with Americans. Many blamed him personally for instituting the 1765 Stamp Act. With Bute County's population growing, support for dividing and renaming the county grew during the mid-1770s. After two years of discussion, the General Assembly decided to divide Bute County along Shocco Creek, with the northern part becoming Warren County and the southern part, Franklin County.

With the incorporation of those two new counties, Bute County ceased to exist. The courthouse that once served that county no longer stands.

JAN 20

An accurate Map of North and South Carolina With Their Indian Frontiers, Shewing in a distinct manner all the Mountains, Rivers, Swamps, Marshes, Bays, Creeks, Harbours, Sandbanks and Soundings on the Coasts, with The Roads and Indian Paths; as well as The Boundary or Provincial Lines, The Several Townships and other divisions of the Land in Both the Provinces; the whole from Actual Surveys by Henry Mouzon and others, 1775.

1840 Launch of Public Schools in North Carolina

On January 20, 1840, North Carolina's first public school opened in Rockingham County.

The Common Law of 1839 authorized counties to hold elections in which voters might vote for or against taxes for public schools. During the elections in late 1839, sixty-one of the sixty-eight counties that were then in existence voted to support school taxes. The remaining seven counties soon followed course. By 1846 every county had at least one public school.

Notice of the opening of the Rockingham school first appeared on February 1, 1840, in the *Greensborough Patriot* and was reprinted the same month in the *Raleigh Standard*. The story did not specify the location of the school but did indicate that the county had been divided up into districts, with more schools to be completed shortly.

Tradition holds that the first school was located in the present Williamsburg community in the southeastern part of Rockingham County, but we may never know the precise location of the first school.

1854 Furnifold Simmons, Democratic Power Broker

On January 20, 1854, Furnifold Simmons, a major nineteenth and twentieth century politico, was born near Pollocksville in Jones County. Simmons would become famous for his five terms in the U.S. Senate and his dominance of the Democratic political machine that then held sway in state politics.

After graduating from what is now Duke University in 1873, Simmons moved to Goldsboro and then to New Bern to practice law. He was elected to his first political position, the U.S. House of Representatives, in 1886. He lost his first bid for reelection to Henry P. Cheatham, an African American.

As the chairman of the Democratic state executive committee in 1892, and again from 1898 to 1907, Simmons gained statewide political prominence and power. He was deeply involved in engineering the white supremacy campaigns of 1898 and 1900.

In the U.S. Senate Simmons was largely responsible for the creation of Fort Bragg during World War I and for the construction of the Intracoastal Waterway. In 1928 he drew national attention for his outspoken opposition to the presidential candidacy of Democrat Alfred E. Smith of New York, favoring Herbert Hoover. He was defeated in the Democratic primary in 1930, largely because he chose not to support Smith.

1881 — Burnt Swamp Association, Set Up in 1881 to Serve American Indians

On January 21, 1881, the elders of three churches met at Burnt Swamp Baptist Church in Robeson County to form what became the Burnt Swamp Baptist Association.

The formation of the group solidified what had been a strong, informal relationship. Burnt Swamp Baptist was founded in 1877 by twenty Lumbee Indians. They received encouragement from two local white Baptist churches, Raft Swamp and Clyburn. Prior to Burnt Swamp's organization, impromptu religious meetings and revivals had been held for two decades, but no organized religion was available to the community.

At their 1885 meeting, Association members resolved to adopt Burnt Swamp Indian Association of the Croatan Indians as their official name, the first in a series of name changes over the years. After years of struggling to gain acceptance, the Association was admitted to the Baptist State Convention in 1929.

The Association was instrumental in the effort to develop schools for Indians in Robeson and surrounding counties. In 1887 members helped organize Croatan Normal School, the forerunner of the University of North Carolina at Pembroke.

Today the Association includes Indian churches in nine counties in North Carolina and South Carolina, as well as in Baltimore. The Association now consists of sixty-nine churches and a mission. The tribal groups represented include the Haliwa-Saponi, Lumbee, Pee Dee, Coharie, Waccamaw-Siouan, and Tuscarora.

1891 — Poached Oysters No Delicacy for Governor Fowle

On January 21, 1891, Gov. Daniel Fowle declared "war" on northern fishermen poaching on North Carolina's deep-water oyster beds. The oyster "pirates" had already depleted the Chesapeake Bay's rich oyster beds during the 1880s. In an effort to meet seafood canneries' growing demands, they had moved their dredging operations into North Carolina.

In 1888 several dredging vessels from Virginia had gathered thousands of bushels of oysters weekly from Hyde County's waters. The following year North Carolina banned non-resident dredging, but there was little enforcement. In 1890 Carteret, Hyde, and Pamlico Counties tried unsuccessfully to oust the oyster pirates using local patrol boats.

Then, in early 1891, a small fleet of illegal oyster schooners were reported in the oyster beds of Pamlico Sound and off the coasts of Hyde and Dare counties. Governor Fowle and the General Assembly quickly passed legislation to stop the out-of-state dredgers and halt the shipping of North Carolina oysters to northern markets.

Fowle sent an armed patrol boat into Pamlico Sound to seize or sink any illegal oyster dredgers. Within three months the oyster "war" was over. Only the captain and crew of one ship were ever taken to trial.

1959 — Lamar Stringfield and the North Carolina Symphony

On January 21, 1959, Lamar Stringfield, the first conductor of the N.C. Symphony, died in Asheville. Raised in Raleigh, Stringfield was the sixth of seven children. His father, O. L. Stringfield, helped establish Meredith College.

After attending college at Mars Hill and Wake Forest, Lamar Stringfield left school in 1916 to join the army. Returning home from tours of duty in Mexico and France, he began serious training in music, both in North Carolina and in New York.

In 1928 Stringfield completed his symphonic suite From the Southern Mountains. Known thereafter as an authority on southern ballads and folklore, Stringfield organized the Institute of Folk Music at the University of North Carolina in 1930 and collaborated with Paul Green on "The Lost Colony Songbook." In 1932 Stringfield helped organize the North Carolina Symphony, which was then headquartered in Chapel Hill. He served as the symphony's conductor from 1932 to 1938.

After his tenure as conductor, Stringfield moved often, residing in Charlotte, Mars Hill, Burnsville, Barnardsville, and Asheville. He remained active as a composer and served as guest conductor for major symphony orchestras across the country.

Lamar Stringfield in the 1930s.

Sheet music and lyrics of the *Star Spangled Banner* (*background*).

JAN 22

1816 Canova Selected to Sculpt George Washington Statue in State Capitol

On January 22, 1816, Thomas Jefferson responded to a letter from North Carolina Congressman Nathaniel Macon seeking a recommendation for a sculptor to create a statue of George Washington for the North Carolina State Capitol. With no hesitation Jefferson named Italian Antonio Canova, "...for 30 years, within my own [knowledge], he has been considered by all Europe as without a rival." Jefferson further recommended that the rendering of the statue be that of a Roman soldier.

The finished sculpture, which arrived in 1821, cost $10,000 and received acclaim nationwide for its beauty and workmanship. An elaborate dedication ceremony was held, and the statue remained in the rotunda of the State Capitol, where in 1825 it was viewed by the Marquis de LaFayette.

When the Capitol burned in 1831, the Carrara marble sculpture was shattered. Pieces were saved and for several years attempts were made to restore the statue. In 1908 an original model of the Washington sculpture was found in the Canova Museum in Italy, and Italian authorities allowed a plaster replica to be made. In 1970 a marble reproduction of the original Canova sculpture was placed in the rotunda of the 1840 State Capitol. It still greets visitors today.

1828 Medical Pioneer Edward Warren

On January 22, 1828, Edward Warren, surgeon general of North Carolina and senior medical officer to the Egyptian khedive, was born in Tyrrell County.

After earning his medical degree, Warren practiced medicine briefly alongside his father before departing for Paris, where he continued his studies. He returned to North Carolina in 1855 but soon left for a professorship of medicine at the University of Maryland.

At the outbreak of the Civil War, Warren again returned to North Carolina to serve the Confederacy. He held numerous appointments throughout the war years, including chief medical officer of Confederate naval forces in North Carolina, medical director of the Confederate Department of the Cape Fear, and surgeon general of North Carolina.

In 1875 Warren accepted the position of chief of medicine for the Egyptian khedive, who occupied a position similar to a governor in the American system. As a result of his own medical issues, Warren left Africa for Paris in 1877 and established a practice in France, where he remained until his death in 1893. An avid writer, Warren left a library of works, ranging from poetry to medical articles concerning the use of hypodermic medication.

1834 Justice for Edgecombe County Slave

On January 22, 1834, Will, a slave belonging to James Battle of Edgecombe County, killed a white man, resulting in the *State v. Will* case, in which the North Carolina Supreme Court protected slaves from a charge of murder when acting in self-defense.

The day started with an argument between Will and a slave foreman named Allen over the possession of a hoe. Tempers flared and Will broke the hoe before going to work at a nearby cotton mill. After learning of Will's behavior, Richard Baxter, Battle's overseer, set off on horseback with his gun. Allen followed with his whip. Confronted by Baxter, Will attempted to flee but was shot in the back. Wounded and running for his life, Will was overtaken. Armed with a knife with poison on the blade, Will fought off Baxter. A deep knife wound to Baxter's arm proved fatal.

After looking at the evidence, Battle believed that Will acted in self-defense and hired two prominent lawyers to insure that Will received justice. The case was appealed to the state Supreme Court, which ruled unanimously that any slave under such provocation could be charged only with manslaughter. This challenged the 1829 *State v. Mann* decision which held that a master's power was absolute.

1919 Littleton College Victim to 1919 Fire

On January 22, 1919, fire consumed a majority of the buildings on the campus of Littleton College in Halifax County. No lives were lost, but the devastation was so complete—damages exceeded $50,000—that the owner could not raise the money to rebuild, and the school closed.

Originally opened in January 1882 as the for-profit Central Institute, the school received a legislative charter that same year. It was conceived as a place for "the intellectual, moral, and religious development and training of young ladies." The all-female institute was affiliated with the Methodist Church.

The institute's first principal was Reverend James Manley Rhodes, himself a graduate of Trinity College. In 1887 Rhodes left the institute for another female college but returned in 1889. Upon his return, Rhodes purchased the college property from the original stockholders. In the intervening year, 1888, the charter had been amended to change the name of the school to Littleton Female College. Rhodes created a two-year program that included such courses as chemistry, physics, stenography, languages, and history. In 1912 the word "Female" was dropped from the name.

Tragically, the fire occurred at the height of the school's popularity.

Littleton Female College student body in 1905.

1844 Renaissance Man William Gaston

On January 23, 1844, William Gaston died. A poet, politician, and lifelong student of the law, Gaston was a leading figure in nineteenth century North Carolina politics. After growing up in New Bern and attending New Bern Academy, he graduated from Princeton in 1798 and was admitted to the bar later that year. In 1800 he transitioned from law to politics, serving in both houses of the General Assembly and in the U.S. House of Representatives.

In 1833 Gaston was appointed to the state Supreme Court, where he championed the abolitionist cause, though he himself was a slaveholder. A Catholic, he helped guide the Constitutional Convention of 1835 to a provision that eliminated a long defunct law prohibiting Catholics from holding public office.

In his twilight years Gaston remained a court justice while occasionally embarking on the lecture circuit. An eloquent speaker and prolific writer, he was often asked to deliver commencement speeches and was popular among philanthropic societies.

Gaston is perhaps best known for his poem "The Old North State," which he penned in 1840. It was later set to music and adopted as the state song in 1927. Gaston County, the city of Gastonia, and Lake Gaston are all named in his honor.

1866 North Carolina Buys Artificial Limbs for Confederate Amputees

On January 23, 1866, the General Assembly passed a resolution asking Governor Jonathan Worth to contract with a manufacturer of artificial limbs to fulfill the needs of the state's Confederate amputees.

North Carolina thus became the first former Confederate state to offer artificial limbs to amputees. The state contracted with Jewett's Patent Leg Company, and a temporary factory was set up in Raleigh. A system was developed whereby the amputees incurred no out-of-pocket expenses in visiting Raleigh for prosthetic fittings.

During the five years that the state operated the artificial limbs program, 1,550 Confederate veterans contacted the state for help. According to records in the State Archives, the artificial-limb program cost the state over eighty-one thousand dollars. After defeat, the loss of thousands of lives, and economic ruin, the state's citizens still had the ability to achieve something noble by repaying, to a degree, those who had literally risked life and limb.

1898 Whatever Happened to Randolph Scott?

On January 23, 1898, Hollywood icon Randolph Scott was born.

Raised in Charlotte, Scott excelled in sports, especially baseball, football, and swimming. After serving in World War I as an artillery observer with the Army, he enrolled at the Georgia Institute of Technology where he played football until an injury caused him to withdraw. He returned to his home state to attend UNC but did not graduate.

Scott worked for a time in his father's accounting firm, but by 1927 he had become interested in acting and moved to Los Angeles. Tall, lanky, and handsome, he worked steadily, primarily, but not entirely, in westerns.

Though it took him nearly 10 years to work his way into A-level movies, he remained a popular star until he retired in 1962. His very name evokes the western film genre.

Scott married twice, briefly to heiress Marion du Pont, and then to Patricia Stillman, with whom he adopted two children. He often returned to North Carolina to visit family and, following his death in 1987, was buried in Elmwood Cemetery in Charlotte.

1950 Light Returns to Cape Hatteras Beacon, 1950

On January 23, 1950, after a 14-year hiatus, the Cape Hatteras Lighthouse once again shone its beacon over the Atlantic Ocean to warn mariners of the dangers of Diamond Shoals. The 208-foot tower had been abandoned because of the encroaching sea, and its signal was temporarily replaced by a light atop a steel structure, known as the skeleton tower, built near the lighthouse site.

At the time of its construction in 1870, the iconic black and white-striped lighthouse was 1,500 feet from the ocean. The lighthouse was constantly at risk from the quickly receding shoreline, but several measures were taken to keep it safe. During the 1930s a Civilian Conservation Corps crew constructed sand dunes and planted grasses that helped to build up the shoreline in the area. Construction of groins, placement of sand bags, and installation of artificial seaweed offshore were also tried at the time, but by 1936 waves had reached the structure's base, forcing the Lighthouse Service to close it.

After being restored in 1950, the lighthouse was threatened once again by the Atlantic during the 1980s, when waters came within 200 feet of its red brick base. Because of its historical and cultural significance, several options for preserving the structure were discussed by scholars, public officials, and lighthouse lovers. After much debate, the 2,800-ton lighthouse was moved 2,900 feet from the shore in 1999.

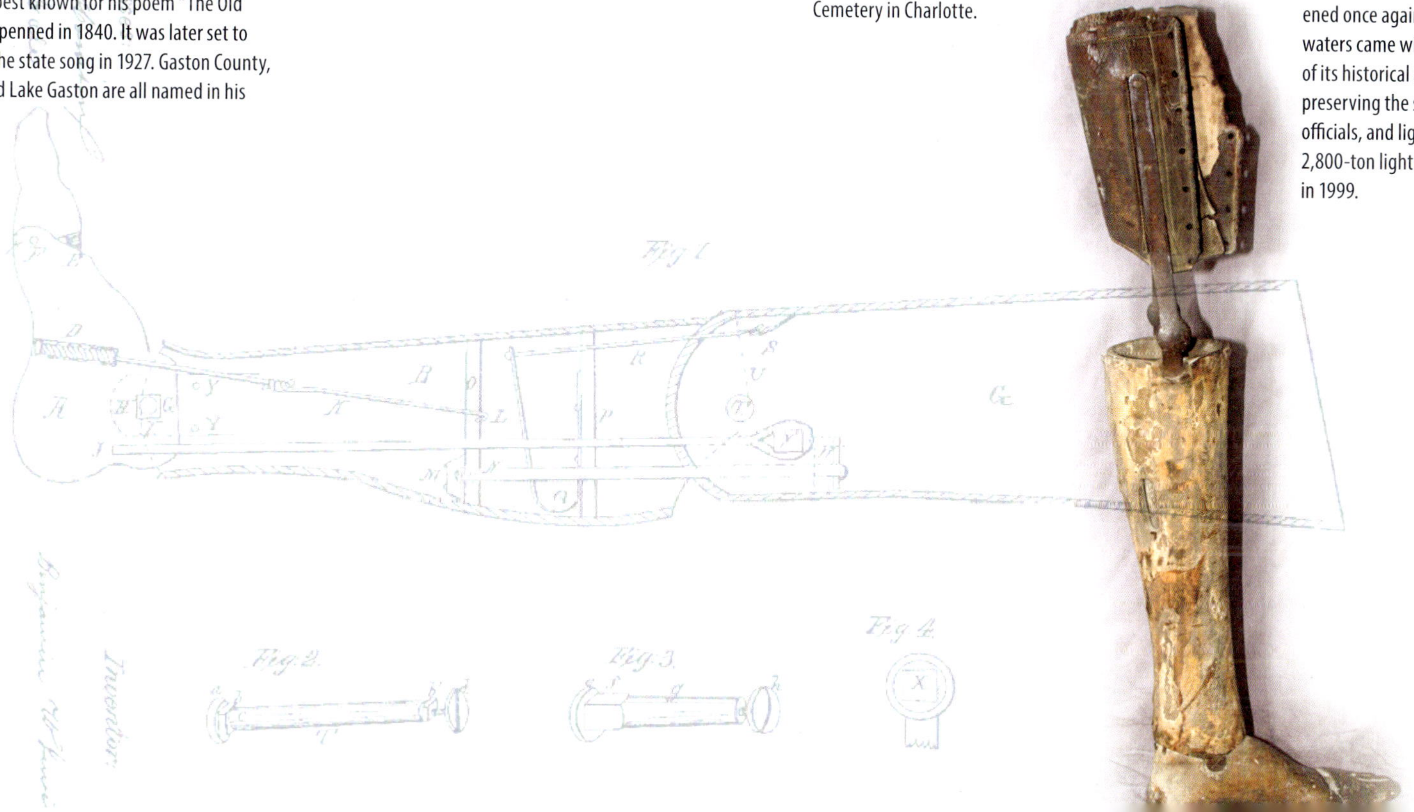

Artificial leg patent.

JAN 24

1759 The 1759 Enfield Riot, Precursor to the War of the Regulation

On January 24, 1759, a group of men from Halifax and Edgecombe Counties rode to Francis Corbin's house in Edenton and seized him during the night. The men were upset because Corbin had extorted money from them when collecting rents for Lord Granville, who controlled the land on which they lived.

Corbin was taken to Enfield, where he was held in jail with his co-conspirator Thomas Bodley. The pair were forced to pay a bond as a guarantee to appear in court in the spring and agree to new rules governing rent and tax collection. They further promised not to sue their captors. During the court session Corbin and Bodley were released after they promised to return all illegal fees and taxes they collected.

Though Corbin eventually was removed from office by Lord Granville, the Colonial Assembly investigated the incident, now called the "Enfield Riot," and punished some of the "rioters" severely, imprisoning several. In response, sympathizers and friends broke the imprisoned out of jail.

Modern historians consider the actions of the Halifax citizens to constitute foreshadowing of the War of the Regulation.

1961 Broken Arrow Incident in Wayne County

On January 24, 1961, a B-52G Stratofortress Bomber carrying two nuclear weapons crashed in rural Wayne County, ten miles northeast of Seymour Johnson Air Force Base. At the height of the Cold War, United States policy was to keep armed aircraft in the air at all times in the event of a conflict.

Internal structural damage had begun inside the right wing during refueling. During preparation for landing at Seymour Johnson, major structural failure of the right wing occurred, and the aircraft exploded at 8,000 feet. Three of the eight-man crew were killed.

As a result of the breakup of the plane, two nuclear weapons were released. Seven of the eight arming, fusing, and firing switches and devices in one bomb automatically actuated. Only a crew-controlled switch prevented a nuclear detonation. Since its parachute deployed, one bomb had only minor damage when it fell about a mile from the crash site. The second bomb fell free, without its parachute deploying, and broke apart on impact.

Because safety interlocks on the weapons failed, having gone through all of the steps to detonate except one, the Goldsboro incident, historians believe, was one of the closest near-disasters of the Cold War.

Photos from the Broken Arrow Incident in Faro, N.C.
Photographs courtesy of the United States Air Force.

1788 Secession Leader Weldon Edwards

On January 25, 1788, Weldon Edwards was born in Northampton County. Though not as ambitious or well-known as many contemporaries, the "venerable Democrat" was a major player in nineteenth century North Carolina politics. His political career extended from the close of the War of 1812 into the Reconstruction era.

After two terms in the state House, the 28-year-old Edwards succeeded his kinsman Nathaniel Macon in his U.S. House seat. After his retirement from the Congress in 1827, Edwards represented Warren County in the state Senate for ten terms. In 1835 he served in the state Constitutional Convention.

An outspoken advocate of Southern nationalism, Edwards was elected president of the Secession Convention that met in Raleigh in May 1861. He presided over that body four times, through May 1862. Edwards "hailed with delight the prospect of separation from the Northern people, whom he despised," according to historian Samuel A. Ashe.

Edward's passion was his Warren County plantation, "Poplar Mount." There he experimented with scientific agriculture, breeding livestock, and cultivating tobacco. He died and was buried at "Poplar Mount" at age eighty-five. Today his house is gone, but outbuildings, trees, and his grave remain.

1942 NFL Star Carl Eller Born in Winston-Salem

On January 25, 1942, Carl Lee Eller, a former professional football star and North Carolina Sports Hall of Fame member, was born in Winston-Salem. Twenty years later, as a University of Minnesota sophomore, he helped lead the Gophers to a 21-3 Rose Bowl victory over UCLA.

The 6-foot, 6-inch, 247-pound defensive standout was a first-round draft pick of both the Minnesota Vikings (NFL) and the Buffalo Bills (AFL) in 1964. Eller signed with the Vikings and for the next fourteen seasons was the left end of a ferocious defensive line often referred to as "The Purple People Eaters." During that time the Vikings won the 1969 NFL championship, claimed three National Football Conference crowns, and played in four Super Bowls.

Extremely quick and mobile for his size, Eller, or "Moose," as he was often called, was one of the most honored defensive players of his time. He was selected to play in six Pro Bowls and earned the George Halas Award as the NFL's leading defensive player in 1971. He finished his career with a single season with the Seattle Seahawks in 1979. Eller was inducted into the North Carolina Sports Hall of Fame in 1991 and elected to the Pro Football Hall of Fame in 2004.

Carl Eller, ca. 1966.

1946 Advocate for African Culture, Orishatukeh Faduma

On January 25, 1946, noted educator Orishatukeh Faduma died in High Point.

Born in the South American country of Guyana to freed slaves from West Africa, Faduma settled in Sierra Leone while he was still in elementary school. Educated there by missionaries, Faduma was baptized with the name William James Davies.

Through his years of teaching and study in Europe, Africa, and America, Faduma became known as a linguist, educator, author, and minister. Interested in political issues and social causes, he was a proponent of African heritage and culture, as evidenced in both his work with the Dress Reform Society, which advocated wearing traditional African garb rather than western jackets for comfort in the African climate, and his adopting the name Orishatukeh Faduma.

From 1895 to 1912, Faduma was pastor and principal at Peabody Academy in Troy, a school for black children founded by the American Missionary Society. Afterwards, he returned to Sierra Leone and taught for a few years before coming back to North Carolina, where he was a professor of Latin, English Literature, and Modern History at Lincoln Academy in Kings Mountain.

Faduma finished his career at the Virginia Theological Seminary and College in Lynchburg, Virginia.

1990 Acclaimed Beauty Ava Gardner, Pride of Grabtown

On January 25, 1990, Johnston County native and world-famous actress Ava Gardner died in her London apartment.

Born on a Grabtown farm, Gardner moved around North Carolina as a child, graduated from high school in Wilson County, and began a program in secretarial studies at what is now Barton College.

Discovered by chance after her brother-in-law posted a photograph in the window of his New York City studio, Gardner was offered a contract with MGM Studios. Since her mother would not allow her to head to Hollywood alone, both Gardner and her sister moved to the West Coast in 1941.

Appearing in mostly minor and nonspeaking roles during the first five years of her career, Gardner saw her profile raised significantly after her 1946 performances in *Whistle Stop* and *The Killers*. She went on to make at least 55 movies, including *On the Beach* (1959), *The Night of the Iguana* (1964), and *Earthquake* (1974). She also achieved notoriety for her marriages to Mickey Rooney, Artie Shaw, and Frank Sinatra.

Gardner moved to Spain in 1955 to escape constant hounding from the press; after nearly a decade there she moved to London, where she spent the final years of her life.

Ava Gardner

JAN 26

1823 Hackney Name Synonymous with Transportation

On January 26, 1823, Willis Napoleon Hackney was born in Nash County. An obituary reported that he began life with no money, but Hackney eventually entered the wagon manufacturing business in Wilson and launched a family dynasty that became synonymous with transportation in North Carolina for nearly a century.

Although his origins are largely unrecorded, sometime around 1854 Hackney became a partner in a Wilson carriage shop with C. L. Parker. He later developed his own business, which was taken over in 1903 by his sons George and W. D. and incorporated as Hackney Wagon Company.

The Hackneys manufactured wagons and carriages from the days of wooden plank roads in the nineteenth century to the development of paved highways in the twentieth. They supplied thousands of wagons to the U.S. military during World War I and would go on to manufacture school buses, refrigerated transportation equipment, and a variety of parts.

Hackney's sons and his grandson Thomas were involved in transportation manufacturing enterprises in Wilson and Washington, North Carolina, that would carry on the Hackney name in various incarnations.

1826 Governor Benjamin Smith Dies a Pauper

On January 26, 1826, former governor Benjamin Smith died. Before becoming governor Smith was elected to state constitutional conventions and the state House and Senate, were he served as Senate Speaker for two terms.

When the University of North Carolina was chartered in 1789, Smith was named a trustee and donated twenty thousand acres of land in present-day Tennessee to the school as an endowment. In 1789 he purchased the tract at the mouth of the Cape Fear River that came to be known as Smith Island. Smithville (now Southport) was established and named in his honor in 1792.

Smith was elected governor in 1810. He served a single term, declining to stand for reelection. Following his governorship he returned to Brunswick. His once enormous wealth, however, was increasingly ravaged by financial misfortunes, personal extravagance, and long-term debt obligations. Over the years Smith had several residences in Brunswick County at Orton, Smithville, and Belvedere. Much of Smith's personal correspondence is marked "Belvedere." It was there that he entertained President George Washington in 1791.

Smith died a pauper in 1826. Initially buried at Smithville, he was later interred in the churchyard of St. Philips at Brunswick Town.

1918 Lilliputian Golf Rooted in Pinehurst

On January 26, 1918, James Barber and his wife gave a garden tea and held a short-course golf tournament for the local ladies of the Advertising Golf League. According to the following week's edition of the *Pinehurst Outlook*, which termed the game "Miniature Golf" in its headline, the course could be "negotiated with a well pitched mashie shot, and bends and curves calling for nice and discriminating slices and pulls."

As with standard golf, the date and location of the invention of miniature golf remains the subject of debate. The Sandhills golf mecca, Pinehurst, is widely believed by many to be the ancestral home of miniature golf in the United States, and the January 1918 game may be one of the first mini golf games played in the country.

Barber, a wealthy New Jersey shipping magnate, built one of the country's first, if not the earliest, "Lilliputian" golf courses at his Pinehurst home. Called "Thistle Dhu," by its owner, the course was constructed sometime between 1916 and 1918. It was designed by amateur architect Edward H. Wiswell and was located on the west side of the Barber's stately mansion amidst its formal gardens.

2002 Loonis McGlohon: North Carolina Was His Home

On January 26, 2002, noted pianist and composer Loonis McGlohon died. Born in Ayden in 1921, he grew up listening to big band music and learning the piano from the church organist. After graduating from East Carolina University, McGlohon moved to Charlotte, where he began working for WBTV, first with a jazz show. He moved up to become the station's music director and producer, among other positions there.

McGlohon is perhaps best known for forming the Loonis McGlohon Trio, which recorded more than two dozen albums and toured the world. His compositions include "The Wine of May" and "Songbird" and have been recorded by scores of performers including Frank Sinatra, Tony Bennett, Judy Garland, and Rosemary Clooney.

An ardent advocate of his home state, McGlohon collaborated with journalist Charles Kuralt on *North Carolina is My Home*, a symphonic work with narration and vocals that has been distributed as a recording, public television broadcast and video, and a coffee table book.

In recognition of his songwriting, McGlohon was honored in 1998 with a tribute at New York's Lincoln Center, where many of the artists who had played with him and sung his songs made appearances. He was inducted into the North Carolina Music Hall of Fame in 1999.

Two Horse Ice Wagon

1778 Death of Governor William Tryon in England, 1788

On January 27, 1788, William Tryon, royal governor of both North Carolina and New York, died. Born in England, Tryon was not formally educated but was boosted by family connections. A professional soldier, he was first commissioned a lieutenant in 1751 and rose through the ranks thereafter.

Tryon was appointed lieutenant governor of North Carolina in 1764 and moved to the colony with his family that year. He assumed the duties of governor in 1765 upon Arthur Dobbs's death. Tryon erroneously believed that the colonists would not object to a tax levied to erect a capitol and governor's residence. The assembly appropriated funds and authorized Tryon to oversee the project, which quickly exceeded the budget.

Some North Carolinians felt that injustices in the colony, including the tax for "Tryon's Palace," corrupt officials ,and lack of representation for the backcountry, needed change. They formed a resistance group known as the Regulators. After several defiant incidents, a special session of the assembly was called, which only caused further agitation. Tryon led militia into the backcountry in 1768 and 1771, defeating the Regulators in the 1771 Battle of Alamance. While on the expedition, Tryon was notified of his transfer to the governorship of New York.

1931 Salisbury's Cheerwine, A Favorite Across the Piedmont

On January 27, 1931, Cheerwine inventor Lewis D. Peeler died in Salisbury.

Born in 1866, Peeler studied at a local Lutheran college and in Virginia before entering business. He tried his hand at a number of different enterprises, including farming and wholesaling, before beginning a soda business in 1913. That year Peeler and other Rowan County businessmen started a bottling franchise with Mint Cola in the basement of his store on Council Street near the train depot in Salisbury.

In 1917 Peeler formed the Carolina Beverage Corporation, using a cherry flavor derived from oil of almond to produce a beverage that used less sugar due to rationing concerns. The sparkling soda, named "cheer" for pleasure and "wine" for its deep red color, inspired the slogan "For health and pleasure."

The company was renamed Piedmont Cheerwine Bottling Company in 1924 to increase brand recognition throughout North Carolina, and Peeler first registered the Cheerwine trademark in 1926. The next year he started another bottling company in Charlotte, which was sold to Sun-Drop Bottling in 1976.

Peeler was active in other businesses throughout his life, becoming manager of the Yadkin Hotel in 1926 and serving as director of the First National Bank of Salisbury.

1993 Gentle Giant Andre Roussimoff Settled in Ellerbe

On January 27, 1993, Andre the Giant, world-famous wrestler and Richmond County resident, died in France.

Born Andre Roussimoff in Grenoble, France in 1946, he suffered from acromegaly, a result of a pituitary disorder that caused his body to over-produce growth hormones. He grew to be 7'4" and 500 pounds. At seventeen Andre moved to Paris, where he was discovered by a wresting promoter. He trained and worked hard at the sport. He enjoyed success in several countries and in a variety of personae before moving to the United States.

In the U.S. he became "Andre the Giant," an immovable force who debuted at Madison Square Garden in 1973. Soon a fan favorite, he was one of the most recognized wrestlers in the business. Andre took advantage of his size when he branched out into acting in the 1970s. He appeared in several television shows, including *The Six Million Dollar Man*, *B. J. and the Bear*, and *The Fall Guy*. His most celebrated role, and his personal favorite, was as Fezzik in the 1987 hit movie *The Princess Bride*.

Andre retired to a ranch in Ellerbe in the south central part of the state, where he enjoyed a peaceful life. His ashes were scattered there after his death.

JAN 27

"Andre the Giant" visiting the Rankin Museum in Ellerbe, N.C. during the late 1980s.

JAN 28

1934 Fire Suppression Stymied at Wrightsville Beach, 1934

On January 28, 1934, a devastating fire destroyed much of Wrightsville Beach, including the legendary Oceanic Hotel.

Just after noon that Sunday, smoke poured out of the Kitty Cottage, a boarding house on the north end of the island. In less than three hours more than one hundred buildings were leveled as the westerly wind took the fire from building to building via wooden-shingled roofs. The handful of permanent residents and the tiny volunteer fire department formed bucket brigades and pushed carts laden with hoses through the sand, but with no fire hydrants it was a lost cause.

Once the wind shifted to the southwest, the flames roared to more than fifty feet high and were so hot they could be felt on Harbor Island, between Wrightsville and the mainland.

The Wilmington Fire Department was called to assist, but with no vehicular bridge to the island, the heavy equipment was placed onto a trolley and, once on the island, sank into the sand as the wooden boardwalks had been burned as well. All that was left on the north end of the island were chimneys, iron bed frames, and dead crabs littering the beach.

1986 Beaufort Native Michael Smith Died in Shuttle Explosion

On January 28, 1986, the Space Shuttle Challenger exploded just 73 seconds after its 11:38 a.m. launch from Kennedy Space Center in Florida.

The seven crew members, including the pilot, U.S. Navy Capt. Michael John Smith of Beaufort, North Carolina, died in the disaster. Investigators later determined that cold weather caused a seal in the craft's right solid rocket booster to fail, allowing pressurized hot gas from the solid rocket motor to reach the external fuel tank. The spacecraft broke apart and disintegrated in a plume of white smoke over the Atlantic Ocean.

The fatal mission (Flight STS-51L), which was to have deployed two satellites into orbit, had received much media attention because it marked the first time a civilian, high school teacher Christa McAuliffe, was allowed to travel in space. After the disaster NASA suspended shuttle flights for two years. The Challenger's remains were recovered from the ocean floor nearly two months after the explosion. Captain Smith was buried in Arlington National Cemetery on May 3, 1986. There is a monument to Smith on the waterfront in Beaufort, and the town's Michael J. Smith Airport is named in his honor.

Challenger crew photo from NASA. Crew members of mission STS-51L stand in the White Room at Pad 39B following the end of the Terminal Countdown Demonstration Test (TCDT). *Left to right*: Mission Specialist, Ellison Onizuka, Teacher in Space Participant, Sharon "Christa" McAuliffe, Payload Specialist, Gregory Jarvis, Mission Specialist, Judy Resnik, Commander, Dick Scobee, Mission Specialist, Ronald McNair, and Pilot, Michael Smith.

1829 Justice John L. Taylor and the Beginnings of the N.C. Supreme Court

On January 29, 1829, John Louis Taylor, the first North Carolina Supreme Court chief justice, died. Born in England, Taylor moved to America when he was twelve. He attended William and Mary College but was unable to complete his studies due to financial problems. He moved to Fayetteville, where he was admitted to the bar in 1788 at age nineteen.

Taylor practiced law in Fayetteville and was appointed to the General Assembly in 1790. In 1798 the Assembly appointed him a judge of the superior courts. By that time he had moved to New Bern. For the following two decades he served as a judge and in 1811 was appointed by all other state superior court judges as their "chief justice." Accordingly, he sold his New Bern properties and moved to Raleigh, where he built his residence, "Elmwood," in 1813.

When the North Carolina Supreme Court was established in 1818, Taylor was elected its first chief justice. Three years later he opened a private law school at his home. Although not a college graduate, he served as a trustee for the University of North Carolina and was awarded an honorary law degree by Georgetown University.

1901 George H. White Delivers "Phoenix" Address

On January 29, 1901, North Carolina Congressman George H. White delivered his now-famous farewell address. White was the fourth of four African Americans to represent North Carolina's Second District in the United States Congress in the late nineteenth century.

He obtained a law license in 1879 and served in the North Carolina House of Representatives and the Senate before being elected to the first of two four-year terms as district solicitor for the Second Judicial District. White moved to Tarboro to run for office in what was known as the "Black Second" Congressional District. Elected in 1896 and 1898, he was the only black representative in Congress at the time. He was attentive to local issues and appointed many blacks in his district to federal positions.

After the passage of legislation disfranchising black voters, White declined nomination to a third term, saying "I can no longer live in North Carolina and be treated as a man." In his farewell speech he stated that "Phoenix-like he (the negro) will rise up some day and come again (to Congress)."

White was the last black member of Congress for twenty-eight years and the last black Southerner in the body until 1973. North Carolina did not see another African American in Congress until Eva Clayton took her seat in 1992.

1920 Nantahala National Forest, Conservation Landmark

On January 29, 1920, President Woodrow Wilson issued a proclamation establishing the Nantahala National Forest.

The area that is now Nantahala has a long history. Explored by early naturalists William Bartram and Andre Michaux, the forest initially included lands in Georgia and South Carolina in addition to those in North Carolina. When the national forests were reorganized in 1936 to follow state boundaries, Nantahala's boundaries were changed to cover more than 500,000 acres in Macon, Jackson, Transylvania, Graham, and Swain Counties adjacent to the Great Smoky Mountains National Park.

Nantahala is the largest of North Carolina's four national forests and features a number of notable attractions, including the Appalachian and Bartram Trails; Whitewater Falls near Cashiers, which are the highest falls east of the Rocky Mountains; and the Joyce Kilmer-Slickrock Wilderness, famous for its 400-year-old trees. Nantahala and the nearby Pisgah National Forest attract more than five million visitors each year.

The name Nantahala comes from the Cherokee language and means "land of the noonday sun."

Portrait of George Henry White, United States Congressman from the Second District of New Bern, Craven County, N. C. (1897–1901).

Entrance to Nantahala National Forest near Sylva, N.C., 1943.

JAN 30

1871 Gov. Holden's Impeachment Trial Began

On January 30, 1871, Gov. William Woods Holden's impeachment trial began. The only Chief Executive in North Carolina history to be impeached and removed from office (and the first in the nation), Holden was a central figure in the state's Civil War and Reconstruction era.

Holden was the editor of the *North Carolina Standard*, a Democratic newspaper based in Raleigh, and used the paper to help lead Zebulon B. Vance to victory in the gubernatorial race of 1862. In 1864 Holden ran against Vance and suffered a humiliating defeat.

On May 20, 1865, President Andrew Johnson appointed Holden provisional governor, though he lost the election to the seat that fall. He made a final bid for governor in 1868 and attained his goal. Vowing to destroy the Ku Klux Klan, he made several decisions that led to racial violence and the imposition of martial law in Alamance and Caswell Counties, effectively ending his political career. Notified that he had been impeached by the House of Representatives, Holden turned the duties of his office over to Lt. Gov. Tod R. Caldwell on December 20. Holden's trial lasted nearly three months. On March 22, 1871, the North Carolina Senate ordered Holden removed from office.

1940 Freakish Weather Alarms Eastern North Carolina, 1940

On January 30, 1940, an iceberg was spotted offshore at Salter Path.

A Works Progress Administration (WPA) worker reported that the iceberg was the size of a small island, extending six feet above the surface of the ocean and moving on a westerly trajectory. Others reported that at Atlantic Beach ice floes had piled up so high in the Bogue Sound at the Atlantic Bridge that gulls were landing on them.

The Harkers Island ferry had to break through ice to continue its run, and a man in Beaufort pulled frozen fish from the water. He got the surprise of his life when he returned from fetching a knife to find that they had thawed and were still alive.

That January had been so cold that the *Beaufort News* declared it the "Ice Age." Temperatures, though cold, were not at record levels. The thermometer dipped down to eighteen degrees on January 20 and to sixteen degrees on the 27th and 28th, though it did rebound to a balmy twenty-one degrees on the 29th. Farther north at Lake Mattamuskeet, so many birds were stranded by the ice-bound conditions that they had to be fed by the superintendent.

1951 J. P. Knapp, Publisher, Outdoorsman, and UNC Benefactor

On January 30, 1951, publisher and conservationist Joseph Palmer Knapp died.

A native of New York, born in 1864, Knapp was the publisher of *Collier's* magazine. His American Lithographic Company pioneered the use of color in newspaper inserts and on baseball cards distributed with tobacco. That connection led to his acquaintance with James B. Duke and the Tar Heel State.

An avid sportsman and co-founder of what became Ducks Unlimited, Knapp settled in Currituck County, where he built a thirty-seven room mansion that would remain his residence from November to April for the rest of his life.

Though a part-time resident, Knapp became a generous member of the community, donating to the local schools. In 1947, at the urging of Governor Gregg Cherry, he extended his generosity to the entire state via a gift of 250 thousand dollars to survey school needs.

Once in North Carolina Knapp also began a correspondence with Albert Coates, founder of the Institute of Government at UNC. Coates persuaded Knapp to fund the construction of a permanent home for the institute. Knapp did not live the see the building completed. After his death, the institute's foundation transferred funds to be matched by the state for the construction.

1956 Ice Hockey's Southern Debut

On January 30, 1956, professional ice hockey debuted in North Carolina.

A week earlier, a fire destroyed the home arena of the Baltimore Clippers, an Eastern Hockey League team. Charlotte representatives convinced the team to play five of their remaining home games at the Charlotte Coliseum. The Clippers' Charlotte debut, in which they played the New Haven Blades, drew 10,363 people to the 9,500–seat venue, with more than three thousand being turned away at the gate. An article in the *Charlotte Observer* described the response: "Thousands of people who didn't know a goalie from a dasher board lined up their cars a mile or so on Independence Boulevard and all the other streets around the Coliseum, trying to get into the place."

The crowd sang *Dixie* before the opening face-off and cheered the Clippers on to a 6–2 victory. The city's enthusiastic response prompted the Clippers to relocate to Charlotte permanently the following season, and they soon changed their name to the Charlotte Checkers. Hockey historian Jim Mancuso calls the relocation of the Clippers "the birth of professional hockey in the South" and credits it with paving the way for the expansion of other hockey leagues into the southern market.

1878 — The Sinking of the *Metropolis*

On January 31, 1878, the vessel *Metropolis* struck the shoals one hundred yards from the beach at Currituck, halfway between two lifesaving stations.

Built in 1861 and originally called the *Stars and Stripes*, the ship was outfitted for naval service in September 1862 and saw action during the Battle of Roanoke Island later that year. The ship was refitted for freight and passenger service but eventually fell into disrepair, rendering it inadequate for the lengthy trips.

Nonetheless, a Philadelphia company chartered the *Metropolis* to transport workmen and supplies to Brazil to build a railroad January 1878. By the time the ship reached the Chesapeake Bay, the cargo was shifting dangerously, causing seams in the hull to leak. On January 31 at 6:45 a.m., the ship hit the shoals. Alarms were sounded and heroic efforts mounted, but to no avail. Of the 245 passengers aboard, eighty-five died in the wreck.

The wreck of the *Metropolis*—combined with that of the USS *Huron* two months earlier— captured the attention of Congress and prompted it to authorize construction of new life-saving stations.

1890 — A Trust to Bust: American Tobacco Company Organized, 1890

On January 31, 1890, the American Tobacco Company was incorporated, creating the world's largest tobacco conglomerate. Driving the creation of this industrial giant was James B. "Buck" Duke of the Durham-based W. Duke, Sons & Co.

Facing tough competition from another Durham-based smoking tobacco firm, W. Duke had decided in 1881 to enter the cigarette business. By leasing newly invented cigarette-rolling machines from the Bonsack Company of Virginia, launching elaborate advertising campaigns, and acquiring many smaller competitors, W. Duke had become one of the nation's top tobacco companies by 1890.

Joining with W. Duke that year to form American Tobacco were Allen & Ginter, W. S. Kimball & Company, Kinney Tobacco and Goodwin & Company. Under James Duke's leadership, American Tobacco grew to monopolize the tobacco market, and in 1907 federal regulators filed an anti-trust suit against the corporation. After much litigation the U.S. Supreme Court ordered it dissolved in 1911.

Duke helped reorganize American Tobacco into three companies: a much smaller American Tobacco, Liggett and Myers Tobacco Company, and P. Lorillard Company. During the 1970s and 1980s American Tobacco began acquiring a variety of non-tobacco products. It renamed itself American Brands in 1986 and later became Fortune Brands.

1921 — The Carroll A. Deering, "Ghost Ship"

On January 31, 1921, the impressive five-masted commercial schooner *Carroll A. Deering* was found wrecked on Diamond Shoals off Cape Hatteras. At the time she was returning to Newport News from a trip to Brazil. Built in 1919 by the G. G. Deering Company in Bath, Maine, the ship was among the last wooden schooners built before their eclipse by iron shipbuilding.

Two days before the discovery of the wreck, the Cape Lookout Lighthouse keeper reported seeing the ship. On the morning of the 31st, the Coast Guard discovered the foundered boat, apparently abandoned.

When the seas calmed four days later and the Coast Guard was able to reach the ship, it was clear the vessel had indeed been abandoned—the crew and their navigational equipment, belongings, documents, and lifeboats were all gone, but interestingly dinner was on the stove, and the captain's cabin was a mess. A few months later the ship was hauled from the rocks and dynamited so it wouldn't be a hazard to mariners in the area.

The mysterious circumstances of the wreck became the subject of investigation, which included a visit to Dare County by the FBI. Various explanations for the wreck surfaced, including the effects of the Bermuda Triangle, Bolshevik pirates, and mutiny. All of these explanations were discredited by investigation, and the cause remains a mystery.

JAN 31

American Tobacco Company plant and offices, ca. 1920s.

1889 Streetcars Debut in the Land of the Sky in 1889

On February 1, 1889, the first streetcar in North Carolina made its debut in Asheville. The first line extended from Pack Square down Biltmore Avenue and Southside Avenue, then was routed west of present-day McDowell Street to a train depot.

The system's roots can be traced to one year prior, when the city authorized a charter for an electric railway that would include lines from Pack Square to various sections of the city. E.D. Davidson, who had designed a Canadian horsecar railway, agreed to build the system in collaboration with Frank Sprague, who engineered the streetcar system in Richmond.

After the initial launch a number of railway companies organized and built streetcar lines to emerging neighborhoods and outlying areas, including the Sulphur Springs resort and Biltmore Village. By 1907 Asheville led the state in streetcar traffic, carrying three million passengers, compared to Charlotte and Wilmington with two million each. By 1915 the street railway reached its peak, operating forty-three cars on eighteen miles of track, including one to the newly opened Grove Park Inn and the surrounding upscale neighborhood.

The system ceased operation in 1934, when it was supplanted by buses.

1960 Landmark Lunch Counter Protest in Greensboro

On February 1, 1960, four African American college students sat down at the lunch counter at Woolworth's Department Store in downtown Greensboro and asked to be served. They were refused, thus launching the sit-in movement that would spread throughout North Carolina and the South. The four freshmen from North Carolina A&T State University who initiated the first sit-in were Ezell Blair Jr. (later known as Jibreel Khazan), Franklin E. McCain, Joseph A. McNeil, and David L. Richmond.

Sit-ins by college students during the next several months forced the integration of businesses in the region. Local media attention led to national coverage, and similar sit-ins began elsewhere in the country, sparking a national call to battle by civil rights activists who endorsed the nonviolent form of protest to demonstrate society's inequities for blacks.

In April 1960 the Student Nonviolent Coordinating Committee, an outgrowth of the sit-in movement, organized at Shaw University in Raleigh. The sit-ins and demonstrations throughout the South slowly led to changes in local attitudes. Nationally, the ultimate consequence of these and other protests was passage of the Civil Rights Act of 1964 and the Voting Rights Act of 1965, both of which assured the legal rights of blacks.

FEB 1

This monument provides a larger-than-life portrayal of Jibreel Khazan (then known as Ezell Blair Jr.), Franklin McCain, Joseph McNeil and David Richmond, four N.C. A&T students who became known as the "Greensboro Four" for their sit-in at Woolworth's department store in 1960. The figures are depicted walking out of Woolworth's after their protest. Photograph courtesy of Dell Upton.

Daring Raid Nets Union Vessel in 1864

Newport Barracks Contested in 1864

On February 2, 1864, Confederate troops engaged the men of the Ninth Vermont Infantry at the Newport Barracks in Carteret County.

The Seventh Regiment North Carolina Infantry built the barracks south of Newport for quarters in the winter of 1861 and 1862. Shortly thereafter the cluster of log huts was captured by Union troops, who added a hospital, headquarters, stables, storehouse, and earthworks. Newport Barracks effectively became a Federal supply depot, since it was located near both the Atlantic Ocean and railroad tracks.

In January 1864, two thousand Confederate troops under the command of Gen. James G. Martin advanced from Wilmington toward Morehead City to support Gen. George E. Pickett's mission to regain control of New Bern. They reached the barracks on February 2. Company D of the Second Massachusetts Heavy Artillery, stationed inside Newport Barracks, prematurely abandoned their posts and retreated as the Confederates advanced. The commander of the Ninth Vermont, after setting fire to the depot, followed suit. The fleeing troops also burned the railroad and road bridges.

The skirmish was largely indecisive, though Martin's men managed to capture thirty Union troops and gather some supplies and equipment from the barracks before they were destroyed. When the Confederate troops learned of Pickett's failure at New Bern, they returned to Wilmington.

On February 2, 1864, the 325-ton federal steamer USS *Underwriter* was captured at New Bern in a well-executed pre-dawn raid.

Led by Cmdr. John Taylor Wood, the raid involved fourteen boats carrying 250 sailors and marines stealthily making their way down the Neuse River from Kinston. Those participating in the mission had been selected from crews of Confederate vessels at Richmond, Wilmington, and Charleston.

The Confederates boarded the *Underwriter* and, following fierce hand-to-hand combat, took control of the gunboat, capturing many of her officers and crew. Fourteen men were killed in the melee, five Confederate and nine Union, including the *Underwriter's* commander.

Because the *Underwriter's* fires were low, the ship did not have enough steam to power it, rendering its capture almost pointless. The Confederates set her afire and headed back up the Neuse River under Union fire from batteries on land, taking the prisoners with them. As the victors made their way away from the burning *Underwriter*, they heard a terrific explosion when fire reached the vessel's arsenal.

The loss of the *Underwriter* late during the Civil War proved that areas under heavy Union occupation were not impenetrable to Confederate raids.

Deep Creek and Thomas's Legion

On February 2, 1864, Union Maj. Francis M. Davidson and the Fourteenth Illinois Cavalry engaged in a skirmish with Thomas's Legion, led by Col. William Holland Thomas, on Deep Creek near Quallatown in modern Haywood County.

Accounts differ as to what occurred that morning, but Union forces apparently surprised the Confederates and overran them. On the Union side two men were killed and another six wounded, while Thomas most likely lost ten killed and thirty-two captured. Eighteen of the Confederates taken prisoner were Cherokee. The captives were imprisoned in Knoxville, where all of the Cherokee took the oath of allegiance to the Union in early March. The event was a turning point in Cherokee allegiance to the Confederacy.

The affair at Deep Creek undermined Thomas's recruiting efforts among the Cherokee. The event coincided with internal conflicts, skyrocketing food prices due to inflation, a harsh winter, and an increase in starvation among Indian families. Thomas attempted to assuage the food shortages by purchasing grain from South Carolina. Nonetheless, the raids into western North Carolina, such as that at Deep Creek, led to the desertion of the Eastern Band from the Confederate cause.

FEB 2

The attack and capture of the USS *Underwriter*.

1834 Wake Forest Institute Opens

On February 3, 1834, Wake Forest Institute opened with an initial enrollment of sixteen students. The school's first building, a simple provincial house, was the home of Dr. Calvin Jones, a founder of the Medical Society of North Carolina, officer in the War of 1812, and long-time trustee of the University of North Carolina.

Jones sold his plantation at Wake Forest to the Baptist State Convention, which established the school. By the end of 1834, seventy-two students were in attendance. The dwelling house was used as the residence of the first president of the college, Samuel Wait, and for classrooms. The carriage house was used as a chapel. Seven former slave cabins—well-made but without windows—were used as dormitories.

In 1946 the trustees of the Z. Smith Reynolds Foundation offered the school, by then Wake Forest College (it became Wake Forest University in 1967), generous funding to move to Winston-Salem. The State Baptist Convention accepted the offer, and construction began in that city in 1951. The original Wake Forest campus was sold to the Southeastern Baptist Theological Seminary in 1956.

The original house, restored it to its 1830s appearance, is now operated as part of the Wake Forest College Birthplace Museum.

FEB 3

1881 Steamboat "Mountain Lily" Plied the French Broad

On February 3, 1881, entrepreneurs chartered the French Broad Steamboat Company, with the objective of ferrying passengers and freight along that river from Asheville to Horse Shoe to Brevard.

Six months later they christened the frame, ninety-foot-long, two-deck excursion boat the *Mountain Lily*. Like its eastern North Carolina counterpart, the CSS *Neuse*, a few years later the *Mountain Lily* met its fate not far from where it was constructed.

Many at the time and since have regarded the venture as folly. The French Broad is a low-volume river that can barely float low draft vessels in any season. In the years before the launch, federal funds had permitted the removal of debris and stumps, which helped make the project more viable.

On August 2 a champagne bottle was broken on the prow of the steamboat, gleaming white with green trim and sporting two staterooms each with a capacity of one hundred. Supporting the vessel were two twelve-horsepower motors. The crowd and brass band enjoyed a barbecue; the captain rang the ship's bell in celebration.

The dream was short-lived. Four years later the ship ran aground and was abandoned. Salvagers used the lumber to construct Riverside Baptist Church in Horse Shoe, where they installed the bell. The two engines were re-purposed to serve local sawmills.

1983 Henry Frye, First African American on the N.C. Supreme Court

On February 3, 1983, Henry Frye was sworn in as North Carolina's first African American Supreme Court Justice. Governor Jim Hunt appointed Frye an associate justice. Then in 1999, in another first, Hunt named Frye to the unexpired term of retiring Chief Justice Burley Mitchell. After Frye lost his electoral bid for a full term as chief justice in 2000, he retired, having served on the state's top tribunal for more than 17 years.

Frye has led a remarkable life. Born the son of a Richmond County farmer in August 1932, he graduated with top honors from North Carolina A&T State University and became a U.S. Air Force captain. Despite his education and service, he was told he had failed the required literacy test when he returned home and attempted to register to vote in 1956. The experience inspired him to become a lawyer.

In 1968 Frye became the first African American elected to the North Carolina General Assembly in the twentieth century. The first bill he introduced was a constitutional amendment abolishing the literacy test. Frye eventually served six terms in the state House and one term in the state Senate before he began his judicial career.

1993 Revered Cherokee Elder, Maggie Axe Wachacha

On February 3, 1993, Maggie Axe Wachacha, Beloved Woman of the Cherokee, died at age 101 in Murphy.

Born in 1894 in Snowbird Gap in Graham County, Wachacha learned to write the Cherokee language as a seven-year-old and, by the time she was ten, was beginning to master midwifery and healing skills her mother and grandmother had already mastered.

In 1935, at age forty-one, Maggie Axe married Jarrett Wachacha, a great nephew of Cherokee leader, Junaluska. For more than forty years she served as the clerk of the Cherokee Tribal Council, while also acting as a midwife and healer. The Wachachas had to walk more than fifty miles from their home to town for each meeting of the council.

In 1986 Wachacha was named one of one hundred American Heroes by Newsweek and received a Distinguished Women of North Carolina Award. She was given the revered Cherokee title of Beloved Woman in 1978.

Throughout her life Wachacha was an indefatigable teacher and promoter of the Cherokee culture, well known for her efforts to preserve and teach the Cherokee language and for her extensive knowledge of traditional foods and plants.

Henry Frye being sworn as a North Carolina Supreme Court Justice in 1983.

1944 — Annie O'Berry, New Deal Administrator

On February 4, 1944, Annie Land O'Berry, administrator of the North Carolina Emergency Relief Administration (NCERA) and president of the Rural Rehabilitation Corporation, died while undergoing treatment for an illness. Born in Edgecombe County in 1885, she lived on the family farm there until she was sent to live with her sister in Littleton after her parents' deaths.

She graduated first in her class from what is now Peace College in Raleigh and went to live with her brother in Kinston. Active in civic organizations and the North Carolina Federation of Women's Clubs, O'Berry demonstrated leadership that garnered the attention of Gov. Angus McLean, who appointed her to the Commission to Study County Government and the North Carolina Historical Commission. In 1930 she was named vice-chair of the state executive committee of the Democratic Party.

In 1933 O'Berry was tapped to lead NCERA, one of the few women to administer a state emergency relief agency. As head of NCERA, she provided relief to many citizens through direct aid and employment. She remained in charge of NCERA's off-shoot, the Rural Rehabilitation Corporation, which provided loans to farmers, until her death.

1946 — Clubwoman and Suffrage Leader Cornelia Jerman

On February 4, 1946, women's suffrage leader Cornelia Petty Jerman died. At the time of her death, the Raleigh *News & Observer* called her the "State's First Woman."

Born in Moore County near Carthage, Jerman moved to Raleigh shortly after her marriage in 1898. She became active in city's social life and was very involved with the Woman's Club of Raleigh and state and national organizations of women's clubs.

Jerman's social involvement soon became political. She helped organize the Raleigh Equal Suffrage League, served as president of the North Carolina Suffrage League, and lobbied the General Assembly extensively for women's right to vote and other causes. She also helped organize and served as president of the Raleigh League of Women Voters.

Becoming active in Democratic Party politics after 1920, Jerman campaigned for Al Smith and Franklin D. Roosevelt in 1928 and 1932, respectively, and was appointed to a position with the federal Internal Revenue Service in Greensboro. She worked in a number of other capacities before her death in 1946.

Annie O'Berry, in an undated portrait.

1805 White Cherokee Chief W.H. Thomas Born

On February 5, 1805, William Holland Thomas, white chief of the Eastern Band of Cherokee Indians, state senator, and Confederate colonel was born in Haywood County.

Thomas was adopted by Yonaguska, principal chief of the Cherokee. He studied the law, became the tribe's attorney in 1831, and was instrumental in arranging for the Oconaluftee Cherokees to remain in North Carolina. In 1839 Thomas was appointed chief. For the next two decades he acted as an advocate for Cherokee rights, stating, "The Indians are as much entitled to their rights as I am to mine."

Thomas was elected to the state senate in 1848 and went on to serve six terms. In 1861 he persuaded the Eastern Band to support the Confederacy. By 1863 he commanded Thomas's Legion, a unit that consisted of two battalions of both white and Cherokee soldiers.

After the war Thomas's personal life began to collapse. He was declared insane in March 1867 and confined to Dorothea Dix Hospital. In 1887 he aided Smithsonian Institute researcher James Mooney in gathering information about the Cherokee. Six years later he died in the Broughton Hospital in Morganton. Thomas's unusual life story was fictionalized by Charles Frazier in his 2006 novel *Thirteen Moons*.

FEB 5

1944 Dunn Favorite Son, General William C. Lee

On February 5, 1944, William Carey Lee, the "Father of the Airborne," suffered a heart attack that ended his military career.

Born in Dunn in 1895, he volunteered for the United States Army during World War I. After the war he remained in the army and was assigned in 1939 to the Chief of the Army's office in Washington, D.C. There he became part of a maverick group of army officers advocating for the development of an airborne army infantry force.

The Army authorized the development of a test platoon of paratroopers and placed Lee in charge. When the Amy raised two airborne divisions, Lee received command of the 101st. He oversaw its development and training and was instrumental in getting airborne and glider operations going at Camp Mackall and Laurinburg-Maxton Army Air Base.

The inclusion of the airborne divisions in the Normandy Invasion in June 1944 was a direct result of Lee's work. Nevertheless, he was unable to participate due to a heart attack, but the members of the 101st Division, the Screaming Eagles, were ordered to yell the name "Bill Lee" as they departed their transports over France in the early morning hours of D-Day.

Lee died in 1948 and is buried in Dunn.

1832 Long Route to Roanoke River Lighthouse

On February 6, 1832, Elizabeth City congressman William Shepard petitioned the House of Representatives for a light station to help guide sailors to safety by the mouth of the Roanoke River.

Two years later Congress appropriated $10,000 for a lightship to operate on the Albemarle Sound. The ship operated through the Civil War but was replaced by a screw-pile lighthouse that operated on whale oil in 1867. That structure, in turn, was damaged by fire and ice in the 1880s.

A larger lighthouse, the one that currently stands, was authorized in 1886 and finished by 1887. It was fitted with a Fresnel lens and continued to operate until 1941, when it was decommissioned by the Coast Guard.

The 1886 Roanoke River Lighthouse changed hands twice in the 1950s, sold for ten dollars each time. Edenton businessman Emmett Wiggins moved the structure to land he owned in the Chowan County town in 1955 and lived in the building until his death.

In 2007 the Edenton Historical Commission purchased the lighthouse and restored it in cooperation with the state of North Carolina. The restored lighthouse opened to the public as part of Historic Edenton State Historic Site in 2012.

Roanoke River Lighthouse

1963 The General Assembly Moves to Jones Street

On February 6, 1963, the General Assembly met in the Legislative Building on Jones Street for the first time. The Assembly had previously met in the State Capitol—now a state historic site—on Union Square since 1840.

As space became increasingly crowded in the State Capitol, a commission was formed in 1957 to acquire land, create plans, and expend funds for the construction of a new building for North Carolina's legislative branch. Architects Edward D. Stone, John Holloway, and Ralph Reeves drew up plans for the building, and bids were received by the end of 1960.

Construction began in early 1961 and was finished by early 1963. The building required more than ten thousand cubic yards of concrete and nearly 150 thousand masonry blocks to complete. The 206 thousand square-foot building also has nearly two miles of water piping and more than fifty-one miles of electrical wire. The building cost about $5.5 million to construct, which translated to about $1.24 for each citizen of North Carolina at the time.

1971 The Wilmington 10 and Firebombing of Mike's Grocery

On February 6, 1971, Mike's Grocery, a mom-and-pop store in Wilmington, was firebombed and burned. It is unclear who was responsible for the arson, which came after a week of increasing racial tension and violence over the desegregation of the city's high schools.

Demanding fairer treatment and a black studies curriculum, black high school students, led by civil rights activist Ben Chavis, began a boycott of classes in late January 1971. The protesters established headquarters at a local church, which became the epicenter of violence after the school board rejected their demands. A racist organization attacked the church in drive-by shootings, and gunfire and arson ensued in the area. Police killed a student protester, and a white supremacist was also killed as he took aim at the church.

About a year later local and state authorities, intent on punishing Chavis, arrested him, eight black high school students, and a white anti-poverty worker on charges related to the arson at Mike's Grocery.

Despite the lack of real evidence tying them to the arson, the prosecutor secured guilty verdicts by using perjured testimony and illegally excluding blacks from the jury. The case garnered national press attention, and in 1976 Amnesty International became involved in an effort to free the Wilmington 10.

Key witnesses recanted their testimony in the late 1970s, and investigatory pieces by *60 Minutes*, the *New York Times*, and others suggested evidence had been fabricated. The Soviet Union even cited the Wilmington 10 as an example of American political imprisonment when Pres. Jimmy Carter criticized that country for that practice in 1978.

The convictions of the Wilmington 10 were ultimately overturned by the U.S. Court of Appeals for the Fourth Circuit in 1980. Gov. Beverly Perdue issued them pardons in 2012.

2010 Swain County's "Road to Nowhere"

On February 6, 2010, Swain County's six-mile "Road to Nowhere" was officially abandoned by the federal government.

The road—called Lakeview Drive—dates back to the 1940s when the federal government and the Tennessee Valley Authority took over land in Swain and Graham Counties and flooded it as part of the Fontana Dam and Great Smoky Mountains National Park projects. The government promised it would build a thirty-mile road to help make up for the loss of access to the area caused by the closure of Highway 288, which was flooded. Shortly after construction began, the project stalled due to environmental issues. Although funding for the work was appropriated later, the road never came to fruition, largely because the cost of its construction was so high.

In February 2010 the National Park Service paid Swain County $52 million, the approximate cost of fulfilling the government's promise in that year, as a substitute for actually finishing the drive. To this day Lakeview Drive provides some of the best views of Fontana Lake, the Tuckasegee River, and the surrounding landscape.

1847 Wilmingtonian Casualty of Mexican War

On February 7, 1847, New Hanover County native Capt. John Henry King Burgwin died of a wound he received while leading an assault during the Taos Revolt, an insurrection of Mexicans and their Pueblo Indian allies against the American occupation of what is now New Mexico.

Earlier that month troops under the command of Col. Sterling Price found rebels holed up in a heavily fortified chapel at Pueblo de Taos. After a fruitless day of artillery fire on the chapel, Burgwin's First Dragoons were ordered to storm it. Burgwin was shot in the chest after having set fire to part of the structure. He lived long enough to see the insurrection quelled but died in Taos of his injury.

Fort Burgwin was established near Taos, N.M. in 1852. The fort, never considered permanent, was utilized during some of the Indian campaigns but was ultimately abandoned by the U.S. military in 1860.

Some of the structures were reconstructed to become the Fort Burgwin Research Center, now a part of Southern Methodist University. There was also a Confederate camp in Wilmington named in Burgwin's honor.

Although his remains were exhumed several times, he is now at rest in Wilmington's Oakdale Cemetery.

1862 Battle of Roanoke Island Commenced in 1862

On February 7, 1862, Federal ships bombarded Fort Bartow, part of the Confederate defenses on Roanoke Island. One of three Confederate earthen forts on the west side of the island, Fort Bartow mounted nine guns. The other two garrisons were Fort Huger and Fort Blanchard.

The three forts were designed to protect the mainland from Federal invasion and to complement obstructions placed in the channel. Of the three forts Bartow was the only one actively engaged in what would become known as the Battle of Roanoke Island.

That battle's first shot was fired from Bartow's guns, and the fort was subsequently bombarded by the Federal fleet for seven hours. The Confederate fleet, under Capt. W. F. Lynch, waited to engage the Federals behind a line of obstructions placed in the Croatan Sound to delay the Federal advance.

After a sharp engagement ended only by darkness, the Confederates were forced to retire due to lack of ammunition. The next day the Union army won the Battle of Roanoke Island, which gave the Federals control of the North Carolina Sound region.

1978 The Power of Flour, Graham's Biscuitville

On February 7, 1978, the Graham-based fast food chain Biscuitville filed to register a trademark for the first time.

Now based in Greensboro, the chain got its start as Pizzaville in 1966, when former flour salesman Maurice Jennings began selling take-out pizzas from two bread and milk stores that he owned in Burlington. The chain expanded to six stores across the Triad region and southern Virginia.

The chain first started selling biscuits to supplement its income and drive more traffic in the morning, and the first biscuit-only store opened in Danville, Virginia, in 1975. Eventually all the chain's Pizzaville locations were converted to Biscuitville stores.

Biscuitville moved its headquarters from Graham to Greensboro in 2007 and today operates more than fifty stores in North Carolina and Virginia. It is still owned by the Jennings family.

FEB
7

The Burnside expedition landing at Roanoke Island, February 7, 1862.

1898 Coleman Manufacturing Company, Landmark African American Business

On February 8, 1898, Warren Coleman and his associates laid the cornerstone for the nation's first black-owned cotton mill in Concord.

Congressman George H. White, himself a civil rights pioneer, was the main speaker at the event. The company represented the first major cooperative effort by North Carolina's African American businessmen.

Coleman was the son of Rufus Barringer, a Confederate general, and Roxanna Coleman, a slave. From meager beginnings he rose to become the wealthiest black man in the state by the 1890s after starting a combination barber shop and candy store and parlaying his success with that enterprise into a large real estate and mercantile business.

With his statewide contacts and a belief in the self-help philosophy of Booker T. Washington, Coleman assembled partners from the state's "black elite" to start the mill. James Walker Hood, John C. Dancy, and Edward A. Johnson were among the men he asked to join him in the project. The company also had white backers, including tobacco magnates Julian Carr and Benjamin Duke.

At its peak the mill employed 300 black workers. Industry-wide economic troubles forced Coleman to resign from the company in December 1903, and Benjamin Duke foreclosed on the mortgage the next year.

Later a section of the mill built by Coleman was operated as a subsidiary of Cannon Mills Company, headquartered in nearby Kannapolis.

1944 WAC Lieutenant Colonel Westray Battle Boyce Long—A Proud North Carolinian

On February 8, 1944, Westray Battle Boyce Long was promoted to lieutenant colonel and became the first WAC to receive the Legion of Merit. Few North Carolina men, and no Tar Heel women, had a more distinguished service record in World War II than Lieutenant Colonel Boyce. In August 1942 she entered training for the Women's Army Auxiliary Corps, which became a part of the Army in September 1943, when the name was changed to the Women's Army Corps (WAC).

In 1943-44 Major Boyce served on Gen. Dwight D. Eisenhower's staff with command over WACs in North Africa. In 1945 she was appointed director of the WAC. Once the war ended, factions within the military split over the WAC's future, but General Eisenhower and Lieutenant Colonel Boyce, who oversaw demobilization, advocated a continued female Army presence. In 1948 the remaining women became a part of the regular Army or Reserves. Boyce retired in March 1947 due to health reasons.

A petite woman with gray hair, Boyce was nicknamed "Webbie." She took pride in her Tar Heel ancestry, keeping portraits and photographs of Battle relatives in her office. She is buried in a family plot near Rocky Mount.

1948 Designer Alexander Julian and Carolina Style

On February 8, 1948, designer Alexander Julian was born in Chapel Hill.

His father owned a menswear boutique, Julian's, downtown near the UNC campus. Growing up visiting and later working in the store, young Julian took a natural career path.

Julian often describes the moment that men's fashion clicked with him. He'd torn the collar of his blue oxford shirt at school and stopped in at his dad's shop to get the tailor to fix it. But instead of a mend, he asked that the collar of a yellow shirt be sewn on. He says he has been designing ever since.

Julian's first store was in Chapel Hill near his father's, but he moved to New York in 1975. There he expanded into producing cloth, furniture, and home goods.

In the late 1980s Julian designed the original, signature teal and purple uniforms for the Charlotte Hornets. In 1990 Dean Smith asked him to update the uniforms for his Tar Heel team.

At age thirty-three Julian became the youngest inductee into the Fashion Hall of Fame. He has won five Coty Awards, the highest honor in the fashion industry. His furniture design garnered him the Pinnacle Award.

Julian has moved his headquarters back to his hometown.

1949 Merci Train, Symbol of Franco-American Friendship

On February 8, 1949, North Carolina's Merci Train car, filled with gifts of gratitude from French citizens, arrived in Raleigh. The French train, with forty-nine cars—one for each state at the time, plus one for Washington, D. C. and the territory of Hawaii to share—was sent in response to the American Friendship Train. That train was sent to France by the United States the previous year and consisted of seven hundred boxcars filled with relief supplies.

The French train cars, built between 1872 and 1885, were designed to hold either forty men or eight horses each—thus their nickname, the "Forty and Eights." The boxcars had been used during both World Wars to transport troops.

North Carolina's boxcar, filled with hundreds of gifts, was received officially in Raleigh by Gov. Kerr Scott. The occasion was festive, with a ceremony and parade to welcome the unusual offering. Following the ceremony many of the gifts, ranging from toys to textiles, from household items to valuable artifacts, were kept at what is now the North Carolina Museum of History. Others were distributed around the state to libraries, school, and other museums.

Today the Merci Train boxcar is restored and on exhibit at the North Carolina Transportation Museum in Spencer.

Lieutenant Colonel Westray Battle Boyce Long in Germany *(left photo, center person)*, 1946.

Portrait of Lieutenant Colonel Westray Battle Boyce Long, undated photograph *(right)*.

1739 Explorer and Artist William Bartram

On February 9, 1739, William Bartram, America's first native-born naturalist, was born near Philadelphia. In 1761 Bartram moved to Bladen County, where his uncle owned a plantation called "Ashwood" on the Cape Fear River. He opened a store and spent his free time exploring the flora and fauna of the region.

Bartram, demonstrating his significant artistic talent, provided patrons in England drawings of American plants and animals as early as 1753. In 1773 John Fothergill, a London physician and proprietor of the largest botanical garden in England, commissioned Bartram to travel through the southeast collecting objects of natural history. That March he set out on the trip outlined in his book, *Travels through North and South Carolina, Georgia, East and West Florida*.

While on his travels in May 1776, in what is now the Nantahala National Forest, Bartram encountered a Cherokee band led by chief Attakullakulla. In his writings Bartram described not only the flora and fauna but also the native Indians, cataloging forty-three towns and villages of the Cherokee nation. He returned to Philadelphia in 1777 after his expedition. His book *Travels*, published in 1791, became the most important description of the southeastern United States during the eighteenth century.

FEB 9

1956 At Point Guard, from Rocky Mount, Phil Ford

On February 9, 1956, basketball legend Phil Ford was born in Kannapolis.

Ford was raised in Rocky Mount, where he graduated from high school in 1974. As a point guard at UNC-Chapel Hill, he led the basketball team to four NCAA tournaments. Ford's accolades during his college career were many. In 1978 he capped off his senior year by winning the coveted John R. Wooden Award, given annually to the country's most outstanding college basketball player. He graduated that year with a degree in business administration.

Ford was the number two pick in the 1978 NBA draft, going to the Kansas City Kings. The following year he was named NBA rookie of the year. During the course of his career, Ford also played professionally for the New Jersey Nets, Milwaukee Bucks, and Houston Rockets.

He was inducted into the North Carolina Sports Hall of Fame in 1991.

Phil Ford at the free throw line at Cameron Indoor Stadium, Durham, 1978.

1854 Noted Educator, Prohibitionist and Civil Rights Leader Joseph C. Price

On February 10, 1854, African American orator and teacher Joseph C. Price was born in Elizabeth City. In 1863 his family moved to New Bern, where he was enrolled in St. Andrew's School. Price, though late in beginning his formal education, made exceptional progress. After completing his own education, he taught in Wilson, becoming the principal at a school there in 1871, but within a few years he returned to school to prepare for the ministry in the A.M.E. Zion Church.

In 1881 Price distinguished himself as an orator, speaking on prohibition and later on education and race issues. On a speaking tour in Europe, Price raised nearly ten thousand dollars to establish a college for blacks in North Carolina. With the additional support of Salisbury residents, he became president of Zion Wesley College (now Livingstone College) in 1882. Price gained national attention while there. In 1890 he was elected president of the Afro-American League and the National Equal Rights Association.

Price's promising life ended abruptly in 1893 after he contracted Bright's disease, a condition affecting the kidneys. He was buried in a mausoleum on the campus of Livingstone College.

Joseph C. Price

1885 The Lumbees and the Road to Recognition

On February 10, 1885, the Indians now known as Lumbees were legally recognized by the General Assembly. The act designated the tribe as Croatan, which reflected the idea of the time that the group was descended from the settlers of the "Lost Colony."

For many years the government pushed the Indians of the Robeson County region to declare themselves either white or African American, but for the Indians state recognition grew critical when the schools became racially segregated in the 1870s. In order for their children to attend public schools, the Indians had to deny their heritage. There were no public schools for Indians.

State recognition led the county to establish a three-part school system, with schools at all levels for the Indians. In 1887 the legislature also established the Croatan Normal School to educate Indian teachers. That school is now known as the University of North Carolina at Pembroke.

Struggling with its own identity and with federal recognition, the tribe adopted a number of names over the years, finally settling on Lumbee. The name comes from the Lumber River, which winds its way through the Indians' traditional homeland.

Lumbee homecoming parade, 1979 (*background*).

1937 Seventies Performer Roberta Flack, Native of Black Mountain

On February 10, 1937, Grammy Award-winning singer, songwriter, and pianist Roberta Flack was born in Black Mountain.

The daughter of two pianists, Flack herself began playing piano at age nine and was heavily influenced by the sound and style of gospel music. She graduated from high school at fifteen and later received a bachelor's degree in music education from Howard University. The unexpected death of her father in 1959 prompted Flack to enter the field of education in order to support her family. Her first teaching job brought her to Farmville, where she taught English and music at an African American school.

Flack continued to pursue music on the side and secured her big break in 1968 when jazz pianist Les McCann sent a copy of one of her performances to Atlantic Records. Flack released her first studio album, *First Take*, with Atlantic Records in 1969. The album initially failed to chart, but subsequent exposure of her music on television and in film pushed Flack to the top of the Billboard 200 and garnered a Grammy in 1972.

Flack won four Grammy awards and her 1973 album *Killing Me Softly* was certified double platinum.

1962 Champion Miler, Jim Beatty of Charlotte

On February 10, 1962, Jim Beatty became the first man to run the mile indoors in less than four minutes.

Born in New York in 1934, Beatty moved to Charlotte with his family when he was four years old. Growing up in the Dilworth neighborhood, he delivered the *Charlotte Observer* for five years. Focused on boxing, the young Beatty decided to start running his paper route to help him train.

Beatty convinced his high school's track coach to let him try running the mile during the last meet of his junior year, discovered his speed, and won the race. In the course of a month he went from never having run a race to winning the state championship in the mile. He went on to run track at UNC-Chapel Hill, where he was a six-time All-American in track and cross country.

Beatty moved to California, where in 1961 he joined the elite Los Angeles Track Club. The next year he broke eleven American records and three world records. Considered the nation's top amateur athlete, he was named the 1962 James E. Sullivan Award winner.

Beatty returned to Charlotte, where he remains an active member of the community. He was an inaugural inductee into the North Carolina Sports Hall of Fame in 1963.

1813 Fugitive Slave & Abolitionist Harriet Jacobs

On February 11, 1813, Harriet Jacobs, fugitive slave, writer, and abolitionist, was born in Edenton. She spent her childhood unaware of her station in life. But when her white mistress, Margaret Horniblow, died in 1825, Jacobs and her brother John were willed to Horniblow's three-year-old niece, Mary Norcom, and thereby came under the control of Norcom's father, Dr. James Norcom.

After suffering years of physical abuse and sexual harassment at the hands of James Norcom, Jacobs fled in 1835 and went into hiding in the attic of her paternal grandmother, Molly Horniblow, a free black woman living in Edenton only a block away from Norcom. According to Jacobs's memoir *Incidents in the Life of a Slave Girl*, published in 1861, Harriet lived in that restricted space for almost seven years until she managed to escape north via Edenton's maritime Underground Railroad.

Jacobs gained her full and legal freedom ten years later. While living as a fugitive slave, Jacobs became an anti-slavery activist and an abolitionist author. By the time of the Civil War, as a free African American woman, Jacobs served as a relief worker dedicated to assisting the newly freed people of her southern homeland.

FEB 11

Drawing of Harriet Jacobs, based on famous photo of her that is owned by Harvard University.

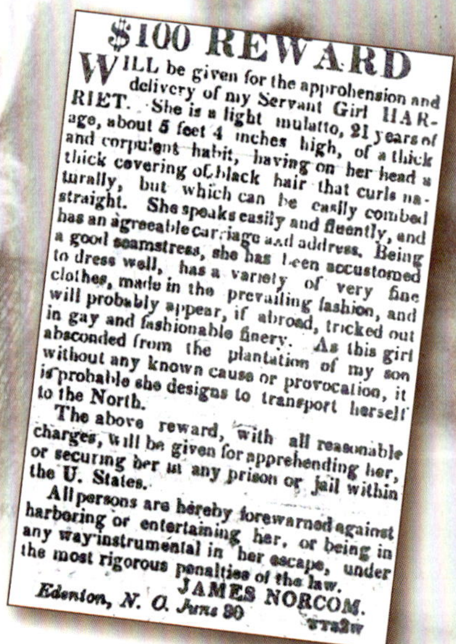

$100 REWARD

WILL be given for the apprehension and delivery of my Servant Girl HARRIET. She is a light mulatto, 21 years of age, about 5 feet 4 inches high, of a thick and corpulent habit, having on her head a thick covering of black hair that curls naturally, but which can be easily combed straight. She speaks easily and fluently, and has an agreeable carriage and address. Being a good seamstress, she has been accustomed to dress well, has a variety of very fine clothes, made in the prevailing fashion, and will probably appear, if abroad, tricked out in gay and fashionable finery. As this girl absconded from the plantation of my son without any known cause or provocation, it is probable she designs to transport herself to the North.

The above reward, with all reasonable charges, will be given for apprehending her, or securing her in any prison or jail within the U. States.

All persons are hereby forewarned against harboring or entertaining her, or being in any way instrumental in her escape, under the most rigorous penalties of the law.

JAMES NORCOM.

Edenton, N. C. June 30

1917 Annie Oakley, Star Attraction at Pinehurst

On February 11, 1917, Annie Oakley exhibited her skills as a markswoman in Pinehurst.

Born Phoebe Ann Moses in Ohio in 1860, Oakley first demonstrated her prowess with a gun while hunting game as a teenager. She was discovered after defeating Frank Butler, a well-known sharpshooter, in an exhibition in Cincinnati in 1876 and married Butler soon thereafter.

In time she became an international celebrity. European royalty adorned her with medals, and she was adopted as "Little Sure Shot" (she was five feet tall) by Lakota Chief Sitting Bull. One of Oakley's favorite routines involved shooting an apple that had been placed on top of her dog Dave's head.

A 1901 train wreck outside Lexington in Davidson County involving Buffalo Bill Cody's Wild West troupe left Oakley temporarily paralyzed and brought an end to that part of her career.

Beginning in 1915 Oakley and her husband wintered at the Carolina Hotel in Pinehurst. There she mingled with society's elite and taught women how to handle guns. She regarded her time in North Carolina as the happiest years of her life, since she was employed only part-time and enjoyed freedom in her schedule and the chance to rest.

In 1918 she was severely injured in an automobile accident in Florida; she died in 1926.

Annie Oakley in 1922.

1919 Senator Lee Overman and the Red Scare of 1919

On February 11, 1919, a subcommittee of the U.S. Senate Judiciary Committee opened hearings on the influence of Bolshevism in America. Chaired by North Carolina senator Lee Overman, originally from Salisbury, the hearings are regarded as a forerunner of the House Un-American Activities Committee of the 1950s.

Overman's committee was formed in 1918, as World War I drew to a close, to investigate the influence of German propaganda. Many Americans were uneasy about the repercussions of the 1917 Bolshevik Revolution in Russia, so in February 1919 a resolution to expand the focus of Overman's committee was passed unanimously by the Senate.

Hearings began shortly thereafter and lasted until March 19. Much of the committee's questioning involved the upheavals caused by the revolution and subsequent civil war and the revolution's potential threat to American capitalism. Anti-Semitic paranoia surfaced regarding the purported prevalence of Jews in Bolshevik ranks. Accusations also circulated of pro-Bolshevism among American university professors and of promiscuity among Bolshevik women.

The committee's final report was released in June 1919. While it provided little concrete evidence of Bolshevik activities in America, it coincided with and inflamed the emerging "Red Scare" panic that swept the nation.

1795 Hinton James, First Student at Chapel Hill

On February 12, 1795, Hinton James became the first student to enter the University of North Carolina.

James, who had walked to Chapel Hill from his home in New Hanover County, was the only student for the first two weeks of the school year. Academically gifted, James helped organize the first literary club and debating society on campus. He was awarded a bachelor's degree in July 1798 as one of the seven students in the university's first graduating class.

After graduation James became an assistant to Hamilton Fulton, a Scottish engineer hired by the state to improve navigation on its eastern rivers. James was put in charge of operations along the Cape Fear River but left in 1807 upon his election to the state legislature. He served three terms in Raleigh before serving as mayor and treasurer of Wilmington and as a magistrate of New Hanover County.

James died in 1847 and was buried at Hopewell Presbyterian Church near Burgaw. A dormitory at the University of North Carolina is named in his honor.

1828 Robert Ransom, Like Brother Matt a Confederate General

On February 12, 1828, Confederate general Robert Ransom Jr. was born in Warren County. Ransom was appointed to West Point, graduating in 1850. The young officer was assigned to Fort Leavenworth, Kansas. Ransom returned to West Point as a cavalry instructor in 1854 but again was posted to the Kansas frontier in 1856. He was promoted to captain in January 1861 but soon resigned to join the Confederacy. Ransom was commissioned captain and ordered to raise a regiment. With his regiment designated the First North Carolina Cavalry, he was promoted to colonel and placed in command.

Ransom was elevated to brigadier general in the spring of 1862 and to major general little more than a year later. In May 1863 he was ordered to assume command of Richmond. Ransom, who battled a number of serious illnesses over the years, fell ill in the summer of 1864 and remained on sick leave for the duration of the war. In 1878 he was hired as assistant to the U. S. civil engineer in New Bern, a job that gave him the opportunity to improve harbors and waterways throughout the Carolinas. He died in 1881 and was buried in Cedar Grove Cemetery, New Bern.

1912 Robeson County at Forefront of Rural Health Movement

On February 12, 1912, Robeson County established the first rural health department in the United States.

State responsibility for public health began in 1877, when the legislature determined that officers of the Medical Society of North Carolina should make up the State Board of Health. That same year the General Assembly directed counties to appoint health boards consisting of practicing physicians, the mayor of the county seat, the chairman of the county commissioners, and the city or county supervisor. Although some local boards did hire superintendents to work as public health practitioners, none created a department to carry out its work.

The county health movement was a direct outgrowth of the battles against hookworm, typhoid fever, and other diseases. In 1911 urban Guilford County became the first county in the state, and the second in the United States, to establish a health department.

Robeson County's health department was the fourth in the country overall, and its roots can be traced to the local health board's hiring Dr. B. W. Page in 1912. In Page's first year he examined forty-five schools, inspected 500 rural homes (quarantining 118), vaccinated 525 schoolchildren, and set up a lecture series.

The Robeson County Health Department was originally located in the basement of the courthouse and has since moved several times.

FEB 12

Robert Ransom, undated portrait.

1941 Durham's "Blind Boy Fuller"

1943 Camp Lejeune and Females in the U.S. Marine Corps

1969 Students Storm Duke's Administration Building

FEB 13

On February 13, 1941, Piedmont Blues musician "Blind Boy Fuller" died in Durham. Fuller was noted for playing a steel-bodied National guitar that was a natural resonator before amplification. Along with Reverend Gary Davis, Fuller dominated the Bull City's blues scene, attracting and influencing many musicians.

Born Fulton Allen in Wadesboro in 1907, Fuller learned guitar and country rag songs from older singers in Rockingham. In his late teens he moved to Winston-Salem, where he played on sidewalks for shift workers in tobacco factories. He became completely blind in 1928 and moved to Durham the next year.

In 1935 Fuller was taken to New York by white merchant J. B. Long for the first of many recording sessions with the American Recording Corporation. He released more than 130 songs on several labels in his five-year recording career. Many of his songs centered on the daily struggles of black tenant farmers and the experiences of those who left the South for the North.

Fuller's repertoire ranged from ragtime to the blues, including "Rag, Mama, Rag," "Truckin' My Blues Away," and "I Want Some of Your Pie." Fuller often recorded with other musicians, including guitarists Floyd Council and Bull City Red and harmonica player Sonny Terry.

On February 13, 1943, the first women to sign up for non-clerical duties enlisted in the Marine Corps Women's Reserve. The Women's Reserve was formed in 1942, when plans were put in place to build a women's cantonment area at Camp Lejeune, consisting of several barracks, mess halls, and other support facilities. Unlike other branches, the Marine Corps did not drastically relax its training regimen or admissions policies for females.

About three thousand women trained elsewhere while facilities were being prepared at Camp Lejeune. The base remained the primary source of female Marines during World War II. During the course of the war, more than twenty-three thousand women enlisted and nearly one thousand held commissions. By the war's end almost eighteen thousand women who trained at Camp Lejeune were on duty, including Eugenia Lejeune, daughter of the general for whom the base is named.

Enlistees were inducted into specialties ranging from cooks and clerks to transport personnel and mechanics. One-third of the women served in aviation-related fields, particularly at the Marine Corps Air Station at Cherry Point. After the war the Women's Reserve was considered expendable and scheduled for elimination. The women's schools were disbanded in September 1945, and the entire reserve was discharged in March 1946.

On February 13, 1969, African American student activists at Duke University occupied the school's main administrative building. The takeover of the Allen Building was sparked by the slowness of racial reform at the university.

Black undergraduates were not admitted to Duke until 1963. In the mid-60s the Afro-American Association formed on campus, influenced by the Black Power movement. By early 1969 the Association and its supporters had become impatient with the progress of promised reform.

Early on the morning of February 13, a group of black students took over a portion of the Allen Building and issued eleven demands for change. White students sympathetic to the protesters soon gathered outside. The administration negotiated with the occupiers and agreed to most of the demands, but gave the protesters only an hour to accept their offer and leave or face arrest.

The students in turn threatened to burn the university's records but eventually complied. The takeover ended as police tear gassed the white students outside. None of the occupiers was expelled from school, though many were put on probation. Continuing frustration with the process of change at Duke led to the creation of the short-lived Malcolm X University in Durham later in the year.

Private First Class Priscilla Goodrich (*left*) and Private Elaine Munsinger (*right*) break down an airplane engine in the Assembly and Repair Department at Marine Corps Air Station Cherry Point.

Private Eleanora Julia Canady takes her turn on sentry duty at Marine Corps Women's Reserve Schools at Camp Lejeune in 1943.

1775 Raleigh's Confederate Soldiers' Home

On February 14, 1775, Janet Schaw, a noted colonial diarist, arrived in Brunswick from the Caribbean.

Born near Edinburgh, Schaw left for the New World in October 1774, beginning her diary, which would later be published as *Journal of a Lady of Quality*, the day after setting sail. After making brief stops in Antigua and what's now St. Kitts, Schaw and her brother set sail for North Carolina.

Though planning to make only a brief stop in North Carolina, they stayed in Brunswick for about a month, then left for a family plantation near Wilmington. As the American Revolution began to heat up in late 1775, Schaw and her family fled to a British warship, then back to Europe.

Schaw would have likely been forgotten if not for her *Journal*, which is considered an excellent portrayal of pre-Revolutionary North Carolina from a Loyalist perspective. The journal is often used by scholars because Schaw's candid observations depict aspects of eighteenth century life that many other sources do not.

1891 Establishment of Raleigh Confederate Soldiers' Home

On February 14, 1891, the North Carolina Confederate Soldiers' Home was established by an act of the General Assembly.

Attempts to establish the North Carolina Confederate Home Association began in 1884, when veterans, led by Senator Zebulon B. Vance, met in Charlotte. The effort did not gain momentum until 1889, when the Confederate Veterans Association of North Carolina was incorporated by the General Assembly.

A temporary building for the Confederate Soldiers' Home was leased briefly at Polk and Bloodworth Streets with funds raised by the Veterans Association, the Wake County Ladies Memorial Association, and the Daughters of the Confederacy. In May 1891 the permanent home at the intersection of Tarboro Road and New Bern Avenue in Raleigh admitted the first occupants. The home sat on the site of the old Pettigrew Hospital, and today is home to the headquarters of the state's Division of Motor Vehicles.

To be eligible, veterans had to have served honorably in North Carolina commands of either the Confederate army or navy. Nearly fifteen hundred men resided at the home, about a third of whom suffered from war-related wounds or disabilities. Most residents were well into their eighties at the time they were admitted. On August 6, 1938, the last resident left the home to move in with family, and the facilities and the buildings, all named for Confederate generals, fell into disrepair.

1943 Maceo Parker of Kinston Brought the Funk

On February 14, 1943, saxophonist Maceo Parker was born in Kinston. Perhaps best known for his work with James Brown, Parker brought funk to the soul music of the James Brown Band. For nearly 20 years Brown's call, "Maceo, I want you to Blow!," summoned his unique sound.

Parker was exposed to music early. His father played at least two instruments, and both his parents sang for their church. His brother was also musical, and the pair joined James Brown's band together in 1964. He has gone on to collaborate with a host of artists including George Clinton, Prince, Ray Charles, James Taylor, the Dave Matthews Band, and the Red Hot Chili Peppers.

Among Parker's many accolades and awards are the 2003 Rhythm and Blues Foundation Pioneer Award, the 2012 Les Victoires du Jazz in Paris Lifetime Achievement Award, and the Icon Award at the North Sea Jazz Festival in Rotterdam.

FEB 14

Maceo Parker performs at the 2016 North Carolina Heritage Awards.

FEB 15

1776 Encampment at Rockfish Creek, Prelude to Moores Creek Bridge

On February 15, 1776, Patriot forces under Col. James Moore camped on Rockfish Creek in Cumberland County.

Nearby more than fifteen hundred Loyalist militia, most of them Scottish Highlanders, gathered under General Donald McDonald at what's now Fayetteville to march to Wilmington. By fortifying the encampment at Rockfish Creek with over one thousand men and five artillery pieces, Moore blocked the Loyalists' most direct route to the coast, forcing them to utilize a narrow bridge at Moores Creek.

There, on February 27, the Loyalists were ambushed by about one thousand Patriots, artillery and rifles, from Col. Richard Caswell's and Col. Alexander Lillington's forces. The Patriots were victorious, killing or wounding at least fifty men and capturing about 850 more.

The Battle of Moores Creek Bridge was a pivotal moment in North Carolina history. Without Loyalist forces to protect the colonial government, the royal system collapsed, allowing Patriot leaders to establish a fledgling state government. The Patriot victory also denied Britain use of North Carolina's ports, which were logistically significant. The battle at Moores Creek is often referred to as the "Lexington and Concord of the South."

Initially a state park, the battlefield at Morres Creek is now managed by the National Park Service.

1898 Fort Macon Garrisoned for Spanish-American War

On February 15, 1898, Charles L. Abernathy, editor of the *Beaufort Herald-Dispatch*, wrote to U. S. Senator Marion Butler to point out that North Carolina's Fort Macon was "in a dilapidated condition with a lone sentry in charge of it. As you are aware our bar has from 18 to 20 feet of water and this port, in the event of a naval engagement, would be of easy access." He also pointed out that other ports along the coast had received defense appropriations "while this one has for some reason been passed by unnoticed."

Ironically, that same night the battleship USS *Maine* exploded in Havana harbor under suspicious circumstances and became an important factor in the United States' decision to declare war on Spain in April. "Remember the *Maine*" became a U.S. rallying cry during the war.

In Beaufort residents were uneasy that Fort Macon, which guarded the entrance to Beaufort Harbor, had not been prepared for possible war. Soon, though, Fort Macon's six remaining Civil War-era cannons were remounted. The fort was garrisoned for the Spanish American War by part of a company of U.S. Artillery and the all-black Third N.C. Volunteers under Col. James H. Young.

Aerial photograph of Fort Macon State Park.

1872 Lowrie Gang of Robeson County, Driven by Revenge

On February 16, 1872, the last robbery by the Lowrie gang took place. The daring raid netted twenty-eight thousand dollars. Days later Henry Berry Lowrie, the leader of the band, disappeared and launched himself into North Carolina legend.

During the Civil War Lowrie and his brothers—Lumbee Indians—hid out in the swamps of Robeson County to escape the forced labor inflicted upon free persons of color. They began to steal from the homes of white people in the area, taking clothing, supplies, and arms. In 1865 Allen and William Lowrie, father and brother of Henry, were executed after capture.

Seven years of violence, including several murders, followed. Among the poor of Robeson County, the gang, which consisted of the Lowrie brothers, some of their cousins, two freedmen, and one poor white man, were regarded as Robin Hood-like heroes. They often shared with area families goods taken in their robberies.

The gang's elusive and violent nature caused great fear among the whites of the area.

In November 1868 Gov. W. W. Holden officially declared Henry Berry Lowrie an outlaw. Holden offered a ten thousand dollar bounty for Lowrie's capture. A white militia hunted for him, but he was never found.

Harper's Weekly-Henry Berry Lowrie illustration.

1924 Henry Bacon, Designer of Washington's Lincoln Memorial

On February 16, 1924, Henry Bacon, Jr., architect and designer of the Lincoln Memorial in Washington, D.C., died.

Born in Illinois in 1866, Bacon moved with his family to Brunswick County in 1876 and then to Wilmington. He attended school in Boston and Wilmington and went on to study at the University of Illinois for a year before moving to Boston to join the architectural firm Chamberlain and Whidden as a draftsman. He progressed quickly from there, winning awards and joining New York's prestigious firm McKim, Mead and White. He studied in Europe during various periods and eventually would partner with James Brite for a time.

Bacon won the commission for the Lincoln Memorial design in 1912 and oversaw its completion. During the next ten years he, somewhat ironically, also served as designer and architect of two of North Carolina's most well-known Confederate monuments: Raleigh's Monument to the Women of the Confederacy and Wilmington's Confederate Monument, working alongside sculptor Francis Herman Packer on the latter project.

His own grave marker was created from drawings found in his desk following his death. He kept close connections to the Wilmington area throughout his life and is buried in the family plot in the city's Oakdale Cemetery.

Henry Bacon, architect of the Lincoln Memorial. Daniel Chester French, sculptor, is on the lower left. Mr. Bacon is on the lower right.

FEB 17

1945 Medal of Honor Recipient Rufus Herring of Sampson County

On February 17, 1945, Roseboro native Rufus G. Herring captained *Gunboat 449* into the bay at Iwo Jima two days before the American invasion of the Japanese-held island. Herring's mission, along with that of six other landing craft infantry units, was to provide covering fire for an Underwater Demolition Team as they conducted reconnaissance of the beach.

On entering the bay, Herring's ship bore the brunt of the Japanese artillery, and two "serious fires" temporarily disabled it. All officers on board except the engineer were killed, wounded or missing.

Herring himself was seriously wounded and began losing strength due to severe bleeding. Despite his critical condition he continued to maintain command of the ship, providing cover for the recon team and eventually steering the crippled ship back to safety. For "conspicuous gallantry and intrepidity at the risk of his life above and beyond the call of duty," Herring was awarded the Congressional Medal of Honor in September 1945.

Life magazine later reported that Herring fell in love with his nurse while recuperating in a naval hospital. The couple married and returned to Roseboro, where he ran a farm and lumber business.

1963 Basketball Superstar Michael Jordan Born

On February 17, 1963, American basketball superstar Michael Jeffrey Jordan was born in Brooklyn, New York. Before his first birthday Jordan's parents moved to Wilmington, where he played three sports at Laney High School and was named to the McDonald's All-America team.

As a UNC-Chapel Hill freshman, Jordan scored the winning basket in the 1982 NCAA title game. In 1984 he was named College Player of the Year and won the first of two Olympic gold medals (the other was in 1992) with the U.S. men's basketball team. After his junior year at Carolina, Jordan entered the NBA draft and was picked by the Chicago Bulls.

His high-scoring, high-flying game quickly made "Air Jordan" an international sports celebrity and marketing marvel. After leading the Bulls to three consecutive NBA championships, Jordan unexpectedly retired in 1993 to pursue a career in baseball. He rejoined the Bulls in 1995 and led them to three more NBA titles before retiring again in 1999. After a two-year hiatus Jordan returned to basketball, playing with the Washington Wizards. He retired for the final time in 2003. Now the primary owner of the Charlotte Bobcats, Jordan is still widely regarded as the best basketball player of all time.

1970 Fort Bragg Murders, 1970

On February 17, 1970, Green Beret surgeon Capt. Jeffrey MacDonald called the Fort Bragg military police. When they got to his apartment, the police found MacDonald injured and unconscious and his wife Colette and their two daughters, Kimberly and Kristen, murdered.

Once revived by the MPs, MacDonald reported that he had been asleep on the sofa and awoke to screams. According to him, there were three men in the living room, one armed with a baseball bat and another with a blade with which they attacked him MacDonald further reported that he saw a blonde woman carrying a flickering light and wearing a floppy hat behind the men. She uttered the words, "Acid is groovy. Kill the pigs," he said.

That night MacDonald was admitted to the intensive care unit of Womack Hospital with life-threatening injuries. In April he was questioned by the Army as a prime suspect in the murders. In October MacDonald underwent a pre-court martial hearing in which the charges were dropped. Then in 1974 a civilian court in Cumberland County began the process of hearing the case. Five years later, MacDonald was convicted of the three murders.

Michael Jordan playing for UNC in 1982 in a NCAA tournament game against rival Georgetown.

1865 Collett Leventhorpe, Englishman Turned Confederate

On February 18, 1865, Collett Leventhorpe was offered a Confederate brigadier general's commission but turned it down. He chose instead to command troops in Raleigh, eventually retreating with the Army of Tennessee and surrendering in Greensboro.

Born in England, where he served in the army and studied medicine, Leventhorpe first came to the United State on a business trip. While vacationing in Asheville he met his future wife, so he continued studying medicine in Charleston and settled in Rutherfordton.

At the outbreak of the Civil War, Leventhorpe offered his services to the state, seeing battle across North Carolina and eventually taking command of the Wilmington area before being transferred again to southeastern Virginia. Severely wounded in the fighting just west of Gettysburg, Leventhorpe was captured and spent nine months in Union prisons. After his release he was placed in command of home guard units in the Piedmont and oversaw actions against Unionists, particularly in Davidson and Randolph Counties.

At the close of war, Leventhorpe moved to New York, where he lived for several years. He eventually returned to North Carolina, settling in the mountains near Lenoir. He died in 1889.

1891 Normal School to Women's College to UNC-Greensboro

On February 18, 1891, the State Normal and Industrial School was chartered. First established as a school for female teachers, it became the Women's College of the University of North Carolina in 1932, joining the University of North Carolina and North Carolina State College as part of the consolidated University System. The State Normal School was built on ten acres in western Greensboro in Guilford County.

The school opened in October 1892 with 223 students and fifteen faculty members. Originally, the school offered degrees in three departments: education, domestic sciences, and business.

Joining the consolidated University System in 1932, the Women's College functioned as the leading college for women in North Carolina throughout the early and mid-twentieth century. Becoming coeducational in 1963, the college was renamed the University of North Carolina at Greensboro. It continued to widen its course offerings, and today, as UNC-G, hosts more than 150 undergraduate and graduate programs in education, the liberal arts, and business.

The integration of men and minority students at UNC-G expanded and diversified the university in the 1960s and 1970s. In 1995 Patricia A. Sullivan became the first female chancellor of UNC-Greensboro.

1927 "Witlings Defame Her": William Gaston and "The Old North State"

On February 18, 1927, the General Assembly adopted "The Old North State" as North Carolina's official state song.

State Supreme Court Justice William Joseph Gaston of New Bern penned the song's patriotic lyrics in the 1830s, when North Carolina was lagging economically behind its neighbors and masses of people were moving away. A dedicated public servant and advocate for internal improvements, Gaston sought to defend North Carolina against accusations of backwardness.

When court was in session in Raleigh, Gaston stayed at the home of Mrs. James F. Taylor. Once when a couple of women in the household returned from a concert by a group of visiting Swiss bellringers, they began to sing and play one of the concert tunes on the piano. Gaston became inspired. At his office on Hargett Street, he wrote several verses of the now-familiar song, adapting it to the melody he had just heard. A chorus of fifty young women first performed the song at the Whig state convention in Raleigh in October 1840.

R. Culver set Gaston's poem to music in 1844, but the arrangement composed in 1926 by Mrs. E. E. Randolph in Raleigh is the version familiar to North Carolinians today.

FEB 18

State Normal and Industrial School Main Building and Brick Dormitory about 1892.

FEB 19

1865 Fall of Fort Anderson to Union Forces

On February 19, 1865, Fort Anderson in Brunswick County was captured by Union forces under the command of Gen. Jacob D. Cox. The fall of Fort Fisher in January had spurred the Wilmington Campaign and virtually assured the capture of the Cape Fear fortifications and Wilmington.

Cox had been directed to move up the west bank of the Cape Fear River and advance on Wilmington from the west. The primary obstacle before the town was Fort Anderson. Designed much like Fort Fisher, it boasted over a mile of earthen fortifications and artillery chambers in addition to batteries that guarded the water approach to the city. The fort made use of the natural terrain, employing swampland and ponds as moats and protective defenses along its battlements.

Cox arrived in front of Fort Anderson on February 16. For two days the opposing forces engaged in heavy skirmishing. On the afternoon of February 18, a large Union force marched around the head of Orton Pond to flank the Confederate stronghold. After a combined bombardment from the river and a land attack, the Confederates realized their position was indefensible, and the post was evacuated in the early morning hours.

1921 Photographer and Conservationist Hugh Morton

On February 19, 1921, developer, conservationist, and photographer Hugh Morton was born in Wilmington.

Morton was instrumental in supporting many of the attractions enjoyed by residents of and visitors to the Tar Heel State. He served as the first president of Wilmington's Azalea Festival and was influential in raising funds to bring the battleship USS *North Carolina* to that port city. He advocated saving the Cape Hatteras Lighthouse by use of artificial seaweed.

Morton is perhaps best known as the developer of Grandfather Mountain, which he inherited in 1952. He was responsible for the construction of the "Mile-High Swinging Bridge," and under his leadership the site grew to become one of the most popular in the state.

He gained notoriety for his fight to keep the Blue Ridge Parkway from crossing Grandfather Mountain and spoiling its aesthetic appeal. The result was the Linn Cove Viaduct, an engineering marvel coursing around the mountain.

Morton was part of the post-World War II era of tourism development in North Carolina and was a friend and colleague of many notables across the state. He took close to a quarter-million photographs, which are now part of the North Carolina Collection Photographic Archives at UNC-Chapel Hill.

He died in June 2006.

1925 Poole Bill and Anti-Evolution Fervor

On February 19, 1925, the North Carolina House defeated the Poole anti-evolution resolution. The proposed resolution, introduced by D. Scott Poole of Hoke County, declared it harmful to the welfare of the citizens for "Darwinism or any other evolutionary hypotheses" to be taught in the schools.

In January 1924 Governor Cameron Morrison denounced two high school textbooks for their inclusion of evolution. Poole's resolution sought to keep all such lessons out of the state's classrooms. William Louis Poteat, a former biology professor, president of Wake Forest College, and a devout Baptist, believed that evolution demonstrated the "divine method of creation." He became an outspoken advocate for keeping it in the curriculum.

Although the House appeared to be quite divided on the issue, when it was put to a vote, the resolution failed by a comfortable margin, sixty-seven to forty-six.

The evolution debate received national attention just a few months later during the Tennessee case that has come to be known as the Scopes "Monkey Trial." The case was in response to a Tennessee law similar to the one defeated in North Carolina.

Re-enactment at Brunswick Town/Fort Anderson State Historic Site

1862 Burning of Winton by Union Troops, 1862

On February 20, 1862, Union troops burned Winton, a small village in Hertford County overlooking the Chowan River.

The previous day six gunboats transporting soldiers from New York and Rhode Island steamed upriver to Winton, intent on destroying a railroad bridge. Confederate soldiers from North Carolina and Virginia opened fire on the vessels. Despite riddling the wheelhouse of the lead gunboat, the USS *Delaware*, the volley did little damage, and the Federal shelling commenced. That night the six gunboats anchored seven miles south of Winton, and Union officers decided that the town of 300 inhabitants should be burned.

The fleet returned to find the town almost completely abandoned. Soldiers, fresh from victory in the Battle of Roanoke Island, landed and took possession of Winton. The invaders burned military goods, along with the courthouse and several private homes; soldiers often ransacked homes before torching them.

Word of the destruction spread fast in newspapers, North and South. Southern editors fueled public outrage. A Norfolk paper proclaimed the action a "vile incendiary." The action at Winton proved to be a precedent for the practice of "total war" embraced by Gen. William Tecumseh Sherman later in the conflict.

1885 Princeville, First Black Town, Incorporated 1885

On February 20, 1885, twenty-two years after Emancipation, freedmen in Edgecombe County incorporated Princeville, the state's first black town.

Its claim to being first in the nation is rivalled only by Eatonville, Florida. Along with James City in Craven County and Roanoke Island in Dare County, the community was among the state's three resettlement colonies for former slaves.

At the close of the Civil War, Union troops occupied the Tarboro area. Former slaves in surrounding counties left their plantations and flocked to the Federal encampment seeking freedom and protection. The future faced by the mostly illiterate, unskilled, and penniless freedmen was uncertain and bleak.

Adopting the name Freedom Hill from a nearby knoll from which Northern soldiers addressed the refugees, the community's first families camped alongside the river and erected crude shanties. White landowners made no effort to evict them from the land, its being so swampy as to be otherwise useless.

In the 1870s the land did change hands, and residents began acquiring lots. One of the buyers was Turner Prince, a carpenter for whom the community was renamed upon its incorporation.

National attention was drawn to Princeville in September 1999, when flooding associated with Hurricane Floyd devastated the area.

1948 Piedmont Airlines Takes Flight

On February 20, 1948, Piedmont Airlines launched its first passenger flight. The flight took off from Wilmington and arrived in Cincinnati after making several stops.

Piedmont Airlines' roots stretch back to 1940, when a struggling aviation company called the Camel City Flying Service was reincorporated by Thomas H. Davis as Piedmont Aviation. Piedmont Aviation's initial focus was training pilots and flight instructors to meet the needs of America's involvement in World War II, but as that conflict wound down, the company sought to change its focus to passenger service.

After problems over a contract, Piedmont Airlines took the federal government's airline regulator, the Civil Aeronautics Board, to court. The case rose to the level of the U.S. Supreme Court and eventually ended in the airline's favor, allowing the first commercial flight to go forward.

The airline grew steadily and acquired a reputation for simultaneously having excellent customer service and bare-bones airplanes and other equipment. Piedmont Airlines was sold to U.S. Airways in 1989.

1980 J. B. Rhine of Duke University, Father of Modern Parapsychology

On February 20, 1980, Joseph Banks Rhine of Durham, a controversial investigator into the paranormal, died. With his pioneering work in parapsychology, Rhine gained national notoriety for himself and Duke University, where he worked.

Born in Pennsylvania in 1895, Rhine received a doctorate in botany from the University of Chicago. He moved to Duke University in 1927, where he began conducting predictive experiments with students. The most common test involved the use of twenty-five cards bearing one of five symbols. The subject was asked to identify cards that had been preselected, in another room or at a greater distance.

In 1934 Rhine published *Extra-Sensory Perception* and coined the term ESP, which later gained wide acceptance. In 1965 Rhine and his wife Louisa cut their ties with Duke and established off-campus the Foundation for Research on the Nature of Man, known today the Rhine Research Center.

Though many were keen to challenge Rhine, many others have credited him with synthesizing the research of his predecessors and advancing a field of inquiry.

FEB 20

Piedmont Airlines airplane at Washington National Airport, 1972.

FEB 21

1764 The Boone Tract in Davie County

On February 21, 1764, famed frontiersman Daniel Boone sold land near what is now Mocksville to settle debts before exploring westward. Aaron Van Cleave, a former ship's captain from New York, paid Boone "80 pounds Proclamation money of the state of North Carolina" for his 640 acres at the forks of the Yadkin River.

The property had been the Boone family's first home in North Carolina. Squire Boone, Daniel's father, had moved his family there from Pennsylvania and acquired the tract along Bear Creek from John Carteret, Earl Granville, in December 1753. Squire Boone sold the tract to his son in October 1759. The original 1764 deed, in which Boone and his wife Rachel, transferred the property to Van Cleave, can still be found in the Rowan County Register of Deeds office in Salisbury. It bears Daniel's signature and Rachel's mark.

Between 1767 and 1775 Boone helped to blaze the Wilderness Road across the Appalachian Mountains via the Cumberland Gap and to lead three expeditions into Kentucky, opening the west for settlement. In 1775 he founded the village of Boonesborough, Kentucky and moved his family there, along with some North Carolina friends and neighbors. That group included five of Van Cleave's sons and his only daughter.

1893 Classical Origins of the State's Motto

On February 21, 1893, the General Assembly adopted *Esse Quam Videri* as the official state motto. Translated from Latin, the phrase means "To be rather than to seem."

The phrase is a quotation from *De Amicitia*, an essay on friendship by the Roman author and politician Cicero, that dates to 44 B.C. Similar sentiments can found in earlier texts by the Greek poet Aeschylus and philosopher Socrates

Noted Halifax County judge and historian Walter Clark first selected the phrase and drafted the bill for the General Assembly to consider. Nash County Senator Jacob Battle first introduced it. At the time of its adoption, North Carolina was one of only a few states across the country, and the only one of the thirteen original states, without an official motto.

Though North Carolina had never had an official motto during statehood, *Quae Sera Tamen Respexit* appeared on the colonial seal. That Latin phrase, which means "Which, though late, looked upon me," referred to the figure of Liberty, which then, as today, also appeared on the seal.

1903 Haywood v. Skinner (1903)

On February 21, 1903, prominent attorney Ernest Haywood shot and killed Ludlow Skinner, the son of a popular Baptist minister, in broad daylight on Raleigh's busy Fayetteville Street.

Several newspaper accounts of the incident say that right before the shooting the pair was spotted arguing on the post office steps and that it was actually Skinner who attacked first, apparently striking Haywood on the side of the head, making him fall. Haywood retaliated by firing two shots. The first caused Skinner to turn away from Haywood, and the second was fatal, hitting Skinner as he staggered across the street.

The dispute seems to have concerned Haywood's quite close relationship with Skinner's sister. Rumors swelled that Skinner's sister and Haywood were secretly married and that she had had a child by Haywood. It's unclear whether the marriage actually occurred.

Initially held without bond, Haywood was eventually released on a ten thousand dollar bail. At his trial in October, Haywood claimed self-defense. After deliberating only fifteen minutes, the jury found him not guilty. The Raleigh community was split on the verdict, with many residents convinced that the trial was fixed in Haywood's favor.

1933 "High Priestess of Soul" Nina Simone Born

On February 21, 1933, Nina Simone, often called the "high priestess of soul," was born in the small town of Tryon in Polk County.

Determined to become one of the first highly-successful African-American concert pianists, Simone spent a summer at the famed Julliard School after graduating from Allen High School in Asheville in 1950. Denied admission to music school in Philadelphia, Simone took menial jobs there.

While on a trip to Atlantic City, New Jersey in the summer of 1954, Simone began to experiment with popular music. Word of her talent spread, and she came into high demand at nightclubs all along the mid-Atlantic coast. After her first album, *Little Girl Blue*, in 1958, her work began to reflect her increasing involvement in the civil rights movement and her close associations with leading African American intellectuals like Lorraine Hansberry and Langston Hughes.

After releasing thirteen albums during the 1960s, Simone hit a rough patch in the 1970s, struggling with a divorce and mental illness. She toured extensively in Europe during the 1980s, and her career began to wind down in the early 1990s. She died in France in 2003.

Nina Simone in concert in France, 1982.

1759 George Burrington, Controversial Colonial Governor

On February 22, 1759, Gov. George Burrington, first royal governor of North Carolina, was murdered in London.

An interesting and controversial figure in the colony during the proprietary and royal periods, Burrington appears in records as contentious, inflammatory, and sometimes violent. At various times he was accused of attempting to blow up colonial chief justice Christopher Gale's house, throwing colonial official Edmund Porter's written defense of his judgeship into the fire, horse theft, and stealing the council secretary's commissioning seals.

Burrington was a man of contrasts, though. Interested in the expansion and promotion of the colony, he traveled and planned for internal improvements, founded what is now Wilmington, and effectively opened the lower Cape Fear area for settlement. In the 1730s Burrington was removed from his royal governorship, just as he had been removed from his proprietary governorship a decade earlier.

He returned to England and remained there until his death, which resulted from an attack during a robbery attempt.

1856 Dorothea Dix Hospital Admits Its First Patient

On February 22, 1856, the new "Insane Hospital of North Carolina"—renamed Dorothea Dix Hospital a century later—admitted its first patient, suffering from "suicidal mania." Previously, families kept mentally ill members at home, or local governments confined them in jails or poorhouses.

Nationwide social reforms during the 1830s and 1840s sparked interest in state-run hospitals for the medical treatment of mentally ill patients. In 1848 mental health crusader Dorothea Dix came to North Carolina and personally lobbied legislators for an asylum. The General Assembly authorized funds in 1849. Construction began in May 1850 on a 182-acre site about a mile southwest of Raleigh. New York architect Alexander T. Davis designed the steam-heated, gas-lighted main building, which accommodated 274 patients.

At its peak, the hospital had nearly twenty-five hundred acres of land, 282 buildings and thirteen hundred employees, who cared for nearly three thousand patients annually. Much of the land was later sold and developed into the State Farmer's Market, North Carolina State University's Centennial Campus, and other projects. In August 2012 Dorothea Dix Hospital closed and moved its last patients to Central Regional Hospital in Butner. In December 2012 the state leased the remaining hospital campus to the city of Raleigh for use as an urban park.

1945 Oliver, North Wilkesboro Native, Sixties Pop Sensation

On February 22, 1945, pop musician William Oliver Swofford, known professionally as Oliver, was born in North Wilkesboro.

A Morehead Scholar, Swofford joined his first band while at the University of North Carolina, but it had no national success. In 1968 he came to the attention of music producer Bob Crewe, who described his voice as "pure, almost like a reed instrument." After recording the song "Good Morning Starshine" from the musical *Hair* but before releasing it, Crewe decided that Oliver would be a better name for the rising star.

The song was a hit in the summer of 1969, climbing to Number 3 on Billboard's Hot 100. During his short musical career Oliver had an additional hit with "Jean" from the movie *The Prime of Miss Jean Brodie*. The song's writer once said that Oliver did not just perform the song well, he "set a standard for its performance." "Jean" rose to Number 2 on the Billboard chart in the fall of 1969.

In the early 1970s Swofford toured hundreds of college campuses and collaborated with Karen Carpenter before leaving the business. His debut album ultimately stayed on the chart for thirty-eight weeks. He died in 2000 in Louisiana.

Dorothea Dix State Hospital Campus, c. 1910.

1911 Avery County, High Country Tourist Beacon

On February 23, 1911, Avery County became the last of North Carolina's 100 counties.

Located on the Tennessee border in the mountainous northwest corner of the state called the "High Country," Avery was formed from parts of neighboring Mitchell, Watauga, and Caldwell Counties. It was named for Col. Waightstill Avery, a Revolutionary War officer and the state's first attorney general.

The county's large stands of Fraser fir trees have made it known as "the Christmas tree capital." A popular tourist destination, Avery County also has become known as the home of Grandfather Mountain, its annual Highland Games, and the Blue Ridge Parkway's Linn Cove Viaduct, a curved, 1,234-foot-long, elevated bridge recognized as one of America's major engineering feats.

The town of Newland, incorporated in 1913 and named for Lt. Gov. William Calhoun Newland, is the county seat. At 3,589 feet in elevation, it is the highest county seat in the eastern United States.

Avery's Beech Mountain ski resort community, which got its start in the late 1960s, became a town in 1981. Located at 5,506 feet in elevation, it is the highest municipality in eastern America and receives nearly one hundred inches of snow each winter.

FEB 23

1955 Good Deed in Durham Launches Literary Career

On February 23, 1955, Reynolds Price met Eudora Welty on a cold, dark railroad platform in downtown Durham. Welty, the Mississippi-bred novelist and short-story writer, was coming to Duke University to give a lecture and lead a writing seminar. Price, a Duke senior English major from Warren County, was eager to meet her. "The world she described seemed so close to my own," he later wrote.

Having learned Welty's train would arrive well after midnight and knowing taxis would be unavailable that late, Price decided to chauffeur the future Pulitzer Prize winner to her hotel in his mother's DeSoto convertible. At the next day's seminar, Welty read Price's short story, "Michael Egerton." Afterward she offered to send it to her agent. "Despite a 24-year-gap in our ages, a friendship was cemented on the spot," Price wrote. That friendship lasted until Welty's death in 2001.

By that time Price had become an award-winning writer and long-time English professor at Duke. Treatment for a cancerous spinal tumor in 1984 left him paralyzed from the waist down. Still, he continued to write and teach. His thirty-seven volumes include poetry, short stories, novels, essays, plays, and memoirs. Price died in 2011 at age seventy-seven.

1983 Buckminster Fuller and Geodesic Domes

On February 23, 1983, Buckminster Fuller was awarded the Presidential Medal of Freedom, the nation's highest civilian award, for his contributions as a geometrician, educator, and architect-designer.

"Bucky" Fuller's application of synergetic geometry to geodesic structures took root at Black Mountain College in Buncombe County. During the 1949 summer session at Black Mountain, Fuller erected, with his students and colleagues, the prototype "Autonomous Dwelling Facility with a Geodesic Structure."

As a guest lecturer at the North Carolina State University School of Architecture from 1949 to1955, Fuller worked with his students to design uses of the geodesic dome for a cotton mill, military installations, and the Ford Motor Company. He patented the structure in 1954. Fuller received an honorary Doctor of Design degree from N.C. State in 1954.

After leaving academia, Fuller served as president of the Raleigh architecture firm Synergetics from 1955 to 1959, where colleagues and students created sustainable commercial domes.

The Buckminster Fuller Institute has now identified more than 300 thousand geodesic domes around the world, ranging from shelters to radar stations to playground structures.

Buckminster Fuller at Black Mountain College, summer 1949.

Richard Buckminster Fuller & Anne Hewlett Fuller Dome Home blueprints, 407 South Forest Avenue, Carbondale, Jackson County, IL (*background*).

1868 Andrew Johnson Impeached, 1868

On February 24, 1868, Andrew Johnson became the first president to be impeached for high crimes and misdemeanors.

Johnson, the seventeenth president, was born in Raleigh in 1808. After apprenticing with a tailor in Raleigh, Johnson moved to Tennessee in 1826 and prospered as a tailor and, later, as a politician. Styling himself an advocate for the common man, Johnson was elected to the Tennessee legislature and served there for several years. He represented the First District of Tennessee in Congress for five consecutive terms, then served two terms as governor of Tennessee. He went on to be elected a U.S. senator.

Abraham Lincoln appointed Johnson military governor of Tennessee in 1862, then named the Southerner his running mate for his successful 1864 re-election campaign. Lincoln's assassination elevated Johnson to the Presidency.

Johnson's greatest challenge as president was leading the nation through Reconstruction. After the Civil War's conclusion, he issued a general amnesty to Southerners, with a few exceptions. Radical Republicans, unhappy with Johnson's national policy, sought to undermine his power and eventually had Johnson impeached. The primary charge related to his removing Secretary of War Edwin M. Stanton from office.

The trial concluded in May 1868 with Johnson's acquittal.

1942 Greenville Long Home to Voice of America

On February 24, 1942, the Foreign Information Service, precursor to the Voice of America (VOA), made its first broadcast from New York City to Europe.

Within months twenty-three transmitters were in place and twenty-seven language services on the air. VOA technical facilities and programming saw vast improvements as America sought to thwart the propaganda of communist bloc countries, which, in turn, sought to jam the broadcasts electronically. International radio became an instrument of American foreign policy.

A key link in the network was built in eastern North Carolina. The facility consisted of three sites west, east, and southeast of Greenville. The sites were chosen to ensure the best "electronic propagation conditions." Programs originating from the Washington studios were beamed via microwave to Greenville, then relayed to Latin America, Europe, and Africa. With its inauguration in 1963, the twenty-three million dollar Greenville operation doubled the VOA's power.

The federal government ceased operations at Greenville in 1989, and one of the sites is now home to the *Queen Anne's Revenge* conservation lab.

FEB 24

An engineer sits at the control console of the Voice of America's (VOA) receiving relay station in Greenville, N.C.. The Voice of America headquarters in Washington, D. C. sent the radio programs to Greenville via microwave, and then the signals were beamed to more than 105 million listeners around the world.

FEB 25

1820 Congressman Felix Walker and Origins of "Bunk"

On February 25, 1820, Rep. Felix Walker delivered a rambling speech in Congress that would be little remembered but for the abuse he took that day.

Walker moved to western North Carolina from what is now West Virginia in 1768. He was a militiaman and took part in the Revolutionary War. Walker served in Congress from 1817 until 1823, and at that time Buncombe County was larger than its present size and comprised the core of his Congressional district.

As a result of the fateful speech, which had little relation to the topic at hand and during which colleagues tried to cut him off, Walker gained a reputation for "speaking for Buncombe." The phrase quickly became short for any sort of spurious or questionable statement. Walker's reputation was discredited and his thoughts dismissed as "bunkum" or "bunk." Walker moved to Mississippi in 1824 and lived there until his death in 1828.

"Bunk," in due course, became part of the American lexicon as a word indicating nonsense. In 1916 Henry Ford, speaking about living in the present, made the oft-quoted statement, "History is more or less bunk."

1870 Hiram Revels and the Genesis of Black Political Representation

On February 25, 1870, Hiram Revels was seated in the United States Senate.

A story, perhaps apocryphal, has it that when Jefferson Davis left the U.S. Congress, fellow Senator Simon Cameron told him, "I believe, in the name of God, that a Negro some day will come and occupy your seat." Cameron's prediction came true, for in 1870 Hiram Rhodes Revels, a native of North Carolina, became the first African American member of Congress, taking Davis's seat representing Mississippi.

Revels was born a free black in 1822 in Fayetteville. The precise location is not known. By 1838, he had moved to Lincolnton. For a few years he worked as a barber's apprentice for his brother, and after his brother's death he managed the shop for a time before moving out of North Carolina to pursue other opportunities.

After leaving the Senate in 1871, Revels served as acting secretary of state in Mississippi in 1873 and, from 1876 to 1882, as president of Alcorn Agricultural College. An ordained African Methodist Episcopal minister, Revels preached and lectured widely. While attending a church conference in Aberdeen, Mississippi in January 1901, he died suddenly. He is buried in Holly Springs, Mississippi.

Hiram Revels

1884 Chatham County "Blood Shower"

On February 25, 1884, Mrs. Kit Lasater, "noted for truthfulness," was walking near her home in the township of New Hope in Chatham County when she heard what she thought was a hard rainfall. Glancing up, she saw only clear sky, but when she looked down, she saw what appeared to be the aftermath of a "shower of pure blood."

None of the liquid had fallen on her, but it had drenched the ground and surrounding trees for some sixty feet (some accounts say yards) in circumference from the spot where she stood. Upon hearing her story, neighbors rushed to see for themselves and, when later interviewed, confirmed Mrs. Lasater's story.

Samples were collected and sent to Dr. F. P. Venable, a professor at UNC, for evaluation. By mid-April he addressed the topic at the Mitchell Scientific Society. In every test performed except one, the conclusion was the same: the samples appeared to be blood. Venable could offer no explanation beyond the results of the tests, suggesting only, "[T]he subject is quite a puzzle and offers a tempting field for the theorist blessed with a vivid imagination."

Similar cases of blood showers have been reported for centuries in various locations around the world.

38 JOURNAL OF THE

of the mass in the bottle. This was poured off and examined. It gave abundant tests for phosphoric acid reduced silver solutions and gave phosphine on heating so that it was seen to consist of phosphoric and phosphorous acids. A strong solution of phosphoric acid was then made and some dry amorphous phosphorus added to it. This gave reactions for phosphorous acid after standing over night and quite strongly on standing three or four days. Some of the phosphorus was then washed well with water and then alcohol. It was then washed with carbon bisulphide, this latter filtered off and washed away and the phosphorous gotten thus quite free from the yellow variety. When this was treated with a strong solution of phosphoric acid, it showed signs of oxidation but the dry powder exposed under a beaker and placed in a damp room was still dry at the end of three months.

"FALL OF BLOOD" IN CHATHAM COUNTY.

F. P. VENABLE.

A singular shower of some red liquid, supposed to be blood, which fell in Chatham on February 25th, 1884, was mentioned in some of the State papers, but little notice was taken of it. Nearly a week after the fall, Dr. Sidney Atwater brought a small specimen of sand soaked with this liquid to the University, to be examined. It was looked upon rather as a joke and no analysis was made for some time. When it was taken up several days afterwards there seemed to be sufficient interest attaching to it to warrant paying a visit to the locality where the matter fell. Meantime nearly three weeks had elapsed, and several heavy rains had fallen, so that when the place was reached (a small negro-cabin in New Hope township, about a quarter of a mile from the Raleigh and Pittsboro road) no vestiges of the matter could be found on the ground, and only one or two marks of drops on the fence. The woman who saw it fall was, however, examined and inquiries were made of the neighbors who visited the spot soon after. The fall came from a cloudless sky, when the wind was so slight as to be almost imperceptible.

An exceprt from F. P. Venable, "'Fall of Blood' in Chatham County." *Journal of the Elisha Mitchell Scientific Society*, 1884 (*right and background*).

1865 Prisoner Exchange at Northeast Cape Fear River, 1865

On February 26, 1865, ten miles northeast of downtown Wilmington, Union and Confederate forces began negotiations that concluded in a total of 8,684 Union soldiers' (including 992 commissioned officers and 120 African American troops) being exchanged for an unknown number of Confederate prisoners of war. Many of the Union troops had been prisoners at Salisbury Prison.

Gen. Ulysses S. Grant informed Secretary of War Edwin Stanton that an agreement regarding prisoners held by the warring armies was at hand. The negotiated agreement was completed on February 16 and word relayed to field officers and prison commandants.

Wilmington fell to Union troops under the command of Maj. Gen. J. M. Schofield on February 22, and the following day he sent word to his Confederate counterpart, Gen. Robert F. Hoke, that he was prepared to receive prisoners of war "at the crossing of the Northeast Cape Fear River, on the main road from Wilmington to Goldsborough."

Schofield assigned Brevet Brig. Gen. Joseph C. Abbott as his special agent of exchange. Abbott reported that the exchange of troops at that site commenced on Sunday, February 26, and took seven days.

1870 Lynching of Wyatt Outlaw and the Kirk-Holden War

On February 26, 1870, Graham town commissioner Wyatt Outlaw, an African American, was lynched by a band of Ku Klux Klansmen.

Outlaw served in the Second Regiment United States Colored Troops during the Civil War. In 1866 he attended the second freedmen's convention in Raleigh and soon after organized the Union League, an organization that aimed to promote loyalty to the United States after the Civil War in Alamance County, as well as a school and church. Outlaw became the target for a Klan mob because he was an effective leader, able to work with both races.

With Klan violence mounting following Outlaw's murder, Gov. William Woods Holden declared a state of insurrection in Alamance and Caswell counties in July 1870. A militia force under George W. Kirk of Tennessee suppressed the Klan in those counties.

Nearly one hundred Klan suspects were arrested during the "Kirk-Holden War," but most were released on technicalities, and none was ever tried. White supremacists gained control of the General Assembly in elections that November and impeached Holden for using the militia against the Klan. He was cast out of office in March 1871.

Superior Court judge Albion Tourgée indicted eighteen Klansmen for Outlaw's murder, but an amnesty bill from the legislature resulted in their never going to trial.

1909 Paper Production Milestone in Roanoke Rapids, 1909

On February 26, 1909, the Roanoke Rapids Paper Manufacturing Company produced the first sulphate-processed kraft paper in the United States. The sulphate name refers to the use of sodium sulphate, or sulphur. Kraft paper has long been used in applications ranging from butcher paper to concrete sacks. It is usually coarse and strong and is often light brown in color.

The pulp mill, constructed between 1907 and 1909, was part of the greater Roanoke Rapids Manufacturing Company, incorporated in 1905. At the outset of production, the mill generated between fifteen and eighteen tons of pulp per day, and that daily amount soon increased to twenty-five tons.

Between 1909 and 1912 the finished product of the paper mill was made from ground wood pulp and sulphate pulp. Kraft paper was manufactured entirely from sulphate pulp after 1912. In 1913 the name of the business was changed to Halifax Paper Company, and improvements were made to the plant in order to boost production to thirty-five tons per day. The company continued to expand and merge over the years and is now a subsidiary of International Paper.

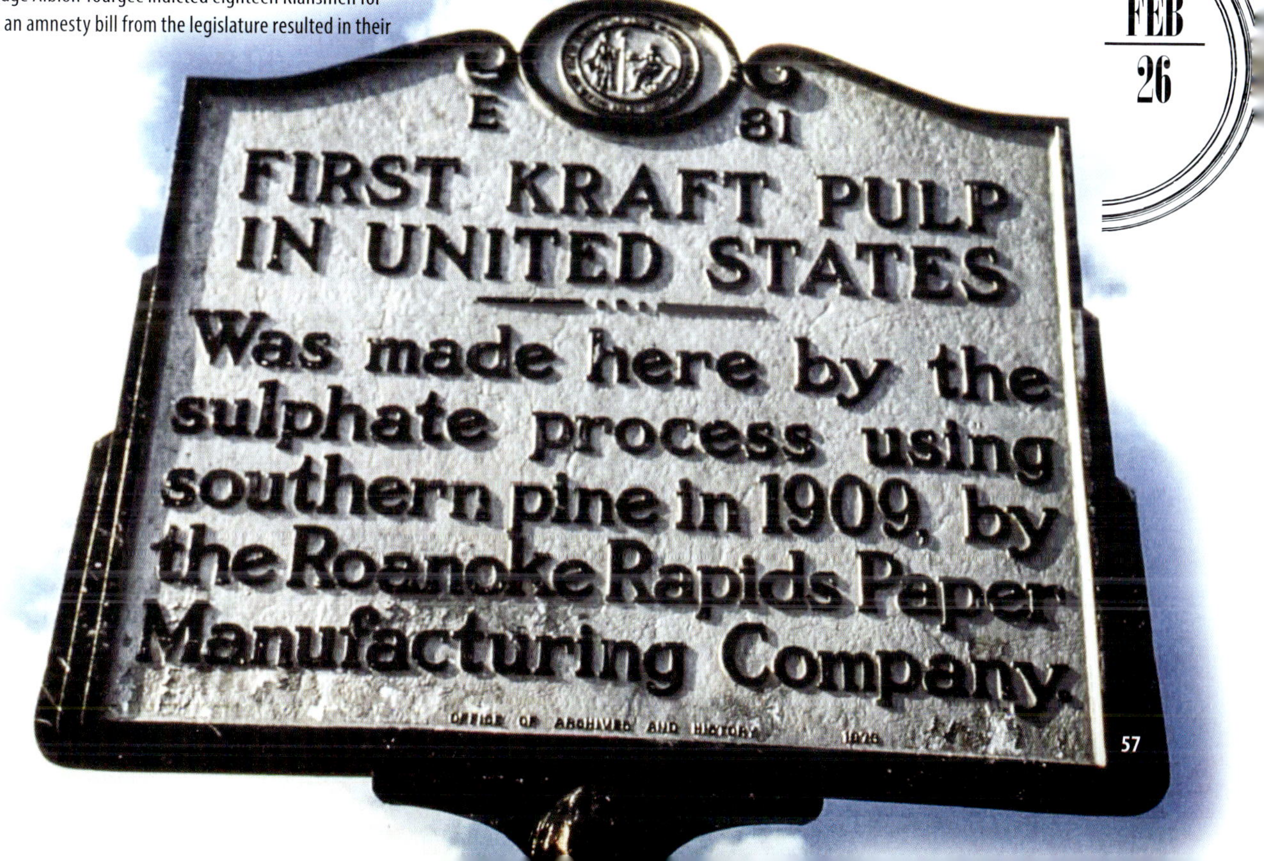

FEB 26

FEB 27

1760 Cherokee Attack on Fort Dobbs

On February 27, 1760, Fort Dobbs (near present-day Statesville) was attacked by a force of more than sixty Cherokee warriors. The fort had been constructed four years earlier to protect the western frontier during the French and Indian War.

Fighting between the British settlers and their former allies broke out in 1759 as settlers were killed in revenge for the murder of several Cherokee the year before. As the only permanent fort on the colony's frontier, Dobbs served as a safe-haven for settlers, and its garrison of soldiers helped to defend the region.

Col. Hugh Waddell, the fort's commander, noted that the Cherokee "found the fire very hot," as ten of his men engaged the Cherokee near the fort around nine o'clock at night. "I ordered my party to fire which we did not further than 12 steps each loaded with a bullet and seven buck shot," Waddell later wrote, adding "They [the Cherokee] had nothing to cover them as they were advancing either to tomahawk or make us prisoners . . .".

Waddell retreated to the fort, and the Cherokee broke off the attack. The combined casualties, killed or wounded, from the brief encounter included twelve Cherokee, two soldiers, and one settler child.

1776 Battle of Moores Creek Bridge, 1776

On February 27, 1776, Loyalist forces commanded by Colonel Donald McDonald discovered a Patriot encampment near Moores Creek that, unbeknownst to them, had been abandoned, although the campfires were left burning.

A Loyalist force of almost two thousand Tories, many of whom were former Scottish Highlanders, prepared to pursue an army believed to be retreating across the narrow bridge over Moore's Creek. At the same time a Patriot force of more than one thousand men commanded by Cols. James Moore, Richard Caswell, and Alexander Lillington greased planks along the bridge and built platforms above the creek to ambush the enemy.

Just after sunrise, the Loyalists, led by Lt. Col. Donald McLeod, stormed the bridge. In the subsequent ambush confusion gave way to slaughter as nine hundred Loyalists were killed, wounded, or captured.

The Battle of Moores Creek Bridge, often referred to as the "Lexington and Concord of the South," was pivotal. Without Loyalist forces to protect the colonial government of Gov. Josiah Martin, the royal system collapsed, allowing Patriot leaders to establish a fledgling state government. The Patriot victory also denied Britain use of North Carolina's ports, which were logistically significant.

1964 Polymath and Centenarian Anna Julia Cooper of Raleigh

On February 27, 1964, black feminist activist, scholar, and educator Anna Julia Haywood Cooper died at age 105.

Born into slavery in 1858 in Raleigh, Cooper graduated from St. Augustine's Normal School, then earned a B.A. and an M.A. in mathematics from Oberlin College in Ohio. She taught for a few years in Raleigh before moving to Washington, D.C., to teach there.

In 1892 she published *A Voice from the South*, one of the first comprehensive statements of black feminism. Her analysis of racism, sexism, and subjugation of black women would echo into the black feminist movements of the twentieth century.

Cooper devoted her life to the advancement of gender and racial equality and higher education of black women, published essays, made speeches, and was active in black women's uplift organizations.

At age sixty-six Cooper became the fourth African American woman in the nation to receive a Ph.D., earning her doctorate from the Sorbonne in Paris. Working well into her nineties, she spent her final thirty years at D.C.'s Frelinghuysen University, a school for working-class black adults.

She is buried in Raleigh.

Moores Creek Bridge, site of one of the first Patriot victories of the American Revolution, fought February 27, 1776.

Photo of Anna Julia Cooper educator and civil rights activist taken in early 1900s.

1869 Governor Thomas Bickett of Monroe and Louisburg

On February 28, 1869, Thomas Bickett, North Carolina's World War I governor, was born in Monroe.

After studying law at UNC, Bickett settled in Louisburg and in 1906 was elected to represent Franklin County in the state House . During his single term in the General Assembly, he made his mark as the sponsor of the "Bickett Bill," which set aside a half-million dollars to help care for the mentally ill.

Drawing attention at the 1908 state Democratic Party convention in Charlotte, Bickett was nominated for attorney general. During his two terms in that office, he successfully defended the state's interests in numerous state Supreme Court cases and five before the United States Supreme Court.

Bickett was elected governor in 1916, the first year primary contests were held. Three months after his inauguration, the United States entered World War I. Though motivating the public to help the war effort became a major focus of his term, he also helped overhaul the state's parole system, expand higher education, reform the tax code, and increase spending on public health. A strikingly successful politician, he saw the General Assembly adopt forty of the forty-eight proposals he made during his term.

Bickett died in December 1921 and is buried in Louisburg.

1935 Driver's Licensing Began

On February 28, 1935, the General Assembly passed the Uniform Driver's License Act, placing in the pockets of authorized drivers the state's official sanction of their being behind the wheel.

The bill, sponsored by Sen.Carroll Weathers of Wake County, was a response to the more than 1,000 deaths on the state's highways since the rise of the automobile thirty years earlier. The automobile age in North Carolina had begun in earnest with the introduction of the "Buggymobile" in New Bern in 1903 and other primitive vehicles soon after.

The 1935 act defined a motor vehicle as "any rubber-tired vehicle propelled or drawn by any power other than muscular." Aircraft, road rollers, street sprinklers, ambulances, baggage trucks, and agricultural and industrial tractors were excluded from the licensing requirement.

Then as now, drivers were required to be at least sixteen years old. Initially no test was required, and only the applicant's word that she or he was experienced and careful was needed. Exams began in 1948.

Today the Division of Motor Vehicles, part of the Department of Transportation, administers the state's drivers licensing program.

1930s Ford

Harnett Basketball Contest in 1964 Had Thirteen Overtimes

1964

On February 29, 1964, Boone Trail High School held off Angier High School to win North Carolina's longest high school basketball game on record, 54-52.

The game, that year's Harnett County high school championship, was played in Campbell University's Carter Gym. That small gym could seat only 947 spectators. There is no known record of how many people attended that day's game.

After the regulation game ended in a 44-44 tie, the two teams duked it out in thirteen overtime sessions, and both teams used only the original five starting players throughout the game, with no substitutions. The teams scored only a combined eighteen points in the thirteen overtime sessions, and there were nine where neither team scored any points.

Boone Trail's Frankie Stewart led all scorers with twenty-nine points. Reportedly, one of the Angier players was so superstitious that the coaches told his teammates not to tell him they were in overtime number thirteen.

The game began at 8:30 p.m. Saturday and ended just before midnight. With the final buzzer, it barely avoided the "no play on Sunday" rule.

FEB 29

The uniforms belonging to the players of the legendary 1964 basketball team were packed in cardboard boxes and forgotten when Boone Trail High School closed in the late 1970s. The uniforms were rediscovered and carefully cleaned in late 2016, then sold to raise funds for a new community center.

MAR 1

1827 Thomas Day of Milton, Premier Furniture Craftsman

On March 1, 1827, Thomas Day ran an advertisement in the local newspaper, the *Milton Gazette & Roanoke Advertiser*, thanking his patrons and advertising his handmade furniture and quality service. Day, a cabinetmaker by trade, was one of North Carolina's most celebrated antebellum craftsmen.

He was born in Dinwiddie County, Virginia in 1801 to free, landowning African Americans. Like his brother John Jr., he followed in his father's footsteps and learned the cabinetmaking trade. Both of the Day sons were well educated.

Thomas and his brother established themselves in the furniture business in Milton by 1823. There, Thomas became a prominent and well-respected citizen of the community. In his almost forty years in Milton, Day built an extraordinary business, employing freedmen and slaves alike to craft stock lines of furniture and to fill custom orders for furniture and interior woodworking.

By 1850 Day had the largest cabinetry shop in North Carolina. He is believed to have died in about 1861 after having suffered financial losses due to the national panic of 1857. The surviving examples of his work are tangible evidence of his skill and accomplishments as a woodworker and craftsman.

1854 North Carolina Wine Pioneer Sidney Weller

On March 1, 1854, Sidney Weller, who introduced the American style of grape culture, died. Weller was born in 1791 in New York. He moved to Virginia in 1828, then further south to Halifax County, North Carolina.

In 1829 Weller purchased about three hundred acres of farm land for $1.50 per acre. Although the land was of poor quality, Weller was a self-proclaimed "book farmer" who read about and experimented with new farming methods. He subscribed to various farm journals and wrote many articles for them. His methods were revolutionary at a time when throngs of North Carolinians were moving southwest in search of better lands. Weller was an advocate of crop rotation, plant propagation, and enriching soil through creative plantings and waste matter.

Among his innovative ventures Weller established a vineyard which by 1840 was the state's largest. At the time, North Carolina was the leading wine producer in America. In 1850 Weller boasted of cultivating more than two hundred types of grapes, although he concentrated on Scuppernong and other native varieties. Weller's property is now Medoc Mountain State Park. Weller named the area Medoc Mountain after a province in Bordeaux, France, famous for its vineyards.

1876 Lewis Redmond, "King of the Moonshiners"

On March 1, 1876, moonshiner Lewis Redmond murdered U.S. Deputy Marshall Alfred Duckworth near East Fork in Transylvania County.

Duckworth was killed while serving a federal warrant on Redmond for the illegal manufacture and sale of distilled liquor. The crime marked the beginning of Redmond's career as the legendary "King of the Moonshiners."

Born in 1854, Redmond grew up during a time when the production of distilled alcohol was an additional source of income for many Southern farmers. In the post-Civil War South many illegal distillers, or moonshiners, attempted to circumvent payment of taxes on their products, leading to conflict with the Federal Bureau of Revenue.

Following Duckworth's death Redmond fled to Pickens County, South Carolina—to an area known as "Dark Corners"—where his moonshining and brushes with the law continued. His activities were fictionalized in a number of publications that gained him national status as a folk hero.

In 1879 he moved to Swain County, where two years later he was captured and tried for violating the revenue law and for criminal conspiracy. He pled guilty and was sentenced to ten years in federal prison. Serving only a few years, he was pardoned in 1884.

Redmond died in Walhalla, South Carolina in 1906.

1898 The Holding Family and First Citizens Bank

On March 1, 1898, the Bank of Smithfield, now known as First Citizens Bank, opened for business.

The bank, Johnston County's first, was founded by Allen W. Smith, who remained president until 1906. The institution became First National Bank of Smithfield before merging with Citizens National Bank to become First and Citizens National Bank. In 1929 the company adopted the now-familiar moniker of First Citizens Bank & Trust Company.

Robert Powell Holding, who joined the bank as an assistant cashier in 1918, became president in 1935. He piloted First Citizens through the Depression and World War II, and by the time of his death in 1957, it was the second largest bank in North Carolina. Holding's three sons continued in their father's footsteps, occupying the key posts of chairman of the board, president, and vice president.

The Holdings elevated First Citizens into one of the largest family-controlled banks in the United States, and the family continues to own the bank today.

Thomas Day furniture from the collection of the North Carolina Museum of History.

Thomas Day residence and workshop (*background*).

MAR 2

1781 Battle of Clapp's Mill, 1781

On March 2, 1781, Patriot forces under Col. Henry Lee, local militiamen, and Catawba Indian allies surprised the Loyalist mounted cavalry of Lt. Col. Banastre Tarleton in a well-planned ambush near Clapp's Mill in Alamance County.

As soon as the confusion caused by the first American volley was brought under control, Tarleton retired to cover and deployed his troops against the Patriots. Coming under heavy fire, the American second line became panic-stricken and retreated. Tarleton chose not to pursue. The British suffered twenty-one casualties, while the Americans had only eight.

Most of what we know about the encounter comes from the account of Joseph Graham, a member of Lee's Legion. Lee and fellow officer Otho Williams apparently planned a major engagement at Clapp's Mill that did not end up happening, but the desired major battle did take place less than two weeks later at Guilford Courthouse.

In 1898 a local historian identified the site of Clapp's Mill about three miles northwest of the site of the Battle of Alamance. Signs of the old dam and millrun were visible in 1898, but evidence of the mill itself had by that time disappeared. Today a reservoir covers much of the site.

1927 Memorial to the Wright Brothers Authorized, 1927

On March 2, 1927, President Calvin Coolidge signed legislation authorizing the Kill Devil Hills National Monument. Five years later, a sixty-foot granite monument was dedicated in Dare County.

The monument itself was built on a ninety-foot sand dune stabilized through the planting of special grasses. The dune was part of a larger natural embankment that the Wright Brothers used to launch gliders in the years leading up to their famed first powered flights in 1903.

Designed to mimic the look of a marine beacon, the monument's double entrance doors each have six panels depicting moments from mankind's attempts at flight. The inscription notes the momentous achievements in the history of flight that the Wright Brothers attained at Kill Devil Hills.

Though the monument's 1932 dedication was expected to draw tens of thousands of people, bad weather kept all but a handful away. Orville Wright attended as the featured guest of honor. In 1953 Congress redesignated the monument as the Wright Brothers National Memorial.

It continues to be one the premiere attractions on the Outer Banks, drawing more than 425 thousand visitors each year.

1936 Agriculture's Voice, the North Carolina Farm Bureau

On March 2, 1936, J. E. Winslow called to order the first meeting of the North Carolina Farm Bureau (NCFB) in Greenville. No records exist to show who was elected to the nonprofit, grassroots organization's first board of directors, but many years later, the Farm Bureau has much to show for its years of service to the state's rural families.

As the unified "voice of agriculture" in North Carolina, NCFB has been—and continues to be—a powerful and effective legislative advocate for Tar Heel farmers at the local, state, national, and international levels. In 1942 farm women became members and gained a voice in affairs by forming what would become the Women's Committee. During its early days NCFB's support helped make Gov. Kerr Scott's Farm-to-Market Roads a reality. More recently it has led the fight for drought relief, transportation regulations, and immigration reform.

In 1953 the organization introduced its first service-to-member program: the North Carolina Farm Bureau Mutual Insurance Company. Today NCFB programs offer its more than five hundred thousand members a wide selection of services and savings, from prescription drug plans to banking services to educational assistance. Based in Raleigh since 1958, the Farm Bureau has offices in all of North Carolina's one hundred counties.

Wright Brothers Memorial, c. 1935.

1868 Cardinal James Gibbons, Roman Catholic Prelate

On March 3, 1868, Rev. James Gibbons was appointed the first vicar of North Carolina. At the time he was the nation's youngest Roman Catholic bishop.

Born in Maryland in 1837 to recent Irish immigrants, Gibbons was forced to return to Ireland with his family shortly after his birth due to financial problems. After growing up there, he returned to the United States and entered seminary. He then worked as a pastor at a Baltimore church and as a chaplain at nearby military prisons before becoming secretary to the Archbishop of Baltimore and eventually getting the North Carolina post.

Although there were few Catholics in North Carolina at the time of his appointment, Gibbons undertook a tour of the state just after arriving in Wilmington in October 1868. He traveled extensively for the rest of his term, serving small Catholic parishes and preaching to larger congregations in Protestant churches as well as in courthouses and other public buildings.

Gibbons went on to serve as Bishop of Richmond and Archbishop of Baltimore before being named a cardinal in 1886. While Archbishop of Baltimore, Gibbons founded the Catholic University of America in Washington, D.C. and often counseled presidents and other public figures.

He died in 1921 and is buried in the crypt of Baltimore Cathedral.

1891 Elizabeth City State University's Beginnings, 1891

On March 3, 1891, legislation passed creating a Normal and Industrial School in Elizabeth City. The school was founded with the express purpose of "teaching and training teachers of the colored race to teach in the common schools of North Carolina."

The bill began in the state House of Representatives and was championed by Hugh Cale, an African American who represented Pasquotank County. Cale, who was a free person of color before the Civil War, had been involved in African American education immediately following the Civil War and served on the Pasquotank County Board of Education.

The Normal School extended its mission under the guidance of its first principal, Peter Weddick Moore. In 1937 it expanded from a two-year program to a four-year teacher's college and received a new name to reflect that change: Elizabeth City Teachers College. The first bachelor's degree was awarded by the school in 1939 in elementary education.

In 1972 the college became part of the consolidated University of North Carolina system and was renamed Elizabeth City State University. To commemorate the school's centennial in 1991, the General Assembly honored Cale and the university with a bill setting a special mock session.

P. W. Horne, far right, with students in 1899.

1915 Mount Mitchell, First Among the State Parks

On March 3, 1915, the General Assembly appropriated twenty thousand dollars to purchase Mount Mitchell. It would become the first of North Carolina's state parks.

At the time the virgin-growth forests rich with balsam and spruce that once dominated the Black Mountains were quickly disappearing because of a thriving timber trade in the area. The effort to preserve the Yancey County mountain from rampant logging came about, in part, from extensive lobbying by Gov. Locke Craig.

At 6,684 feet Mount Mitchell is the highest peak east of the Mississippi River. It was named for Elisha Mitchell, a science professor who first visited the area around it as part of the North Carolina Geological Survey. In the 1830s and 1840s, he took barometric pressure readings from the state's tallest peaks and used mathematical formulas to determine their elevations. Until Mitchell's calculations New Hampshire's Mount Washington, only 396 feet shorter than Mitchell, was thought to be the tallest peak in the east.

In an unfortunate twist of fate, Mitchell died while exploring the mountain that bears his name in 1857, when he slipped and fell from a cliff, drowning near a waterfall now known as Mitchell Falls.

One hundred years later, the North Carolina State Park System is thriving. It now preserves nearly 220 thousand acres of North Carolina's natural beauty at seventy-four parks, recreation areas, natural areas, lakes, rivers. and trails and attracts millions of visitors each year.

1923 Guitar Virtuoso "Doc" Watson—A Late Bloomer

On March 3, 1923, Arthel Lane Watson, known to the world as "Doc" Watson, was born in Watauga County. The sixth of nine children, as an infant Watson developed an eye infection that left him blind, and he was sent to attend the Governor Morehead School in Raleigh.

His parents sang and encouraged their son's interest in music. Virtually self-taught, he mastered harmonica, banjo, and guitar at an early age. It was his guitar playing that garnered the greatest attention due to his unique style. In 1953 he was playing with a band that often did not have a fiddle player. Watson taught himself to play the fiddle parts on his guitar, often at breakneck speeds.

Although he had been playing locally for years, Watson was not discovered nationally until the 1960s during the folk music revival. In 1961 he and several other musicians played in Greenwich Village. That led to other concerts, and Watson was invited to perform at the Newport Folk Festival in 1963 and 1964.

Watson never claimed to be a purist; he played music that he liked, and he had eclectic taste. During his long career he won eight Grammys and, in 1997, the National Medal of Arts.

Mount Mitchell as seen from Mount Craig.

MAR
4

1825 Lafayette Visits Town Named in His Honor

On March 4, 1825, the Marquis de Lafayette visited Fayetteville, a town named for him in 1783, staying at the home of Duncan McRae, on the site of the present Cumberland County Courthouse.

Lafayette was a close confidant of George Washington and one of the great heroes of the Revolutionary War. He returned to the United States at age sixty-eight on a celebratory tour, and although he originally planned to visit only New England and the mid-Atlantic, he extended his trip to the southern states as well, including North Carolina. While in North Carolina, Lafayette was hosted by his namesake town for one night at McRae's home.

Before arriving in Fayetteville, Lafayette stayed at the Indian Queen Inn in Murfreesboro, visited the Rocky Mount home of Henry Donaldson, and attended a banquet at the Eagle Tavern in Halifax. He also traveled to Raleigh, where he visited Gov. Hutchins Burton and William Polk, a veteran of the Revolutionary War.

Fayetteville, incorporated in 1783, was one of the first towns in the newly independent United States named for the Marquis.

1861 Elizabeth Keckley, From Hillsborough to the White House

On March 4, 1861, successful African American dressmaker Elizabeth Keckley met soon-to-be First Lady Mary Todd Lincoln for the first time at the Willard Hotel in Washington, D.C.

It was the day of Abraham Lincoln's inauguration, and Mrs. Lincoln was too busy with plans for the festivities to talk with Keckley, who was recommended by a friend. After a brief meeting at the White House the next day, she hired Keckley.

The two women quickly developed a close friendship, and Keckley even assisted the President with his clothes and hair before public appearances.

In 1868 Keckley published her memoir, *Behind the Scenes: Or 30 Years a Slave, and Four Years in the White House*. Though Keckley claimed she wrote the book to help support the widowed Mary Lincoln financially, its publication created a rift between the two women that would never be healed.

Born a slave in Virginia around 1820, Keckley came to Hillsborough with her master's son in 1835. After thirty-seven years in slavery she purchased her freedom and that of her son George in 1855 and left an abusive husband in 1860 to move to Washington, where she started her dressmaking business.

Keckley died in Washington, D.C. in 1907.

1911 "Muley Bob" Doughton of Ways and Means

On March 4, 1911, Congressman Robert Lee Doughton launched a forty-two-year career in the United States House of Representatives. He served twenty-one successive terms in Congress before voluntarily retiring in 1953, just short of his ninetieth birthday.

Born in Alleghany County in 1863, he was named for the Confederate general under whom his father served. A farmer by trade, Doughton began a career in public service with his appointment to the state Board of Agriculture in 1903. He then served in the state Senate in 1908 and 1909, before being elected to Congress in 1910.

In Congress Doughton was appointed to the powerful House Ways and Means Committee. He would eventually work his way up to chair the committee and went on to hold that post for eighteen years, longer than any other member. Often called "Muley Bob," since he was famous for his stubbornness, Doughton was an expert on tax policy. He also took great pride in his role in the preparation and passage of the Social Security Act of 1935, and he was instrumental in the creation of the Blue Ridge Parkway, the ground for which was broken in his home county in 1935.

Doughton died in 1954 in his home in Laurel Springs.

Dress attributed to Elizabeth Keckley (*left*), worn by Mary Todd Lincoln (*on right*).

1728 William Byrd II and the 1728 NC/VA Survey

On March 5, 1728, delegates from North Carolina and Virginia met to survey the border between the two colonies.

Virginia's and Carolina's early settlers intermingled in the early colonial period, as colonists trickled south in search of good land to grow crops and establish homesteads. Explorer John Lawson began surveying a boundary between Carolina and Virginia but was unable to complete the task.

The border remained vague until 1728, when the survey, led by Virginian William Byrd II of Westover, was conducted. The group defined the line from the coast to about 240 miles inland in what is now Stokes County. The survey was completed in 1749, when Thomas Jefferson's father, Peter, began in Stokes County and finished the line in what is now Ashe County. The borders were often disputed and additional surveys were called to settle claims.

Generally speaking, surveyor's reports are mundane, but Byrd penned a journal of the expedition with exceptional literary merit. It was widely published in two forms, candidly chronicling the people and places on both sides of the line. Both versions of Byrd's account are entertaining and offer a rare and humorous glimpse into life and travel in colonial America.

1756 Surgeon, Governor Nathaniel Alexander of Charlotte

On March 5, 1756, Nathaniel Alexander, physician, congressman, and governor, was born in what is now Mecklenburg County.

While not much is known about his early life, Alexander graduated in 1776 from the school that is now Princeton University. He earned a degree in medicine and was commissioned as a surgeon in the North Carolina Continental Line in 1778, serving for the duration of the war.

In addition to practicing medicine, Alexander was a Mason and was active in establishing a lodge in Charlotte. He entered politics in 1797, when he was elected to the state House of Commons, representing Mecklenburg County. He served in both houses of the General Assembly and was elected to Congress in 1803 but resigned in 1805, when he was elected governor of North Carolina.

Called a "scholar and a true patriot," Alexander as governor attempted to settle the lingering border dispute with Georgia and was an early advocate of education and internal improvements.

He lost the gubernatorial election in 1807 and died less than a year later in March 1808. He was buried in the First Presbyterian Church Cemetery in Charlotte.

1974 A Look Back at Streakers

On March 5, 1974, at the end of "Streak Week," students at the University of North Carolina at Chapel Hill loosely organized the American Streaker Society. In celebration, and under a banner proclaiming "Home of the World Champion Streakers," about nine hundred naked students marched across campus through a crowd of six thousand onlookers, accompanied by the University pep band.

Western Carolina University laid claim to the first major streak of the short-lived fad, making North Carolina the streaking epicenter of the nation. All of the major universities in the state and large numbers of the smaller universities and colleges had streaking events on their campuses. Authorities reacted in many different ways to the campus fad, from amused tolerance to hostile arrests and threats of expulsion.

A North Carolina state senator said that he was mulling over the efficacy of introducing a Streaker Ban Bill. It was unnecessary, however, since the fad stopped almost as suddenly as it had begun.

Streak Week streakers behind Wilson Library in 1974.

MAR 6

1836 Defender of the Alamo, Micajah Autry

On March 6, 1836, North Carolina native Micajah Autry died defending the Alamo. Autry was born in Sampson County around 1794 and grew up in Cumberland County.

In 1823 Autry moved to Tennessee, where he practiced law and tried his hand as a merchant. In Jackson, Tennessee he met David Crockett, whom some believe influenced Autry's decision to investigate the Texas frontier. Autry set out for Texas with a companion in late 1835 and sent a series of remarkably descriptive letters home to his wife. Those letters survived, and one is on display at the Alamo to this day. In that letter he states, "I go the whole Hog in the cause of Texas. I expect to help them gain their independence and also to form their government, for it is worth risking many lives for." A postscript to the letter reads, "Col. Crockett has joined our company."

In Texas Autry and Crockett enlisted in the Volunteer Auxiliary Corps and arrived at the Alamo in February. Autry was likely among the first to die in the Mexican siege of the mission.

FRANK LESLIE'S ILLUSTRATED NEWSPAPER.

GEN. GEORGE SYKES, U. S. A.

THE SINKING OF THE CELEBRATED STEAMER PETERHOFF.

THE MUSIC-STAND IN THE BALL OF THE 3D ARMY CORPS.

1863 Monticello-Peterhoff Encounter, 1863

On March 6, 1863, only one week into blockading duty, the USS *Peterhoff* met an untimely end south of New Inlet near Confederate-held Fort Fisher.

The incident was the result of a misunderstanding. Off-duty blockading vessels were not supposed to travel inside the blockading lines at night, but the wooden-hulled, screw steamer USS *Monticello* violated that rule while heading to Beaufort for refueling and, in the process, mistook the *Peterhoff* for a blockade runner. The *Monticello* rammed the *Peterhoff*, and in less than a half hour the latter lay on the bottom of the sea.

The audacious captain of the *Monticello*, Lt. Cmdr. William B. Cushing, was not held responsible, nor was the ship's commander, Acting Volunteer Lt. Thomas Pickering, though Pickering later was put on another assignment. The ensign who was in charge of the deck at the time of the incident was blamed for "irresponsibility and carelessness."

One hundred years later the wreck of the USS *Peterhoff* was discovered by recreational divers. Cannons and other artifacts recovered in 1974 can be seen at area museums. The site of the *Peterhoff* wreck is now listed on the National Register of Historic Places.

North Carolina has more Civil War shipwrecks than any other state.

1970 Nabs for a Nickel, No More

On March 6, 1970, Lance Crackers produced the last of its trademark five-cent items.

The company was formed in Charlotte in 1913, largely by accident, when food broker Phillip L. Lance got stuck with five hundred pounds of Virginia peanuts that he couldn't use. Instead of simply returning them to the farmer, Lance roasted the nuts and sold them in small bags for a nickel.

Inspired by his initial success, Lance soon moved his business out of his home and into a factory on Charlotte's College Street, where he both roasted peanuts and made peanut butter. His wife Mary and daughters are credited with first spreading peanut butter between two crackers around 1915.

Lance's company began making its own crackers in 1938, though candy was actually its primary product through World War II. Lance vending machines first appeared in 1954, and the company went public in 1961. Through this entire time all of the company's individually-packaged products were sold for five cents.

Though the price of many of its products changed in 1970, the company continued to be successful, expanding into grocery stores in 1982 and acquiring several competitors. In 2010 Lance merged with Synder's of Hanover to become the second largest salty snack maker in the United States.

Illustration of the sinking of the USS Peterhoff, 1864.
From *Frank Leslie's Illustrated Newspaper*, April 2, 1864.

MAR 7

1887 Croatan Normal School, Forerunner of UNC-Pembroke

On March 7, 1887, the General Assembly passed legislation allowing the construction of a secondary school for the Robeson County Indians then called the Croatan and now known as the Lumbee. First known as the Croatan Normal School, the institution's main goal was to train Indians to become school teachers.

In 1909 the campus moved to its present location. As the curriculum expanded and four-year degrees were offered, the school changed its name to Pembroke State College for Indians. The campus officially became part of the University of North Carolina on July 1, 1972, as a result of consolidation leading to the creation of a sixteen-campus system. The name change to University of North Carolina at Pembroke became official in 1996.

In 1972 a campaign to save "Old Main," the white-pillared centerpiece of the campus, drew national press coverage. The building, a symbol of Indian education and social progress, was restored in 1979. Once primarily an all-Indian school associated with the Lumbee tribe, the university today serves a multi-racial student body.

In 2005 the General Assembly passed a law that recognized UNC-Pembroke as "North Carolina's Historically American Indian University."

1903 The Historical Commission and "History for All the People"

On March 7, 1903, the General Assembly established the North Carolina Historical Commission.

First based in the northeast corner of the Capitol's second floor, the Commission's most important obligation was to collect, edit, and publish documents to make those records, both public and private, available to the citizens and to assure their preservation.

R. D. W. Connor, who later became the first Archivist of the United States, was the commissioner's first secretary. His successor in 1934 was populist historian Christopher Crittenden, who held the reins until 1968 and who promoted "History for All the People" as the commission's goal.

In 1943 the agency's name was changed to the Department of Archives and History, better describing its function, importance, and permanence. In 1955 the legislature transferred most state historic sites to the agency.

In 1968 the department's administration, the state archives, and the Museum of History moved into a new building at 109 East Jones Street. With the reorganization of state government in 1971, the agency became part of the new Department of Cultural Resources.

Today the Office of Archives and History is an agency of the North Carolina Department of Natural and Cultural Resources and includes diverse programs, museums, and sites that promote the state's long history.

1914 "Babe" Ruth Gets His Nickname in Fayetteville

On March 7, 1914, George Herman Ruth Jr. hit his first home run as a professional baseball player and gained the nickname "Babe" in Fayetteville.

Ruth began playing baseball in his native Baltimore at age nineteen. Jack Dunn, manager of the Baltimore Orioles, recognized his talent and signed him to his first professional contract. A few weeks later the team headed to Fayetteville en route to Florida for spring training.

While in Fayetteville the players learned that Dunn had legally adopted Ruth to keep him with the Orioles. That, combined with Ruth's playing on the elevators at the Lafayette Hotel, resulted in the older players teasing him as "Dunn's baby," later shortened to "Baby" and "Babe."

In the last inning of the exhibition game at the Cape Fear Fair Ground, Ruth hit a long home run. He described that moment: "I hit it as I hit all the others, by taking a good gander at the pitch as it came up to the plate, twisting my body into a backswing and then hitting it as hard I as I could swing." Ruth later commented, "I got to some bigger places than Fayetteville after that, but darn few as exciting."

Babe Ruth, in Fayetteville, March 7, 1914, the day he began his career with the Baltimore Orioles by hitting a home run.

MAR 8

1705 Bath Becomes North Carolina's First Incorporated Town

On March 8, 1705, Bath, the first town in the colony of North Carolina, was incorporated. Bath was a thriving town of vital importance to the fledgling colony. The first town lots, recorded and acknowledged in court on October 1, 1706, were those belonging to Christopher Gale, the first Chief Justice of the colony. The following year Bath added a gristmill and the colony's first shipyard. Other North Carolina firsts in Bath include the public library, St. Thomas Church, and the post road.

Bath became the colony's first port in 1716 but was later overshadowed by ports that were geographically more suitable. The General Assembly met in Bath in 1743, 1744, and 1752. In 1746 the town was considered for becoming the colony's capital. It was home to colonial governors Robert Daniel, Thomas Cary, Charles Eden, and Matthew Rowan.

When the Beaufort County seat was moved to Washington, twelve miles away, Bath lost much of its trade and status, becoming the quiet, rural town that it is today. Bath's original town limits today encompass a historic disctrict that includes the Historic Bath State Historic Site.

1865 Sherman's Troops Camped at Laurel Hill

On March 8, 1865, Gen. William T. Sherman, traveling with the 15th Corps, crossed the state line and entered what is now Scotland County. Orders went out that Union troops should treat North Carolinians less harshly than South Carolinians, who were blamed for starting the war.

Other parts of the Union army had entered North Carolina the previous day. Heavy rain and poor roads made for difficult travel. On the night of March 8, Sherman's party camped at Laurel Hill Presbyterian Church near Laurinburg, home to one of the many congregations founded by Scots settlers in the Cape Fear region in the eighteenth century.

At camp, Sherman made plans to advance on to Fayetteville and Goldsboro. Sending communications to fellow Union officers in Wilmington, he ordered that a boat be sent up the Cape Fear River to meet him in Fayetteville.

While near Laurel Hill, a contingent of Union troops destroyed the Murdock Morrison gun factory, a supplier of Confederate weapons. Other troops ransacked the meeting place of the Richmond Temperance and Literary Society in Wagram. On their way out of the area, Sherman's soldiers are said to have used pews from the church to build a bridge across Jordan's Creek.

1865 Battle of Wyse Fork on the Eve of Bentonville

On March 8, 1865, the Battle of Wyse Fork began near Kinston.

The first day of action would prove to be the high point for Confederate forces. More than thirteen thousand Union forces under Maj. Gen. Jacob D. Cox were intent on moving up the rail line from New Bern through Kinston to Goldsboro to unite with Gen. William T. Sherman and open a supply route through eastern North Carolina. Around 12,500 Confederate troops under Gen. Braxton Bragg entrenched on Southwest Creek sought to impede Union progress. The two forces clashed there, and the ensuring battle lasted three days.

The Battle of Wyse Fork involved one of the largest concentrations of troops ever on North Carolina soil. The armies engaged were exceeded in size only by those at the Battle of Bentonville, which would occur just over a week later.

More than 225 Confederates were taken prisoner and an unknown number left dead or dying on the field. Total Union casualties for the three days were fewer, with fifty-seven killed and 265 wounded. As a delaying maneuver, the battle was a success for the Confederates.

St. Thomas Church, Bath.

1891 Birthday for N.C. A&T State University

On March 9, 1891, North Carolina Agricultural and Technical State University was founded as a land grant institution for African Americans. The school, originally named the Agricultural and Mechanical College, was established as a result of the Second Morrill Act, enacted by Congress in 1890, which mandated separate colleges for the "colored race."

Initially the college shared space with Shaw University but eventually moved to its permanent home in Greensboro with the assistance of Dewitt Clinton Benbow, a Guilford County businessman and philanthropist, and Charles H. Moore, an African American educator and businessman.

In 1915 the state legislature changed the name to Agricultural and Technical College. The college became a university in 1967 and took its current name, and in 1972, N.C. A&T became a constituent institution of the University of North Carolina system.

Today N.C. A&T has more than ten thousand students and awards degrees in bachelor's, master's, and doctoral programs with a strong emphasis on engineering, science, and technology. It awards more degrees in engineering to African Americans than any other university in the country and is the second-largest educator of minority agricultural graduates nationwide.

1903 Dougherty Brothers and Appalachian State University

On March 9, 1903, the General Assembly granted brothers B.B. and D.D. (short for Blanchard Barnard and Dauphin Disco) Dougherty a charter for the Appalachian Training School for Teachers.

The school had its roots in the Doughertys' Watauga Academy, which they established in 1899 to train public school teachers for jobs in western North Carolina. With both brothers at the helm, B. B. Dougherty was considered head of school, while D. D., was the principal.

D. D. served as the budding school's business manager and head trustee until June 1929, when he died of a heart attack on the first day of registration. The original library on the campus is named in his honor.

B. B. remained president of the college until his retirement in 1955. He died two years later at age eighty-seven. During his nearly sixty years of service to the school, the Appalachian Training Schoolhad grown from a small teaching college with a single two-year degree program to a regional center for higher education with a four-year bachelor's program and a graduate school.

Twelve years after B. B.'s retirement, the state legislature changed the school's name to Appalachian State University. The campus has been a part of the UNC system since 1972.

1965 Federal Legislation Boost for Appalachia

On March 9, 1965, after receiving bipartisan backing in Congress, the Appalachian Regional Development Act was signed into law by Pres. Lyndon B. Johnson.

The bill was introduced to reverse economic disparities existing in Appalachia—the mountainous region stretching from Mississippi to New York—where thirty percent of people lived in poverty, income lagged nearly twenty-five percent behind the national average, and residents were leaving their homes to find better employment opportunities.

The Appalachian Regional Development Act called for creation of the Appalachian Regional Commission, a federal-state economic partnership formed to build up local economies and to foster sustainability in the Appalachian region.

Membership is made up of governors from the thirteen Appalachian states and a federal leader appointed by the president. Local participation takes place through smaller councils and commissions that serve multi-county regions.

The Commission's key goals are to strengthen the economy through investment, to prepare a workforce through education, to improve infrastructure in the region, to sustain and capitalize on the unique natural and cultural aspects of the area, and to prepare leaders for the future by encouraging collaboration and continued economic development.

Of the 320 counties covered by the Appalachian Regional Commission, twenty-nine are in North Carolina.

1966 Speaker Ban Law Challenged At UNC-Chapel Hill

On March 9, 1966, Herbert Aptheker attempted to speak to students near the Confederate monument at UNC-Chapel Hill. The campus police chief escorted him a short distance away to a spot technically off-campus. There Aptheker, a historian and member of the Communist Party, spoke to two thousand students from the sidewalk outside the rock wall that separates the campus from Franklin Street.

The speech came almost three years after the state legislature passed on June 26, 1963, "An Act to Regulate Visiting Speakers at State Supported Colleges and Universities," otherwise known as the Speaker Ban law. The action came just weeks after students joined others in Raleigh to advocate civil rights. The Speaker Ban forbade from speaking at a state school any known Communist, anyone who advocated overthrow of the government, or anyone who exercised Fifth Amendment rights when questioned on related topics. Passage of the law came with very little debate on the last day of the legislative term.

Administrators, faculty, and students loudly protested the infringement of First Amendment rights, but it was not until 1968 that the law was declared unconstitutional.

MAR 9

North Carolina A&T College band, 1941 (*left*).

Herbert Aptheker, Communist party member, on campus in Chapel Hill before deilvering anti-Vietnam lecture under Speaker Ban, March 9, 1966 (*right*).

1764 Fort Dobbs Decommissioned, 1764

On March 10, 1764, Gov. Arthur Dobbs consented to a request from the Assembly of North Carolina that all remaining military stores at Fort Dobbs be removed.

The fort, named in honor of the governor, was the only permanent frontier fort in the colony of North Carolina. It served as the military headquarters for a company of approximately fifty men and as a safe haven for settlers during the French and Indian War. The post had not been garrisoned with soldiers since December 1761.

Walter Lindsay, a local militia officer, served as caretaker for the fort between 1761 and 1764. With the global war between France and England over and the alarms caused by Pontiac's Rebellion in the north quieted, Fort Dobbs quickly deteriorated. It was described by the next governor, William Tryon, as "a ruin" in 1766.

Today the archaeological site of Fort Dobbs is preserved and operated as one of North Carolina's state historic sites. It hosts several living history events throughout the year, and plans are underway to reconstruct the blockhouse fort.

1865 Kilpatrick's "Shirt-Tail Skedaddle"

On March 10, 1865, Confederate Gen. Wade Hampton surprised Union Gen. Hugh J. Kilpatrick at Monroe's Crossroads. Kilpatrick's Third Cavalry Division was protecting the left flank of Gen. William T. Sherman's army as troops headed north.

On the night of March 9, Kilpatrick's division camped at Monroe's Crossroads, in what is now Hoke County. Confederate cavalrymen led by Hampton approached the camp from behind and found the rear of it completely defenseless. They retreated to plan a surprise attack.

The next morning Kilpatrick woke up early and stepped outside the house in his nightshirt. At that point Confederate cavalrymen charged through the camp. Groggy Federal soldiers rose from their bedrolls, clumsily took their weapons, and headed for shelter. Still only in his nightshirt, Kilpatrick ran across the yard in his bare feet, mounted a horse, and escaped.

In just a few minutes the Confederates had overrun the camp. Union troops regained control when a lieutenant reached the unguarded Confederate artillery pieces and fired them into a mass of Confederates. By 9:00 a.m., the Confederates had retreated.

Today the battlefield site is an artillery impact area at Fort Bragg. The gravestones of Union and Confederate soldiers who lost their lives that day are hidden throughout the woods.

1918 Edenton Residents Rally to Save Historic Home

On March 10, 1918, Edenton residents formed the Cupola House Association, the earliest community preservation effort in North Carolina. The association hoped to save the Cupola House from further decline after the owners sold interior woodwork to the Brooklyn Museum.

Originally built for Francis Corbin in 1758, the Cupola House is widely considered one of North Carolina's most significant early dwellings. In 1777 Corbin's heirs sold the home to Dr. Samuel Dickinson, whose heirs lived there for 141 years. Over time the house fell into disrepair as family funds became more limited, and the environment took its toll.

After the association was formed on March 10, funds were solicited from local residents, and the association was able to buy back a portion of the woodwork the very next day. By April 25 the association had acquired the house and most of its property. In time the association was able to restore the house, which was used as a county library, tearoom, and museum.

The Cupola House became a National Historic Landmark—the highest status that the National Park Service bestows on historic buildings—in 1971.

1948 Zelda Fitzgerald Casualty of Hospital Fire, 1948

On March 10, 1948, the central building of Highland Hospital in Asheville was destroyed by fire, which swept from the facility's kitchen through the dumbwaiter to all four floors. Nine women, including Zelda Fitzgerald, wife of author F. Scott Fitzgerald, were killed.

Rescue attempts saved eleven women, but others were trapped on the upper floors. According to one employee, she and her supervisor first rushed to save the patients considered helpless, hoping that the others would save themselves. Two women brought down by firemen died within a short while. All of the city's fire equipment was called out to fight the fire, along with most of the off-duty personnel.

Originally known as "Dr. Carroll's Sanatorium," Highland Hospital was founded by psychiatrist Dr. Robert S. Carroll and treated people with mental and nervous disorders and addictions. In 1939 Carroll gave his facility to the Neuropsychiatric Department of Duke University.

Duke closed the unit in the 1980s, and the complex is now an office park and shopping plaza.

1865 End of Story for CSS Neuse

On March 11, 1865, the Confederate ironclad CSS *Neuse* was scuttled in the Neuse River, just downstream from Kinston, to prevent its capture by advancing Union forces. Following the Battle of Wyse Fork, fought three days earlier, Gen. Braxton Bragg ordered the gunboat's commander, Capt. Joseph Price, to use his vessel to hold off Union Gen. Jacob D. Cox's force while the Confederate Army evacuated the town and retreated west toward Goldsboro. The ship was then to be destroyed.

The CSS *Neuse* had been partially constructed at what is now Seven Springs, starting in October 1862. It was floated downriver to Kinston in the summer of 1863, where it was outfitted with armor plating, engines, and guns. The project was delayed numerous times, but the *Neuse* was launched in April 1864 and commanded to steam downriver to assist an attempt to recapture Union-occupied New Bern.

Unfortunately the ship ran aground and never made it downriver again until being called into action in March 1865. Following Gen. Bragg's orders, once the evacuation of Kinston was complete, the crew of the *Neuse* set it ablaze and left it to sink. By March 13 the crew was in Halifax awaiting their next assignment.

Gunboat Commander of the CSS *Nuese*, Captain Joseph Price.

1879 Convict Labor Constructed Swannanoa Tunnel

On March 11, 1879, the Western North Carolina Railroad's Swannanoa Tunnel opened. The tunnel opened the region to growth and freed it from its previous isolation.

Authorized by the General Assembly in 1855, construction of the tunnel was spurred by a drought in 1845. The drought resulted in a total crop failure on mountain farms, and pack trains and loaded wagons were unable to provide frontier families with enough food to carry them through to the next crop.

By the beginning of the Civil War, all but seventy miles of the route into Asheville was complete. During Reconstruction the state secured four million dollars in bonds for the completion of the project, but construction was delayed after key players embezzled some of the funds. It did not resume until 1877.

The General Assembly approved the use of five hundred convicts as laborers, and 125 men lost their lives in the course of the work. Though the tunnel was holed through in March 1879, it wasn't until October 1880 that the tracks were clear and the first train from Salisbury entered Asheville.

1936 Burlesque Advertisement Prompts Lawsuit

On March 11, 1936, the *Greensboro Daily News* ran a racy ad for a burlesque show that was appearing in town for two days. Pictured in the ad were two scantily clad young women, one of whom was Winston-Salem native Nancy Flake. While she was not identified by name in the ad, the young radio entertainer and big band vocalist was hurt and embarrassed by the improper use of the photograph that had been taken by Columbia Broadcasting Company for its advertising use.

When the image ran in the newspaper, many of her relatives and her parents' friends saw it and questioned the family about their daughter's association with the burlesque show. Since, at nineteen, Flake was considered a minor, her mother contacted a lawyer, who filed a suit in Forsyth County District Court for invasion of privacy. Even though the newspaper ran a retraction, the case was decided in Flake's favor, and she was awarded sixty-five hundred dollars for being exposed to ridicule and contempt.

On appeal the North Carolina Supreme Court ordered a new trial, but the lawyers involved signed a final judgment that awarded Flake one dollar for damages, plus court costs.

1795 John Carruthers Stanly, Black Master of New Bern

On March 12, 1795, John Carruthers Stanly was freed from slavery in New Bern through a petition of his owners, Alexander and Lydia Stewart.

Generally acknowledged to be the son of prominent New Bern merchant John Wright Stanly and an enslaved African woman, Stanly was born in 1774. He received a good education, trained as a barber, and was generally treated with kindness by his owners.

Able to work as a barber while still enslaved, Stanly was earning a considerable income and was well-known in the community by the time he was freed at age twenty-one. He soon began to buy property, both in New Bern and the surrounding rural areas, and purchased the freedom of his wife and children. Stanly continued to prosper and became one the richest men in Craven County in the period, dealing in property, renting some of his land, planting cotton, and manufacturing turpentine.

As his wealth grew, Stanly began to purchase slaves of his own to meet the increased demands for labor created by his businesses. At one point he owned more than 160 slaves, making him one of the largest slaveholders in the area and the largest black slaveholder in the South.

Stanly died in 1846.

MAR 12

1865 Fayetteville Arsenal Torched by Sherman's Troops

On March 12, 1865, Union troops under the command of Gen. William Tecumseh Sherman set fire to the Fayetteville Arsenal complex as they marched through North Carolina. The United States Arsenal at Fayetteville was built in 1838. During the Civil War it produced rifles, ammunition, and gun carriages for the Confederacy and was vital to the Confederate war effort.

When President Abraham Lincoln asked North Carolina governor John W. Ellis to help suppress rebellion in neighboring states in April 1861, Ellis quickly pledged his loyalty to the Confederacy and ordered all federal property seized. On April 22 the arsenal was surrendered, and Ellis transferred it to the Confederacy. Samuel A. Ashe oversaw improvements made to the arsenal in 1863, including the construction of buildings used for manufacturing and support of the facility.

Given the importance of the arsenal, Sherman was drawn to Fayetteville in March 1865. His troops invaded the town and set fire to the complex; personnel and equipment had been evacuated the day before. The Arsenal House, built in 1862, is the only surviving structure from the arsenal.

Arsenal Park is now part of the Museum of the Cape Fear Historical Complex.

1944 Secret Basketball Game of 1944

On March 12, 1944, an all-white team from Duke University's medical school faced off against an all-black team, the Eagles, from what is now North Carolina Central University in a secret, interracial basketball game.

At the time strict segregation laws criminalized racial interaction and fostered a dangerous environment for those who violated them, prompting the participants to take extreme caution in planning and attending the event. Coaches kept school administrators in the dark and barred the doors to the Eagles' gym.

The two teams played cautiously at first, worried that a foul might morph into a fight. But by the second half the jitters subsided, and the teams focused on just playing the game. When the clock ran down, the Eagles, who had lost only one game that season, emerged victorious. The final score was 88-44.

The two teams then mixed their squads and played a second game. One Duke player told his family, "[W]e sure had fun and I especially had a good time, for most of the fellows playing with me were Southerners. . . . And when the evening was over, most of them had changed their views quite a lot."

1952 Herman Baity, Worldwide Champion of Clean Water

On March 12, 1952, North Carolina native Herman Baity became chief engineer and director of sanitary engineering for the World Health Organization (WHO) in Geneva, Switzerland.

Born in rural Davie County in 1895, Baity attended the University of North Carolina, where he was particularly interested in hydraulic and sanitary engineering. He received a Rockefeller Foundation grant to study at Harvard, where in 1928 he received the nation's first doctorate in sanitary engineering.

Baity returned to Chapel Hill, where he worked at the forefront of sanitary engineering worldwide. In the 1930s he served as an engineer with the State Board of Health and as state director of the Public Works Administration, which was part of the larger New Deal package of programs. Baity's interests broadened beyond North Carolina in the late 1930s and 1940s as he served as a consultant on national and international projects.

Working with the newly-formed WHO from 1952 until 1962, Baity traveled throughout the world promoting sanitary water treatment and management. His diligent and impassioned work improved water quality at home and abroad.

Drawing of the U.S. Arsenal in Fayetteville, N.C.

MAR 13

1821 Burke's Waightstill Avery, First Attorney General

On March 13, 1821, North Carolina's first attorney general, Waightstill Avery, died in Morganton.

A native of Connecticut, the Princeton-educated Avery came to North Carolina by way of Edenton in 1769 and was granted permission to practice law in the state. While living in Charlotte in 1772, Avery was elected to the provincial assembly.

He was a signer of the 1775 Mecklenburg Resolves, which declared all laws of the British Crown void and suspended authority of the King and Parliament.

Instrumental in establishing North Carolina's early statehood, Avery served on the committee to draft the state's first constitution and literally wrote most of the document. He attended the first meeting of the General Assembly held in New Bern in 1777 and while there was appointed North Carolina's first attorney general.

For his part in the revolutionary cause, Lord Charles Cornwallis had Avery's office set afire.

Married with four children, Avery joined his family in Burke County at Swan Pond plantation after the Revolution. Between 1782 and 1796 he served several terms in the state House of Commons and one senate term.

Avery was known for his manners, gentlemanly demeanor, and his adherence to colonial-style dress.

1937 Camp Butner's Namesake, Henry Wolfe Butner

On March 13, 1937, Maj. Gen. Henry Wolfe Butner, a native of Surry County and commander of the First Artillery Brigade in World War I, died. Butner received the Distinguished Service Medal and the Silver Star among other commendations for his wartime service. He was also briefly the commander at Fort Bragg.

An Army camp named in Butner's honor opened in August 1942. Located on approximately forty thousand acres in Granville, Person and Durham Counties, it served as a combat infantry facility and site of training exercises for nearly thirty thousand soldiers during World War II. The rolling farmland terrain was used for a range of exercises, including rehearsals of gas attacks, the use of camouflage, and river crossings. German and Italian prisoners of war were brought to Camp Butner, where they served as cooks and performed various other duties.

At the war's close the temporary quarters were bulldozed, and most of the land was returned to its former owners. Today the grounds house a variety of state and federal facilities, including several mental health facilities, multiple correctional institutions, state-owned farms, and a National Guard training facility.

1953 Carl Kasell and Charles Kuralt Help Launch WUNC-FM

On March 13, 1953, UNC-Chapel Hill students Carl Kasell and Charles Kuralt stepped up to the microphone for WUNC's inaugural FM broadcast.

After getting its start as a student-run AM station in the 1940s, the station made its transition to the FM band with future broadcasting greats Kasell and Kuralt. The station went on a six-year hiatus in 1970, after being taken off the air by technical difficulties, and returned in 1976 as a professionally-run National Public Radio affiliate.

Since its return WUNC has produced several long-running programs—many of which have been broadcast nationally— including *Back Porch Music*, *The People's Pharmacy*, and *The State of Things*.

Both Kasell and Kuralt went onto distinguished careers in broadcasting. Wilmington-born Kuralt is perhaps best known for his long career with CBS, working on *The CBS Evening News with Walter Cronkite* and as the first anchor of *CBS News Sunday Morning*. Goldsboro native Kasell was the news announcer for NPR's *Morning Edition* from its inception in 1979 through 2009, and was the official judge and scorekeeper on the news quiz show *Wait Wait... Don't Tell Me!* for many years.

Charles Kuralt (*left*) and Kent Jackson (*right*) doing a radio dramatization during the dedication ceremonies for WUNC Radio," March 13, 1953. UNC-Chapel Hill Chancellor R. B. House seated, holding paperwork behind Mr. Kuralt and Mr. Jackson.

1787 Edenton's Hugh Williamson, Signer of the Constitution

1862 Ambrose Burnside and the Fall of New Bern, 1862

1984 Wildlife Preserve on the Alligator River

On March 14, 1787, Dr. Hugh Williamson was appointed a delegate to the Constitutional Convention. Williamson was born in 1735 in Pennsylvania. After studying medicine in Philadelphia and Europe, he opened a medical practice in Philadelphia and tinkered with astronomy and natural sciences in his spare time.

In 1773 while enroute to England, Williamson's vessel stopped in Boston, where he witnessed the turmoil caused by the Stamp Act and the Boston Tea Party. In London Williamson relayed the news to the Privy Council that if the government did not alter its course, civil war or revolution was imminent. While in Britain Williamson also became close friends with Benjamin Franklin and wrote a letter to Britain's chief justice entitled "Plea for the Colonies."

In late 1777 Williamson settled in Edenton. He volunteered his services to Gov. Richard Caswell and began vaccinating North Carolina Continental troops for smallpox. He was soon appointed surgeon general of the entire North Carolina militia.

Before becoming surgeon general, Williamson had pursued a political career and represented the state at the Constitutional Convention in Philadelphia. A strong Federalist, he worked hard for the ratification of the Constitution. Williamson later wrote *A History of North Carolina*, the first post-Revolutionary history of the state.

MAR 14

On March 14, 1862, the Battle of New Bern was fought. It was the second of three major engagements in an expedition led by Union Gen. Ambrose Burnside. The first was at Roanoke Island in early February. After capturing the Island and securing the region, Burnside set his sights on New Bern, a strategic port.

The advance on New Bern was a strategic success and provided a boost to Burnside's reputation. He threw all available resources into the effort. Leaving a single brigade to guard Roanoke Island, Burnside's fleet sailed on March 11, stopping at Hatteras, where they were joined by an additional thirteen gunboats, amassing a combined force of eleven thousand men. On March 12, sailing in two parallel lines, the fleet entered the Neuse River.

Anchoring at the mouth of Slocum's Creek, the force shelled the shoreline and disembarked early on the morning of March 13. No Confederates were posted there, but sentries upriver set bonfires to announce the Federals' approach. Despite thick mud Burnside's army pressed on to New Bern, encountering token resistance from Confederate forces along the way. The town fell to Union soldiers the next day and remained occupied for the rest of the war.

On March 14, 1984, the Alligator River National Wildlife Refuge was established on mainland Dare and Hyde Counties to protect and preserve the forested wetland habitat called "pocosin" and its associated wildlife species.

In the late 1970s biologists were growing concerned by the rapid loss of wetlands in eastern North Carolina as pocosins were drained, and old-growth cypress and Atlantic white cedar trees were destroyed for logging and farming operations. Several conservation organizations and state and federal agencies worked together to preserve these fragile wetlands.

The Prudential Life Insurance Company donated the refuge's first 118 thousand acres, and congressional appropriations eventually allowed it to expand to the more than 150 thousand acres it covers today. The preserved area is bordered by the Alligator River and Intracoastal Waterway; Albemarle Sound; Croatan and Pamlico Sounds; and the Long Shoal River and corporate farmlands.

In 1986 the U.S. Fish and Wildlife Service initiated the Red Wolf Recovery Program to reestablish the endangered red wolf population in the wild. Today about one hundred red wolves roam the refuge. It is also an important habitat for black bear, American alligators, river otters, and the endangered red-cockaded woodpecker. Two hundred species of birds have been recorded in the refuge.

The Fish and Wildlife Service has also launched a number of projects designed to restore habitat and monitor wildlife populations, including restoring historic water levels, banding wood ducks on the refuge, and replanting Atlantic white cedars.

The refuge is open to the public year-round for hiking, kayaking, photography, birding, fishing, and hunting in season.

Alligator River National Wildlife Refuge (*right and background*).

1781 Quaker Meeting House Skirmish Prior to Guilford Courthouse

On March 15, 1781, British and American forces skirmished near the New Garden Meeting House just hours before the larger Battle of Guilford Courthouse.

In the predawn hours Gen. Charles Cornwallis's British army advanced north, intent on closing in on Gen. Nathanael Greene's position near Guilford Courthouse. Greene had placed troops out in advance positions to the south and west to give him fair warning of any potential attack.

When the front line of the British army, led by Lt. Col. Banastre Tarleton, encountered Lt. Col. "Light Horse" Harry Lee's troops just north of the meeting house, British and American dragoons slammed into each other in a narrow lane. Sabers clanged and shots echoed as horses and men crashed to the ground. After the initial clash the British cavalry were pushed back, across what's now the Guilford College campus to the meeting house, where they were joined by infantry units. The two sides exchanged fire twice more before American forces retired north towards Greene's army.

The primary effect of the New Garden skirmishes, totaling roughly two-and-a-half hours, was that Greene had time to position his main army and prepare his men, many of whom were inexperienced militia, for battle.

1781 Battle of Guilford Courthouse, Prelude to Yorktown

On the day of March 15, 1781, American and British forces clashed near Guilford Courthouse. The battle was the culmination of several months of hard campaigning by the armies of Nathanael Greene and Lord Charles Cornwallis.

Early in the day Greene deployed his army in three lines. The first and second lines were North Carolina and Virginia militiamen, with Greene's Continental soldiers composing the third. Veteran Virginia and North Carolina riflemen and Continentals were also posted on the flanks of the first line.

After a thirty-minute artillery barrage by both sides, the British broke through the first and second lines, but suffered severe casualties in the advance. Despite their losses, Cornwallis's army pushed on to the third line, where they engaged the Continental soldiers.

Unwilling to risk the destruction of his army and realizing that he had inflicted massive casualties on the British, Greene withdrew his forces; the battered British did not pursue. Twenty-seven percent of Cornwallis's army lay dead or wounded on the field. By comparison, Greene lost only six percent of his force, the majority of whom were some North Carolina and Virginia militiamen who fled shortly after the battle began.

In October Cornwallis surrendered his army to George Washington at Yorktown.

1941 Blossom of Dogwood Tree Official State Flower

On March 15, 1941, the General Assembly designated the dogwood as the state flower. In choosing the dogwood the General Assembly called the bloom "a radiantly beautiful flower which grows abundantly in all parts of this State."

Four species of dogwood are native to North Carolina. *Cornus florida*, the flowering dogwood, grows on a tree, can be found during spring in most parts of the state, and is the flower with which most people are familiar.

Cornus racemose, the grey dogwood, grows on a bush and can be found in the northern Piedmont. *Cornus asperifolia*, the roughleaf dogwood, is found along the southeast coast. The alternate-leaf dogwood, *Cornus alternifolia*, was once found in the Piedmont but now can be seen only in the mountains.

The dogwood is also both the official state tree and flower of Virginia and the state tree of Missouri.

1962 Recovery of the *Modern Greece* 100 Years After Its Sinking

On March 15, 1962, archaeologists began diving for the wreck of the blockade runner *Modern Greece*. The wreck, which had been hidden on the sea floor for nearly one hundred years, was discovered after a storm uncovered it. Divers found much of the vessel and its cargo intact. Historians and archaeologists with the state of North Carolina and U.S. Navy teamed up to recover more than 11,500 artifacts from the site.

The British-owned steamer *Modern Greece* ran aground near Fort Fisher while attempting to run the federal blockade in June 1862. The crash came after the vessel was pursued by U.S. Navy ships for three days. It was heavily laden with war materiel for the Confederacy and civilian goods. Although a portion of the cargo was salvaged by the crew, the vessel was intentionally sunk with most of its cargo still aboard.

Work on the site had a profound effect on the field of underwater archaeology. When private companies started trying to salvage artifacts, the state stepped in, asserting North Carolina's sovereign right to unclaimed shipwrecks. Research on the *Modern Greece* also led the state to establish one of the nation's first underwater archaeology programs.

MAR 15

Nathan Henry, Assistant State Archaeologist and Conservator, holds an Enfield rifle recovered from the *Modern Greece*.

MAR 16

1780 Sailors Beware on Old Quork's Day

On March 16, most likely in the 1780s, an odd and offbeat mariner from Ocracoke Island known as Quawk or Quork went to sea in his small fishing skiff despite warnings of impending foul weather. He never returned. The sailor was said to be a loner and was, by some accounts, the sole survivor of a shipwreck on the island. He was called Quork because of his voice, which was said to be like that of the "quawk," the colloquial name for the black-crowned night heron.

The day became known as Old Quork's Day, a day of bad luck or misfortune for seamen, who might fall victim to quick-forming storms that could catch an unwary mariner. On Ocracoke Island and as far south as Carteret County, cautious fishermen and old salts still stay ashore on March 16, for only the foolhardy go out on Old Quork's Day.

North Carolina storytellers and raconteurs have kept Quork's tale alive for more than two hundred years. In Morehead City during the 1970s, "Old Quork's Day" was held as a promotional activity on a Saturday in mid-March to open the vacation season.

1916 Last Whale Killed Off North Carolina Coast

On March 16, 1916, the last whale killed by North Carolina fishermen was caught near Cape Lookout.

Whaling was practiced in North Carolina since the colonial era, and the first evidence for whaling in North Carolina comes from a 1666 commercial whaling license issued by Peter Carteret, the assistant governor of the Carolina colony. The industry quickly became prosperous, with English and Scottish settlers setting up fisheries up and down the coast to catch and process whales for their meat, oil, and bone. North Carolinians played an active role in this industry, although their participation was most often shore-based rather than oceanic.

By the early twentieth century, as Americans turned to gasoline and kerosene for their heating and lighting needs and to synthetic substances for greasing, whale oil fell into disuse, and the shore-based whaling industry collapsed.

Undated photo of fishermen in a shad boat in Manteo, N.C.

"Whale Fishing in North Carolina," in *Bulletin of the North Carolina Department of Agriculture*, 14 (April, 1894). Image from H. H. Brimley (*background*).

MAR 17

1775 Richard Henderson and the Transylvania Company

On March 17, 1775, Richard Henderson's Transylvania Company purchased much of the land that is now Kentucky and Tennessee from the Cherokee through a treaty signed at Sycamore Shoals on the Watauga River.

Born in 1735 in Granville County, Henderson became a lawyer and was appointed associate justice of the Salisbury District Superior Court. As early as 1764, Daniel Boone acted as an agent for Henderson's land company. Henderson retired from the bench in 1773 and organized what became the Transylvania Company in order to develop lands on the Trans-Appalachian frontier. He established the colony of Transylvania with the settlement of Boonesborough on the Kentucky River, though Virginia, North Carolina, and the Continental Congress all refused to recognize Transylvania's attempts to become the fourteenth colony.

Without federal recognition, the Transylvania Company eventually lost control of the land. Henderson continued to engage in land speculation and later led a group of settlers into the Cumberland Valley in Tennessee. There he founded French Lick, known today as Nashville.

1829 Bishop John England Dedicates St. Patrick's, 1829

On March 17, 1829, Roman Catholic Bishop John England consecrated Saint Patrick's Church in Fayetteville. The consecration was the first for a Catholic church in North Carolina. The following week England traveled to Beaufort County, where he dedicated St. John's in Washington, the first Catholic church built in North Carolina.

Bishop England directed the Catholic Church in the Carolinas for much of the antebellum period. He arrived from Ireland in 1820 at the age thirty-three to take charge of the Diocese of Charleston. Before his arrival small enclaves of Catholics in larger towns met in private homes and the church buildings of other faiths and were served on occasion by itinerant priests. Owing in no small measure to England's energy and steadfastness, the church took hold in North Carolina.

Catholic churches were later built in Raleigh, New Bern, Wilmington, Charlotte, and Edenton, all before the Civil War. The state remained part of the Diocese of Charleston until 1868, when a new vicariate was created, with Rev. James Gibbons installed as the first vicar apostolic.

1865 John Sprunt Hill of Durham, Credited with Rural Credit Unions

On March 17, 1865, John Sprunt Hill, an early leader in the credit union movement, was born on a farm near Faison.

After finishing high school at age twelve and working for several years, Hill entered the University of North Carolina in 1885. Upon graduation he returned to Duplin County to teach before heading off to New York City, first to study law and then to establish a law practice.

A marriage to the daughter of a Durham industrialist brought Hill back to North Carolina, where he established Durham Bank and Trust Company and served as its president until 1932. He later founded Home Savings Bank, forerunner of Central Carolina Bank, and served as its head until late in his life.

In 1913 Hill traveled to Europe to study rural credit systems and returned to the United States eager to implement similar enterprises at home. He addressed farmers' organizations and Congressional committees on the subject. In 1915, soon after passage of enabling legislation by the legislature, the state's first credit union opened in the Lowes Grove community of southern Durham County.

A lifelong philanthropist, Hill contributed generous sums for the expansion of the UNC campus and established an endowment fund for the North Carolina Collection of the UNC Library.

1967 Glory Days at Winston-Salem State University, 1967

On March 17, 1967, the Winston-Salem State University Rams bested the Southwest Missouri State University Bears 77–74 at the NCAA Division II national men's basketball championship game in Evansville, Indiana.

In so doing WSSU became the first historically black college in the nation to win a national championship.

That championship was the highlight of a 30-1 season for the Rams and represented a comeback from the Rams' third-place finish in the CIAA tournament behind North Carolina A&T and Howard.

WSSU player Vernon Earl "The Pearl" Monroe, who would later go on to a stellar pro career with the Baltimore Bullets and New York Knicks, largely led the team to victory and earned honors as NCAA Division II Player of the Year and NCAA Tournament Most Outstanding Player honors as a result.

Hall of Fame winning coach Clarence "Big House" Gaines, who coached men's basketball at WSSU for nearly fifty years, also earned top honors as NCAA Division II College Coach of the Year.

Winston-Salem State National Basketball Championship team, 1967. Coach Clarence "Big House" Gaines is at the podium and Earl "The Pearl" Monroe is second from the right behind the table.

1863 Women in Salisbury Riot for Bread

On March 18, 1863, a group of about fifty women, all wives and mothers of Confederate soldiers, participated in what would become known as the Salisbury Bread Riot.

The women blamed speculators for driving up the prices of necessary items during the Union blockade. Struggling to provide for their families, they banded together against the businesses that they suspected of speculating and demanded government prices for goods.

Michael Brown, the owner of a local store, recalled that when he refused to deal with them, the women attempted to break down his storeroom door with hatchets. Finally he decided to give them ten barrels of flour if they would leave. By the end of the day, the women had obtained "twenty three barrels of flour, two sacks of salt, about half a barrel of molasses and twenty dollars in money."

The group later wrote to Gov. Zebulon Vance to explain their unpleasant, but justified, actions. The *Carolina Watchman*, a local newspaper, commented on the event but did not place blame on the women. The editors instead blamed the ineffectiveness of the government in providing enough food for the families at home. This event ultimately led to better rationing of government resources to aid Civil War soldiers' families.

1942 Marines Begin Flight Operations at Cherry Point, 1942

On March 18, 1942, flight operations began at the Marine Corps Air Station Cherry Point in Craven County with the landing of a Grumman J2F "Duck" amphibian.

The base was established just a few years earlier, after the Marine Corps conducted a search up and down the U.S. East Coast for a suitable site for an air station. After Congressman Graham Barden helped secure forty million dollars for construction in 1941, the base grew quickly, becoming a self-contained city of twenty thousand within a few months.

As the U.S. involvement in World War II ratcheted up, so did the size and scope of Cherry Point. It was the home of the Third and Ninth Marine Aircraft Wings during the war and has been the home of the Second Marine Aircraft Wing since 1946.

Troops from Cherry Point have taken part in every major military engagement since 1941, and the base is the largest Marine airfield in the world today.

2003 Authorities Seize Copy of the Bill of Rights

On March 18, 2003, a sting operation resulted in the recovery of North Carolina's copy of the Bill of Rights from a group of antiques dealers.

The return of the document ended an odyssey that began in 1865, when it was taken from the State Capitol in Raleigh by Union soldiers occupying the building. During the 140 years that it was missing, it came up for sale several times, but the state refused to pay for its own property. In 2003 an offer to sell a copy of the Bill of Rights came to the National Constitution Center in Philadelphia. When its experts recognized the document as North Carolina's copy, they notified the state.

A sting operation was organized by the FBI and the U.S. Attorney's Office. A meeting was set up to close on the purchase of the document. A check for four million dollars was brought to the meeting, but the document was not. Once the seller was satisfied with the closing documents, he had the manuscript brought into the room. Once the document was verified, authorities entered and seized it.

After five years of litigation, the Bill of Rights was declared the rightful property of North Carolina. It now resides in a vault at the State Archives.

North Carolina Highway Patrol officers holding North Carolina's copy of the Bill of Rights after escorting and returning it safely to the N. C. State Archives.

MAR 18

1865 Last Stand in the Carolinas at Bentonville

On March 19, 1865, at Bentonville, a Confederate army led by Gen. Joseph E. Johnston attacked the left wing of Union Gen. William Tecumseh Sherman's army. Gen. Robert E. Lee had directed the Confederates to make a stand in North Carolina to prevent Sherman from joining Gen. Ulysses S. Grant in front of Lee's army at Petersburg, Virginia.

Union Gen. Henry Slocum, initially not realizing that he faced an entire army, pushed forward, but was driven back throughout the afternoon. Confederates led by Gen. D. H. Hill were able to flank Slocum's troops, pouring devastating fire upon them. Johnston continued his assaults throughout the evening but pulled back upon realizing that the right wing of Sherman's army, marching from Fayetteville, would arrive soon.

Sherman's army of sixty thousand men was divided into two wings: half in the left wing marching through Averasboro and Bentonville and half in the right wing marching on a parallel route to the southeast. Sherman's objective was Goldsboro, where forty thousand additional troops and supplies would reinforce his army. After initial success on March 19, the Confederates were unable to subdue the Union army, and early on March 22 they withdrew. The Union Army did not pursue.

Engraving of the Battle of Bentonville, April 22, 1865.

1946 Automatic Pilot Advances Credited to George Holloman

On March 19, 1946, George Holloman, a pioneer in the field of aeronautical engineering and unmanned flight, died in a plane crash.

The Northampton County native developed a keen interest in radio early on. After graduating from high school, Holloman went to work with the Marconi Company, later the Radio Corporation of America, developing radio designs. He returned to North Carolina and enrolled at what is now N.C. State University, earning a degree in electrical engineering. Holloman joined the ROTC program at State, and after graduation he received a commission as a second lieutenant in the Army and transferred to the Army Air Corps.

Holloman eventually became head of one of eleven Instrument and Navigation laboratories, overseeing in that role the development of unmanned flight and automatic pilot and landing systems. In 1937 he engineered and oversaw the first automatic landing of an airplane, flying in the machine as a passenger.

Four years later, with war clouds looming off in the distance, the Air Corps developed a new laboratory at Wright Field in Dayton, Ohio called the Special Weapons Unit. Holloman was given command of the unit. At Special Weapons he continued to oversee the development of automatic piloting systems, advanced bombsights, and unmanned flying vehicles until his death.

1793 Turkey's Talons Tied to Jurist's Demise

On March 20, 1793, Samuel Spencer died.

Spencer was a member of North Carolina's colonial assembly, the state's de facto executive during the Revolutionary War, a trustee of the University of North Carolina, a colonel in the militia, and a superior court judge. He voted against the new federal constitution because it did not yet have a Bill of Rights.

The judge also played a major role in the landmark legal case *Bayard v. Singleton*, the first instance in which a court declared an act of the post-revolutionary North Carolina General Assembly unconstitutional.

Spencer had a most unusual death—by turkey. At age sixty he was napping outside on his porch, wearing a red cap. His bobbing head was then taken for a challenge by a turkey, which attacked the judge with such violence that he was thrown from his chair.

Spencer died a few days later from either from injuries sustained in the fall, or from an infection from the scratches.

1862 Husband and Wife Side-By-Side in the Confederate Army

On March 20, 1862, Malinda Blalock disguised herself as a young man and enlisted in the Confederate army. Malinda and her husband Keith were Unionists from Watauga County. Keith was pressured by recruiters to join the Confederate army, which he did with the intention of deserting into federal lines at the first opportunity.

Stories differ as to whether Keith was aware of Malinda's intentions, but the more romantic version is that Keith looked over at the private walking next to him and did a double-take when he recognized his wife, who had cut her waist-length hair and donned baggy men's clothing to become "Sam" Blalock. Sam Blalock, purportedly Keith's brother, was described as "a good looking boy aged 16."

Keith and Malinda served in Company F of the Twenty-Sixth Regiment and shared a tent in Kinston during training. Malinda performed all the duties of a soldier and did not raise suspicions. When Keith realized that they would not easily be able to desert, he obtained a medical discharge by creating a severe rash, rubbing poison oak or sumac all over his body. At that point "Sam" revealed her secret and was discharged. Keith was soon pursued as a deserter.

Malinda Blalock (*right*) in an undated photograph holding a picture of her husband Keith.

1840 Raleigh and Gaston Railroad Completed, 1840

On March 21, 1840, work was completed on the Raleigh and Gaston Railroad. A week later the Raleigh depot received twenty bales of cotton from Petersburg, Virginia, the line's first commercial shipment on record. In June 1840 a "Grand Celebration" was held in Raleigh to commemorate two milestones, the new railroad and the new State Capitol.

Experiments in the 1830s with horse-drawn rail cars preceded the state's first self-propelled railroad, the Raleigh and Gaston line. Gaston in Halifax County was its northern terminus and Raleigh its southern end point. Slaves were leased to lay the rails on heavy wooden planks. Setbacks with financing and materials delayed the railroad's completion.

Throughout North Carolina in the 1840s, the sound of the locomotive horn was heard, signifying a new era of unprecedented prosperity. The benefits of the Raleigh and Gaston line were apparent immediately. The train allowed for quick transportation of goods and provided new jobs. The Confederacy used the Raleigh and Gaston heavily during the Civil War.

In 1900 the railroad was incorporated into the larger Seaboard Coast Line Railroad. The Seaboard building stands today on Salisbury Street in Raleigh as a reminder of the beginnings of rail transportation in the state.

1865 Third Day at Bentonville

On March 21, 1865, Union and Confederate forces fought the third and final day of the Battle of Bentonville in southern Johnston County.

Three days prior Confederate Gen. Joseph E. Johnston attempted to strike and overwhelm the left wing of Major Gen. William T. Sherman's Union armies advancing northward to Goldsboro. When the surprise attack failed, both sides settled into heavy skirmishing as Johnston began pulling his embattled Confederate forces across a single bridge at Mill Creek.

On March 21 Union Major Gen. Joseph Mower of the Seventeenth Army Corps was able to find a gap in the Confederate left and pushed his infantry division through to threaten Johnston's retreat route. Confederate Lt. Gen. William J. Hardee was able to gather together a Confederate force to strike at Mower's regiments and removed the threat to the Confederate route of retreat. Unfortunately, Hardee's son, Willie, was severely wounded during the attack on the advancing Federals.

The next day Johnston completed his troops' retreat across Mill Creek, and General Sherman continued his advance to Goldsboro. Willie Hardee was taken back to Hillsborough, where he died and was buried.

1949 Freedom Riders Surrender in Hillsborough

On March 21, 1949, the Freedom Riders surrendered at the Orange County Courthouse in Hillsborough and were sent to segregated chain gangs.

In 1946 the U.S. Supreme Court declared that segregation on interstate buses and trains was unconstitutional, though segregation was still widely practiced across the South. The Congress of Racial Equality (CORE) decided to test compliance with the court's ruling across the South by having interracial groups of protesters travel on Greyhound and Trailways buses. This "Journey of Reconciliation," as it was dubbed, began in April 1947, and the protesters who participated became known as the "Freedom Riders."

In Chapel Hill in April 1947, four riders, including one of the organizers, Bayard Rustin, were arrested and later went to trial. In 1949 Rustin and two white protesters surrendered and were sent to segregated chain gangs. Rustin published journal entries about the experience. His writings, as well as the actions of the "Journey" riders in April 1947, in time inspired Rosa Parks's nonviolent protest in 1955 and the Freedom Rides of 1960–1961.

1966 Textile Humidifiers Specialty for Agnew Bahnson

On March 21, 1966, textile manufacturer Agnew Hunter Bahnson died.

Born in Salem in 1886, Bahnson attended UNC before starting to work in the textile business. He started out as an apprentice at Mayo Mills in Mayodan, then moved to Loray Mills in Gastonia, where he fixed loom machines.

His first supervisory job came in 1909, when he became superintendent of a Greensboro mill, and after working with a mill in Virginia for a time, he returned to North Carolina, where he led Arista Mills in Winston-Salem. He assumed leadership roles in other mills, too, consolidating some of their operations.

Bahnson's brother Frederic patented several pressure regulators and humidifiers for use in textile plants in the 1910s and 1920s, and the brothers formed the Normalair Company in 1915 to manufacture and sell those devices. The company was renamed the Bahnson Company in 1925, and it continues to operate to this day.

Bahnson was a lifelong supporter of the Moravian Church, which first brought his ancestors to the Triad region, and of Salem College.

Raleigh and Gaston Railroad Roundhouse and Rail Yards, Raleigh, N.C., ca. 1895.

MAR 22

1862 Carolina City, Union Encampment, Confederate Target

On March 22, 1862, Union Gen. John G. Parke occupied and set up his headquarters at Carolina City, a small village of about one hundred inhabitants just west of Morehead City.

With the previous successes at Roanoke Island and New Bern, Union commanders set their sights on Fort Macon at Beaufort Inlet. Morehead City, just across the sound, was a strategic target, since it was the terminus of the Atlantic and North Carolina Railroad. Beaufort was also captured and occupied. Union forces used the Carolina City location as a launching point to ferry weapons and supplies across the sound to Bogue Banks.

Parke and the Union troops selected Hoop Pole Creek, about five miles west of Fort Macon and directly across the sound from Carolina City, as their landing site on the banks. On April 11 the first skirmish took place between the Union landing force and the detachments from the fort. Union troops set up artillery positions on the banks leading up to the fort and began bombarding the fort on April 25.

In the end Fort Macon's commander, Col. Moses J. White, posted the white flag. Today the campus of Carteret Community College and the Crystal Coast Civic Center mark the approximate location of Carolina City.

1882 Governor O. Max Gardner and the Great Depression

On March 22, 1882, Gov. Oliver Max Gardner, whose political organization known as the "Shelby Dynasty" dominated state politics for a generation, was born in Cleveland County.

Gardner took office as governor only months before the stock market crash of 1929, and the Great Depression that followed presented Governor Gardner with many unforeseen challenges. One of his many initiatives was to promote his "Live-at-Home" program to encourage the planting of crops for subsistence.

To help alleviate budget crises in counties across the state, Gardner authorized a study of state government, which recommended a massive shift of power to Raleigh, with the state taking responsibility for roads and schools. He counted the consolidation of the public universities in Chapel Hill, Raleigh, and Greensboro as his proudest achievement, and, in this as in other efforts, his moves were opposed by special interests and required all his leadership abilities to come to fruition.

The next four governors, including his brother-in-law Clyde R. Hoey, came to office with his backing. In 1947 Gardner was named Ambassador to Great Britain but died hours before he was to sail for London.

1892 Ramble On, Charlie Poole

On March 22, 1892, Charlie Poole, banjoist extraordinaire and founder of the old-time music pioneers known as the North Carolina Ramblers, was born in Randolph County. At an early age he moved to Spray (now Eden in Rockingham County) and over the course of his short life achieved near-legendary status. Although he died in 1931, before reaching age 30, his star continues to rise to this day.

Partnering with two neighbors, Poole made some of the first known country music records. His high-pitched vocal style was a hit. The Ramblers's fan base extended from the Piedmont cotton mills all across the nation. Music historian Bill Malone concluded, "No string band in early country music equaled the Ramblers' controlled, clean, well-patterned sound."

Poole had smashed his right hand in a childhood baseball accident, leaving his fingers curled and leading him to favor a three-finger banjo picking style. Stories about his drinking, rambling, and carousing are widespread. His style of living prefigured that of Hank Williams a generation later. In recent years re-releases of his works, featuring songs such as "Can I Sleep in Your Barn Tonight, Mister" and "Don't Let Your Deal Go Down," have reached new audiences.

Charlie Poole and the North Carolina Ramblers, musicians, Charlie Poole (*left*), Posey Rorer (*middle*), and Norman Woodlief (*right*).

MAR 23

1713 Culminating Battle of the Tuscarora War, 1713

On March 23, 1713, the Tuscarora Indian stronghold known as Neoheroka fell to colonial militiamen. As a result of the action, 950 Indians were killed or captured.

As European settlers encroached on Indian land to meet the needs of the growing colony of North Carolina, tensions escalated between the two groups. In 1711 the Tuscarora, who controlled most of the land between the Neuse and Roanoke Rivers, began a war with the colonists. In 1713 the government of North Carolina appealed to South Carolina for assistance. That colony sent Col. James Moore, who marched his combined force of North and South Carolina militia and allied Indians to Neoheroka. He had been informed that the Tuscarora had placed their largest concentration of warriors at a fort there on a branch of Contentnea Creek in what is now Greene County.

Archaeological investigations of the fort have revealed a series of interconnected bunkers and tunnels supplied by large quantities of provisions. The fort covered an acre and a half and had high palisades.

The fall of Neoheroka signaled the end of concerted Indian resistance to colonists. By the end of the Tuscarora War, approximately two hundred whites and one thousand Indians had been killed, with an additional one thousand Tuscarora sold into slavery and more than three thousand others forced from their homes.

1862 Siege of Fort Macon, 1862

On March 23, 1862, Union forces under Brig. Gen. John G. Parke began the siege of Confederate-held Fort Macon. At the time the fort was commanded by Col. Moses J. White of Mississippi and was defended by fifty-four pieces of artillery and a garrison of five companies.

In January 1862 a Federal force under Maj. Gen. Ambrose Burnside arrived off the North Carolina coast. After taking Roanoke Island in February and New Bern in March, Burnside's next objective was Fort Macon. After White refused to surrender on Parke's arrival, Parke laid siege to the fort with the support of the Union's blockading squadron.

In mid-April Burnside arrived with reinforcements to take direct command of the siege. On April 25 the fort was bombarded from both land and sea. Although cannon blasts from Union ships did little damage because of the fort's strong seaward defenses, the land bombardment did major damage. White surrendered the next day.

The fall of Fort Macon gave the Federals access to the sea via Beaufort and Morehead City, strengthening their control over much of eastern North Carolina.

The fort was constructed by the federal government from 1826 to 1834 to guard Beaufort Harbor and was seized by North Carolina militia only two days after shots were fired on Fort Sumter.

1896 Beginnings of Spencer Shops

On March 23, 1896, the Southern Railway Company broke ground on a new repair facility in Spencer. The Rowan County community was chosen as the location of the new shop complex because it was halfway between Atlanta and Washington, D.C. The shops were named in honor of Southern's first president, Samuel Spencer.

Initially Spencer Shops included a fifteen-stall roundhouse, a machine shop, and a blacksmith shop. More buildings were constructed over the next twenty years, the most impressive being the Back Shop, which covered the length of two football fields. In 1924 the original roundhouse was replaced by a thirty-seven-stall facility. At its peak, three thousand people worked at Spencer Shops.

One of the first U.S. rail systems to experiment with diesel-electric locomotives, Southern retired its last steam engine in 1953. This began the decline of Spencer Shops, with employment there dropping steadily through the 1950s and 1960s. The shops were eventually closed in the late 1960s.

Historic Spencer Shops is now the site of the N.C. Transportation Museum, one of twenty-seven state historic sites. It interprets all forms of transportation history in North Carolina from dugout canoes to airliners.

An interior photo of Spencer Shops, Back Shop, ca. 1904, and current location of the N.C. Transportation Museum.

FRANK LESLIE'S ILLUSTRATED NEWSPAPER

NEW YORK, MAY 17, 1862.

The Surrender of Fort Macon, April 26, 1862, from *Frank Leslie's Illustrated Newspaper*, May 17, 1862.

MAR 24

1663 Carolina's "Birth Certificate"

On March 24, 1663, King Charles II granted a charter for land in America to the Lords Proprietors, who were eight of his closest supporters during the Restoration of 1660.

Since a permanent English settlement in the New World was important, the king gave broad powers to the proprietors. These powers guaranteed political and religious freedoms to the inhabitants of Carolina, which stretched from the Atlantic Ocean to the South Seas, encompassing an area roughly from the middle of Albemarle Sound to what is now the Georgia/Florida border.

Inhabitants of the new colony claimed many of the same rights as English citizens, including the right to import and export goods, the right to be tried in Carolina for a crime committed there, personal and property rights, and a basic form of religious freedom. In 1665 another charter was issued, which amended the 1663 document and moved the northern boundary to include the prosperous and more populous Albemarle Sound region. It is likely that no more than two of the proprietors ever saw any of their Carolina lands, and their control over the colony was unstable.

Regardless, many of the charter's provisions became the basic principles upon which American freedom is based.

First page of the Carolina Charter.

1853 William R. D. King Elected Vice President of the United States

On March 24, 1853, William R. D. King was elected vice president of the United States.

Born in Sampson County, King distinguished himself early on as an excellent student, graduating from UNC in 1804 at age 18. He moved to Fayetteville to study law and established his own practice in nearby Clinton a year later. He entered politics in 1808 as a member of the North Carolina House of Commons at age 22, and was elected to United States Congress in 1810. There he allied himself with prominent politicians of the time including Henry Clay and John C. Calhoun.

In 1818, King left North Carolina for Alabama, where an abundance of inexpensive, yet fertile, land offered significant profits. In 1819, King helped draft Alabama's state constitution and was elected to the United States Senate, where he served for 20 years.

Shortly after being elected in 1853, King traveled to Cuba to ease his tuberculosis. His health forced him to become the first and only vice president to be sworn into office while on foreign soil. Soon after his return to America, King succumbed to his illness before ever reaching the District of Columbia.

William Rufus Devane King

1862 Rosenwald Schools and George Davis of Johnson C. Smith University

On March 24, 1862, African American educational leader George E. Davis was born in Wilmington. Davis was the primary organizer and fundraiser for the Rosenwald schools movement in North Carolina.

After graduating from the forerunner of Johnson C. Smith University, Davis became that school's first black professor. He earned his doctorate over time, while teaching science and sociology, and was named dean of the faculty in 1905. He stepped down in 1921 to take on the task of implementing the Rosenwald program in North Carolina.

Sears, Roebuck, and Company president Julius Rosenwald established a fund in 1917 to finance public school buildings for African Americans in the rural South. Educational facilities for blacks in the South at the time were sorely substandard, usually much worse than counterpart white schools.

Between 1917 and 1932, more than fifty-three hundred Rosenwald Schools were constructed in fifteen states. Of that number 813 were built in North Carolina, more than in any other state.

Davis crisscrossed the state to raise funds in mostly impoverished communities. In 1932 he reported having raised more than 660 thousand dollars in matching funds since 1917. In exchange for money from the Rosenwald Fund, local communities were expected to raise a matching amount, and white-dominated school boards were expected to commit to maintenance.

Davis retired in 1935 at age seventy-three. He died in 1959.

1524

Verrazzano Anchors Off the Carolina Coast

On March 25, 1524, an expedition under Giovanni da Verrazzano anchored off the Outer Banks. The voyage marked the first European exploration of the North Carolina coast. Verrazzano sought a northward sea route to Asia's lucrative markets on behalf of Francis I of France.

Usually identified as a native of Florence, Verrazzano was a navigator before being commissioned by King Francis to look for a new route to Asia in 1523. He reached the North American coast with one of his four original vessels sometime in March 1524, and probably first explored the Bogue Banks area. After a brief excursion southward he returned and explored the Outer Banks, anchoring twice and encountering some of the native peoples when going on land. The geography convinced him that the Outer Banks were an isthmus beyond which lay the Pacific.

After leaving what's now North Carolina, Verrazzano explored the coasts of New York, Rhode Island and Maine. He returned to France convinced that these more northward shores were part of one continent distinct from Asia.

Although he was the first European to explore much of the North American coast, his findings were not immediately followed up on by other explorers. On a later voyage to the Caribbean, he was killed and eaten by Carib Indians.

1758

Richard Dobbs Spaight Born in New Bern

On March 25, 1758, Richard Dobbs Spaight, North Carolina's first native-born governor, was born in New Bern. Orphaned young, he received his preparatory education in Ireland and is thought to have graduated from the University of Glasgow.

Returning to North Carolina during the early stages of the Revolution, Spaight served as a military aide to Gov. Richard Caswell, though his energies and ambitions were directed more toward politics than warfare.

As a prominent Federalist leader, Spaight was one of five delegates from North Carolina to the Constitutional Convention in Philadelphia in 1787. Following an active role in the Convention, he signed the Constitution and argued forcefully for its ratification. In 1792 Spaight was elected governor. Twice reelected, he served the maximum three consecutive terms.

Spaight was the first governor to convene the General Assembly in Raleigh. Much of his role as Chief Executive was played against the backdrop of war between England and France. Other issues during Spaight's administration included the negotiation of lingering border disputes with South Carolina and the threat of Cherokee uprisings in the mountain region. In 1795 he presided over the official opening of the University of North Carolina.

1918

Howard Cosell, North Carolinian: Like Him or Lump Him

On March 25, 1918, television sportscaster Howard Cosell was born Howard William Cohen in Winston-Salem. Before he turned three, his family moved to Brooklyn, N.Y., where he later changed his surname to Cosell to reflect his Polish roots. He studied law at New York University, passed the state bar in 1941, and served in the U.S. Army in World War II.

After the war Cosell practiced law in Manhattan and hosted a Saturday-morning ABC radio show featuring Little Leaguers interviewing major leaguers. He became a full-time ABC sportscaster in 1956, first gaining fame as a boxing announcer. He went on to co-anchor *Monday Night Football*, for which he is now best known.

With his staccato style of speech and trademark "tell-it-like-it-is" approach, Cosell transformed sports broadcasting, winning fans and detractors alike. He wrote four best-selling books, made several movie cameos, and was inducted into the American Sportscasters Association Hall of Fame in 1993.

Diagnosed with cancer in 1991, Cosell died at seventy-seven of a heart embolism in 1995. The next year he was posthumously awarded an Emmy for lifetime achievement in sports.

Howard Cosell in a 1975 publicity photo for *Monday Night Football*.

MAR 26

1722 Charles Eden Dies Near the Town Named in His Honor

On March 26, 1722, Gov. Charles Eden died. Shortly after Eden's death the town nearest his home, known as "the Town on Queen Anne's Creek," was renamed Edenton in his honor.

Eden was governor of North Carolina during a period of progressive change. Although there are few surviving records, he is generally credited with the improvements made during his administration. Eden's early life is even more of a mystery than his colonial career. There are no records of his activities, public or private, prior to his 1713 appointment as governor of North Carolina.

An assembly that Eden called in 1715 passed various far-reaching governmental reforms. The contemporary legal code was revised, taking aim at widespread disturbances that occurred during previous administrations. With the objective of enhancing trade, immigration and communication, several transportation issues were addressed, including plans to improve existing roads, build new roads, and establish shipping channels. Though a a leader in his church and a devout Anglican, Eden tolerated religious diversity and ensured that the colony's laws reflected that.

In 1889 Eden's remains and gravestone were moved to St. Paul's Churchyard in Edenton.

1749 William Blount, a Founding Father of Tennessee

On March 26, 1749, signer of the Constitution and early political leader William Blount was born in Bertie County.

Blount served in the Continental Army as paymaster before being elected to six terms as a state representative and senator. He went on to accept a position with the Continental Congress and later served in both state conventions called to consider adopting the U.S. Constitution.

A supporter of handing the state's western lands over to the federal government, Blount became territorial governor of what's now Tennessee. After leaving North Carolina Blount worked as the federal Superintendent of Indian Affairs and helped found the state of Tennessee, chairing the convention that drafted the Volunteer State's first constitution in 1796.

When Tennessee was admitted to the Union in 1796, Blount was elected to the U.S. Senate, but the following year he was expelled from that body for having been involved in a scheme to incite the Creek and Cherokee to aid the British in conquering Spanish-held West Florida.

After leaving Congress Blount was elected to the Tennessee state senate and chosen its president at its first session in December 1797. He died in Knoxville in 1800.

1758 A Moravian Tradition, the Sunrise Service

On March 26, 1758, the first Sunrise Easter Service at Bethabara was held on Manakes Hill, north of what is now Winston-Salem. Though the sunrise service can now be found across many different Christian denominations, it got its start in Germany as a distinctly Moravian tradition.

An account of the time described the service: The congregation was awakened early with music, and as they sang, the sun broke through a bank of clouds, throwing its clear beams upon the scene.

The typical Moravian sunrise service begins with a brass choir waking the congregation before the first part of the liturgical service, which is held within the church. The entire congregation then moves to a nearby Moravian cemetery, where the second part of the liturgy is read while the sun rises over the graves as a symbol of Christ's resurrection.

The Moravians had come to the area that is now Forsyth County in 1753 from Pennsylvania in search of a large tract of available land suitable for farming. They had settled in Pennsylvania after a failed settlement attempt in Georgia and after being largely forced to leave their ancestral homelands in central Europe.

Though they had planned a community centered around farms, their first settlement at Bethabara grew to a town that included a church, gristmill, saw mill, tannery, pottery, distillery, and other crafts shops by the end of 1756.

From Bethabara the group quickly fanned out across today's Forsyth County, establishing the settlements of Bethania, Salem, Friedberg, and Friedland.

1830 Baptists Get It Together in Greenville, 1830

On March 26, 1830, the North Carolina Baptist State Convention was organized at a home in Greenville. The organization had its roots in the North Carolina Baptist Missionary Society, formed in 1811 as an outlet for planning missionary work. It eventually came to be known as the Benevolent Society.

The founders of the Baptist State Convention created two other related institutions once the convention was operational. The statewide Baptist newspaper, the *Biblical Recorder*, was established in 1833, and Wake Forest College came into existence the following year. The Baptist Female University, now Meredith College, opened with the convention's support in 1899.

Today the Baptist State Convention offers an outlet for cooperative missionary work as well as guidance to church leaders and administrative staff. Resources include instruction and guidelines for general operations and advice for churches. The state convention also assists groups in forming new Baptist congregations in the state. The Baptist State Convention operates educational facilities, children's homes, retirement homes, and a credit union, as well as missionary and support programs. Its home office is in Cary.

Easter Sunrise Service at Bethabara Moravian Church, April 1938.

1911 Pisgah National Forest Established, 1911

On March 27, 1911, the first land purchased under the newly enacted Weeks Act created Pisgah National Forest.

The Weeks Act, named for Massachusetts Congressman John Weeks, allocated nine million dollars in federal funds for the purchase of six million acres of land in the eastern U.S., which was to be used specifically for conservation.

Named for Buncombe County's Mount Pisgah, which in turn was named for the peak from which the Bible says Moses viewed the promised land, the national forest's history is deeply connected with that of the neighboring Biltmore Estate. German experts hired by George Vanderbilt to manage Biltmore's lands founded the nation's first school of forestry in the area in 1898, and the bulk of the forest's land came to the federal government in 1915, when Edith Vanderbilt offered to sell 86,700 acres of Biltmore property for a relatively small sum to ensure that the land was preserved.

Today the forest includes more than 510 thousand acres that stretch across fifteen counties in the western part of the state.

1931 General Assembly Consolidated UNC

On March 27, 1931, the General Assembly consolidated what is now UNC-Chapel Hill, N.C. State University, and UNC-Greensboro into the University of North Carolina system. The streamlined system was intended to reduce inefficiency and redundancy in higher education.

For more than 125 years the only campus of the University of North Carolina, chartered in 1789, was at Chapel Hill. Beginning in 1877 the General Assembly began to support other institutions of higher education with diverse purposes. After the initial creation of the multi-campus University in 1931, more schools were brought into the fold in 1969. In 1971 legislation was passed bringing the state's ten remaining public institutions on board.

As of fall 2012 the entire system had more than 175,000 students across all of its campuses. It now includes historically black institutions, a school formed to educate American Indians, colleges established to prepare teachers for the public schools, and a training school for performing artists.

1950 Modernist Giant George Matsumoto

On March 27, 1950, George Matsumoto was licensed to practice architecture in North Carolina. Known for his Modernist designs, Matsumoto was one of the founding faculty members of N.C. State's School of Design in 1948. Born in 1922, he grew up in San Francisco. He studied architecture at the University of California at Berkeley, Washington University in Saint Louis, and Cranbrook Academy of Art in Michigan.

In 1952 Matsumoto began construction of his own house in Raleigh, extending the living space visually into the wooded hillside. The Matsumoto House, a designated Raleigh Historic Landmark, is on the National Register of Historic Places.

He returned to San Francisco in 1961 to teach at Berkeley and later opened a successful private practice with commissions in commercial, educational, and recreational work, as well as campus and community planning. He was elected a fellow of the American Institute of Architects.

North Carolina has the third largest collection of Modernist houses in America, the residential building style Matsumoto helped initiate. The George Matsumoto papers and drawings are now held by N.C. State's D. H. Hill Library.

2013 Judaculla Rock, Cherokee Petroglyph of Prominence

On March 27, 2013, Judaculla Rock, a soapstone boulder in Jackson County, was added to the National Register of Historic Places.

Though commonly identified simply as a boulder covered with ancient and mysterious engravings, Judaculla Rock is the best-known and largest example of an American Indian petroglyph that can be found in North Carolina.

The petroglyphs, or rock art, at Judaculla were carved intermittently within the Late Woodland to Late Mississippian periods from about 500 to 1700 A.D. The rock itself is actually one of several petroglyph boulders within a fifteen-acre area. It is an archaeological site of great significance.

The site is also a landscape component of a prominent Cherokee legend that chronicles the vast supernatural and physical realm of a creature known as Judaculla. Cullowhee, six miles from the rock, is believed to be a shortened and anglicized form of Judaculla-whee, meaning Judaculla's Place.

Today Judaculla Rock is managed by Jackson County, which received the property in 1959 as a donation from the Parker family, very conscientious caretakers who still own the surrounding lands. The Eastern Band of the Cherokee is a principal partner in efforts to protect, enhance, and celebrate the site.

MAR 27

Judaculla Rock with markings filled with chalk for visibility, ca. 1935–1940.

MAR 28

1865 Stoneman's Cavalry Drove Old Dixie Down

On March 28, 1865, Maj. Gen. George Stoneman's troops marched through Blowing Rock. Union cavalry under Stoneman, commander of the Union army District of East Tennessee, conducted one of the longest cavalry raids in history.

About five thousand men under Stoneman's command entered North Carolina with a mission "to destroy and not to fight battles" in order to expedite the close of the Civil War. Stoneman's raid coincided with the raids of Gen. William T. Sherman in the eastern sections of the state. Stoneman divided his men and sent detachments throughout the region, securing the destruction of factories, bridges, and railroad lines. The army relied heavily on local citizens for food and supplies, often emptying local storehouses.

Stoneman's raids in North Carolina lasted from late March until May. The men marched more than one thousand miles during the raid, and historians credit the expedition with assuring the death of the Confederacy. The march is considered such a success because it captured artillery pieces and took thousands of prisoners while destroying Confederate army supplies and blocking a line of possible retreat for both Lee and Johnston's armies.

1880 Körner's Folly, Architectural Wonder in Kernersville

On March 28, 1880, Körner's Folly opened to the public.

Furniture designer, decorator, and painter Jule Gilmer Körner began construction on the house in 1878 as a showcase for his work. He continually added new designs to the building, and when he died in 1924, renovation plans were found on his drawing table.

The elegant structure on Main Street in Kernersville has twenty-two rooms spread over three floors and seven levels. No two parts of the house are exactly alike. Ceiling heights range from five and a half to twenty-five feet; there are fifteen fireplaces, numerous cubbyholes and trap doors, and a unique air distribution system with pivoting windows. Körner also built a house on the property for Clara, the servant who raised him. Born a slave, she was purchased by his Quaker father in order to free her.

In addition to being used as a residence and being open for tours, the building has a long legacy as a performing arts venue for the Triad community. Körner's wife Polly Alice established the Juvenile Lyceum in the building in 1896 so that children in the community would have a space to stage performances. In 1897 Jule renovated the third-floor billiard room into a theater space adorned with cupid-themed murals painted by Caesar Milch. Called Cupid's Park Theater, it is said to be the first private little theater in America and is still used for community productions.

1914 Lexington Landmark Erlanger Mills

On March 28, 1914, Erlanger Mills began production in Lexington. The company was conceived of in 1911, when New York textile magnates Abraham and Charles Erlanger needed a source of cotton fabric for their BVD underwear factory in Baltimore, Maryland. Lexington businessmen convinced the brothers to build a plant near their town.

The Erlangers bought 250 acres north of Lexington, laid out a mill and model village, and began construction in 1913. The mill complex initially included a brick mill building housing 25,600 steam-powered spindles and 680 looms, a large weave shed, picker room, cotton warehouse, water tower, and reservoir.

By the 1920s the grid-plan village encompassed 325 houses, two churches, schools, a hotel, hospital, clubhouse, company store, and even a dairy. Erlanger residents also benefitted from a community poultry yard, piggery, greenhouse, cannery, and their own athletic teams. After the village was annexed by Lexington, executives sold village houses to their employees during the 1950s. In 1972 the Erlanger family sold the mill to Gastonia's Parkdale Mills Inc. Parkdale spent millions to modernize the mill, which currently manufactures cotton and cotton-blend yarn.

The village was listed on the National Register of Historic Places in 2008.

Körner's Folly, a home built by Jule Gilmer Körner, labelled by many of his neighbors as the strangest home in America, Kernersville, N. C.

Aerial view of Erlanger Mills, Incorporated, showing mill buildings and the surrounding mill village, Lexington, N. C., ca. 1940 (*background*).

1795 Joel Lane, Key to Raleigh's Establishment

On March 29, 1795, Patriot, planter and prominent Raleigh resident Joel Lane died.

Born in Halifax sometime in the early 1740s, Lane is believed to have been a descendant of early settlers of Jamestown. After serving as justice of the peace and sheriff in Halifax County, Lane acquired several thousand acres of land in what is now Wake County and moved there sometime in the late 1760s.

After arriving in what is now Raleigh, Lane quickly established himself as one of the area's leading citizens. He represented it in the General Assembly in 1770 and 1771, introducing the bill that established Wake County as separate from Johnston County. He helped select the sites for the new county's courthouse and prison, and it is believed that the first Wake County court session was held in his home in 1771.

Lane went on to serve more terms in the General Assembly, hold various local offices, fight under Gov. William Tryon in the War of Regulation, and represent the Wake area at two constitutional conventions, but he is now perhaps best known for selling the land on which Raleigh would be built to the state in 1792.

His home is now operated as a museum.

1862 Burnside's Troops Extended Occupation to Bogue Banks

On March 29, 1862, Union forces led by Gen. John G. Parke landed unopposed on Bogue Banks at the mouth of Hoop Pole Creek.

With successes in 1862 at Roanoke Island and New Bern, Union commanders set their sights on Fort Macon, built between 1826 and 1834 to protect Beaufort Inlet. Garrisons had manned the facility at irregular intervals leading up to the Civil War, usually only during periods of international tension. Consequently, the masonry fort had begun to deteriorate by the 1860s.

Morehead City, just across the sound, was a strategic target since it was the terminus of the Atlantic and North Carolina Railroad. The only significant Confederate force still operating on the coast between Wilmington and Norfolk was defending Fort Macon. Gen. Ambrose Burnside selected Parke to capture the fort. Early on, Parke hoped but failed to compel the Confederates to surrender without resistance. He set up his headquarters in Carolina City, a village of about one hundred inhabitants just outside Morehead City. Forces on both sides amassed their weapons, and the siege lasted for more than four weeks.

In the end the fort's commander, Col. Moses J. White, surrendered. Given the intensity of the firing, casualties on both sides were remarkably light.

1982 Championship Win #1 for Dean Smith

On March 29, 1982, UNC basketball coach Dean Smith and his Tar Heels won the school's first national title since 1957. The Tar Heels took on the Georgetown University Hoyas in New Orleans in the final game of the National Collegiate Athletic Association basketball tournament that year.

Expectations for the Tar Heels had been high since the team lost in the NCAA championship game the previous year. The starpower of the 1982 UNC team also raised the hopes of fans, with key players Sam Perkins and James Worthy returning from the previous season and being joined by freshman guard Michael Jordan.

The game was close the entire time. The team in the lead was never ahead by more than a few points, with the lead shuttling back and forth between Tar Heels and Hoyas the whole night. With thirty-two seconds left in the game, the Tar Heels were behind. Smith called for a time out, and whatever was said in huddle seemed to work, because when the Tar Heels took the court again, Jordan took a jump shot giving them the lead and the win, 63 to 62.

Smith coached the UNC Tar Heels for a total of thirty-six seasons and took the team to the NCAA tournament twenty-five times; he earned one more national championship title in 1993 and seventeen ACC titles.

MAR 29

University of North Carolina Tar Heels men's basketball player Michael Jordan cutting basketball net at NCAA Final Four, likely in 1982 after the finals against Georgetown University held at the Louisiana Superdome in New Orleans.

1811 Warrenton's Architect-Builder Jacob Holt

On March 30, 1811, Jacob W. Holt, notable carpenter, builder and contractor, was born in Virginia.

Holt moved to Warrenton in 1844 and established one of the state's largest antebellum building firms. Drawing on popular architectural books, he developed a distinctive style that mixed elements from the Greek Revival and Italianate schools. In addition to the more than twenty buildings known to be his work, as many as seventy more are attributed to Holt and his shop, and his work is seen by historians as representative of mid-nineteenth century North Carolina architecture as whole.

Holt's arrival in Warrenton coincided with a larger cultural renaissance in the area. The completion of the Raleigh and Gaston Railroad in 1840 and the expansion of the slavery-based tobacco-growing plantation economy generated new wealth in the region, and planters and merchants created a market for larger houses and public buildings than the previous generations had constructed.

Warren County became in the antebellum era one of the richest counties in the state. Holt and his associates transformed the old town, building new churches, a new courthouse, and many new houses within about fifteen years, as well as many plantation houses and country churches in the surrounding rural areas.

MAR 30

1929 Feds Take Control of the Dismal Swamp Canal

On March 30, 1929, the federal government acquired the Dismal Swamp Canal for five hundred thousand dollars.

Originally authorized by the General Assembly in 1790, a private company that used slave labor was hired to construct the canal. Work began in 1793, and though the canal was finished by 1805, only small boats could traverse its course.

Between 1839 and the beginning of the Civil War, the canal was widened and deepened. A system of locks was built so that ships could be raised or lowered in the waterway. The locks were improved with masonry, enabling larger boats to pass through. Between 1896 and 1899, the masonry locks were replaced with timber ones. During the Civil War, the canal had fallen into disrepair, but it reopened in 1899.

Today the canal runs nineteen miles long, sixty feet wide and nine feet deep. Supervised by the Army Corps of Engineers, it is part of the Intracoastal Waterway, which stretches along the Atlantic and Gulf coasts.

1929 Loray Mill Walkout, 1929

On March 30, 1929, workers at the Loray Mill in Gastonia began a walkout. Two days later they called a general strike. At the time the five-story building covered more than a half-million square feet and was the world's largest factory under one roof. Labor unions targeted it for organization because of its size, and the Rhode Island owners caused resentment by erecting a tall fence around the property and pressing for greater productivity.

The National Textile Workers Union, widely acknowledged to be under Communist influence, exploited the situation by sending activists to Gastonia. They argued that winning North Carolina was the key to the labor movement's advancement in the South, and winning the Loray Mill was the key to winning North Carolina.

The strike dragged on through the summer and fall of 1929. O. F. Aderholdt, Gastonia's chief of police, was shot and killed in June. Ella May Wiggins, a ballad singer and union sympathizer, was killed in September. The strike and associated violence dealt a setback to union efforts, bolstering anti-union sentiment both locally and, owing to the wide press coverage, across the state and region.

Renovations commenced in 2013 to rehabilitate the mill and transform it into apartments and retail and office space.

Dismal Swamp Canal showing a typical scene with buildings lining shoreline and boats.

1862 Vincent Colyer, Freedmen's Friend

On March 31, 1862, Vincent Colyer was appointed Superintendent of the Poor for the Union's Department of North Carolina. Stationed in the occupied town of New Bern, Colyer immediately set about employing African Americans as skilled laborers to work on fortifications for the town. He managed to have three sets of earthworks constructed during his brief tenure.

Colyer set up schools to educate African Americans but ran afoul of Edward Stanly, who was serving as the military governor of North Carolina. Stanly was under orders to restore North Carolina to the Union as it was before the secession movement, and in Stanly's view that meant that educating blacks was illegal. Colyer successfully appealed to President Lincoln, who disagreed with Stanly's stance.

Colyer produced a detailed accounting of his time as Superintendent that highlights the breadth of activities performed by African American men. In addition to working military construction, these men served as scouts and spies.

After the Civil War Colyer became a successful artist, noted especially for his paintings of the American West.

1933 Civilian Conservation Corps Established

On March 31, 1933, the Civilian Conservation Corps (CCC) was established to provide work relief to men ages eighteen to twenty-five. In North Carolina the CCC had sixty-six camps, employing nearly fourteen thousand men in forty-seven counties.

One of the earliest of North Carolina's camps was Camp John Rock in Pisgah Forest. Plans were laid for the installation as early as April 1933, and men began arriving from Fort Bragg on May 5 to construct barracks and other buildings. Eventually 220 workers were assigned to the unit. Their major projects included fish and fawn rearing, road building and maintenance, trail improvement, reforestation, and forest conservation. Their work is evident today throughout Pisgah National Forest. The camp closed in 1936, and the program was abolished by Congress in 1942.

Directed by Army officers and foresters, the CCC was famous for its semi-military discipline. Dismissed by some as "Roosevelt's tree army," the CCC initiated site development and improvements in nearly twenty-one hundred national, state, and private forests and parks across the United States. By the end of its run, three million men were hired by the CCC at an average salary of thirty-five dollars per month.

1934 Songwriter John D. Loudermilk of Durham

On March 31, 1934, songwriter John D. Loudermilk was born in Durham.

Loudermilk learned to play instruments at the Salvation Army church he attended as a child, and his mother taught him to play a cigar box ukulele built by his father. At age thirteen he performed on Durham radio station WTIK as Little Johnny Dee, his recording name on the Colonial label.

While working as a handyman for WTVD, the station let Loudermilk perform "A Rose and a Baby Ruth" on air. He had written the song first as a poem and later set it to music. After George Hamilton IV recorded a version in 1956, Loudermilk's career began to take off.

Loudermilk's star continued to rise after his 1957 recording of "Sittin' in the Balcony" made the Top 40. The song made the Top 20 when it was covered by Eddie Cochran later that same year.

As his career progressed, he found more success as a songwriter than as a performer. He wrote country and pop music hits for the Everly Brothers, Chet Atkins, Paul Revere & the Raiders ("Indian Reservation"), The Casinos ("Then You Can Tell Me Goodbye"), and Johnny Tillotson ("Talk Back Trembling Lips").

Loudermilk was inducted into the Nashville Songwriters Hall of Fame and the North Carolina Music Hall of Fame. He died September 21, 2016 and was buried in Tennessee.

1973 Carowinds Opens on NC/SC Border

On March 31, 1973, Carowinds, near Charlotte, opened to the public.

Miss North Carolina and Miss South Carolina cut the ribbon at the opening ceremony. Young Charlotte resident Jimmy Henderson, waving a giant ticket, led about three thousand visitors into the park in a parade reminiscent of the opening of Disneyland in California.

Many had waited since before dawn to be among the first admitted at 10 a.m. That first day drenching rain fell on the park, which straddles the state line between North and South Carolina, yet despite the less than ideal conditions more than six thousand people came through the park's main gates.

Carowinds, the dream of Charlotte developer E. Pat Hall, was spread over seventy-three acres and at the time of its opening was larger than Disneyland, Astroworld in Houston, or Six Flags Over Georgia in Atlanta. Construction cost more than thirty million dollars and took about three years to complete.

A golden concrete state line runs through the park. Two weeks before the opening, the legislatures of both states met at the park in a joint session.

CCC Camp John Rock, Transylvania Co.

APR 1

1888 Once "Largest Manufacturer of Towels in the World"

On April 1, 1888, Concord's steam-powered Cannon Manufacturing Company, predecessor of Cannon Mills, produced its first yarn.

Founded by James W. Cannon the year before, the steam-powered, four-thousand-spindle manufacturing facility took raw cotton, spun the yarn, then wove it into a finished product called Cannon Cloth. The inexpensive cloth was popular for making shirts and pillowcases. By 1890 Cannon was focusing his operation on towels. Initially the flat weave towel was designed to be completed at home, with the purchaser cutting and hemming the fabric to desired sizes.

In 1906 Cannon bought six hundred acres of land a few miles north of Concord. He built a planned community that included rental houses and a school. The community became the town of Kannapolis. Around that same time Cannon began to produce a more absorbent towel made out of terry cloth. By the end of the World War I, the company was the nation's largest towel producer.

Cannon expanded his textile holdings, and in 1928 he consolidated nine plants into the Cannon Mills Company. Eventually part of Fieldcrest and later Pillowtex, the Kannapolis-based operations of Cannon Mills closed in 2003.

1937 Origins of Archaeology at Town Creek

On April 1, 1937, Lloyd Frutchey, a Montgomery County farmer, conveyed one acre of land containing a Mississippian-era Indian mound to the state of North Carolina for excavation, interpretation, and protection. The area was known as Frutchey State Park until the 1940s, when its name was changed to Town Creek.

Significant work did not get underway to excavate the mound area until November 1939, when the project was approved as a Works Progress Administration program. Some of the best archaeological work performed at the site came during the WPA years, but World War II effectively shut down operations there. Joffre Coe, the original archaeological supervisor of Town Creek and chief archaeologist at UNC, resumed his great interest in the area after the war. Coe worked on the Town Creek project for more than fifty years.

In 1955 Town Creek Indian Mound became one of North Carolina's first State Historic Sites under the Department of Archives and History. It remains the only site dedicated to interpreting the lives of American Indians. Town Creek includes the preserved mound, as well as two reconstructed temples, a burial hut, and a mortuary hut.

1987 Tar Heels Say No to the Mobro Garbage Barge

On April 1, 1987, WRAL-TV in Raleigh broke the "Gar-barge" story.

The story began a year earlier when Alabama businessman Lowell Harrelson proposed to alleviate overcrowding in a Long Island landfill by sending garbage to landfills across the South via barges. A parcel in Jones County was selected as the site for the first transfer of waste, and more than three thousand tons of garbage set sail aboard the *Mobro 4000* in late March 1987, bound for the port in Morehead City.

After the story broke, local residents quickly became incensed at the prospect of New York's garbage being dumped in pristine coastal North Carolina. A state environmental official spotted a bedpan in the trash, leading the load to be classified as medical waste.

The state Department of Human Resources secured an injunction blocking Harrelson from offloading the garbage, and soon the barge was headed to Louisiana. After it was turned away there and by five other states and three counties, the town of Islip, which had originally sent most of the garbage, agreed to take the load.

The *Mobro's* six-thousand-mile, five-month odyssey captured the attention of the nation. Dan Rather called the shipment "the most watched load of garbage in the memory of man."

Spinning frames at the Cannon Manufacturing Company Cotton Mill at Kannapolis, N. C.

Town Creek Indian Mound depicting an entire view of the Town Creek Indian Mound located in southern Montgomery County. The Pee Dee Indians migrated here in the eleventh century and built their main village around 1300 A.D. This site has researched by archaeologists since 1937 (*above and background*).

1759 Venus Flytrap-Dobbs's "Catch Fly"

On April 2, 1759, Gov. Arthur Dobbs penned a letter to his naturalist friend Peter Collinson in England. The words that he wrote would begin the annals of the Venus Flytrap: "We have a kind of Catch Fly sensitive which closes upon anything that touches it, it grows in the Latitude 34 but not in 35°—I will try to save the seed here."

Dobbs, originally from Ireland, was the Royal Governor of North Carolina from 1754 to 1763. In 1758 he moved to Brunswick, where he made his home at a plantation he called Castle Dobbs. His time as governor was difficult, and he found himself increasingly at odds with the North Carolina Assembly. Dobbs found solace in his exploration of the natural history of North Carolina.

Though it is known and cultivated throughout the world, the Venus Flytrap is native only to a small area of the Coastal Plain in North and South Carolina, mostly within a seventy-five-mile radius of Wilmington. The General Assembly adopted the Venus Flytrap as the official State Carnivorous Plant in 2005.

1931 Horace Kephart and the "Back of Beyond"

On April 2, 1931, naturalist and writer Horace Kephart was killed in a car crash near Bryson City. He was riding in a taxi with another author, Fiswoode Tarleton, when the car plunged from the highway and overturned three times. Both Kephart and Tarleton were killed instantly.

A former librarian, Kephart came to the Great Smoky Mountains in 1904, seeking solace, and spent the rest of his life there, writing about the environment and outdoor life. By 1913 he had published three books on self-reliant living and the natural world. He was an early advocate of the mountain region and tirelessly promoted the creation of the Great Smoky Mountains National Park. Though born in Pennsylvania and raised in the Midwest, he lived in a remote cabin on Hazel Creek and in Bryson City in Swain County for much of his later life.

Kephart wrote many books and articles about southern Appalachian culture and the natural environment of the area he had adopted as his home, which he heralded as the "Back of Beyond." His book *Our Southern Highlanders*, published in 1913, is the classic work on the region.

Kephart is buried in Bryson City on a hill overlooking the Great Smoky Mountains. Western Carolina University holds many of his papers.

APR 2

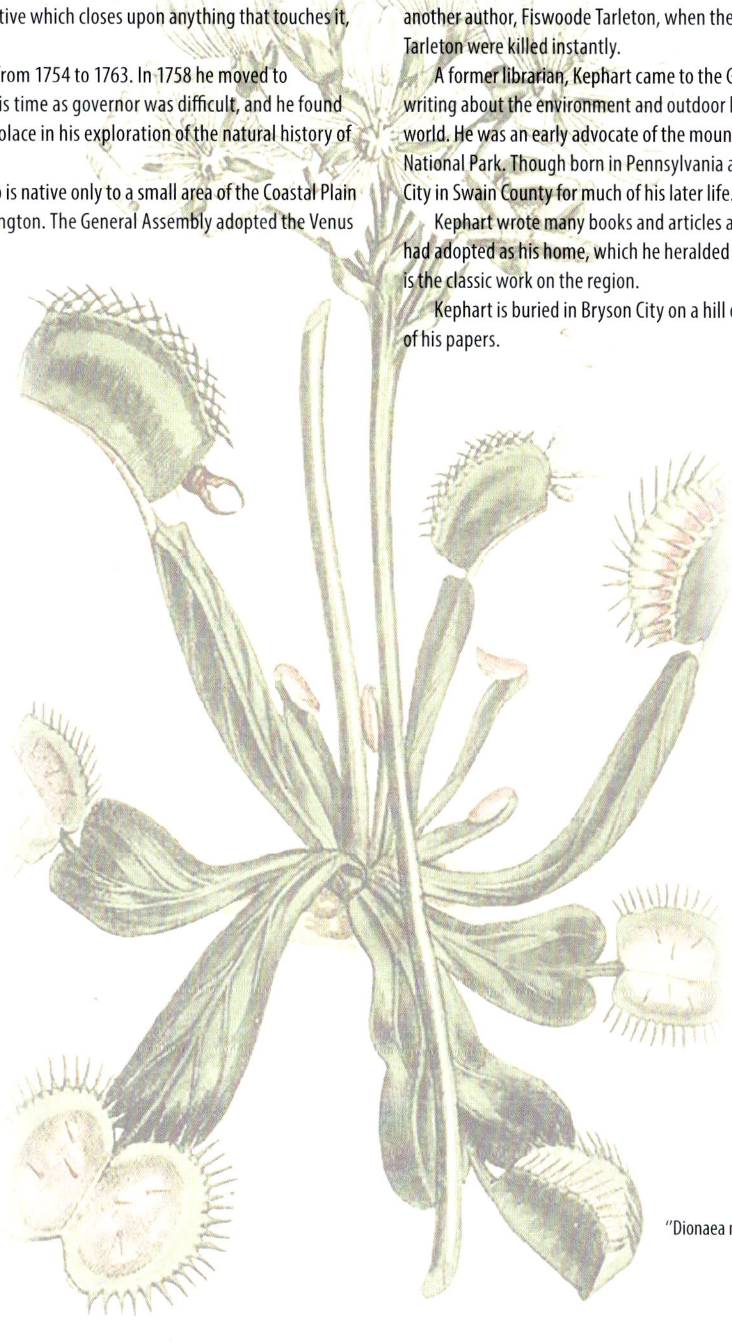

"Dionaea muscipula." A drawing of a Venus Flytrap by William Curtis (1746–1799).

APR
3

1730 The Nikwasi Treaty

On April 3, 1730, Scotsman Sir Alexander Cuming was present at a meeting of Cherokee leaders at the council house at Nikwasi.

With Cuming's support and apparent influence among the Indians, local headman Moytoy was selected "Emperor of the Cherokee." Moytoy and Cuming then persuaded those present to pledge their allegiance to King George II. In a ceremony of friendship and possibly of political adoption, the Indians presented Cuming with the "Crown of Tannassy," a dyed possum-hair headdress. It is likely Moytoy and the other leaders believed that the gesture would create a link between the Cherokee and the British.

Shortly thereafter Cuming and a group of Cherokee representatives traveled to England, where they presented the king with the Crown, some eagles' tail feathers, and scalps. The group included the young warrior who would become known as Attakullakulla, or Little Carpenter. The Indians were then coerced into signing "Articles of Friendship and Commerce."

Cuming petitioned to be made an official ambassador to the Cherokee, but his request was denied. He left interesting memoirs of his time among the Indians, including a tale that he was crowned King of the Cherokee, but scholars have more recently reinterpreted the events to include the Cherokee perspective.

1930 Thomas Built Buses Since 1930

On April 3, 1930, Thomas Built Buses, the High Point company now recognized internationally for building bright yellow school buses, was incorporated.

The company was the brainchild of Canadian native Perley A. Thomas. With only an elementary school education Thomas took correspondence courses in engineering and learned about streetcar manufacturing in Detroit. He became chief engineer of the Kuhlman Car Company in Cleveland, Ohio and moved to High Point in 1909 to become chief engineer of the Southern Car Company.

After that firm failed, Thomas started a streetcar repair business in 1916. The company eventually began manufacturing streetcars and continued to do so for cities across the country as the Thomas Car Works. One even inspired the title of Tennessee Williams's *A Streetcar Named Desire*. As an assurance of quality, each of his streetcars bore an engraved "Thomas Built" plaque.

In 1936 Thomas won his first state contract to build schoolbuses. His use of all-steel construction and a rear safety door secured the company's future. Thomas died in 1959, and the family-owned company became part of the Freightliner LLC group in 1998.

With several foreign factories and about sixteen hundred employees worldwide, Thomas Built Buses now builds nearly fourteen thousand vehicles annually.

1946 Thomas Dixon and the Genesis of Birth of a Nation

On April 3, 1946, Shelby native Thomas Dixon Jr., whose novel was the basis for the film *Birth of a Nation*, died.

Educated locally and at Wake Forest, he won a scholarship to graduate school at The Johns Hopkins University. In Baltimore he fell in love with theater and soon moved to New York to pursue an acting career. His disappointing experience there led him home to Shelby, where he studied law.

Dixon was elected to the General Assembly in 1884 and passed the bar after serving in the legislature for a single session. Tiring of law, he became a Baptist minister. In 1895 he left the ministry to become a nondenominational speaker, soon achieving fame as a lecturer and earning as much as one thousand dollars per engagement.

In 1901 Dixon wrote his first novel *The Leopard's Spots*, calling for the exclusion of blacks from American society and for reconciliation between North and South. He wrote two more novels with similar messages and in 1905 adapted one of them into a play entitled *The Clansman*.

D. W. Griffith went on to adapt the play still further into the landmark motion picture *Birth of a Nation* in 1915.

1973 Mast General Store, Now in Its Second Century

On April 3, 1973, the Mast General Store was added to the National Register of Historic Places. After a century as a landmark in the mountain community of Valle Crucis, today it is an iconic symbol of the heyday of country stores and their role in the life of rural communities.

Henry Taylor, originally a clock salesman from Davidson County, began the store as the Taylor mercantile business in the mid-1800s. By the early 1880s he operated two general stores opposite each other on North Carolina Highway 194, then known as the Caldwell Watauga Turnpike. In 1898 he partnered with W. W. Mast, and the store's name changed to Taylor and Mast.

Mast took sole ownership of the business in 1913, changing its name to the Mast Store. Like Taylor before him, Mast expanded the business as the community grew, serving residents' need for goods and a community center. The store sold local items traded by residents, including wild ginseng, which reportedly made its way to markets in China.

The Mast family owned the store until the 1970s. Then struggling to stay afloat, it closed in 1977. In 1980 the business reopened under new ownership in the original Taylor and Mast Store building in Watauga County.

A 1936 Guilford County school bus built by Perley Thomas.

1928 Rosenwald Schools and Berry O'Kelly

On April 4, 1928, the completion of the four thousandth Rosenwald school project—two additions to the Berry O'Kelly School in the Method community of Wake County—was celebrated.

The school was able to add two buildings, one with a large classroom and administration space and a second featuring a shop for teaching the trades, thanks to the generosity of local businessman Berry O'Kelly and former Sears Roebuck & Co. CEO Julius Rosenwald. The additions transformed the school into a fully developed campus with more than eight buildings, which included dormitories and dining halls.

Originating during Reconstruction as a Freedmen's village west of Raleigh, Method experienced significant development in the 1890s and early twentieth century due in large part to the efforts of Berry O'Kelly, a successful businessman who had a strong interest in the improvement of educational opportunities for rural black children.

O'Kelly devoted much of his philanthropy to the school that adopted his name. Through his association with Booker T. Washington, O'Kelly met Julius Rosenwald, who was inspired by Washington to provide financial assistance for the construction of more than fifty-three hundred schools for African Americans across the South.

The Berry O'Kelly School, acclaimed as the best school for black children in North Carolina, drew students from across the state. Today the shop building, a playing field, and a gymnasium survive as part of the Method Park and Community Center.

1929 National Guard Called Out to Suppress Strike

On April 4, 1929, the National Guard was called out by Gov. O. Max Gardner to suppress a strike at the Loray Mill in Gastonia. Organized in 1900, the mill was the largest in North Carolina at the time. Employing more than two thousand workers at its peak, the mill was also reported to be the largest factory under one roof in the United States.

Because of the mill's size, the United Textile Workers of America targeted it and formed a local chapter there in 1919. On March 30, 1929, workers began a walkout, with a general strike on April 1. The union sent activists to the mill, and the strike began to draw national press coverage, lasting through the summer and into the fall.

Violence escalated and in June, Gastonia's chief of police, O. F. Aderholdt, was shot and killed. In September mill worker Ella May Wiggins, a ballad singer and Union sympathizer, was killed. Wiggins had been a focus and inspiration during the organizing drive. More violence followed her death, setting back union organizing efforts substantially and creating a wave of anti-union sentiment across the state.

The Loray Mill historic district is listed on the National Register of Historic Places.

1946 A Place for H. H. Brimley: N.C. Museum of Natural Sciences

On April 4, 1946, H. H. Brimley died.

Visitors to the North Carolina Museum of Natural Sciences in downtown Raleigh encounter one exhibit that is distinctly different from all the rest. It is the cluttered office of Herbert Hutchinson Brimley, the museum's original curator and first director. Brimley's tenure at the museum stretched from 1895 until his death more than fifty years later.

Brimley and his brother Clement emigrated from England to America in 1880 and shortly thereafter opened a taxidermy shop in Raleigh. They quickly gained reputations as two of the South's leading naturalists.

Their first work for the state was to create an exhibit on waterfowl and fishes for the State Exposition of 1884. The Department of Agriculture, which oversaw the display, found the exhibit too valuable to discard. The department found a more permanent place in its halls for the exhibit and, in time, found a more permanent place for Brimley, too, as the exhibit's curator and director of the museum it began.

Once simply the State Museum, the institution has been the N.C. Museum of Natural Sciences since 1986. One of North Carolina's most popular attractions, the museum now averages more than seven hundred thousand visitors per year.

1983 Valvano's Championship Stuff of Memories for Wolfpack

On April 4, 1983, the North Carolina State University Wolfpack won the NCAA Men's Basketball Championship in Albuquerque, New Mexico.

After a series of unlikely and often last-minute wins that began during the Atlantic Coast Conference tournament weeks earlier, the "Cardiac Pack," under the leadership of head coach Jim Valvano, culminated its run with a barnburner over the University of Houston Cougars. The Cougars were nicknamed "Phi Slama Jama" for their expertise in slam-dunking basketballs over the heads of opponents, so chances were slim that the underdog Wolfpack would pull off the upset.

One *Washington Post* sports reporter wrote, "Trees will tap-dance, elephants will drive at Indy and Orson Welles will skip lunch before North Carolina State finds a way to beat Houston." But find a way they did. Both State's first and last baskets were dunks, and that last shot came just as the buzzer sounded, clinching the victory for the Pack, 54–52.

The images of Lorenzo Charles making the basket and Coach Valvano running around the court looking for someone to hug have become iconic in sports culture, and both are fitting tributes to two extraordinary individuals who are no longer with us.

APR 4

H. H. Brimley in his museum workshop examining a bird having undergone taxidermy, ca. 1940.

NCSU wins 1983 NCAA Basketball Championship. Coach Jim Valvano cuts down the net in Albuquerque, New Mexico.

APR 5

1919 Pope Air Force Base Gets Its Name

On April 5, 1919, the Camp Bragg Flying Field was renamed in memory of First Lt. Harley Halbert Pope, the first officer assigned to the post. Pope had been killed when the Curtiss JN-4 Jenny he was flying crashed into the Cape Fear River earlier that year.

In the early years activity around Pope Field was so slow that pilots were asked to buzz the area to scare away grazing deer before landing. In the 1920s the facility's primary uses were observation and balloon and bombing training. A major expansion occurred in the 1930s with a runway extension, installation of lighting, and construction of a new headquarters building and two hangars. During World War II the field was used primarily for troop carrier training. Throughout those years Pope Field remained under the auspices of the Army. After the Army Air Force became a separate branch of the military in 1947, Pope became a base.

Troops from Pope have been deployed in many major conflicts, including the Vietnam, Gulf, and Iraq Wars, as well as military actions taken in the Congo, the Dominican Republic, Grenada, Panama, and Somalia. In 2011 Pope Air Force Base was absorbed into Fort Bragg, once again becoming Pope Field.

1976 Jim Hunt Takes the Stage, 1976

On April 5, 1976, James Baxter Hunt Jr. announced his intention to run for governor of North Carolina.

With sixty-five percent of the vote, Hunt handily won the 1976 election. He served as governor for a record-breaking sixteen years—with an eight-year break between two sets of consecutive four-year terms.

During Hunt's administration North Carolina became a model of educational reform and the growth of technology. He set higher standards for teachers and students and sought to raise teacher salaries. A signature part of Hunt's agenda was helping young children grow and develop. To that end he advocated for the establishment of the Division of Child Development and created the non-profit SmartStart to provide assistance to preschoolers.

Hunt also sought to position North Carolina as a center of technology. He helped start the N.C. School of Math and Science in Durham and worked to found the Microelectronics Center of North Carolina in order to give companies and students the opportunity to work with technology and expand the economy.

After a generation in the public eye, Hunt left office in 2001 as one of the most familiar actors ever on the stage of North Carolina politics.

1986 Sci-Fi and Horror Master Manly Wade Wellman

On April 5, 1986, author Manly Wade Wellman died in Chapel Hill.

Born in 1903 in the African nation of Angola, where his father was a medical officer, Wellman returned to the United States with his family when he was six. After receiving degrees from what is now Wichita State University and Columbia Law School, he moved to North Carolina in 1947.

Wellman's prolific career as a professional writer began in 1927, when he worked as a newspaper reporter and submitted stories to pulp fiction magazines. He primarily wrote nonfiction, focusing on the Civil War, historical crime and other subjects. His fiction included juvenile historical adventures set in the Carolinas during the American Revolution and the Civil War, mysteries, and science fiction.

Wellman's best-regarded writings are in the genres of fantasy and horror. Their inspiration often derived from Appalachian or Native American folklore. His best-known character was Silver John, a balladeer whose wanderings in the mountains brought him into conflict with various supernatural entities.

Wellman taught creative writing at the University of North Carolina in the 1960s. He received numerous awards for both his fiction and nonfiction. Following his death Wellman was cremated and his ashes scattered in his Chapel Hill yard.

2000 Petty Patriarch Passes

On April 5, 2000, stock car racing legend and NASCAR pioneer Lee Petty died in Greensboro. He was eighty-six.

It wasn't until age thirty-five that Petty began his racing career, driving a borrowed 1946 Buick Roadmaster in NASCAR's first "strictly stock" race in June 1949 in Charlotte. That same year Petty established a garage in a repurposed reaper shed on his family's farm in Randleman. Over the course of his career, Petty claimed fifty wins, including three NASCAR championships and the top spot at the inaugural Daytona 500 in February 1959.

A serious wreck during a 1961 qualifying race at Daytona left Petty with a punctured lung and a badly broken leg. He recovered but participated in only six more races before his retirement in 1964. Though his racing days were behind him, Petty continued to manage his garage. Eventually he was joined by his sons, Richard and Maurice, and grandson, Kyle. Known as Petty Enterprises, the complex grew to sixteen buildings, including racing workshops and fabrication facilities.

Petty's son Richard went on to become a seven-time NASCAR champion and claimed a record two hundred career victories, including seven Daytona 500 wins.

Gov. James B. Hunt talking to schoolchildren in his office, 1984.

"Pope Field Hangars Fort Bragg, N.C." in Durwood Barbour Collection of North Carolina Postcards.

1917 Camp Greene, Charlotte's Massive WWI Installation

On April 6, 1917, the United States entered World War I. That summer Maj. Gen. Leonard Wood, who was charged with selecting sites for new military camps, visited Charlotte as part of a tour of prospective sites in North Carolina. Wood chose Charlotte as the site for Camp Greene, a twenty-three-hundred-acre military training facility for the United States Army.

Named for Revolutionary War hero Nathanael Greene, the camp was constructed in ninety days, and by December it was a temporary home to nearly sixty thousand soldiers.

The camp boosted Charlotte's flagging economy, and the city's population of forty-five thousand witnessed a major increase in jobs and wealth, as restaurants, shops, and other amusements directed at the soldiers were constructed. Unfortunately, the camp also spread communicable diseases. The winter of 1917 proved incredibly harsh as hundreds of soldiers and citizens succumbed to pneumonia. The influenza epidemic of the following year also struck the camp and city.

The men who trained at Camp Greene and deployed to France saw some of the heaviest fighting of the war. At the war's end the camp was dismantled, and it was closed officially in June 1919.

1959 Bayard Wootten, Esteemed Photographer, of Chapel Hill and New Bern

On April 6, 1959, pioneering photographer Bayard Wootten died in New Bern.

Born in New Bern in 1875, Wootten left the area to attend college in Greensboro and then teach. She returned to New Bern to help family members. Once back she did design work to support her family, eventually creating Pepsi-Cola's first trademarked logo. She embraced photography in 1904, and after displaying her first photograph that year, orders for her work began to roll in.

After working for the National Guard as photographer and director of publicity, she turned to aerial photography in 1919, taking pictures of New Bern and the Neuse River.

Wootten moved to New York, and after a brief stint there and running a statewide portrait photographic service, she settled in Chapel Hill in 1928. She would remain there until her retirement in 1954. During her time in Chapel Hill, she received frequent invitations to exhibit her work and assembled popular slide presentations based on her architectural and landscape photography. She also illustrated books for UNC Press, Houghton Mifflin, and J.B. Lippincott during that time.

Shortly after her retirement she returned to New Bern, where she died five years later.

APR 6

Postcard shows an aerial view of Camp Greene, about 1918.

Photographer Bayard Wootten with camera in front of cypress tree in Great Lake, Craven County, NC, 1909.

1850 Oak Ridge, Military Prep School in Guilford County

On April 7, 1850, citizens in northwestern Guilford County met and appointed a board of trustees to erect a schoolhouse. The school would eventually become Oak Ridge Academy, the first coeducational military high school in the nation.

Three years later the school opened with a traditional curriculum and sixty-three male students. In 1861 and 1862 the entire student body and faculty enlisted in the Confederate army, which necessitated the school's closing. Set to reopen in September 1865, the school's main building burned the night before classes were to resume. The school was moved to nearby cabins and private homes.

Many senior students volunteered for service during World War I, and the U.S. Army began recruiting graduates for service as officers. In 1926 the Army organized a Junior Reserve Officer Training Corps there.

The school changed its name to Oak Ridge Military Academy in 1971, and that same year the school became the first military academy in the United States to admit females. Women had attended the school's secondary courses since about 1929 but never in a military capacity.

In 1983 the 101-acre campus became a historic district on the National Register of Historic Places.

APR 7

1910 Surfers Catch a Wave in Wrightsville Beach

On April 7, 1910, the Honolulu *Pacific Commercial Advertiser* published a letter that Wrightsville Beach resident Burke Haywood Bridgers had written to the national magazine *Colliers* requesting information about building surfboards.

Bridgers wrote to *Colliers* in response to Alexander Hume Ford, founder of the Outrigger Canoe and Surfboard Club in Hawaii, who penned an article for the magazine the previous year encouraging readers to try the sport.

Bridgers wrote that people in Wrightsville Beach tried out surfing during the summer of 1909 without great results. The Lumina Pavilion, then one of the area's premiere attractions, hosted a "surf board riding contest" over Labor Day, in fact.

Bridgers went on to describe the kinds of boards that the locals were using and the nature of the Atlantic Coast surf. The surfboards he described were built with local juniper wood, a traditional favorite of boat and ship builders, as it is resistant to wood-boring worms.

It is impossible to claim a "first" in East Coast surfing, but Bridgers's experiments certainly would have been among the earliest appearances of surfboards in the Atlantic Ocean. The surfing in the Wrightsville Beach area in the early 1900s is the earliest documented in the state of North Carolina.

Recently Wrightsville Beach was named as one of the top twenty surfing towns in the world by *National Geographic*.

Postcards from 1922 showing surfers in Wilmington, N.C.

1808 Poor Naomi Wise, "Sacrificed to the Beast in Man"

On April 8, 1808, Jonathan Lewis was arrested for the murder of Naomi Wise. Wise, an orphan, cook, and occasional field hand noted for her beauty and her innocence, lived in the household of William Adams in Randolph County. Lewis was a frequent visitor to the Adams house.

Courting Naomi while promising marriage to another woman, Lewis led the pregnant Wise to the Deep River and pushed her off a bluff, drowning her. Jailed in Asheboro, he escaped and made his way to Ohio. He was eventually tracked down by a bounty hunter and returned to North Carolina, where he was acquitted of murdering Wise for lack of evidence. Legend has it that he confessed to the crime on his deathbed.

Much of what we know of the murder comes from an account by Braxton Craven, president of nearby Trinity College, who researched the story. Craven based his 1851 retelling of the crime on the memories of local residents. Lewis, by Craven's account, was a "merciless wretch, a hyena."

The site of Wise's death came to be known as Naomi Falls. The story was brought to people nationwide largely through the folk ballad, "Naomi Wise," which was a favorite of Doc Watson's. Like "Tom Dooley" and "Frankie and Johnny," the song relates the story of a North Carolina murder with drama and pathos.

1928 Karastan Rugs, Product of Carolina

On April 8, 1928, the first machine-made oriental design rug came off the loom in Leaksville in Rockingham County. Branded Karastan, the process used to make the rug replicated the detailed craftsmanship of a hand-woven rug.

The Karastan method has its roots in 1912, when retailer Marshall Field acquired several textile mills in Rockingham County. His employee Eugene Clark, a New England inventor, began to modify a spool Axminster power loom in 1926 to pull pile yarns through the back, making it possible to weave up to fifty colors with a soft feel and hand-knotted appearance on both sides.

The advanced manufacturing process led to Karastan rugs becoming known as "mystery rugs." At the 1933-34 World's Fair in Chicago, more than five million people walked on a large Karastan traditional Persian-patterned rug, which, when cleaned, displayed its original luster, earning the brand a reputation for producing "wonder rugs."

Karastan expanded to produce carpets woven with its innovative Kara-loc process and on computer-controlled Van de Wiele Wilton looms. Now a subsidiary of Mohawk Industries, Karastan still makes wool rugs in Eden and is the only U.S. maker of Axminster spool rugs.

1946 Baseball Legend "Catfish" Hunter

On April 8, 1946, famed baseball player James "Catfish" Hunter was born in Perquimans County.

Though Hunter excelled in a variety of sports in high school, his pitching skill stood out. Word spread fast, and soon major league scouts began to make the trip to Hertford to see him play. Though wounds from a hunting accident jeopardized Hunter's prospects in the eyes of many professional scouts, the Kansas City Athletics had faith in the young pitcher and signed him to a contract.

Hunter was an immediate success with Kansas City, earning his first major league victory in July 1965 in Fenway Park in Boston. He pitched a perfect game against the Minnesota Twins after the Athletics moved to Oakland in 1968. After a contract dispute in 1974, he left the Athletics for the New York Yankees. He was the highest paid pitcher in baseball when he signed with the Yankees in 1975. After retiring from baseball in 1979, Hunter returned to his native Herford, where he lived until his death in 1999.

Hunter's numerous accolades include spots in the National Baseball and North Carolina Sports Halls of Fame, five World Series titles, and eight All-Star team appearances.

1959 Tryon Palace Opens in New Bern

On April 8, 1959, the restored Tryon Palace opened to the public.

Interest in rebuilding the parts of the Palace that were lost in a 1798 fire was shown as early as 1925, but it wasn't until 1945 that Gov. R. Gregg Cherry appointed a commission to study the idea and organize restoration efforts. Maude Moore Latham, a New Bern native who had played in the Palace ruins as a child, served as the commission's chair and committed substantial amounts of her own money to the project.

The commission acquired the site of the original Palace with money from the General Assembly, and in 1951 the Boston firm that had restored Colonial Williamsburg in Virginia was hired to help with the restoration.

Two original copies of drawings of the palace done by its first architect, John Hawks, extensive historical research, and substantial archaeological evidence guided the work. Workers located the building's original foundations as construction began. As the excavations progressed, interior designers were aided by the discovery of pieces of marble, brass, molding, and glass.

The restoration's total cost came in at around three and a half million dollars, and after its re-opening Tryon Palace quickly became one of the most visited historic sites in the state.

APR 8

Reenactment in restored Tryon's Palace main building at New Bern, N.C.

APR 9

1585 Lane Expedition Sails to America

On April 9, 1585, Sir Ralph Lane sailed with 107 colonists to America.

A native of Devonshire, England, Lane entered the service of Queen Elizabeth I in 1563. After serving as a courtier, soldier, and sheriff, he was invited by Sir Walter Raleigh to command an expedition to America. By the end of June 1585, that expedition had arrived at Wococon (now Ocracoke) on the Outer Banks. A colony was established there, with Lane as the governor.

The colony later moved to Roanoke Island and established Fort Raleigh. In 1586 Lane and a group of colonists explored the Choanoac Indian country and the Chowan River. Thomas Harriot, a mathematician and scientist, and John White, an artist, were members of the expedition. Raleigh had sent Harriot to study the native inhabitants and explore the region's plants, animals, and minerals. White was hired to make maps and paint watercolors. Their findings were preserved in a book, *A Briefe and true report of the new found land of Virginia*.

By June 1586 the colony's supplies were running short. Sir Francis Drake arrived on June 11, and the discouraged Lane and other colonists abandoned the colony and boarded Drake's ships to return to England.

1862 W. H. Thomas's "Legion of Indians and Mountaineers"

On April 9, 1862, William Holland Thomas joined the Confederate army and brought his Cherokee recruits with him.

Thomas's Legion, as Thomas and his men came to be known, was a Civil War unit unlike any other. Made up of both whites and Cherokee, the Legion fought in western North Carolina, Tennessee, and Virginia.

A native of Waynesville, Thomas became close to the Cherokee at an early age and was adopted into their tribe. He studied law and successfully represented the tribe against the federal government during Andrew Jackson's Indian removal efforts.

At the outbreak of the Civil War, Thomas recruited soldiers from the mountains of North Carolina and Tennessee to serve in the Confederate army. His Legion was made up of several infantry and artillery units, including an Indian Battalion. After fighting throughout the region, Thomas's Legion was given the task of protecting the local people in the North Carolina mountains, a task made especially difficult by the high concentration of active Union sympathizers in the area.

Toward the end of the war, Thomas negotiated the surrender of his troops in Waynesville. When his men returned home, the region was still a no-man's-land with pro-Union and pro-Confederate factions skirmishing throughout the area.

1896 Latecomer Strikes Gold at Reed, 1896

On April 9, 1896, the last large gold nugget was found at Reed Gold Mine, the focal point of the nation's first gold rush. The discovery came ninety-seven years after John Reed first found a large nugget on his land.

Gold from the Reed property realized more than two million dollars in sales by 1824. By the late 1800s the mine had been mostly exhausted, and the prospectors who worked it had departed for other places like Colorado, Alaska, and California.

Jake Shinn, though, hadn't lost hope. On April 9 Shinn struck something hard only three feet underground. He ran off to clean what he had hit and see what he found, ignored by the fellow miners around him, who were used to many false alarms. When he returned, it was clear that he was holding a twenty-two-pound gold nugget. He eventually sold the nugget for around forty-eight hundred dollars, which would be more than one hundred thousand dollars today.

Mining at Reed continued to dwindle until the last operation closed in 1964. The property was acquired by the state in 1971 and opened as a state historic site in 1977.

Gold in a pan from Reed Gold Mine in Midland, N.C.

1872 Mycologist Moses A. Curtis of Hillsborough

On April 10, 1872, prominent botanist, author, and Episcopal priest Moses A. Curtis died in Orange County.

Born in Massachusetts, Curtis attended Williams College before beginning his ministry in Wilmington. He soon moved to Raleigh to teach at St. Mary's School and worked at a parish in Washington for a short time before going to St. Matthew's Church in Hillsborough in 1841. He would remain there for much of the rest of his life.

A dedicated priest and talented musician and composer, Curtis is best known for his contributions to botany, particularly in the field of mycology, the study of fungi. He was widely considered a national authority on the subject at the time and corresponded with other well-known scientists of the day, including Asa Gray, H. W. Ravenel, William Sullivant, Edward Tuckerman, and A. W. Chapman. He contributed to numerous publications and regularly identified specimens harvested on expeditions by others.

Curtis reported eating forty different species of mushrooms collected within two miles of his house and believed that if people had a better knowledge of edible fungi, food shortages for Southern armies during the Civil War would have been less severe.

He is buried at St. Matthew's in Hillsborough.

1922 Radio Broadcasting Began in North Carolina

On April 10, 1922, WBT in Charlotte received a broadcast license, becoming the first commercial radio station in North Carolina. Advances in radio took place in three North Carolina cities in 1922. In Raleigh on the campus of what is now N.C. State University, engineers installed a transmitter and initiated experimental broadcasts in March 1922. Regular transmission began on October 16, the day before the State Fair. Later that year the campus registered the call letters WLAC, but the following year the station left the air after campus funds were no longer available.

In Charlotte initial broadcasts began on March 25, in the kitchen of radio enthusiast Fred Laxton. Within weeks WBT had set up a studio in the Independence Building downtown. In Asheville WFAJ, owned by the local newspaper, began broadcasts on May 4 but failed the following year. WBT was thus the only startup that prospered.

WPTF in Raleigh originated as WFBQ in October 1924. Later known as WRCO, that station adopted its present call letters in November 1927. FM radio broadcasts in North Carolina began in 1942.

WBT radio station taken between 1920 and 1930.

1924 Kenneth Noland and Abstract Art

On April 10, 1924, abstract artist Kenneth Noland was born in Asheville. Noland devoted much of his career to the genre of color field abstraction. He studied and painted the interaction of contrasting and complementing colors. His most famous paintings feature a circle or chevron pattern that contains a distinct array of colors.

After a four-year stint in the Air Force, Noland enrolled at Black Mountain College, not far from his hometown. The experimental liberal arts college challenged students to learn through their own creative approach. During his time at Black Mountain College, Noland learned Professor Josef Albers's color theory and was greatly influenced by geometric abstractionist Ilya Bolotowsky. From Black Mountain he went on to Paris to study with artist Ossip Zadkins in 1949 before returning to the United States and teaching in Washington, D.C. and New York for the remainder of his career.

Noland's work has been shown around the world. It has been said of Noland that he was "one of the great colorists of the 20th century," and that "he invented a new kind of American abstraction based on the primacy of color."

1952 Unraveling the Mysteries of Psywar

On April 10, 1952, the United States Army moved the Psychological Warfare Center and School from Fort Riley, Kansas, to Fort Bragg, where it remains to this day.

The term "psychological warfare" originated during World War II, although the practice has been around since human beings first engaged in conflict with each other. Alexander the Great, Ghengis Khan, and other historic military leaders often spread exaggerated rumors of their own armies' prowess and savagery to intimidate enemies.

Any dissemination of propaganda to targeted enemy groups with the intention of sapping their morale and willingness to fight could be considered psychological warfare.

As communications grew more sophisticated, soldiers needed superior skills to employ effective psychological warfare. To accommodate this increasing complexity, the training program at Fort Bragg has evolved into its current form, the John F. Kennedy Special Warfare Center and School (JFKSWCS).

JFKSWCS chooses elite recruits for advanced, intense education in unconventional special operations techniques and tactical skills that can shape foreign political milieus. Soldiers are trained in world languages, international cultural norms, and methods for using information to influence the activities of governments and individuals.

1865 Stoneman's Troops Cross Shallow Ford

On April 11, 1865, as part of Stoneman's Raid, troops under the command of Col. William J. Palmer split from the main force and skirmished with Confederate forces at Shallow Ford. The ford is a landmark on the Yadkin River and is rich in history. In the mid-1700s immigrants used Shallow Ford as a crossing point on the river for the Great Wagon Road. That route, along an ancient Indian trading path, extended from Pennsylvania to Georgia. Essentially a rock-bottomed section of the river, the ford was also where Lord Charles Cornwallis led his troops across the Yadkin River in 1781.

During the closing months of the Civil War, Gen. George Stoneman led about five thousand troops through western North Carolina in one of the longest cavalry raids in history. He sent detachments throughout the region, securing the destruction of factories, bridges, and railroad lines.

After a brief foray into southwestern Virginia, Union troops turned southward to North Carolina. Stoneman divided his forces, sending a detachment to destroy textile factories and rail lines farther south, while his other men marched to Shallow Ford.

APR 11

1896 Governor Thomas Holt, Textile Magnate, Friend of Education

On April 11, 1896, industrialist and Progressive Era governor Thomas Michael Holt died at age 64.

Born to a prominent Alamance County family of textile manufacturers, Holt worked in his family's factories while climbing the political ladder. He got his start in politics as an Alamance County commissioner, before serving in both houses of the General Assembly and rising to the post of Speaker of the House.

Holt was lieutenant governor when Gov. Daniel Fowle died in office in 1891, so the state's top job fell to him. He served as governor until 1893, filling out Fowle's term. He chose not to seek re-election for health reasons.

Throughout his career, Holt was interested in education. He helped found, among other institutions, two colleges in Greensboro and what's now N.C. State University. He was also active in business and agriculture, serving as the North Carolina Railroad Company's president, directing the North Carolina State Fair, and transforming his family's business into one of the leaders in the textile industry.

He died at his family home in Haw River and is buried in Graham.

Thomas Holt portrait.

1900 Charles B. Aycock and His Mixed Legacy

On April 11, 1900, Charles B. Aycock was unanimously nominated as the Democratic candidate for governor of North Carolina.

Aycock practiced law and co-founded the *Daily Argus* newspaper in Goldsboro, but it became clear that politics was his true passion. He distrusted the Republican Party, which supported African American involvement in government, and endorsed the idea that politics should be reserved for the white race.

As he sought to build a political reputation, Aycock worked tirelessly on behalf of the public schools, believing that education was the key to social change. After serving as a federal prosecutor, he toured the state in 1898, pressing his views on race and education in a statewide series of debates with Populist Cyrus Thompson.

Aycock handily defeated his Republican opponent in the general election, and his inauguration in 1901 launched a seventy-two-year Democratic hold on the state's highest elected position. As governor, Aycock touted the "Dawn of a New Day" and continued to press for educational progress. He also advocated strongly for child labor reform and temperance laws but met mixed success on those initiatives with the legislature.

His restored birthplace in Wayne County is now a state historic site.

1967 The North Carolina Arts Council: Advancing the Arts

On April 11, 1967, the North Carolina General Assembly created the North Carolina Arts Council as a statutory agency.

Established in 1964 by executive order of Gov. Terry Sanford, the Arts Council began its work by documenting architecture, design, visual arts, crafts, theatre, music, dance, opera, creative writing, communications, film, concert series, school programs, statewide organizations, local arts councils, and support of the arts throughout the state.

Phillip Hanes, Jr. chaired the state's effort to advance the arts, in conjunction with the National Arts and Cultural Development Act, which led to the establishment of the National Endowment for the Arts.

The state Arts Council quickly built on the seventeen local arts councils and more than two hundred arts organizations already working in North Carolina, organizing poetry readings throughout the state, beginning an artists-in-schools program, and supporting nonprofit arts organizations and exemplary artists through grants.

Today a strong arts infrastructure provides opportunities for citizens to experience the arts in their own communities, reflecting and sharing the state's diversity. New initiatives include literary, Blue Ridge Music, and African American Music cultural tourism guides, additions to the model arts education program, A+ Schools, and the creation of an arts-based economic development, the SmART Initiative.

Billboard from the North Carolina Arts Council awareness campaign in 1979.

1776 Halifax Day Celebrates Embrace of Independence

On April 12, 1776, eighty-three delegates to North Carolina's Fourth Provincial Congress, meeting in Halifax, unanimously passed a resolution now known as the Halifax Resolves.

The resolves advocated severing North Carolina's ties with England and indicated support for independence for all American colonies. North Carolina became the first colony to commit such intentions to paper, striking the first blow for an independent America.

As the colonies joined forces to oppose British legislation, citizens initially asserted their rights as Englishmen against unfair taxation and exploitation. When events such as the Boston Tea Party in 1773 prompted British occupation of Massachusetts, North Carolina and other colonies began to dissolve ties with England and create new systems of local government.

At the Fourth Provincial Congress a committee led by Cornelius Harnett was appointed to draft a document declaring North Carolina's support for American independence from England. Eight days after the congress convened, the Halifax Resolves were created.

Today at least two original copies of the Halifax Resolves exist. One can be found in the State Archives. The other, sent to North Carolina's delegates to the Continental Congress, is held by the National Archives.

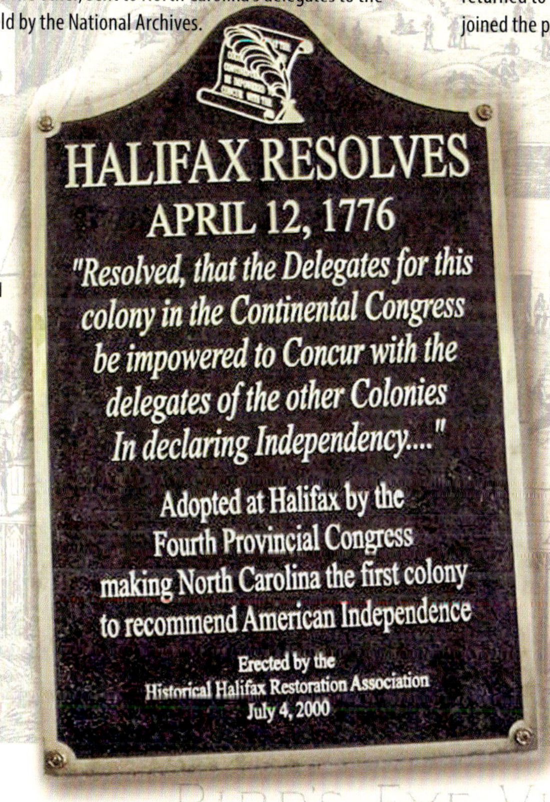

Halifax Resolves plaque located in the State Capitol.

1865 Stoneman in Salisbury, Liberator and Scourge

On April 12, 1865, Union Gen. George Stoneman and his forces burned the already abandoned Salisbury Prison, as well as the town's other public buildings, industrial structures, and supply depots as part of a raid through western North Carolina.

The raid began on March 24, when Stoneman led six thousand cavalrymen from Tennessee into western North Carolina and southwestern Virginia to disrupt Confederate supply lines by destroying sections of the Virginia & Tennessee Railroad, the North Carolina Railroad, and the Piedmont Railroad. He also sought to liberate Union prisoners-of-war held in Salisbury, cut off avenues of retreat available to Confederate armies, and encourage Unionists in western and central North Carolina to rise up.

Stoneman struck Boone on March 28, then divided his force and sent part of it into Virginia. On April 12 the Federals occupied Salisbury. Stoneman moved west the next day, dividing his command again. Other than a fight at Swannanoa Gap, Stoneman and his cavalrymen encountered only bushwhackers and isolated groups of Confederate soldiers.

Stoneman's forces approached Asheville on April 23, negotiated a truce, then rode through the streets on April 26. Two days later part of Stoneman's force returned to Asheville to loot. Other elements either continued to Tennessee or joined the pursuit of Confederate Pres. Jefferson Davis into Georgia.

1960 Sports Journalists Honored in Salisbury

On April 12, 1960, the first National Sportscasters & Sportswriters awards program was held in Salisbury, where those in attendance formed the National Sportscasters and Sportswriters Association. The group added a Hall of Fame two years later.

The idea for the National Sportscasters and Sportswriters Association started with local restaurant owner Pete DiMizio, who appreciated the regional sports media and decided to honor them. He hosted a banquet for them at his restaurant in 1953. The event launched the North Carolina Sportscasters and Sportswriters Association, and after DiMizio's death in 1958, a small group of Salisbury citizens continued and expanded upon DiMizio's dream. The association went national the next year.

Today the association is dedicated to honoring, preserving, and celebrating the legacy of sportscasters and sportswriters in the United States, with the knowledge that what they do helps American fans form lifelong connections to sports. The organization also develops educational opportunities for those who are interested in pursuing a career in sports media.

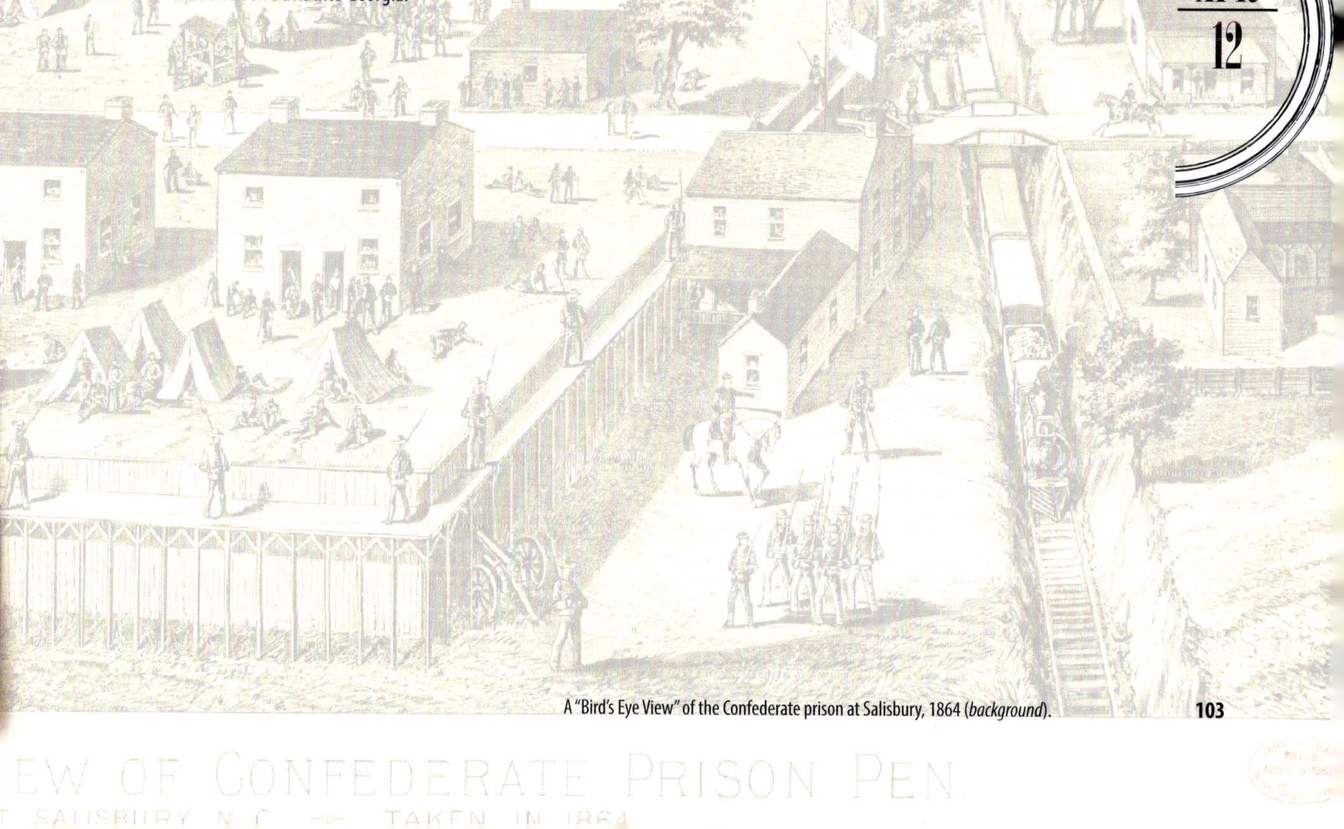

A "Bird's Eye View" of the Confederate prison at Salisbury, 1864 (*background*).

1865 Fall of Raleigh

On April 13, 1865, the state capital fell to Union forces under the command of Gen. William T. Sherman. The day before, seeing that Raleigh's capture was imminent, Gov. Zebulon B. Vance crafted plans to surrender the city, with the hope of sparing it from the destruction suffered by other southern capitals captured by Sherman's army.

Vance appointed commissioners to carry a notice of surrender to Sherman's headquarters. Among them was former governor David L. Swain. The commissioners delivered the notice but were delayed overnight. Unaware of the delay, Vance left Raleigh and gave additional instructions for the surrender to Raleigh's mayor William Harrison.

At the southern edge of Raleigh, Harrison and others met Union cavalry commander Gen. Hugh Judson Kilpatrick. While Swain waited at the Capitol, they offered the surrender of Raleigh, promising no military resistance in exchange for protection of the city. The agreed-upon terms were almost undone by a lone Texas cavalry officer who fired on Kilpatrick's men. In the scuffle that followed, Kilpatrick's men captured and hanged the officer. When order was restored, Union soldiers occupied and secured Raleigh.

1909 William Briggs and His Cigarette Machine

On April 13, 1909, William Briggs patented the first automatic cigarette manufacturing machine.

Born in Maine, Briggs came to North Carolina by way of New York and New Jersey. Settling first in Fayetteville and then in Winston, he worked in a machine shop there before perfecting a machine that could produce three hundred thousand cigarettes a day in 1898.

Briggs formed his own company and began to market his machines to the R.J. Reynolds Company, which used them to compete with its much larger rival, the American Tobacco Company.Briggs quickly sold his machines and the related intellectual property to a Japanese company and was soon thereafter sued by United Cigarette, a larger manufacturer of tobacco machinery in Virginia, for patent infringement. After successfully defending the suit in an Asheville court, Briggs was hired by United Cigarette. He would go to invent a more efficient machine for them.

The new company moved Briggs to Virginia, where he lived the rest of his life. His other inventions include the first return carriage for a typewriter and a stamp vending machine. He died in 1918.

1947 Journey of Reconciliation, 1947 Civil Rights Protest

On April 13, 1947, a mob attacked civil rights protesters at the bus station in Chapel Hill. Earlier that year the Congress of Racial Equality laid plans to test the enforcement of a Supreme Court decision that declared segregation on interstate buses and trains unconstitutional.

On April 9 eight African American and eight white members of the group set out from Washington, D.C. on Greyhound and Trailways buses in what was billed as the "Journey of Reconciliation." A few days later the buses arrived in Chapel Hill, where the organizers met with students and townspeople. As the buses prepared to depart on April 13, two blacks refused to move to the rear. Upon subsequently leaving the buses, several of the protesters were attacked and arrested.

In May those who had been arrested went on trial and were sentenced. Organizer Bayard Rustin and two white protesters surrendered at the courthouse in Hillsborough and were sent to segregated chain gangs. Rustin published journal entries about the experience. His writings, as well as the actions of the "Journey of Reconciliation" riders, in time inspired Rosa Parks' nonviolent protest in 1955 and the Freedom Riders of 1960–1961.

APR 13

Bayard Rustin (*center*) speaking with (*left to right*) Carolyn Carter, Cecil Carter, Kurt Levister, and Kathy Ross before a demonstration in 1964.

1861 Fort Macon, Contested Ground during the Civil War

On April 14, 1861, a militia company from Beaufort, acting on its own, boated over to Fort Macon, near Atlantic Beach, and seized the fort in the name of the state from a lone Union army caretaker.

Only two days after the firing on Fort Sumter, North Carolina had not yet left the Union to join the Confederate States of America. By the time North Carolina did secede on May 20, Fort Macon was securely in state hands with hundreds of Confederate soldiers making it ready for war. Over the next year the fort was armed with fifty-four heavy cannons.

The Confederacy did not manage to hold the fort for long. In April 1862, after an extended siege led by Union Brig. Gen. John G. Parke, Fort Macon's Col. Moses J. White surrendered the garrison to Union forces. The fall of Fort Macon closed the port of Beaufort to the Confederacy. The seizure was part of the Burnside campaign, which saw much of coastal North Carolina fall into Union hands.

1942 Enigma Machine Plucked from Its Watery Grave

On April 14, 1942, the destroyer USS *Roper* sank the German submarine *U-85* off the Outer Banks between Wimble Shoals and Cape Hatteras.

By January 1942 there were about nineteen German U-boats patrolling the Atlantic coastline, with two or three hiding at Diamond Shoals at any given time to attack ships as they rounded Cape Hatteras. At the height of what is now called the Battle of Torpedo Junction, the Germans were sinking a ship nearly every day; between freighters, tankers, and passenger ships the losses were tremendous.

At the same time the American military was learning how to detect and defeat the U-boats. The first hit was on *U-85*. Navy divers surveyed the area near the wreck and attempted to salvage the ship, but efforts were not successful. Since men were needed elsewhere, the submarine was left to the elements.

The wreck was explored by recreational divers for many years. In July 2001 divers salvaged the submarine's Enigma machine. The Germans used this complex coding device for secret communications, especially for divulging locations of enemy vessels and supply convoys. Although it is still being conserved, the stable parts of the machine are on display at the Graveyard of the Atlantic Museum in Hatteras.

1989 Hysteria Over Day Care in Edenton

On April 14, 1989, the first arrests were made in Edenton in what would become known as the Little Rascals Day Care case. The case came amidst a nationwide flurry of prosecutions of daycare workers for alleged "satanic ritual abuse" of children.

Twenty-nine students at the Little Rascals center accused twenty adults, including Edenton's mayor and the sheriff of Chowan County, with 429 instances of sexual and physical abuse over a three-year period. The childrens' descriptions of those events were mind-bending. Some described incidents involving space ships, hot air balloons, pirate ships, and trained sharks.

As in similar cases from across the country, the children's stories were concocted through sessions with investigators and therapists, many of whom used leading and suggestive questioning techniques. Prosecutors did not produce evidence or eyewitnesses. Today social scientists consider the scandal a "moral panic," and it has been compared to a witch hunt.

In the most notorious of the Little Rascals trials, the defendant was convicted on ninety-nine counts and sentenced to twelve consecutive life terms in prison. The court of appeals overturned the convictions of all seven defendants in 1995. The Little Rascals case is said to have been the state's longest and costliest criminal trial.

Enigma machine recovered from the German submarine, *U-85*, off the Outer Banks in July, 2001.

APR 15

1853 Daniel Kanipe, Survivor of Custer's Land Stand

On April 15, 1853, Daniel Kanipe, one of two survivors of Custer's battalion at the Battle of the Little Bighorn, was born in Marion. In 1872 he enlisted in Company C, Seventh United States Cavalry and briefly served with the occupation forces in Lincolnton.

In 1876 Lt. Col. George A. Custer led the Seventh Cavalry into present-day Montana, eventually reaching a large Native American encampment along the Little Bighorn River. Underestimating the number of warriors within the camp, Custer decided that a frontal assault was the best strategy. He chose to ride directly towards the Native position with his own battalion, leaving Capt. Frederick Benteen's battalion in reserve.

Kanipe and John Martin were sent to relay messages to the pack train and to Benteen. With the destruction of Custer's column imminent, Benteen held his battalion back and refused to allow the couriers to return to battle.

Kanipe was often called upon to relate his experience at Little Bighorn. He became a noted celebrity among admirers of the "Old West" and researchers of "Custer's Last Stand." His recollections became the basis for many of the twentieth century accounts of the battle.

1861 Governor Ellis and Building Confederate Sentiment

On April 15, 1861, North Carolina Gov. John Ellis responded to President Abraham Lincoln's call for troops with the often quoted statement: "You can get no troops from North Carolina."

Although North Carolina as a state had seemed moderate during the Secession Crisis of 1861, Ellis had worked behind the scenes to align North Carolina with the budding Confederate government. In February 1861 citizens of the Old North State rejected a call for a Constitutional Convention to even consider the secession question.

Southern state after Southern state declared for secession in early 1861, following South Carolina's declaration in December 1860. President Lincoln inherited a nation at the breaking point, and he ordered the Federal fort in Charleston harbor to be resupplied. South Carolina forces prevented the effort and fired on Fort Sumter. Lincoln then issued a call for troops to put down the rebellion.

Ellis considered Lincoln's call to arms an unacceptable power grab, and he immediately ordered state troops to seize the Federal forts in North Carolina as well as the Federal arsenal at Fayetteville. He called the General Assembly into session two weeks later and rushed through a bill that called for a secession convention and authorized Ellis to send troops to Virginia. North Carolina left the Union just a few weeks later.

Though Ellis' pithy sentence is often quoted, the full text of his reply to Lincoln lays out a number of Constitutional justifications for secession that were popular at the outset of the war.

1960 SNCC's Raleigh Roots

On April 15, 1960, about 150 student leaders from ten states met at Shaw University in Raleigh for the "Southwide Leadership Conference on Nonviolent Resistance to Segregation." The meeting took place just two months after the Woolworth sit-ins in Greensboro had launched the protest effort.

The session was designed to consolidate isolated sit-in efforts and map strategy. It was organized by the Southern Christian Leadership Conference, whose executive director, Ella Baker, was a Shaw graduate. The conference created the "Temporary Student Nonviolent Coordinating Committee" headquartered in Atlanta.

The weekend's keynote speaker, the Reverend James Lawson of Nashville, criticized established older groups such as the NAACP for moving too slowly and acting too conservatively. The Reverend Martin Luther King Jr. spoke to a large group in Memorial Auditorium, urging students to adopt the nonviolent philosophy of Ghandi and face jail time for peaceful protest if necessary.

SNCC ("Temporary" had been dropped from the organization's title) members were the "shock troops" and frontline leaders in the civil rights movement, especially in Mississippi in the summer of 1964. John Hope Franklin called them "probably the most courageous and the most selfless" of the civil rights workers.

SNCC promotional literature depicting the interracial nature of the group and buttons that were worn by civil rights activists.

1846

Ill-Fated Donner Party Included North Carolinians

On April 16, 1846, the eighty-seven men, women, and children known as the Donner Party set out from Sangamon County, Illinois, on their ill-fated journey to California.

Already running behind schedule and facing an early winter when they reached the Sierra Nevada Mountains, the group saw its situation made worse by an enormous blizzard, with snow as high as sixteen feet, that trapped them in place for five months. So desperate was their situation that some members resorted to cannibalism. Before the winter was over, forty-six of the group had died.

George and Jacob Donner, who led the group, were Rowan County natives. The Donners moved from North Carolina to Kentucky, then to Indiana and Illinois. George was elected leader of the group, and so the party bore his name.

George's wife Tamsen Eustis was a well-educated woman from Massachusetts who also had a North Carolina connection. She was an administrator at Elizabeth City Academy before moving to Illinois and meeting George. Unfortunately, George, Tamsen, and Jacob Donner all perished in the cruel winter of 1846–47. When rescuers did come, Tamsen refused to leave her husband, who was dying from an infected wound. Tamsen's three daughters and two stepdaughters were all rescued and survived.

1849

Physicians Form Professional Alliance, 1849

On April 16, 1849, the Medical Society of North Carolina was established after several state legislators who were also physicians called for a state medical convention.

The organization wasn't the first statewide group for doctors. An earlier association had been chartered by the General Assembly in 1799 but was no longer meeting by 1805. The new organization's goals were largely the same as its predecessor's: to unite physicians across the state, represent their interests, and help professionalize the practice of medicine.

Edmund Strudwick, an Orange County native and surgeon, was the group's first president. He had an excellent reputation, having served in the General Assembly and Congress. He also helped establish UNC's medical school, and aided in the construction of Dorothea Dix Hospital.

The society's first goals were creating stricter educational standards for students entering medical school, starting a medical journal, pushing for more concrete vital-records laws, and founding a state licensing board for doctors.

The group, now called the North Carolina Medical Society, has continued to meet annually since 1849, except for a few years during the Civil War and World War II. It now has more than ten thousand members statewide.

1953

Luck's Canned Foods Originated in Seagrove

On April 16, 1953, Seagrove's Mountain View Canning Company was incorporated. Before the year was over, the business would change its name to Luck's.

Founded in 1947 by Alfred Spencer and Ira Luck, the company's original purpose was to can homegrown vegetables and farm raised meat. The first commercial product produced at the two-story cinderblock cannery was Mountain View Beef and Gravy.

Pinto beans, Great Northern beans, and black-eyed peas—all home-style with pork seasoning—were added to the company line in 1950 and 1951. When Luck's Beans sponsored the country group Tommy Floyd and the Blue Ridge Buddies for a series of short musical spots syndicated on television stations in the Southeast, it helped the canned legumes grow in popularity.

In 1967 Luck's merged with American Home Products. Then in 2000 Lucks was acquired by food processing giant Con Agra, and the production of the canned beans moved to Tennessee. The Seagrove cannery ceased operations two years later.

Luck's Beans continue to be canned and sold today with their signature yellow label, although they are now produced in Tuscon, Arizona by the Arizona Canning Company, which purchased the line in 2011.

1958

W. Kerr Scott, Squire of Haw River

On April 16, 1958, Governor, United States Senator and state Commissioner of Agriculture W. Kerr Scott died. He was born in the Haw River community of Alamance County. Scott remained a farmer and dairyman with close ties to his home and church for all of his life.

After working as an agricultural agent in Alamance County and serving as master of the North Carolina State Grange, Scott fulfilled a promise made to his father by successfully running for state agriculture commissioner in 1936. As commissioner, Scott was a leading proponent of rural electrification and led the successful fight to rid the state of Bang's disease among cattle. He forced manufacturers of feed and fertilizer to eliminate sawdust and sand from their products.

Scott was elected governor in 1948. During his four-year administration, the state paved more roads than had been paved up to 1949. Scott also directed the utilities commission to extend electricity and telephone service to rural areas.

In 1953 Scott left Raleigh to return to his farm at Haw River. The following year he was elected to the U.S. Senate, where he served on the Agriculture Committee and helped frame legislation to finance the interstate highway system.

APR 16

The Donner Lake Pass in the Sierra Nevada Mountains of California, 1870s.

APR 17

1865 Startling News at Initial Bennett Place Meeting

On April 17, 1865, Gen. William Sherman met with Gen. Joseph Johnston to discuss terms of surrender for Johnston's forces. They met at the home of James Bennett near what was then a rail stop, Durham Station. Once alone, Sherman handed Johnston a telegram that bore the news of Abraham Lincoln's assassination.

Accounts differ on the Confederate general's reaction. Sherman later said that Johnston broke out in large beads of sweat and expressed hope that the Union officer did not suspect the assassination plot to have been organized by the Confederate government. Johnston later recalled saying to Sherman that Lincoln's death "was the greatest possible calamity to the South."

Remarkably, Sherman managed to keep the news in the telegram from his own men. Only the telegraph officer knew of the information, and Sherman swore him to silence. Sherman had just returned from a meeting with Lincoln and Gen. Ulysses S. Grant, where the topic was the terms of peace.

With the news Sherman offered Johnston what he thought was Lincoln's terms for peace. Those terms, in the wake of the assassination, were deemed too generous and rejected. Sherman and Johnston would meet again on April 26 to complete the surrender process.

1937 Co-Op Leads the Way to Rural Electrification

On April 17, 1937, the first switch was thrown at the Eason-Tarboro substation, jumpstarting rural electrification efforts in North Carolina.

As part of his New Deal, Pres. Franklin D. Roosevelt created the Rural Electrification Administration (REA) in May 1935 with the dual goals of helping rural areas get electricity and providing work to the unemployed. High startup costs and anticipated low returns on investments made existing electric companies unenthusiastic about entering rural markets, so communities turned to cooperative ventures instead.

North Carolina's first co-op, the Edgecombe-Martin County Electric Membership Corporation, or EMC-EMC, was formed by citizens in the northeastern part of the state. After the corporation received a thirty-two thousand dollar loan in June 1936, work quickly began to bring electricity to the region. The switch was thrown on April 17 at the Eason-Tarboro substation and electricity began to flow. The plant is still in operation today.

North Carolinians had been interested in rural electrification long before the EMC-EMC. The state actually established its own Rural Electrification Authority in April 1935, one month before Roosevelt's REA. North Carolina's progressive attitude toward rural electrification helped to make the EMC-EMC more than a flash in the pan.

1968 Prelude to Attica: Prison Riot in Raleigh, 1968

On April 17, 1968, inmates at Central Prison in Raleigh began a riot.

The riot started as a peaceful protest, with roughly five hundred inmates "sitting-in" in an attempt to get prison officials to listen to their grievances. They were upset about restricted visiting hours and poor living conditions in the aging facility.

When the prisoners were ordered to return to their cells, a violent riot began in an open yard. Inmates threw torches, which started fires that damaged several buildings. Prisoners with homemade weapons attacked the staff. Riot-control officers were called in and ordered to open fire. Guards shot down from the walls. Six inmates were killed and more seventy-five people, including two state troopers and two corrections officers, were injured.

Today Central Prison still houses male prisoners with sentences over twenty years. Major renovations in the 1980s included the destruction of the original castle-like building. The prison also now provides inmates with a mental health facility, therapy sessions, worship groups, and educational opportunities.

The facility has not had another inmate riot since 1968.

Rural Electrification Administration (REA) erects telephone lines in rural areas.

1791 Washington's Tarboro Layover, 1791

On April 18, 1791, Pres. George Washington arrived in Tarboro. He was met at the Roanoke River by Col. John B. Ashe, who escorted him into town. The procession was welcomed by a salute from a single cannon.

While in town, the president was entertained at the home of Maj. Reading Blount. After a single night's stay Washington left Tarboro for Pitt County. In his diary he remarked that the town of "Tarborough" was "more lively and thriving" than Halifax.

Washington's stay in Tarboro was part of tour of the southern states that he embarked on in early 1791, after establishing a site for the new "Federal District" along the Potomac River. The tour was part of his effort to visit every state during his term of office.

After leaving Virginia and crossing the Roanoke River, Washington's first stop in the Old North State was Halifax. From there the president's carriage tour took him through Tarboro, Greenville, New Bern, Trenton, and Wilmington before heading to South Carolina. On his return trip Washington came back into North Carolina near Charlotte and traveled northward, visiting Salisbury, Salem, and Guilford Court House.

1853 Vice-President William R. King a North Carolinian

On April 18, 1853 William Rufus Devane King—senator, diplomat, and vice president of the United States—died.

Born in Sampson County, King distinguished himself early on as an excellent student, graduating from the University of North Carolina in 1804, at age eighteen. He moved to Fayetteville to study law and established his own practice in nearby Clinton a year later. He entered politics in 1808 as a member of the North Carolina House of Commons at age twenty-two and was elected to United States Congress in 1810. There he allied himself with prominent politicians of the time including Henry Clay and John C. Calhoun.

In 1818 King left North Carolina for Alabama, where an abundance of inexpensive, yet fertile, land offered significant profits. In 1819 he helped draft Alabama's state constitution and was elected to the United States Senate, where he served for twenty years. He was elected vice president in March 1853. Shortly after his election, King traveled to Cuba to ease his tuberculosis. His health thus forced him to become the first and only vice president to be sworn into office while on foreign soil.

Soon after his return to America, King succumbed to his illness before ever reaching the District of Columbia.

Engraving of William Rufus Devane King, 1852.

1862 Battle of South Mills, April 1862

On April 18, 1862, Federal forces landed in Camden County to begin a two-day march and fight directed at finding and destroying the locks on the Dismal Swamp canal system. Closing that system would prevent Confederate naval forces from sending ships from a shipyard in Virginia to Albemarle Sound.

The landing action, now known as the Battle of South Mills, involved about three thousand Union soldiers commanded by Gen. Jesse L. Reno and nine hundred Confederates commanded by Gen. Ambrose R. Wright. The battle was part of the Burnside Expedition, which had the wider goal of reclaiming northeastern North Carolina for the Union.

After the Federal troops landed and moved toward locks on the canal, one group of men took a wrong road on the advice of their guide. That misstep led to an unplanned ten-mile march, and by the time the stray group reunited with the larger force, they found their fellow soldiers hotly engaged by entrenched Confederates.

The confusion prevented Union troops from reaching the locks, so the Federal forces broke off the engagement allowing the Confederate troops to retreat from the scene. Both sides claimed victory—Union forces for retaining the field of battle, the Confederates for preventing the locks' destruction.

Purportedly, Federal forces executed the guide who took the circuitous road.

1927 Asheville Launching Pad for "Singing Brakeman," Jimmie Rodgers

On April 18, 1927, Jimmie Rodgers—one of country music's first superstars—got his big break on Asheville radio station WWNC.

Born in 1897 near Meridian, Mississippi, James Charles Rodgers liked to yodel and won an amateur talent contest at age thirteen. That same year he became a railroad water boy. In March 1927 Rodgers moved to Asheville, working as a railway brakeman and doing other jobs until he and friend Otis Kuykendall began performing live weekly on WWNC. The duo soon added other musicians and billed themselves as the Jimmie Rodgers Entertainers.

In August 1927 Victor Records recorded Rodgers doing two songs. One, "The Soldier's Sweetheart," became an instant hit. Another hit, "Blue Yodel," quickly followed. By 1929 Rodgers was a star. He appeared in a short film, "The Singing Brakeman," toured the Midwest with humorist Will Rogers, and recorded with a young trumpeter, Louis Armstrong.

By the time he returned to Asheville in December 1929, the "Father of Country Music" had been living with tuberculosis for five years. He died in 1933. Rodgers in 1961 became the first performer inducted into the Country Music Hall of Fame.

APR 18

1585 Wanchese and Manteo Conclude Visit to London, 1585

On April 19, 1585, Algonquian Indians Wanchese and Manteo set sail aboard the English vessel The *Tyger* to return to the Roanoke Island region. The Indians had sailed to England in 1584 with Arthur Barlowe and Thomas Harriot. They caused a sensation when they were presented at the English Court.

While in England they were hosted by Sir Walter Raleigh at the Durham House. There they met with Thomas Harriot and, over the course of several visits, taught him the Algonquian language. Wanchese, unlike Manteo, was not curious to learn English.

Wanchese remained suspicious of English motives and the English in general and eventually considered himself a captive rather than a guest. These ill feelings would cause trouble for the colonists once he returned to Roanoke.

The *Tyger* raided Spanish shipping lines during the voyage to America and forcibly exchanged goods with Spanish traders on Puerto Rico, where the ship waited to reunite with its fleet. From there the vessel continued on to Roanoke, arriving near Ocracoke Inlet in June 1585.

Wanchese slipped away from English control in early July. He urged resistance to the settlers, setting himself at odds with the English and Manteo.

1813 States' Rights Champion, Governor and Senator David Reid

On April 19, 1813, David Settle Reid, governor and member of both houses of Congress, was born in Rockingham County.

Reid was raised in a community that in time became the town of Reidsville, named for Reid's father. After first holding public office as a state senator at age twenty-two, Reid won his second bid to the U.S. House of Representatives at age thirty. Reid was elected governor in 1850, calling for sensible internal improvements, support for public schools, and states' rights.

Reid's two terms as governor were marked by expanded internal improvements, appointment of Calvin H. Wiley as the first superintendent of the Common Schools, initiation of a statewide geological survey, and confirmation of land titles held by the Cherokee Indians who had remained in North Carolina.

In late 1854 the General Assembly elected Reid to fill a vacancy in the U.S. Senate. Reid in turn transferred his duties as governor to Warren Winslow. Reid served only one term in the Senate, where he championed the defense of states' rights.

After being defeated for reelection in 1858, Reid retired to private life. He suffered a severe stroke in 1881 that left him paralyzed. He fought failing health for a decade before dying in 1891. He is buried in Reidsville.

1877 Agricultural Research Stations Date to 1877

On April 19, 1877, the first agricultural experiment station opened in a one-room chemistry lab at UNC. It was the first such station in the South and the second in the nation.

A movement had been building to found the research station since 1885, when the General Assembly directed the Board of Agriculture to begin acquiring land and machinery for it. The actual legislation establishing the station, with a focus on research that would aid in plant nutrition and develop new fertilizers, was passed in February 1877.

In 1889 management of the station was transferred to what is now N.C. State University. The change was the result of the federal Hatch Act, which sent federal funds for agricultural research to the states through land grant colleges. At the same time the N.C. Department of Agriculture began establishing "test farms" across the state to try different crop, fertilizer, and soil combinations and discover which crops were best suited to particular regions.

The program has continued to grow, and today the N.C. Department of Agriculture and Consumer Services and N.C. State University operate eighteen research stations around the state.

Planting the first fruit tree on the experimental farm of the North Carolina State Horticultural Society, Southern Pines, N.C., 1895. From the *Annual Report of the North Carolina Agricultural Experiment Station*, 1896.

1791 Warm Welcome in New Bern for President Washington

On April 20, 1791, George Washington visited Tryon Palace in New Bern during his Southern Tour.

The federal government was new in 1791 and so was the presidency. Washington had been elected only two years before in February 1789, and North Carolina had become part of the Union in November of the same year.

Like any political move, the formation of the United States was seen with much skepticism from citizens and government leaders. Washington's tour of the southern states allowed him to explore the nation he led, giving him the opportunity to promote national unity among its people. In his diary Washington reported details about the geography of the states, their exports such as tobacco, and the attitudes of the citizens.

Washington's visit was warmly received by New Bernians. During his two-day stay the president dined at Tryon Palace and attended a "dancing assembly" with about seventy ladies. He also visited many of New Bern's well-known citizens including John Wright Stanly, John Sitgreaves, and Richard Dobbs Spaight.

Leaving New Bern on April 22, Washington headed south toward Wilmington.

1898 Hydroelectric Power Introduced, 1898

On April 20, 1898, the Fries Manufacturing and Power Company transmitted electrical power thirteen miles from the generating plant to the Fries-owned Arista textile mill. The transmission, which originated near the Yadkin River bridge west of Clemmons in Forsyth County, was North Carolina's first long-distance transmission of electricity.

Long interested in the use of electricity to power industrial machinery, Henry Fries of Salem founded the company to harness the hydroelectric capability of the river. Construction on the power plant began in 1897, and it soon became known as Idol's Hydroelectric Station, after a ferry that was once located on the same site. The dam built for the station was 482 feet long, and the reservoir covered about thirty-five acres. The flow of the dam generated about twenty-five hundred horsepower. The station later provided power for other textile and grain mills, fertilizer plants, the Winston-Salem electric railway, electric street lights, and wood and metal working shops in Winston-Salem.

Fries sold his power company in 1913 to Southern Public Utility Company, which was purchased by Duke Power in 1914. Duke Power, now Duke Energy, operated the Idols station until 1996. The station burned two years later.

1945 Asheville Engineer Charles Waddell

On April 20, 1945, pioneer electrical engineer Charles E. Waddell died.

Waddell grew up in Asheville and was educated at Bingham Military School before teaching himself electrical engineering. He worked as superintendent of the Asheville fire alarm system when he was only fourteen years old. He continued his engineering training in New York and Maine.

Waddell returned to Asheville to start his own business, and one of his company's first projects was the development and installation of an electrical heating system for the Biltmore House. From 1901 on, Waddell was the electrical consultant for the Vanderbilt estate.

Biltmore wasn't Waddell's only project. He went on to build hydroelectric power plants for Weaver Electric Company and served for many years as a director of the business, which later became the North Carolina Electric Company. Skilled beyond electrical engineering, he also designed a bridge over the Swannanoa River at Biltmore—one of only two area bridges to hold up in the flood of 1916. He was instrumental in the industrialization of western North Carolina, overseeing large projects for Champion Fiber Company and American Enka Corporation, among others.

An active patriot during World War I, Waddell served as an engineering consultant for the state and federal governments. His genius and influence helped shape industrialization across the state and region.

1971 The Beginnings of Busing

On April 20, 1971, the Supreme Court issued its opinion in the *Swann v. Charlotte-Mecklenburg Board of Education* case, allowing for school desegregation by busing.

In 1965 attorney Julius L. Chambers filed suit on behalf of ten pairs of African American parents who contended that the Charlotte-Mecklenburg Board of Education's assignment plan did not sufficiently eliminate the inequalities of the formerly segregated system. The board tried to redo the assignment plan, but the plaintiffs argued that decades of discrimination could be undone only through extensive busing. Federal district court judge James B. McMillan agreed.

Disagreements between the board and McMillan on the specifics of the plan landed the case in the Fourth Circuit Court of Appeals, which affirmed McMillan's decision, with qualifications. The school board and plaintiffs appealed to the U.S. Supreme Court, which unanimously reaffirmed the ruling in April 1971.

Though the decision was initially quite divisive in the community, many Mecklenburg residents eventually began to take pride in their new schools, and some observers have linked the city's growth and prosperity in the 1980s to the school board's continued commitment to full integration.

African American and white school children on a school bus, riding from the suburbs to an inner city school, Charlotte, 1973.

1864 Myrtle Grove Sound Third Site for State Salt Works

On April 21, 1864, the state salt works in New Hanover County were attacked by Federal forces, and about a third of the site was destroyed.

An important ingredient for the preservation of the meat, salt was essential for the security of the food supply during the era. Salt works were established in Currituck County and near Morehead City, though both were captured by the Federal troops who controlled much of northeastern North Carolina by the end of 1863.

For the remainder of the war, state salt production was anchored in the Wilmington area, where numerous private salt works had previously operated.

The state bought 220 acres near Myrtle Grove Sound for its works, and soon began assembling the required furnaces. In November 1862 Gov. Zebulon B. Vance reported two hundred kettles in operation, producing twelve hundred bushels of salt per day. At the peak of production, the facility was putting out eighty-five hundred bushels each day.

Late in the war Gen. W. H. C. Whiting, the Confederate commander at Fort Fisher, suspended state salt works operations in the Cape Fear region, and the principal center of production shifted to the mountains of Virginia.

APR 21

1941 Charlotte Airport Dedicated

On April 21, 1941, New York City Mayor Fiorello LaGuardia dedicated what is now the Charlotte Douglas International Airport in front of a crowd nearly ten thousand local residents.

The airport has its roots in Morris Field, which was constructed in 1936 with funds from the Works Progress Administration at the urging of local business leaders. With the U.S. entry into World War II in 1941, the Army Air Corps took control of the field and transformed it into an airbase to support several large military facilities in the Charlotte region.

In May 1946 the Air Corps vacated Morris Field. Charlotte officials then converted the base's structures into apartment buildings to relieve the postwar housing shortage. The airport is named after Mayor Ben E. Douglas, who was instrumental in the completion of the airport project.

1972 Moonwalker Charles Duke's Rare Distinction

On April 21, 1972, Charlotte-born Charles M. Duke became at age thirty-six the youngest man to walk on the moon.

After graduating and receiving a commission from the U.S. Naval Academy in 1957, Duke embarked on a career as an Air Force pilot. His dedication to aeronautics and advanced education at MIT made him an ideal candidate for NASA, which selected him and eighteen others in April 1966 to form Astronaut Group Five. Before visiting space himself, Duke served as the capsule communicator for the Apollo 11 crew, the first crew to land on the moon. The Earth-based capsule communicator's job was to keep constant contact with the crew in space.

During the Apollo 16 mission Duke was the lunar module pilot alongside mission commander John Watts Young and command module pilot Thomas K. Mattingly. On April 21 Duke and Young stepped out onto the lunar surface, becoming two of only twelve people ever to walk on the moon. They spent seventy-one hours in the Descartes Highlands, a rugged region of the moon. In just over twenty hours of moonwalks, the pair carefully surveyed the Moon's surface, collected samples, and deployed scientific equipment.

Official NASA portrait of Mr. Duke, 1971.

Astronaut Charles M. Duke Jr., lunar module pilot, collecting lunar samples at Station No. 1 during the first Apollo 16 extravehicular activity (EVA), at the Descartes landing site.

1861 Fayetteville Arsenal Surrendered, 1861

On April 22, 1861, the U.S. Arsenal at Fayetteville surrendered to a force of state militia troops roughly a month before North Carolina seceded from the Union.

At the time of the firing on Fort Sumter ten days earlier, the Fayetteville Arsenal was guarded by a company of the Second U.S. Artillery. On April 22 those U.S. soldiers were confronted with a large force of nearly one thousand state militia troops reinforced with artillery.

Former governor Warren Winslow, acting as an agent for Governor John Ellis, negotiated the surrender of the post, which allowed the Federal soldiers to leave with their equipment but forced them to turn over the arsenal's equipment to the state. By April 27 the Union artillerymen were able to get transportation to Wilmington, and by May 7 the company had arrived at Fort Hamilton in New York City.

During the Civil War the arsenal manufactured small arms for the Confederacy with machinery shipped from Harpers Ferry, Virginia shortly after secession. One of the arsenal's better-known products was the "Fayetteville Rifle," a copy of the US 1855 rifle.

Union Maj. Gen. William T. Sherman retook the arsenal in March 1865 and had the installation destroyed.

1865 Confederate Cabinet Met in Charlotte

On April 22, 1865, the Confederate Cabinet held the first of a series of meetings in Charlotte to determine its final official actions as an organized government. The Confederate Cabinet began its journey south on April 2, when Gen. Robert E. Lee recommended that the Confederate Capitol, Richmond, be evacuated due to the advance of Lt. Gen. U.S. Grant's spring offensive.

Confederate Pres. Jefferson Davis and his fellow cabinet members traveled first by rail to Greensboro. On April 12, President Davis conferred with Confederate Gen. Joseph E. Johnston and other officials concerning potential surrender negotiations with Union Maj. Gen. William T. Sherman. The Cabinet then moved south to Charlotte, arriving there on April 19.

Davis and his cabinet held their final meetings in the branch office of the Bank of North Carolina on Tryon Street, which served as the final center of the Confederate government. Faced with the inevitability of defeat, Davis adjourned his government and planned to escape southwest overland to Mexico, where he could establish a government in exile. On May 10 Davis and his wife Varina were captured near Irwinville, Georgia.

1953 Tar Heel Junior Historians Learn, Boost State History

On April 22, 1953, the General Assembly established the Tar Heel Junior Historian Association program to advance the study of North Carolina history in public and private schools.

Administered by the North Carolina Museum of History, the association enrolls about eight thousand students in grades four through eight each year. The highlight of the program comes each spring when students gather at a convention in Raleigh to share projects and conduct competitions.

Educators William H. Cartwright and J. C. McLendon were the driving force behind the creation of the program. They studied junior history programs in other states and met with Christopher Crittenden, then director of the state Department of Archives and History, to sketch out a plan for the program.

In 1961 the association first issued the *Tar Heel Junior Historian* magazine, which is still published. The North Carolina History Quiz, later renamed the Christopher Crittenden State History Quiz, was started in 1976.

When state history was reintroduced as a separate eighth grade course in 1988, the association's enrollment increased exponentially, and in 1995 the Tar Heel Junior Historian Gallery opened in the new Museum building in downtown Raleigh, giving the association a permanent space to display student work.

1954 Librarian of Congress Lawrence Mumford of Pitt County

On April 22, 1954, Pres. Dwight D. Eisenhower nominated Lawrence Quincy Mumford for the post of Librarian of Congress. Mumford was the eleventh person to hold the office and the first trained as a professional librarian.

Born near Ayden in Pitt County in December 1903, Mumford began his education in a one-room schoolhouse and continued at Duke, where he received an M.A. in English in 1928. He earned a B.S. in library science from Columbia the following year.

He worked first at the New York Public Library, at the same time doing work for the Library of Congress, before moving to the Cleveland Public Library, where he became director in 1950.

Confirmed by the Senate in July 1954, Mumford began his tenure at the Library of Congress under a dark cloud for the institution and its leadership. At his confirmation hearings Congress expressed dissatisfaction with the library's increasing public service role as a national library beyond its original mission as Congress's legislative library.

Despite this and other tensions Mumford's twenty years at the Library saw extraordinary growth in its appropriations, completion of the Madison Building, adoption of the first computer-readable format for library catalog records, and continued expansion of its national role.

Mumford retired from the Library in December 1974 and died in Washington, D.C. in August 1982.

APR 22

A student examines a scale model of the Charles B. Aycock Birthplace by the Mount Olive Tar Heel Junior Historian Club, first place winner in the arts division, 1966.

1864 Robert F. Hoke, Victorious at Plymouth, Promoted

On April 23, 1864, Robert Frederick Hoke, then only twenty-seven years old, became the youngest major general in the Confederate States Army. He was promoted days after leading a successful campaign to recapture Plymouth in Washington County.

Early in April Brigadier General Hoke and his division had been given the task of recapturing Plymouth, which would reopen the Roanoke River to Confederate operations. Hoke was assigned his own division from the Army of Northern Virginia, which was reinforced with additional troops and assisted by the newly commissioned ironclad, the CSS *Albemarle*.

Beginning on April 17 Hoke moved his ground troops against the Federal garrison at Plymouth, while the *Albemarle* attacked Union gunboats stationed in the river. After the sinking of the USS *Southfield*, Hoke was able to besiege the river town and force the Union garrison to surrender on April 20.

Confederate Pres. Jefferson Davis wired a telegram to Hoke to congratulate him for his victory. Within that message was Hoke's promotion to major general. He and his division would finish the war fighting at other North Carolina engagements, including Fort Fisher, Wyse Fork, and Bentonville before surrendering in Durham in April 1865, while serving under Confederate Gen. Joseph E. Johnston.

APR 23

1929 Winston-Salem's Reynolds Building, 1929

On April 23, 1929, the newly completed twenty-two-story office building for the R. J. Reynolds Tobacco Company in Winston-Salem was officially opened for business. The public enjoyed access to the retail and commercial shops on the lower levels off the elevator lobby, including a barber shop, restaurant, pharmacy, telegraph office, and a railway ticket office.

When the skyscraper opened, the Reynolds Company occupied half of the building, and insurance firms, brokerage firms, attorneys, architects, and developers leased the other half of the space.

Reynolds president Bowman Gray Sr. commissioned New York City architects R. H. Shreve and William F. Lamb to design the dramatic corporate headquarters in the popular Art Deco style. The two-million-dollar, limestone-faced tower became the tallest building in the South, surpassing the 1923 Jefferson Standard Building in Greensboro.

Shreve and Lamb, with new partner Arthur Harmon, went on to design Manhattan's Empire State Building, completed in 1931. The two buildings share a sleek, streamlined exterior with a distinctive stepped-ziggurat roofline.

Postcard of R.J. Reynolds Tobacco Co. Building, Winston-Salem, also known as, "The Camel City."

1932 Major Depression-Era Loss at Wingate

On April 23, 1932, the Administration Building of what's now Wingate University was destroyed by fire.

At the time the building housed the college library and chemistry labs, classrooms, an auditorium, and offices. The library, which had more than five thousand volumes at the time, and the chemistry labs were totally destroyed.

The building was valued at fifty thousand dollars, and the loss was only partially covered by insurance. Some equipment and furniture in the building were saved, as were the surrounding buildings. The fire began in the boiler room, even though the furnace had not been lit for several days.

Firefighters from Monroe and Marshville tried to save the building, but a lack of water pressure and the chemicals from the lab hampered their progress. Another fire that night destroyed the W. A. Chaney Building nearby. An investigation into a break-in there led to suspicions that that fire was set on purpose. There were suspicions, too, that the Wingate fire was intentionally set, but its cause remains undetermined.

The board of trustees voted quickly to have a new building erected before classes began the next year and began fundraising. Local Baptist churches helped as much as they could in the Depression-strapped times.

1985 U.S. Senator Sam J. Ervin, Jr. of Watergate Fame

On April 23, 1985, former U.S. senator and Watergate Committee chairman Sam J. Ervin Jr. died of respiratory failure at North Carolina Baptist Hospital in Winston-Salem. He was eighty-eight.

Born in Morganton, Ervin graduated from UNC in 1917 before serving in France during World War I. After earning a law degree from Harvard University in 1922, he returned to his hometown to practice law and years later still described himself as an "old country lawyer."

A Democrat, Ervin won election to three terms in the General Assembly, was appointed to Congress, and served on the North Carolina Supreme Court before beginning a twenty-year career in the U.S. Senate in 1954. Considered a strict constitutionalist, Ervin defied ideology or party lines. He sat on the committee that censured Senator Joseph McCarthy in the 1950s, led filibusters against civil rights laws while simultaneously advocating for civil liberties in the 1960s, and opposed the Equal Rights Amendment in the 1970s.

His folksy humor, distinctive accent, and Southern charm made "Senator Sam" a national figure during the televised Watergate hearings in 1972–73. Ervin retired in 1974 and again returned to his hometown, where he wrote three books and continued to practice law.

Senator Sam Ervin displaying the tremendous amount of correspondences received in his office, 1971.

1776 Salt Works Established to Support Revolutionary War Effort

On April 24, 1776, North Carolina's Provincial Congress ordered that a salt works be established in the colony for Revolutionary War use.

Before the war North Carolina and other southern colonies had relied largely on salt imported from Great Britain to preserve their meats, flavor their foods, and feed their livestock. It was a vital commodity. At the war's outbreak in 1775, Great Britain had severed all trade with the fledgling American government, causing fear of a salt shortage. To ensure availability, the Provincial Congress initially set price caps on salt, rationed the existing supply, and offered bounties to encourage its manufacture.

Not until April 1776, when the colonial government authorized four men to spend up to two thousand British pounds of public funds to establish a salt works, did work begin. Robert Williams and Richard Blackledge both began salt works near Beaufort that spring. Williams's operation at Gallant's Point, which used solar evaporation, soon failed. But Blackledge's plant on Core Creek succeeded, using a furnace to boil saltwater in iron pans until the water evaporated and only the salt remained.

Although Blackledge died in 1777, his salt works continued to operate throughout the Revolutionary War.

1776 Herring and Devane's Gun and Bayonet Factory

On April 24, 1776, prominent patriots Richard Herring and John Devane founded a gun factory on the Black River north of Wilmington in what's now Sampson County.

Money to build the factory, buy some of the initial materials needed, and pay the workers was provided by the colonial government. The one thousand British pounds the government allocated would be worth about forty thousand dollars in today's money. Records indicate that the factory produced simple muskets with 3-foot, 8-inch barrels and one-and-a-half-foot bayonets.

Documents from the period indicate that the objective was to produce guns at a cost of no more than five pounds apiece. The bayonets were to include a "trumpet mouthed" loop at one end. The point of the factory was to ensure a well-armed local militia.

The factory made about one hundred muskets and a few rifles and smooth-bore guns before being destroyed by forces loyal to the Crown. Five other gun factories, located in and around New Bern, Edenton, Halifax, Hillsborough, and Salisbury, operated during the Revolutionary period.

1837 L. L. Polk, Agricultural Reformer

On April 24, 1837, Leonidas LaFayette Polk, founder of *The Progressive Farmer* and president of the National Farmers' Alliance, was born in Anson County.

Polk attended Davidson College and served in the Confederate army before advocating for farmers' rights. In 1877 he was named the state's first agriculture commissioner by Gov. Zebulon B. Vance.

After founding *The Progressive Farmer* in 1886, one of the nation's oldest and most widely read agricultural periodicals, Polk used the publication to promote the creation of a land grant university, separate from the University of North Carolina. In 1889 his vision became a reality when what is now N.C. State opened. He also used the *Farmer* to advocate for the creation what is now Meredith College, founded in 1891.

After helping found the Farmers' Alliance in North Carolina and assuming a high position in it, Polk became a leader of the new Populist Party, which soon gained strength nationally in the South and the West. He quickly became the Populists' presidential nominee but died in June 1892 before the general election.

In 1995 Polk's house, a two-story gingerbread Gothic structure, was purchased by the Leonidas L. Polk House Foundation and moved to its present location on North Blount Street in Raleigh.

L. L. Polk, 1878.

APR 25

1862 Endor Ironworks Saved from the Forces of Nature

On April 25, 1862, the Endor Iron Company was chartered. Two months later the investors purchased the Deep River plantation of Alexander McIver and constructed a smelting furnace on it.

It is likely that the furnace supplied the Confederate arsenal at Fayetteville in addition to small nearby arms factories. The iron works changed hands twice before a Maryland manufacturer purchased Endor and, with a local partner, invested heavily in the operation. By 1872 their Cape Fear Iron and Steel Company was one of the South's largest and best equipped iron furnaces.

Two years later it was determined that local mineral deposits were smaller than had been estimated. By 1876 the company had ceased operation. Though most of the machinery was dismantled and removed, the furnace continued operating until 1896 on a smaller scale, serving only local manufacturers.

With cooperation from the Triangle Land Conservancy and the financial support of the nonprofit Railroad House Historical Association, the original structure is now being prepared for stabilization and ultimately restoration, with plans for greater public access and appreciation of this important chapter of North Carolina industrial history.

Endor Iron Furnace (*left* and *background*), Cumnock vicinity, Lee County, December 1978.

1908 Edward R. Murrow, Legendary Journalist

On April 25, 1908, famed CBS broadcaster Edward R. Murrow was born in Greensboro.

Though its ties to the area were strong, the Murrow family moved to Washington state while Edward was still young. There Murrow enrolled at Washington State College, where he had the opportunity to go to Washington, D.C. as president of the National Student Federation.

In 1935 Murrow became "director of talks" for CBS Radio. With tensions mounting in Europe, he was dispatched there two years later. Hitler's annexation of Austria in 1938 began Murrow's rise to fame. His broadcasts during the Battle of Britain, beginning each evening with "This is London," are legendary.

Murrow began *See It Now* on CBS Television in 1951. His signature on that series was his sign-off: "Good night and good luck." Perhaps the most noted episode of the program came in March 1954, when Murrow took on Senator Joseph R. McCarthy. The program is credited with significantly contributing to McCarthy's downfall.

1932 Meadowlark Lemon, Basketball's Court Jester

On April 25, 1932, Meadow Lemon III was born in Lexington County, South Carolina. He moved to Wilmington at age six.

A fan of basketball from an early age, Lemon used to tell the story that his first basketball ensemble was a hoop made from an onion sack and a coat hanger with a Carnation milk can as a ball. After seeing the famed Harlem Globetrotters in a movie theater newsreel, he ran home to tell his father that he planned to join the team. In 1954 he did just that.

Lemon changed his name to Meadowlark in the late 1950s, but he was also widely known as the "Clown Prince of Basketball." Though a slick player with phenomenal ball-handling skills and a long-distance hook shot that rarely missed the hoop, it was his cheeky comedy on the court that propelled him into the spotlight.

The best-known Globetrotter, Lemon became a television star, portraying himself in television shows like *Gilligan's Island* and in cartoons, including *Scooby Doo*.

Lemon retired from the Globetrotters in 1979, became an ordained minister in 1986, and established Meadowlark Lemon Ministries in 1994.

Inducted into the North Carolina Sports Hall of Fame in 1975 and the Naismith Memorial Basketball Hall of Fame in 2003, Lemon died in 2015.

Meadowlark Lemon (*right*), formerly with the Harlem Globe Trotters, warming up for a game on the flight deck of the aircraft carrier USS *Ranger*, 1988.

APR 26

1865 Negotiations at the Bennett Place

On April 26, 1865, the largest troop surrender of the Civil War took place on farm of James and Nancy Bennett in what was then Orange County.

Ten days earlier two worn adversaries, Union Maj. Gen. William T. Sherman and Confederate Gen. Joseph E. Johnston, along with their escorts, rode out to meet and negotiate the terms for the surrender. By chance, the Bennett farm was located half-way between the Union forces positioned in Raleigh and the Confederate forces encamped in and around Greensboro.

The two generals asked permission to use the farmhouse to conduct their meeting. The Bennett family, already touched by the war with the loss of both of their sons and a son-in-law, retreated to the separate kitchen building to allow the generals to use the house. After several days of negotiations, which were complicated by the assassination of Pres. Abraham Lincoln, Johnston surrendered his army. Johnston's forces included all Confederate troops in North Carolina, South Carolina, Georgia, and Florida, totaling nearly ninety thousand soldiers. The mustering out of the Confederate army took place in Greensboro in early May, where paroles were issued to the soldiers.

Bennett Place became a State Historic Site in 1961.

1942 The Marines of Montford Point

On April 26, 1942, the United States Marine Corps opened Montford Point at Camp Lejeune, specifically for the training of African American recruits.

Before Pres. Harry Truman's 1948 executive order that ended segregation in the armed forces, blacks who served did so in segregated units, like the one at Montford Point. In that era of strict segregation, interaction between white and black Marines during training was practically nonexistent.

The larger base, Camp Lejeune, had been established one year earlier as part of the mobilization for World War II. Shortly after that time the Corps constructed barracks and support facilities, including a chapel, mess hall, steam plant, and recreational area on the sixteen-hundred-acre peninsula that became Montford Point.

More than nineteen thousand black Marines served in World War II, all in units trained at Montford Point. Among the units organized there were the Fifty-First and Fifty-Second Defense Battalions, which were dispatched to the Pacific but saw no combat action, and eleven ammunition and fifty-one depot companies, which did see action. The Fifty-First Battalion Band, led by musician Bobby Troup, lent to the sense of esprit de corps.

The facility became obsolete after Navy Secretary Francis Matthews ordered the end of racial division in the Navy and Marines in June 1949.

1956 Malcolm McLean, Containerization Innovator

On April 26, 1956, at the port of Newark, New Jersey, Malcolm McLean watched a giant crane swing his newly invented shipping containers onto a ship. As the ship steamed off toward Houston, Texas, the era of container shipping had begun.

Born in 1914 in Robeson County, McLean rose from humble roots to build a business empire. He began by driving a truck as a teenager and owned one of America's largest transportation companies by the time he was in his mid-thirties.

He had the idea for a shipping container as early as 1937, when he was still driving his own truck. After sitting for a whole day at a New Jersey port waiting for workers to unload his truck and put the goods on a ship, he wondered why there wasn't a truck-trailer that could be lifted onto a ship or onto railroad wheels without anyone touching the contents.

The success of his 1956 endeavor led to a company called SeaLand, now a part of Maersk. By the mid-1960s McLean's SeaLand had built container-handling facilities in many U.S. ports, and after the company's technology was used by the government during the Vietnam War, it spread throughout the world.

McLean died in 2011 in New York City.

The Unity Monument at Bennett Place.

Montford Point Marine inductees at Camp Lejeune using a field telephone and two-way field radio, 1943 (*left*).

1584 The First of the Roanoke Colonies

1855 Benjamin Duke and the "Dukes of Durham"

1916 Baseball Hall of Famer Enos Slaughter of Roxboro

1935 "Big Hugh" Bennett, the "Father of Soil Conservation"

APR 27

On April 27, 1584, Capts. Arthur Barlowe and Philip Amadas sailed from the west coast of England in two ships "well furnished with men and victuals" to begin a four-month exploration of the New World.

The expedition was the first English exploration of Roanoke Island and was commissioned by Sir Walter Raleigh. The report Barlowe produced on the expedition was written for Raleigh's benefit.

After sailing through the Caribbean via the Canary Islands, the group arrived at present-day North Carolina in July 1584. First landing somewhere between Ocracoke Island and Oregon Inlet, the party made their way to Roanoke Island in smaller boats.

The expedition developed friendly relationships with Native Americans through trade, gift exchanges, and mutual hospitality. The goodwill fostered between the groups led the Algonquian Indians Manteo and Wanchese to return to England with the group when they departed toward the end of the year.

The wealth of information provided by Amadas and Barlowe and the fascination in England with Manteo and Wanchese encouraged Raleigh in his plans to colonize North America.

Barlowe's report of the expedition describes the region and people in vivid, admiring detail. John White, a member of the mission who would be the governor of the ill-fated "Lost Colony," added pictures of the Native Americans as well. A phrase describing North Carolina's soil captures the spirit of the document well:

> *"the most plentifull, sweete, fruitfull*
> *and wholesome of all the worlde."*

The text was ultimately published in 1589 in *The Principall Navigations Voiages and Discoveries of the English Nation* by Richard Hakluyt, who used Barlowe's admiring words to help encourage colonization.

Theodorus de Bry's (*background*) engraving of the Native American village of Secoton, which accompanied the text of Thomas Hariot's book of 1588, *A Briefe and True Report of the New Found Land of Virginia*.

On April 27, 1855, Benjamin N. Duke was born on the Duke family farm north of Durham.

Often sickly as a child, Duke didn't let his health get in the way of helping with the family tobacco business, which began shortly after the end of the Civil War. He became a partner in the business when it was incorporated in 1878 and treasurer of the American Tobacco Company in 1890 when the Duke organization became part of that enterprise.

Duke was the primary member of the family engaged in setting up Erwin Mills, the Dukes' foray into textiles, and he went onto to serve as president of a number of the family's other holdings.

Not as able a businessman as his brother Buck, Ben Duke took to managing his family's philanthropic efforts after working with Buck to found what is now Duke Energy. After his father financed what would become Duke University, Ben helped steer the school through its early days and was the primary link between the university and the family.

Ill during most of the last two decades of his life, Duke gave large portions of his fortune to his wife and children before dying in 1929.

Duke Homestead State Historic Site interprets the early home, factories, and farm where Duke family first grew and processed tobacco.

On April 27, 1916, Hall of Fame baseball player Enos Slaughter was born near Roxboro to a farm family.

As a child Slaughter honed his strength and skill with farm work, hunting rabbits with rocks, and playing sports. He also developed a lifelong passion for baseball by watching Durham Bulls games. Slaughter began his pro career with a St. Louis Cardinals farm team, the Martinsville Redbirds, and it was while playing with the Virginia team that his tireless hustle earned him the nickname "Country."

Slaughter entered the majors with the Cardinals in 1938 and stayed with them until 1953, before playing for a number of other teams including the New York Yankees. He competed in five World Series and ten All-Star Games. At various times he led the National League in triples, double plays by an outfielder, and RBIs.

Though a standout player in many respects, Slaughter's reputation was marred by his racial attitudes. In 1947 he tried to get Cardinal players to strike in protest of Jackie Robinson's presence on the Dodgers' roster. Though the strike attempt failed, Slaughter intentionally spiked Robinson in a later game.

Slaughter retired from playing in 1959 but managed a few minor league teams and coached briefly at Duke. He died in 2002.

An autographed photograph of Enos Slaughter with an unbuttoned uniform as a result of a confrontation during a game, ca. 1950's.

On April 27, 1935, Hugh Hammond Bennett of Anson County became director of the Soil Conservation Service, a position he held until his retirement in 1952. "Big Hugh," as he came to be known, grew up in the drainage basin of the Pee Dee River and became aware of the woeful effects of soil erosion at an early age. He is widely credited with selling the benefits of soil conservation to a dubious public.

The solution to the nation's agricultural problems, according to Bennett, was preservation of the topsoil, accomplished by means of terracing, cover and strip cropping, contour plowing, grassed waterways, and crop rotation, among other methods. The "Dust Bowl," which devastated the American prairie lands in the mid-1930s, increased the urgency of his work. Widely respected for his expertise, Bennett advised on projects in Alaska, Brazil, Cuba, South Africa, and other places around the world.

For fifty years Bennett worked with the federal Department of Agriculture, rising to the leadership role in the Soil Conservation Service. In his native Anson County he established the Brown Creek Soil Conservation District in 1937. It was the first organization of its kind in the nation. Today those who continue the work to preserve the soil honor Bennett as the "father of soil conservation."

1911 Carnival Worker Preserved, Abandoned in Laurinburg

On April 28, 1911, Cancetto Farmica, died in Laurinburg.

Farmica, a musician, was murdered after an argument with a fellow carnival worker when he was hit on the head with a tent stake. The carnival and the attack took place in McColl, just over the border with South Carolina, but the injured man was taken to the hospital in nearby Laurinburg. Farmica was operated on but died about twelve hours later. The body was removed to the McDougald Funeral Home in that town.

The story becomes somewhat murky after that. Some say that a decision was made not to try the case due to the expense and the fact that both men were foreigners. Others say that the assailant was actually acquitted. Regardless, Farmica's body was left at the funeral home where it had been embalmed.

A couple of weeks after the death, Farmica's father came to the funeral home, paid an installment to have his son buried, and promised to send the rest. He was not heard from again, so Farmica's body remained in the funeral home for sixty-one years, until it was finally buried in 1972 in Hillside Cemetery in Laurinburg.

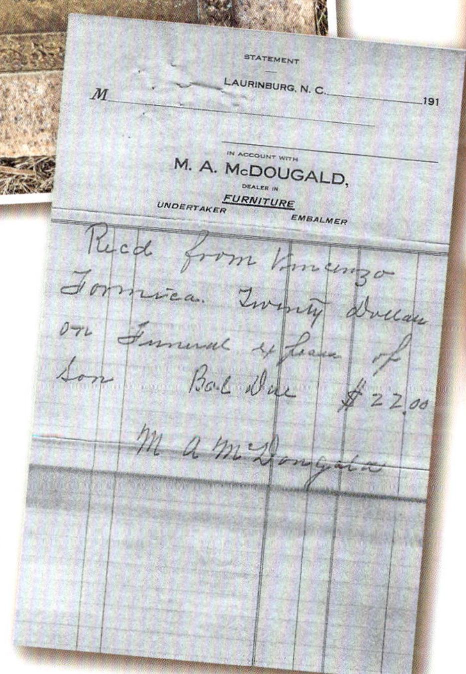
STATEMENT

M ______ LAURINBURG, N. C. ______ 191

IN ACCOUNT WITH
M. A. McDOUGALD,
DEALER IN
FURNITURE
UNDERTAKER EMBALMER

Rec'd from Vincenzo Formica. Twenty Dollars on Funeral expense of Son Bal Due $22.00

M A McDougald

Cancetto Farmica's gravestone (*above*) and receipt of partial payment from Vincenzo Farmica, his father (*right*). An outstanding balance of $22 was not received and Cancetto Farmica was not buried until sixty-one years later.

1993 "Jimmy V." Mourned by NCSU Fans

On April 28, 1993, Jim Valvano died of cancer at age forty-seven.

Valvano was born in Queens, New York, played basketball at Rutgers University, and had several coaching positions before coming to North Carolina State as head coach in 1980. In a series of inspiring and improbable last-minute victories, he led the Wolfpack to the championship of the men's NCAA basketball tournament in 1983. *Sports Illustrated* included the achievement as one of the top ten sporting events of the twentieth century.

In 1992 Valvano was diagnosed with terminal cancer. In the final months of his life, he helped establish the Jimmy V Foundation for Cancer Research, whose motto, "Don't Give Up. . .Don't Ever Give Up!" reflects Valvano's eternal optimism. His last public appearance occurred when he received the Arthur Ashe Award for Courage from ESPN in March 1993.

Broadcast of his inspirational speech at the ESPY awards ceremony has become an annual tradition on the network and has helped the V Foundation raise over 120 million dollars for cancer research—a fitting legacy for a man who inspired a nation both on and off the basketball court.

Coach Jim Valvano on the sidelines in a game versus Duke, 1981.

APR 29

1864 Pitt County Native Dies at Andersonville Prison

On April 29, 1864, forty-three years old Pvt. Howell Turnage of Company I, Thirty-Fifth United States Colored Troops, died from the effects of chronic diarrhea while incarcerated at the infamous Confederate prison at Andersonville, Georgia.

The Pitt County native was one of three black Union soldiers from North Carolina to die in the prison. A farmer by trade, Turnage enlisted with the Thirty-Fifth USCT, the first black regiment organized in the state, at New Bern in May 1863 for a term of three years. He was captured in February 1864 during the Battle of Olustee in northern Florida.

In March 1864, the month after the prison's opening, Turnage was among the first black prisoners of war to arrive at Andersonville. Contaminated water supplies and nutritional deficiencies, stemming from the overcrowded nature of the camp, greatly affected the health of the prisoners. The conditions resulted in the deaths of close to thirteen thousand Union soldiers—a death rate of nearly thirty percent.

Of the estimated one hundred black POWs held at Andersonville, twelve perished during captivity, including two other black North Carolina natives, William Morse and Warren Norfleet. Morse, Norfleet, and Turnage are all buried in Andersonville National Cemetery on the former site of the prison.

1951 NASCAR Great Dale Earnhardt

On April 29, 1951, Dale Earnhardt was born in Kannapolis. His father Ralph was a competitive driver on the NASCAR Modified, Sportsman, and Grand National circuits. Dale dropped out of school in ninth grade to pursue a career in racing, following in his father's footsteps.

Earnhardt made his stock car debut in 1975 at the Charlotte Motor Speedway, finishing twenty-second. He drove sporadically, without a full-time sponsor until 1979, when Richard Osterlund chose him for his team. He won at Bristol in his sixteenth start and went on to place in the top five in eleven races during the season. His performance earned him Rookie of the Year honors. The following year he won the first of the seven Winston Cup Series titles he would collect over the course of his life.

Known for his aggressive driving style and often called "The Intimidator," Earnhardt dominated the sport through the 1980s and early 1990s. Aside from his seven Winston Cup and three IROC titles, he was also named American Driver of the Year twice and National Motorsports Press Association Driver of the Year five times.

Dale Earnhardt was killed in the final lap of the Daytona 500 on February 18, 2001, at age forty-nine.

1956 "King of the Hill" at Chimney Rock

On April 29, 1956, the first Chimney Rock Hill Climb took place. Hill climbing is an uphill motorsport in which drivers compete against the clock.

Organized by the Morse family, then owners of Chimney Rock Park, and the Sports Car Club of America, the hill climb ran in the spring and sometimes the fall of each year. While the length of the course changed over the years from 2.7 miles during the early years to 1.8 miles later on, the goal of the race always was to be crowned "King of the Hill."

The narrow winding access road to the top rose from eleven hundred to twenty-two hundred feet above sea level in less than three miles and often sent drivers over the edge. In later years the race to the top took less than two minutes, but during the course of run, no one was ever seriously hurt. The thirteen hairpin turns were always lined with spectators, and the event attracted repeat drivers and enthusiastic crowds.

Unfortunately, the park, usually a tranquil place where people could view wildlife and serene beauty, became anything but that on race weekends, filling with raucous crowds and loud, fast cars.

Safety and liability issues finally ended the race in 1995.

1975 The Fall of Saigon and Ambassador Graham Martin

On April 29, 1975, the last Americans, including Ambassador Graham Martin, were evacuated from Saigon just hours before the city fell to the communists. A few days earlier Pres. Gerald Ford declared that the Vietnam War was "finished as far as America is concerned."

Although military involvement in Vietnam had come to an end, the U.S. still had to evacuate all the Americans who remained. It was the biggest helicopter rescue of its kind in history—an eighteen-hour operation that carried more than one thousand Americans and well over five thousand Vietnamese to safety.

Born in Mars Hill in 1912, Martin served as a U. S. Army Intelligence Officer during World War II. He began his diplomatic career in 1947 in Paris and served as the U.S. Representative to the United Nations and as the American Ambassador to Thailand and to Italy before he was appointed Ambassador to South Vietnam in 1973.

The helicopter that carried Martin to safety is on display at the Flying Leatherneck Aviation Museum in San Diego.

Martin died in 1990 and is buried at Arlington National Cemetery.

Russ Roland at the Chimney Rock Hill Climb, 1975.

President Ford meeting with Secretary of State Henry Kissinger, Army Chief of Staff General Frederick Weyand, and Graham Martin, Ambassador to Vietnam, in the Oval Office, March 1975.

1864 The Siege and Burning of Washington, April 1864

On April 30, 1864, Federal troops partially burned the town of Washington in Beaufort County.

Washington was first occupied by the Federals in March 1862, following the fall of New Bern. Although many of the inhabitants fled before troops arrived, those who remained were generally strong supporters of the Union.

In March 1863 Confederate Maj. Gen. D. H. Hill laid siege to the town in an unsuccessful effort to recover it for the Confederates.

As a result of Confederate Brig. Gen. Robert F. Hoke's capture of Plymouth on April 20, the Federal garrison received orders on April 26 to evacuate Washington. Hoke's forces laid siege to the town on April 27. Beginning that night and continuing for the next three days, as Union troops withdrew from Washington, they looted and vandalized the town.

As the last of the Federal forces prepared to board ships on the afternoon of April 30, fires broke out across the town. At least half the settlement was destroyed, leaving many of the inhabitants destitute and homeless.

The conduct of the departing Northern garrison was harshly condemned by both the Confederates and by Brig. Gen. Innis Palmer, Federal commander of the District of North Carolina.

1963 African Diplomat Denied Service in Raleigh, 1963

On April 30, 1963, Angie Brooks and Allard Lowenstein attempted to have lunch together at two restaurants in downtown Raleigh, but they were denied service because Brooks was African.

Brooks, Liberia's United Nations ambassador and a Shaw University graduate, was in Raleigh to deliver a speech at N.C. State University. After the speech Lowenstein, a professor at the university, invited the ambassador to lunch. The pair, with a few students in tow, visited the S & W Cafeteria and the Sir Walter Coffee Shop. Despite her diplomatic credentials, Brooks was refused service at both. In fact, the manager at the coffee shop went so far as to say that he would not serve Brooks but could offer her a job as a cook or waitress.

The media was soon alerted, and the press was on hand to report the story. The incident brought national attention to North Carolina, and Gov. Terry Sanford issued an apology to Brooks on behalf of the state.

Since Lowenstein had chosen restaurants that were frequented by state officials, many believed he was an agitator who wanted to stir up controversy. Although he had been aware that the establishments were segregated, he denied staging the event.

SHELLING OF REBEL BATTERIES IN THE WOODS OPPOS. WASHINGTON.N.C APRIL.16th 1863

WASHINGTON, ON THE TAR RIVER, NORTH CAROLINA.—From a Sketch by Byron S. Heath, U. S. S. Louisiana. Castle Island.

MAY 1

1814 Johnston Blakeley, War of 1812 Hero, Lost at Sea

On May 1, 1814, the USS *Wasp* set sail with a crew of 173 men and orders to harass British merchant ships. The ship's successes were many, and the ship's captain, Johnston Blakeley, was described as "a brave and discreet officer" and his ship as "one of the most successful of our cruisers."

Blakeley was awarded a gold medal for his victory over the HMS *Reindeer* and was promoted to captain. He never learned of his promotion since the *Wasp* was lost at sea. The ship is believed to have sunk in an Atlantic storm, since no British ship reported destroying the prized vessel. The last known sighting of the ship was by the Swedish vessel *Adonis* on October 9.

Blakeley's widow, Jane Ann, gave birth to their daughter, Maria, in January 1815. The following year the state of North Carolina voted to bestow upon his widow a sword in honor of her husband's service, but she suggested instead that a silver tea service be given to Maria. An elegant service was crafted by Anthony Rasch of Philadelphia in 1818 and presented to the child. The Blakeley tea service is now in the collection of the North Carolina Museum of Art.

1845 North Carolina Among First to Establish School for the Blind

On May 1, 1845, North Carolina's school for the blind, the Governor Morehead School, opened in Raleigh. Originally conceived by Gov. John Motley Morehead in 1843, the school became a reality in January 1845, when the General Assembly approved an act to provide for the education of deaf and blind persons.

Four months later the school opened in a building two blocks west of the State Capitol, with four teachers and twenty-three deaf students between the ages of eight and thirty-two. The school's students became the first in America to produce a newspaper made for and by the deaf, and for a brief time during the Civil War, they worked for the war effort, making musket parts.

After the war efforts were made to address the needs of African Americans with disabilities, and a separate school opened in 1869. In time enrollment at the white school exceeded the facility's capacity, and the legislature funded a separate school for the deaf in Morganton, which opened in 1894.

In 1963 administrators changed the name of the original Raleigh facility to the Governor Morehead School, and in 1971 operations of the white and black schools were consolidated.

Musicians Doc Watson and Ronnie Milsap are among the school's best known alumni.

1928 Air mail Introduced in North Carolina

On May 1, 1928, North Carolina's first airmail delivery arrived at the small airport in Greensboro known as Lindley Field.

Pitcairn Aviation was given a contract to fly an airmail delivery route between New York and New Orleans, and Greensboro was one of five stops along the route. Pilot Sid Malloy landed at 8:15 p.m. with two bags of mail and took three bags of mail with him when he left for his next stop in Atlanta.

Lindley Field had been open for only a year at that time. National hero Charles Lindbergh and the *Spirit of St. Louis* drew large crowds to the field's opening ceremony in 1927. He visited Lindley Field as part of a three-month tour promoting air flight that took him to forty-eight states and eighty-two cities. As a result of his visit, interest in the use of airmail intensified.

Lindley Field was closed during the Depression because of a decline in service and substandard facilities. It was a project of the Works Progress Administration during the mid-1930s and re-opened in 1937. The facility, now known as Piedmont-Triad International Airport, has grown into a major hub for both transportation and commercial shipping.

1935 Gas Chamber in Use at Central Prison After 1935

On May 1, 1935, the state Senate approved a bill making lethal gas the method of execution in North Carolina. It replaced electrocution, which was used until that time.

Charles Peterson, a Spruce Pine physician who served as a member of the General Assembly during the first half of the twentieth century, was the primary advocate for the change. Raleigh's *News & Observer* described bringing about the change as his "pet project."

Doctors and dentists testified before the legislature's Joint Committee on Penal Institutions that lethal gas was a more humane method of execution than electrocution, and a bill Peterson wrote was quickly sent to and approved by both houses of the General Assembly.

A lethal gas chamber was constructed at Raleigh's Central Prison by December 1935, with many across the state seeing the change as a positive technological innovation.

Allen Foster, who had been convicted of rape in Hoke County, was the first to be executed by lethal gas. His January 1936 execution demonstrated that the change in method was not necessarily positive. Because prison officials kept the temperature in the gas chamber near freezing, the gas failed to work effectively, and Foster didn't die for eleven minutes and convulsed violently in the process.

Death row inmates could choose between lethal gas and lethal injection until 1998, when the General Assembly made lethal injection the only method of execution in the state.

The Governor Morehead School's original campus on Caswell Square, Raleigh, in 1875.

1863 Friendly Fire Killed Stonewall Jackson

On May 2, 1863, Confederate Lt. Gen. Thomas "Stonewall" Jackson was wounded by several volleys of gunfire from the Eighteenth North Carolina Troops during the Battle of Chancellorsville in Virginia.

From April 30 to May 6, the Battle of Chancellorsville was fought between the Union Army of the Potomac and the Confederate Army of Northern Virginia in Spotsylvania County, Virginia. Confederate Gen. Robert E. Lee sent Jackson and his Second Corps to attack the Union right flank. The attack proved successful, but by early evening the Confederate assault began to lose its momentum.

In an effort to restart the advance, Jackson and his staff rode out on the Plank Road to reconnoiter the Union positions in the darkness. While returning, Jackson and his staff rode into the picket line of the Eighteenth North Carolina, who responded to a perceived possible attack with successive volleys. Jackson was struck three times. Four members of his staff were killed and another three wounded.

While in the hospital Jackson contracted pneumonia after the amputation of his left arm and died on May 10.

1892 Discovery of Calcium Carbide Process

On May 2, 1892, in Spray (now Eden), Canadian chemist Thomas L. Willson accidentally produced calcium carbide and acetylene with an electric-arc furnace. In August Willson applied for a patent for the new process.

By 1897 acetylene was competing with electricity in providing lighting, especially in rural areas and those places where gasoline was unavailable. Portable acetylene generators provided light to mines, bicycles, automobiles, and railroads. Willson developed the acetylene gas buoy as a maritime navigational aid; it was used worldwide. Oxygen was also combined with acetylene to allow for faster welding and cutting of metals.

In August 1894 Willson and his business partner James Turner Morehead sold the patents for utilizing calcium and acetylene in lighting to the Electrogas Company but kept the manufacturing rights. That same month Morehead, using borrowed money, completed the first commercial calcium carbide plant by expanding the Spray operation.

The plant burned in 1896. Morehead later built a larger plant in Virginia. A factory in West Virginia made ferro-alloys using methods developed at Spray. Morehead eventually sold the rights to the Union Carbide Company, which was formed in 1898. That company eventually became Union Carbide Corporation, which was acquired by Dow Chemical in 2001.

1929 Link Wray, Guitar Innovator, Renowned for "Rumble"

On May 2, 1929, Fred Lincoln Wray, Jr., better known as Link Wray, was born in Dunn. Wray developed an interest in music at a young age and during the 1940s started playing in a western swing band. After launching a solo career, Wray became popular in the late 1950s. "Rumble" from 1958 was one of his first big hits. He is still widely remembered for it today, since it was one of the first songs to feature the guitar effect of distortion. It was said that "Rumble" was banned from radio airplay because it was feared that the instrumental would initiate youth violence. The song proved popular, though, and spent ten weeks on *Billboard's Top 40* list, rising as high as Number 16.

Wray continued putting out new music into the late 1980s, then spent the last years of his life in Denmark. He died in 2005 in Copenhagen.

Wray's unique style of playing paved the way for heavy metal, punk, and grunge. He is on *Rolling Stone* magazine's list of "100 Greatest Guitarists" and is credited with influencing guitar players such as Jeff Beck, Jimmy Page, Pete Townshend, and many others.

MAY 2

Link Wray at The Tractor Tavern in Seattle, Washington, 2005.

MAY 3

1775 John Harvey of Harvey's Point

On May 3, 1775, John Harvey, Speaker of the Assembly, moderator of the Provincial Congress, and a politically powerful Revolutionary era leader, died in Perquimans County.

While he had long been in delicate health, he actually died of injuries received from a fall from his horse. He was buried at his home on the shores of Albemarle Sound in a large tomb that has since washed into the sound. It was last seen, covered in barnacles, in 1908.

Born about 1724 to a privileged family, Harvey entered the political arena by the time he was twenty-one. He served as a justice, member of the Assembly, speaker of the Assembly and member of the revolutionary Committee of Correspondence, the body appointed to communicate with other colonies concerning Crown policies deemed detrimental to America, before the advent of the Revolutionary War.

Harvey first adopted the cause of resistance to the tyrannies of the British Crown after the the British government imposed new taxes on the American colonies under the Townshend Acts. Historian R. D. W. Connor called Harvey the "Father of the American Revolution in North Carolina."

1856 Age of Duelling Ends in the Old North State

On May 3, 1856, the last recorded duel between North Carolinians, and one of the last duels in the South, was fought. Joseph Flanner and William Crawford Wilkings, both of Wilmington, battled just across the border in South Carolina. The duel resulted in Wilkings's death.

Duelling was relatively rare in the colonial South, though British and French officers made the practice more popular in the region during the Revolutionary War. The first recorded duel was fought between two British naval officers in Brunswick in March 1765. The first recorded duel between native North Carolinians was fought in Wilmington in July 1787.

The practice reached its peak of popularity in the early 1800s with the famed Stanly-Spaight Duel, in which John Stanly killed former governor Richard Dobbs Spaight. The General Assembly reacted to the incident by banning dueling. The law was largely unenforced, and the state's political elites continuing to use duels to resolve rivalries into the second half of the nineteenth century. Gradually though, public opinion began to shift against duels, and the practice faded into history.

1918 Stephen B. Weeks, State's First Professional Historian

On May 3, 1918, Stephen Beauregard Weeks died at age fifty-three. A native of Pasquotank County, Weeks became the state's first professionally-trained historian to earn his living specifically from his skills as a historian.

Weeks graduated second in his class at UNC in 1886. He went on to earn master's and doctoral degrees from the school's Department of English before entering Johns Hopkins University to focus on history. There he learned primary-source research and historical objectivity.

Weeks graduated with a doctorate in history from Johns Hopkins in 1891, then joined the faculty of Trinity College, now part of Duke University, in Randolph County. There he established the Department of History and Political Science and the Trinity College Historical Society. At Trinity Weeks founded modern historical scholarship in North Carolina. Though he resigned from Trinity after only two years, he continued to work in education and editing for the rest of his life.

Weeks was a prolific writer and is credited with more than two hundred books and articles. He avidly collected material related to North Carolina, amassing a collection of over nine thousand items. At his death the University of North Carolina purchased that collection and used it to supplement the special collections now housed in Wilson Library.

"The Duel" by E.W. Kemble, 1887.

1932 Wing Walker and Daredevil Bonnie Rowe

On May 4, 1932, Bonnie Rowe, legendary wing walker, was killed performing a stunt in Lawrenceville, Georgia. He was thirty-seven years old. He had almost been killed two years before in Lenoir when, upon opening, his parachute split in two places.

Rowe, who had his roots in North Carolina and had lived in Charlotte, had moved about a year before his death. Married to Alexander County native Florence Pool, Rowe had met her when he was hurt performing a stunt in Gastonia. She nursed him while he recovered. The two were married soon after, much to the surprise of Pool's Taylorsville community.

A World War I Navy veteran, Rowe starred in Mabel Cody's Flying Circus and performed more than twelve thousand jumps. He was known for performing other stunts, too, including running along the top of a speeding train to grab a ladder hanging from an airplane overhead.

The *Charlotte Observer* reported that at his death Rowe was hanging from the undercarriage of a plane, lost his grip, and plunged to the ground. Although Rowe's widow and son remained close to their family in North Carolina, they lived in Georgia for the rest of their lives.

1959 Randy Travis and His Route to Country Music Stardom

On May 4, 1959, country music star Randy Travis was born in Union County. Raised on a Marshville turkey farm, Travis began playing guitar at age ten, discovering what would become a lifetime love of country music.

As an adolescent, Travis had several run-ins with the law and dropped out of high school at fifteen. To help put him back on track, Lib Hatcher, owner of a Charlotte club where Travis performed, adopted him. With her help Travis focused seriously on his music career and moved to Nashville.

Warner Brothers Records signed Travis in 1985. His first hits included "1982" and "On the Other Hand." Travis's second album, *Always and Forever*, released in 1987, proved his staying power in the country music spotlight.

The authenticity and traditional approach Travis gives to his music distinguishes him as a country music legend. His style is said to be strongly influenced by the legendary Hank Williams. Fellow musicians, including Garth Brooks and Clint Black, now claim they looked to Travis for inspiration.

Travis has won many accolades in his long career, including six Grammys, seven Academy of Country Music Awards, and nine American Music Awards.

1981 Acclaimed Dramatist Paul Green

On May 4, 1981, Paul Green died. Among North Carolina's most revered writers, Green, born in Harnett County, began study at the University of North Carolina in 1916. After service in World War I, he returned to Chapel Hill and taught there until 1944, when he resigned to devote himself to fulltime writing.

Plays were Green's favorite art form but he also wrote short stories, novels, and poetry. In 1927 he was awarded a Pulitzer Prize for the play *In Abraham's Bosom*. His signature achievement was development of the outdoor drama (or "symphonic drama," as he termed it). Green's best-known production, *The Lost Colony*, opened on Roanoke Island in 1937 and runs every summer.

Over time Green wrote sixteen such symphonic dramas, with productions staged in Florida, Virginia, Kentucky, and Texas. Green's many honors include a designation by the General Assembly in 1979 as the state's Dramatist Laureate.

Outside the arts Green demonstrated from an early age sympathy and compassion for African Americans and the underprivileged. He was a lifelong champion of human rights and a dedicated opponent of war, lynching, capital punishment, chain gangs, and prejudice. His last home was "Windy Oaks," south of Chapel Hill.

Randy Travis, 2007.

Paul Green at work, 1939.

1864 Ironclad Raleigh Ran the Cape Fear River Blockade

1864 The CSS *Albemarle* and the Battle of Batchelor's Bay

1913 Clarence Steppe, Founder of Wayside Nurseries

1972 Reverend Gary Davis, Durham Blues Legend

MAY 5

On May 5, 1864, the CSS *Albemarle*, an ironclad ram, crossed Batchelor's Bay and fought seven Union warships.

Upon entering Albemarle Sound, the *Albemarle*, under command of Capt. J. W. Cooke, and her escort vessels were attacked by four double-ended steamers and three smaller gunboats under Capt. Melancton Smith. The Confederate ram entered battle late in the day. Leading the first line of attack was the Union flagship, the *Mattabesett*. The *Albemarle* returned fire, destroying the launch and cutting away some of the standing and running rigging.

The Federal steamer *Sassacus* then struck the ironclad. The crew of the *Albemarle* responded with a one-hundred-pound shot through the starboard boiler of the Union vessel and into her wardroom. The scalded men managed to free the ship as they drifted out of range. All parties then withdrew. Only by throwing butter, lard, and bacon into the boilers was it possible for the crew of the *Albemarle* to raise enough steam to return to Plymouth.

On May 5, 1864, Flag Officer William F. Lynch decided to take the war to the enemy, using the recently completed Richmond-class ironclad CSS *Raleigh*.

Built at J.L. Cassidey and Sons shipyard on Eagle's Island in the Cape Fear River opposite Wilmington, the *Raleigh* measured 172 feet long. It was protected by two layers of two-inch iron plate and armed with four Brooke rifles, two 6.4-inch and two seven-inch.

After being commissioned on April 3, the ironclad was placed under the command of Lt. Pembroke Jones. When Lynch gave his orders on May 5, the *Raleigh* steamed out into the Atlantic and made contact with several Union vessels.

The ensuing engagement was shrouded in darkness and marked by confusion. Because of its slow speed, the *Raleigh* was unable to mount a serious attack on the Federal ships. Flares and gunfire alerted the rest of the blockading squadron, but most commanders, unaware of the ironclad's presence, assumed a blockade-runner had been cornered.

For the rest of the night, the *Raleigh* steamed blindly through the blockading squadron, unnoticed by the Federals. It returned to the Cape Fear River the next day but ran aground shortly thereafter and was lost.

On May 5, 1913, Clarence Steppe, noted landscape nurseryman, was born at Dana in Henderson County.

Known throughout his life as "Kit," Steppe graduated from high school in McDowell County and attended Lenoir-Rhyne College before earning a diploma from the American Landscape School and working for the National Park Service through the 1930s.

Steppe earned degrees in nuclear engineering and political science from the University of Tennessee and served with the U.S. Army Corps of Engineers and the Navy during World War II. Between 1946 and 1951 he worked with the North Carolina Division of State Parks.

In 1951 Steppe founded Wayside Nurseries on US 64 east of Raleigh, and in time he received fifteen national awards for landscape engineering. He held a patent for the Pink Sachet, a flowering dogwood tree.

The North Carolina Farm Bureau headquarters, Balentine's Cafeteria in Cameron Village, and Quail Corners Shopping Center were among his commissions in Raleigh. He also landscaped portions of the Research Triangle Park, the campus of St. Andrews Presbyterian College in Laurinburg, Charlottetown Mall in Charlotte, and the grounds of Reynolds Tobacco Company in Winston-Salem.

On May 5, 1972, legendary bluesman Rev. Gary Davis died. Renowned as a finger-style ragtime guitar player, he influenced generations of players.

Davis got his start as a popular street musician in Durham in the 1930s, where he was known as "Blind Gary Davis." Ordained as a minister of the Free Baptist Connection Church in Washington, North Carolina in 1913, he began to tour as a singing gospel preacher.

Davis recorded with Blind Boy Fuller in New York in 1935. His "Piedmont style" of the blues was akin to the music performed later by Brownie McGhee and Sonny Terry who first became popular in the 1940s. As his popularity grew, Davis toured the folk and blues revival circuits, playing jumbo Gibson acoustic guitars. His students included David Bromberg, the Grateful Dead's Bob Weir, and the Jefferson Airplane's Jorma Kaukonen. His finger-picking guitar style influenced many other musicians, including Jerry Garcia, Ry Cooder, Dave Van Ronk, Taj Mahal, and Bob Dylan.

In addition to being a performer and teacher, Davis was a prolific composer of both religious and secular music. He incorporated John Phillips Sousa marches, spirituals, and square dance music into intricate guitar instrumentals. Songs associated with Davis include "Baby, Can I Follow You Down," "Candy Man," "Cocaine Blues," and "Samson and Delilah."

Photo of the CSS *Albemarle* from *The Photographic History of the Civil War: The Navies* (Vol. 6, 1911).

1818 Maiden Voyage of Otway Burns's Prometheus, 1818

On May 6, 1818, eleven years after Robert Fulton's invention of the steamship, Otway Burns launched a similar vessel in North Carolina.

Burns, known for his privateering during the War of 1812, built the *Prometheus* at his waterfront lot at the mouth of the White Oak River in Swansboro. He attracted the attention of North Carolina newspapers as he strove to launch his *Prometheus* before the *Henrietta*, another steamship built that year in Fayetteville. The *Prometheus* entered service on the Cape Fear River by the summer of 1818, shortly before the *Henrietta*.

Fulton's vessel operated on a route between Smithville (now Southport) and Wilmington, which took about four hours and cost passengers one dollar each way. Two of the most famous of the passengers on the *Prometheus* were Pres. James Monroe and Secretary of War John C. Calhoun, who rode the steamship to inspect Fort Johnston in April 1819.

1944 The "Rice Diet" and Duke University

On May 6, 1944, the *Journal of the American Medical Association* cited a study on the effect of what would become known as the "Rice Diet" in treating heart disease. Walter Kempner of Duke University presented the results at an AMA conference later that year.

Kempner documented decreases in heart size, improved kidney function, and a reversal of high blood pressure when patients ate a diet limited to rice and fruit. The prescribed diet contained only fifty milligrams of sodium and limited its calories from fat and protein to less than five percent each.

The regimen successfully treated disease without drugs. Its beneficial effects were dramatic, not only on kidney disease and hypertension, but also on cholesterol, cardiovascular disease, congestive heart failure, and diabetes. Kempner found that the low fat content of the diet also enhanced weight loss.

Patients who adopted the diet, known as Ricers, lost weight because it was so low in calories and fat. Kempner was one of the first doctors to recognize obesity as a disease as serious as hypertension, although his results were questioned at first. Patients began making pilgrimages to Kempner's Duke University clinic, transforming the hospital into an internationally-known institution.

1976 Andrews Geyser at Old Fort

On May 6, 1976, the town of Old Fort in McDowell County rededicated its once nationally-known Andrews Geyser.

The Western North Carolina Railroad Company constructed the geyser around 1885 as a feature of its ritzy Round Knob Hotel and as a tribute to the men who died while building the railroad from Old Fort to Asheville. Engineers dammed a mountain spring and laid a pipeline downhill to create the gravity-generated fountain, which, at its prime, could spew water 250 feet into the air.

Railroad passengers enjoyed seeing the man-made waterspout as trains looped around thirteen miles of track and passed through seven tunnels while ascending Old Fort Mountain and crossing the Eastern Continental Divide. After fire destroyed the Round Knob Hotel in 1903, the geyser fell into disrepair.

Wealthy New York banker and philanthropist George Fisher Baker rescued it in 1911 and had it redesigned and moved across Mill Creek. At that time it was named in honor of his friend and Southern Railroad's vice president, Alexander Boyd Andrews.

In 1975 Southern Railway, WNCRC's successor company, deeded Andrews Geyser to the town of Old Fort, which restored and rededicated it a year later. It now is part of a town park.

MAY 6

1865 Martin's Surrender at Waynesville

1915 Owen Hill Kenan, Survivor of the *Lusitania* Sinking, 1915

1942 Evelyn Whitlow, Army Nurse

1964 "War on Poverty" Photo Op in Rocky Mount, 1964

MAY 7

On May 7, 1865, Confederate Gen. James Green Martin surrendered the Army of Western North Carolina at Waynesville, nearly a month after Appomattox.

The surrender followed a skirmish at White Sulphur Springs between Confederate troops under William Holland Thomas (commonly known as Thomas's Legion) and Union troops under Lt. Col. William C. Bartlett. Thomas's Legion surprised the Union troops who retreated to Waynesville, with Martin advancing since he was likely unaware of Confederate Gen. Joseph E. Johnston's surrender at Durham on April 26.

When a truce was called the next day, almost a month after Appomattox, Martin surrendered his forces. On inspecting his former brigade in late 1864 and complimenting it on its efficiency, Robert E. Lee said that "Gen. Martin is one to whom North Carolina owes a debt that she can never repay." After the war Martin moved to Asheville, where he practiced law until his death in 1878.

Though the last engagement of the Civil War was fought in Texas about a week later, popular belief maintained that the "last shot" of the Civil War was fired in Waynesville, and a monument was dedicated to that effect in 1923.

On May 7, 1915, the German submarine U-20 fired a single torpedo at the luxury liner RMS *Lusitania*, striking the hull at 2:10 p.m. Wilmington resident Owen Hill Kenan was onboard, making his way to Deck A when the torpedo hit its target.

A second, more powerful explosion followed the first, causing the ship to list severely. Kenan waited for the ship to level off a bit, donned a lifejacket, and leapt off the starboard side. The sinking ship immediately pulled him down. Debris swirled all around him, sunlight gave way to darkness, and ever-increasing depth squeezed him to the brink of unconsciousness.

When the suction finally stopped, Kenan began to fight for the surface, popping up directly beneath one of the ship's smoke stacks. Again he went down, the smokestack pushing him deeper and deeper until he lost consciousness. When he opened his eyes again, the ship had completely disappeared. Four hours later Kenan was plucked from the water, one of only 761 survivors.

In May 1916 Kenan joined the American Ambulance Field Service, transferring later to the Medical Corps, where he spent the remainder of his war service on a relief mission to Russia and Turkey.

On May 7, 1942, Evelyn Whitlow was among the seventy-seven Army and Navy nurses captured following the fall of the Philippines.

The Whitlow family of Leasburg, in Caswell County, saw six of their twelve children (four sons and two daughters) enter the service during World War II. Evelyn was the first of the family to join the military. In May 1940 she enlisted in the Army Nurse Corps (ANC) as a second lieutenant. Whitlow was serving as a nurse in the Philippines when Pearl Harbor was attacked on December 7, 1941.

Known as the "Angels of Bataan and Corregidor," the captured nurses were the first group of American women taken prisoners of war. For three years she remained in Santo Thomas, a Japanese internment camp outside Manila, until being liberated on February 3, 1945. After the war she left the ANC, married a fellow POW from Santo Thomas, and moved to California. Whitlow died at age seventy-eight in 1994.

On May 7, 1964, Pres. Lyndon Johnson, accompanied by Gov. Terry Sanford, visited the home of tenant farmer William David Marlow near Rocky Mount to promote the president's "War on Poverty" initiative.

The fifteen-minute visit was essentially a photo opportunity to launch Johnson's tour of Appalachia. There have been questions over the years as to why Rocky Mount, not particularly close to the mountains, was selected, though many have assumed it has something to do with the town's name.

Though the Nash County family that hosted Johnson didn't live in Appalachia, it certainly met the rest of the criteria for people to be helped by the president's programs. Marlow lived with his seven children, his wife and his mother-in-law. A World War II veteran, he suffered from a chronic back injury and earned less than fifteen hundred dollars per year.

To emphasize the family's living conditions for the visiting journalists and politicians, the Marlows were instructed to hang a load of laundry on their clothesline and to keep their children barefooted. After the visit the family struggled with the stigma of poverty. Having never thought of herself as poor, Mrs. Marlow later wrote to the president, "We have just found out that we are the joke of a whole nation."

Pocket watch (*background* and *front cover*) from the RMS *Lusitania*. The RMS *Lusitania* was a British ocean liner that a German submarine sank in World War I, causing a major diplomatic uproar. The sinking of the *Lusitania* caused a storm of protest in the United States because 128 American citizens were among the dead.

President Lyndon Johnson (*center*) visits with the Marlow family of Rocky Mount as part of his poverty tour in 1964. Also in the group are U.S. Rep. Harold Cooley and Agriculture Secretary Orville Freeman and Gov. Terry Sanford and Lynda Bird Johnson.

1751 William Lenoir, Frontier Patriot

On May 8, 1751, Revolutionary War-era leader William Lenoir was born in Virginia. Lenoir first worked as a teacher and founded several schools before he became a surveyor and moved westward to take advantage of opportunities along the frontier.

Just after his move the Revolutionary War broke out. Lenoir answered the call to duty, serving in the militia, most notably at the Battle of Kings Mountain, with his service extending until he resigned during the War of 1812.

In addition to military service and success as a planter, Lenoir was very active in government. He was appointed justice of the peace and served in both houses of the state legislature for nearly two decades. As a delegate to the state ratifying conventions of 1788 and 1789, Lenoir voted against the U.S. Constitution because it did not include a bill of rights.

Lenoir went on to run unsuccessfully for governor and for both houses of Congress before his death in 1839. Lenoir County, the town of Lenoir, and Lenoir Hall at UNC, where he was one of the first trustees, are all named in his honor.

His home, Fort Defiance, is a now a popular privately-run historic site in Caldwell County.

1875 Medical Pioneer Susan Dimock Casualty at Sea, 1875

On May 8, 1875, Susan Dimock, the first female member of the North Carolina Medical Society, drowned off the coast of England. Hers was one of 336 lives lost when the SS *Schiller* hit rocks in heavy fog. The Washington, North Carolina native was en route to Europe, where she planned to further her education.

Born in Beaufort County in 1847, Dimock lived there through the occupation of Washington by Union troops in 1862. Her father, a native of Maine, operated the Lafayette Hotel and housed Union troops during the occupation.

From a young age Dimock associated with S. S. Satchwell, who lived across the street. Dr. Satchwell was a strong influence on her, allowing her to attend to patients and make house calls with him, eventually inspiring her to enter the medical profession. He shepherded her honorary membership in the Medical Society.

Dimock moved to Massachusetts but attended medical school at the University of Zurich after being rejected by Harvard.

She became a resident physician at one of the earliest hospitals for women, the New England Hospital for Women and Children. There she worked as a surgeon and developed a practice in obstetrics and gynecology.

1953 Birth of the Atlantic Coast Conference, 1953

On May 8, 1953, the Atlantic Coast Conference (ACC) was created during a meeting of representatives from the Southern Conference in Greensboro. The ACC's initial members were Clemson, Duke, the University of Maryland, the University of North Carolina, N.C. State, the University of South Carolina, and Wake Forest. The University of Virginia was accepted as a member later that year. Wallace Wade, the former Duke football coach, who was commissioner of the Southern Conference, agreed to serve as the ACC's interim commissioner as well. Jim Weaver, the athletic director at Wake Forest, was named commissioner the following year.

The seven schools decided to pull out of the Southern Conference for two primary reasons. First, the Southern Conference's seventeen-institution membership made scheduling games in all sports very difficult. Additionally, the Southern Conference had banned post-season bowl games due to gambling and financial scandals, but some of the schools disputed the ban. The nascent conference elected to allow schools to play in bowl games as long as they did not profit greatly from their participation.

A number of names were proposed for the new conference including Dixie, Tobacco, Blue-Gray, and the Southern Seven. Duke's Eddie Cameron ultimately suggested the name that stuck: Atlantic Coast Conference.

MAY 8

Dr. O. K. Cornwell (*left*), faculty chairman at the University of North Carolina, and Dr. J. T. Penney (*right*), faculty chairman at the University of South Carolina, are seen looking over plans made for the Atlantic Coast Conference in 1953.

1771 Gunpowder Raid by Black Boys of Cabarrus

On May 9, 1771, nine young men from what would become Cabarrus County raided a British convoy carrying gunpowder to Gen. Hugh Waddell's militia. The attack happened on Phifer's Hill just north of Concord.

The men disguised themselves as American Indians before they blew up two wagons worth of gunpowder. They already had darkened their skin as part of their disguises, and the explosion of the powder coated them with additional soot, blackening their faces and earning them the moniker, the "Black Boys of Cabarrus."

At the time of the raid, royal Gov. William Tryon and his troops attempted to suppress the Regulator uprising near Hillsborough, and Waddell was en route to assist Tryon. The powder the Black Boys blew up had been intended to be used on Regulators, so their efforts likely saved future lives.

The Regulators viewed the Black Boys as heroes, but Governor Tryon most assuredly did not. He pardoned some of the Regulators after the failed uprising, but not the Black Boys, instead labeling them criminals and fugitives.

The Black Boys hid out in Georgia until the Mecklenburg Resolves in 1775, after which they joined other colonists in fighting the British.

1777 John Butler, Militia District Commander

On May 9, 1777, John Butler was appointed commander of the Hillsborough District militia.

Butler had settled in Orange County in the early 1760s and was elected sheriff in 1770. When the Revolution began, he was appointed to the Hillsborough committee of safety and later commanded the Orange County militia at Moores Creek Bridge. In 1776 the government divided the state into six military districts. Butler's command put him in charge of militia regiments from Caswell, Chatham, Granville, Orange, Randolph, and Wake Counties.

Though he held his command for the next seven years, Butler did not have a stellar military career. While he acted quite courageously in every engagement in which he was involved, he was no great tactician. One soldier who served under him described him as just "an old man in a hunting shirt."

During the "Tory War" in the early fall of 1781, Butler took an active part in trying to capture David Fanning. In September 1781 he engaged Fanning's forces at Lindley's Mill in an attempt to rescue Gov. Thomas Burke and other political prisoners. After heavy fighting, Butler retreated, letting Fanning escape to Wilmington.

Butler's home at "Mount Pleasant" is now the site of a golf course.

1942 U-Boat Survivors Added to POW Camp Rosters

On May 9, 1942, the U.S. Coast Guard sank German U-Boat 352 off the Outer Banks. Thirteen German sailors died and thirty-three were plucked from the water. They were taken to Fort Bragg and confined as prisoners of war. During the course of the war, thousands of POWs, mostly German and Italians, were captured and sent to camps in North Carolina.

Most of those POWs were brought to North Carolina from abroad. Fritz Teichmann was a member of the German Luftwaffe (the air corps) and was captured in Sicily in July 1943. He was held as a POW at Camp Butner in Granville County. Giuseppe Pagliarulo, a soldier in Benito Mussolini's Italian army, was captured in Tunisia in May 1943 and held at Camp Sutton in Monroe.

So many POWs were brought to the state that some were sent from larger military bases to smaller branch camps. These smaller camps housed up to five hundred men each and were located in sixteen communities around the Tar Heel state, including Whiteville, Roanoke Rapids, Williamston, and Hendersonville. There they were placed on compulsory work details and sent out to cut pulpwood, dig ditches, wash dishes, and pick apples. Their employers—farmers, loggers, and restaurant owners—knew of the camps, but otherwise their presence was relatively secret.

MAY 9

U.S. Coast Guard Cutter *Icarus* arriving at Charleston Navy Yard with prisoners of war from the U-boat, *U-352*, on May 10, 1942.

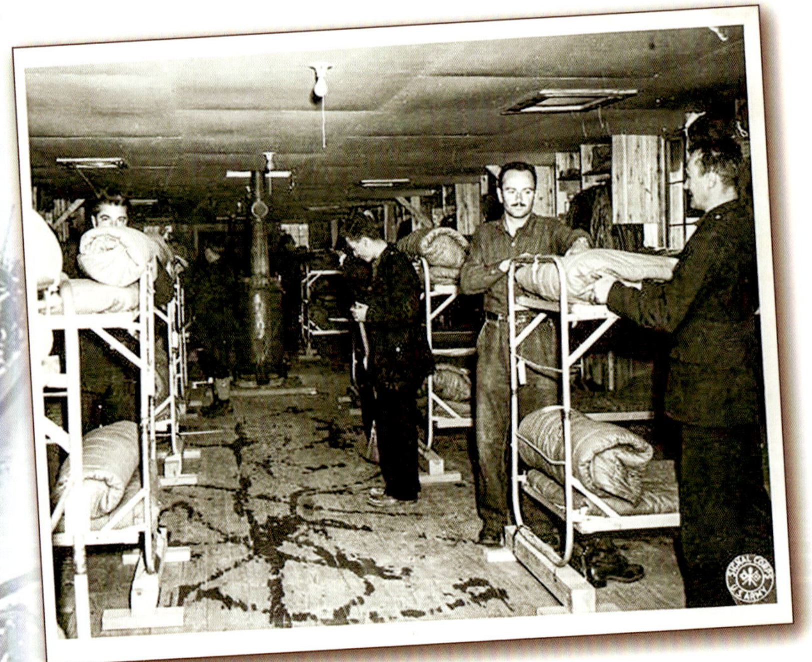

Italian POWs at Camp Butner during World War II.

1838 Military Order Beginning of the Trail of Tears

On May 10, 1838, Gen. Winfield Scott issued a proclamation to the eastern Cherokee, by order of Pres. Martin Van Buren, to evacuate their ancestral homeland. The subsequent military-enforced migration to what is now Oklahoma became known as the Trail of Tears.

The events leading to the migration were set in motion eight years earlier in 1830 with the passage of the Indian Removal Act by the U.S. Congress. The act gave the president authority to exchange unsettled land west of the Mississippi River for Indian land in existing states.

In 1835 an unauthorized group of Cherokee leaders entered into the Treaty of New Echota in Georgia with the federal government, giving all Cherokee territory in the South to the federal government in exchange for land in the west. Chief John Ross petitioned the Senate, with more than fifteen thousand Cherokee signatures, not to ratify the treaty. His effort was to no avail; the treaty was ratified in 1836.

Two years later in 1838, with the Cherokee still occupying their lands, General Scott issued the ultimatum to evacuate, backed by more than five thousand troops. His May 10 proclamation read in part:

"Cherokees! The President of the United States has sent me, with a powerful army, to cause you, in obedience to the Treaty of 1835, to join that part of your people who are already established in prosperity, on the other side of the Mississippi. . . . The full moon of May is already on the wane, and before another shall have passed away, every Cherokee man, woman and child . . . must be in motion to join their brethren in the far West."

Cherokee people were initially placed in internment camps in western North Carolina, where many died before the tragic exodus.

1865 James Jones of Raleigh, Valet of Jefferson Davis

On May 10, 1865, James H. Jones, valet to Confederate Pres. Jefferson Davis, was captured along with Davis near Irwinsville, Georgia, after warning him of the approaching federal troops.

Jones had stayed awake through the night to alert Davis and his party to any Union forces on the horizon. Upon being captured, Jones was taken with Davis and the rest of the group to prison at Fort Monroe near Norfolk, Virginia, though Jones was released less than a month later. Jones returned to Raleigh, where he was living before meeting the Davises. He became a pillar of the black community there, going on to attend two freedmen's conventions, serving as a city alderman and working for several railroad companies. He also helped found the state's first black military company.

Jones was native of either Warren or Wake County and was working as bricklayer and plasterer in Raleigh in 1862, when Davis's wife Varina fled to the city to escape approaching Union troops. Jones was recommended to Mrs. Davis, who hired him as a servant before she returned to Richmond later that year.

Jones called the former president of the Confederacy "my best friend" after learning of his death in 1889.

1876 Juliana Busbee and Jugtown

On May 10, 1876, Julia Adeline Royster was born in Raleigh.

After studying art and photography she changed her name to the more artistic Juliana and in 1910 married artist Jacques Busbee, also of Raleigh. Her dedication to art led her to become art department Chair of the Raleigh Women's Club in 1911 and chair of the state federation of women's clubs in 1915. In both roles and in her other philanthropic work, she devoted her efforts toward both promoting North Carolina's handicraft traditions and advocating social good.

In 1915, while judging a county fair in Lexington, Mrs. Busbee became enamored with a farmer's entry, apples displayed in a dirt dish. The discovery of native pottery led her and her husband to establish Jugtown Pottery in Seagrove in 1921. With her effervescent personality and savvy marketing skills, she tirelessly promoted Jugtown's pottery in a rustic atmosphere, fostering appreciation for and desire to own Jugtown's wares.

Today collectors still seek out Jugtown Ware, realizing the vision of artistic entrepreneurs Juliana and Jacques Busbee, devoted to preserving North Carolina's pottery traditions.

1949 The First Planetarium in the South

On May 10, 1949, the Morehead Planetarium opened on Franklin Street in Chapel Hill. It was the first planetarium in the South, the first on a university campus, and the sixth to be built nationwide.

The planetarium was primarily a gift of John Motley Morehead III, an 1891 graduate and founder of Union Carbide Corporation. Construction took seventeen months and cost three million dollars, making the building the most expensive in the state at the time. It was supervised by Harvard astronomer Harlow Shapely and designed by the architects who worked on the Jefferson Memorial.

From the late 1950s to the late 1970s, the planetarium became a hub of NASA's astronaut training program. The facility was used primarily to help astronauts learn to navigate by the stars in case computerized navigation systems failed. The program ended largely because of advances in the technology of those navigation systems.

In 1973 the planetarium added an observatory with a telescope managed by UNC-Chapel Hill's Department of Physics and Astronomy, and in 1984 it became one of the first planetariums in the nation to use computer animation in its shows.

MAY 10

Juliana Busbee by the sale cabin at Jugtown, 1937.

Dedication of Morehead Planetarium at the University of North Carolina at Chapel Hill.

1898 Worth Bagley of Raleigh, Casualty of the Spanish-American War

On May 11, 1898, in a battle at Cárdenas, Cuba, Ensign Worth Bagley of Raleigh became the first naval officer and first North Carolinian killed in the Spanish-American War. The sinking of the USS *Maine* on February 15, 1898 led to a declaration of war on Spain by the United States. North Carolina met Pres. William McKinley's call for troops by establishing three regiments.

Born in Raleigh in April 1874, Worth Bagley graduated from the United States Naval Academy in 1895. He achieved the rank of ensign in July 1897 and in November was appointed inspector of the new torpedo boat *Winslow*. When she went into commission the next month, Bagley became her executive officer. In April 1898 the *Winslow* was mobilized, with the fleet, for operations in Cuban waters.

On the morning of May 11, the ship went with two others to force open the entrance to the harbor of Cárdenas. The *Winslow* was fired upon by a Spanish gunboat, and a battle ensued. The ship was disabled and was hauled out of range of the Spanish guns. Just as the engagement ended, Bagley and four sailors were killed by a shell.

MAY 11

1970 Oxford Murder Sparked Violent Protests

On May 11, 1970, Henry Marrow, a twenty-three-year-old African American Vietnam veteran, was murdered in Oxford. Marrow was approaching Robert Teel's store to buy a Coca-Cola when he spoke to a young white woman. Teel, his son, and his step-son interpreted the exchange as offensive, so they chased Marrow from the store parking lot, beat, and fatally shot him.

Oxford had remained segregated, and violence against blacks in the town was met with a blind eye. Marrow's murder served to unite the African American community, already outraged by years of Jim Crow oppression.

Mobs rioted and destroyed several local businesses, including Teel's. After Marrow's funeral mourners marched to the town's Confederate monument and held a rally for civil rights. Marrow's cousin, Benjamin Chavis, organized a boycott of white-owned businesses. Despite the outrage an all-white jury returned a not-guilty verdict on all counts against the Teels in the trial for Marrow's murder.

Historian Timothy B. Tyson, who was a ten-year-old boy living in Oxford at the time of the murder, explored Marrow's death and its effects on the community in his award-winning 2004 book *Blood Done Sign My Name*.

A group of deputized citizens awaiting the "not guilty" verdict in August of 1970.

1842 St. Mary's School True to Its Nineteenth Century Roots

On May 12, 1842, the first classes got underway at Saint Mary's School in Raleigh.

Established through the vision and fundraising efforts of Episcopalian minister Aldert Smedes and his wife Sarah, the school for women was converted from a similar institution for young men built in 1831. Smedes and his wife greeted the new students at the door, and from then on the couple acted more like family than faculty to the students.

Albert Smedes personally interviewed each student for admission, and though most students came from prosperous families throughout North and South Carolina, Smedes would grant scholarships to girls whose families were unable to provide tuition. He understood that the education of young women, as well as the confidence and skills it confers, was essential for coming generations.

The school offered a junior college program until 1997 but shuttered that program to focus on high school and college preparatory classes, which it continues to offer.

The school's entire twenty-three-acre campus is listed on the National Register of Historic Places, and its iconic Gothic Revival style campus chapel, designed by architect Richard Upjohn in 1857, continues to be a Raleigh landmark to this day.

1876 State's First Jewish House of Worship, Temple of Israel

On May 12, 1876, North Carolina's first Jewish synagogue, the Temple of Israel, was dedicated in Wilmington. The Jews of Wilmington were part of the second wave of immigrants who arrived in the United States from Germany, and they worked primarily as artisans, merchants, and storekeepers. In 1855 Jews set aside a Hebrew section of Oakdale Cemetery in the city. As the community grew in the mid-1800s, Jews in the area began to need a house of worship.

The initial plans for a synagogue were interrupted by the Civil War. About forty families came together in 1872 to set plans for the church. Soon afterwards they affiliated with the Union of American Hebrew Congregations. A local chapter of B'nai B'rith, a Jewish service organization, was founded in 1874. Samuel Sloan of Philadelphia was retained as the synagogue's architect, and plans were developed for a distinctive building in the Moorish Revival style. Construction began in 1875 and was completed the next year.

Rabbi Samuel Mendelsohn presided over the dedication in 1876. He went on to lead the Temple of Israel congregation until 1922. Eric Meyers, director of Duke University's Center for Judaic Studies, said of the synagogue, "It represents one of the high points of Southern Jewish culture."

1954 Former Governor Clyde Hoey Died at His U.S. Senate Desk, 1954

On May 12, 1954, Clyde Hoey died in his office in the U.S. Capitol.

A native of Shelby, Hoey married Bess Gardner, sister of Gov. O. Max Gardner, and is counted as part of the "Shelby Dynasty," which dominated state government for two decades. Hoey served as governor from 1937 until 1941. Until his bid for governor, he concentrated on his law practice and worked as a lobbyist.

Like his predecessors, the conservative Hoey gave priority to a balanced state budget and exhibited little enthusiasm for the New Deal, which by the late 1930s was no longer a major political force in North Carolina.

In 1944 Hoey defeated former governor Cameron Morrison in a race for the U.S. Senate. His election secured his place in history as only the second North Carolinian to serve as governor, in both houses of the state legislature, and in both houses of Congress.

Today Hoey is remembered for his oratory, courtly manner, long white hair, and distinctive style of dress, which included a swallow-tail coat, striped pants, a wing collar, high-topped shoes, and a flower in his lapel.

Gov. Clyde Hoey with the governor's car in front of the mansion, 1937.

Temple of Israel in Wilmington.

MAY 13

1830 Birthday of Zeb Vance—the State's Champion

On May 13, 1830, Zebulon Baird Vance was born in the Reems Creek area of Buncombe County. Raised in Asheville, Vance studied at the University of North Carolina. After setting up a law practice in Asheville, he launched his political career. Known for his personality and oratorical skills, Vance served as a state senator, U.S. congressman, governor, and U.S. senator.

Initially an opponent of secession, Vance cast his lot with his state and region after Pres. Abraham Lincoln's call to arms. Vance raised his own company and was later elected colonel of the Twenty-Sixth Regiment.

Though the war raged on, politics was never far from Vance's mind. The Conservative Party selected the popular colonel as its candidate for governor in 1862. The election resulted in an overwhelming victory for Vance.

On his birthday in 1865, Vance was arrested in Statesville by Federal cavalry as he attempted to flee the approaching Union army. He was imprisoned in Washington, D.C. for two months. No charges were ever brought, and he was eventually released.

On May 13, 1961, Vance's 131st birthday, the Gov. Zebulon B. Vance Birthplace State Historic Site in Weaverville was dedicated and opened to the public.

Painting of Zebulon Vance, 1877–1879.

1846 The Mexican War Erupts, 1846

On May 13, 1846, United States president and North Carolina native James K. Polk signed a declaration of war on Mexico.

At the time of the 1844 election, many Americans advocated an expansionist vision of the nation's future, popularly known as "Manifest Destiny." Complicating the issue was a growing dispute over the possible expansion of slavery into any territories acquired by the United States.

Controversy centered on the possible annexation of the Republic of Texas, which had revolted against Mexico in 1836. As Texas was a slaveholding republic, its potential incorporation was a political flashpoint. Polk ran on a platform advocating annexation of the Lone Star State.

Upon taking office in March 1845, Polk signed an annexation treaty with Texas. Tensions simmering between the U.S. and Mexico over the Texas boundary came to head in April 1846, when fighting erupted between Mexican and U.S. forces in the disputed zone. The resulting Mexican-American war led to the U.S. conquest of all Mexican territory north of the Rio Grande. The conflict also began a series of increasingly heated controversies over whether that territory would become slave or free, culminating in the Civil War.

1913 Winston and Salem Merged, 1913

On May 13, 1913, the town of Salem and the city of Winston merged to form the new city of Winston-Salem through the election of a new unified city board.

The two municipalities that would eventually become Winston-Salem came from strikingly different backgrounds. Salem traced its lineage back to 1753, when it was established by Moravian Bishop August Spangenberg. Winston, named for Joseph Winston, was created in 1849 as the county seat for newly formed Forsyth County.

In 1879 the two towns attempted to unite through legislation passed by the General Assembly, but the use of "Salem" as the city's new name led the citizens of Winston to withdraw their support in the referendum to authorize the merger. In the years following this first attempt at unification, the local post office was renamed "Winston-Salem" to reflect the closeness of the two communities.

In 1913 a second effort was made to unite the two communities through legislation, and another referendum was taken to the voters of both municipalities. This second attempt proved successful, and Winston-Salem was formed that May.

1976 It's a Shell of a Building

On May 13, 1976, the iconic Shell Service Station on East Sprague Street in Winston-Salem was added to the National Register of Historic Places.

Built by R.H. Burton in 1930, the station was one of eight constructed around Winston-Salem that year in an effort by the Shell Company and its local affiliate, Quality Oil, to boost marketing in North Carolina. The Sprague Street station is the only one of those eight still in existence.

The building's design was modeled on the logo of Royal Dutch Shell Oil at the time, and the structure was built by first boxing in the interior office, then adding a wire frame in a shell shape around it. Concrete was then poured on the wire like stucco, giving the building its distinctive shape. The station reflects the literalism of the era's advertising, and it is a great example of the Pop architecture that became popular around the time.

After the structure was used as a lawn mower repair shop and had fallen into disrepair, Preservation North Carolina raised funds to bring the landmark back to its original condition in the late 1970s.

Shell Station in Winston Salem.

1873 North Carolina Press Association Founded, 1873

On May 14, 1873, a group of male journalists representing newspapers across North Carolina met in the Goldsboro courthouse and established the North Carolina Press Association "for mutual benefit and protection."

The group elected Joseph A. Engelhard, editor of the *Wilmington Journal* and chief instigator of the new organization, its first president. One of the NCPA's early initiatives was to impose regulations on advertising, as the claims of some Victorian-era patent medicine companies had become a point of contention among newspaper professionals.

Throughout its history, NCPA has striven to protect the public's right to know by pushing for open government and by defending First Amendment freedoms. The association has also promoted the business interests of Tar Heel newspapers, recognized achievement in the industry through awards and scholarships, and effectively supported public improvement projects such as better roads and schools.

For decades upon decades, NCPA's members have convened annually to discuss important issues facing the press, including privacy, access to government meetings, court photography, political advertising, and libel laws.

Today the organization's members include daily and community newspapers, as well as special-interest and online news publications, and companies that provide equipment, supplies, growth opportunities, and materials to the newspaper industry.

1889 Mount Airy, "Granite City"

On May 14, 1889, the North Carolina Granite Company was founded in Surry County by Thomas Woodroffe. It has been in continuous operation since. Now known as the North Carolina Granite Corporation, it operates the world's largest open-faced granite quarry.

The site has produced granite for many high-rise buildings and even for the Singapore subway system. Its granite has been used to create several notable structures, including the Fort Knox Bullion Depository in Kentucky, the Wright Brothers Monument at Kitty Hawk, the Centennial Olympic Plaza in Atlanta, and the World War II Memorial in Washington, D.C.

The granite is also popular for curbing, especially in northern states that use salt in winter, since salt breaks down concrete curbs in short order. Other uses for the product include tombstones and mausoleums. Waste granite, the small bits that are left over from extraction and from fabrication, is crushed for road construction and landscape use.

Located on the Ararat River near Mt. Airy, the active quarry covers more than two hundred acres and is estimated to have enough granite to continue extraction at the current rate for five hundred more years. The quarry is the source of Mt. Airy's "Granite City" nickname.

1932 Inaugural Concert for the North Carolina Symphony, 1932

On May 14, 1932, the North Carolina Symphony played its first concert at Hill Hall on the campus of UNC. The concert included music by Wagner, Beethoven, Tchaikovsky, and others, and featured forty-eight musicians from around the state under the direction of conductor Lamar Stringfield. The symphony had its origins earlier that year as a work relief project of Franklin D. Roosevelt's New Deal and became the first symphony orchestra to receive state aid with the passage of what became known as the "Horn Tootin' Bill" in 1943.

Today the North Carolina Symphony is a first-class, professional orchestra with sixty-five members led by Music Director Grant Llewellyn, based at Meymandi Concert Hall in downtown Raleigh. In addition to classical series in Raleigh, Chapel Hill, Fayetteville, New Bern, Southern Pines, and Wilmington, it also features a Pops Series, Young People's Concerts, and the annual Summerfest outdoor concert series at Cary's Booth Amphitheatre.

Always the "people's orchestra," the symphony has an especially strong legacy of music education, with more than three million school children reached since it began its children's concerts series in 1945. Each year the symphony puts on more than fifty educational programs in nearly as many communities across the state.

The North Carolina Symphony performing in a school gymnasium as part of their educational outreach.

1886 Blockade Runner John N. Maffitt

On May 15, 1886, John Newland Maffitt, captain of several Confederate blockade runners, died.

Born at sea in 1819, Maffitt split his formative years between northern schools and his uncle's home near Fayetteville. At age thirteen Maffitt was commissioned a midshipman in the United States Navy and spent fifteen years with the U. S. Coast Survey, experience that proved invaluable during his time as a blockade runner.

Following the bombardment of Fort Sumter in April 1861, Maffitt resigned his commission in the Navy and received a commission as a lieutenant in the Confederate States Navy. After a two-month stint in command of blockade running operations out of Nassau, Maffitt assumed command of the CSS *Florida* and was promoted to the rank of commander. At the helm of the *Florida*, Maffitt shifted his attention to raiding merchant vessels during an eight-month cruise, capturing twenty-three ships.

Maffitt is credited with making the Confederacy's last run of the blockade, which took place after Gen. Robert E. Lee's surrender. Obeying final orders from the Confederate government, Maffitt delivered the *Owl* to agents in England, where he remained until 1868.

With his career at sea largely over, Maffitt retired to a farm near Wrightsville Beach.

MAY 15

1918 St. Augustine's Bishop Delany and His Carolinas-Wide Charge

On May 15, 1918, Henry Beard Delany became the first black Episcopal bishop in North Carolina and only the second in the United States. A native Georgian who grew up in Florida, Delany came to North Carolina in 1881, when he enrolled at St. Augustine's Normal School (now St. Augustine's University). He remained at the school teaching courses, overseeing facility construction, serving as vice principal, and after he was ordained an Episcopal priest, as the school chaplain.

Delany was elected bishop "in charge of Negro work" and served in that capacity broadly across North and South Carolina. His work is credited with improvement in the quality of life among African Americans in the South. At his death he was memorialized as having risen "to a position of eminence in which he had won not only the esteem of his white colleagues throughout the country but also their love."

Two of Delany's daughters, Sarah and Elizabeth, became famous in the 1990s for their book *Having Our Say: The Delany Sisters' First 100 Years*. The book was later adapted into a play and film.

Henry Beard Delany seated outside St. Augustine's University Chapel, Raleigh.

1950 Raleigh Broadcaster Tangled with Former First Lady

On May 15, 1950, W. E. Debnam published *Weep No More, My Lady*, his response to former First Lady Eleanor Roosevelt's newspaper column earlier that year.

In her nationally-distributed "This Day" column, Mrs. Roosevelt, the liberal stalwart and defender of her husband's legacy, wrote concerning her recent visit to North Carolina that she was "not so sure that there are not signs of poverty and unhappiness that will gradually have to disappear if that part of the nation is going to prosper."

Debnam, a Raleigh native, had spent a lifetime in journalism, including several years at the *Standard-Laconic*, his family's weekly in Snow Hill. During World War II he covered the war in the Pacific for Raleigh radio station WPTF, tagging each broadcast with "This is Debnam."

After the war he stepped into his news commentary role. First on the radio and then in a widely-circulated sixty-page softcover book, he took Mrs. Roosevelt to task. He attributed the South's weak economy to Sherman's destructive campaign during the Civil War and to the "tragic era" of Reconstruction. Race relations, Debnam contended, were better in the South than in northern cities.

Debnam's book reached a ready audience, selling a half-million copies at fifty cents each.

1771 Gov. Tryon Takes on the Regulators at Alamance

On May 16, 1771, the Battle of Alamance was fought. The two opposing forces were colonial militia, under the command of Gov. William Tryon, and a band of frontier citizens known as Regulators, who raised arms against corrupt practices in local government.

Tryon's force of eleven hundred men marched into Regulator country to subdue the uprisings. About two thousand Regulators, armed with old muskets and makeshift weapons, organized near Tryon's camp. Messages were exchanged, with the governor demanding immediate and complete surrender of the Regulators and the Regulators petitioning the governor for reforms.

Nothing came of the negotiations, and on the morning of May 16, Tryon ordered his forces to march. Tryon sent messages offering surrender terms while his militia marched slowly forward, but the Regulators rejected them all. The governor's artillery began the engagement, followed by concentrated musket fire from the militia. The Regulators prevailed for a while before retreating into the woods. Eventually Tryon ordered a charge, which drove the Regulators from their positions.

Nine Regulators were killed, more than two hundred wounded and between twenty and thirty taken prisoner. Nine of Tryon's men were killed, and another sixty-one were wounded. Though the Battle of Alamance quieted the Regulators, the effects of their calls for reform eventually reverberated.

1804 Women's Education in North Carolina Began at Salem

On May 16, 1804, Salem Academy opened the doors of its new dormitory, South Hall, to students and officially transitioned from a day school to a boarding school.

The Moravians had established the all-girls' school in 1772 soon after the first women trekked five hundred miles from Bethlehem, Pennsylvania to join the community at Salem. One of their number, Elisabeth Oesterlein, became the first teacher at the school. The unmarried women of Salem, known as "single sisters," governed the academy during this early period.

The Moravians believed women and other disenfranchised groups of the time deserved an education. As early as 1785, records indicate the inclusion of African-American students, and in the 1820s the daughter of a Cherokee chief attended the school.

By the late nineteenth century Salem Academy began awarding college degrees. Eventually the academy and the college split into two separate institutions, although they still share the same campus.

Salem Academy and College both remain all-female, though some continuing education programs for men over age twenty-three are offered. The American Council on Education recognizes Salem College as the oldest such institution strictly for women in the United States.

1961 Corbitt, Major Manufacturer of Trucks, Based in Henderson

On May 16, 1961, Richard Corbitt, a well-known truck builder, died.

Corbitt began in business as a tobacco merchant in the 1890s before creating the Corbitt Buggy Company in 1899. Initially building horse-drawn buggies to haul agricultural products, Corbitt's company began to produce passenger cars and trucks, and later buses and military vehicles.

The company adopted assembly-line production, and that, combined with successful marketing efforts, transformed the small Henderson operation into the leader in North Carolina's auto industry. Though the Corbitt Company made the state's first commercially produced automobile, a motorized buggy, in 1907, the most successful products it offered were trucks. It built the first of those in 1909.

Trucks continued to be the bestselling vehicles produced by Corbitt, thanks in large part to sizable contracts with the state Highway Department and U.S. military. The company is also notable for furnishing the state's first motorized school bus, which it delivered to the Pamlico County school system in 1917.

Corbitt's cars and trucks sold well in the South, but the company was unable to keep pace with the mass-production operations in Detroit. When Corbitt retired in 1952, the company lost its momentum and ceased production soon after.

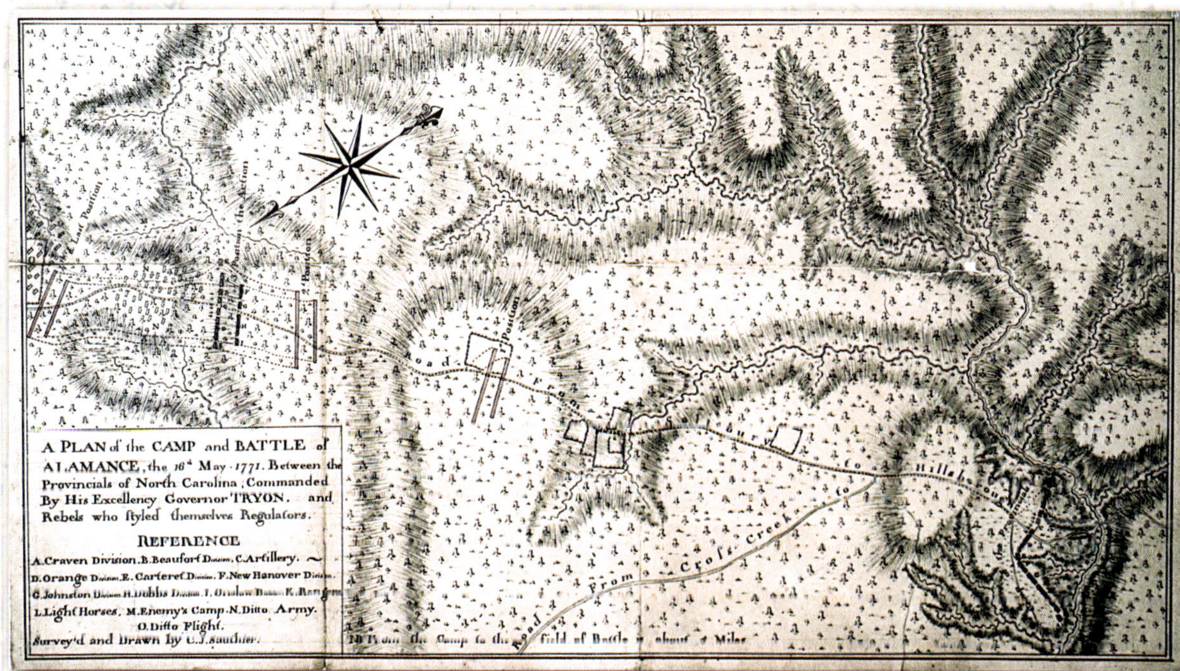

A Plan of the Camp and Battle of Alamance, the 16th May 1771. Between the Provincials of North Carolina, Commanded by His Excellency Governor Tryon and Rebels who styled themselves Regulators.

1771 Regulator James Few Hanged

On May 17, 1771, James Few was hanged.

Few, a carpenter from Orange County, was part of the Regulator Movement, a colonial rebellion that predated the American Revolution. Fed up with corrupt officials, the Regulators took on royal Gov. William Tryon and his forces at the Battle of Alamance, where they were defeated. Few was taken prisoner after the battle, and Tryon had him executed without a trial.

Exactly why he was executed is a matter of debate. Tryon claimed Few was hanged to satisfy his troops' thirst for Regulator blood after the battle, though others claim that corrupt Hillsborough official Edmund Fanning demanded Few's death for his role in destroying Fanning's house the previous year. Still others say Few was driven mad by Fanning's transgressions with Few's fiancé.

Whatever the reason, after the battle Tryon's forces destroyed the Few family farm. The family moved to Georgia, where James's brother, William Few Jr., became a member of the Continental Congress, a U.S. senator, and a judge.

After the Battle of Alamance, the Regulator movement largely dissipated, with most of its leaders either going into hiding or moving away.

MAY 17

1906 Textile Executive Stuart Cramer and Air Conditioning

On May 17, 1906, North Carolinian Stuart Cramer coined the term "air conditioning."

Though not particularly skilled as a textile executive, Cramer contributed significantly to the cotton mill industry by using his engineering and invention skills. In 1895 he established his textile business and over the next ten years designed and equipped more than 150 (or roughly a third of all) cotton mills in the South. Cramer invested his profits back into his own mills, especially those in the community, Cramerton, that came to bear his name.

Though he got his start in cotton, Cramer is best known for the role he played in the development of air conditioning. The holder of more than sixty patents, he pioneered humidity control and ventilating equipment for cotton mills and installed scores of such systems in plants across the South. In a paper read before an American Cotton Manufacturers Association convention, Cramer was the first to use the term "air conditioning."

Though credit for the invention of air conditioning does not belong to one person, the biographer of industry giant W. H. Carrier attributes eleven technological advances and "outstanding work which later had a large part in the air conditioning industry" to Cramer.

1956 Olympic Medalist Leonard No Match for Camacho

On May 17, 1956, Olympic gold medalist and professional boxing champion Charles Ray "Sugar Ray" Leonard was born in Wilmington.

Leonard spent the majority of his formative years in the suburbs of Washington, D.C., where, as a teenager, he discovered his love of boxing. At age twenty he dominated opponents in the 1976 Olympics in Montreal and took home a gold medal in the sport. Though he had originally planned to retire following the Olympics and go to college, his father's mounting medical bills and the birth of his son persuaded Leonard to pursue boxing professionally.

In February 1977 Leonard fought the first of forty professional bouts, defeating Luis "The Bull" Vega and claiming a forty thousand dollar prize. He went on to claim world titles in five different weight classes.

Despite his retirement in 1991, Leonard returned to the sport at age forty to fight Hector "Macho" Camacho. The match was an embarrassing loss for Leonard and proved to be his last. Nevertheless, he finished his career with a record of thirty-six wins, three losses, and one draw. Twenty-five of his wins were knock-outs.

Sugar Ray Leonard at the Sheraton Resort in Palm Beach Gardens, Florida, May, 1989. Leonard was training in an outdoor tent for his upcoming fight with Tommy "Hit Man" Hearns.

1795 Joseph McDowell, Not to Be Confused with Joseph McDowell

On May 18, 1795, Revolutionary War veteran Joseph McDowell died in Burke County at age thirty-eight.

The only son of "Hunting John" McDowell, a pioneer of Scotch-Irish descent who arrived in western North Carolina in the mid-1700s, Joseph was born on the family plantation, Pleasant Gardens, in what was then Burke County.

Because McDowell had a cousin of the same name, he was referred to as "Pleasant Gardens Joe" so as not to be confused with "Quaker Meadows Joe." During the American Revolution both men enlisted in a military unit under the command of their kinsman Charles McDowell and fought at the Battle of Kings Mountain.

There are discrepancies as to which Joseph led the troops at Kings Mountain, but it is most likely that Maj. Joseph McDowell (Pleasant Gardens) was under the command of Col. Joseph McDowell (Quaker Meadows).

Following the war McDowell practiced law and served in the state legislature, as a delegate to two Constitutional Conventions, and as an early member of the Board of Trustees of the University of North Carolina.

He married Mary Moffett, and they had three children, John, James, and Annie. McDowell County is named in his honor.

1947 North Wilkesboro and the Roots of NASCAR

On May 18, 1947, the North Wilkesboro Speedway opened its doors to a crowd of more than ten thousand spectators, who watched Fonty Flock win the first official race held there. The 5/8-mile oval dirt track was well-known for challenging the best of drivers.

Stock car racing fans and scholars have long acknowledged that the roots of the National Association for Stock Car Auto Racing (NASCAR) are closely tied to the tradition of illegal moonshine production. Races between "runners" evolved into spectator events. The North Wilkesboro Speedway was among the first tracks recognized by NASCAR during its inaugural year of 1949. NASCAR's first finale took place there, with the crowning of the first points champion, Robert "Red" Byron, in October 1949.

The speedway often has been called "The House that Junior Built," in tribute to racing legend Junior Johnson, who began his career there at age sixteen. Johnson earned four of his fifty career NASCAR victories there and continued his success on the track as a team owner.

The last NASCAR race at North Wilkesboro, won by Jeff Gordon, was held on September 29, 1996, with more than sixty thousand fans in attendance.

1948 Episcopal Bishop of Alaska Installed in Raleigh, 1948

On May 18, 1948, William J. Gordon Jr. was consecrated Episcopal bishop of Alaska. At the time he was, at thirty years old, the youngest priest in the United States ever elevated to such a post. The ceremony at the Church of the Good Shepherd was only the third consecration to take place in Raleigh.

Since 1943 the native of Rockingham County had served as a missionary in Point Hope, Alaska. In 1949 Gordon earned his pilot's license and became known as the "Flying Bishop of Alaska." Before he got a plane, Gordon had traveled about six thousand miles by dogsled to minister to the Arctic villages.

His journey to visit all of the churches in his diocese was thirty-five hundred miles long and took three months to complete by boat. Once he began flying to visit his churches, he logged over a million miles in the small plane purchased for him with money raised by the women of the Episcopal Church.

The Bishop strongly believed in the rights of Alaskan native people and fought for the development of native clergy. He is buried in Point Hope, Alaska, where he first ministered, in a grave marked with whale jawbones, a high honor in the Arctic.

MAY 18

Pro All Stars Series (PASS) South events, 2011.

Aerial photo of North Wilkesboro Speedway, 2017

MAY 19

1865 Rough Justice in the Backcountry, 1865

On May 19, 1865, Confederate vigilantes led by Capt. R. M. Sharpe began the siege of Fort Hamby in Wilkes County.

A simple log house that between eighteen and thirty Union army deserters called home, the fort took its name from its previous occupants, a group of "disreputable" women. The men used it as a staging point to plunder homes in Wilkes, Watauga, Caldwell, and Alexander Counties and to murder people who had been left defenseless by the war. Led by a man with the surname Wade, the band of deserters benefited from the lack of law and order in the region that followed Lee's surrender in April 1865.

After a twenty-two-man group of former Confederate soldiers unsuccessfully tried to capture Wade and his associates, Sharpe led two companies of local men to try to eliminate the group. Shots were fired back and forth all day and into the night. Only after two men set fire to the house did Wade and his men finally ask to surrender. Sharpe's reply was "We will shoot you."

Wade managed to escape, but four of his men were captured, tied to a stake, and executed. Inside the house the victors found a wealth of stolen goods. Once the valuables had been removed, the house was burned to the ground.

1955 Elvis Upstages, Excites in Raleigh

On May 19, 1955, Hank Snow's All Star Jamboree tour, featuring a new young talent named Elvis Presley, ended at Memorial Auditorium in Raleigh. It marked the beginning of the end of the touring relationship between the headliner, Faron Young, and featured player Presley.

Before intermission each show included a new talent portion in which Presley took the stage, with the headliners performing after intermission. Young later recounted that each night of the tour Elvis got bigger and wilder crowds. As the tour progressed, fans began to shout for more of Elvis during the other performances, and he was called back for encore after encore. In the early days of the tour. Col. Tom Parker, as booking agent, actually paid teenagers five dollars apiece to scream for Presley and sent the publicity photographs to the newspapers in the next cities on the tour.

Other tour performers later recalled how much they discounted Presley and his odd onstage behavior. Most country singers thought that he was a fad who would quickly fade, but Presley soon found himself the headliner, and few established stars would agree to perform with him on a tour.

Elvis Presley promoting Jailhouse Rock, 1957.

2008 Texas Oilman Enriched the State, the University

On May 19, 2008, Walter Royal Davis of Midland, Texas; Manteo; and Chapel Hill died. The oil magnate turned philanthropist, a native of Elizabeth City, never attended a college class in his life but donated generously to North Carolina schools, other favorite causes, and those in need of help.

As a young man Davis engaged in the rough-and-tumble of the oil business and served a ninety-day federal prison sentence in 1948 for failure to file income taxes. By 1952 he had launched a highly successful trucking operation to haul crude oil from wells to refineries. He parlayed those profits into real estate and, combined with his winnings at the blackjack and gin rummy tables, became fantastically wealthy. Over the course of his life, he was married six times to four different women.

Thoroughly Texan and a friend of both Presidents Bush, Davis did not forget the Tar Heel State. He retired to North Carolina and formed strong political and personal friendships, notably with legislator Marc Basnight.

Louisburg College, Methodist University, and churches and schools in Elizabeth City benefited from his gifts. As a trustee of UNC-Chapel Hill, he guided thirty-two million dollars in state proceeds from utility sales to the construction of a library, completed in 1984, that bears his name.

1861 Secession Vote and Realigned Allegiance

On May 20, 1861, North Carolina delegates unanimously voted to approve an Ordinance of Secession from the United States. Only three months earlier, in February, North Carolinians by popular vote refused to call a convention to consider a secession ordinance. The vote in May made North Carolina's action the last legislative vote to secede.

Between February and May much happened that shaped the delegates' decision. After South Carolina passed a secession ordinance in December 1860, one attempt after another to stem the secession crisis failed. North Carolinians adopted a "watch and wait" attitude after the election of Pres. Abraham Lincoln.

The April 12 bombardment of Fort Sumter by the budding Confederate government prompted Lincoln to call for troops to put down the rebellion. Deeming such a call an illegal use of Federal power, Gov. John Ellis replied that Lincoln would get no aid from North Carolina.

Ellis called for a convention. The delegates debated the wording of the resolution but not the outcome. Divided sentiments expressed earlier were not voiced, and the vote to pass the resolution became unanimous. Shortly thereafter the state aligned with the Confederacy.

1929 Highway Patrol Outfitted in Morehead City

On May 20, 1929, the first candidates for the North Carolina State Highway Patrol reported to Camp Glenn in Morehead City.

Charles D. Farmer, superintendent of equipment for the State Highway Commission, was selected to serve as captain and commanding officer. Nine lieutenants, one for each of the state's highway division districts, were appointed to assist in the administration of the patrol. The plan was to hire twenty-seven patrolmen, three for each district. A total of sixty-seven applicants were selected to attend the first highway patrol training school.

The courses for the first class of cadets included motor laws, pistol marksmanship, and geography of North Carolina. After six weeks the students with the best records were appointed to the Highway Patrol. The novice patrolmen were issued uniforms and motorcycles. The nine lieutenants received Ford coupes, and Charles Farmer was given a Buick. The entire group embarked on a statewide tour in order to engender support for and confidence in the new program. The 1,028-mile tour took the men from Beaufort to Asheville and back to Raleigh, with many stops along the way.

Concluding at the State Capitol, all thirty-seven members of the force took their oaths of office and reported for duty.

1956 Tweetsie's Track to Blowing Rock

On May 20, 1956, Gov. Luther Hodges proclaimed "Tweetsie Homecoming Day" to celebrate the return of the East Tennessee & Western North Carolina Railroad's No. 12 steam locomotive to North Carolina for refurbishing.

Nicknamed "Tweetsie" because of its high-pitched whistle, the narrow-gauge, coal-fired "ten-wheeler" hauled freight and passengers between Johnson City, Tennessee and Boone, North Carolina from 1919 to 1940, when floods washed away part of its tracks.

In 1952 railroad enthusiasts bought Tweetsie to operate the Shenandoah Central Railroad in Harrisonburg, Virginia. After Hurricane Hazel's destruction there in 1954, they optioned the locomotive to Hollywood actor Gene Autry. Unable to transport the sixty-ton engine to California, Autry sold it for one dollar to Blowing Rock developer Grover Robbins Jr. in 1956. That's when Robbins brought Tweetsie back to North Carolina for refurbishing in the Carolina & Northwestern Railway's repair shop in Hickory.

Just over a year later, with large crowds on hand, the locomotive was loaded onto a flatbed truck for the trip up the mountain to Blowing Rock, where it was installed as the main attraction of the new Tweetsie Railroad Theme Park. Now listed on the National Register of Historic Places, Tweetsie still operates regularly, offering family fun for new generations.

Gov. Luther Hodges at the "Tweetsie Homecoming Day," May 20, 1956.

MAY 21

1870 Murder in Yanceyville Sparks "War"

On May 21, 1870, J. W. Stephens, a state senator and Freedman's Bureau agent, was murdered by Ku Klux Klansmen in the basement of the Caswell County Courthouse in Yanceyville.

On that Saturday there was a political rally near the courthouse. One of the people in attendance was J.W. "Chicken' Stephens," despised by the local Ku Klux Klan chapter for his progressive attitudes towards blacks. Gov. William W. Holden had tasked Stephens with investigating suspected Klan members, the same Klan members who had marked Stephens for death. Lured into the basement of the courthouse, Stephens was ambushed and stabbed; his body was left on a woodpile.

The murder, along with that of black town commissioner Wyatt Outlaw in Graham earlier that year, led Governor Holden to declare martial law in Alamance and Caswell Counties. Holden, believing the area to be in a state of insurrection, called up the militia to occupy the area and settle the racial violence. The episode, which has become known as the Kirk-Holden War, led to Holden's impeachment and removal from office in 1871.

1940 Hiwassee Dam, Five Years in the Making

On May 21, 1940, the Hiwassee Dam in Cherokee County generated power for the first time. The dam was built by the Tennessee Valley Authority and was one of the largest construction projects in the state at that time.

The TVA was one facet of the sprawling New Deal plan created by Pres. Franklin D. Roosevelt, and its goal was to bring electricity, economic development, and flood control to the Southern Appalachian region. To achieve those aims, it recommended building dams and reservoirs along the Tennessee River and its main tributaries. The Hiwassee and Fontana Dams were built in western North Carolina as part of that effort.

Work on the Hiwassee project began in July 1936, and it took a crew of sixteen hundred men nearly four years to complete. The building of the dam and reservoir led to the creation of Hiwassee Lake, which is still used today for recreation.

At the time of construction, the overspill dam was the nation's tallest at 307 feet. The final cost of construction came in at 16.8 million dollars, which would be about 282 million dollars if built today.

1957 Here's to the Land of the Longleaf Pine

On May 21, 1957, the General Assembly adopted an official state toast.

The toast was first read by the Rev. Walter W. Moore in May 1904 in Richmond, Virginia at a banquet hosted by the North Carolina Society of Richmond. Moore's toast came from "The Old North State," a poem, written by Leonora Monteiro Martin, which was reportedly commissioned for the event. Martin, a writer who had lived in North Carolina, resided in Richmond with her husband, Harry Culver-Martin, at the time.

Beginning in May 1904 lines from the poem appeared in newspapers in accounts of tributes and toasts given at other occasions. The poem became almost instantly ubiquitous in association with patriotic and nostalgic feelings for the state, and within a few years it appeared on postcards and in anthologies.

In the 1930s Mary Burke Kerr, a music teacher in Sampson County, composed music for Martin's poem, and in 1933 the General Assembly officially recognized Kerr's composition with a resolution and requested that WPTF, a Raleigh radio station, begin to play a recording to acquaint North Carolinians with it.

From that point generations of North Carolina school children learned the song before the General Assembly officially recognized the combined creations of Martin and Kerr as the state toast in 1957.

2007 Chimney Rock Acquired by the State, 2007

On May 21, 2007, the state of North Carolina purchased Chimney Rock Park in western Rutherford County from the Morse family, which had owned and operated the tourist attraction for more than a century.

Two months later the General Assembly merged the thousand-acre park with neighboring Hickory Nut Gorge State Park and renamed the entire 5,942-acre tract Chimney Rock State Park. The new state park was named after the 315-foot granite spire that overlooks Lake Lure and offers spectacular views of the fourteen-mile gorge carved by the Rocky Broad River.

In 1902 Dr. Lucius B. Morse, a Missouri physician diagnosed with tuberculosis and looking for a healthier climate, bought sixty-four acres on Chimney Rock Mountain, including the "Chimney" and cliffs, from Jerome B. "Rome" Freeman. Freeman already had built a stairway to the mountaintop and opened it to the public in 1885.

Over the years the Morse family constructed a 258-foot elevator shaft inside the mountain, opened a gift shop and snack bar at the top, and developed a nature center and hiking trails, all while expanding the park's size.

Chimney Rock in the 1940s.

North Carolinians Readied for Spanish-American War, 1898

1898

On May 22, 1898, the First North Carolina Regiment was dispatched to Camp Cuba Libre in Jacksonville, Florida for service in the Spanish-American War.

The regiment was raised earlier that month, and the troops trained at Camp Bryan Grimes in Raleigh. The camp was established near the State Fairgrounds after the Raleigh Chamber of Commerce donated land for it along Hillsborough Street, then on the western outskirts of the city. The camp consisted of nearly three hundred tents, laid out in rows. Eventually, as the camp took in more volunteers, Camp Dan Russell was established on the fairgrounds to accommodate the Second Regiment.

After arriving in Florida, the troops stayed there throughout the war, which ended in August 1898, and were subjected to poor conditions, mass desertions, and lack of supplies. The only service abroad the unit would see was four months of a guard duty in Cuba between December 1898 and March 1899.

North Carolina's other two regiments during the war were plagued by outbreaks of disease and dismal conditions. They were stationed in several locations around the southern U.S. but did not go to Cuba.

National Park Status for Great Smoky Mountains, 1926

1926

On May 22, 1926, Pres. Calvin Coolidge signed the bill that established the Great Smoky Mountains National Park. The process had been difficult, taking many years and much negotiation before the park became one of the fifty-nine in the national system.

The idea to create a park in the mountains of North Carolina and Tennessee started in the late 1890s. Initially there was a debate over whether to make the public land preserve in this area a national park or a national forest. The main difference is that in a national forest, timbering of the land is permissible, while in a national park, scenery and resources are protected.

Once Coolidge signed the bill establishing the park, supporters had to find the funds to purchase an initial 150 thousand acres before the Department of the Interior would assume responsibility. By 1928 ten million dollars had been raised by individuals, the North Carolina and Tennessee legislatures, private groups, and a campaign by school children. Thousands of small farms and homesteads as well as large timber corporations had to be bought out.

The park was dedicated in 1940, and today it is the nation's most visited park.

Jennette's Pier: A Nags Head Institution

1939

On May 22, 1939, work began on Jennette's Ocean Pier in Nags Head, the first fishing pier on the Outer Banks.

The 750-foot wooden structure was built by Elizabeth City's Warren Jennette Sr., who purchased the former site of Camp Weaver, a WPA transient camp that housed workers who built sand dunes in the area. Some buildings were converted into overnight accommodations for fishermen.

The pier opened for business that summer with a snack bar, bait stand, guest rooms, and restrooms for the public. Located across from Sam and Omie's restaurant and near Whalebone filling station, the pier helped establish the business district in South Nags Head.

Jennette's Pier suffered damage from sea worms, nor'easters, hurricanes, and even a wayward shipwreck, and was rebuilt a number of times. But it was Hurricane Isabel in 2003 that caused its final demise. A new one-thousand-foot state-of-the-art green pier with educational exhibits, wind turbines, and concrete pilings was built to replace the old pier.

The new Jennette's Pier was dedicated in May 2011, with Gov. Beverly Perdue taking part in the opening celebration. It is now a facility of the North Carolina Department of Natural and Cultural Resources.

Jennette's Fishing Pier featured on "The Outer Banks of North Carolina, Nags Head" North Carolina Postcard Collection.

1810 Kenan Progenitor James Kenan

On May 23, 1810, Revolutionary-era military and political leader James Kenan died.

Born on his family's plantation near what's now the town of Turkey, Kenan was elected sheriff of Duplin County when he was twenty-two. He displayed strong leadership early, assembling a group of volunteers to go to Wilmington in vocal opposition to the British Stamp Act.

After serving in the colonial assembly and provincial congress, Kenan joined the Duplin militia at the outset of the Revolutionary War. He helped lead a group of volunteers against Scottish loyalists at the Battle of Creek Bridge in 1776 and rose through the ranks to become brigadier general for the Wilmington District shortly after the war ended.

Kenan served more than 10 terms in the state legislature after independence and was prominent in the state's political scene, acting as a member of the 1788 and 1789 state constitutional conventions, becoming a member of UNC's original board of trustees, and sitting on the council of state under Richard Caswell.

Active in the Freemasons, Kenan was the first Master of the original Masonic lodge in Duplin County.

MAY 23

1840 Architect David Paton Hired, Dismissed at State Capitol

On May 23, 1840, David Paton, supervising architect of the State Capitol, was dismissed just as the structure was nearing completion. While the exterior was designed by New York architects Ithiel Town and Alexander Jackson Davis, Paton, from Scotland, took over the project in September 1834 and played a critical role in refining and shaping the final design of the building and its impressive interior.

Paton's interior changes made the building more functional while also making its appearance more ornate. His work was appreciated by the commissioners tasked with overseeing the building's construction and by Raleigh citizens for most of his nearly six years of work on the Capitol.

Paton claimed that his services as architect were performed under his private contract with Town and Davis, over and above his work for the state as construction superintendent. The commissioners increased his salary from three dollars to five dollars per day, but eventually tensions drove the commissioners to let Paton go.

Jackie "Moms" Mabley, ca. 1944.

1975 Moms Mabley, Boundary-Breaking Comedian from Brevard

On May 23, 1975, the comedian known to the world as "Moms" Mabley died in a White Plains, New York hospital.

Born Loretta Mary Aiken in Brevard around 1897, Mabley was the granddaughter of a former slave. She left home as a teenager and joined a minstrel show based in Pittsburgh, beginning a sixty-year career that included work in everything from African American vaudeville to Broadway to television and the movies. Mabley also released more than twenty comedy albums during her lifetime.

Throughout her career Mabley performed in many of the nation's top venues, including Carnegie Hall and the Kennedy Center, and broke gender and racial barriers by becoming the first female comic to perform at New York's Apollo Theater in 1940. Her television performances included appearances on the Merv Griffin, Johnny Carson, Flip Wilson, Mike Douglas and Smothers Brothers shows.

Mabley is best remembered for her brilliant stand-up comic persona, a grumpy lady dressed in bright and crumpled housedresses, who delivered sly double-entendres tackling such topics as race and sex with expert timing and ad-libbing.

1987 Vietnam Monument at State Capitol Dedicated 1987

On May 23, 1987, the North Carolina Vietnam Veterans Memorial was dedicated on the grounds of the State Capitol in Raleigh. Entitled *After the Firefight*, the memorial honors the more than 206 thousand men and women of the state who served in the Vietnam War.

Designed by Abbe Godwin of Colfax in Guilford County, the monument depicts two soldiers carrying a wounded comrade to a nearby landing zone to await medical help. The clothing and equipment of the soldiers portrayed were sculpted from items loaned by Vietnam veterans.

During the four years she worked on the project, Godwin immersed herself in the conflict, collecting artifacts, reading histories and literature from the period extensively, and talking to Vietnam veterans.

The monument was the first on the Capitol grounds to be authorized since the World War II-era and is the first to be designed by a woman. It is also the first on Union Square to depict an African American.

The North Carolina Vietnam Veterans Memorial on the grounds of the State Capitol in Raleigh by Abbe Godwin entitled "After the Firefight."

1768 Short, Active Life of St. Philips Church at Brunswick Town

On May 24, 1768, St. Philips Anglican Church at Brunswick Town on the Cape Fear River was dedicated.

Efforts to construct the church began in 1754, but it sat unfinished until 1759, when Gov. Arthur Dobbs proposed to make it "His Majesty's Chapel in North Carolina." Construction of St. Philips was funded initially through two lotteries and the sale of goods from the captured Spanish privateer, *La Fortuna*. Rev. John McDowell became the full-time minister for St. Philips Parish and received a small house and three hundred acres of land nearby.

Construction was delayed many times and for many reasons, but Dobbs continued to push the project. In 1763 the seventy-three-year-old governor married fifteen-year-old Justina Davis in the still unfinished church. When he died in 1765, he was buried inside the structure.

Gov. William Tryon also took an interest in the church's completion, seeing the project through to its finish in 1768. The parish was never very large, and the church was not destined for a long life. Much of it was destroyed when the British sacked the town in 1776; only the four walls remain.

Ruins of St. Philips Anglican Church at Brunswick Town, prior to 1953 (*above*).

St. Philips Church in 2012 (*right*).

1775 Last Royal Governor Ruled from Offshore

On May 24, 1775, Josiah Martin, the last royal governor of North Carolina, fled Tryon Palace under cover of darkness.

In 1774 delegates to North Carolina's First Provincial Congress recommended that counties form committees of safety, a move to supplant royal authority. Fearing that the cannons on the palace grounds might be used in an insurrection, Martin had them removed in May 1775.

Abandoning the palace, Martin went from New Bern to Fort Johnston, at the mouth of the Cape Fear River, where several English warships lay at anchor. He described the fort as "a wretched little place." Receiving reports that the Wilmington Committee of Safety planned to attack the fort and seize him, Martin took refuge on the HMS *Cruizer*, which was resting offshore. It was a wise move, since five days later the militia, in Martin's words, "wantonly in the dead hour of night set on fire and reduced to ashes the houses and buildings within the Fort."

The *Cruizer* would remain Martin's headquarters through the summer and fall. From aboard the ship on August 8, he issued his "Fiery Proclamation," denouncing the safety committees.

1923 Dramatist Lula Vollmer, Acclaimed for *Sun-Up*

On May 24, 1923, Moore County native Lula Vollmer's play *Sun-Up* premiered on Broadway. Her first and most successful drama, *Sun-Up* depicted people of the southern mountain region. She donated her royalties of more than forty thousand dollars to help educate them.

Born in 1898 and educated at what later became Asheville College, Vollmer went to New York after graduation in 1918 to try to sell the play. Although she worked for the Theatre Guild as a box-office clerk, the Guild joined other producers in rejecting *Sun-Up* until it was produced at the Provincetown Theater. Subsequently it was performed in Chicago, London, Amsterdam, Paris, and Budapest.

In 1925, *Sun-Up* was published in book form. Between 1923 and 1946, Vollmer wrote many other plays, among them *The Shame Woman*, *The Dunce Boy*, *Trigger*, and *Sentinels*, although none had the commercial success of her first.

Except for Paul Green, Vollmer had more plays produced in New York than any other North Carolina dramatist. Grant Wood, famous for his painting *American Gothic*, was scene designer for one of her early works.

Vollmer also wrote a variety of radio serials and in later years wrote short stories for the *Saturday Evening Post*, *Collier's*, and other magazines.

Lula Vollmer, circa 1922–23.

MAY 25

1673 A Female Lawyer in the 1600s

On May 25, 1673, Ann Durant became the first woman to act in the capacity of an attorney in North Carolina.

At a proceeding held at the home of council member Francis Godfrey, Durant represented Andrew Ball in his successful effort to recover wages due him for work aboard a ship. On at least twenty other occasions she appeared before colonial courts on behalf of herself, her husband, or others. She frequently appeared to collect debts owed to her store.

Durant's court appearances were not the first display of her self-reliance. After marrying George Durant in Virginia in January 1659, the couple moved to their "southern plantation," settling on the peninsula today known as Durant's Neck. George Durant served in various capacities in the colony, including Speaker of the Assembly and Attorney General.

In her husband's frequent absence Ann Durant ran their plantation, often providing accommodations for officials attending meetings of the Assembly and Council held at their house. Prisoners were also sometimes held at the Durant home, and it was on their tract that North Carolina's first public structures, stocks, and pillories, were built. She also raised nine children.

1857 Entombed at Sea in a Cask

On May 25, 1857, Nancy Adams Martin died at sea. Her body was placed in a cask of alcohol to preserve her remains until the ship reached port.

Affectionately known as "Nance" by her family, Martin was the daughter of Wilmington businessman Silas H. Martin. A sea captain and shipper by trade, Silas planned a trip around the world, and his eldest son John and daughter Nance accompanied him on the voyage. It would be an ill-fated journey for the Martins.

Nance took ill about three months into the trip and quickly succumbed to the sickness. The only means of preserving her body for later burial was to store it in a cask of rum. The thought of her body sloshing around in a cask was too much for her father and brother, so they decided that a chair would be placed in the cask, nailed in place, and Nance seated and tied onto the chair to keep her from swishing around.

The voyage continued and tragedy struck again. John was swept overboard and lost at sea. Upon returning to Wilmington, Silas had Nance buried. Rather than disturb the remains, her family buried her in the cask in the port city's Oakdale Cemetery.

1860 Daniel Barringer's Mining Efforts Cratered

On May 25, 1860, influential geologist Daniel Moreau Barringer Jr. was born in Raleigh.

In 1902 Barringer became intrigued by a crater in Northern Arizona, known today as Barringer Crater, that was surrounded by scattered deposits of meteoritic iron. He immediately recognized the crater as the result of a meteorite's impact.

The meteorite that formed the crater was 150 feet wide, weighed three hundred thousand tons, and was travelling at a speed of twenty-six thousand miles per hour when it struck the earth's surface fifty thousand years ago. The impact left a crater measuring three quarters of a mile wide and 750 feet deep.

Barringer incorrectly assumed the meteorite could be found beneath the crater's floor and began a mining operation to harvest the ten million tons of iron he assumed was there. In 1929, after twenty-six years of mining without result, scientists determined the meteorite in question hit with such force that it vaporized on impact, meaning no substantial iron deposits were present beneath the crater's surface. Barringer's investors abandoned the project, which at its end had a total cost of 600 thousand dollars with 120 thousand of them coming out of Barringer's own pocket. The news may have been too much for Barringer, who died three months later of a massive heart attack.

Rustic cross grave of Nancy Adams Martin in Oakdale Cemetery (*left*).

1864 Torpedo Blast Felled Union Soldiers, 1864

On May 26, 1864, a deadly torpedo explosion occurred at Batchelor's Creek, about eight miles west of New Bern. For the Union forces stationed there, the losses were devastating. Initial reports claimed that forty soldiers were killed in an accident while unloading the last four of thirteen torpedoes from a train car. The torpedoes were intended to complete the blockade of the Neuse River.

When the last of the four weapons was offloaded, a log struck the cap of one, and it exploded, setting off a chain reaction. Newspaper accounts said it sounded like a thousand pieces of artillery firing and could be heard twenty miles away. Members of the 132nd New York Volunteers were waiting for mail to be unloaded at the time and took the brunt of the explosion.

Body parts were scattered for a quarter of a mile, and two buildings were destroyed. Twenty-eight soldiers and about twenty former slaves, who were working civilian jobs, were killed. While they waited for coffins to be sent from New Bern, hardtack boxes were used to collect body parts. Many of the dead are buried at New Bern National Cemetery.

1884 The Watauga Club and the Origins of N.C. State University

On May 26, 1884, the Watauga Club was founded.

Comprised of a number of influential young leaders under age thirty, including William Joseph Peele, Josephus Daniels, and Walter Hines Page, the progressive organization championed several causes that its members hoped would set the state on a positive course.

Improved roads, more effective farming and agricultural techniques, and better schools were all touted by the club as it attempted to bring the state into a more modern era. But perhaps the most important and successful of the group's goals was the establishment of the North Carolina College of Agriculture and Mechanical Arts. That institution was founded three years later in 1887 and went on to become North Carolina State University.

The Watauga Club remains in existence today and includes about two dozen members, most of whom are influential leaders in the Raleigh area. North Carolina State University commemorates the club each year with its Watauga Medal. Two or three outstanding people are chosen to receive the honor, which "recognize[s] individuals who have rendered significant and distinguished service to North Carolina State University."

1908 North Carolina Voters Approve Prohibition

On May 26, 1908, North Carolina voters approved a prohibition on the sale of alcoholic beverages statewide. North Carolina was the first state in the nation to approve such a measure and did so by the wide margin of sixty-two to thirty-eight percent.

Restrictions and regulations related to the sale and use of alcohol existed in North Carolina since the early 1700s, but the temperance movement, with its calls for statewide prohibition, was not full in swing until the mid-1800s. During the Civil War the legislature prohibited the use of various crops to make alcoholic beverages because the crops were needed for food. Throughout the late 1800s the General Assembly gave local communities the option to ban alcohol and also began passing special legislation prohibiting saloon licenses in particular areas of varying sizes.

The Prohibition enacted by voters in 1908 went into effect in January 1909. The Eighteenth Amendment to the U.S. Constitution became effective in 1920, making it illegal to manufacture, sell, or transport intoxicating liquors in the United States. Nationwide Prohibition ended with the passage of the Twenty-First Amendment in 1933. North Carolina was one of only two states that refused to ratify the repeal.

Richmond County Sheriff and a crowd of onlookers as they curiously observe captured whiskey stills that were destroyed at the courthouse in Rockingham, Richmond County, June 1909.

1949 "Foxy Brown," "Jackie Brown" Star Pam Grier

On May 26, 1949, actress Pam Grier was born in Winston-Salem.

Grier's father was an Air Force mechanic, keeping the family constantly on the move, so it was in Colorado that her acting career got its start. Spotted by an agent at Colorado's preliminary to the Miss Universe pageant, Grier accepted the agent's offer to come to Hollywood to try to make it in the film industry.

After making her debut on the silver screen in the 1971 film *Big Doll House*, Grier quickly became a staple of the so-called "Blaxploitation" genre of films—films geared toward urban black audiences whose plots and characters relied heavily on black stereotypes. She played the starring role in *Foxy Brown*, perhaps the best-known movie of the genre.

In the 1980s and 1990s Grier acted in several blockbuster, more mainstream movies and began working in television as well. In her later career she is perhaps best known for playing the title character in Quentin Tarantino's 1997 movie *Jackie Brown*, and she continues to work in movies and television to this day.

Grier was the first black woman to appear on the cover of *Ms.* magazine in August 1975, and *Ebony* included her on its list of the "100 Most Fascinating Women of the 20th Century."

MAY 26

1862 Brief Return to Native State for Edward Stanly

On May 27, 1862, Pres. Abraham Lincoln appointed Edward Stanly military governor of North Carolina.

Born in New Bern, Stanly served in the state legislature and practiced law in Beaufort County before being elected to Congress in 1837. After losing his third bid for re-election he returned to the state legislature and also briefly served as state attorney general.

He moved to California after losing the Whig nomination for North Carolina governor in 1848.

Stanly fiercely opposed the secessionist movement in California and believed that North Carolina was tricked into joining the Confederacy, so he volunteered to return to the Tar Heel State to work for peace.

Stanly found few friends back home in New Bern. Those on the Confederate side viewed him as a traitor, while many Unionists were angry that he wouldn't authorize schools for African Americans. Outraged at Lincoln for issuing the Emancipation Proclamation, which he believed would make peace between North and South impossible, Stanly resigned from his post less than nine months after taking it.

He returned to California, where he died in 1872.

1863 W. D. Pender, One of Lee's Lieutenants

On May 27, 1863, William Dorsey Pender was promoted at only twenty-nine years old to major general in command of a division of Confederate Gen. A.P. Hill's Third Corps.

Born in in 1834 in what is now Wilson County, Pender graduated from the U.S. Military Academy at West Point. From 1856 to 1860, he saw active service on the frontier in New Mexico, California, Oregon, and Washington state. At the outbreak of the Civil War, Pender resigned his commission, choosing to fight for his native state.

Pender was first elected colonel of the Third North Carolina Volunteers and then transferred to become commander of the Sixth North Carolina Troops. In combat at Seven Pines, Pender performed so valiantly that he received a promotion to brigadier general. While commanding his brigade, Pender was wounded at Malvern Hill, Second Manassas, and Fredericksburg. He took over command of A.P. Hill's division at Chancellorsville after Hill was wounded.

Two months after Chancellorsville, Pender led the division in Lee's invasion of Pennsylvania. While leading his division in an assault on Cemetery Hill at Gettysburg, he was struck by a piece of artillery shell. He later suffered a botched amputation of his leg. The procedure ruptured an artery, and he bled to death.

1925 Coal Mine Explosion Rocks Chatham County

On May 27, 1925, the Carolina Coal Company experienced a massive explosion at Coal Glen in Chatham County. An eyewitness recounted that the first boom of the explosion that morning split the air, smoke began to fill the sky, and women began to scream. People knew immediately what had occurred, and rescue efforts began very quickly. By nightfall five thousand people waited silently at the mouth of the mine for word of survivors.

Almost as quickly, the explosion became headline news across the country. While some of the miners were from communities in other states, just about everyone in the small village of Farmville knew at least one of the dead. Fifty-three victims died in the worst mining disaster in North Carolina history. It took five days to remove the bodies from the mine.

The Carolina Coal Company was established in 1921 near the Chatham County village of Farmville. Coal Glen was about two miles east of another operation known as Cumnock Mine. In a *News and Observer* article written shortly after the explosion, the event was erroneously called the Cumnock Mine Disaster. The 1955 disaster is still often referred to by that name, but it is more accurately called the Coal Glen Explosion.

1942 Navy Muscians Broke Color Barrier

On May 27, 1942, in Raleigh a group of forty-four black musicians, many of them affiliated with North Carolina A&T, enlisted at general rank in the Navy. The date is important, since official Navy histories date the integration of the service on June 1, 1942, placing this group at the forefront of efforts to integrate the Navy.

During World War I the only African Americans to serve in the Navy did so as cooks and stewards. During World War II Pres. Franklin Roosevelt pressed Navy Secretary James Knox to integrate his forces. The UNC campus at Chapel Hill had been selected as the site for one of the nation's five Naval Pre-Flight Schools. Officer training there commenced on May 23, 1942. The forty-four new black recruits trained in Norfolk, but they were assigned to serve in Chapel Hill and played their first concert on July 31.

Since the men could not sleep or eat alongside the white enlistees, they dined and bunked at what is now Hargraves Recreation Center, about two miles from campus. Their duties included marching to campus each day to play as flags were raised and returning each evening to play "Taps." In May 1944 the band was transferred to Pearl Harbor. Many of the members took up postwar careers as music educators.

U.S. Navy B-1 Band playing while the American flag is raised at the UNC Pre-Flight School.

Coal Glen mine within days of the explosion. A rescue train from West Virginia can be seen behind the men on the right.

1845 John Reed and the North Carolina Gold Rush

On May 28, 1845, John Reed, the owner of the property where the first documented discovery of gold in the United States took place, died.

In 1799 Reed's son Conrad found a seventeen-pound yellow rock in Little Meadow Creek. Conrad brought it home where it was used as a doorstop for years. The elder Reed made several unsuccessful attempts to discern the rock's value. In 1802 a merchant in Fayetteville paid the family $3.50 for it. Later Reed discovered that the rock was in fact gold and that the merchant received thirty-six hundred dollars from its sale.

After turning a substantial profit selling nuggets found along the creek, in 1803 Reed ventured into a partnership to purchase slaves to search for gold. The venture was rewarded with a twenty-eight-pound nugget, the discovery of which sparked an era of gold fever.

The Reed Mine helped establish North Carolina's mining industry twenty years before the California gold rush. So much gold was discovered in the Charlotte area that in 1837 the Federal government established a branch United States Mint there to transform it into currency. In recognition of the mine's contribution to state history, the Reed Gold Mine is now a state historic site.

1900 Wadesboro Prime for Viewing of 1900 Solar Eclipse

On May 28, 1900, a total solar eclipse occurred.

Though the eclipse's path could be tracked across the Southeast, roughly from New Orleans, Louisiana to Norfolk, Virginia, scientists determined that Wadesboro in Anson County was the best place in North America to view it.

Scientific expeditions were mounted from some of the world's preeminent astronomy programs, including Princeton University, the University of Chicago, the Smithsonian Institution, and the British Astronomical Association. S. P. Langley and C. A. Young, two of the founders of modern astronomy, were also there.

According to the *Anson Independent*, a local newspaper, the public came out in droves. Extra trains, including a special excursion train from Charlotte, brought out hundreds of people, and by the time the eclipse's effects were beginning to be seen around 7:30 a.m., the streets were packed and people were vying for better viewing spots on top of and out the windows of buildings.

The same local newspaper described the total eclipse itself as lasting for less than a minute and a half and recorded that though a large crowd was on hand, it was nearly silent during that entire time. The paper also mentioned that the drop in temperature from the shadow caused by the eclipse was quite significant.

1965 Cross Burnings by Ku Klux Klan, 1965

On May 28, 1965, members of the Ku Klux Klan burned crosses on the grounds of courthouses and city halls in thirteen North Carolina cities and towns large and small across the Coastal Plain and Piedmont, including Burgaw, Currie, Elizabethtown, Henderson, Oxford, Roxboro, Salisbury, Southport, Statesville, Tarboro, Ward's Corner, Whiteville, and Wilmington. The coordinated cross burning was part of a wider wave of violence undertaken by the KKK in reaction to the growing civil rights movement sweeping the nation and state.

Just months later the U.S. House of Representatives' Un-American Activities Committee found that North Carolina had the largest Klan presence of any state in the Union, with more than six thousand members organized into at least 112 local chapters and scores more sympathizes. The Klan had even set up a booth at the State Fair.

Despite the violence and tension Gov. Terry Sanford continued to quietly lead business and other community leaders toward desegregation, not by calling for changes in law, but by setting up programs like the Good Neighbor Council, which encouraged fair employment practices to improve race relations.

Map showing the path of the solar eclipse of 1900 in Wadesboro (*background*).

Solar eclipse of 1900 in Wadesboro (*left*).

MAY 29

1664 Barbadians Upon the Cape Fear

On May 29, 1664, settlers from Barbados under John Vassall disembarked on the Cape Fear River. They established a settlement called Charles Town after King Charles II of England on the river's west bank north of Town Creek.

Vassall, a merchant from Barbados, had organized a colonizing company under the patronage of Sir John Colleton, one of the eight Lords Proprietors of the Carolina Charter of 1663. After explorations conducted by William Hilton, a division occurred within the company. Vassall's faction backed a Cape Fear site, while another under John Yeamans favored Port Royal in what is now South Carolina.

Vassall pushed ahead with his project, and by 1666 there were about eight hundred settlers in the colony. Meanwhile Yeamans's son William negotiated an agreement with the Proprietors securing governorship of the colony for his father. Now a knight, Sir John Yeamans sailed for Carolina but on arrival focused on developing a Port Royal colony.

Charles Town declined in neglect and isolation, while Colleton's death in 1666 deprived the Cape Fear colonists of their advocate. By 1667 Charles Town was deserted. Yeamans and a band of Barbadians established a new Charles Town on the Ashley River in 1670, which today is Charleston, South Carolina.

1831 Citywide Fire in Fayetteville, 1831

On May 29, 1831, much of Fayetteville burned to the ground.

Starting in a kitchen on the northwest corner of Market Square, the fire's starting point near the town's center was part of the reason it caused so much destruction. Though townspeople began trying to extinguish it around it noon, the fire continued to spread rapidly, destroying many of the nearby structures, including the building where the state had ratified the U.S. Constitution.

The town's fire engine was unable to contain the blaze and, indeed, was itself destroyed in the flames. All nearby was destroyed, and the streets became a chaotic mess of people trying to save family members and possessions as the fire roared through town.

After four hours the inferno was quenched but not before incinerating more than six hundred buildings, including hundreds of homes, a school, two hotels, 105 stores, two banks, and all but one of the city's churches.

Although many people were injured and almost everyone displaced, no one was killed. Private donations poured into town once news of the disaster spread, with over one hundred thousand dollars collected and distributed to the people of Fayetteville.

Many of today's older buildings in the city, such as the Market House, are ones built after this spectacular fire.

1888 Belk's Rooted in Monroe

On May 29, 1888 the first Belk department store opened under the name "New York Racket" in Monroe. The store was founded by William Henry Belk, only twenty-five at the time. Belk used all 750 dollars of his life savings, a five hundred dollar loan and three thousand dollars in consigned merchandise to launch the operation.

The store stayed in business largely because of Belk's innovative sales techniques. He insisted that prices be clearly labeled and that no haggling or credit be allowed. The store opened early and closed late to accommodate working-class customers and consistently relied on slim profit margins and a high sales volume.

After a few years of success, Belk convinced his brother John to join the business as a partner. When John came onboard, the store became Belk Brothers. As the success of the business grew, so did its footprint. New locations opened across the Charlotte region in the late 1800s and early 1900s, many of which were partnerships between the Belk brothers and trusted former employees.

1893 Waldenses Settle in Burke County

On May 29, 1893, the first Waldensian settlers arrived in Burke County. The Waldenses are a Christian sect founded in the twelfth century. For many years the group was confined to a rugged area in the Cottian Alps along the boundary between Italy and France.

During the nineteenth century many Waldenses emigrated to North and South America to form missionary colonies, not because of religious persecution, but because their small strip of land in the Alps was overcrowded. The largest North American Waldensian settlement was the one that grew up on ten thousand acres of land in Burke County. It was named Valdese, which is Italian for Waldenses.

Valdese became a hub of the American textile industry in the early twentieth century. The Waldensian Hosiery Mill was established in 1901 and the yarn factory, Valdese Manufacturing Company, in 1913. The establishment of a variety of factories, banks, and stores solidified the prosperity of the mountain community.

Since 1967 an outdoor drama, *From this Day Forward*, has been performed each summer by Valdese's Old Colony Players. The saga features authentic costumes and folk dances that highlight the heritage of North Carolina's Waldensian settlers.

Carolina sheet of Popple's great twenty sheet map of North America, 1733, (*background*).

1803 Slavery and Persistence: Lunsford Lane of Raleigh

On May 30, 1803, Lunsford Lane was born into slavery in the household of Sherwood Haywood, a Raleigh banker.

The Haywoods acknowledged Lane's intelligence, ambition, and talent for business. As a boy Lane began to pursue entrepreneurial ventures in Raleigh. He developed a variety of enterprises that included selling commodities he kept in a rented warehouse and operating a successful tobacco business, where he invented a unique pipe and a popular tobacco blend.

Savings enabled him to purchase his freedom in 1835 and move to Massachusetts, where he published *The Narrative of Lunsford Lane*. There he worked to raise money to free his family.

Lane's 1842 *Narrative* provides an account of the extremely rare occurrence of an enslaved man's managing to develop a highly successful business despite the oppressive constraints of a legal and social system that took away his right to the products of his own mind and time. His book recounts his awareness of the need to be invisible and play within the rules despite his growing disillusionment with the immoral legal and social system that conspired against him, even after he purchased his freedom.

Returning to Raleigh in 1839 as a free man, Lane purchased a home and continued his tobacco business, aiming to free his family. He was soon banished under a law preventing the immigration of free blacks into the state. Returning again in 1842 to free his family, he was arrested for being an abolitionist.

Lane eventually freed his wife, mother, and seven children, and the family made their way to Massachusetts, where he spent the rest of his life working and lecturing on abolition. He died around 1863, although the location is unknown.

Lunsford Lane

1935 George Denny and the Beginnings of Talk Radio

On May 30, 1935, *America's Town Meeting of the Air* debuted on the radio. The show, America's first political talk program, was hosted by Washington, N.C. native, George V. Denny Jr.

With dreams of being an actor, Denny moved to New York after attending UNC. Finding no work in the theater, Denny worked briefly in outreach at Columbia University before being hired by the League for Political Education, which at that time focused primarily on hosting political lectures.

Denny eventually rose to become the organization's director and pitched the idea of a radio show featuring guests with opposing viewpoints debating the major issues of the day. As the moderator, he formatted the show like an old town hall meeting in which audience members could engage with the guests. That format gave the show its energy and popularity.

The show's first episode was called *Which Way America: Fascism, Communism, Socialism or Democracy?* and was picked up by only eighteen stations. After six episodes, NBC agreed to carry the program across its network, and at its peak *America's Town Meeting of the Air* attracted more than three million listeners weekly.

Denny served as the program's moderator until 1952. The program left the air in 1956.

1971 Gertrude Weil of Goldsboro Remembered for Social Activism

On May 30, 1971, Gertrude Weil died at age ninety-one. A humanitarian, social reformer, and philanthropist, Weil was born in 1879 in Goldsboro to department store owners Henry and Mina Weil. The Weils were members of a wealthy Jewish family who settled in North Carolina about 1865.

After graduating from Smith College in 1901, Weil traveled extensively and turned her energies toward social reform. By 1920 she helped found the North Carolina Suffrage League, the North Carolina Federation of Women's Clubs, and the North Carolina League of Women Voters. She also helped establish the Wayne County Health Department. Additionally, Weil served as president for the North Carolina Association for Jewish Women but worked tirelessly for interfaith activities and initiatives.

Civil rights became her focus in the 1950s and 1960s, when she funded a park and swimming pool for African Americans and founded the Bi-Racial Council in 1963. During her lifetime Weil received many awards, including the Smith College Medal, given to alumnae who "exemplify in their lives and work the true purpose of a liberal arts education."

Just weeks before Weil's death in 1971, North Carolina finally ratified the Nineteenth Amendment, which granted women suffrage, fifty years after it had become the law of the land.

Gertrude Weil (*far left*) with a group of suffragettes, ca. 1920.

1775 Mecklenburg Resolves, Bold Step Toward Independence

1870 Cotton Planter Patented by N.C. Inventor

2003 Fugitive Bomber's Run Ended in Murphy

MAY 31

On May 31, 1775, a committee led by Thomas Polk met at the Mecklenburg County Courthouse, in the heart of Charlotte at present-day Trade and Tryon Streets, to adopt the Mecklenburg Resolves.

Unlike the widely disputed legitimacy of the "Mecklenburg Declaration of Independence," the authenticity of the resolves is not in question. This was a radical set of resolutions, denying the authority of Parliament over the colonies and investing that power in the Provincial Congress, which was meeting that same week in New Bern.

In the absence of an operational new government, the resolves set some basic tenets. Anyone who received or exercised a commission from the Crown was deemed an "enemy to his country" and subject to arrest. The county's militia companies were ordered to arm themselves and maintain vigilance.

The Mecklenburg Resolves were published in full in the *North Carolina Gazette* in June 1775 and received wide circulation. Others took note, and similar resolves were adopted in Wilmington on June 19, Fayetteville on June 30, and Pitt County on July 1.

This was all a prelude to the Halifax Resolves, signed by delegates to the Fourth Provincial Congress on April 12, 1776, voicing support for independence for all colonies.

On May 31, 1870, Richmond County inventor James Lytch was awarded a patent for the Eclipse Lytch Cottonseed Planter.

Exhibited at agricultural fairs in North Carolina, South Carolina, and Georgia, Lytch's planter became the instrument of choice in the South. The planter could be purchased for twelve dollars. In 1872 Lytch received a medal from the Cape Fear Agricultural Association for his work with cotton planting. He also received an award at the International Cotton Expo in Atlanta in 1881. According to the inventor, one thousand of his planters were in use by 1880.

Among Lytch's other inventions were a cotton scraper, cider mill, and fertilizer distributor. He also developed a door check for stopping doors, gates, and window shutters, as well as a greaser for buggy axles.

After James Lytch's death in 1890, his son, Daniel, continued to produce the popular cotton planter in a manufacturing facility near the family home in the X-Way community of what is now Scotland County.

James M. Lytch

On May 31, 2003, fugitive Eric Rudolph was captured in Murphy. Indicted in 2000 for deadly bombings in Atlanta at the 1996 Olympics and in Birmingham in 1998, Rudolph fled into North Carolina's Nantahala Forest. Often described as a survivalist, he was familiar with the area since he had been raised in the rugged region. An initial massive search for Rudolph proved unsuccessful.

On the day he was found, about 3:00 a.m. rookie police officer Jeffrey Postell spotted someone with what appeared to be a gun behind a grocery store. When the figure began to run away from him, Postell called the sighting in, left his patrol car, and drew his weapon.

A man came out of hiding and surrendered but did not identify himself. Two other law enforcement officers responded to Postell's call, and one, a Cherokee County sheriff's deputy, thought the man resembled Rudolph.

At the detention center, the three officers found the FBI Most Wanted poster and compared it to the man before them. After hiding out for five years, Eric Rudolph was arrested, pled guilty to the bombing charges, and is now serving four life sentences in a maximum security prison in Colorado.

Eric Rudolph mug shot.

1586 Tragic End to Native-Newcomer Encounter

On June 1, 1586, Algonquian chief Pemisapan was decapitated by Edward Nugent, a member of Ralph Lane's Roanoke Island colony.

Originally known as Wingina, Pemisapan was a well-respected regional leader in the Algonquian tribe on Roanoke Island and the adjacent mainland in the 1580s. Although he and his people helped the English colonists on Roanoke at first, Pemisapan came to the same conclusion that many native chieftains would in future years: the Europeans intended to take over by any means, including violence.

Realizing the English had superior weapons and numbers, Pemisapan joined with other tribal leaders to fight together to drive the Ralph Lane colony away from Roanoke.

When an Algonquian hostage revealed the plot to the English, Lane assembled men to pursue Pemisapan. Lane lured him into an open area, so Lane and other colonists could shoot at him, and though wounded in the initial volley, Pemisapan ran into the woods. Nugent and another colonist pursued him and returned later carrying his head.

Algonquian Indians later killed George Howe, a close advisor to the Roanoke Island governor, John White, as revenge for the murder of Pemisapan. Fearing the consequences of their actions, the tribe abandoned their capital town and moved inland.

1898 The Vanderbilts of Biltmore Marry in Paris

On June 1, 1898, Biltmore Estate owner George Washington Vanderbilt wed American socialite Edith Stuyvesant Dresser in a civil ceremony in Paris. The next day the couple exchanged vows again during a religious ceremony in Paris's American Cathedral with much of society's elite present.

After a four-month European honeymoon the Vanderbilts came home to Asheville, and Edith became "mistress of Biltmore," assuming day-to-day management of America's largest house. The new bride quickly endeared herself to estate workers, delivering food and medicine to their families when needed, and bringing gifts when babies were born. The Vanderbilts' own child, Cornelia, was born in 1900.

Already actively involved in the community, George helped establish the Biltmore Forest School—America's first institute for scientific forestry—while Edith started a school to teach young women housekeeping skills. In 1901 the couple created Biltmore Estate Industries to help area residents learn to make and sell traditional crafts. After George died in 1914, Edith continued to support local causes. She also served as the first female president of the North Carolina Agricultural Society and of the State Fair.

In 1925 Edith married Rhode Island Sen. Peter Gerry. She died in 1958 at age eighty-five.

1944 Polio Outbreak and the "Miracle of Hickory"

On June 1, 1944, the first case of polio, in what would become a devastating epidemic, was diagnosed in Catawba County. Within twenty-four hours, six cases were identified in the county and sixty-eight others in the region.

"At this moment," according to an article in the national magazine *Coronet*, "the town of Hickory became great—for all time." Meeting in a high school auditorium, Hickory leaders mobilized efforts, seeking help from the state and from the National Foundation for Infantile Paralysis but relying primarily on local resources.

A local fresh air camp was evacuated, and, with contributed materials and labor, fifty-five hours later a full-scale hospital was constructed, equipped, and staffed. It was called the Hickory Emergency Infantile Paralysis Hospital. Specialists traveled to Hickory from Harvard, Yale and Johns Hopkins to help. Various treatments were employed, among them iron lungs and "hot pack" therapies.

Over the course of nine months, 454 patients were treated at the facility, frequently called the "Miracle of Hickory." The remaining patients were transferred in March 1945 to Charlotte Memorial Hospital, where beds had become available. Lincoln County native Harlan Boyles, who would go on to serve as state treasurer for twenty-four years, was a patient at the hospital when he was fifteen.

Many patients returned to Hickory for a fiftieth anniversary reunion in 1994.

1977 Death Penalty Debated, 1970s

On June 1, 1977, a revision to the law, which reestablished the death penalty for first-degree murder, became effective in North Carolina.

Capital punishment's roots in North Carolina extend all the way back to the colonial era, but it wasn't until 1910 that the state took over administration of the practice from the counties and began using electrocution instead of hanging. Asphyxiation by lethal gas, which was promoted as more humane by several legislators in the 1920s and 1930s, became the preferred method in 1936.

In 1972 the U.S. Supreme Court ruled that the death penalty was unconstitutional under the Eighth Amendment because its imposition was arbitrary. That led the N.C. Supreme Court to rule that the death penalty for murder, rape, arson, and burglary would be mandatory. That ruling, in turn, was struck down by the U.S. Supreme Court in 1976, and the convictions of 120 people then on death row were vacated.

Though the General Assembly reauthorized the practice in 1977, the next execution did not take place in North Carolina until 1984. Inmates could choose death by lethal gas or by lethal injection until 1998, when lethal injection became the only authorized method.

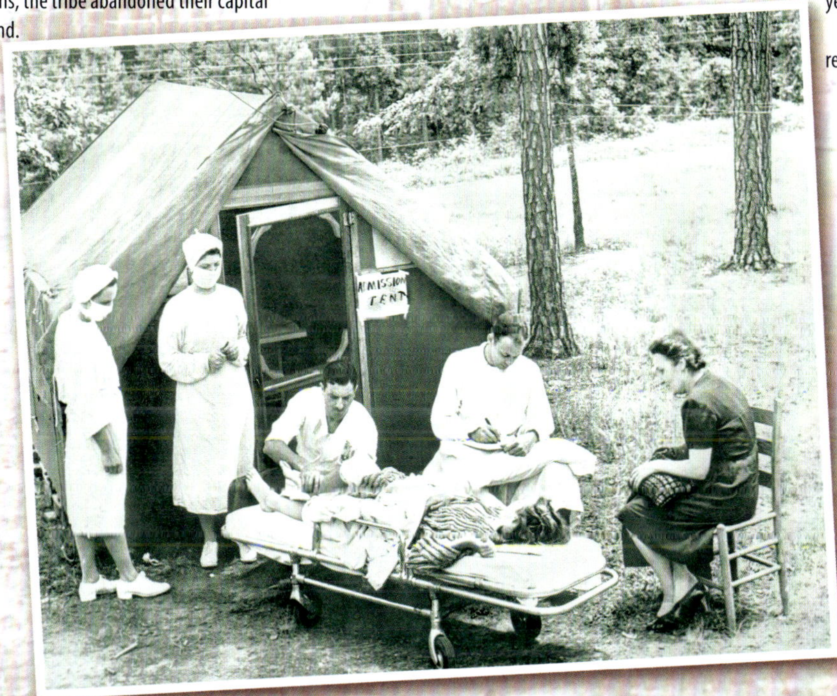

Patient being examined outside an admission tent at the Hickory Emergency Polio Hospital.

JUN 2

1690 Competing Claims to Governorship, 1690

On June 2, 1690, John Gibbs issued a declaration claiming his right to the governorship of Carolina and called on the people to obey him.

After Gov. Seth Sothel was banished earlier that year, Gibbs proclaimed himself chief executive of the colony, basing his claim on the Fundamental Constitutions of Carolina adopted by the Lords Proprietors in 1669, despite Philip Ludwell's having arrived in the colony in the spring of 1690 with a governor's commission from the Lords Proprietors. Ludwell set up his government, but Gibbs was determined not to leave the governorship. Gibbs referred to Ludwell as a "rascal, impostor and usurper" and said that he would fight anyone to keep Ludwell from the governor's office.

The next month Gibbs and some supporters entered the Pasquotank precinct court and broke it up. Gibbs forbade the holding of a court without its first receiving a commission from him. The force seized two magistrates, took them as prisoners, and held them captive on Gibbs's Virginia plantation. Upon hearing this, the Albemarle council sent the militia to stop this rebellion, but the militia refused to enter Virginia without permission from that colony's government.

Gibbs and Ludwell both went to England to make their claims before the Lords Proprietors. The proprietors upheld Ludwell's commission.

1863 Civil War Origins of "Tar Heel"

On June 2, 1863, in an article in the semi-weekly Raleigh newspaper the *North Carolina Standard*, the nickname "Tar Heel" appeared—one of the first known uses in print. Describing battle actions from a month earlier, Sgt. George W. Timberlake reported, "The troops from other States call us 'Tar Heels.' I am proud of the name, as tar is a sticky substance, and the 'Tar Heels' stuck up like a sick kitten to a hot brick, while many others from a more oily State slipped to the rear, and left the 'Tar Heels' to stick it out."

A number of different oral traditions suggest multiple possible origins for the nickname. Some tales suggest colonial origins, but the more persistent anecdotes date the term to the Civil War.

The term is most commonly associated with Gen. Robert E. Lee, who is said to have exclaimed "God Bless the Tar Heel boys." Lee's statement was made when he heard of an exchange in which a North Carolina soldier, hearing a jeer of "Tar Heel," responded that if the other states' soldiers had had some tar on their heels, the North Carolina troops would not have had to retake the battle line.

1935 Duke Chapel Dedicated, 1935

On June 2, 1935, Duke Chapel was dedicated in Durham.

The chapel's iconic design was the work of Julian Abele, a prominent African American architect from Philadelphia who designed much of Duke's West Campus, and since Duke University is rooted in the Methodist tradition, Abele planned the chapel for the campus's center.

Construction began on the building in October 1930 after university leaders fitted a strongbox of photos and publications inside its cornerstone. It ultimately took five years and cost $2.3 million, which would be more than $39.4 million today. The bluestone of the building's exterior was quarried near Hillsborough.

Though not officially dedicated until June 1935, the chapel's first major use was for Duke's 1932 commencement ceremony. At that point many of the windows had not been installed, and the interior was largely unfinished.

Today Duke Chapel stands a majestic 210 feet tall at the center of Duke's West Campus. A fifty-two-hundred-pipe Flentrop organ and a fifty-bell carillon, both added since the first round of construction was completed, are two of the building's most distinctive features.

Duke Chapel (*foreground and background*)

1905 Lumina, Storied Beacon at Wrightsville Beach

On June 3, 1905, Lumina, a pavilion on Wrightsville Beach known as the "Fun Spot of the South" opened for the first time.

Lumina had its roots in February 1905 when the Consolidated Railways Light & Power Company purchased a train track along the waterfront. On the land it purchased, the company constructed the pavilion to promote beach tourism and better accommodate the patrons of its trolley line.

The ground floor featured dressing rooms, refreshment stands, and various amusements. The second level was primarily a dance floor with a balcony and band shell for the orchestra and a restaurant. The third floor housed a fifteen-foot-wide promenade overlooking the dance floor.

Lumina quickly became a mecca for excursions from all across North Carolina and beyond. Incandescent lights inside and out made the pavilion a beacon. In the era of silent films, a screen was erected on tall pilings on the beach alongside the pavilion, Though the style of music changed over the years, music always dominated the scene. Writer Lewis Philip Hall even claims that it was at Lumina that the shag was invented in 1928.

The pavilion was condemned in 1972 and demolished a little over a year later.

1909 Couldn't Eat Just One: Potato Chip Magnate Herman Lay

On June 3, 1909, snack food tycoon Herman Lay was born in Charlotte.

An entrepreneur from a young age, Lay first sold Pepsi at age eleven to spectators at the city baseball park across the street from his Greenville, South Carolina home. He translated that pursuit into a job as a peanut vendor in the park.

His first foray into the world of potato chips came in the early 1930s, when he interviewed for a job at Barrett Potato Chip Company in Atlanta, distributor of Gardner's Potato Chips. At the time he decided not to take the job because he doubted that there was a future in the potato chip business.

Lay later accepted the chip job, and in time became a distributor for Barrett's in Nashville, Tennessee. In 1939 he purchased Barrett's potato chip factories in Atlanta and Memphis and changed the name to H. W. Lay and Company. He eventually bought the remaining Barrett plant in Florida and then started three new factories of his own, including one in Greensboro.

In the 1950s Lay expanded his product variety and area by purchasing other snack food companies. In 1961 he merged Lays with Texas-based Frito Company. Lay spearheaded the merger of Frito-Lay with Pepsi in 1965, creating the mega-corporation, PepsiCo.

Lay retired from the snack food industry in 1980 and died two years later.

1933 *Our State* Magazine Makes Its Debut

On June 3, 1933, the first issue of *The State* magazine hit newsstands across North Carolina.

The brain child of Carl Goerch, an eastern North Carolina newspaper publisher and radio broadcaster, the magazine was an instant success despite the tough economic times. The first issue was almost entirely written and edited by Goerch, and roughly twenty-five hundred copies of it were printed. Each copy cost ten cents.

Goerch envisioned the publication as a weekly statewide survey that would increase people's love for North Carolina. He tirelessly traveled from the mountains to the coast and back again to develop that product, collecting stories and subscribers until he sold the magazine in 1951.

Bill Sharpe, the magazine's second owner, switched the publication schedule from weekly to monthly. W. B. Wright, who owned the magazine from 1965 to 1987, focused on business and historical stories and began to feature the work of prominent North Carolina writers.

After Shaw Publishing briefly owned the publication, Bernard Mann bought it in 1996 and changed its name to *Our State*. The magazine remains a staple in North Carolina homes today and has a monthly circulation of more than 150 thousand.

1985 The Bizarre "Bitter Blood" Murders

On June 3, 1985, a Chevrolet Blazer driven by Fritz Klenner exploded during a police chase in Summerfield, north of Greensboro. Klenner, a native of Reidsville, was a suspect in the murders of three people in Winston-Salem and two in Kentucky. Also in the Blazer were Susie Newsom Lynch and her sons John and Jim.

Klenner, who had deceived and manipulated family and friends for years—pretending for years to be a medical student at Duke to please his father, later adding service in the CIA to his imagined resume—had become romantically involved with Lynch, his first cousin, after she divorced. The murders appear to be rooted in the couple's belief that Lynch's ex-husband and other family members were conspiring to take the boys from her.

Klenner is suspected of having killed his cousin's former mother-in-law and her daughter in Kentucky in 1984 in an attempt to make the ex-husband appear to have mafia ties. In mid-May 1985 he killed Lynch's parents and grandmother in their Winston-Salem home, with assistance from a misguided friend who believed he was "auditioning" for the CIA.

With law enforcement closing in on the couple a few weeks later, Klenner loaded his Blazer with weapons and rigged it to explode. Lynch's remains were found in a nearby culvert, blown apart by the bomb that must have been under her seat. One of the Kentucky detectives located Klenner, barely alive, in a ditch. Hoping for a confession, the detective leaned an ear toward Klenner, who gurgled blood and died. Evidence later revealed that the young boys had been poisoned with cyanide and shot in the head by their mother prior to the explosion.

The story of Klenner and his crimes is chronicled in *Bitter Blood: A True Story of Southern Family Pride, Madness, and Multiple Murder*, a bestselling book by Jerry Bledsoe, who wrote for *Greensboro's News and Record* at the time.

"Lumina, Best Dancing Pavilion on South Atlantic Coast, Wrightsville Beach, near Wilmington, N.C."

Greensboro News & Record

Vol. 95, No. 155 — Greensboro, N.C., Tuesday Morning, June 4, 1985 — 25 Cents

4 killed, 3 hurt in chase, explosion

Murders, shooting, evacuation linked

Police officials stand by body of suspect and search among the scattered debris from the vehicle explosion

Article from the *Greensboro News and Record* recounting the "Bitter Blood Murders" of 1985.

JUN
4

1835 Constitutional Convention Gaveled In, 1835

On June 4, 1835, a convention called to modify the North Carolina Constitution of 1776 opened at the First Presbyterian Church in downtown Raleigh.

The main impetus to change the state constitution was a growing divide between the eastern and western parts of the state. By 1830 more North Carolinians lived in the western part of the state, but eastern interests continued to dominate the General Assembly.

A special election was held in April 1835 to select 130 delegates to attend the convention in Raleigh.

After about five weeks of debate and votes, a slate of constitutional amendments was adopted. The main changes made by the convention had to do with elections and who could hold certain offices.

Under the new constitution, free African American men, who had previously been able to vote, were disenfranchised. Elections for the General Assembly shifted from being held annually to every other year, and the way each chamber's membership was apportioned changed. Balloting for governor shifted from the legislature to popular vote, the governor's term was extended from one to two years, and all Christians, not just Protestants, became eligible to hold public office.

After the 1835 convention North Carolina's state constitution wouldn't be completely overhauled again until Reconstruction.

1904 Master of an Art Form, Potter Ben Owen

On June 4, 1904, potter Ben Owen was born in Moore County.

Owen learned to turn clay from his father, potter and farmer Rufus Owen, and by age sixteen he was a proficient potter who produced lead-glazed utilitarian earthenware for his father and for neighboring shops.

In 1923 Owen was hired as the second known potter to work at the newly built Jugtown Pottery. Under the guidance of Jugtown founders Jacques and Juliana Busbee, Owen developed a classic pottery style that blended old and new forms, incorporating the principles of restraint and simplicity inherent in both native folk and Oriental traditions.

Owen was the sole potter at Jugtown from the early 1930s until 1959, when he left to found the Old Plank Road Pottery. He produced the same forms and glazes until his retirement in 1972. His son and grandson revived his work, opening Ben Owen Pottery to produce pottery based closely on his unique style.

Owen's work has been widely exhibited across the state, nation, and world. His pieces can be found in the permanent collections of the Mint Museum of Art, North Carolina Museum of Art, Smithsonian Institution, Metropolitan Museum of Art, and the Louvre, among many others.

Ben Owen, as a young man, creating a piece at his potter's wheel.

1924 Baker Roll, a Census of the Eastern Band of Cherokee Indians

On June 4, 1924, the United States Congress passed an act aimed at terminating the Eastern Band of Cherokee Indians.

Indian Agent Fred A. Baker was tasked with preparing an official roll of all members of the Eastern Band. The roll anticipated a final allotment of land and granting of United States citizenship to the Indians. Now known as the Baker Roll, it was to be the final conclusive list of the Band's membership.

Baker visited Indian households, much like a census-taker, and recorded information on each individual including name, birth date, and percentage of Eastern Cherokee blood. Controversies arose due to the number of people included on the roll and the amount of land that could be allotted to each. The Cherokee were also facing difficulties registering to vote—clerks refused to acknowledge citizenship until the allotment issue was resolved.

Ultimately the Indians decided that it was prudent to keep the tribal lands in trust with the government, and in 1931 Congress voted not to act on the tribal assets. The Baker Roll was amended, with many people of questionable descent removed. The roll stands today as tantamount to being acknowledged as a member of the Eastern Band of Cherokee Indians.

1777 Edenton Patriot, Edward Vail

On June 5, 1777, Edward Vail, colonial statesman and brigadier general of the Edenton District militia, died at age sixty.

Vail's public life began in 1754, when he helped raise troops in the French and Indian War and fought in the conflict in Virginia. Though Vail and his troops supported Gov. William Tryon in the campaign against the Regulators in 1771, he, like many others who supported Tryon in the earlier conflict, subsequently became a supporter of the Revolution.

Vail represented Chowan County in the colonial assembly frequently between 1754 and 1774. A well-respected member of his community and the colony overall, Vail was appointed in 1768, 1773, and 1774 to serve as a member of North Carolina's Committee of Correspondence, along with other prominent revolutionaries including Cornelius Harnett, John Harvey, and William Hooper. Work on the committee brought Vail in contact with leaders from other colonies who sought to increase communication among the diverse and far-flung population in an effort to unify the colonies.

Vail remained active in the militia throughout his life and in 1776 was appointed brigadier general of the Edenton District militia.

1910 Greensboro Writer O. Henry

On June 5, 1910, writer William Sidney Porter, known to the world by the pseudonym O. Henry, died.

Born in 1862 in Greensboro, Porter was raised by an aunt who educated him until he turned fifteen, when he began work in his uncle's pharmacy. In 1882 Porter left Greensboro for Texas, where he worked as a ranch hand, an experience that would later manifest itself in his writing.

Over the next fourteen years, Porter worked various jobs in Austin, Texas, including stints as a bookkeeper, draftsman, and bank teller, all the while writing short stories, sketches, and humorous pieces for several newspapers.

In 1896 Porter moved to Houston for a newspaper job. Once there, he was indicted by an Austin court on charges of embezzlement stemming from his tenure as a bank teller. He fled to Honduras but subsequently was arrested, convicted, and ordered to serve five years in prison. While incarcerated, he had time to engage in serious writing, and by the time he was released for good behavior in 1901, Porter had had several works published. In 1902 he moved to New York City and wrote more than one hundred stories in less than two years.

He moved to Asheville in 1907, where he lived until his death.

1918 U-Boats Active Off N.C. Coast in Both World Wars

On June 5, 1918, attacks by German U-boats began off the North Carolina coast. The raids were the first against the state by a foreign government since the War of 1812, and the initial assault lasted for four days. During that time one German submarine, U-151, sank four Allied ships.

Two other German ships launched attacks off the Outer Banks during World War I. U-140 claimed four more ships, including the Diamond Shoals lightship, which sank in early August. U-117 arrived off the North Carolina coast a few weeks later and laid mines north of Cape Hatteras that would result in the sinking of the British steamship *Mirlo*. U-117 sank another ship before returning home. The submarine raids finally ended when an armistice was signed in November 1918.

The damage done during World War I would ultimately prove minor compared to that done during World War II. Attacks began off North Carolina's shores almost immediately after the America's entry into the conflict in December 1941 and continued at intense levels until the U.S. Navy began to strengthen antisubmarine defenses in the summer of 1942.

During World War II more than eighty ships were sunk or damaged off North Carolina's coast.

William Sydney Porter, also known as "O. Henry."

JUN 6

1765 Nutbush Address Published

On June 6, 1765, George Sims published the Nutbush Address. The document, entitled "An Address to the People of Granville County," set forth in graphic language the abuses of power that the people of the Piedmont region were forced to suffer under colonial rule. The address specifically mentioned excessive taxes, high rents, unfair fees, and fraudulent accounting of public funds. Its particular target was Samuel Benton, political kingpin of colonial Granville.

Sims was a schoolteacher living in that portion of Granville County known as Nutbush, which was roughly what is now Vance County. With wide circulation of the Nutbush Address, public temper in the "Granville District" became increasingly agitated. Regulator leader Herman Husband quoted from the address and used it to his advantage when he later wrote about the Regulator movement.

One historian wrote that the Nutbush Address represents "the first recorded mutterings of the troubles that grew into the War of the Regulation."

1795 Long-time Unionist Lawmaker Bedford Brown

On June 6, 1795, long-time lawmaker Bedford Brown was born in Caswell County.

Remembered as a politician who dedicated himself to the preservation of the United States before, during, and after the Civil War he feared the most, Brown was elected to the North Carolina House of Commons when he was only twenty years old. After serving four terms in the House, Brown was elected to the state Senate in 1828 and was chosen as speaker soon after. He was elected to the United States Senate the following year.

Brown's ten-year tenure in Congress ended in 1840, when his Unionist views found him out of favor with the Calhoun Democrats of the South. Brown lived in Missouri and Virginia until returning to his Caswell County home in 1855.

Catching a second wind, Brown returned to politics with election to the state Senate in 1858, where he served until 1864. In the fall of 1868, Brown was once again elected to the state Senate, but partisan politics prevented his attendance.

Known as an ardent Unionist, Brown considered secession "the greatest political calamity that can befall the people of any nation." Brown died at his home in December 1870, two years after his political career came to an end.

1920 Babies Hospital, Seaside Resort Facility, Opened 1920

On June 6, 1920, Wilmington physician J. Buren Sidbury opened Babies Hospital on the sound just across from Wrightsville Beach. Sidbury chose the location because he believed that seaside breezes had curative powers and were especially good for expectant mothers. Similar seaside resort hospitals could be found in Virginia Beach and Atlantic Beach, New Jersey at the time.

The original cottage that housed the hospital burned in 1927 and was replaced by a building that featured twenty-two rooms, a spacious ward, and a rooftop garden. It remained the state's only pediatric care facility until Duke Hospital opened in 1930.

From 1942 until 1967, Babies Hospital operated a nurses training program. A third floor was added and a dormitory for nurses was constructed.

Patient use peaked in 1967, and although the hospital primarily served the eastern Carolinas, it was not unusual for patients to be referred from other states up and down the East Coast. In 1978 the board of directors closed the hospital since the need for a specialized facility had by then diminished. Progress in the treatment of children's diseases had replaced the efficacious sea breezes.

The building was demolished in 2003 over the objections of preservationists.

1928 "The Squire of Turkey Creek," Bascom Lamar Lunsford

On June 6, 1928, Bascom Lamar Lunsford kicked off the first Mountain Dance and Folk Festival, an annual tradition that continues "along about sundown" to this day in Asheville. That event spawned similar festivals far and wide. Pete Seeger attended the gathering in 1935 and thereafter dedicated his life to folk music.

The festival was initially held in conjunction with Asheville's Rhododendron Festival but split off to become a separate event in 1930. It was committed to presenting the participants with dignity and to showcasing the authentic culture of the region in a time when popular culture portrayed the music and musicians who created it as "hillbillies."

Billed as the "Minstrel of Appalachia," Lunsford was an avid collector and promoter of traditional mountain music and thus a natural choice to start the festival. In the course of song collecting, he claimed to have spent time in more homes between West Virginia and Alabama "than anybody but God." It was his native region, which he loved and where he sought to preserve the old-time ways. He was born in Mars Hill but moved in 1925 to Turkey Creek in Buncombe County.

Lunsford is widely known for his rendition of "I Wish I Was a Mole in the Ground," a plaintive tune that has amused and puzzled listeners for generations. He penned "Mountain Dew" and performed for the Roosevelts, King George, and Queen Elizabeth in 1939.

Lunsford recorded his "memory collection" of 350 songs for the Library of Congress in 1949. He was an eccentric, sporting a starched white shirt and black bowtie as symbols of defiance against the prevalent hillbilly stereotype.

Bascom Lamar Lunsford (*far left*) and two "Alabama visitors" at the Mountain Music Festival.

1771 First Burial in God's Acre

On June 7, 1771, the first burial in God's Acre, the cemetery of the Salem Moravian Congregation, took place when the body of John Birkhead was laid to rest.

God's Acre is the common name for Moravian cemeteries, most of which are divided into large squares separated by pathways. The identical stones in the churchyard are all white marble and recumbent. Their uniformity, except for the names, is symbolic of the Moravian belief in the equality of all in the eyes of God. In accordance with the eighteenth century choir system, men and women are buried on opposite sides of the main path, just as the Brethren and Sisters sat at worship.

Salem Congregation's God's Acre, in Winston-Salem, is the largest in North Carolina. It contains more than six thousand graves. It is used by the thirteen Moravian churches that form the Congregation. Birkhead's grave is in the second square on the right through the central arch of the cemetery.

Amid the hustle and bustle of a busy city, God's Acre provides a calming place in which to admire the quiet beauty and serenity of the humble surroundings.

1801 Stephen Lee and His Asheville School

On June 7, 1801, educator and Civil War soldier Stephen Lee was born. Lee operated a Buncombe County school, highly regarded in the region for its academic rigor, from 1846 until 1879.

At the outbreak of the Civil War, Lee was elected colonel of both the Fifteenth and Sixteenth North Carolina Troops but chose to command the latter regiment. Taking command in June 1861, Lee led his regiment against Union forces led by George McClellan in the western Virginia campaigns of the summer and fall of 1861. In the winter of 1861 and 1862, the Sixteenth was assigned to a brigade of Georgians and South Carolinians stationed at Dumfries, Virginia.

The sixty-one-year-old Lee resigned from the Confederate army in February 1862, citing "old age, and swelling of the legs," but his time away from the military would prove short. He returned to Buncombe County and began teaching but in 1864 organized many of his students and local elderly men into a reserve unit called the Silver Greys. The Silver Greys and about 250 other locals fought Union troops in an engagement known as the Battle of Asheville in April 1865.

After the war Lee resumed teaching.

1969 Private Dan Bullock, USMC, Youngest Vietnam Casualty

On June 7, 1969, Private First Class Dan Bullock, a rifleman in the U.S. Marine Corps, was mortally wounded by a burst of enemy small arms fire. He died shortly thereafter. He was only fifteen years old.

At the time he was killed, Bullock was scurrying about to bolster the ammunition supply of the Second Platoon of Company F at An Hoa Combat Base outside Da Nang in South Vietnam. The base was under active assault by the North Vietnamese.

Raised in Goldsboro, Bullock was big for his age and thus able to carry off a deception when enlisting. His mother died when he was eleven, and he moved with his father to New York, to the Williamsburg section of Brooklyn.

At age fourteen, he altered his birth certificate, changing the year of his birth from 1953 to 1949, and enlisted in the Marines. Training at Parris Island was tough, but he survived with the help of fellow Marines. He had been in Vietnam for just three weeks when he was killed. A week later the *New York Times* broke the news about Bullock's age, and the Defense Department has confirmed that he was the youngest of the war's fifty-eight thousand American casualties.

Public attention came to his story in 2000, when television talk show host Sally Jesse Raphael purchased a headstone for his grave in Goldsboro.

1973 Tortoises Take Up Residence at the Zoo

On June 7, 1973, two Galapagos tortoises became the first residents of the North Carolina Zoo in Asheboro, slated to open the following year.

The huge reptiles, native to the Galapagos Islands off the coast of Ecuador, were purchased by the North Carolina Zoological Society from Evelia Burr of Concord, whose late husband had hatched them from eggs. The pair, considered endangered species, cost five thousand dollars.

The public was enlisted to help find monikers for them in a "Name the Tortoises Contest." More than two thousand entries were submitted, and a Raleigh woman had the winning suggestion with the names Tort and Retort. The four-hundred-pound tortoises, both in their twenties, were housed in a temporary enclosure until permanent quarters could be built.

The idea for the North Carolina Zoo was first proposed by the Raleigh Jaycees in 1967. The Jaycees and other community leaders led a statewide fundraising campaign to convince North Carolinians of the need for a zoo, and a site in Randolph County was selected. The zoo opened temporary exhibits in 1974 before moving into its permanent home in 1979.

The North Carolina Zoo is the largest "natural habitat" zoo in the world, and it remains a popular destination.

JUN 7

"God's Acre" cemetary of the Salem Moravian Congregation.

JUN 8

1868 Wilmington's Robert R. Taylor, Pioneer Black Architect

On June 8, 1868, architect Robert R. Taylor was born in Wilmington.

Taylor learned construction from his father Henry, the son of a white slave owner and a black mother, who was a successful builder.

Taylor worked for his father until entering MIT in 1888, where he was the school's first black architecture student. While at MIT, Taylor met Booker T. Washington. Their friendship drew him to the Tuskegee Institute in Alabama, where he went to work after graduating in 1892.

At Tuskegee Taylor designed and oversaw the construction of forty-five campus buildings and drew up plans for many others. The campus chapel, completed in 1898, is considered his crowning achievement. He continued to work at Tuskegee as an architect and director of "mechanical industries" until his retirement to Wilmington in 1935, except for a brief three-year stint in Cleveland around the turn of the twentieth century.

Two highlights of Taylor's career his 1929 trip to Liberia to plan the "the Tuskegee of Africa" and his appointment to the Mississippi Valley Flood Relief Commission by Pres. Herbert Hoover.

Taylor remained active in North Carolina's civic and religious life until his death in 1942. He is buried at Pine Forest Cemetery in Wilmington.

1917 Bavarian Village Constructed by POWs in Hot Springs

On June 8, 1917, the first of twenty-three hundred Germans arrived by train at Hot Springs to begin life in a World War I internment camp. Their civilian merchant ships had been docked in various American ports two months earlier when the United States entered the war. At that time the government seized the German vessels and declared their officers and crews "alien enemies."

Unable to return the men home while war was raging, the government leased the luxurious Mountain Park Hotel in Hot Springs to house them. Each of the hotel's two hundred steam-heated, electric-lighted bedrooms accommodated between three and five German officers, while rows of barracks and accessory buildings were constructed on the resort's grounds and golf course to house crew members.

When not farmed out for lumbering or road building projects, homesick internees inside the barbed-wire-enclosed camp created a Bavarian village—including houses, a church, and even a carousel—using driftwood from the French Broad River, tin cans, and other materials. They also crafted furniture, grew gardens, and played sports. A German brass band provided concerts for the townspeople every Sunday afternoon.

After living in the camp for seventeen months, many internees developed close friendships with local families. Some returned to visit after the war ended.

1933 Clayton's William E. Dodd, Minister to Hitler's Germany

On June 8, 1933, William Edward Dodd, a Johnston County native, was appointed ambassador to Germany amid rising tensions in Europe.

Born in 1869 near Clayton, Dodd studied history at what's now Virginia Tech, earning a master's degree in 1897. Shortly thereafter, he sailed for Germany and entered the University of Leipzig to pursue a Ph.D. in history. Dodd returned to America in 1899 and later taught history at Randolph-Macon College and the University of Chicago, where he became a nationally-renowned expert on the history of the Old South before taking up his diplomatic assignment.

Dodd's tenure as ambassador to Germany coincided with the rise of the Nazi Party. Having run afoul of the State Department in 1937 for writing materials critical of the Nazi-controlled government, Dodd was recalled the following year. He returned to his farm in Virginia, where he died of pneumonia in 1940.

During the Nuremburg Trials in April 1946, Dodd's detailed diary was used as evidence against Hjalmar Schacht, Adolph Hitler's minister of economics and president of the Reichsbank. Having been arrested by the Germans during the war and serving time in a concentration camp, Schacht ultimately was acquitted of the war crimes charges.

Robert R. Taylor as a student at MIT, ca. 1890.

William E. Dodd, June 10, 1933

JUN
9

1864 Blockade Runner Grounded Off Bogue Banks

On June 9, 1864, the SS *Pevensey*, a Confederate blockade runner, was run aground at Pine Knoll Shores by the Union supply ship *New Berne*. At the time the *Pevensey's* crew was disoriented, thinking they were much closer to Cape Fear than they actually were.

To prevent Union capture of the supplies on board, the crew exploded the ship's boilers, then escaped to shore, where they were captured and taken to Fort Macon. One crew member was apprehended before even making it that far. The *Pevensey*, an iron-hulled sidewheel steamer, was typical of the type of vessel used to run the Federal blockade during the Civil War. The ship had successfully run the blockade at Cape Fear four times before she was lost.

Though the *Pevensey* is less well preserved than other blockade runner wrecks in the Cape Fear region, people can actually see a portion of it from the beach, making it a special curiosity. The wreck has captivated beachgoers for years and is known locally as the "Iron Steamer." It was studied extensively by the Office of State Archaeology in 2000.

1953 North Carolina's Texas Pete, Cousin to Louisiana's Tabasco

On June 9, 1953, the trademark "Texas Pete" was registered to the TW Garner Company of Winston-Salem as a hot sauce for use on prepared foods. Made from hot red peppers, vinegar, and salt, "Texas Pete" was first used commercially in 1936 as a spicier version of the Garner family's popular barbeque sauce.

Thad Garner got the original barbeque sauce recipe from a restaurant he bought at age sixteen. That sauce was made in the family kitchen and peddled throughout the state by his father Sam. Joined by brothers Ralph and Harold, the "four Garners" built a successful food business, which continues to thrive on the site of original Garner family home.

"Texas Pete" was chosen to evoke the spicy Mexican inspired foods of Texas. "Pete" comes from Harold's nickname. In the 1930s, with cowboys being popular movie icons, the Texas Pete trademark represented independent self-reliance. During World War II Texas Pete and other Garner products were sold to the U.S. government as soldier rations. "Texas Pete" was also used as the name of a cartoon villain in the 1980s BBC *SuperTed* cartoon.

The Garner foods trademark was originally only for the sauce, though the family later expanded to produce Texas Pete hot dog chili, honey mustard, seafood cocktail, green pepper sauce, Worcestershire sauce, and Buffalo wing sauce.

1978 Asheville's Robert Moog, Father of the Synthesizer

On June 9, 1978, Robert Moog incorporated Big Briar, his musical instrument company in Asheville. In 1963 Moog, an engineer, had invented the Moog synthesizer that made him famous.

As a teenager Moog had been interested in the theremin, an obscure musical instrument that produced, via hand waving in an electromagnetic field, the strange, ethereal sounds that were used in many of the science fiction films of the 1950s. At age fourteen he built one and with his father's help turned it into a business, R. A. Moog Company, which was incorporated in the state of New York in 1954.

An amateur musician, Moog was fascinated by electronic instruments and intrigued by the emerging world of electronics. He attached circuits to a keyboard and, in doing so, invented a much more affordable and portable synthesizer.

In spite of the successes, the company, which was eventually renamed Moog Music, fell on hard times due to Moog's lack of business experience. He sold his trademark and worked as an engineer for the company that bought Moog Music until he established Big Briar. Moog reacquired his trademark, changing the name of the company back to Moog Music, Inc. in 2002.

Each year Moogfest, originally in Asheville but in Durham since 2016, celebrates electronic music.

Thad W. Garner in front of a large display of his Texas Pete Original Hot Sauce.

1786 Slaves Bound for Somerset Place Arrive, 1786

On June 10, 1786, the brig *Camden* arrived in Edenton, importing eighty Negroes from West Africa. The slaves were brought to North Carolina by a group known as the Lake Company, a venture founded to promote rice cultivation on the edge of Lake Phelps in what is now Washington County. At the time importation of slaves was still legal.

Formed by three prominent men from Edenton, the Lake Company sought to use slave labor to dig a canal from Lake Phelps to the upper reaches of the Scuppernong River, thus accessing Albemarle Sound. Eventually, Josiah Collins would be the sole owner of the Lake Company.

The Lake Company slaves completed the canal, which was six miles long, twenty feet wide, and between four and six feet deep, in 1788. The swampland was transformed into a prosperous plantation, which Collins named Somerset Place. By the 1790 census he owned 113 slaves.

Today Somerset Place is a state historic site.

1861 Henry Lawson Wyatt, Dead at Bethel, 1861

On June 10, 1861, Henry Lawson Wyatt lost his life at the Battle of Bethel in Virginia.

It was the first battle of the Civil War, and Wyatt was among the first casualties. A member of the Edgecombe Guards, part of the First North Carolina Infantry, Wyatt was mortally wounded as he dashed across an open field with four others. A volley ripped through the squad and all hit the ground. Wyatt was shot and seen to have "a clot of blood on his forehead as large as a man's fist." His fellow soldiers found him still breathing and carried him to a hospital in Yorktown. He weakened through the evening, and the following morning the nineteen-year-old carpenter died.

Wyatt's compatriots escorted his body to a boat that carried him up the York River. From there, his remains travelled by rail to Richmond, where he was interred at Hollywood Cemetery, the first of roughly eighteen thousand Confederate burials at that cemetery.

As early as 1866 Wyatt was hailed as the Confederacy's first war casualty. Others pointed to earlier deaths in smaller actions, setting a stage for a debate that rages to this day. Wyatt defenders have countered by recognizing him as the first casualty in a line of battle.

1946 Car Accident Claims Jack Johnson, 1946

On June 10, 1946, Jack Johnson, the first African American heavyweight champion boxer, died at St. Agnes Hospital in Raleigh.

Johnson won the boxing title in 1908 in Australia. Immediately after his victory the public cried for a "great white hope," in other words, a white man to defeat Johnson. In 1910 Jim Jeffries, the champion from 1899 to 1905, was coaxed out of retirement to fight Johnson. In what was one of the most publicized events in the history of sports, Johnson defeated Jeffries easily. Upon the public outcry that Jeffries was past his prime, Jeffries responded that he couldn't have beaten Johnson, even at his best. Johnson went on to successfully defend his belt for seven years.

For most of his life, Johnson was passionate about sports cars. Passing through North Carolina in 1946, his car struck a utility pole south of Franklinton. He was taken to the closest hospital that accepted black patients, St. Agnes, where he died of his injuries. Appropriately, the occupation listed on the sixty-eight-year-old's death certificate was prize fighter.

Jack Johnson, 1909.

Jack Johnson peers through the steering wheel of his Thomas Flyer automobile, 1909.

1719 Tobias Knight, Charged with Accessory to Piracy

On June 11, 1719, colonial official, attorney, and judge Tobias Knight died.

While he appears in North Carolina records as early as 1710, it wasn't until two years later that he figured prominently as the secretary and collector of the colony. He soon was beset by a series of scandals. The first came when Knight was accused of stealing from the Church after refusing to repay a debt, which Gov. William Glover had accrued and which many felt was Knight's responsibility on behalf of his wife, Catherine Glover Knight. Catherine was Governor Glover's widow.

A more significant scandal came later and involved the notorious pirate Blackbeard. After Blackbeard's death some of his slaves were tried in Virginia. They testified that Knight had worked with the pirate. Charged as an accessory to piracy, Knight was tried in 1719. As an attorney, he spoke on his own behalf and convinced Gov. Charles Eden and the council of his innocence. In spite of that, Knight resigned as the colony's chief justice and was accused again, this time along with Governor Eden and others, of collusion with pirates.

Before he could be investigated further, Knight died after a long illness.

1937 Eleanor Roosevelt Visits Penderlea, 1937

On June 11, 1937, Eleanor Roosevelt kicked up her heels with the homesteaders at Penderlea.

The First Lady visited Pender County to check on the progress at one of her husband Franklin's premier homestead sites. Hugh MacRae of Wilmington first had the idea, during the depths of the Depression, to create a model farm community at Penderlea on a grand scale. He had experimented with similar communities across southeastern North Carolina early in the twentieth century.

The intention at Penderlea was to build the "best planned rural community in the world." A tract of ten thousand acres was set aside, land was cleared, and homes and a community center were built. MacRae disagreed with those in Washington as to how Penderlea should be managed, and in May 1934 the entire program was federalized.

Though Roosevelt and his New Dealers were pursuing similar programs across the country, no other rural project was as large as Penderlea. The original goal of five hundred twenty-acre farms was never met. A total of 142 units were leased but, by 1941 few of the original homesteaders remained.

Memories of the experiment remain vivid at Penderlea, where a large community building remains, and a museum interprets that page in history.

A family working in a field at Penderlea, 1950.

1838 U.S. Army Rounds Up Cherokees, 1838

On June 12, 1838, Gen. Winfield Scott ordered troops to begin rounding up Cherokee Indians for internment at Fort Butler, near what is now Murphy, and eventual forced relocation to Oklahoma.

The order was part of a larger effort led by Scott at the behest of Pres. Martin Van Buren to remove the Cherokee from Tennessee, Georgia, Alabama, and North Carolina as authorized under the Indian Removal Act of 1830. Scott was personally involved in the action in southwestern North Carolina because the Army believed the area was most likely to be a center of conflict.

After a week the troops had arrested more than two-thirds of the local Cherokee population, and by early July nearly twenty-five hundred Cherokee were in custody. Those and approximately 12,500 others would ultimately make the journey westward on the Trail of Tears between October 1838 and March 1839, while about three or four hundred Cherokees hid out in North Carolina, laying the foundation for the purchase of the Qualla Boundary property and the establishment of North Carolina's Cherokee Reservation.

The Eastern Band of Cherokee was not formally granted freedom to live in North Carolina until 1866 and was not recognized as a separate entity from the Cherokee living in Oklahoma until 1868.

JUN 12

1886 Hanes Brand Began in Winston-Salem

On June 12, 1886, James G. Hanes, founder of the Hanes knitwear enterprise, was born in what's now Winston-Salem.

Following his 1909 graduation from the University of North Carolina, Hanes returned to Forsyth County and joined the family textile business. His factory, Hanes Hosiery Mills, became the world's largest manufacturer of women's nylon seamless hosiery. He was known to have said, "Nature gives you seamless legs; Hanes gives you seamless nylons." In 1965 Hanes Hosiery Mills Company merged with P. H. Hanes Knitting Company to become the internationally known Hanes Corporation.

In addition to his work with the family business, Hanes served on the board of directors for organizations including the Norfolk and Western Railway, the New York City-based Savoy Hotel, Hanes Dye and Finishing Company, the National Association of Manufacturers, and Wachovia Bank and Trust Company. He also took an active role in local government, most notably serving for four years as mayor of Winston-Salem and for twenty-two years on Forsyth County's Board of Commissioners.

At his death in 1972, James G. Hanes willed his stately English manor-style home and the adjoining thirty-two-acre estate to the Southeastern Center for Contemporary Art.

1942 Seymour Johnson Field Transferred to U.S. Army Air Force

On June 12, 1942, the U.S. Army Air Force took over Seymour Johnson Field for use as a training center.

In 1941 the Works Progress Administration built a municipal airport south of Goldsboro; the dedication was held one week before the attack on Pearl Harbor. The field was named for Seymour Johnson, a Goldsboro native, U.S. Naval Academy graduate, and test pilot for Grumman Aircraft, who died in a crash shortly before the war.

At the peak of its strength, the field hosted twenty-seven thousand troops. During the course of the war more than 250 thousand troops trained there. The 326th Fighter Group arrived in 1943, and in 1944 basic training of F-4 pilots became the field's primary mission. At the close of the war, it functioned as a separation center. In May 1946 it was deactivated.

In April 1956, the U.S. Air Force reopened the facility as Seymour Johnson Air Force Base following a successful campaign by Goldsboro community leaders. Today the base is home to the F-15 Strike Eagle. It is the only Air Force base named for a naval officer.

First Lieutenant Benjamin D. Moore, Jr., Lead Pilot of the B- 17 Bomber, Squadron B, 536th Army Air Force Base Unit, United States Army Air Force, during World War II, in uniform. The photograph was taken at Seymour Johnson Field about 1945.

1903 A. J. Tomlinson's "Fields of the Wood"

On June 13, 1903, Ambrose Jessup Tomlinson spent much time in prayer at the "fields of the wood" in Cherokee County and had a revelation that the local Holiness church was the Church of God as prophesized in the Bible.

Tomlinson, born in Indiana in 1865 and known to most as "A.J.," made his living as a Quaker Bible salesman. He traveled widely before settling in the mountains of North Carolina to spread the word of his adopted Holiness church. There he published a monthly religious tract intended for the "speedy evangelization of the mountain districts of North Carolina, Georgia, Tennessee and the world."

Tomlinson's joining the church after praying on the mountain in June 1903 is believed by members to have begun the restoration of the true Church of God. He became a charismatic leader of that congregation and others soon after. In 1907 the organization took the name Church of God and within a few years joined the Pentecostal movement.

In 1940 Tomlinson established a monument in Murphy at the site of his revelation from God. Before he died in 1943, he inscribed into the hillside in rock the "world's largest Ten Commandments." Now known as Fields of the Wood, the site is a Bible park operated by the Church of God of Prophecy.

1905 Lesley Riddle, Collaborator with the Carter Family

On June 13, 1905, African American old-time musician Lesley Riddle was born in the Silvers Gap community north of Burnsville. Riddle learned to play blues and gospel songs on the guitar after losing most of a leg in an accident at a cement plant. He had to adjust his picking techniques to use only his thumb, index finger, and little finger after losing two fingers in a shotgun accident.

A.P. Carter, patriarch of the famous Carter family, first heard Riddle play and sing in Kingsport, Tennessee in 1927 and quickly recruited him to help advance the Carter family's fame. Carter and Riddle visited African American communities and churches throughout Appalachian Tennessee, Virginia, and North Carolina to find new songs for the Carter Family. Riddle would memorize the tunes and words before returning to teach the songs to Sara and Maybelle Carter. "Mother Maybelle" learned her trademark guitar techniques from Riddle, including using a pocketknife for slide guitar work.

Riddle never made a living at music; he worked as a shoeshine boy, presser, and school crossing guard. In the 1960s he accompanied Mike Seeger and the New Lost City Ramblers on the folk festival circuit.

Riddle is celebrated by an annual festival, Riddlefest.

Brownie McGhee and Lesley Riddle, 1920s.

1929 Bob Scott Followed Father Kerr Into Executive Mansion

On June 13, 1929, Gov. Robert W. Scott was born in Alamance County to a family active in the state's political and social life.

After attending school at Duke and N.C. State, Scott returned home to manage his family's dairy farm. He served in the Army's Counter Intelligence Corps in Asia before being elected the state's lieutenant governor in 1964.

Elected to the state's top job in 1968, Scott became the second governor in North Carolina history (after Richard Dobbs Spaight Jr.) to follow his father into office. Scott's signature achievement was a reorganization of state government and a realignment of the state's system of higher education. He consolidated more than three hundred state agencies and offices into seventeen cabinet-level departments and centralized the state's public universities in one system. Scott also helped institute a kindergarten program, increased vocational education in high schools, and resolved conflicts arising from court-ordered busing to achieve racial integration.

At the close of his term as governor, Scott became vice president of the N. C. Agribusiness Council. He went on to co-chair the Appalachian Regional Commission, to unsuccessfully challenge Gov. James B. Hunt Jr. in the Democratic primary for governor in 1980, and to serve as president of the state's community college system.

Scott's governorship marked the end of a seventy-two-year Democratic monopoly on the office.

1940 USS *North Carolina* Launched

On June 13, 1940, the USS *North Carolina* (BB-55) was launched at the Brooklyn Navy Yard, beginning a highly decorated career. Commissioned on April 9, 1941, the ship became the first of ten fast battleships to join the fleet in World War II. The *North Carolina* and her sister ship, *Washington*, comprised the North Carolina Class of battleships.

At the time of her commissioning, the *North Carolina* was considered the world's greatest sea weapon. Armed with nine sixteen-inch guns in three turrets and twenty five-inch .38-caliber guns in ten twin mounts, the *North Carolina* proved a formidable weapons platform.

During World War II the *North Carolina* participated in every major naval offensive in the Pacific theater, including the Battles of Guadalcanal, Marshall Islands, Luzon, Iwo Jima, and Okinawa, earning fifteen battle stars along the way. In all, the USS *North Carolina* carried out nine shore bombardments, sank an enemy troopship, destroyed at least twenty-four enemy aircraft, and assisted in shooting down many more. Although the Japanese claimed six times that the USS *North Carolina* had been sunk, she survived many close calls and near misses and by war's end had lost only ten men in action and had sixty-seven wounded.

1838 The Pulaski Explosion, 1838

On June 14, 1838, a boiler on the steamship *Pulaski* exploded while the ship was off the North Carolina coast.

The vessel was bound for Baltimore from Savannah. She carried a crew of about thirty-six and close to 150 passengers, many of whom were killed immediately by the scalding steam. Others drowned or perished when struck by falling wreckage. Two of the Pulaski's small boats with survivors made it to shore the following day, landing in Onslow County.

Of the passengers who were not either killed instantly or made it to the lifeboats, many floated on two large chunks of the wreck, while others drifted on pieces of furniture lashed together or small shreds of debris. After four days drifting in the open sea, twenty-three people were taken off a portion of the wreck by the schooner *Henry Camerdon*. Those survivors shared that they had seen another group that morning, and the ship headed in the direction indicated, where it found and saved another seven people.

Two of the survivors, who had drifted together on pieces of wreckage for a number of days, had plenty of time to get to know one another and, after experiencing each other's knack for enduring, became engaged at sea.

JUN 14

1864 Civil War General and Episcopal Priest Leonidas Polk

On June 14, 1864, Confederate Lt. Gen. Leonidas Polk was killed at Pine Mountain, Georgia. While he was observing the Union's position with Gens. Joseph E. Johnston and William J. Hardee, a shell fired by Federal artillery struck Polk in the left arm, traveled through his body, and exploded on a nearby tree. Nearly cut in half, he died instantly.

Born in 1806 in Raleigh, Polk was the second cousin of James K. Polk, the eleventh President of the United States. Shortly after Leonidas Polk graduated from the U.S. Military Academy at West Point, he resigned his commission to attend Virginia Theological Seminary. He became an Episcopal priest in 1831 and worked his way up the church hierarchy to become Bishop of Louisiana in 1841.

Despite limited military experience, Polk was appointed a major general by his West Point classmate and Confederate president Jefferson Davis in 1861. This made him one of the most controversial leaders in the Confederate Army. Nevertheless, in 1862 he was promoted to lieutenant general. His relationship with other officers was often strained, if not adversarial, but his men always loved him. Polk often ministered to his troops, putting on his robes over his uniform.

1908 John Scott Trotter, Arranger for Bing Crosby and Charlie Brown

On June 14, 1908, arranger, composer, and orchestra leader John Scott Trotter was born in Charlotte.

A piano student from a young age, Trotter began playing piano professionally with Hal Kemp's band after meeting Kemp as a student at UNC. At the end of his first year, Trotter left college to continue with the band, serving as its arranger as well as the pianist. In 1936 Trotter left Kemp's band and began orchestrating for Bing Crosby, an association that would last for almost twenty years.

In the 1950s Trotter, known for his easy-going style and large physical size, began working in television, first as music director for the *George Gobel Show* and later on several specials for Crosby.

Trotter later directed the music for the Charlie Brown specials and movies, receiving nominations for both an Oscar and a Grammy for *A Boy Named Charlie Brown*. He is credited with the idea of using the trombone for the teacher's voice, which became a hallmark of the animated movies.

Trotter died in 1975 in Los Angeles and is buried in Sharon Memorial Park in Charlotte.

1918 USS Cyclops, Lost at Sea, 1918

On June 14, 1918, following a ninety-day search operation, the U.S. Navy declared the crew and passengers of the USS *Cyclops* dead. Of the 293 souls on board, six were North Carolinians: Junius L. Dellinger, Leonard Calvert Day, George Henry Allred, Isaac P. Dancy, Robert Hardy Powers, and Robert Earl Riddle.

The *Cyclops* was last seen on March 4 at Barbados and was heading toward the port of Baltimore at half speed because of engine trouble. Radio contact with the ship was lost that same day. In April, more than a month after the *Cyclops's* disappearance, Navy officials finally released the ship's overdue status to the Associated Press. French and American vessels searched trade routes between the two ports but found no trace of the ship or its passengers.

Rumors regarding the ship's fate spread rampantly in the media. Sabotage by the ship's German-born commander, capture at sea, a German submarine attack, and a sudden hurricane were all cited as possible causes for its disappearance. The true reason for the ship's loss remains a mystery to this day, though many modern investigators have surmised that the over-loaded ship, which had a documented problem with extreme side-to-side tipping, quickly sank in rough seas.

Explosion of the *Pulaski*.

1838 John Chavis, Revered Antebellum Preacher and Teacher

On June 15, 1838, John Chavis, an African American teacher, preacher, and Revolutionary War veteran died.

Born sometime around 1763, Chavis had an extensive education for the time period, likely the best education of any African American of his day in North Carolina. In 1778 Chavis enlisted in the Fifth Regiment of Virginia, serving for three years with the Patriots. Honorably discharged, he studied at what is now Washington and Lee University.

Between 1801 and 1807 Chavis did mission work for the Presbyterian Church among slaves throughout the southeastern United States. He moved to Raleigh in 1809, where he began preaching as a part of the Orange County Presbytery. It was around this time that Chavis began his school, where he taught white students during the day and black students in the evening.

In 1832 free blacks lost many of their rights in North Carolina, and Chavis lost his freedom to preach and to teach. He published his only written work in 1833, a sermon entitled "An Essay on Atonement." The piece was successful and widely read and helped to supplement his income during the final years of his life.

1970 The Mixed Fortunes of the Land of Oz

On June 15, 1970, the Land of Oz theme park opened on Beech Mountain in Avery County.

The park, based on the book and movie *The Wizard of Oz*, was the brainchild of entrepreneur Grover Robbins, the same man who opened Tweetsie Railroad. It featured costumed characters reminiscent of the movie, with a recreation of the city of Oz, complete with a yellow brick road. In its early years the theme park attracted many visitors, and experienced much success.

That began to change in December 1975, when a fire caused major damage to many of the park's structures. The park experienced financial troubles and attendance declined. It closed in 1980.

The property was abandoned for several years until the landowner restored the park in the late 1990s. A few former employees decided to hold an "Autumn of Oz" festival to commemorate their days of working at the park. The festival became an annual event.

Today the Land of Oz is used primarily as a venue for special events and private parties. Individuals can also rent the facility and spend a night in Dorothy's house.

Land of Oz characters during the 1970–1971 season.

1987 G. W. Creef and the Shad Boat

On June 15, 1987, the shad boat was designated as North Carolina's official state historical boat.

The legislation was introduced by Sen. Marc Basnight of Dare County, the state's easternmost county, which in addition to bordering the ocean is flanked by a number of sounds where shad boats were employed by local fishermen.

The design originated with boat builder George Washington Creef Sr., who crafted the vessel in his boat building shed on Roanoke Island in the years following the Civil War. Shad boats were used to retrieve fish from pound nets and were particularly suited for navigating the shallow sounds and weathering unpredictable wind shifts.

Shad boats were built from native white cedar, which grows in abundance on the Dare County mainland and is prized for its light weight and ability to resist rot. These small watercraft featured a rounded hull and were powered by three sails—a main sail, jib, and topsail.

The advent of the gasoline engine and the rising price of materials caused shad boats to fall out of vogue by the 1930s.

1988 *Bull Durham* Premiered

On June 15, 1988, *Bull Durham* premiered. The film, starring Kevin Costner, Susan Sarandon, and Tim Robbins, was a blockbuster hit, grossing more than fifty million dollars in North America alone. *Sports Illustrated* put it at the top of its list of the greatest sports movies of all time.

The film centers around the Bulls, Durham's minor league baseball team. "Crash" Davis, played by Costner, is brought in to help prepare "Nuke" LaLoosh (Robbins) for the Major Leagues. Baseball groupie Annie Savoy (Sarandon) initially becomes involved with Nuke but finds herself increasingly attracted to Crash.

The phrase "Bull Durham" has its origins in the post-Civil War era. Durham tobacco industrialist John R. Green based his tobacco advertising on a popular brand of mustard made in Durham, England that featured the head of a Durham bull on its label. The tobacco was widely advertised and became one of the most recognized American products of the late 1800s and early 1900s.

Bull Durham brought national attention to both the famous tobacco name and the Durham Bulls.

JUN 15

Shad Boat Construction Shed, Roanoke Island, N.C., about 1907 (*background*).

JUN 16

1783 Miranda's Plans for Tryon Palace Recovered

On June 16, 1783, Francisco de Miranda visited Tryon Palace. The Venezuelan revolutionary soldier, scholar, and world traveler evaded political arrest in Havana, Cuba by coming to the United States.

Arriving in New Bern on June 10, he stayed in a local tavern for about a month. Miranda, a lifelong journal keeper, recorded his thoughts and impressions of places he visited. Regarding his trip to New Bern, he mentioned a barbecue held in town to celebrate the end of the Revolution. Attended by common folk, gentry, and government officials, the event, in Miranda's eyes, was democracy in its purest sense.

Miranda's journals now reside in an archives in Caracas. When research began for the restoration of Tryon Palace in the 1940s, historians consulted them and found a reference to the original drawings of the garden but not the drawings themselves. In 1991 researchers renewed efforts to obtain copies of the drawings and finally succeeded.

Despite the landmark find, the documentary evidence in the drawings was not straightforward and conflicts with other historical evidence about the Palace gardens. The decision was made not to alter the current landscape until additional research was done, and none of the historic garden plans has ever been implemented at the Palace.

1903 "Brad's Drink," now Pepsi-Cola, Stirred Up (in) New Bern

On June 16, 1903, the U.S. Patent Office registered the trademark of New Bern pharmacist Caleb Bradham's new soft drink, Pepsi-Cola.

Fond of concocting fresh syrup flavors to mix with soda water at his drugstore's soda fountain, Bradham had developed the formula for his new beverage in 1893. His friends initially dubbed it "Brad's Drink." But in August 1898 Bradham renamed his product "Pepsi-Cola" after two of its ingredients: pepsin, a digestive enzyme, and kola nut extract. Other ingredients were sugar, vanilla, and "rare oils."

Working in his pharmacy's back room, Bradham launched the Pepsi-Cola Company and incorporated it in 1902. He first applied to register "Pepsi-Cola" as a trademark on September 23 of that year. The application, approved in 1903, described his product as "flavoring syrup for soda water." At first he mixed the syrup and sold it exclusively to soda fountains. Then, realizing that a ready-to-drink beverage might appeal to more people, he began bottling and franchising Pepsi-Cola in 1905. On April 15, 1905, he applied for a second Pepsi-Cola trademark for a "tonic beverage." Registered a year later, that trademark was renewed and is currently owned by the multinational corporation, PepsiCo, Inc., of Purchase, N.Y.

1939 Billy "Crash" Craddock, Rockabilly to Country

On June 16, 1939, country music star Billy "Crash" Craddock was born in Greensboro.

Craddock grew up in a very musical family. His parents and twelve siblings enjoyed singing and playing instruments together. He earned his nickname "Crash" during his years as a running back for his high school football team.

While coming of age in Greensboro, Craddock was musically influenced by Lefty Frizzell and Little Jimmy Dickens. He was also inspired by the music and career of Elvis Presley. When he decided to pursue music after high school, his parents were very encouraging and supportive.

By the early 1950s Craddock was on his way to stardom. He debuted as a "teen idol" with Columbia Records and enjoyed some success with rockabilly and pop songs. He began to focus more on country music in 1971, when he signed on with Cartwheel Records, but his style remained up-tempo, influenced by his years as a rock musician.

Craddock reached legendary status during the 1970s and 1980s. "Rub it In," "Dream Lover," and "Sweet Magnolia Blossom" were among his major hit singles. His cover of Tony Orlando's "Knock Three Times" was his first Number One record.

Tryon Palace Historic Sites and Gardens.

JUN 17

1742 Prominent Patriot William Hooper

On June 17, 1742, William Hooper, one of North Carolina's three signers of the Declaration of Independence, was born. Hooper grew up in Boston and attended Harvard before moving to Wilmington and opening a law office there in 1764. Within a few years he was active in politics.

In 1774 Hooper wrote to a friend that the colonies' independence would not be far off, and within a few weeks he was selected to play a central part in it. At the First Provincial Congress in North Carolina, Hooper was elected as one of the colony's three delegates to the Continental Congress. He remained in Congress for the next few years. Although absent when the Declaration of Independence was voted on, he signed his name to the document on August 2. The next year he helped with devising the North Carolina state seal.

In April 1777 Hooper resigned from Congress and returned to Wilmington, which he represented in the General Assembly for several more years. When the British took Wilmington in January 1781, the family fled to Hillsborough.

Hooper died at age forty-eight in 1790. A nineteen-foot statue at the Guilford Courthouse National Military Park memorializes Hooper, whose remains were moved there in 1894.

1864 Explosives Advanced by Gabriel Rains during the Civil War

On June 17, 1864, Brig. Gen. Gabriel Rains was appointed chief of the newly created Torpedo Bureau of the Confederate army.

Born in New Bern in 1803, Rains graduated from the U.S. Military Academy at West Point in 1827. He began experimenting with mines, then called "torpedoes," in 1839 during the Seminole War. At the outbreak of the Civil War, he resigned his commission and offered his services to the Confederacy.

Rains continued to develop his "infernal machines" for use on land and in waterways throughout the war. Many officers in both the Union and Confederate armies thought torpedoes constituted an improper form of warfare, but Rains defended his use of explosive devices as a means to discourage a night attack by an enemy, to defend a weak point of a line, and to check enemy pursuit.

While in service in Richmond, Rains began to formulate plans for the torpedo defense of Confederate ports. Impressed with the plans, Pres. Jefferson Davis directed him to put them into operation. Rains was first sent to Vicksburg, Mississippi, then to Charleston, South Carolina and Mobile, Alabama.

Rains's torpedoes were a great success, providing an effective deterrent to Union naval attack and sinking about fifty-eight Union vessels in all.

1961 The Vagabond Players and Robroy Farquhar

On June 17, 1961, the Flat Rock Playhouse in Henderson County's village of Flat Rock was named the State Theater of North Carolina.

The venue is home to the Vagabond Players, the oldest Equity acting troupe in the state. The ensemble formed in 1937 in New York City under the direction of Robroy Farquhar. In 1940 the Vagabond Players made their way south to North Carolina and performed for two summer seasons in a converted grist mill, the Old Mill Playhouse, near Highland Lake.

Following World War II the troupe resumed performing in a schoolhouse near Lake Summit that had been renovated into a theater for use by the Carolina Players. In 1952 the Vagabond Players purchased a lot in Flat Rock and began staging plays under a fifty by eighty-five-foot tent erected on the site.

The current playhouse, built in 1956, seats five hundred people. Through the years tens of thousands have enjoyed performances. Acclaimed one of the top summer theaters in the nation, the Flat Rock Playhouse is where many actors, actresses, directors, and stagehands have honed their craft.

Today the Flat Rock Playhouse season runs nine months, from April through December, and features drama, musicals, comedy, and children's performances.

1986 God Bless Kate Smith

On June 17, 1986, Kate Smith, "The Songbird of the South," died of complications from diabetes at Raleigh Community Hospital.

A native of Greenville, Virginia, the singer renowned for her rendition of Irving Berlin's "God Bless America" spent the final years of her life in the Capital City near her sister Helena Steele. While living in Raleigh, she resided in a quiet cul-de-sac off Millbrook Avenue.

For an earlier generation Smith represented all that was good and right about America. Her professional recording career began in 1925, and she became a major star of radio. She was a large woman and could belt out songs, such as her personal theme "When the Moon Comes Over the Mountain," like nobody's business.

A professional hockey team, the Philadelphia Flyers, played her recording of "God Bless America" before a game in 1969. As it brought them a victory that night, they made it a team tradition and brought Miss Smith to the arena, where she created near pandemonium and provided the Flyers with an assist on their road to the Stanley Cup.

The U.S. Postal Service issued a stamp featuring Smith in 2010.

Brigadier General Gabriel J. Rains, circa 1860.

Flat Rock Playhouse, circa 1961 *(background)*.

Actors performing in *There Goes the Bride* at Flat Rock Playhouse *(far right)*.

JUN 18

1866 He Met Her on the Mountain and There He Took Her Life

On June 18, 1866, the body of Laura Foster was found in a shallow grave in Wilkes County.

She had last been seen on May 25 riding a horse down Stony Fork Road. Tom Dula, who had liaisons with both Foster and Ann Melton, was charged with her murder. She had been stabbed in the chest and reportedly was pregnant at the time of her death. Dula, a Confederate veteran, was returned to North Carolina from Tennessee, where he had fled.

Ann Melton and Tom Dula were brought to trial for murder during the fall term of Wilkes County Court, but a change of venue removed the trial to Iredell County. Dula was convicted, but Melton was found not guilty. The North Carolina Supreme Court overturned Dula's conviction. He was tried again in January 1868 and was once again convicted. This time the verdict was sustained by the Supreme Court. Dula was hanged in May 1868 in Statesville.

The subjects of mountain folk ballads sung even before his execution, Dula and Laura Foster were immortalized in the bestselling song, "The Legend of Tom Dooley," recorded by the Kingston Trio in 1958.

1867 Phantom Pain: N.C.'s Limb Replacement Program

On June 18, 1867, the state-run artificial limbs factory in Raleigh closed due to a lack of business. The state had been operating the plant through Jewett's Patent Leg Company for about eighteen months in order to fulfill the needs of the state's Confederate amputees.

North Carolina was the first of the former Confederate states to offer artificial limbs to its maimed citizens. The temporary factory was set up in Raleigh near a railroad terminus. A system was developed whereby the amputees bore no out-of-pocket expenses in visiting Raleigh for prosthetic fittings.

During the operation of the artificial limbs program, 1,550 Confederate veterans contacted the state for help. According to records in the State Archives, the total cost of the program to the state was over eighty-one thousand dollars. After defeat, the loss of thousands of lives, and economic ruin, the state's citizens still had the ability to achieve something noble by repaying, to a degree, those who had literally risked life and limb.

1875 St. Mark's, Episcopal Landmark in Wilmington

On June 18, 1875, the Right Reverend Thomas Atkinson, Bishop of the Diocese of North Carolina, consecrated St. Mark's Church in Wilmington. The congregation was the first Episcopal Church for African Americans in North Carolina.

The church can trace its roots to late 1869, when Rev. Charles Otis Brady was called to lead a new Episcopal Church for an exclusively black congregation. The worshipers initially selected the name St. Paul's but soon after adopted St. Mark's. The new congregation purchased a lot at the corner of Sixth and Mulberry Streets and began raising money for the land and the future church building.

People from around the nation contributed to the campaign, and construction on the church began in March 1871. Although the structure was not fully finished, the first church service was held in the new building in December of that year.

St. Mark's became part of the Episcopal Diocese of North Carolina as a mission in 1872. The original church building, at 220 North Sixth Street, has been extensively renovated and is still in use.

St. Mark's Church in Wilmington.

1771 Regulators Hanged in Hillsborough

On June 19, 1771, six Regulators were hanged in Hillsborough following the Battle of Alamance on May 17.

The hanging represented a culmination of the War of Regulation and the "backcountry" rebellion by Orange County Regulators. Like many of those throughout the colonies discontented with the control of and taxation by the British government, the Regulators wanted the Currency Act of 1764 and the Stamp Act of 1765 repealed.

As both sides anticipated confrontation, Regulators sent petitions to Governor Tryon, then camped out on Alamance Creek with fourteen hundred troops on May 14 and May 16. Tryon rejected the Regulators' terms, and a battle broke out until the Regulators retreated.

Several Regulators were captured and tried. After the trial Tryon pardoned six men and sent the others—Benjamin Merrill, Robert Matear, James Pugh, and two other unrecorded men—to be hanged not far from the courthouse in Hillsborough. Their exact burial location is unknown.

The site of the hanging was memorialized in 1963 by a marble slab monument erected by the N.C. Society of the Colonial Dames in America and placed next to the historic Hughes Academy schoolhouse in Hillsborough.

1949 Springs Altered Race History

On June 19, 1949, NASCAR held the first race in its top division at a three-quarter-mile dirt track at the Charlotte Speedway. Today nothing remains of that old track. Interstate 85 sits atop one of its banks, though a highway historical marker on Little Rock Road marks the place.

The race's promoter, Bill France, intended that the race provide a test of driving skill in cars similar to those actually driven by fans. The more than thirteen thousand attendees confirmed France's conviction that people would flock to see late-model sedans race. Glenn Dunnaway finished first, but his victory did not stand. Officials conducting a post-race inspection found altered rear springs, disqualified Dunnaway, and declared second-place finisher Jim Roper the winner. It was later revealed that the springs had been modified in a manner common to cars used to haul moonshine.

The success of the race led France to promote seven more "Strictly Stock" races that year, forming the foundation for what would become NASCAR. The original Charlotte Speedway would continue to be an important stop for the tour until construction of the new, larger track near Concord in 1960.

2006 Revelry Ensues After Stanley Cup Victory, 2006

On June 19, 2006, the Carolina Hurricanes won their first ever National Hockey League championship.

The Stanley Cup win came after the Canes defeated the Edmonton Oilers 3–1 in front of a sold-out crowd in the last game of a seven-game series. In addition to the team's victory, twenty-two-year-old rookie goaltender Cam Ward was recognized with the Conn Smythe Trophy, given to the most valuable player in the playoffs, for his stellar performance in relief of veteran netminder Martin Gerber.

The Stanley Cup triumph kicked off two days of celebration in Raleigh, with Gov. Mike Easley declaring June 20 "Carolina Hurricanes Day" and urging North Carolinians to wear the Hurricanes colors of red and black in support of the team. A victory parade held at the RBC Center, now the PNC Arena, drew thirty thousand fans and was covered live by WRAL.

A second parade was held in downtown Raleigh the next day, ending with a celebration at the State Capitol. Even the General Assembly paid homage to the victors, holding a special joint session, where legislators greeted head coach Peter Laviolette, Hurricanes players, and the Stanley Cup with enthusiastic applause.

The Hurricanes' 2006 Stanley Cup win was North Carolina's first professional men's sports championship.

World 400 Charlotte Speedway.

JUN 20

1780 Militias Battle at Ramsour's Mill, 1780

On June 20, 1780, at the Battle of Ramsour's Mill, Col. Francis Locke and his Patriot force stormed the defenses of the Loyalist militia led by Maj. John Moore. Farmers, not soldiers, determined the outcome of most Revolutionary War battles fought in North Carolina, as most of the skirmishes and battles were fought between Loyalist and colonial militias. Few participants had ever received formal military training.

In hopes of supplementing Lord Cornwallis's British force at Camden, South Carolina, Moore had gathered a force of thirteen hundred Loyalists near Derick Ramsour's mill in what is now Lincoln County. Knowing this, Patriot militias mobilized and began marching to the mill, launching their attack at dawn nearly a week later.

The fighting at Ramsour's Mill soon degraded into little more than a killing field, primarily because of lack of military discipline. Though the Loyalists outnumbered the Patriots almost four-to-one, many of them ran from the field. Each side lost around 150 men, but the Patriots prevailed since they had uprooted the Loyalists from their position. The battle was indecisive at best, but was illustrative of how the Patriot militia played a significant role in the war throughout the South.

1886 Thomas F. Price, Co-Founder of the Maryknoll Fathers

In June 20, 1886, Thomas F. Price was ordained a Catholic priest and assigned to St. Paul's Church in New Bern. He served as pastor there for nine years before departing for Raleigh, where he became the head of Sacred Heart Church.

While in Raleigh, Price became involved in missionary works and founded Nazareth House, an orphanage. In 1904 and again in 1910, Price lectured about his missionary methods at the meetings of the Catholic Missionary Union and developed the concept of establishing a permanent American seminary for foreign missionaries.

The school was ultimately developed at a site in Maryknoll, New York, and in 1915 received a "Decree of Praise" from Pope Pius X. Following World War I Maryknoll priests departed for their first assignment in southern China. Price went with them, but a year later he died from complications associated with appendicitis.

He was buried initially in Hong Kong, but in 1936 his remains were returned to Maryknoll, where they are interred at the chapel of the Mother House of the Missionary Society.

1921 Market Boosts Furniture Industry

On June 20, 1921, the Southern Furniture Exposition opened in High Point.

Designed by William Rose and costing more than one million dollars to construct, the ten-story building housed more than 249 thousand square feet of exhibition space. At the opening market seven hundred dealers sold more than two million dollars worth of merchandise.

High Point emerged as a furniture manufacturing center as early as 1900 owing to the nearby supply of lumber. In 1900 there were thirty-three furniture plants in the city; by 1904 there were 107. High Point's proximity to transportation, the availability of a large labor force, its abundance of quality lumber, and strong community support fueled its success.

The market, established in 1909 as a modest local effort, was reorganized in 1921 as the Southern Furniture Exposition. It was renamed the International Home Furnishings Market in 1989, and since 2001 it has been known simply as the High Point Market.

Today the semi-annual furniture market draws as many as eighty thousand attendees and encompasses 180 buildings across the city, though its core remains the original 1921 structure, with many additions. It is the biggest furniture market in the world, drawing more people than the next four largest furniture markets combined.

Southern Furniture Exposition building in High Point, 1940.

1913 Parachutist Tiny Broadwick of Vance County

On June 21, 1913, Tiny Broadwick became the first woman to jump from an airplane. Remembered as the "First Lady of Parachuting," Broadwick still holds a place in the *Guinness Book of World Records* for her achievements as a parachutist.

Born Georgia Ann Thompson, she was married at twelve, a mother at thirteen, and abandoned by her husband soon thereafter. After attending a carnival in Raleigh and seeing Charles Broadwick parachute from a balloon, Thompson joined his "World Famous Aeronauts." Soon after she became Broadwick's adopted daughter and took his surname.

At just over four feet tall, Broadwick was nicknamed "Tiny." She thrilled audiences by jumping from a swing attached to a balloon. As the novelty wore off for crowds, the Broadwicks moved their act to flying machines.

After her first jump in 1913, Tiny demonstrated Charles's pack parachute for Army officials in 1914, who were impressed with what they called the "life preserver of the air." She retired from parachuting in 1922, after completing more than eleven hundred jumps.

Broadwick is the only female member of the Early Birds of Aviation, and her parachutes are housed at the North Carolina Museum of History and the Smithsonian Institution.

1933 George Masa, Great Smokies Photographic Artist

On June 21, 1933, businessman, naturalist, and photographer George Masa died.

He was born Masahara Iisuka in Japan in the early 1880s; little is known about Masa's early life. After his father's death, Masa immigrated to the United States and studied engineering at the University of California before moving to North Carolina to work at the Grove Park Inn in Asheville.

In Asheville Masa joined the Carolina Mountain Club and was exposed to the area's spectacular scenic beauty. Though it is unclear how he learned photography, he became quite skilled as a lensman. He went to work for a photography studio and eventually became its proprietor.

Masa is best known for extensively photographing and mapping the Blue Ridge Mountains, often in concert with his friend, naturalist and author Horace Kephart. Together the pair tirelessly promoted the region and its people, and they were instrumental in the creation of the Great Smoky Mountains National Park.

Masa presented a book of his photographs of the region to Grace Coolidge, wife of Pres. Calvin Coolidge and a frequent visitor to the area, who helped spur the founding of the park.

Many of Masa's photographs, maps, and other personal papers are now held by the Buncombe County Public Library, UNC-Asheville, and Western Carolina University.

1963 The School of the Arts, Pride of Winston-Salem and North Carolina

On June 21, 1963, what's now the UNC School of Arts (UNCSA) was chartered by the General Assembly as the nation's first public arts conservatory.

The idea for the school, known until 2008 as the North Carolina School of the Arts (NCSA), came from then Gov. Terry Sanford and Asheville-born author John Ehle. In addition to providing a $325,000 appropriation, the 1963 legislation established an advisory board of nationally-renowned artists to select a site for the school. The board sought a community that would be engaged with the school, and the citizens of Winston-Salem responded by raising more than $850,000 for the new institution in a two-day phone drive.

High school and undergraduate level classes began in September 1965 on the old campus of Winston-Salem's Gray High School. The school's first chancellor was composer and Julliard School instructor Vittorio Giannini.

A $1.5 million challenge grant from the Ford Foundation helped NCSA expand its offerings, and the school became part of the UNC system in 1972. Throughout the 1980s NCSA continued to expand its offerings, adding its first graduate program in 1982.

Today UNCSA is one of the nation's premier creative and performing arts conservatories, offering programs across five disciplines—dance, design and production, drama, filmmaking, and music.

Tiny Broadwick *(above)* with a parachute on her back.

Tiny Broadwick *(left)* with an open parachute.

JUN 22

1892 The Aberdeen and Rockfish, an Independent Rail Line

On June 22, 1892, the Aberdeen and Rockfish (A&R) Railroad Company was organized by Moore County resident and Civil War veteran John Blue.

Blue sought to build the line because he needed a way to transport to market the timber and turpentine he was harvesting from his large holdings in the Aberdeen area. Construction began almost immediately after Blue established the company and continued into the early 1900s. The line reached its original terminus in Rockfish, a small community in Hoke County, in 1902.

As the company's logging business began to decline, the railroad began two extensions, one southwest from Raeford to Wagram, and another northeast from Rockfish to Fayetteville. The first extension was ultimately sold, but the second proved successful and remains part of the Aberdeen and Rockfish line to this day. A&R did away with its passenger service in 1921, but continued a rail motor bus service commonly called the "jitney" to handle mail and carry passengers until 1950.

The A&R line was a vital link for carrying passengers and freight to Fort Bragg during World War II and continued to innovate throughout the twentieth century. It was among the first railroads to use diesel power for freight trains, harness radio for train operations, and computerize its accounting systems.

Today the company's forty-six miles of track are still owned and operated by Blue's descendants despite the widespread consolidation across the industry.

1905 Duke Energy Brings Power to the Piedmont

On June 22, 1905, the Southern Power Company was incorporated in New Jersey by Benjamin and James Duke, two sons of tobacco industrialist Washington Duke, and two other partners. Southern Power changed its name to Duke Power in 1924, then became Duke Energy in 1997 after merging with another company.

The company can trace its origins to the 1890s, when the Duke brothers began to experiment with generating electricity. Its first power station, on the Catawba River, was established in 1900 to power textile mills near Rock Hill, South Carolina. Duke Power originally focused on generating electricity for industrial customers and didn't initially intend to service residential customers. It wasn't long, though, before local pressures from the Charlotte region, upstate South Carolina, and the Triad drew the company into the residential business. Duke Power's early advances in harnessing hydroelectric power and connecting existing electrical grids played an important role in the industrialization of North Carolina's Piedmont.

The company today is a diversified utility and pipeline company that is listed in the Fortune 500 and provides service to customers across the Southeast and Midwest.

1974 Society's Work a Boon to Genealogical Research

On June 22, 1974, the North Carolina Genealogical Society was organized in Raleigh.

The group grew out of the North Carolina Literary and Historical Association when in 1973 an exploratory committee met to discuss forming a genealogical section within their organization. Instead, the group decided that interest and momentum were strong enough to launch a separate group dedicated to promoting and encouraging genealogical research in North Carolina.

The society regularly produces two publications, the quarterly *North Carolina Genealogical Society Journal*, containing articles of genealogical value and abstracts of unpublished records, and a bi-monthly newsletter, which includes information about local genealogical societies, genealogical events and workshops, and a section for making family history inquiries.

The society also sponsors a variety of educational and instructive conferences, workshops, and webinars and has helped publish several key genealogical reference works over the years, including the landmark *North Carolina Research: Genealogy and Local History*, edited by Helen F. M. Leary. Its members serve the community by volunteering to abstract and index original documents and to provide other helpful research to individuals in their genealogical quests.

Aberdeen and Rockfish RR engine # 35, Aberdeen, N.C., Aug., 1947.

1895 R. Stanhope Pullen, Philanthropist and Benefactor

On June 23, 1895, Raleigh's R. Stanhope Pullen, an astute capitalist who conducted business on his own terms, died. Pullen was widely known for the generous gifts he gave to North Carolina.

Born in the Wake County community of Neuse in 1822, Pullen moved to Raleigh in 1852. There he managed the finances of his widowed aunt Penelope Smith. Smith made Pullen her principal heir, then his investments in real estate made him a wealthy man.

In 1872 then-closed Peace Institute (now William Peace University) was mortgaged to Pullen. He organized a new charter and offered most of the stock to the Presbyterians. As a member of Edenton Street Methodist Church, he was the largest donor of the money that paid for a new church structure.

Pullen in 1887 donated eighty acres to Raleigh for a park, now named Pullen Park in his honor. In that same year he gave land next to the park for the North Carolina College of Agricultural and Mechanic Arts (now North Carolina State University). R. T. Gray and Pullen also donated the original ten acres for the Normal and Industrial School in Greensboro (now the University of North Carolina at Greensboro).

1954 Historic Halifax, a Public-Private Partnership

On June 23, 1954, 150 people met to organize a nonprofit association to save, restore, and preserve historic sites in Halifax. The group came to operate under the title of the Historical Halifax Restoration Association.

The historic area in Halifax saw capital improvements in 1955 and 1956, with a three-thousand-dollar grant made by the state to the association, which, in turn, purchased the town's Old Jail, refurbished it, and established a museum in the facility. After years of collaboration between the association and the state, Historic Halifax was designated a state historic site in 1965. Over the next four years the Restoration Association transferred about twenty-five acres of land to the state. In 1970 Historic Halifax was listed on the National Register of Historic Places.

More than sixty years after it founding, the Historical Halifax Restoration Association remains in existence and lends support to the Historic Halifax State Historic Site. With their combined efforts the area continues to grow with restoration of buildings within the area.

1957 Landmark Sit-Ins Before Woolworth's

On June 23, 1957, the Royal Ice Cream Sit-Ins began in Durham.

The Royal Ice Cream Company had a doorway on one street with a "White Only" sign and one on another street marked "Colored Only." A partition divided the restaurant in two. To protest, a local minister and six young African Americans went to Royal Ice Cream and took up booths on the white side. The manager called the police, who charged them with trespassing.

Found guilty of trespassing the next day, each of the protesters was fined ten dollars plus court costs. On appeal the case went to Durham County Superior Court, and a jury trial was held. An all-white jury rendered a guilty verdict on each defendant. The case was then appealed to the N.C. Supreme Court, which upheld the law regarding segregated facilities. Attorneys appealed the decision to the U.S. Supreme Court, which refused to hear the case.

The Royal Ice Cream Sit-Ins helped lay the foundation for the 1960 Greensboro sit-ins, which sparked the national movement for civil rights.

JUN 23

Durham pastor and civil rights leader Douglas E. Moore gives communion to five of the local youths who sat-in at the Royal Ice Cream Company shop in 1957.

1749 James Davis of New Bern, Fit to Print

On June 24, 1749, James Davis, a printer trained in Williamsburg, Virginia, printed the first official publication for the colony of North Carolina.

Although printers had been active in some colonies for more than a hundred years, North Carolina was slow in acquiring a public printer. The establishment of a press in the colonial capital at New Bern was due in large part to the actions of the royal governor, Gabriel Johnston.

North Carolina delayed acquiring an official press for three reasons. First, the provincial government liked to control the distribution of information and feared challenges to its authority. Second, North Carolina did not have the dense, urban population necessary to finance the large investment required to get a printing press. Third, presses in Williamsburg and Charleston made it easy to farm out print requests to neighboring colonies.

Complaints by Governor Johnston in 1736 prompted the Assembly to begin the process of hiring a printer and acquiring the press. In 1747 Johnston appointed James Davis to the position of public printer. His first task was likely the printing of currency. Davis printed the *Journal of the House of Burgesses of the Province of North Carolina* in 1749, the colony's first official publication.

JUN 24

1933 Celtic Sam Jones of Wilmington and the NBA

On June 24, 1933, legendary Boston Celtics player Sam Jones was born in Wilmington. During his twelve seasons with the Celtics, Jones and his team won ten championships.

Basketball was always a part of Jones's life. He played the game in high school, then at North Carolina Central University. During his college career, he caught the eye of Red Auerbach, the coach of the Boston Celtics. At N.C. Central, Jones studied and prepared to teach high school, and by the time he graduated, he had a job offer. But teaching was not Jones's destiny. He was the first draft pick for the Celtics and the eighth overall pick in the 1957 NBA draft.

Jones began to gain national recognition during the 1961-1962 season, earning the nickname "Mr. Clutch." As a guard for the Celtics, he was known for his great dedication, amazing accuracy in shooting, and speed and agility on the court.

Jones retired in 1969, and shortly thereafter the Celtics officially retired his jersey number, 24. He went on to coach at Federal City College and N.C. Central and worked as an assistant coach with the New Orleans Jazz.

He was inducted into the NBA Hall of Fame in 1983.

2004 New American Tobacco Campus Takes Shape

On June 24, 2004, GlaxoSmithKline became the first business to move into the newly renovated and re-purposed American Tobacco Campus, ushering in a new era for downtown Durham.

Originally the home of W. T. Blackwell & Company's factory, which dates to 1874, the campus was considered the world's largest tobacco factory at one time. The Blackwell company was purchased in 1899 by Washington Duke, who transformed it by introducing automated production, starting the iconic Lucky Strike brand, and consolidating it with his other holdings to create the American Tobacco Company.

The campus became a National Historic Landmark in 1977 and sat vacant and deteriorating for several years after American Tobacco ceased cigarette manufacturing there in 1987. Capitol Broadcasting Company began to express interest in rehabbing the facility in the late 1990s. After the city and county of Durham, the A.J. Fletcher Foundation, and the Center for Community Self-Help committed to pitch in on the project, construction began.

The two hundred million dollar project helped jumpstart the revitalization of downtown Durham. Today the dynamic campus features a stunning water feature, grassy areas for enjoying concerts, and several popular restaurants. Anchor tenants included North Carolina Public Radio, Duke University, Burt's Bees, and the Durham YMCA.

The restored American Tobacco Campus.

1781 Thomas Burke Chosen Governor

On June 25, 1781, Thomas Burke was chosen by the General Assembly to serve as North Carolina's third governor under the constitution of 1776. At the time of Burke's appointment, the state was ravaged by war and on the brink of anarchy. Government on both the state and county levels had almost completely broken down.

Burke took extraordinary measures to reform the militia, increase essential revenues, banish intractable Loyalists, and defend against renewed British attack from both Virginia and South Carolina. Acting on his own authority, he established special courts and assumed for himself veto power over legislative acts.

Less than three months after assuming office, Burke's frantic efforts came to an end in Hillsborough when he and several other state officials and officers of the Continental Line were taken prisoner by the Loyalist leader David Fanning. Transported south to Wilmington, then to Charleston (technically it was still Charlestown), Burke was released on parole after an ordeal of two months. Fearing that his life was in danger, he escaped from his very loose confinement and returned to North Carolina and the governorship, thereby violating both his parole and the code of honor in the eyes of many contemporaries.

When the embittered Burke convened the General Assembly in April of 1782, his rather ambiguous offer to retire from public office was accepted almost without remark. Having served only ten months as governor, two of those as a prisoner, he returned to Hillsborough a ruined and deeply disillusioned man. He died less than two years later.

1876 Marion's Daniel Kanipe, Survivor of Custer's Last Stand

On June 25, 1876, Lt. Col. George A. Custer led the Seventh Cavalry under his command on an attack against an Indian encampment at Little Big Horn. The incident is now commonly known as "Custer's Last Stand." Custer's troopers were quickly encircled by the Native Americans under Chief Sitting Bull, who were expecting them, and Custer and 265 of his men were killed in under an hour.

Marion native Daniel Kanipe and one other soldier were the only two from Custer's battalion to survive Little Big Horn. The two were sent to relay messages to Capt. Frederick Benteen and others in the train of pack mules supplying the unit. Seeing Custer's mistake, Benteen held his battalion back and refused to allow the couriers to return to battle.

Kanipe remained in the reconstituted Seventh Cavalry until receiving his discharge in 1877. He returned to North Carolina, where he operated a farm in McDowell County. He went back to the Little Bighorn battlefield in 1908 on a publicity tour to raise money to preserve the graves there.

Often called upon to relate his experience at Little Bighorn, Kanipe became a celebrity among admirers of the "Old West" and researchers of "Custer's Last Stand." His recollections became the basis for many of the twentieth century accounts of the battle.

1948 W. C. Chance Protested Segregated Rail Cars, 1948

On June 25, 1948, Parmele native William Claudius Chance was ejected from an Atlantic Coast Line Railroad passenger train car in Emporia, Virginia for refusing to move to a car for black passengers.

Chance was a well-respected educator in Martin County, having established and operated the Parmele Industrial Institute. He was returning home to Parmele from the Republican National Convention, held in Philadelphia that year, when he was instructed to leave a "white car" at the stop in Emporia. When he refused, Chance was arrested for disorderly conduct.

After the incident Chance sued the Atlantic Coast Line and conductor Alva S. Lambeth for twenty-five thousand dollars. A jury in Richmond initially determined the railroad had committed no crime in ejecting Chance from the train but awarded him a sum of fifty dollars for wrongful arrest.

With the support of the NAACP, Chance appealed the case to the Fourth U. S. Circuit Court, where the initial decision was overturned in January 1951. The court determined that the Atlantic Coast Line's enforcement of Jim Crow laws on their passenger lines was an unconstitutional burden on interstate commerce.

Chance's case served as a foundation for later cases that desegregated interstate travel.

1963 Speaker Ban Roiled UNC-Chapel Hill Campus

On June 25, 1963, on the last day of the session, the General Assembly rushed through the Speaker Ban law.

The bill, formally known as An Act to Regulate Visiting Speakers, prohibited speeches on state campuses by members of the Communist Party, persons advocating overthrow of the state or federal constitution, and individuals who had pleaded the Fifth Amendment about related topics.

The target of the ban was UNC-Chapel Hill. In many people's minds, UNC was associated with liberals, the left, and Communism. In the weeks before the vote, students from Chapel Hill carried their protests about civil rights to the Capitol and the Sir Walter Raleigh Hotel, where most lawmakers lived while in session.

The reaction of the campus to the ban was one of surprise and outrage. There were also fears that the school might lose its accreditation. UNC Pres. William Friday, supported by the trustees and student leaders, used his skills to seek repeal or modification of the law. The heart of the matter was the First Amendment and the importance of open debate and free thinking in a democracy.

In 1968 a three-judge federal district court ruled the measure unconstitutional and a violation of free speech rights.

JUN 25

Daniel Kanipe marker and house.

1857 Hinton Rowan Helper, Critic of Slavery

On June 26, 1857, the *New York Daily Tribune* published an advertisement touting a new book, *The Impending Crisis of the South: How to Meet It*. The author was Hinton Rowan Helper, born in Davie County. The book, which denounced slavery in no uncertain terms, caused a sensation.

Helper argued that an economic system based on enslavement only slowed the South's growth, and he illustrated the various ways in which the region lagged behind the North. Going yet further, he denounced slave owners as "robbers, thieves, ruffians and murderers" and argued that slaves should gain freedom by violence if necessary.

In his native state Helper became a villain of the highest order. His book was outlawed, and anyone found owning a copy could be imprisoned. In 1857 editor James G. Bennett handed Pres. James Buchanan a copy saying, "There is gunpowder enough in that book to blow the Union to the devil." *The Impeding Crisis* further polarized American politics and helped get Abraham Lincoln elected in 1860. Next to *Uncle Tom's Cabin*, no book was more important in stimulating sectional strife.

Helper's childhood home, built in 1818, is a National Historic Landmark.

JUN 26

Woodcut portrait of Hinton Rowan Helper.

1862 Montfort Stokes Wounded at Elyson's Mill

On June 26, 1862, Col. Montfort Sidney Stokes of the First Regiment, North Carolina State Troops, was mortally wounded in an engagement at Elyson's Mill, Virginia. He died eleven days later in a Richmond hospital.

Stokes was born in Wilkes County in 1810. His grandfather had served with Gov. William Tryon during the Regulator rebellion, and his father was a major general during the War of 1812, governor of North Carolina from 1830 to 1832, and later a U.S. Senator.

Stokes was appointed a midshipman in the Navy in 1829, training at the Norfolk Navy Yard and the Norfolk School. His naval career lasted ten years before he returned to Wilkes County to become a farmer. After serving in the Mexican-American War, he returned to farming again, serving on the Council of State at the same time.

At the outbreak of the Civil War, Stokes volunteered for the Wilkes Valley Guards and was chosen first lieutenant. He saw service at Goldsboro and in Virginia. Following his death, he was buried in the family cemetery on the banks of the Yadkin River.

1974 Bar Code, Retailing Innovation, Product of IBM and RTP

On June 26, 1974, a scanner at a supermarket in Troy, Ohio scanned a pack of chewing gum. It was the first product to be checked out by the Universal Product Code, an invention largely credited to Research Triangle Park scientist George Laurer.

The first barcodes were developed by New Jersey engineer N. Joseph Woodland in the late 1940s and early 1950s, but the technology wasn't brought into use largely because the scanners necessary for checkout systems to work were too expensive to produce.

In 1973 a group of supermarket executives decided some sort of universal symbol and system needed to be adopted to make checking out of stores faster. They formed a "Symbol Selection Committee," developed a set of specifications, and invited companies to pitch ideas. Though RCA had already successfully demonstrated a technology to the committee, IBM, where Laurer worked, submitted a surprise bid.

Laurer had the advantage of having not worked on a similar project before and was thus able to tackle the problem with fresh eyes. He adapted Woodland's bullseye-shaped design into the now universally recognizable rectangular bar code.

The committee unanimously adopted Laurer's symbol and code in 1973, which they named the Universal Product Code, or UPC.

9 781234 567897

JUN 27

1760 Cherokee Clash with British Along Frontier, 1760

On June 27, 1760, Chief Occonostota, leading a band of Cherokee warriors, attacked British forces near what's now Franklin in Macon County, pushing them back into South Carolina.

When the French and Indian War broke out in 1754, the Cherokee allied with the British against the French. By 1758, though, relations between the Cherokee and British had soured. A dispute that year over stolen horses touched off an escalation of hostilities between the two groups, culminating with the British murder of several chiefs who had traveled to Charleston to negotiate peace in 1759.

Following the deaths of the would-be peacemakers, the Cherokee tribes united in their efforts to resist the British in the Carolinas. As part of their strategy, they laid siege to Fort Loudon in eastern Tennessee. Col. Archibald Montgomery and his men responded by burning the Cherokee villages along the trading path near the Keowee and Oconee Rivers.

The Anglo-Cherokee War would last until 1762, when the two nations came to an uneasy peace.

1857 The Death of Elisha Mitchell

On June 27, 1857, Elisha Mitchell, exploring the Black Mountain range, slipped and fell to his death in a deep pool at the bottom of a sixty-foot waterfall. Search parties were organized, and the body was discovered several days later by "Big Tom" Wilson.

Wilson was an extraordinary tracker and guide. He was also noted locally as a skilled bear hunter and storyteller. Wilson located Mitchell's trail and tracked him to the place where he fell. Since the pocket watch Mitchell had been wearing was broken at 8:00, it has been assumed that was likely the time of his death.

In 1835 Mitchell announced that a peak in the Black Mountains was the highest in the eastern United States. He estimated its height at 6,672 feet, only twelve feet short of the present official height. A "controversy of major proportions" ensued in the 1850s between Mitchell and Thomas L. Clingman, who called into question the accuracy of the earlier observations and measurements. Mitchell died in an effort to set the record straight.

Initially interred in a cemetery in Asheville, Mitchell's remains were later moved to the top of the mountain which now bears his name.

1862 The *Modern Greece* Ran Aground

On June 27, 1862, the British-owned steamer *Modern Greece* ran aground near Fort Fisher while attempting to run the Federal blockade.

The crash came after the vessel was pursued by U.S. Navy ships for three days. It was heavily laden with war materiel for the Confederacy and civilian goods. Although a portion of the cargo was salvaged by the crew, the vessel was intentionally sunk with most of its cargo still aboard.

The first salvage operations on the wreck site took place in July 1862, when Confederate officials removed several of the artillery pieces from the vessel for use at Fort Fisher. One hundred years later, in the early spring of 1962, a fierce storm removed the sand covering the wreck. A recovery of artifacts was mounted by the state, and that, in turn, spawned legislation in 1967 establishing that North Carolina had a sovereign right to unclaimed shipwrecks off the coast.

The recovery of artifacts from the *Modern Greece* and the 1967 legislation also led to the creation of the North Carolina Underwater Archaeology Branch and spurred conservation methods that underpin the science of underwater archaeology to this day.

1963 Wilkes to Watauga Wagon Train Commemorated Carolina Charter

On June 27, 1963, more than 150 people in mostly nineteenth century garb and nearly twenty-five wagons pulled by livestock departed from a Wilkes County farm for a three-day, thirty-five-mile journey to Boone.

The Daniel Boone Wagon Train, as it was called, was intended to commemorate the Carolina Charter's three hundredth anniversary. Designed to recall a 1773 trip that famed frontiersman Daniel Boone took through the area, the "reenactment" was more a reflection of the 1960s than it was of 1773 or of 1663, the year the Carolina Charter was granted. In fact, it seems that organizers drew more upon *Wagon Train*, a popular TV show of the time.

Likely more spectacle than history, the journey actually ended up being relatively difficult, mostly because of bad weather, uncooperative animals, and a number of unfortunate accidents. Despite that fact the Wagon Train became an annual event and grew in size for much of the rest of the decade.

The Wagon Train was cancelled in 1974 due to increasing rowdiness but saw a brief revival in the 1980s.

The *Modern Greece* grounded. Courtesy of the North Carolina Museum of History.

1799 Paint Rock, Cherokee Pictograph in Madison County

On June 28, 1799, land agent and mapmaker John Strother measured the American Indian pictographs on Paint Rock in Madison County. Strother wrote in his diary for that day that the vertical formation was 107 feet tall and noted, "Pictures of some human's – wild beasts fish & fowls were to be seen plainly made with red paint."

Paint Rock was created approximately five thousand years ago during the Archaic Period. Its creators used pigments of exceptional quality and complex design made from ingredients that were clearly local. The rock outcropping, which features red and yellow markings, straddles the North Carolina-Tennessee border and has long been a landmark for travelers.

Paint Rock sits in a gorge along a road. Archaeologists suggest that Paint Rock may have been a major travel route for Native Americans through the mountains and a natural crossing over the French Broad River. The panel of Paint Rock on the North Carolina side of the border displays alternating red and yellow rectilinear lines painted against the vertical cliff face. Archaeologists have suggested the paints may have been created as a road marker, for use in healing rituals, or for a combination of both, since healing pilgrimages to the nearby hot springs may have been popular.

Campfires and weathering over the centuries have damaged the pictographs. In 2004 images on the rock panels were formally recorded, and archaeologists did more mapping and sampling in 2006 to support conservation and management.

JUN 28

1969 A Hollerin' Contest in Sampson County

On June 28, 1969, the first National Hollerin' Contest was held in Spivey's Corner in Sampson County.

The contest is the product of the farm culture of the Sandhills region. Before the advent of the telephone, yelling loudly, or hollering, was the primary way farmers and neighbors communicated in rural North Carolina. As new technologies made communication easier, the practice began to disappear.

The idea for the contest grew out of a conversation on a local radio program. The contest's two goals were to preserve agricultural heritage and to attract tourists to a struggling region. Though Spivey's Corner had only about fifty residents in 1969, the first contest attracted between two and three thousand visitors and garnered national media attention from North Carolina's own Charles Kuralt and others. The contest's first winner was seventy-year-old Dewey Jackson. For his prize-wining rendition of "What a Friend We Have in Jesus" Jackson earned an appearance on *The Tonight Show* and a congratulatory letter from Pres. Richard Nixon.

The annual contest was suspended in 2016.

1973 The Dogwood, the Cardinal, the Plott Hound, the Emerald

On June 28, 1973, the General Assembly designated the emerald as the state's official precious stone.

Emeralds are a variety of the mineral beryl. Beryl is colorless in its pure state, but chromium turns beryl green. The aquamarine is blue beryl, and there are also yellow, light green, red, and pink varieties. Beryl, in all its variety of colors, is found among mica, quartz, and feldspar, all of which are abundant in the North Carolina mountains.

North Carolina is rich in minerals. More than three hundred varieties have been found—more than in any other state. It also has the largest emerald deposits found in the United States. Most of the mining operations for the gem are in Alexander and Mitchell Counties.

In 2012 the Nature Research Center at the North Carolina Museum of Natural Sciences acquired four of the largest emeralds ever found in North America. Surprisingly, all four of the gems were found on the same property and three were found on the same day. One of the stones, known as the Carolina Emperor, is a whopping sixty-four carats.

"Paint Rock near Asheville," in North Carolina Postcard Collection.

1837 Nathaniel Macon, Advocate of Checks on Government

1905 "Moonlight" Graham and His Place in Baseball Lore

1987 Carrboro's Libba Cotten, Composer of "Freight Train"

1990 Governor Martin and His Campaign Promise to Complete I-40

On June 29, 1837, one of the most prominent and influential politicians of the nineteenth century, Nathaniel Macon, died at his plantation in Warren County. In a long and distinguished political career Macon held various positions but was always an advocate for the agricultural, social, and economic values of North Carolina.

Born in late 1758, Macon received a rudimentary education at a makeshift school in Bute (now Warren) County. After studying at what is now Princeton University, he joined the New Jersey militia at the outbreak of the Revolutionary War. At the war's end he returned to North Carolina and was elected to the state Senate. Macon went on to serve twelve terms in the U.S. House of Representatives and two in the U.S. Senate. He was known for a simple, blunt, and unreserved political philosophy that reflected his modest upbringing. An ardent Anti-federalist, he was wary of a large federal government that strayed from the guideposts of the Constitution.

Macon retired from politics at age 70, choosing to spend his remaining days at his plantation. Fort Macon, Macon County, Macon, Georgia, and Virginia's Randolph-Macon College are all named in his honor.

Drawing of Nathaniel Macon.

On June 29, 1905, Cumberland County native "Moonlight" Graham played in his first and only Major League Baseball game. His story came to national attention after being incorporated into the 1989 hit film *Field of Dreams*.

Born Archibald Wright Graham in Fayetteville in 1879, Graham was raised there and in Charlotte, where he honed his baseball skills, playing with family and friends. He went on to a stellar career playing baseball at UNC and began playing with a Charlotte minor league team while still studying medicine in Chapel Hill. After stints with several minor league teams in North Carolina and New Hampshire, Graham signed with New York Giants in February 1905, while simultaneously taking more medical courses at the University of Maryland.

In his only major league appearance, Graham played two innings as a right fielder. No ball was hit in his direction, and he was on deck to bat when the game ended. Graham returned to the minor leagues shortly after that June 1905 game, then moved to Chisholm, Minnesota, for a job as a doctor in 1911, staying there until his death in 1965.

A decade later, author W. P. Kinsella happened to notice Graham's story in *The Baseball Encyclopedia* and included it in his 1982 novel *Shoeless Joe*, upon which *Field of Dreams* was based.

"Moonlight" Graham with the UNC baseball team photo, 1900. Third from the right *(circled)*.

On June 29, 1987, folk music legend Libba Cotten died.

Cotten taught the world "Freight Train," "Shake Sugaree," and a host of other songs. Her "parlor ragtime" style was no less elegant for the guitar being turned upside down and the thumb and finger roles being reversed.

Cotten was born in 1893 in an area that would eventually become Carrboro and grew up near the railroad tracks on what is now called Lloyd Street. She wrote "Freight Train" at age eleven. Her early biography reads much like those of most of the people around her: hard work punctuated by frolics, music, marriage, church, and family.

She eventually moved to Washington D.C., where she found employment with composer and folklorist Ruth Crawford Seeger. While working for Seeger's family, Cotten idly picked up a guitar and revealed herself to be precisely the kind of native player they held up as an ideal. By then she was over sixty years old.

Seeger's son Mike made a project of recording her songs, releasing a Folkways record of them to great acclaim. Cotten ceased domestic work and spent the rest of her life as a traveling entertainer.

On June 29, 1990, Gov. Jim Martin dedicated the final segment of Interstate 40, a 2,554-mile highway that stretches from Wilmington to Barstow, California. The first Interstate-funded construction on I-40 nationwide had taken place in Haywood County more than three decades earlier.

Nearly three thousand people attended the opening ceremony at the interchange of I-40 and North Carolina 50/55 just outside of Newton Grove, where nine hundred pounds of barbecue and a descent by Fort Bragg's Green Beret Sport Parachute Team were also part of the fun. The day's festivities continued with an ice cream social at a rest area west of Warsaw and a final ceremony at Wilmington's Grace Baptist Church not far from the eastern end of the interstate.

Though an extension of I-40 through Raleigh to Wilmington appeared in the final Interstate System map adopted by the Eisenhower administration, opposition to the Raleigh-to-Wilmington stretch remained strong through the early 1980s. Major pushes by Gov. Jim Hunt, local officials, and Wilmington-area state legislators were no match for the opposition led by U.S. Sen. Jesse Helms.

Martin finally turned the tide after he was elected governor in 1984, and construction began to move forward. The final price tag for the 122-mile Raleigh-to-Wilmington project was $417 million.

The benefits of the project, which cut an hour off the travel time between Raleigh and Wilmington, were realized fairly quickly. In the first decade following I-40's opening, tourist spending in New Hanover County increased by more than fifty-two percent, according to a study done by the state Department of Commerce.

JUN 30

1814 — Capture of the Legendary *Snap Dragon*, 1814

On June 30, 1814, Otway Burns's privateering ship *Snap Dragon*, temporarily under the command of Capt. W. R. Graham, was captured by the British near, Halifax, Nova Scotia. Burns was at home in North Carolina suffering from rheumatism.

The vessel mounted six guns and was carrying seventy men at the time it was seized. It was on its fourth privateering voyage and had recently captured the schooner Linnet, laden with fish and oil, and another schooner full of fruit.

Burns had *Snap Dragon* outfitted for privateering through the sale of stock. Hefty subscribers came from New Bern and Beaufort. Burns, who was born near Swansboro, made three lucrative privateering runs on his ship during the War of 1812, two to the West Indies and one to Nova Scotia. The prizes and captures he brought into North Carolina were reported in several newspapers, and stories were told of Burns's adeptness at sea as well as his ability to lead men.

The village of Otway in Carteret County bears the captain's name, as does the Yancey County town of Burnsville. *Snap Dragon* was the most successful North Carolina privateer during the war period.

1863 — African American Troops Organize in New Bern, 1863

On June 30, 1863, the Thirty-Fifth United States Colored Troops Regiment officially mustered in New Bern. The organizing and recruitment of North Carolina's African-American troops had already been underway for nine months.

In July 1862 Congress issued both a Second Confiscation Act and a Militia Act. This legislation allowed Pres. Abraham Lincoln to use as many African-Americans as he deemed necessary to suppress the South and to use them in whatever way he thought best to accomplish that end. The use and treatment of African-Americans varied, and men were frequently assigned fatigue duty rather than combat, but Lincoln did authorize African-Americans to assume combat roles in the January 1863 Emancipation Proclamation.

That May, General Order No. 143 established a Bureau of Colored Troops and required that all future regiments be designated as United States Colored Troops. North Carolina units had begun organization under Corps d'Afrique designations and as state-named regiments but entered into Federal service as United States Colored Troops.

1963 — Freedom Rallies Begin in Williamston, 1963

On June 30, 1963, a month of protests known as "Freedom Rallies" began in Williamston.

The seat of Martin County on the Roanoke River was a "hotspot" of the civil rights movement, and Green Memorial Church, a Disciples of Christ church rooted in the Holiness tradition, was the epicenter. Discontent had simmered in the area since the 1957 acquittal of white men charged with the murder of a local black man.

Protesters, keenly aware of the civil rights movement sweeping across the South, made it their goal to desegregate schools and the public library. Local woman Sarah Small and Golden Frinks of Edenton, a friend of Martin Luther King Jr., organized the efforts. As the protests continued, the Southern Christian Leadership Conference held biweekly nonviolence training sessions at the church.

Protests continued for thirty-two consecutive days and involved as many as four hundred people, many of them children and teenagers, who sang and prayed at the church before marching uptown about a half-mile to the courthouse. State troopers and local deputies kept close watch over the nonviolent summer rallies.

Rallies were suspended temporarily after Gov. Terry Sanford's office organized interracial meetings but resumed in the fall when twelve white ministers and seminarians from Boston joined the effort. The fall protests were more violent, with protesters throwing bottles and the police using electric cattle prods on at least one occasion, but they ended following Pres. John F. Kennedy's assassination in November.

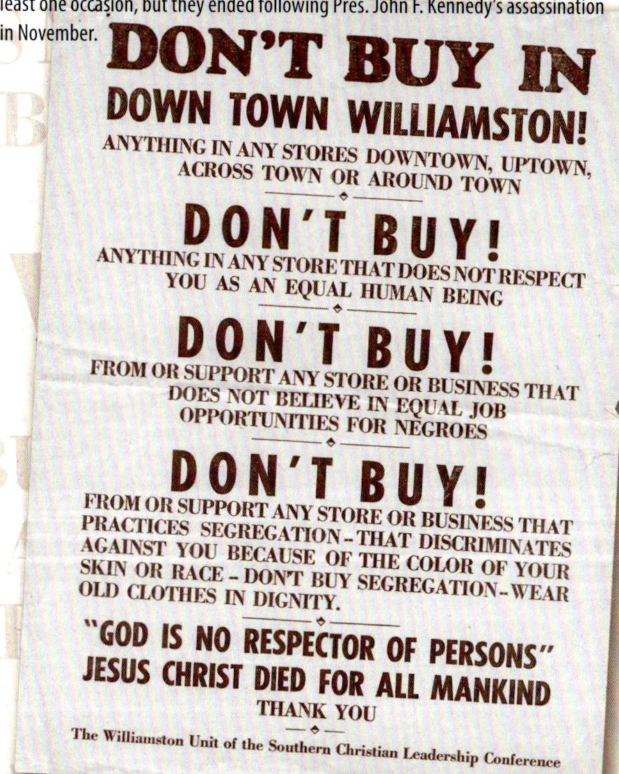
DON'T BUY IN
DOWN TOWN WILLIAMSTON!
ANYTHING IN ANY STORES DOWNTOWN, UPTOWN, ACROSS TOWN OR AROUND TOWN

DON'T BUY!
ANYTHING IN ANY STORE THAT DOES NOT RESPECT YOU AS AN EQUAL HUMAN BEING

DON'T BUY!
FROM OR SUPPORT ANY STORE OR BUSINESS THAT DOES NOT BELIEVE IN EQUAL JOB OPPORTUNITIES FOR NEGROES

DON'T BUY!
FROM OR SUPPORT ANY STORE OR BUSINESS THAT PRACTICES SEGREGATION – THAT DISCRIMINATES AGAINST YOU BECAUSE OF THE COLOR OF YOUR SKIN OR RACE – DON'T BUY SEGREGATION – WEAR OLD CLOTHES IN DIGNITY.

"GOD IS NO RESPECTOR OF PERSONS"
JESUS CHRIST DIED FOR ALL MANKIND
THANK YOU

The Williamston Unit of the Southern Christian Leadership Conference

1909 North Carolina's 4-H Clubs Rooted in Ahoskie

On July 1, 1909, I. O. Schaub, a North Carolina State University researcher, organized the first Corn Club in Ahoskie. The club was eventually recognized as North Carolina's first 4-H Club.

The 4-H Club movement grew out of an effort from what was essentially the Cooperative Extensive Service of the U.S. Department of Agriculture. Seaman A. Knapp, who worked for USDA, set up demonstration farms across the South during the late 1800s and early 1900s to convince farmers to diversify their operations and plant other crops besides cotton.

Knapp saw the importance of getting youth involved early in this work, and he developed the Corn Club concept to teach boys the latest farming techniques on one-acre plots of land. His concept was quickly adopted by other agriculture leaders, including Schaub, Jane McKimmon, and G. W. Herring.

The 4-H movement picked up more momentum in 1914 after Congress passed the Smith-Lever Act, which more permanently established the Cooperative Extension. That in turn led to more personnel to organize the clubs. The clubs also expanded to include livestock and crops other than corn.

Today 4-H has more than ten thousand established programs across North Carolina and more than seven million participants nationwide.

1939 McDowell County's "Wondrous Splendors"

On July 1, 1939, Linville Caverns, North Carolina's only show cave, opened to the public. The caverns became an overnight success, as their development coincided with construction of the Blue Ridge Parkway in McDowell and Avery Counties in 1938.

The natural limestone cave sits at the base of Humpback Mountain and showcases colorful mineral formations resulting from the effects of acidic water as it has moved through the shady dolomite for millions of years. Development of the site, led by Marion businessman J.G. Gilkey, began in 1937, and electric lights were installed to illuminate the features that continue to change in the active cavern.

In 1859 young Fayetteville naturalist and school teacher Henry Colton published one of the earliest accounts of exploring the cave. He wrote of the "wondrous splendors of that hidden world" that could be found in the caverns, from the arctic cold water to the formations, which he called the "grandest of nature's stony tapestry." He noted the caverns' inhabitants included bats, mice, and a "perfect grasshopper, petrified and covered with a crust of lime."

Linville Caverns has operated as a private enterprise since 1939 and remains open to the public today.

1950 Outdoor Drama at Cherokee Revived

On July 1, 1950, the outdoor drama *Unto These Hills* premiered to a capacity crowd at the Mountainside Theater in Cherokee.

The pageant tells the story of the Cherokee people from their first encounter with European explorers in the 1540s through the period of forced removal from their homeland and subsequent journey to Oklahoma in the late 1830s. The trip became known as the Trail of Tears because numerous people suffered and died along the way.

Unto These Hills was written by Kermit Hunter and directed by Harry Davis. For many years it was enormously popular, but when later compared with true Cherokee history, came up lacking. Locals lost a connection to the play and stopped identifying with it. Attendance dwindled.

In 2006 the play underwent a major overhaul under the direction of American Indian playwright Hanay Geiogamah. Additional revisions followed, and now, although many reminisce about the original version, *Unto These Hills* better reflects the history, culture, and traditions of the Cherokee people.

The play is still performed each summer in Cherokee and draws upwards of thirty thousand people a year.

1985 Pauli Murray Broke Barriers

On July 1, 1985, lawyer, professor, writer, and outspoken civil and women's rights activist Anna Pauline "Pauli" Murray died.

Born in 1910, Murray grew up under the care of her aunt in Durham. In 1938 Murray applied to the University of North Carolina to study sociology. Her application, defying state laws which required "separate but equal" institutions, garnered national attention. Her unsuccessful campaign for admission was the first time that she lived her lifelong saying: "One woman with a typewriter constitutes a movement."

Murray was admitted to Howard Law School in 1941, where she experienced discrimination due to her gender rather than her race. She would later wonder whether her race or gender was the greater obstacle to her career.

Murray was a prolific writer. In 1951 she published *State's Laws on Race and Color*, which Thurgood Marshall called "the Bible for civil rights lawyers." Her second book, *Proud Shoes*, a biographical account of her maternal grandparents, was published in 1956.

In 1977 Murray became the first African American female Episcopal priest in the United States and held her first Eucharist at the Chapel of the Cross in Chapel Hill, where her grandmother had been baptized as a slave.

JUL 1

For 18 years Robert Bushyhead played the character, Elias C. Boudinot, in the production *Unto These Hills*.

Pauli Murray

JUL 2

1829 The "Sable Orator" and Poet, George Moses Horton

On July 2, 1829, Raleigh printer Joseph Gales published George Moses Horton's *The Hope of Liberty*, the first book by an African American published in the South. Horton's life story, and the account of how he became a published poet while enslaved, is compelling.

Horton was an infant when his owner, William Horton, moved from Northampton County to Chatham County. By all reports, and given the fact that he could travel freely, George endured a relatively mild bondage. He walked on weekends to Chapel Hill, where he sold fruit and was prodded into reciting poems for UNC students.

Over time he became known as the "sable orator," as he signed his works and made friends, including UNC Pres. Joseph Caldwell. It was Caldwell's wife who helped Horton first get published. Other volumes of his work appeared in 1837 (*Poems by a Slave*), 1845 (*The Poetical Works of George M. Horton*), and 1865 (*Naked Genius*). In 1866 he moved to Philadelphia, after which little is known about his life.

Interest in Horton's work has increased in recent years, earning him the honor of being among the fifteen inaugural inductees into the North Carolina Literary Hall of Fame in 1996.

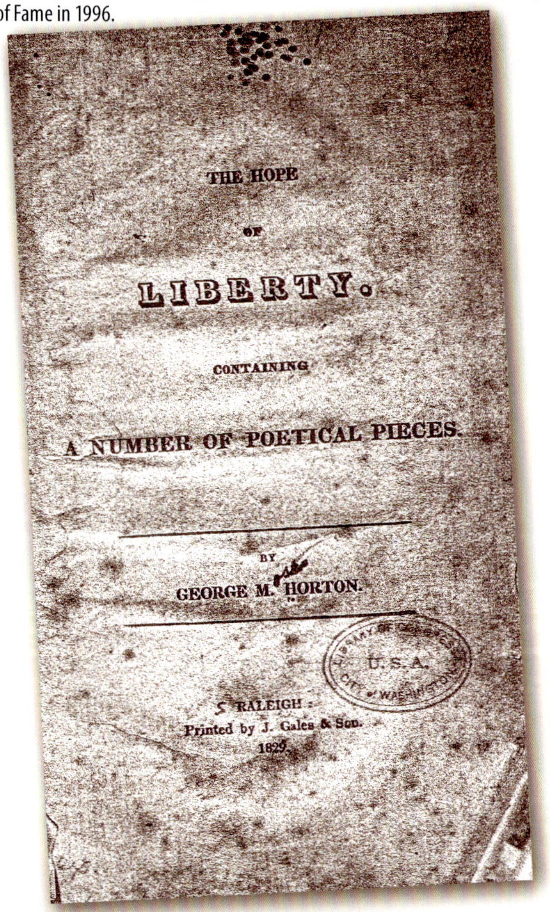

THE HOPE
OF
LIBERTY.
CONTAINING
A NUMBER OF POETICAL PIECES.
BY
GEORGE M. HORTON.
RALEIGH:
Printed by J. Gales & Son.
1829.

1831 Bechtlers Advertise Their Coins, 1831

On July 2, 1831, an advertisement appeared promoting gold coins minted by the Bechtler family in Rutherford County.

From about 1803 until California's gold strikes of 1848, North Carolina led the nation in gold production, which was a key industry in the state. About fifty mines were operating in the western part of the state by the 1830s.

Christopher Bechtler, his son Augustus, and a nephew, also Christopher Bechtler, moved to North Carolina in 1830. The elder Bechtler first opened a jewelry shop in Rutherfordton but soon saw that the lack of currency in western North Carolina was stifling the regional economy.

Experienced metalworkers, the Bechtlers built a press, and soon were striking \$2.50 (quarter-eagle) and \$5 (half-eagle) coins north of Rutherfordton on Hollands Creek. The following year they began to strike gold \$1 coins. Private mints met with mixed success, based on the quality of the product that they generated and on the public's perception of the purity of the gold.

The elder Christopher Bechtler died in 1842 but the mine continued to operate. The younger Christopher Bechtler moved the minting business into Rutherfordton soon after.

The Bechtler Mint ceased operations around 1849, after having struck about \$2.25 million in coins.

1935 First ABC Store Opens in Wilson

On July 2, 1935, the state's first Alcoholic Beverage Commission—ABC, for short—store opened in Wilson to an excited public. The store offered legal alcohol in the state for the first time in twenty-six years. On its first day of operation, shoppers purchased 825 bottles of liquor at a total cost of \$1,003. There were no reports of rowdiness or drinking on the premises, as had been predicted by prohibitionists.

Prohibition had been in effect in North Carolina since 1909, after voters approved a ban on the sale of alcoholic beverages in a referendum. North Carolina was the first state in the nation to approve such a measure and did so by the wide margin of sixty-two to thirty-eight percent.

The rest of the nation joined North Carolina in 1920 with the passage of the Eighteenth Amendment, which made it illegal to manufacture, sell, or transport intoxicating liquors anywhere in the country. The amendment was repealed in 1933, and North Carolina was one of only two states that refused to ratify that repeal.

In 1935 the General Assembly passed laws that granted local options for the sale of alcohol and set up the system of Alcoholic Beverage Control Boards to administer retail shops.

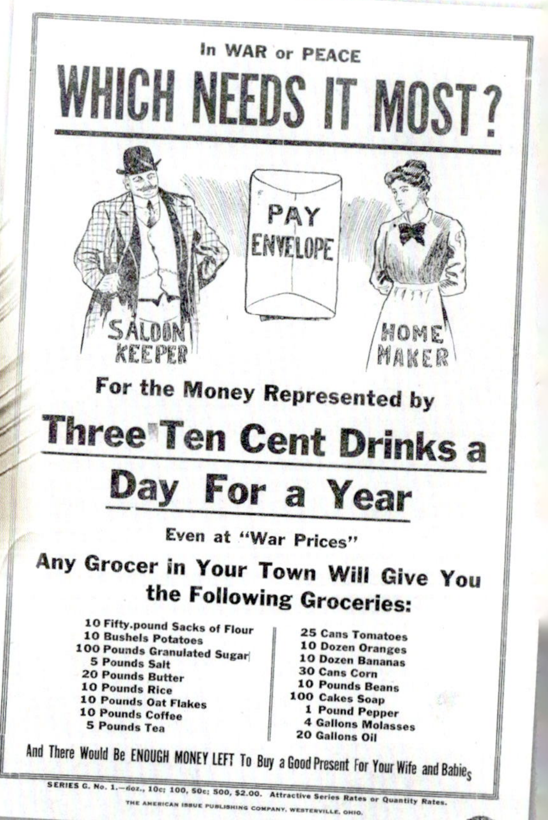

Prohibition poster *(far right)* depicting a pay envelope, saloonkeeper, and homemaker, showing list of groceries that could be purchased with the money instead of used for alcoholic beverages.

1863 I.E. Avery's Words for His Father, the "Letter from the Dead"

On July 3, 1863, thity-four-year-old Lt. Col. Isaac E. Avery of the Sixth North Carolina State Troops died from mortal wounds received the previous day. Shot in the neck and partially paralyzed during the Battle of Gettysburg, the Burke County native was unable to speak.

Avery fell alone while leading his men in an attack on Cemetery Hill. He had taken command of Brig. Gen. Robert F. Hoke's brigade after Hoke himself was wounded at Chancellorsville. Avery was the only man mounted and, once found, was carried from the field. Clutched in his hand was a small bloodstained piece of paper that has become one of the treasures of the State Archives of North Carolina.

Though right handed, Avery was forced to write with his left because of paralysis. His letter said, "Major, tell my father that I died with my face to the enemy. IE Avery". Maj. Samuel McDowell Tate, a friend from Burke County to whom the message was addressed, remained with Avery until he died. The short letter contains words long on duty and sentiment and has been featured in many books and documentaries about the Civil War. It has become known as the "Letter from the Dead."

Major

Isaac Avery's last letter home, written on the Gettysburg Battlefield on July 3, 1863.

1929 North Carolina Veterans Honored at Gettysburg, 1929

On July 3, 1929, the North Carolina Monument at Gettysburg National Military Park was dedicated. The monument commemorates the thirty-two North Carolina regiments involved in the action at the Battle of Gettysburg in early July 1863 and notes that one out of every four Confederate soldiers who died during the engagement was a North Carolinian.

The statue depicts four Confederate soldiers leaning forward in a charging position. One of them kneels down and points toward the enemy in the front. It was designed by Gutzon Borglum, who is most famous for sculpting Mount Rushmore. Borglum used photographs of Orren Smith of Warren County, a North Carolina veteran who died in 1913, as his model for the color bearer and developed the likenesses of the other three soldiers depicted from photographs of Confederate veterans.

More than fourteen thousand North Carolinians fought at Gettysburg as part of the Army of Northern Virginia, making the Tar Heel state's contingent second only to Virginia's in size. Over six thousand North Carolinians, more than forty percent of those fourteen thousand, died in the conflict.

Additional monuments were erected to the Twenty-Sixth and Forty-Third North Carolina Infantry Regiments at Gettysburg in 1985 and 1988, respectively.

1981 Look a-Yonder Comin': "Orange Blossom Special" and Ervin Rouse

On July 3, 1981, Ervin Rouse, composer of "Orange Blossom Special," the "unofficial anthem of bluegrass," died. Plagued by alcoholism and mental illness, he was living on the edge of the Everglades and playing local taverns occasionally for tips.

Born in 1917 in Craven County, Rouse left home at age eight to play in vaudeville shows. For a time he and his brother followed an evangelist and used their musical skills to energize audiences.

In Florida Rouse became acquainted with the Orange Blossom Special, a passenger train operated from New York to Miami on the Seaboard Air Line Railway from 1925 to the early 1960s. The song, with its interplay of fiddle and harmonica, evoked the train's sound and speed.

Recorded first by Chubby Wise, the song was brought to wide attention in 1942 by Bill Monroe and returned to the charts in 1965, when a version by Johnny Cash was released. When the "Man in Black" revived the song, Rouse took the stage to share the acclaim in one show. Cash supported him directly and through royalties.

The song endures and has been featured in the film *Urban Cowboy* and the TV series *Benny Hill*. The *Atlanta Journal-Constitution* named "Orange Blossom Special" one of one hundred "Songs of the South."

JUL 4

1833 Cornerstone Laid at State Capitol, 1833

On July 4, 1833, builders laid the cornerstone of the State Capitol on Union Square. The ceremony kicked off construction that would last for seven years and cost $532 thousand, a massive sum for the era. The Capitol that stands today was not the first in Raleigh. The original Capitol building, completed in 1794, burned in 1831.

Several architects contributed to the neoclassical design of the current building, including Ithiel Town, Alexander Jackson Davis, William Nichols Jr., and William Strickland. Scottish-born David Paton ultimately supervised much of the construction, though he was dismissed before the project was completed. The exterior walls are built of granite quarried in southeastern Raleigh and hauled to the site on the horse-drawn Experimental Railroad, the state's first railway.

The Capitol housed all of North Carolina's state government until 1888, when the Supreme Court Building, now the Labor Building, was completed across Edenton Street. The General Assembly left the Capitol and moved into the State Legislative Building in 1963.

The Capitol became a National Historic Landmark in 1973. It is now one of twenty-seven state historic sites and is open to the public for tours.

1878 The Saluda Grade, Steepest Mainline Rail Grade in the U.S.

On July 4, 1878, the first train to travel the Saluda Grade railway passage arrived in what's now the town of Saluda in Polk County.

Construction of the railway passage began in 1877 under the direction of Capt. Charles W. Pearson. The railway was intended to link Salisbury, Murphy, and Knoxville, Tennessee and, most importantly, to provide a connection between Asheville and Spartanburg, South Carolina.

While railroad builders used tunnels to snake through the steep climbs found elsewhere in the North Carolina mountains, near Saluda they decided to the face the steep inclines head-on and built straight up the rugged terrain. The engineering feat that made the project possible was unprecedented in the 1870s, and construction proved so dangerous and resulted in so many causalities that it sparked an investigation by the General Assembly.

Until taken out of service by Norfolk Southern in 2001, the Saluda Grade was at 4.7% the steepest operating mainline grade in the United States. Throughout the passage's long history, it was famous for its many runaway train accidents.

1937 *The Lost Colony* Opens

On July 4, 1937, *The Lost Colony* debuted on Roanoke Island. Written by Pulitzer Prize-winning playwright Paul Green, the symphonic play was the first outdoor drama. Although it was meant to last only one season, *The Lost Colony* has become the longest-running theatrical production of its kind in the nation.

Roanoke Island residents commissioned Green to write and produce a play to commemorate the 350th anniversary of the birth of Virginia Dare in 1937. While Green was busy writing the play, residents constructed the Waterside Theater using Works Progress Administration funds and labor supplied by the Civilian Conservation Corps. WPA funds were also used to hire out-of-work professional actors from New York to play the leads.

The Lost Colony opened to a packed house and, despite the economic hardships of the time, drew good crowds through the remainder of the summer. When Pres. Franklin D. Roosevelt attended on August 18, the anniversary of Virginia Dare's birth, the resulting national attention that resulted ensured that the production would return for a second season.

In 2013 *The Lost Colony* was awarded a Tony for Excellence in Theater.

1986 Craft Brewery Industry Launched in Manteo, 1986

On July 4, 1986, North Carolina's first microbrewery opened.

Weeping Radish Brewery in Manteo was the first in what is now a long list of craft breweries in the state.

Founder Uli Bennewitz came to North Carolina in the early 1980s and decided to open a microbrewery similar to those he had seen in Bavaria. At that time it was illegal in North Carolina for a brewery to sell beer directly to consumers. Working with state leaders Bennewitz helped change the law to allow microbreweries to sell their beer onsite.

Since its beginning Weeping Radish has brewed beer according to Bavaria's Reinheitsgebot Purity Law of 1516, which states that beer must be brewed using only four ingredients: hops, malt, yeast, and water.

As North Carolina's craft beer culture has grown, so has Weeping Radish's business. A new, larger location opened in Grandy in 2001 and includes a restaurant, butcher's facility, and farm, as well as a larger brewery. Though the original Manteo location closed in 2007, the Grandy brewery continues to be a popular stop for visitors heading to the Outer Banks.

Lillian Prince (as Queen Elizabeth), Andy Griffith (as Sir Walter Raleigh), and Barbara Griffith (as Eleanor Dare), in Paul Green's *The Lost Colony* as performed in Manteo in 1950.

1865 From Old Capitol Prison to U.S. Capitol: Zebulon B. Vance

On July 5, 1865, ex-Confederate governor Zebulon Baird Vance was paroled on his honor from his imprisonment at the Old Capitol Prison in Washington, D.C.

As the end of the Civil War unfolded in North Carolina, Vance played an important role. Fleeing west in front of Gen. William T. Sherman's army, Vance stopped in Greensboro and met with Gen. Joseph Johnston. When Johnston traveled to Charlotte to meet with Confederate Pres. Jefferson Davis, Vance followed, then returned to Greensboro after agreeing to have no further obligations to the Confederacy. He contacted Union Gen. John Schofield and offered to surrender himself, though Schofield declined to arrest him, saying he had no orders to do so. Vance informed Schofield that he would return to his home in Statesville.

Vance's stay in Statesville was short-lived. He arrived home on May 4 only to be arrested on the orders of Gen. Ulysses S. Grant on May 13. By May 20 he was in Washington. While he was imprisoned, his wife's health, usually fragile, took a bad turn. Provisional Gov. William Holden sent a telegram on July 4 noting her ill health and asking for Vance's release.

After the war Vance practiced law in Charlotte. He was prevented from taking the U.S. Senate seat to which he was elected in 1870 by the Fourteenth Amendment, but he worked behind the scenes to develop the Conservative Party until he was eligible for office in 1872.

He was elected governor again in 1876 but vacated that office with two years left in his term in 1879 to join the U.S. Senate. He would serve there until his death in 1894.

Zebulon Baird Vance

1916 Joffre Coe, Father of North Carolina Archaeology

On July 5, 1916, widely respected archaeologist Joffre Coe was born in Greensboro.

Coe developed his interest in archaeology early, spending time exploring the outdoors with his paternal grandfather when he was young and corresponding with prominent anthropologists during his teenage years. Graduating from high school in Florida in 1933, Coe returned to North Carolina and helped form the Archaeological Society of North Carolina. He enrolled in Brevard College in 1934 and transferred to UNC shortly thereafter. While there, Coe undertook several major projects, including a survey of thirty-two Indian sites in Transylvania County and the first systematic archaeological excavation at an Indian site in the North Carolina Piedmont. During his college years he also began work that he would continue for the rest of his life at Town Creek Indian Mound in Montgomery County.

After graduating from UNC, Coe enlisted in the Army in 1942 and worked as a war photographer and intelligence officer. He received his graduate degrees in anthropology from the University of Michigan and joined the faculty at UNC. His dissertation has become a classic work in American archaeology, and he is now considered one of the foremost authorities on the archaeology of eastern North America.

Joffre Coe

JUL 5

JUL 6

1896 Rayon Key to Success of Burlington Mills and Spencer Love

On July 6, 1896, textile industrialist J. Spencer Love was born in Massachusetts.

Though Love's family roots were in North Carolina, he remained in New England until finishing his studies at Harvard and serving a brief stint in the Army during World War I. After he was unable to find work in Boston, Love moved to Gastonia and joined his grandfather and uncle in the textile business.

Love owned the Gastonia Cotton Manufacturing Company briefly in the late 1910s and early 1920s but sold it and moved to Burlington, where he set up a new textile operation. He had a penchant for experimentation and took a gamble on producing a new product, rayon.

That move helped Love's Burlington Mills expand and evolve into Burlington Industries, the largest textile manufacturing company in the world and among the nation's fifty largest corporations in the 1960s.

Beyond his business pursuits Love was active in industry groups, civic organizations, and state politics throughout his life. He died in 1962 and is buried in Greensboro.

J. Spencer Love

1935 Flightless Birds Race in Brevard, 1935

On July 6, 1935, a race between two ostriches was held on Main Street in downtown Brevard. Each bird was ridden by a young woman. According to the *Transylvania Times*, a local newspaper, the two jockeys, Billie Dean and Amie Register, rode without bridles, saddles, or any other equipment.

Accounts of the race vary, but an article in the *Times* before the race said that each 350-pound bird would be blindfolded while the jockey mounted it and that folks weren't exactly sure what would happen after the blindfolds were removed, though the hope was that the birds would race down Main Street toward a railroad bridge and maybe reach thirty-five miles per hour.

The race's victor has been lost to history, but one account mentions that one of the ostriches got off track and ran into a Ford Model T, knocking the rider unconscious, though she soon recovered.

The entire event was a traveling show that had originated in Florida, where, again according to the *Times*, fourteen thousand people had turned out at a racetrack in Miami to watch the race. The paper mentions that Brevard was the eleventh town outside of Florida where the ostrich races had been held.

1977 "Bo Time" Began in 1977

On July 6, 1977, the first Bojangles' Famous Chicken 'n Biscuits restaurant opened in Charlotte.

The quick-service restaurant was founded by Jack Fulk and Richard Thomas. It was a walk-in location with no seating and was located in what was then a lesser visited part of Charlotte. The location was Fulk's way of proving the quality of his food, and it came to be very successful, indeed. Bojangles offered a brand of seasoning that stood out from the rest.

First franchised in 1978, the regional chain of quick-service restaurants quickly grew. Its success is mostly attributed to Fulk, a Davidson County native, who showed innovation and perseverance and always tried to adhere to the highest standards of quality.

The restaurant has been enormously popular, achieving near legendary status across the Southeast. In 2008 the *Wall Street Journal* named Bojangles one of only eight restaurant chains in its elite "25 Franchise High Performers." Today Bojangles boasts more than five hundred stores in ten states, Washington, D.C., and two foreign nations.

Ostrich Race! DON'T MISS IT!

Something New, Novel and Different

FREE! Race Down Main Street Saturday, July 6, 2:30 P. M.

Begins at B. & B. Feed Store---Ends at Fire Station

Brevard merchants are sponsoring a show by the

KATHERINE REID OSTRICH TROUPE

Birds on display Friday and Saturday on lot rear of Esso Station on Broad Street.

Sponsored by the following firms:

Hayes Motor Co.
McCrary Auto Service
Clemson Theatre
Whiteway Dry Cleaners
The Fashion
Ward's News Stand
Hawkins' Fruit Store
Central Market
City Market
Long's Drug Store
Philipp's Bakery
R. F. Tharp Plumbing Co.
R. H. Plummer & Co.
Dutch Oven Food Shop
Brevard Pharmacy
Dixie Cleaners
Trantham's Dept. Store
Ruth's Beauty Parlor
Macfie Drug Store
Taylor's Peach Store
M. A. Mull Pool Room
The Canteen Cafe
Esso Service Station
The Gift Shop
A&P Tea Co.
Austin's Studio
Poinsette Cafe

B&B FEED & SEED CO.
We furnish feed for Ostriches

Photo by Eadweard Muybridge (*background*).

Advertisement from the *Transylvania Times*.

1833 Sir Archie and the North Carolina Roots of Thoroughbred Racing

On July 7, 1833, Sir Archie, arguably the greatest thoroughbred in North Carolina history, died at age twenty-eight.

Sir Archie was the foundation sire of champions Timoleon, Man O'War, Seabiscuit, and Secretariat. In the era before Kentucky became the nation's center of horse racing and equine culture, North Carolina established a considerable reputation for raising thoroughbred winners. For several generations Virginia and North Carolina horses dominated tracks throughout the country.

Foaled in Cumberland County, Virginia, at an early age Sir Archie came to the attention of the nation's first great trainer, Warrenton's William Ransom Johnson. He bought the horse for fifteen hundred dollars and described him as "the best horse I have ever seen." After Sir Archie won races in Richmond and Petersburg, Johnson was hard pressed to find competition.

In 1809 former governor and UNC founder William R. Davie purchased the horse for five thousand dollars and soon thereafter put him out to stud. Sir Archie's offspring became the next generation of champion thoroughbreds. From 1817 to 1833 he was quartered at the "Mowfield" plantation in Northampton County, and he is buried on the grounds there.

1861 Gubernatorial Succession Early in the Civil War

On July 7, 1861, Gov. John Ellis died and Henry Toole Clark was elevated to fill the position.

Ellis, elected to the office in 1858 and 1860, was in command in April 1861 when Pres. Abraham Lincoln requested troops to put down the insurrection. After answering the president, "You can get no troops from North Carolina," Ellis ordered state troops to seize all Federal forts and the Fayetteville Arsenal and sent a telegram to Confederate Pres. Jefferson Davis indicating that the state would support the Confederacy. Shortly after North Carolina seceded from the Union, Ellis succumbed to tuberculosis.

Clark was elected to the state Senate in 1850 and was returned in every election through 1860. His high character and strong moral values commanded the respect of both parties, and he was elected president of the senate in 1858 and 1860. When Gov. John Ellis became seriously ill in June of 1861, it fell upon Clark, as president of the senate, to assume the duties of the chief executive. His position was made official by Ellis's death in July.

1863 The Home Guard, Peacekeepers During the Civil War

On July 7, 1863, the North Carolina General Assembly passed legislation to create the Home Guard.

By 1863 the Civil War had become an internal crisis for the state of North Carolina. Large sections of Piedmont and western North Carolina were openly opposed to both the Confederate government and the administration of Gov. Zebulon Vance. There was strident opposition to the Confederate Conscription Acts, which allowed large slave owners to be exempted from military service, and heavy taxes were being levied to pay for the war effort.

In an effort to deal with lawlessness, the Home Guard was created to provide an emergency police force. White men between the ages eighteen to fifty who were exempted from the conscription laws were automatically enrolled in these units. The units were then classified first, second, or third class, depending on the physical condition of the men enrolled. All counties had at least one home guard unit, which could be called into service for three months at a time for the "public defense."

By the end of the war, eight regiments were formed, comprising roughly twelve thousand men. These units rounded up deserters, attempted to maintain law and order within communities, skirmished with invading Union forces, and guarded Federal prisoners.

JUL 7

JUL 8

1885 "Goat Gland Doctor": A Legendary Con Man

On July 8, 1885, John Romulus Brinkley was born in Jackson County.

In 1908 Brinkley left his job in North Carolina as a telegraph operator and moved to Chicago, where he entered medical school, but soon dropped out. Brinkley then set up his first practice in Greenville, South Carolina, nevertheless. From there he moved to Arkansas and secured a degree from "Eclectic Medical University," which would probably be called a "diploma mill" today. His rise to fame commenced in 1922 with his development of an operation whereby the sex glands of goats were transplanted into the bodies of impotent men.

Brinkley's ownership of radio station KFKB in Milford, Kansas helped him to publicize his treatment. Officials of the American Medical Association denounced Brinkley as a charlatan, but that scarcely dented the rush of business to his hospital. In 1933 he moved to Del Rio, Texas, where he founded XERA, the world's most powerful radio station, across the border in Mexico. At the height of his success, Brinkley had a net worth of twelve million dollars. The press touted him as the "Kansas Ponce de Leon" and the "Goat Gland King." The target of many lawsuits, he died bankrupt in 1942.

1979 Film Screening Prelude to Klan/Nazi Shooting, 1979

On July 8, 1979, members of the communist Greensboro Workers Viewpoint Organization (WVO) protested a screening of the white supremacist film *Birth of a Nation* held by the Ku Klux Klan at the town hall of the small Rowan County town of China Grove.

The Greensboro communist group opposed the Klan because it divided working people by their race, thereby, in WVO's view, distracting them from the struggle for workers' rights. When the WVO learned of the screening, it immediately began to organize a protest march.

The march culminated in a standoff between armed KKK members, who stood in front of the town hall, and WVO members and others, who marched past chanting anti-Klan slogans while waving bats and sticks. WVO members burned a Confederate flag in front of the building, while local police defused the situation by forcing Klan members to return inside.

The march is significant because it kicked off hostilities between the WVO, which later became the Communist Workers Party, and the Klan. The conflict would come to a head in the "Death to the Klan" march and shooting in Greensboro in November of that year.

John R. Brinkley, 1921.

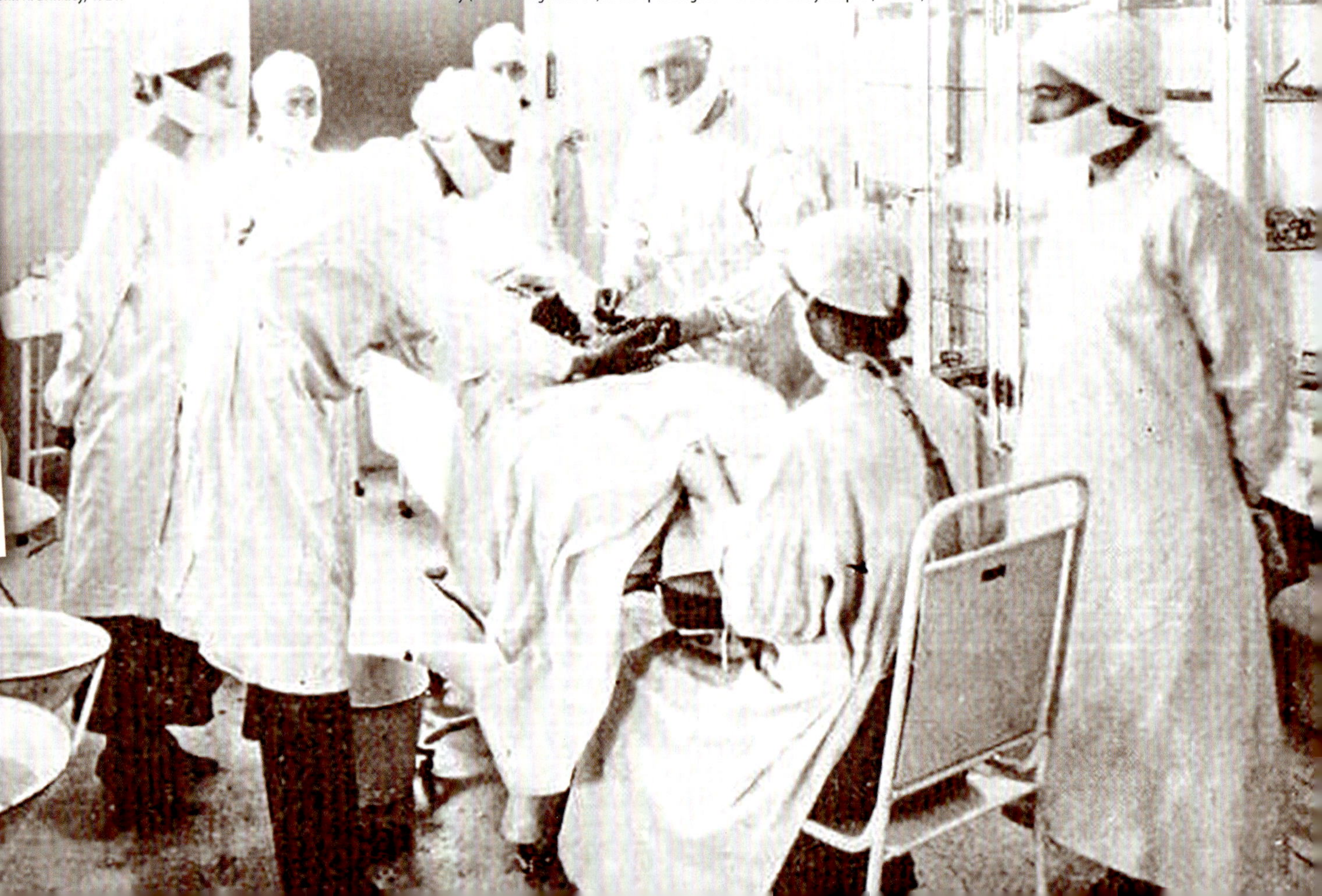

John R. Brinkley (*below with glasses on*) in the operating room at the Brinkley Hospital, Milford, Kansas.

1807 Lutheran Leader J. G. Arends

On July 9, 1807, minister, educator, and founder of the North Carolina Synod of the Lutheran Church J. G. Arends died in Lincolnton.

Born in Germany in 1740, Arends arrived in Rowan County in 1773 to become a Lutheran teacher. When the minister who served the area left in 1774, Arends was ordained to take his place.

Arends traveled extensively throughout the western part of North Carolina ministering to those who otherwise had no pastoral care. By the end of his ministry, he had served nineteen churches, most of which he helped establish. Although many in the Lutheran Church in North Carolina were supportive of the Crown, Arends dedicated himself to the cause of American independence.

Responding to the "outburst of intensive religious activity" and the "alarming deterioration of both faith and morals" during the revivalism known as the Second Great Awakening, Arends and other Lutheran ministers in North Carolina saw the need to organize and bring authority to the Lutheran Church. They met in Salisbury in May 1803 to form the North Carolina Synod of the Lutheran Church. It was only the third Lutheran synod in America, and Arends was elected the group's first president.

He died four years later.

1933 Tarboro's "Cool Pool"

On July 9, 1933, the Tarboro Town Council approved the purchase of a refrigeration unit for the town's municipal pool. The council's action was in response to the unseasonably hot summer that year in eastern North Carolina. The town had just recently put in an Olympic-sized pool for residents to enjoy, but the water in the pool was kept too warm by the weather and the activity of the swimmers.

The council asked Frick and Company of Waynesboro, Pennsylvania to design and install a refrigerating unit in the pool. The company did so, and by mid-August the device was installed at a cost of nearly three thousand dollars. Some of that money may have come from the federal government as part of Depression-era economic development programs.

Nicknamed "The Cool Pool," it drew large crowds of swimmers and played host to a number of state and regional meets during the 1930s and 1940s. A national meet was held there in 1943, with Gov. J. Melville Broughton as the honored guest.

By the 1970s the pool was closed. It is believed to have been the first and only refrigerated pool in the nation.

1945 Root Boy Slim and Blues Based Mayhem

On July 9, 1945, Foster McKenzie III, known to punk music fans as Root Boy Slim, was born to a fishmonger in Asheville.

The family moved to Washington, D.C. while McKenzie was still a boy. He was in and out of private academies, including the Sidwell Friends School, throughout his youth before being accepted at Yale University. While studying in New Haven, McKenzie formed his first band, Prince La La and the Midnight Creepers.

As a budding musician McKenzie idolized outsiders like Captain Beefheart and placed a premium on shocking his audiences, performing in ermine capes and silver hot pants. He boasted that his band was never asked to make a return engagement. At Yale McKenzie pledged Delta Kappa Epsilon. George W. Bush, one year younger and then president of the chapter, reportedly banned the musicians from playing the fraternity house.

A new lineup, Root Boy Slim and the Sex Change Band, signed with Warner Brothers and released their best-known song, "Boogie 'Til You Puke," in 1978. Their brand of blues maintained a hardcore cult following, especially in the D.C. area.

McKenzie died in Orlando, Florida in 1993 and is buried at Calvary Episcopal Church In Fletcher.

A swimmer, believed to be Carolyn Perrest, at the Tarboro swimming pool, May 1939.

JUL

10

1920 Wry Television Journalist David Brinkley a Wilmingtonian

On July 10, 1920, broadcaster David Brinkley was born in Wilmington.

Brinkley got his start reporting with the *Wilmington Morning Star* in 1938. After serving briefly in the Army, he was hired by the NBC radio network as a news writer, partly for his knack for "writing for the ear." In 1956 he paired with Chet Huntley to cover the Republican and Democratic national conventions. The two proved so popular that NBC tapped them to anchor the evening television news program *Huntley-Brinkley Report*. The program went on to become the top-rated evening newscast of the 1960s. Brinkley reported from Washington, D.C., Huntley from New York. In 1981 Brinkley went to work for ABC and hosted a Sunday morning interview program *This Week with David Brinkley*.

The title of his 1995 book, *David Brinkley: 11 Presidents, 4 Wars, 22 Political Conventions, 1 Moon Landing, 3 Assassinations, 2,000 Weeks of News and Other Stuff on Television and 18 Years of Growing Up in North Carolina*, reflects the breadth of his career.

Among Brinkley's accolades are ten Emmys, three George Foster Peabody Awards, and the Presidential Medal of Freedom. Brinkley died at his home in Texas in 2003 at age eighty-two. He is buried in Wilmington's Oakdale Cemetery.

1930 Serial Prison Escapee Meets His Demise

On July 10, 1930, Otto Wood made his final escape from Central Prison. To this day, no one knows how he did it.

On the lam for six months, he was finally recognized by Salisbury police as he walked through town on December 31. In a bold move Wood drew a gun on the officers and got into their car, demanding that they drive out of town. When the officers drew their guns, a shootout ensued, and Wood was killed on the street.

During his lifetime Wood was a legend for both his felonious ways and his numerous escapes from jail—the final one was his eleventh. During one of his incarcerations, he wrote a short autobiography, entitled *Life History of Otto Wood, Inmate, State Prison*. From 1923, when he began a sentence for murder, he escaped about once per year until in 1926 he was placed in solitary confinement.

Wood's autobiography convinced many of his sympathizers that he was a reformed man. Removed from solitary, he escaped again. Wood was well known as a wily criminal throughout the state and nation, and his story was followed gleefully in the press. In the end, his notoriety was his undoing.

David Brinkley in the newsroom of ABC's Washington, D.C. bureau, about 1987.

JUL 11

1851 Millie-Christine, the "Carolina Nightingale"

On July 11, 1851, the conjoined twins Millie and Christine McCoy were born into slavery in Columbus County.

Bright, engaging, and talented, the twins soon attracted the notice of legendary nineteenth century showmen, including P.T. Barnum. A bizarre series of sales, kidnappings, and custody battles ensued, blighting the twins' early years until their mother and her owner tracked them down in England and returned them to the United States.

Their unusual situation highlights the cruel absurdities of slavery laws: Their mother could plead for the twins' return as a free woman in English courts, but on American soil she and the girls were considered property.

After the Civil War Millie-Christine took their new-found freedom on the road, with Millie singing alto and Christine soprano while they danced and played the piano in a traveling circus. Audiences knew them as the "Carolina Nightingale." They traveled around the world, learned several languages, and even visited Queen Victoria, who gave them matching brooches.

After earning twenty-five thousand dollars each show season, Millie-Christine purchased the farm where their family had labored as slaves and built a large house, where they retired. They passed away within hours of each other in 1912 and rest in a double coffin under a tombstone inscribed "A soul with two thoughts. Two hearts that beat as one."

1851 North Carolina Railroad Boosts the Piedmont Economy

On July 11, 1851, construction on the North Carolina Railroad began in Greensboro. A crowd of thousands attended, which the local paper judged to be the largest gathering in the town's history.

Former Speaker of the N.C. House of Commons Calvin Graves, who sacrificed his political career by casting the deciding vote in favor of the railroad, had the honor of turning the first spade of soil. Those assembled filled a chest to serve as a time capsule. Five years later two track-laying crews met midway between Jamestown and Greensboro, where a legislator and railroad backer drove the final spike.

The railroad was the longest in the state up to that time. Running from Charlotte to Goldsboro for 223 miles, it became a key factor in Greensboro's prosperity and industrial growth. During the Civil War it helped the city establish itself as a storehouse and rail center for the Confederacy. Civilian refugees and wounded soldiers were transported and sheltered there.

Greensboro was not alone in benefiting from the railroad, though. It spurred growth all along the route and aided the development of several towns including Durham, Burlington, High Point, and Thomasville.

1879 Gaston Means, Con Man, Swindler, and Hoax Artist

On July 11, 1879, private detective, bootlegger, and all-around con man Gaston Means was born in Concord.

The son a prominent lawyer, Means attended UNC and worked as a schoolteacher and traveling salesman before moving to New York City to work as a private detective in 1911. For the next twenty years he was involved in a variety of dubious activities, from stealing money from a widow to advancing the German government's interests in the U.S. while America was still neutral during World War I.

Among his most famous hoaxes was his publication of the book *The Death of President Harding*, which falsely asserted that Harding had a been a central player in all the scandals of his administration and accused First Lady Florence Harding of murdering the president. Another was his involvement in the Lindbergh baby case, where he swindled a wealthy heiress out of thousands of dollars by insisting he could recover the child. He gained national infamy when FBI Director J. Edgar Hoover wrote an article about him for *The American Magazine* in which he called Means "the most amazing figure in contemporary criminal history."

It was the Lindbergh case that ultimately brought him down. In its aftermath Means was captured, convicted of grand larceny, and sent to Fort Leavenworth, Kansas to serve a fifteen-year sentence. He died there in 1938.

The HBO series *Boardwalk Empire* included a character based on Means's life.

1979 Ill-Fated Windmill Just Outside Boone

On July 11, 1979, Boone celebrated "Windmill Day" with a street festival to dedicate NASA's Mod-1, the world's largest megawatt industrial windmill on Howard's Knob.

The windmill was installed on the forty-four-hundred-foot peak as part of a program run by NASA and the U.S. Department of Energy to study wind power in response to the petroleum shortages of the 1970s OPEC oil embargo. The mammoth steel structure—140 feet tall, 200 feet wide across the blades, and weighing more than 350 tons—had propellers supplied by Boeing and a generator by General Electric. The Blue Ridge Electric Membership Corporation ran the project locally to return electricity, anticipated to power five hundred homes, to the energy grid.

A harbinger of the project's fate, the winds blew only about six miles per hour that first day, requiring manual rotation of the propeller blades. The windmill was soon plagued by terminal structural issues, inconsistent winds, and negative public perception from complaints of noise, disrupted television reception, and wasted public dollars. Too costly to repair, the windmill was dismantled and sold by the federal government in 1983.

The windmill had also become the centerpiece of pranks by Appalachian State University students. In one account TV news cameras were met by students dressed in sheets, calling themselves "Wooshies" who worshipped the god Nay-zuh.

Gaston Means in court. Means has his head tilted toward the camera.

1813 Southern Banks Fell to British in War of 1812

On July 12, 1813, a British fleet under the command of Adm. George Cockburn continued the invasion of the Outer Banks that had begun the night before. Before the day was over, the British had taken Ocracoke and Portsmouth Islands.

The invasion, which was part of the War of 1812, was the most serious attack on North Carolina during the course of that war. Cockburn's fleet included a seventy-four-gun man-of-war, three frigates, a brig, three schooners and several transport vessels carrying nearly three thousand British soldiers and marines

The British plundered the islands of "200 head of cattle, 400 sheep, and sixteen hundred fowls of various kinds." The troops paid the inhabitants for what they took, but at prices far below actual value. The Redcoats took customs collector Thomas Singleton's "papers in his library" and "tore up his law books."

Though the British took two privateers, a revenue cutter managed to escape their grasp, reach New Bern, and alert the rest of the state to the attack. That, in turn, allowed state militiamen to march on and guard coastal towns.

The British fleet sailed for Nova Scotia on July 16 but warned locals that the entire North Carolina coast remained under a British blockade. There is no evidence that the fleet ever returned to enforce it.

JUL 12

1833 "Die With It in You!": The Execution of Frankie Silver

On July 12, 1833, "Frankie" Silver was hanged in Morganton after being convicted of killing her husband Charlie with an ax and hacking his body into pieces. The murder occurred just before Christmas in 1831.

Though at first Frankie claimed that Charlie had gone hunting, his family suspected foul play when he did not return for Christmas. A search party found no sign of him, and the mystery seemed unsolved until a neighbor found pieces of bones and human teeth among the ashes in the fireplace inside the Silvers' Mitchell County cabin. More human remains were discovered beneath the floorboards, buried in the yard, and hidden in a stump.

Frankie was arrested for first-degree murder, though little hard evidence was presented during the two-day trial. The jury found her guilty, and the judge sentenced her to execution by hanging. She was eighteen years old and the mother of an infant daughter.

Since the law at the time did not allow women to testify in court, Silver never told her story before a judge. Even at the gallows, when she started to speak her last words, her father shouted to her from the crowd, "Die with it in you, Frankie!" Sadly, she did.

1913 The Grove Park Inn and Its Host of Prominent Guests

On July 12, 1913, the Grove Park Inn opened on Sunset Mountain near Asheville. Secretary of State William Jennings Bryan delivered an opening address officially welcoming guests and indicating that the inn was "built for the ages."

The brainchild of Edwin W. Grove, a Missouri pharmacist often called the "father of modern Asheville" because of the extensive development work he did in the city, the inn was designed by Fred L. Seely. Seely was an adherent of the Arts and Crafts movement, and that's evident in the inn's distinctive architectural style.

Construction on the building with its original 156 guest rooms took less than a year, thanks to the large crew of four hundred laborers and twenty Italian stonemasons, who worked ten-hour days to ensure the project's speedy completion.

Over the years the inn has hosted a number of notable personalities, including Pres. Franklin D. Roosevelt, writer F. Scott Fitzgerald, and exiled Philippine Pres. Manuel L. Quezon, who established the headquarters of a government-in-exile for the Philippines at the inn.

An extensive renovation in the 1980s increased the hotel's size to include 510 guest rooms, forty meeting rooms, two ballrooms, four restaurants, a full-service sports center, and a number of other facilities. It continues to attract guests from around the world.

The Grove Park Inn.

JUL 13

1767 Tryon Mountain Along the Indian Boundary, 1767

On July 13, 1767, a public proclamation made official a new boundary line delineating the western frontiers of the province of North Carolina from the Cherokee hunting grounds. The boundary mandated that white settlers west of the line should remove themselves by January 1768 and that anyone wishing to trade with the Cherokee must obtain a license from the governor.

In 1766 John Stuart, superintendent of Indian affairs for the southern colonies, pressed Gov. William Tryon to enter into negotiations with the Cherokee regarding extension of the boundary line. Tryon appointed commissioners to conduct the survey and mounted a personal military expedition to take part in the negotiations. The Cherokee were flattered to receive the governor's visit and gave him the title "Great Wolf of North Carolina."

The commissioners began their work in June 1767 at the Reedy River in South Carolina. From there, with the assistance of the several Cherokee, they surveyed a line fifty-three miles north to a tree atop the peak that the Indians called the "great Mountain" and that the commissioners renamed Tryon Mountain.

It was agreed that the boundary would extend in a straight line into Virginia, but that that portion would, by necessity, remain unsurveyed.

1908 Homegrown Raleigh Powerhouse, CP&L

On July 13, 1908, the Carolina Power & Light Company (CP&L) was chartered.

The corporation, with a customer base primarily in Raleigh, was the result of a merger of the Raleigh Electric Company, the Central Carolina Power Company, and the Consumer Light and Power Company. Within a few years CP&L owned or controlled local power companies in Oxford, Henderson, Asheville, and Goldsboro.

In the early part of the twentieth century, electric streetcar systems operated by companies that would become part of CP&L were an integral part of the utility's business and played an important role in the development of suburban neighborhoods in Asheville and Raleigh. After World War I the company benefited from the demand created by the proliferation of electrical appliances once considered luxury items, such as refrigerators, washing machines, and stoves.

To generate power for electricity, CP&L used coal, oil, and water until the 1960s, when the company built its first nuclear power plant in South Carolina. It also constructed costly nuclear plants in Brunswick and Wake Counties before scaling back its production of nuclear energy.

In 2000 CP&L merged with Florida Progress Corporation to form Progress Energy, and Progress in turn merged with Charlotte-based Duke Energy in 2012.

1937 Krispy Kreme Makes its Debut in Winston-Salem

On July 13, 1937, Vernon Rudolph began making yeast-raised doughnuts in a rented building in Winston-Salem.

Rudolph used a secret recipe he had bought from a New Orleans French pastry chef. The name "Krispy Kreme" had come with the recipe, and Rudolph decided to keep it. He initially sold his glazed confections to local grocery stores, but when people started asking to buy his fresh, hot doughnuts, he cut a hole in the bakery's wall and began selling them directly to customers.

By the 1960s Krispy Kreme stores had spread throughout the Southeast. To improve the made-from-scratch doughnuts' consistency, Rudolph built a mix plant and developed a dry dough that was delivered to each store. He also hired engineers to design Krispy Kreme's own doughnut-making equipment. With increased efficiency and new doughnut flavors, the company continued to grow.

After Rudolph died in 1973, Beatrice Foods Company bought Krispy Kreme, but some early franchisees bought the company back in 1982. By 1999 Krispy Kreme had expanded nationwide. The company went public in April 2000 and opened its first international store in Canada in 2001. Today Krispy Kreme has more than five hundred stores across the United States and in twenty-one countries worldwide.

1974 John Harris Hang Glides from Grandfather Mountain, 1974

On July 13, 1974, John Harris became the first person to hang glide from the sixteen-hundred-foot high rock pinnacle of Grandfather Mountain. Harris managed to convince Hugh Morton, the mountain's owner, to let him make the daring attempt during the mountain's annual Gathering of the Scottish Clans.

Harris flew about fifteen hundred feet, landing safely on the golf course below, and soon afterwards the heyday of hang gliding at the mountain began. In 1975 the U.S. Open Hang Gliding Tournament was held at Grandfather Mountain, and it continued to be held there until 1986. By then the gliders had become more efficient, making for increasingly longer and faster flights, so that there were inadequate safe landing areas around the heavily forested mountain. Flying was suspended from the peak in 1986 after a series of accidents.

Like Wilbur and Orville Wright, Harris was a native Midwesterner inspired by North Carolina's Outer Banks. He relocated to the Tar Heel State in the early 1970s for work as an engineer and became captivated by the fledgling sport of hang gliding, spending his free time on Jockey's Ridge. While living at the coast he started a kite and hang gliding business, Kitty Hawk Kites, that remains in operation today.

JUL 14

1863 Carolina Cavalier J.J. Pettigrew Mortally Wounded at Falling Waters

On July 14, 1863, Confederate Gen. James Johnston Pettigrew was fatally wounded by a gunshot to the stomach in a skirmish at Falling Waters, Maryland. Born in 1828 in Tyrrell County to a wealthy planter family, he entered the University of North Carolina at age fourteen and graduated as valedictorian in 1847.

In 1856 Pettigrew was elected to the South Carolina legislature, but his arguments against a series of bills that called for reopening the foreign slave trade ensured his defeat in the next election. After the outbreak of the Civil War, Pettigrew was elected colonel of the Twenty-Second North Carolina Infantry, which he led until he was severely wounded at Seven Pines in May 1862. Taken prisoner, he survived his wounds and was repatriated. For his courage, Pettigrew was promoted to brigadier general.

In May 1863 Pettigrew's brigade joined Gen. Robert E. Lee's Army of Northern Virginia for the Pennsylvania Campaign. Between July 1 and 3 he led his men at Gettysburg and participated in Pickett's Charge. Eleven days later Pettigrew was shot in the stomach.

He died three days later in West Virginia and is buried at his family's plantation.

1879 Silas McDowell, Originator of the Thermal Zone Concept

On July 14, 1879, Silas McDowell, prolific self-taught scientist and originator of the concept of the thermal belt, died.

Originally from York, South Carolina, McDowell attended school at Asheville's Newton Academy and then began work as a tailor in Charleston. He returned to the North Carolina mountains in 1823 and bought a farm in what's now Macon County. There, in Franklin, he began a long career of farming, viticulture, and horticulture, including an extensive apple production operation that developed many new varieties.

McDowell applied science to all his endeavors, published articles on agriculture, and began to develop a theory of thermal belts from his observations. In 1861 he published his best-known article, "Theory of the Thermal Zone," in which he postulated the thermal belt, a mountainside temperate zone ideal for growing crops. McDowell also made contributions to botany, guiding a number of the day's prominent botanists in explorations of the state's mountains. His wide-ranging interests also included mineralogy, geology, and zoology.

In his later years McDowell retired from farming and turned to history, literature, and poetry, penning biographies of prominent local people and accounts of historical events, and writing poetry recalling his youth and the mountain landscape.

1916 So Great the Devastation in 1916 Flood

On July 14, 1916, the worst flood in western North Carolina's history occurred after six days of torrential rain. In one twenty-four-hour period the region saw more than half of a normal year's total rainfall. The twenty-two inches of rain that fell that day set the record for the most rainfall in a single day in the United States.

Because the ground was saturated, most of the water immediately filled streams and rivers, causing them to reach flood stage in just a few hours. Eighty people lost their lives and the property damage surpassed twenty-two million dollars, one million of that in Asheville alone. Asheville and Hendersonville were completely cut off from the outside for weeks. Railroad tracks that were not destroyed had their supports washed out from under them, leaving tracks eerily suspended over mud-covered ravines—895 miles of track were rendered useless.

Everyone was taken by surprise at the speed with which the water rose. People were stranded in trees when their cars or homes were overwhelmed and they had nowhere else to go. Industrial plants along the rivers were swept away and landslides engulfed homes.

For most of western North Carolina the 1916 flood remains the benchmark for disasters.

French Broad River at Asheville during the flood of 1914. The remaining spans of Smith's Bridge, in foreground, collapsed soon after this photograph was taken.

1816 Henry Gatling and His Flying Machine

On July 15, 1816, Henry Gatling, inventor of an early flying machine and brother of Richard Gatling of Gatling gun fame, was born in Hertford County.

In interviews Gatling claimed the flight of the turkey buzzard as his inspiration. The bird, he observed, could soar for long intervals with only slight wing movements. To try to mimic this method of flight, he developed a flying machine with hinged triangular wings that could be moved with wires.

Gatling installed hand-cranked engines with blower-type wooden blades in front of each wing. The blades blew air to the underside of the wings to keep the plane aloft until necessary momentum was achieved. Anticipating the ground maneuvering needs of aircraft, Gatling placed large wooden wheels at the front and a smaller one under the tail of his "aeroplane." The completed contraption was about eighteen feet long with a fourteen-foot wingspan.

Gatling performed a number of ground and air trials of his airplane in the summer and fall of 1873. Eyewitnesses to the machine's first (and only) trip through the air in 1873 recalled an approximately hundred-foot flight from a raised platform, with the plane descending rapidly, suggesting that it was actually more of a "glide" than a "flight." The descent left the machine badly damaged, and Gatling never made the repairs necessary to attempt further flights.

The flying machine garnered wide press attention in 1872 and 1873. One article claimed that it was "destined at some future day to eclipse the famous gun [his brother's], and fly triumphant over time, space, and water." There is little doubt that the statement reflects the inventor's aspirations on both counts.

Gatling was murdered on his property in September 1879. The airplane, which had been stored in a barn, was destroyed by a fire in 1905.

A group of enthusiasts in Murfreesboro have built what they believe to be an accurate replica of the Gatling flying machine.

1938 Good Times for Ernie Barnes of Durham

On July 15, 1938, football player, painter, and all around Renaissance man Ernie Barnes was born in Durham.

As a child, Barnes began to draw as an antidote to bullying. He later developed physical discipline and became captain of Durham's then segregated Hillside High football team, receiving an athletic scholarship to what's now N.C. Central University in 1956. At Central Barnes studied art, but he left in 1959 before graduating to play professional football for six years.

Nicknamed "Big Rembrandt," Barnes kept a sketchbook with him on the field and turned the physical and emotional violence of the game into paintings. He also became known for depictions of people, often African Americans, engaged in everyday life, but with their eyes symbolically closed. His work is evocative and tangible, fusing elongated sculptural forms of the human body with vibrant color, movement, and emotional intensity.

Barnes's paintings appeared on the sitcom "Good Times" as the work of the show's character JJ. *The Sugar Shack*, a well-known painting, appeared in the show's credits and later became the cover image for Marvin Gaye's album *I Want You*.

In addition to his work as a painter and athlete, Barnes wrote books, co-created a TV special, and appeared in a number television programs and films, including episodes of "Good Times". He died in Los Angeles in 2009.

1949 "Uncle Jim" Patterson and WBT Sign-On, 1949

On July 15, 1949, announcer Jim Patterson signed on Charlotte's WBTV, the first television station in the Carolinas, two months ahead of WFMY in Greensboro, which signed on in September 1949. The Charlotte studio at that time was in the Wilder Building on Tryon Street, the present site of the Marriott Hotel.

WBTV and WFMY in 1949 were owned by Jefferson Standard Broadcasting Company, an affiliate of the life insurance company of the same name. The company filed an application for a Charlotte license with the Federal Communications Commission in December 1947. A construction permit arrived two months later, and work proceeded on an antenna atop Spencer Mountain in Gaston County. At the time there were only twelve television stations in the nation, mostly in larger cities.

Test patterns began running on Channel 3 on July 1, 1949. Station owners set up a viewing party in the Charlotte Armory, and thousands packed the venue for three days beginning on July 15. At that time the number of television sets in the area was less than a thousand; that count was up to eighty-five hundred by year's end. In 1955 WBTV moved to its present location.

Ernie Barnes in his studio.

Ernie Barnes unveiling his painting "In Remembrance" in Philadelphia, 2002.

JUL
16

1813 A Little-Known Episode of the War of 1812

On July 16, 1813, a British Royal Navy fleet departed Ocracoke Island, bringing to an end a little known episode of the War of 1812.

The fleet appeared off the coast on July 11. Under the command of Adm. George Cockburn, the expedition landed at Ocracoke and Portsmouth as part of a surprise attack. The British invaders plundered the islands of hundreds of livestock. Their objective was to take New Bern and the state's interior.

The United States Revenue Cutter *Mercury*, built at Ocracoke in 1807, usually policed the inner coast, enforcing state customs laws under the leadership of Capt. David Wallace. On receiving word of the invasion, the *Mercury* set course for New Bern to deliver a warning of the fleet's presence. Several of the British ships chased but failed to overtake the *Mercury*, which escaped very narrowly by running up all its sails.

The timely warning allowed the state to prepare a defense, thus preventing a full-scale invasion. As news reached the mainland of the threat, militia units from across the state gathered at New Bern. British commanders abandoned their mission once the advantage of surprise had been compromised.

The U.S. Revenue Service was the forerunner of the U.S. Coast Guard.

1857 Stonewall Jackson Wed in Lincoln County, 1857

On July 16, 1857, Thomas "Stonewall" Jackson married Mary Anna Morrison at "Cottage Home," the Morrison family's Lincoln County.

The couple first met through Morrison's sister, Isabella, who was married to D. H. Hill, a faculty member at what's now Washington and Lee University in Lexington, Virginia. Jackson, who had previously attended West Point and fought in the Mexican-American War, was on the faculty of the Virginia Military Institute, also in Lexington.

Married not long after their meeting and the death of Jackson's first wife, the couple were said to be deeply devoted to one another and to have had a happy home despite the death of their first child. They were not married long before they were separated by the advent of the war in 1861. After Jackson's death at the Battle of Chancellorsville, Mary returned to Lincoln County and never remarried.

Though Mary was said to not approve of her husband's nickname "Stonewall," since she thought it didn't accurately reflect his character, she came to accept it and be highly regarded as his widow throughout North Carolina and the rest of the former Confederacy. She was often visited by Confederate veterans and received military honors at her death in 1915.

1978 State Treasurer Edwin Gill, "Mr. Integrity"

On July 16, 1978, long-time state treasurer Edwin Gill died in Raleigh. Gill was known as "Mr. Integrity" during his more than thirty years of service as a public finance official.

Born in Laurinburg in July 1899, Gill opened a law practice there in 1924 after attending what's now Duke University in the early part of the decade. He represented Scotland County in the legislature for one term before working as Gov. O. Max Gardner's private secretary.

Gill became the first head of the North Carolina Paroles Commission in 1933 before serving as the state's Commissioner of Revenue, his first financial post, for much of the 1940s. He was a federal internal revenue collector for the state from 1950 until 1953, when he was appointed state treasurer.

After that initial appointment, Gill was consistently re-elected and remained the state treasurer for five consecutive terms until he retired in 1977. Under his direction the state attained the highest possible credit rating, reflecting his saying, "In North Carolina, we have made a habit of good government."

An avocational painter, he served on the boards of the North Carolina Arts Council, the North Carolina Museum of Art, and the State Art Society. He was considered a "respectable" pianist and organist. An avid reader, he collected books and donated to libraries.

He is buried in Laurinburg.

1711 Thomas Cary and Tumult of the Proprietary Period

On July 17, 1711, Thomas Cary was exiled from Carolina after a failed uprising that is now known as Cary's Rebellion.

With support from the Anglican establishment that dominated the colony's political scene at the time, Cary was appointed Governor of the Province of Carolina in 1705.

While the Quakers sent a representative to England to convince the Lords Proprietors to oust Cary, he tapped William Glover as his deputy and left to pursue business interests in South Carolina. Glover, supported by residents of the Albemarle region, was elected chief executive in 1707.

Cary had a change of heart in 1708 and switched his allegiances to the Quakers, who, along with the residents of Bath, saw him as a better alternative to Glover. Cary and his supporters regained control of the government and remained in power until 1711 when Edward Hyde, who had been appointed governor in England by the Lords Proprietors, arrived in North Carolina to claim the governorship of the colony and called for Cary's arrest.

Hyde sent a force to capture Cary at his home but was unsuccessful. Cary retaliated by outfitting a ship and sailing into Albemarle Sound with the intent of overthrowing the government. Royal marines dispatched from Virginia put down the rebellion, and Cary was taken back to England, where he was held for a year before being released without further punishment.

He returned to Bath where he died a few years later.

1752 Royal Governor Gabriel Johnston in Office for 18 Years

On July 17, 1752, colonial-era governor Gabriel Johnston died.

Johnston served in the colony's top job for eighteen years, holding the post longer than any governor in North Carolina's history down to the present day. Perhaps even more remarkable, due to problems collecting the rents and taxes that paid his salary, he was left uncompensated for thirteen of those years.

Johnston was born in the Scottish Lowlands, before being educated at the Universities of Edinburgh and St. Andrews. Sometime around 1728 he moved to London, where he lived in the home of Spencer Compton, Baron Wilmington, who was president of the Privy Council, which was a panel of king's closest advisers.

Named governor of North Carolina in 1733, Johnston didn't arrive at his post until October of the following year. He advocated for the establishment of Newton in 1735 and later renamed the town Wilmington in his patron's honor.

Johnston's term saw many changes in North Carolina, including its first printer and thus the first newspaper and printed laws, new agricultural techniques, and the building of several forts. North Carolina's population also tripled during his term, thanks in part to Johnston's efforts in encouraging immigration, especially from his native Scotland.

1967 Bebop and Avant Garde Jazz Master, Saxophonist John Coltrane

On July 17, 1967, legendary jazz saxophonist and composer John Coltrane died.

Born in 1926 in the small Richmond County town of Hamlet, Coltrane and his family family moved to High Point by the time he was three years old. Coltrane's love of music developed early, and he played both clarinet and saxophone in high school. After graduating from high school, Coltrane moved to Philadelphia to attend music school.

He made his professional debut in 1945 and collaborated with Dizzy Gillespie, Thelonious Monk, and Miles Davis on milestone recordings before forming his own group in 1960. Though he died at age forty, Coltrane released nearly fifty studio albums and almost twenty singles during his career.

He is perhaps remembered best for spanning genres and audiences while establishing avant-garde jazz and also achieving popular success. One measure of Coltrane's significance is the fact that he has been the subject of at least four biographies.

1970 Festival Rocked Iredell County Community, 1970

On July 17, 1970, the "South's Woodstock" opened at Love Valley. The rock festival swelled the small Western-themed community of about one hundred people to almost two hundred thousand.

Located north of Statesville, Love Valley was the creation of Andy Barker in 1954, who had always wanted to live like a cowboy in an Old West town. The idea of the rock festival was Barker's, and he charged five dollars a person for the three-day event.

While the festival could not draw the band lineup of Woodstock, which the Iredell County event was modeled after, the headliner was the Allman Brothers Band. Young and on the rise, the band played several sets during the weekend festival, and documentarians captured it in about twenty minutes of film. Several local bands, including Kallabash of Greensboro, were also on the program. Organizers had hoped to do a documentary like the one made at Woodstock, but lack of funds meant that they were able to capture only parts of each band's performance.

In spite of some locals' dire worries about illegal and immoral behavior, the weekend passed without major incident, and the festival in the valley lived up to its name.

Love Valley rock concert, 1970.

JUL 18

1585 Sixteenth Century Vengeance on Roanoke Island

On July 18, 1585, the Indian village of Aquascogoc was burned by men from the second of three Roanoke Voyages.

The voyagers on the second expedition left England in April 1585 with the goal of establishing a new colony on Roanoke Island. After arriving on the Outer Banks in June, a detachment of colonists, with the Native American Manteo as their interpreter, explored the mainland and visited several villages, including Pomeiok, Aquascogoc, and Secotan.

All but one of the boats of the detachment returned to the settlers' camp at Wococon on July 18. The remaining boat took Capt. Philip Amadas, Manteo, and a few others back to Aquascogoc to "demand a silver cup which one of the Savages had stolen from us."

It is unclear exactly what transpired at Aquascogoc—whether the Indians denied having the cup or whether they thought the English were taking back a gift. The leader of the village apparently promised the cup's return in an effort to stall the English long enough for the women and children to escape. After noticing the people clearing the village, Amadas reacted with unconscionable violence. It was written that his men "burnt, and spoyled their Corne, and Towne, all the people being fledde."

Not a month had passed into the attempted colonization of the "New World," when the English committed the first act of violence against the natives. It is believed that Aquascogoc was southeast of modern-day Belhaven in Beaufort County.

1670 John Lederer, Trailblazer

On July 18, 1670, German-born explorer John Lederer ended his trip through the Carolina Piedmont north of what's now Roanoke Rapids. Lederer's expedition predated the much better-known trip led by naturalist John Lawson by thirty years.

Trained as a physician in Hamburg, Lederer arrived in Virginia in 1669, where Gov. William Berkeley encouraged him to search for the Pacific Ocean. His journey helped allay many of the colonists' fears about the backcountry.

Lederer began his search with twenty-one militiamen and a Susquehanna Indian guide. Afraid of getting lost, the group pursued a straight compass course, ignoring several known Indian paths and encountering numerous natural obstacles. After twelve days of laborious path-cutting, the militiamen turned back, leaving Lederer and the guide to continue alone.

Together the pair demonstrated that explorers could survive in the wilderness among native peoples and that large armed expeditions such as those undertaken by Spaniards a century earlier were not necessary for exploring the interior.

The militiamen who deserted Lederer spread stories that discredited him. Claims related to his journey were doubted and scorned. Lederer moved to Maryland in shame but in time regained his reputation.

His accounts remain widely studied today by cartographers, historians, and ethnologists.

1918 Valorous Service by S.I. Parker in World War I

On July 18, 1918, Union County World War I soldier Samuel I. Parker advanced directly into machine gun fire, killing the gunner with his pistol. The incident took place near Soissons in northern France and earned Parker one of only two Medals of Honor awarded to North Carolinians for World War I service. The Medal of Honor is the military's highest honor and is awarded for gallantry above and beyond the call of duty.

Parker was a descendant of both early Supreme Court Justice James Iredell and Gov. Abner Nash. He left UNC for military service just prior to graduation in 1917. As a member of the First Infantry Division of the American Expeditionary Force, he served on the front lines in France. Samuel J. Ervin, one of his classmates at UNC and later U.S. senator, served in the same unit.

After the war Parker worked in textile mills. Pres. Franklin D. Roosevelt presented the Medal of Honor to him in 1936 in a White House ceremony attended by Douglas MacArthur. During World War II Parker trained troops at Fort Benning, Ga..

Second Lt. Samuel I. Parker, 1918.

1963 Scourge of Poverty Target of North Carolina Fund

On July 18, 1963, Gov. Terry Sanford announced the establishment of the North Carolina Fund, an interracial antipoverty initiative that predated and anticipated Pres. Lyndon B. Johnson's "War on Poverty." Sanford laid out his course in a speech at N.C. A&T State University in April 1963, rejecting segregation and proclaiming, "We must move forward as one people, or we will not move forward at all."

The governor and his aides, principally novelist John Ehle, crafted a plan, using nonprofit and federal money, to promote objectives without legislative interference. Startup funds, in the amount of 2.5 million dollars, came from the Z. Smith Reynolds and Mary Reynolds Babcock Foundations. A boost came from the Ford Foundation, in the amount of seven million dollars. Over the course of five years, federal funds totaling another seven million dollars, were routed to the Fund.

George Esser directed the effort, with the assistance of hundred of student volunteers. Headquarters were set up in a former auto dealership in Durham, but the focus was statewide and not entirely urban. Special focus went to four mountain counties, Watauga, Avery, Mitchell, and Yancey.

Over time the project became a political target, and while the Fund did not succeed in eliminating poverty, its ideals inspired subsequent efforts and activists.

JUL 19

1816 Anti-Slavery Sentiment Sparks Quaker Organization

On July 19, 1816, twenty-three delegates from four Quaker meetings organized the North Carolina Manumission Society in Guilford County.

The delegates represented 147 members in local societies. The antislavery organization alternated between Quaker meeting houses at Centre and Deep River until it disbanded after 1834. Female auxiliary societies were added beginning in 1825. Members met resistance from many quarters and had difficulty retaining printers for their handbills and other publications.

The Manumission Society was the chief antislavery society in antebellum North Carolina. Little is known about the separate North Carolina Abolition Society organized in 1824. Though the impact of the Manumission Society's activities on state politics is generally considered small, one of its major achievements was colonizing 420 slaves in Liberia.

After 1830 participation in the society declined, mostly due to the westward migration of its members and the rise of the more radical abolitionist movement. The Manumission Society's final meeting was held in 1834 before legal and other pressures forced the society to disband. Many of its members turned their abolitionist energies toward working for the Underground Railroad.

1906 Cherokee Wrestler and Chief

On July 19, 1906, Osley Bird Saunooke, super heavyweight wrestler and Chief of the Eastern Band of Cherokee Indians (EBCI), was born in Cherokee.

Professional wrestling was a natural fit for Saunooke, who served in the Marine Corps, stood six feet, six inches tall and weighed more than 350 pounds. During the Depression, he began wrestling and his rise in the sport was quick. In 1937 he became the Super Heavyweight Champion of the World, and he went on to hold that title for fourteen years. When he retired from the wrestling in 1951, Saunooke had fought 5,217 matches all over the country.

He then changed gears quickly. Saunooke was elected Principal Chief of the EBCI almost immediately, serving in that capacity from 1951 to 1955 and again from 1959 to 1963. He is widely credited with turning the Cherokee's home in western North Carolina into a model reservation and is often praised for working closely with the federal and state governments to ensure greater autonomy for the Cherokee.

Respected for his leadership abilities, Saunooke was the first Indian east of the Mississippi River elected to an office in the National Congress of American Indians. He died in 1965.

1937 Country Music's International Ambassador, George Hamilton IV

On July 19, 1937, country music star George Hamilton IV was born in Winston-Salem. While a student at UNC, the young Hamilton recorded "A Rose and a Baby Ruth" at the independent Chapel Hill label, Colonial Records. The song eventually became a gold record.

Hamilton left Chapel Hill for Nashville to pursue a career in country music and was invited to join the Grand Old Opry in 1960. Later that year he signed a record contract with RCA. His fame quickly rose, and in 1963 he topped the *Billboard* Country chart with "Abilene."

After his popularity declined in America in the 1970s, he began travelling internationally and had events in the Middle East and Eastern Europe. The activities earned Hamilton the nickname of "The International Ambassador of Country Music." In 2010 Hamilton was inducted into the North Carolina Music Hall of Fame. He died in 2014.

1982 Justice at Nuremburg: Judge Fitzroy Donald Phillips

On July 19, 1982, former Superior Court Justice Fitzroy Donald Phillips died in Rockingham. He was one of two North Carolina judges who participated in the second phase of trials of former Nazi officials at Nuremberg, Germany (the other was Richard Dillard Dixon).

Phillips was born in Laurinburg in 1893, where he practiced law after studying at UNC. After service in the American Expeditionary Force in the World War I, he was elected mayor of Rockingham. In 1923 he was elected solicitor of the Thirteenth Judicial District, a role similar to that of district attorney, and eleven years later he was elected a Superior Court justice for the same district.

Following the major war crimes trials held before the International Military Tribunal in Nuremberg in 1945 and 1946, the United States established military courts to try lesser Nazi officials. In November 1946 Phillips resigned his judgeship to serve as one of the three judges of what was called Military Tribunal II, the venue for two trials in 1947. The tribunal met again in 1948 to hear additional details concerning the second case. Afterwards, Phillips returned home to serve as Superior Court judge before retiring in 1962.

The Nuremburg trials collectively established the precedents for the successful prosecution of war criminals.

Osley Bird Saunooke, 1954.

George Hamilton IV onstage at the Grand Ole Opry, 2007.

JUL 20

1777 Cherokees Seek Peace After Rutherford Expedition

On July 20, 1777, the Overhill Cherokee Indians signed a treaty of peace and ceded their lands east of the Blue Ridge Mountains. The meeting between Indian representatives and commissioners from North Carolina and Virginia took place at Long Island in the Holston River in Tennessee and produced what has since come to be known as the Treaty of Long Island of the Holston.

White settlers had long been encroaching on Cherokee tribal lands, and after the Indians' demand in 1776 for the withdrawal of settlers was met with no action, the Cherokees began to attack frontier settlements. Citizens of the backcountry were alarmed. Griffith Rutherford, brigadier general of the Salisbury District militia, called for volunteers to conduct an expedition against the Cherokee. The Indians, having gotten word of the expedition, abandoned many of their settlements. Rutherford's men burned whatever was left behind.

Rutherford concluded his campaign in October 1776, having effectively neutralized the threat of the Cherokee in North Carolina. As refugees, surviving over the winter on wild game, nuts, and fruits, the remaining Cherokee agreed to discuss peace terms the following year.

1813 Surveying of the State Boundary and the Block House Near Tryon

On July 20, 1813, representatives from North Carolina and South Carolina met near the present-day town of Tryon and marked the state boundary at a prominent building of the period known as the Block House.

The event was designed to help resolve a series of bitter boundary disputes. The Proprietary province of Carolina had been divided into two separate colonies as of 1712, but no official boundary was specified for many years.

An initial agreement in 1730 called for the boundary to start thirty miles south of the mouth of the Cape Fear River and run northwest parallel to the river. Surveys in 1735 and 1737 brought the diagonal line beyond the settled regions to a remote meadow that was thought to lie on the thirty-fifth parallel.

As early as 1750, the Block House site stood as a prominent landmark along the line between the Carolinas, although technically three hundred feet within South Carolina. It was used as a trading post and fortification.

In 1764 another survey began at the same meadow where the line had ended in 1737. Additional work on the boundary started in 1772. After years of disagreements, both states finally accepted the 1764 and 1772 survey lines in 1813, reasoning that what each state lost in one survey was made up for by the other.

Border disputes have continued into the modern era, and after more than twenty years of debate over minor adjustments, the Carolinas reached a final border agreement in 2016.

1863 Rocky Mount Mills Burned by Union Troops, 1863

On July 20, 1863, Union cavalry led by Gen. Edward Potter torched Rocky Mount Mills, the second cotton mill operation in North Carolina after the short-lived Schenck-Warlick Mill in Lincoln County.

Manufacturing began in Rocky Mount in 1818 on a twenty-acre tract at the falls of the Tar River. The mills were initially operated by Joel Battle and two partners, but by 1825 Battle was the sole proprietor.

Built from local granite, the facility, housing cotton and grist mills, was three stories plus a basement. Slaves and a few free African Americans supplied the labor from the earliest days until about 1852, when the Battles began to substitute white workers, many of them women and children. By that time local slaveowners were less inclined to hire their slaves out for factory work.

After the Civil War Battle rebuilt the mills on the original foundation. The new brick building, burned in 1869, and Battle again rebuilt the mills.

When Rocky Mount Mills closed in 1996, the facility was believed to be the oldest operating cotton mill in the South. It now comprises a local historic district and is undergoing redevelopment.

1892 Sensational 1890s Murder in Winston-Salem

On July 20, 1892, Ellen Smith was fatally shot by Peter DeGraff near the Zinzendorf Hotel in Winston-Salem. The murder became the subject of a popular turn-of-the-century ballad, "Poor Ellen Smith."

A maid in the home of a Winston-Salem merchant, Smith became pregnant while romantically involved with DeGraff, a local ladies' man and ne'er-do-well. The child was stillborn or died after birth during a visit to Smith's family in Yadkin County. On that visit Smith was allegedly accompanied by DeGraff, who denied that the child was his.

DeGraff subsequently broke off the relationship and threatened to shoot Smith if she attempted to contact him again. On July 17 the two had a major quarrel at the home of Smith's employer. Tensions cooled the next day, and DeGraff sent Smith a note telling her that he loved her and asking to see her on evening of the twentieth. Smith's body was found the morning of July 21, when individuals were directed to the site by a man who was apparently DeGraff himself.

DeGraff soon fled and lived under an assumed name in Mt. Airy but returned in June 1893 and was arrested. At the trial the accumulated evidence pointed convincingly towards DeGraff, who pled innocent, as the killer.

Convicted, DeGraff was executed in 1894. He confessed to the murder in front of a large crowd of onlookers right before he was executed.

A postcard showing Rocky Mount Mills in 1909.

1669 Precepts for Colonial Government Set, 1669

On July 21, 1669, the Lords Proprietors signed and sealed the Fundamental Constitutions of Carolina. The document, perhaps written by John Locke, who served as secretary to one of the Proprietors, established a framework of government for the nascent colony.

While the document recognized the Church of England, it also promoted religious tolerance. It attempted to set up an orderly feudal system with landed gentry, freemen, "leet-men" (similar to serfs), and slaves.

The Proprietors were given authority to grant titles, but not titles that existed in England, so they came up with landgrave (a title used in central Europe) and cacique (a term used for chiefs by some Caribbean natives). The Constitutions proposed a relatively low threshold for giving property owners the right to vote.

The complex document, with 111 often impractical provisions, was never popular among the residents of Carolina. One element of the Constitutions that came to fruition was the Palatine Court ,which operated in the colony for about fifty years and was in some ways a precursor to our modern legal system.

1778 Hillsborough Convention Fails to Ratify Constitution

On July 21, 1788, 270 delegates convened in Hillsborough for what would become a two-week debate on ratifying the national Constitution drafted in Philadelphia in 1787. The Anti-Federalist delegates outnumbered their Federalist colleagues by a margin of two-to-one.

The Federalists wanted to strengthen the powers of the federal government in order to help the country keep from dissolving. They argued that the powers granted to the federal government in the Articles of Confederation were not sufficient. On the other side the Anti-Federalists were suspicious of the federal government and did not want self-rule to come under fire from a government that could intrude on state and individual rights.

Knowing that they would likely lose, members of the Federalist minority brought a stenographer to the convention to record their arguments for publication in hopes of changing public opinion in the future. The debate resulted in the delegates voting 184 to 84 to neither ratify nor reject the Constitution, and North Carolina was not part of the Union until the 1789 Fayetteville Convention. One of the major reasons why North Carolina didn't ratify the Constitution was its lack of a Bill of Rights.

1930 Modest Beginning for Duke University Hospital

On July 21, 1930, Duke University Hospital opened to patients after three years of construction.

The idea for the hospital can be traced back to 1925, when industrialist James B. Duke made a four million dollar bequest to establish a medical school, nursing school, and hospital to help improve healthcare in the Carolinas. Duke's dream was to create what he hoped would become the best medical institution between Baltimore and New Orleans.

Although Durham already had two hospitals, Watts and Lincoln, Duke would be unique in offering specialized medical care, and with four hundred beds it would be by far the largest hospital in the city's history. Some experts were skeptical about the idea of a medical facility of that size in Durham, arguing that the area was not densely populated enough to support it.

But patients were willing to travel. On the hospital's first day, seventeen of them were registered. The number continued to grow at an extraordinary rate and by 1932 over then thousand patients had been treated.

While it began as a regional hospital, today the Duke University Medical Center is recognized as one of the top healthcare organizations in the country, known for its commitment to education, research, and innovation.

Duke hospital opened in 1930.

1900 Planter and Politician Elias Carr

On July 22, 1900, Elias Carr, planter and former governor, died at "Bracebridge Hall," his home in Old Sparta for most of his life.

Born in 1839 to early settlers and planters in Edgecombe and Nash Counties, Carr was orphaned with the death of his mother in 1840 and his father in 1843. He was raised by an aunt and uncle in Warren County, where he received his early schooling before finishing his education at UNC and the University of Virginia.

Carr was an enlightened farmer, and his use of scientific methods in his varied agricultural endeavors made him very wealthy. In 1887 he became the first president of the North Carolina Farmer's Association, and as such he became well-known throughout the state.

After gaining significant political experience with the Farmer's Alliance, Carr was nominated for governor by the Democratic Party in 1892 and won the office. His single term in the state's top job was marked by progressive policies and efficient management, and he advocated for many of the same things he championed before entering the political sphere, including better roads and more funding for rural schools.

After his term, Carr retired to "Bracebridge Hall," where he died a few years later.

1967 Prolific Poet Carl Sandburg

On July 22, 1967, American poet, journalist, biographer, and folk musician Carl Sandburg died at Connemara, his antebellum home in Flat Rock, where he wrote a third of his works and spent the last twenty-two years of his life.

Born in January 1878 to Swedish immigrants in Galesburg, Illinois, Sandburg left school after the eighth grade. He worked numerous odd jobs and hoboed his way across the West before serving in the Spanish-American War. Afterward, he attended Lombard College in his hometown but never graduated. In 1908 Sandburg married Lillian Steichen. They had four daughters.

As a family man, Sandburg settled into journalism, writing for the *Chicago Daily News*, while still pursuing his poetry. By 1945, when the family moved to Flat Rock, Sandburg had published several volumes of poetry, written five children's books, and received two Pulitzer Prizes: one for *Corn Huskers* and another for *Abraham Lincoln: The War Years*. He won a third Pulitzer Prize in 1951 for his *Complete Poems*.

Connemara's 264 acres offered plenty of space for Mrs. Sandburg's prize-winning goats and plenty of solitude for the poet. There, in an upstairs garret, Sandburg wrote, and in a downstairs bedroom, he died at age eighty-nine.

1996 Vermont Royster, *Wall Street Journal* Sage

On July 22, 1996, Vermont Connecticut Royster, a journalist affiliated with the *Wall Street Journal* for sixty years, died.

Born in 1914 in Raleigh, Royster was not the only one in his family to have unusual first and middle names. His great-grandfather started the tradition of naming people after places, and relatives had such names as Arkansas, Delaware, Iowa, and Michigan.

A graduate of UNC, where he began his writing career as a reporter for the *Daily Tar Heel*, Royster moved to New York in 1936 and found part-time work as a writer for the *Journal* for $15 a week. He quickly worked his way up the paper's ranks, leaving only for a brief stint in the Navy during World War II. As editor from 1958 until 1971, Royster set the *Journal's* political policy, aligning it closely with business interests and the resurgent conservative movement.

In 1971, upon retirement from full-time employment at the *Journal*, Royster returned to UNC as a Kenan Professor in the School of Journalism. His autobiography, *My Own, My Country's Time*, was published in 1983. His column, "Thinking Things Over," remained a staple of the *Journal* until his last year, 1996.

Among his many achievements, Royster received two Pulitzer Prizes, journalism's highest honor, in 1953 and 1984. He was awarded the Presidential Medal of Freedom by Pres. Ronald Reagan in 1986.

Carl Sandburg with his guitar singing folksongs after an evening of poetry.

Carl Sandburg's home, Flat Rock, North Carolina *(background photo)*.

1840 From Slavery to Capitol Hill, John Hyman of Warren County

On July 23, 1840, John Hyman, the first African American to represent North Carolina in the United States Congress, was born into slavery in Warren County.

Though eventually sold away from his family and sent to Alabama, Hyman made his way back home at the close of the Civil War. With an aptitude for public speaking and politicking, he became a delegate to the second state Freedman's Convention in 1866, to the first Republican state convention in 1867, and to the state Constitutional Convention in 1868. In that same year he started the first of the several terms he would serve in the state Senate.

Hyman was defeated in his first run for Congress in 1872. Two years later he was elected, but he failed to obtain his party's nomination in 1876. During his single term in Washington, Hyman supported legislation to secure and protect civil rights, especially suffrage privileges.

After leaving public life, Hyman returned to Warrenton, where he farmed and operated a grocery store. He was constantly in debt and was forced to sell all his real estate in 1878. Around 1880 Hyman left North Carolina for Washington, D.C., where he worked as an assistant mail clerk until his death in 1891 at age fifty-one.

John A. Hyman

1868 Universalists and Inman Chapel Near Canton

On July 23, 1868, western North Carolina's first Universalist congregation was organized in Haywood County after traveling preacher Benjamin F. Strain converted a handful of citizens. Universalists, also known as Hell Redemptionists, were a denomination whose beliefs were based on a benevolent God and salvation as opposed to damnation.

Strain granted a Universalist license to Jonathan Plott, who in turn designated Haywood native James Anderson Inman to serve as the congregation's permanent pastor. With assistance from the North Carolina Universalists Conference, which was organized in 1896, a chapel was built in 1902 and named for Inman, who donated much of the construction funds.

Following Inman's death in 1913, the chapel reverted to management by the Universalists' Women's National Missionary Association (WNMA). Though it had almost dispersed by 1921, when Hannah Jewett Powell became regional denominational representative, the congregation flourished under Powell's leadership. After Powell's retirement in 1942, the congregation of Universalists declined and the WNMA closed the chapel and community center in 1957. The Universalists merged with the Unitarians in 1961 to become the Unitarian Universalist Church. A congregation was established in Asheville in 1969.

The Inman Chapel has undergone restoration and is used by the Inman family for homecoming gatherings.

1985 Kay Kyser: "C'mon Chillun! L'es Dance!"

On July 23, 1985, James "Kay" Kyser, popular radio personality and bandleader, died in Chapel Hill. Born in Rocky Mount in 1905, Kyser attended the University of North Carolina where he was an exuberant head cheerleader and the class president. Also known as the "Ol' Professor of Swing," Kyser became the most wild and grandiose bandleader of the swing era.

In the 1930s Kyser toured with his band, Kay Kyser's Kollege of Musical Knowledge, through much of the Midwest. By the next decade it garnered national attention and had eleven Number One hits. Although he never learned to play an instrument, Kyser was a top-notch entertainer and went on to appear in over a dozen movies, co-starring with actors such as Lucille Ball and John Barrymore.

In 1941 Kyser performed live at camp shows for U.S. military personnel, predating other famous performers such as Bob Hope. He retired suddenly in 1950, withdrawing to Chapel Hill, where he remained until his death. In 1999 he was inducted into the North Carolina Music Hall of Fame.

Kay Kyser at the microphone, N.C. State College, on October 18, 1941.

JUL 24

1859 Antacid Inventor Had Chapel Hill Ties

On July 24, 1859, Isaac Emerson, the "Bromo-Seltzer King," was born in Orange County.

Emerson enrolled at UNC, working with a local druggist while pursuing a degree in chemistry, which he received in 1879. He married and moved to Baltimore, where he established several drugstores and began experimenting with the headache remedy that he eventually patented as Bromo-Seltzer.

To produce and market his product, Emerson created the Emerson Drug Company in 1891. His remedy became wildly successful due in large part to his marketing genius. He advertised the product across the county and the world.

In 1911 he oversaw the construction of the Emerson Bromo-Seltzer Tower, a fifteen-story skyscraper in Baltimore. The tower originally had a fifty-one-foot-tall, rotating, and glowing blue Bromo-Seltzer bottle at its top. The bottle was eventually removed, but the tower remains a well-known landmark, now housing artists' studios and a fire department.

Emerson was deeply involved in Maryland's naval reserves and personally financed a naval squadron during the Spanish-American War. He also donated the money to build UNC's first sports stadium in 1914, which remained in use until 1971.

1874 Politician and Prize-Winning Poet John Charles McNeill

On July 24, 1874, poet John Charles McNeill was born in Wagram.

He spent a blissful childhood in Scotland County before attending Wake Forest College. After studying law his junior year, McNeill graduated as valedictorian of his class in 1897 and received a master's degree in English two years later.

At twenty-six he moved to Lumberton, where he established himself as an attorney, although he preferred journalism and poetry to the drudgery of law. It was in Lumberton that he began submitting material, including poems, to a weekly newspaper.

Elected to the state Senate in 1903, McNeill continued to pen poems, a number of which were published in *Century Magazine* and the *Charlotte Observer*. He joined the staff at the *Observer* in 1904. Already an established poet, he became a roving journalist, covering interesting stories all over the state. In October 1905 McNeill won first place in the competition for the inaugural Patterson Cup, the first literary contest held in North Carolina. The achievement brought McNeill the unofficial title of "North Carolina's Poet Laureate."

McNeill died at age thirty-three. His boyhood home has been restored and is open to the public at Temperance Hall in Wagram.

1894 Truman Adviser Kenneth Royall of Goldsboro

On July 24, 1894, Kenneth Royall, the last United States Secretary of War and the first Secretary of the Army, was born in Goldsboro.

After graduating from Harvard Law School in 1917, Royall joined the Army. He served in France from August 1918 until he was wounded in February 1919. At that time Royall returned to Goldsboro and began practicing law.

In June 1942 he retired from his legal practice, by then located in both Goldsboro and Raleigh, in order to accept a commission as a colonel in the U. S. Army, managing the War Department's legal services. Royall was soon promoted to brigadier general and in 1945 he was appointed under-secretary of war and received the Distinguished Service Medal. Pres. Harry S. Truman selected him to be Secretary of War in July 1947.

Two months later, with the formation of the Defense Department, that position was eliminated, and Royall was designated Secretary of the Army. He held that position until he resigned in April 1949. Later that year Royall became a partner in a New York City law firm, where he worked until 1968.

Royall retired to Raleigh and died in 1971. He is buried in Goldsboro.

Kenneth C. Royall painting by Alfred Jonniaux, 1949.

1924 Catholic Leader Leo Haid of Belmont Abbey

On July 24, 1924, Leo Haid, abbot and founder of Belmont Abbey, died.

Born in Pennsylvania in 1849 as Michael Haid, he attended school at the nearby Benedictine abbey. He entered the Benedictine order as a novice in 1868 and assumed the religious name Leo. Formal vows as a monk and priest followed four years later. He worked as a teacher and chaplain until 1885, when the church promoted him to the abbacy of Maryhelp in North Carolina.

With its few dilapidated buildings, poor farm, and small staff, Maryhelp needed strong management. Though young and untested in leadership, Haid vastly improved and exponentially expanded Maryhelp, constructing many fine buildings, making the farm productive, increasing the number of monks to seventy and welcoming several hundred students. It became known as Belmont Abbey in 1913, and its success helped Catholicism become more accepted in North Carolina.

Dedicated to his post, Haid almost turned down his election as titular bishop of Messene and vicar-apostolic of North Carolina, only agreeing to the promotion when his superiors allowed him to continue as abbot. His accomplishments gained him a reputation as a skilled orator, writer, and church leader, especially in the area of Benedictine education.

He served as abbot and bishop until his death.

Engraving of Haid from Samuel A. Ashe's *Biographical History of North Carolina from Colonial Times to the Present*, (1905).

JUL 25

1729 North Carolina Became a Royal Colony

On July 25, 1729, North Carolina became a royal colony when the Lords Proprietors sold the colony to King George II. South Carolina had become a royal colony ten years earlier, setting the stage for North Carolina to follow suit.

The English crown, long dissatisfied with proprietary and corporate colonies, had begun the process of converting those colonies to royal control in the 1680s. North Carolina's sale was the culmination of legal proceedings initiated in 1706 by Queen Anne. Having never made a profit from the colony, most of the proprietors sold their shares back to the crown. Only Sir George Carteret, Earl of Granville, refused to sell his shares, creating the Granville District across the entire top portion of the colony.

The sale of North Carolina was the beginning of a prosperous time for the colony. During the next forty years the colony grew rapidly. The governance of the colony remained largely unchanged. The powers and duties of the governor, Council, Assembly, courts, and local officials remained the same as before. The king simply replaced the proprietors as the head of administration, improving the colony's stability and efficiency of administration drastically and allowing for strong growth.

1780 Horatio Gates's Brief Revolutionary Command

On July 25, 1780, Maj. Gen. Horatio Gates assumed direct command of the American forces in the Southern Military Department at their campsite on the Deep River in Randolph County.

Born in 1727 or 1728 in England, Gates served in the British army before settling in the colonies. In 1775 he volunteered for the Continental Army and served as a staff officer before receiving field command.

In September and October 1777 Gates commanded an army that defeated a British invasion from Canada at Saratoga, New York. The victory led to a military alliance with France and propelled Gates to the forefront of American military heroes. His ascent was accompanied by controversy, due to his ambitions and his reputation as an overly cautious commander.

Influenced by faulty intelligence indicating an opportunity for a quick victory, Gates embarked on a campaign in South Carolina along a route lacking in food to support his army. On August 16 his exhausted and underfed army was routed by the British at Camden, South Carolina.

Nathaniel Greene was soon selected to replace Gates, who never received another field command. He retired from the army in 1784 and died in New York City in 1806.

Horatio Gates, major general of the American forces, 1780.

1960 Sit-in Victory in Greensboro, 1960

On July 25, 1960, Greensboro lunch counters opened to sitting customers of all races for the first time. The event was the culmination of a brief and intense desegregation campaign by black activists that sparked similar actions throughout the country.

In February of that year, four students from North Carolina Agricultural and Technical State College began a sit-in at the lunch counter of the downtown Woolworth's, demanding equal service with white customers. The original demonstrators, Ezell Blair Jr., Joseph McNeil, Franklin McCain, and David Richmond, were joined on succeeding days by more and more protestors, and the campaign they began spread to other stores.

After six days stores closed, and the protesters declared a moratorium to negotiate with civic leaders. Similar protests spread throughout the South, while supporting demonstrations were launched in the North.

Negotiations failed, and the demonstrations resumed in April. Stores that refused to seat black customers at their lunch counters were picketed. By the end of June, store managers gave up, as the boycott was hurting their businesses.

New negotiations brought agreement that blacks could eat at Greensboro lunch counters. The successful outcome of the campaign marked an important state and national milestone in the on-going civil rights struggle.

1981 Guy Owen and the Flim-Flam Man

On July 25, 1981, N.C. State University professor and writer Guy Owen died at age fifty-six.

Born in Clarkton in Bladen County, Owen grew up on a tobacco farm. Years of clerking at his father's general store provided the author with much eventual grist for his creative mill.

Owen enrolled at UNC in 1942, and after taking a three-year break from his studies for service in World War II, he earned bachelors and doctoral degrees in English. Brief teaching stints followed at Davidson and Elon Colleges, then Stetson University in Florida, before he joined the faculty at N.C. State in 1962.

He found his greatest acclaim as the author of *The Ballad of the Flim-Flam Man*, the tale of an aging confidence man. A bestseller, the book was adapted into a film in 1967 starring George C. Scott. Mordecai Jones, the protagonist, appeared in two other books by Owen.

Today Owen is also remembered for his courses at N.C. State. He edited several anthologies of state and regional fiction, lectured and conducted workshops across the state, and helped shape the state's eventual literary renaissance.

A recipient of the North Carolina Award in 1971, Owen was one of the inductees into the North Carolina Literary Hall of Fame in 1996, its inaugural year.

JUL 26

1864 Robert C. Anderson, Presbyterian Leader at Montreat

On July 26, 1864, Dr. Robert C. Anderson was born near Martinsville, Virginia.

After attending Hampden-Sydney College and Union Theological Seminary, both in Virginia, Anderson was ordained a Presbyterian minister in 1890. From that year until 1911, he pastored four different churches, including one in North Carolina.

In 1911 Anderson became president of the Mountain Retreat Association (MRA) of Montreat. John Collins, a Congregationalist minister from Connecticut, had started the association nearly fifteen years earlier with the goal of building a Christian retreat where people could gather for physical and spiritual renewal.

It was Anderson who truly brought Collins's vision to fruition and created much of what's now the Montreat Conference Center. During his nearly forty-year tenure at the helm of the group, MRA founded a small school for girls, saw it grow into a four-year college, and completed construction on much of the current campus, including Anderson Auditorium.

Anderson also turned around the association's financial fortunes, initiating a successful capital campaign and promoting the facility in a more focused way to both attract more visitors and give the center a larger role in the Presbyterian Church's mission work.

In addition to welcoming visitors for more than a century, the center played an appropriate role as a testing ground for new doctrinal ideas and fostered racial justice.

Anderson died in 1955 and was buried in Charlotte.

1926 Home for Durham Bulls Dedicated, 1926

On July 26, 1926, the Durham Bulls' El Toro Park was dedicated. Judge Kenesaw Mountain Landis, the first Commissioner of Baseball, stole the show that day by riding onto the field on the team mascot, a real bull. Gov. Angus McLean was also on hand for the festivities. The park was the home field for the Bulls, a local Class-D farm team for the Cincinnati Reds.

In 1933 the City of Durham purchased the park with the help of a donation from local banker and attorney John Sprunt Hill and renamed the facility Durham Athletic Park. The stadium burned in June 1939, but a new concrete and steel grandstand that seated one thousand spectators was constructed within weeks.

During the off season the rest of the stadium was rebuilt, again funded by Hill. The reconstructed Durham Athletic Park opened in April 1940. It was that stadium that was featured in the 1988 blockbuster film, Bull Durham.

In 1995 the baseball team moved down the road to Durham Bulls Athletic Park, leaving their old stadium for municipal uses such as festivals and other sporting events.

1962 Hang Glider Adapted for Water Use, 1962

On July 26, 1962, Thomas Purcell Jr. demonstrated the FlightSail glider at Lake Waccamaw.

The Columbus County flight was the first water-based use of the glider, which had been adapted by Purcell from technology created by aviation pioneer Francis Rogallo. The aircraft was a single-seat open-cockpit, parasol-winged glider, with skids to facilitate water takeoffs and landings.

Purcell, who studied at North Carolina State, got a job after graduating at Bensen Aircraft Corporation, a gyrocopter manufacturer near the Raleigh-Durham Airport. He later opened his own company, Flight Dynamics, which designed and sold plans for a variety of aircraft.

Purcell thought up his designs after reading magazine articles about the glider technology invented by Rogallo, often called the "father of hand gliding."

NASA, which had previously been interested in Rogallo's work, began to take an interest in Purcell's as well. He visited NASA in 1961 to demonstrate the FlightSail glider, which the nation's space agency thought could be used as a substitute for traditional parachutes for the Gemini program.

Though NASA ultimately decided to use regular parachutes for Gemini, the Flightsail system and others like it are still remembered as massive improvements in glider technology, and Purcell marketed his technology for recreation throughout the 1970s.

A model of the FlightSail that Purcell flew at Lake Waccamaw is among the holdings of the North Carolina Museum of History.

Durham Bulls' El Toro Park

1812 The "Prince of Politicians," Thomas L. Clingman

On July 27, 1812, Thomas Clingman was born at Huntsville, in what is now Yadkin County. Clingman is known for both his service as a U.S. Senator and Confederate general and for boosting the development of western North Carolina. The highest peak in the Great Smoky Mountain range is named Clingman's Dome in his honor.

Clingman served in the state House of Representatives, state Senate, and U.S. House of Representatives before being appointed to fill a vacated U. S. Senate seat in 1858. He was the last Southerner to leave the Senate in 1861.

During the Civil War Clingman rose quickly to the position of brigadier general. Despite his unremarkable military career, he was prevented from returning to political office due to the provisions of his amnesty.

Clingman worked to promote the popularity of western North Carolina, publicizing the region through writing and lectures. For more than ten years, He and Elisha Mitchell engaged in a fierce debate about which peak was the tallest in North Carolina. In 1858 geographer Arnold Guyot, having determined that what would become Mount Mitchell was thirty-nine feet taller, named Clingman's Dome for its proponent.

2009 Homegrown Jihadists Arrested in Raleigh, 2009

On July 27, 2009, seven men were arrested in Raleigh and accused of plotting to wage "violent jihad" outside the United States.

The alleged ringleader was Daniel Patrick Boyd, who recruited men, including two of his sons, to commit terrorist activities abroad. In the 1980s and 1990s Boyd had traveled to Pakistan and Afghanistan, where he "received military-style training in terrorist training camps for the purpose of engaging in violent jihad."

The men arrested were attempting to make their way to the Middle East to join a terrorist organization. They failed and, in doing so, were arrested by the federal government. The men were all American citizens who had been radicalized at some point in their lives. Several of the members had been talking about waging some form of jihad for years, and many people who knew them were not surprised by the arrests.

In 2011 Boyd plead guilty to one count of conspiracy to provide material support to terrorists and one count of conspiracy to commit murder, maiming, and kidnapping overseas. He later testified in court against some of his co-conspirators.

Thomas L. Clingman, politician and Confederate general, circa 1860.

1863 Confederates Repulse Union Army at Boon's Mill, 1863

On July 28, 1863, a skirmish was fought at Boon's Mill near Jackson. It marked the end of a Federal raid against Weldon, a major railroad hub linking the Deep South to Richmond.

The operation began three days earlier, when infantry under Maj. Gen. John G. Foster landed near Winton on the Chowan River. The next day they advanced toward Murfreesboro and defeated a Confederate force at Potecasi Creek.

The Union advance was slowed when a cavalry column under Col. Samuel P. Spear assigned to strike Weldon was delayed after losing a pontoon bridge in a storm. That, in turn, gave the Confederate military time to dispatch Brig. Gen. Matt Ransom's brigade from Petersburg as reinforcements.

Ransom established a position at Boon's Mill with the few companies that had arrived at that point. In the meantime Spear reached Winton and headed for Weldon. Ransom and his staff were almost captured as they encountered the Federals but raced back to their line. Spear made little effort to take the position, and the confrontation settled into an artillery duel that was ended by a storm.

Casualties were light on both sides. Spear retreated, and the railroad line was safe again for the moment.

JUL 28

1918 Tobacco Magnate R.J. Reynolds

On July 28, 1918, Richard Joshua Reynolds, founder of one of North Carolina's most prosperous corporations, died after a battle with pancreatic cancer. Born in 1850, Reynolds grew up in a large and affluent Virginia family. His upbringing gave him many opportunities for education and for learning the family's tobacco business.

In 1874 Reynolds decided to venture into business for himself, purchasing a town lot in Winston. There he built a factory with railway connections. In his first year of operation, he manufactured about 150 thousand pounds of Southern flat plug chewing tobacco. By the 1890s his annual production was in the millions of pounds.

In the late 1880s Reynolds revolutionized the chewing tobacco industry with the addition of saccharine to his flue-cured chew. He introduced his Prince Albert smoking tobacco in 1907, and in 1911 he followed up with his Camel cigarette, the first genuinely American cigarette and the first to be mass produced. The R. J. Reynolds brands and products became driving forces in the tobacco industry.

Reynolds amassed great wealth and found philanthropic ways to share it. His descendants have followed his philanthropic example, with charitable foundations in North Carolina and beyond.

1951 Political Utility Player, Ambassador Capus Waynick

On July 28, 1951, Capus Waynick of High Point was appointed United States ambassador to Colombia.

Before entering the political arena, Waynick worked as a newspaper reporter and later served as editor, publisher, and part owner of the *Greensboro Record* and as editor of the *High Point Enterprise*.

His first political service came with terms in the N. C. House of Representatives and Senate during the early 1930s. For the rest of that decade, he held a few short-term public service jobs, including serving as chairman of the State Highway Commission.

Active in the Democratic Party in North Carolina, Waynick was tapped to serve as the ambassador first to Nicaragua and later Colombia. He was also called upon by Pres. Harry Truman to launch the Point Four Program, which was aimed at aiding and revitalizing underdeveloped nations.

After a brief retirement to High Point at age seventy-three, Waynick was enlisted by Gov. Terry Sanford to become his special aide for racial affairs. The elder statesman traveled across North Carolina calling for the end of "second class citizenship" for African Americans.

Frequently honored for his public service, Waynick was the recipient of honorary degrees and distinguished awards. Despite having been a college dropout, he was widely applauded for his extraordinary intellect and his ability to master any task required of him.

Waynick married Elizabeth Hunt McBee in 1915. They lived on the twenty-four-acre Fieldstone Farm near High Point, where Waynick maintained his own golf course. He died on Sept. 7, 1986, and is buried in High Point's Oakwood Cemetery.

1995 Screenwriter's Tapes Sought by Simpson Attorneys

On July 28, 1995, Forsyth County Superior Court Judge William Z. Wood Jr. ruled against O. J. Simpson's attorneys, holding that aspiring screenwriter Laura Hart McKinney did not have to turn over her taped interviews with Los Angeles police officer Mark Fuhrman and others.

Professor McKinney of the North Carolina School of the Arts, who was working on a screenplay and novel about women police officers, conducted the interviews about the work of LAPD officers between 1985 and 1994. She had amassed about thirteen hours of tapes in which Fuhrman repeatedly used racial slurs and made remarks about police brutality, planting of evidence, and harassment of female officers.

Fuhrman later became a central figure in the O. J. Simpson trial after he found a bloody glove at the murder site on Simpson's estate. Simpson's defense team argued that the glove was planted and sought to use the tapes to bolster their argument, as well as to prove that Furman perjured himself by denying his use of racial slurs.

The following month Simpson's North Carolina lawyers, Kenneth B. Spaulding and Joseph B. Cheshire V, successfully appealed the decision to the North Carolina Court of Appeals on the grounds that it interfered with the defendant's right to a fair trial.

Capus Waynick reviews construction progress on the Blue Ridge Parkway in Wilkes County in August 1936.

1781 Attack at House in the Horseshoe

On July 29, 1781, Phillip Alston and a small band of patriot militia were besieged at the Alston home by forces loyal to the king under the command of David Fanning. The attack occurred in the early morning hours. Trapped in his house, Alston ordered his men to barricade the doors and windows. Fanning posted his men along a split-rail fence outside the home, and for several hours the men exchanged fire, with no side gaining a real advantage.

As her house was being riddled by bullets, Temperance Alston, Phillip's wife, was level-headed enough to hide her children in the chimney, standing them on a table so that their bodies were behind the brickwork. Just as Fanning was considering retreating, his men found a small wagon in Alston's barn. He ordered it loaded with hay and set it afire with the purpose of pushing it into the house. In an effort to save the lives of everyone inside, Temperance Alston cautiously stepped out and negotiated a surrender.

The Alston house, near the Moore County town of Carthage, is now known as the House in the Horseshoe and is a North Carolina State Historic Site.

Re-enactment at Alston House

1924 Launch of Rayon Production, Burlington Mills

On July 29, 1924, Burlington Mills, owned by entrepreneur J. Spencer Love, began operations.

Initially Love struggled with sales, but his luck began to change as soon as he began experimenting with the newly-created synthetic yarn called rayon. Burlington Mills produced an incredibly popular rayon blend bedspread, the success of which allowed Love to diversify into other rayon products, including draperies and cloth for garments. During this time Love built new facilities and purchased old cotton mills for conversion to rayon production.

In the late 1930s Love, on the advice of an associate, began to advertise his goods. Burlington Mills was marketed as the manufacturer of the best quality rayon fabric available—fabric that would not shrink or fade. By 1955 the business had been renamed Burlington Industries and had expanded to weaving the new synthetic fabrics nylon, acrylic, and polyester. Toward the end of the twentieth century, the company operated 130 manufacturing plants with 65 thousand employees in sixteen states and seven foreign countries and had earned the title of largest textile corporation in the world.

Still, it wasn't immune to the economic challenges affecting the textile industry at-large in the Tar Heel state. Burlington Mills declared bankruptcy in 2001 and was absorbed into the massive International Textile Group in 2004.

JUL 30

1863 Wild's African Brigade

On July 30, 1863, Gen. Edward Wild departed New Bern with his "African Brigade" for the coast of South Carolina.

Wild's First North Carolina Colored Volunteers (NCCV), along with some soldiers from the Fifty-Fifth Massachusetts Volunteers, were among the ten thousand reinforcements requested by Gen. Quincy A. Gillmore, who was in command of Union forces attempting to attack Charleston. Ordered to depart in light marching order, the men of the regiment left their baggage and personal belongings behind in New Bern.

The First NCCV, raised by Wild in North Carolina, saw service mainly beyond the state's borders. The regiment became the Thirty-Fifth United States Colored Troops (USCT), fighting all of its battles and skirmishes in South Carolina and Florida, including the action at Battery Wagner, later made famous in the movie *Glory*, before seeing Reconstruction-era service at Charleston.

Though difficult to track, evidence suggests that few members of the "African Brigade" returned to North Carolina after the war, and many likely remained in locations where they had served during the war.

1952 Crackdown on Klan, 1952, Nets Grand Dragon

On July 30, 1952, Thomas L. Hamilton, Grand Dragon of the Association of Carolina Klans (ACK), was sentenced to four years in prison for kidnapping and assaulting Evergreen Flowers, an African American woman from Chadbourn.

Hamilton's arrest in May 1952 was in many ways the culmination of a larger crackdown on the Ku Klux Klan in Columbus County and Horry County, South Carolina by federal, state, and local state authorities that had been underway since the beginning of the year. Hamilton and the mob he led apparently targeted Flowers because a Klansman claimed that he saw her husband Will have sex with Bessie Page, a white woman who was Flowers's neighbor in Chadbourn.

After first pleading not guilty in the case, Hamilton changed his plea to guilty on the first day of his trial on July 22. From prison, where he would ultimately serve only seventeen months of his four-year sentence before being paroled, Hamilton wrote, in a letter repudiating the organization in which he played such a central role, "All my friends everywhere should disband the Ku Klux Klan . . . . I am through with [it] and believe all my former associates will best serve themselves and society as a whole by taking a similar stand."

After leaving prison in 1954, Hamilton and his wife returned to their native South Carolina, where they lived with their daughter. Hamilton, later ordained a Baptist minister, died in 1976.

The *Tabor City Tribune* and *Whiteville News Reporter*, two weekly newspapers in Columbus County, were awarded the 1953 Pulitzer Prize for Meritorious Public Service for their coverage of the case and their role in helping to bring down the Klan's strong presence in the area.

1965 Asheville Fascist and Presidential Candidate William Dudley Pelley

On July 30, 1965, American fascist and anti-Semite William Dudley Pelley died. A writer, novelist, and screenwriter from Massachusetts, he turned to politics and religion after two harrowing events, his own near-death experience and the country's Great Depression.

Pelley spent the 1930s in Asheville, where he developed his "Liberation Theology," a combination of elements of Christianity, fascism, nationalism, theocracy, and socialism. In Asheville he established Galahad Press, through which he published his radical magazine *New Liberator*. In 1932 he founded Galahad College, where he further promoted his political and economic theories. The following year he organized the Silver Legion of America, better known as the "Silver Shirts," a group modeled on Hitler's Brown Shirts. He ran for president in 1936 as a candidate of the Christian Party.

Convicted of fraud in North Carolina, Pelley moved to Indiana in 1940. Arrested in 1942 and charged with sedition and treason, he spent the rest of the 1940s in federal prison.

After his release in 1952, Pelley lived the rest of his life in Noblesville, Indiana, developing and publishing works about another religious philosophy he called "Soulcraft." It was based on UFOs and later on Pelley's reported contact with the souls of famous historical figures.

Veterans of the 35th United States Colored Troops, formerly the 1st North Carolina Colored Volunteers, gathered for a reunion in Plymouth, circa 1905.

1924 Son and Namesake of Confederate General Key to NCSU Growth

On July 31, 1924, noted academic Daniel Harvey Hill Jr. died.

Born in Davidson in January 1859, Hill earned bachelor's and master's degrees from Davidson College and taught at Georgia Military College before joining the first faculty at what's now N.C. State University in 1889 as an English professor. He stayed on at the Raleigh university for twenty-nine years and was instrumental in helping the budding college grow.

In addition to his duties on the English faculty, Hill worked as the college's bursar, bookkeeper, and secretary of the faculty. He helped begin the library at N.C. State and served as the school's first librarian on a part-time basis for ten years. He was elected N.C. State's vice president in 1905, then served as its president from 1908 to 1916.

An active writer and historian, Hill penned the North Carolina volume for the 1899 series *Confederate Military History*. He went on to write history books for young people, a textbook on agriculture, and a two-volume history of North Carolina during the Civil War.

The D. H. Hill Library, the main library on the N.C. State campus, is named in his honor.

1949 J. C. B. Ehringhaus, Governor, 1933–1937

On July 31, 1949, Depression-era governor John Christoph Blucher Ehringhaus died.

Born in Elizabeth City in 1882, Ehringhaus represented Pasquotank County in the General Assembly and served as the modern-day equivalent of a district attorney before becoming governor.

Ehringhaus is probably best remembered for balancing the state's budget during the turbulent times of the Great Depression. He improved management of the state's public schools, ensured that no teachers lost their jobs or pay, and made certain that the schools kept functioning eight months a year with busing and textbook rentals.

Ehringhaus cut the state budget and returned the government to fiscal stability, while increasing its power with the introduction of a state sales tax to fund the public school system. He reorganized the prisons to make them self-sufficient and left the state with a five million dollar surplus.

An advocate for farmers, Ehringhaus closed the state's tobacco markerts in 1933 and traveled to Washington, D.C. to demand the federal government set higher prices for the crop. He publicly supported Franklin D. Roosevelt's New Deal programs but did little to help implement them.

Ehringhaus's popularity declined in the mid-1930s, and he returned to his law practice in Raleigh after his term.

1970 A Possum Is Pardoned By Gov. Scott

On July 31, 1970, Slow Poke the Possum was granted executive clemency by Gov. Bob Scott in a ceremony at the State Capitol.

Slow Poke was an ordinary opossum who won a "prettiest possum" competition at the Spivey's Corner Hollerin' Contest in 1970. The winning possum was to be given to the governor, so on July 16, 1970, Slow Poke, his owner, hollerin' champ H. H. Oliver, and beauty contest winner Margaret Ann Wilkes visited Scott. When Wilkes confided to the governor that she had never eaten possum, Scott immediately invited her to a possum banquet in the Executive Mansion, with Slow Poke as the main course.

Hundreds of calls and letters from an indignant public protested the governor's proposed possum feast, leading to Scott's granting the possum clemency. Slow Poke was turned over to the North Carolina Wildlife Commission and later released at the Raven Rock State Park.

Governor Scott was unrepentant. "I shall not be thwarted in my appetite for possum," he proclaimed. The governor was true to his word. A few years later Scott served possum at a black-tie affair at the Executive Mansion.

JUL 31

Slow Poke is granted clemency at the State Capitol. *Left to right:* Gov. Bob Scott, Tom Ellis, "Miss Possum" Margaret Ann Wilkes and Larry Barnes of the state Wildlife Commission.

AUG
1

1776 Leading Patriot Touts Declaration in Halifax, 1776

On August 1, 1776, Cornelius Harnett read what would become known as the Declaration of Independence to a crowd in Halifax. It was the first public reading of the document in North Carolina.

Harnett was president of the North Carolina Council of Safety and had served as chairman of the committee that in April of 1776 produced the Halifax Resolves, a formal declaration of North Carolina's support for independence from Britain.

After the Declaration had been adopted by the Continental Congress on July 4, the manuscript was taken to the shop of John Dunlap, official printer of the budding American government. According to the National Archives, it's unclear how many copies Dunlap made that night, but twenty-six are still around for us to see. Those first copies of the document, often called "Dunlap broadsides" were dispatched the following day to members of Congress, committees of safety, commanders of the Continental Army, and others. It was a Dunlap broadside that Harnett shared with the residents of Halifax.

Since it was a point of state pride that North Carolina was the first colony to commit intentions of independence to paper with the Halifax Resolves, many deemed it appropriate that the Declaration should be read there first.

1828 Crucial Rally to Support Railroads, 1828

On August 1, 1828, more than two hundred people gathered at the home of William Albright in what is now Alamance County to respond to UNC president Joseph Caldwell's pleas for a state-supported railroad. The meeting led to increased public interest in internal improvements, which in turn created more interest in the Industrial Revolution and in the progress of the state as a whole.

Caldwell, a mathematician, advocated for the railroad in a series of publications known as the "Carlton Letters," detailing his ideas about the advantages, costs, and routes that the state should pursue. He hoped to see a central railroad from New Bern to Asheville created, providing access to the west and a boost to industry. The letters had wide circulation, especially for the time, and were influential in developing public interest.

In 1840 the Wilmington and Weldon Railroad was established, inaugurating a 161-mile route between Wilmington and Weldon, in Halifax County, via Goldsboro and Rocky Mount. At the time the railroad was the longest in the world and exemplified the success of railroad development in North Carolina. The capstone to rail development was the North Carolina Railroad, the groundbreaking for which took place in Greensboro in 1851.

These improvements in transportation helped North Carolina shed its reputation as the Rip Van Winkle State.

1880 Cherry Hospital Expanded Mental Health Care

On August 1, 1880, the first patient enrolled at what is now Cherry Hospital in Goldsboro. The hospital was set up to serve North Carolina's black population.

Mental health care in North Carolina can be traced to Dorothea Dix's appeals to the legislature in 1848 and the opening in 1856 of the hospital in Raleigh that bears her name. In 1883 the state opened what is now Broughton Hospital in Morganton to serve the western region. A commission study in 1937 sharply criticized care at the mental hospitals in the state, and most of the older buildings were replaced in the 1930s and 1940s.

The site in Goldsboro was selected in part because it was near the center of the state's black population. Originally known as the "Asylum for the Colored Insane," the institution's name was changed in 1959 to Cherry Hospital to honor former governor R. Gregg Cherry. The hospital remained segregated until 1965, when in order to comply with the Civil Rights Act of 1964, the state's mental institutions were integrated.

Today Cherry Hospital maintains an association with the School of Medicine at East Carolina University and serves patients from thirty-eight eastern counties.

1952 Lowe's and Homegrown Home Improvement

On August 1, 1952, Lowe's Home Improvement was incorporated.

The chain can trace its roots to 1921 when I. S. Lowe founded a hardware store in North Wilkesboro. His son, Jim Lowe, and son-in-law, Carl Buchanan, took over the store after his death, but the two disagreed on whether to expand the business, and Buchanan ultimately bought out Lowe.

Buchanan recognized the post-World War II building boom that was coming to the country and narrowed Lowe's focus to selling only hardware, appliances, and building materials (at the time hardware stores tended to sell a lot of general merchandise). He quickly tied the company's reputation to low prices by buying products directly from manufacturers and operating on very slim profit margins to keep prices down.

Buchanan's model took off, and by 1960 Lowe's had fifteen stores and thirty million dollars in annual sales. The company continued to grow quickly in the 1960s and 1970s by focusing on selling primarily to contractors. After a new chairman took over in 1978, the hardware chain began marketing directly to the general public.

Still based in North Carolina, Lowe's is one of the nation's fifty largest companies, according to *Fortune*. It operates nearly two thousand stores across the United States and Canada and had revenues of more than fifty-two billion dollars in 2014.

The original Lowe's store on C Street, North Wilkesboro.

1781 Britons Under Craig Rout Militia, 1781

On August 2, 1781, British forces clashed with the North Carolina Militia near Wilmington in a skirmish now known as the Battle of Rockfish.

In the months following his January 1781 capture of Wilmington, British Maj. James Craig issued a proclamation threatening the loss of life and property to all who would not swear loyalty to King George III. When the period for taking the oath expired largely unheeded, Craig began to devastate the territory around Wilmington.

On August 2 his troops found their path through Duplin County blocked by a Militia force under the command of former state governor Richard Caswell and Thomas Kenan. The militiamen were posted behind breastworks bordering the bank of Rockfish Creek.

A skirmish ensued, ending when the militiamen ran out of ammunition and were forced to withdraw under a barrage from the British artillery. Casualties were slight, with perhaps sixty militiamen killed and another thirty captured.

Craig continued his marauding and recruited three hundred Tories. His local success was negated by the surrender of the main British force in the South under Lord Cornwallis at Yorktown, Virginia on October 19.

Craig evacuated Wilmington on November 19.

1953 James Larkin Pearson Appointed Poet Laureate

On August 2, 1953, Gov. William B. Umstead appointed James Larkin Pearson of Wilkes County the state's second Poet Laureate, succeeding Arthur Talmage Abernethy. Pearson was born in 1879 in a log cabin on Berry Mountain near the community of Boomer. Education was not a priority for his family, and he worked in the fields, composing in his head.

Journalism would be Pearson's bread and butter for much of his life. He worked first for *The Yellow Jacket* in Moravian Falls and later for the *Charlotte Observer*. In time he returned to Wilkes County, where he began publishing a monthly paper, *The Fool-Killer*. His aim was for the paper "to make a fellow laugh right big and to cram a truth down his throat while his mouth was open." *The Fool-Killer* had a readership of fifty thousand at its peak.

The *News and Observer* of Raleigh wrote of Pearson in 1934: "More than any other living North Carolinian he has put the life of the people into poetry, made it tangible and beautiful and easily seen." Pearson died a few days shy of his 102nd birthday and held the Poet Laureateship to his death. His library and press were acquired by Wilkes Community College.

1958 Legendary Percy Flowers, "King of the Moonshiners"

On August 2, 1958, the *Saturday Evening Post* profiled Percy Flowers of Johnston County, labeling him the "King of the Moonshiners." Throughout his career Flowers managed to stay just out of reach of the law and developed a reputation as a local Robin Hood.

Born in 1903, Flowers grew corn and tobacco on his nearly five thousand acres, like many others in the region. Unlike most others, he began to use some of his corn for making illegal liquor, concealing the stills and spirits in his tobacco barns.

Flowers's first brush with the law came in 1935, when he and his brothers assaulted a federal treasury agent. His brothers served time for the incident, but Flowers was sprung after only three days when a judge stayed his sentence. His attorney argued that twenty-two sharecropper families were dependent on Flowers for their livelihood.

A bigger bust came in 1957, when agents searched and padlocked his store, seizing his safe and its contents, which reputedly included large amounts of cash. The jury deadlocked over the charges, but the judge found Flowers guilty of contempt for publicly berating another agent in the courthouse lobby. Six months in the federal penitentiary followed, the longest sentence he faced.

Flowers farmed well into the 1970s and died in 1982.

Moonshine bust, Johnson County, 1951.

AUG 3

1790 Federal Judge John Stokes Appointed by George Washington

On August 3, 1790, John Stokes was named the first federal judge for the district of North Carolina.

Born in March 1756 in south central Virginia, Stokes entered military service at the outbreak of the Revolutionary War and became a captain in February 1778. He served throughout the northern campaigns of Washington's army, fighting at Brandywine, Germantown, and Monmouth. He was severely wounded in action at Charleston.

After the war Stokes moved to Halifax to live near his brother Montfort Stokes. He operated law offices in Rowan and Montgomery Counties and tutored several law students, including Andrew Jackson. After marrying in 1788, Stokes moved close to what is now Cooleemee in Davie County and became one of the original trustees of the University of North Carolina in 1789.

Stokes also entered politics, getting elected to the General Assembly in 1789. Later that year Stokes took part in the constitutional convention in Fayetteville. A staunch Federalist, Stokes was appointed to the North Carolina federal judgeship by George Washington after William R. Davie turned down the post.

Stokes's career as a judge lasted only one term. He died in October 1790 while riding home from his first court appearance in New Bern. Stokes County, created in 1789, is named in his honor.

1940 Bearded Lady, Featured in Freaks, at Circuses

On August 3, 1940, an article about North Carolina native Lady Olga, considered the world's greatest bearded lady, was published in *The New Yorker*. The profile, written by literary journalist Joseph Mitchell, himself a native North Carolinian, recounted with a sweet solemnity Lady Olga's life from her birth as Jane Barnell in 1871 in Wilmington.

Barnell had a tragic childhood. She was sold by her mother to a passing circus at a young age before ending up in an orphanage. Retrieved by her father and sent to live with her grandmother in Mecklenburg County, she met a man there who convinced her to grow her beard once again and join the circus.

So at age twenty-one, and this time by her choice, she became Lady Olga. Though she was popular in the circus, it wasn't until she played a bearded lady in Tod Browning's infamous 1932 film *Freaks* that she gained wider recognition.

The New Yorker article articulates the often conflicting feelings that Barnell had about her long career in circuses, carnivals, and fairs, as well as her opinion of sideshows. Mitchell recounted her life simply, and his powerful prose leads the reader to know, as Lady Olga knows, that the real freaks are not those standing behind the curtain, but those watching from in front of the curtain.

Lady Olga's last circus performance was with the Ringling Brothers in New York City in 1938, though she continued making public appearances until her death in 1951.

Lady Olga (a.k.a the "Bearded Lady")

1857 James Dobbin of Fayetteville, Secretary of the Navy

On August 4, 1857, Secretary of the Navy James Dobbin died.

Born in 1814 in Fayetteville, Dobbin entered the University of North Carolina at age fourteen and graduated with honors in 1832. He returned to Fayetteville where he studied law, launched his law practice, and became active in local politics. Unwittingly nominated for Congress and ultimately elected to the body in 1844, Dobbin refused to run again in 1846. He later served in the General Assembly, rising to become Speaker of the House in 1850.

Influential in the presidential nomination and election of Franklin Pierce, Dobbin was awarded with an appointment as Secretary of the Navy. He worked to reform and expand the Navy, making it a more efficient and effective military branch. A firm believer in a strong Navy as insurance for peace, Dobbin put eighteen ships, including six steam-powered frigates, into service during his tenure. He supported exploratory voyages, including Commodore Matthew Perry's expedition to Japan, which resulted in an 1854 trade treaty with that country.

The four years that Dobbin spent as Secretary of the Navy took a heavy toll on his fragile health. He died just five months after leaving office and is buried in Fayetteville.

The USS *Dobbin*, named in his honor, was damaged at Pearl Harbor during the 1941 attack.

1937 Anson County Home to Soil Conservation Landmark

On August 4, 1937, North Carolina Secretary of State Thad Eure issued a certificate setting up the Brown Creek Soil Conservation District, the first of its kind in the nation. That summer, farmers in Anson County voted overwhelmingly to formally establish a district of more than 120 thousand acres, much of it badly eroded. The Brown Creek District, part of the drainage basin of the Pee Dee River, included the birthplace of Hugh H. Bennett, widely credited, most recently in a Ken Burns documentary, as the "father of soil conservation."

In every sense of the term, this was a grassroots effort. During the depths of the Depression, rural areas across the nation suffered profoundly from the effects of soil depletion. Sheet erosion was the primary problem, and preservation of the topsoil was the key to solution. Soil conservation brought the land back through techniques like terracing, planting of cover crops such as kudzu, strip cropping, contour plowing, and crop rotation, among others. Conservation districts were created throughout the United States, and Bennett and his team of specialists worked with the farmers in the districts for an effective program.

Over the course of a fifty-year career, Bennett advised on projects in Alaska, Brazil, Cuba, and South Africa, among other places.

1942 Camp Butner and Axis Prisoners of War

On August 4, 1942, Camp Butner, a forty-thousand-acre military training facility, officially opened. The camp spanned parts of Durham, Granville, and Person Counties and was large enough to accommodate more than thirty thousand troops.

As the war progressed, Camp Butner's mission evolved to include the housing of prisoners of war. It served as one of two principal prison camps in North Carolina, the other being Fort Bragg. Italian prisoners were the first to arrive at Butner, their numbers swelling in time to roughly three thousand. They remained there until Benito Mussolini's regime dissolved in September 1943, and German prisoners soon took their place.

Camp Butner's prisoners attempted a number of escapes, but only one can be considered successful. On August 4, 1945, Lt. Kurt Rossmeisl, a German linguist, donned plain clothes and dark glasses before calmly walking out the camp's front entrance. Considered by some to the "most dangerous" of the nation's escaped prisoners at the time, Rossmeisl remained at large in the U.S. until he surrendered in Cincinnati in May 1959. That year, the Toledo *Blade* ran a six-part series by Rossmeisl in which he described his escape, his new life in Chicago, and his eventual surrender.

AUG 4

Opening day at Camp Butner, 1942.

AUG 5

1889 Fast Start for Predecessor of Western Carolina University

On August 5, 1889, Cullowhee Academy, a private school that was the predecessor of Western Carolina University, opened with an enrollment of eighteen. The school quickly prospered and closed the year with one hundred students.

The school's second principal, Robert Lee Madison, was a strong proponent of teacher education and proposed that the General Assembly give money to an existing high school in each congressional district so that a normal school could be opened to train prospective teachers. The legislators chose to fund only Cullowhee, giving fifteen hundred dollars to Madison to get the program started. Although not fully-funded at the time, Madison's idea, called the "Cullowhee Experiment," became the model for the state's regional colleges.

Improvements to the campus were funded by the legislature in 1901, and the school's name was changed to Cullowhee Normal and Industrial School in 1905. It began operating as a junior college in 1913 and continued growth facilitated the transition to a four-year college in 1925.

Rechartered in 1929, the school became Western Carolina Teachers College, a four-year, degree-granting institution. In 1953 the name changed again to Western Carolina College, to better reflect the institution's liberal arts programs and graduate courses. The college gained university status in 1967, adopting its ultimate name, Western Carolina University.

1940 Wolfpack Quarterback, Roman Gabriel

On August 5, 1940, Roman Gabriel, Jr. was born in Wilmington. Gabriel gained fame as the quarterback for N.C. State from 1959 to 1961, where he was a two-time All-American, and a two-time ACC Player of the Year.

Gabriel gained fame as the quarterback for N.C. State from 1959 to 1961, where he was a two time All-American and a two time ACC Player of the Year. His skill as a quarterback led him to set numerous passing records at N.C. State. As a result, his jersey was officially retired in 1962. In 1989 he was inducted into the College Football Hall of Fame.

After his stellar college career, Gabriel was the No. 2 draft pick for the Los Angeles Rams in 1962. He played sixteen seasons in the NFL with the Rams and Philadelphia Eagles, earning the NFL Most Valuable Player Award in 1969 and spots in the Pro Bowl four times. Gabriel retired from football in 1978 and eventually returned to his native North Carolina. For seven seasons he was a game analyst with the Carolina Panthers Radio Network.

While playing in Los Angeles, Gabriel took advantage of his dark good looks and his proximity to the entertainment industry to have a brief career in the movies and television. His best-known role was as the adopted Indian son of John Wayne in *The Undefeated*.

His dark complexion led some to believe he was actually American Indian but his lineage was Filipino American on his father's side and Irish American on his mother's.

Cullowhee Normal and Industrial School around 1924. The buildings shown are (from left to right) the Cullowhee Baptist Church, Madison Building, the Steam Plant, Davies Hall, the Music and Arts Building, Joyner Building and Moore Dormitory, and the Cullowhee Methodist Church.

1918 World War I U-Boat Casualty Off Cape Hatteras

On August 6, 1918, while anchored off Cape Hatteras, Diamond Shoals Lightship No. 71 was shelled by a German submarine. The lightship, which had just sent a wireless message about the submarine's shelling of the USS *Merak*, served as a beacon at sea to warn mariners of the dangerous shoals that formed off the coast.

As a result of the blows, the ship quickly sank. The lightship's crew of twelve rowed ten miles to shore in a small lifeboat. "We succeeded in getting away and never did mortal man row as we did that afternoon," the chief engineer later recounted. The lightship was quickly replaced by another that was kept to use as a backup.

The German submarine that took the ship down, *U-140*, also claimed the Standard Oil tanker *O.B. Jennings* a hundred miles off the Virginia coast and the four-masted schooner *Stanley M. Seaman* off Cape Hatteras in each of the two previous days. Following the sinking of the lightship, the submarine was spotted just a half mile off the North Carolina coast in a busy shipping lane.

By sinking American merchant vessels, Germany hoped to hinder important trade along the Atlantic coast. Taking out the lightship would further disrupt navigation.

1944 Ace George Preddy of Greensboro: Cripes A'Mighty

On August 6, 1944, Greensboro native George E. Preddy Jr., the top P-51 Mustang ace during World War II, downed six planes on a single day, earning a Distinguished Service Cross, the nation's second highest award, in the process.

Preddy was a barnstormer pilot before the war. He tried three times to become a naval pilot but was rejected because of health problems. The Army Air Corps accepted Preddy, placing him on a waiting list for a cadet class. In 1940 he joined the National Guard, and he received his wings in December 1941.

In July 1942 Preddy was involved in a midair collision during training. Following a three-month recovery, he returned to the United States and was eventually assigned to a squadron that was sent to Great Britain. He shot down his first plane in December 1943.

His squadron received P-51 Mustangs in April 1944, and Preddy named his the *Cripes A'Mighty*. That same year he became the temporary commander of the 487th Fighter Squadron.

While flying in pursuit of a German plane during the Battle of the Bulge, Preddy was accidentally shot down by friendly ground fire. He is buried at the Lorraine American Cemetery in France.

1945 *Enola Gay* Bombadier Thomas Ferebee of Mocksville

On August 6, 1945, Maj. Thomas Wilson Ferebee, a U.S. Army Air Corps bombardier and Mocksville native, dropped the atomic bomb on Hiroshima, Japan.

The twelve-man crew aboard the B-29 bomber, the *Enola Gay*, took off for Hiroshima at 2:00 a.m. from Tinian Island in the western Pacific. Ferebee, then twenty-six and a veteran of sixty-four combat missions, was napping and initially did not hear the pilot, Col. Paul Tibbets Jr., brief the crew about their top-secret mission.

Approaching Hiroshima, Ferebee activated the plane's automated Norden bombsight, centered its crosshairs on the Aioi Bridge, and called "bomb away." It was 8:15 a.m. The nine-thousand-pound bomb, nicknamed "Little Boy," tumbled from the plane's belly and sped six miles to its target below. Forty-three seconds later, the bomb detonated, instantly killing seventy thousand people. Many others died later from radiation.

On August 9 another bomber crew dropped a second atomic bomb on Nagasaki, Japan. Six days later the Japanese government surrendered unconditionally, ending World War II.

Ferebee retired from the U.S. Air Force in 1970 and died in 2000. He never expressed regret about dropping the A-bomb, maintaining that it saved more lives than it took by ending the war sooner.

Preddy signing his "Form 1" document, as pilots did to inform their crew chiefs regarding the condition of their fighter aircraft and performance following a mission. The photo was taken following Preddy's return to his base at Royal Air Force Base Bodney in England on August 6, 1944.

AUG 7

1906 Triple Lynching: Dark Day for Justice

On August 7, 1906, three black men were lynched in Rowan County for their supposed role in the murder of five members of a locally prominent farm family, the Lyerlys, a month earlier.

Though forensic evidence in the case was scant, authorities arrested six of the Lylerlys' tenants after neighbors reported hearing the family fighting with their sharecroppers earlier in the week. The accused—Mitchell Graham, also known as Nease Gillespie; his son, John Gillespie; Jack Dillingham and his wife, Della; George Irvin; and Nease's half-brother, Henry Lee Gillespie—were taken to Charlotte for their own protection while awaiting trial.

Three of the group—Nease Gillespie, John Gillespie, and Jack Dillingham—were brought to trial on August 6. At sundown after that first day of court, a mob that would ultimately grow to about three thousand people gathered on the steps of the jail in Salisbury. Though local officials tried to ease the growing unrest, the crowd broke past them and emerged from the jail with the three men in tow. Gov. Robert Glenn called out the state militia in an attempt to prevent further violence, but they arrived too late to intervene.

Just after midnight on August 7, the three were hanged. Then the crowd shot at their dead bodies.

The incident garnered worldwide press coverage and sparked widespread outrage over increasing racial violence. Though four were ultimately arrested for the three murders, only one man, George Hall of Montgomery County, was tried and convicted for his role in the crimes.

Hall was sentenced to fifteen years of hard labor, an oddity for those convicted in lynching cases in the post-Reconstruction South.

1914 Kiffin Rockwell of the Lafayette Escadrille

On August 7, 1914, Kiffin Rockwell of Asheville set sail for France.

He had volunteered for the French army after war had broken out and Pres. Woodrow Wilson issued a neutrality proclamation for the United States. As members of the French Foreign Legion, he and his brother were severely wounded. After recovering from the thigh injury that ended his infantry service, Rockwell became one of the first Americans to join the newly formed Lafayette Escadrille, an American volunteer aerial combat squadron.

In May 1916 Rockwell became the first American to shoot down an enemy plane. He was one of four North Carolinians who flew for France in World War I. For the next four months he participated in every mission his squadron was assigned.

On September 23, 1916, during his first mission after returning from leave, Rockwell engaged in a dogfight with a German plane. He was shot in the chest, making him the second-ever American killed in aerial combat. Rockwell was memorialized and honored in France and the United States, including being awarded the Cross of the Legion of Honor posthumously.

1945 Fred Kirby, Mojo Nixon, and "Atomic Power"

On August 7, 1945, country singer and WBT radio personality Fred Kirby of Charlotte wrote the hit song "Atomic Power."

Kirby was so moved by the news of the dropping of the atomic bomb on the Japanese city of Hiroshima the previous day that he was inspired to write the song comparing God's power to that of the bomb and warning against misuse of such power. Described as "the song that really started the fad for atomic bomb songs," "Atomic Power" was recorded by numerous artists over the years, including Kirby himself. Later versions also included references to Nagasaki, which was bombed on August 9, 1945. The best-selling version, released in 1946, was recorded by the Buchanan Brothers of Georgia, but the advent of the Cold War and concern over possible nuclear annihilation kept the song's message relevant for many years.

In the 1990s Jello Biafra, former lead singer for the Dead Kennedys, and North Carolina native Mojo Nixon included a version of "Atomic Power" on their collaborative album *Prairie Home Invasion*.

1972 Rocky Mount Man Inducted into Baseball Hall of Fame

On August 7, 1972, Negro League ballplayer and Rocky Mount native Walter Fenner "Buck" Leonard was inducted into the National Baseball Hall of Fame.

Born in 1907, Leonard was forced to quit school at age fourteen, since there was no high school for black students in Rocky Mount at the time. To help support his mother and five siblings following his father's death, young Leonard worked at a local hosiery mill, as a shoeshiner, and later for a railroad, while playing semi-pro baseball for the Rocky Mount Elks and Rocky Mount Black Swans.

The loss of his job during the Great Depression prompted Leonard to focus on professional baseball fulltime. He eventually made his way to the Pennsylvania-based Homestead Grays.

Fans and analysts alike heralded Leonard, an extraordinary first baseman and hitter, as the "black Lou Gehrig." Alongside power slugger Josh Gibson, he helped to lead the Grays to nine consecutive Negro League championships. In 1950, with seventeen years and a career batting average of .320 under his belt, Leonard retired to Rocky Mount.

Buck Leonard was the first National Baseball Hall of Fame inductee from North Carolina.

Buck Leonard and Commissioner Bowie Kuhn at the Baseball Hall of Fame induction ceremony.

1740 Second Governor Post-Statehood, Abner Nash

On August 8, 1740, Abner Nash, a politician and zealous advocate for the Patriot cause, was born.

From 1774 to 1776, Nash was a delegate to each of North Carolina's five provincial congresses, while also serving as a member of the Provincial Council. He served in both houses of the fledgling General Assembly before being elected governor in 1780. As chief executive, Nash drew upon every resource to support the national war effort while protecting North Carolina against British attack from the south.

In August 1780 the disastrous defeat of Patriot forces at Camden rendered North Carolina much more open to invasion by Cornwallis's army. Eventually the tide of war began to turn following the Battles of King's Mountain and Guilford Courthouse, but the exhausted and frustrated Nash had no desire to serve longer in a position he considered untenable. When nominated for reelection in June of 1781, he asked that his name be withdrawn from consideration.

Nash lived out his years near New Bern.

1908 Mary Reynolds Babcock, Patron of the Arts and Education

On August 8, 1908, Mary Reynolds was born in Winston to tobacco magnate R. J. Reynolds and his wife Katherine.

Both of her parents had died by the time she was fifteen, so Reynolds and her three siblings were left in the care of their uncle Will Reynolds at Reynolda, the family homeplace in Winston-Salem. After studying art in France, Mary Reynolds returned to the United States and in 1929 married investment banker Charles Babcock.

The couple lived in Greenwich, Connecticut before buying up the Reynolds siblings' interests in Reynolda. In 1936 Babcock inherited thirty million dollars from her father's estate, making her one of the wealthiest women in America.

After using some of the money to renovate Reynolda, Babcock turned her interests to philanthropy. In 1951 she and her husband donated more than three hundred acres to Wake Forest University, allowing the college to move to Winston-Salem from Wake Forest and construct an entirely new campus. A few years later, she established with twelve million dollars a charitable foundation that continues to support Wake Forest University, the arts, and social welfare.

Babcock died in New York City in 1953. In keeping with one of her lifelong passions, Reynolda House is now a celebrated museum of American art.

1974 Project Azorian and Cold War Espionage

On August 8, 1974, the CIA and U.S. Navy recovered a portion of the Soviet submarine *K-129* from the bottom of the Pacific Ocean, using the purpose-built ship *Hughes Glomar Explorer*. The sub, armed with three nuclear-armed ballistic missiles, had sunk six years earlier. The operation, known as Project Azorian and personally approved by Pres. Richard Nixon, was largely the brainchild of Carl E. Duckett, a Swannanoa native and the CIA's deputy director for science and technology at the time.

Massive cost overruns, the high probability of failure, and a détente between Moscow and Washington threatened to cancel the project, but Nixon and his national security team remained convinced that extensive intelligence could be gleaned from the operation, and it moved forward. The cover story for the mission was a seafloor manganese mining expedition by one of Howard Hughes's varied businesses.

Finally arriving near the *K-129* wreck in July 1974, recovery operations began on August 1 under almost constant surveillance from two nearby Soviet ships. After the sub's remains were secured in the *HGE's* massive hull, the ship sailed for Hawaii on August 9.

Many details of the project remain classified, so it has been difficult to gauge the project's success. But since most of the parts of ship that would have had significant intelligence value, including the ballistic missiles, fell back to the ocean floor, many consider Project Azorian largely a failure.

Photograph of Mary Reynolds Babcock taken about 1934 by Ira L. Hill.

AUG 9

1751 State's First Newspaper Issued in New Bern, 1751

On August 9, 1751, James Davis issued the *North-Carolina Gazette*, the first newspaper to appear in the colony.

The newspaper wasn't Davis's first foray into publishing; he had established the colony's first printing press two years earlier in New Bern. In that capacity he printed currency and various official publications.

The newspaper, unlike modern print papers, did not have headlines or much local news. It focused mostly on international news and the arrivals and departures of ships. The *Gazette* was supposed to have been published weekly, but from the issues that survive, it appears to have had no regular schedule and wasn't published at all between 1759 and 1768.

A terrible storm destroyed Davis's print shop in 1769, forcing him to salvage what equipment he could and rebuild his business. The Revolutionary War also presented Davis with problems in regularly issuing his *Gazette*, making it difficult for Davis to get paper and forcing his son, who was his assistant, to serve in the army.

Davis served as the colony's public printer until 1782, and he kept issuing the *Gazette* until just before his death in 1785. The paper appeared in another form between 1786 and 1798, when it was used by another printer to promote the Bill of Rights and other causes.

1949 Winston-Salem Pacesetter for Arts Councils

On August 9, 1949, the first locally-established arts council in the United States was formed in Winston-Salem.

The Junior League of Winston-Salem brought national community arts consultant Virginia Lee Comer to town in 1943 to study the cultural life of the community. Her strategy for cultural planning was to build connections between the community and its arts activities.

Seed money of seventy-two hundred dollars was set aside by the Junior League in 1946, and in 1949 representatives from twelve cultural groups convened to form the arts council. The council's stated purpose was to serve those members and to plan, coordinate, promote, and sponsor the opportunity for, and the appreciation of cultural activities in Winston-Salem and Forsyth County.

The Arts Council of Winston-Salem and Forsyth County today works to make Winston-Salem the "City of the Arts," where center-city revitalization efforts rely on the arts as an economic-development resource. The Council has helped develop new arts organizations, established a united arts fund, and constructed an arts center. Its comprehensive cultural program has received national acclaim and gained support for the arts from local business.

More than four thousand local arts agencies across the country now work to build the presence of the arts to enhance their community's quality of life, including seventy-four local arts councils in North Carolina.

1953 Clyde McPhatter of Durham, Influential Rhythm and Blues Performer

On August 9, 1953, Clyde McPhatter and the Drifters recorded "Money Honey" at Atlantic Studios in New York City. The song was a huge success, remaining on the rhythm and blues charts for twenty-three weeks and peaking at Number 1. In 2010 *Rolling Stone* ranked it the 252nd greatest song of all time.

Born in Durham in 1932, McPhatter got his start in music in the Baptist church where his father was minister. After his family moved to New Jersey, McPhatter won an amateur night at Harlem's famed Apollo Theater and caught the attention of doo-wop singer Billy Ward, who invited McPhatter to join his group.

McPhatter started a group of his own in the early 1950s, and together they quickly produced a number of hits, including a doo-wop version of Bing Crosby's "White Christmas." After a stint in the Army, he embarked on a solo career and tracked up more successes including "Treasure of Love."

Though he continued to record new music in the early and mid-1960s, McPhatter became disillusioned with the music industry and moved to England. His career continued to decline in large measure because of his battle with alcoholism.

He died in 1972 and was inducted posthumously into the Rock and Roll Hall of Fame in 1987.

2003 Pisgah Covered Bridge Rebuilt After Flood

On August 9, 2003, a flood washed away the Pisgah Covered Bridge. Spanning the West Fork Branch of the Little River in the Uwharrie National Forest south of Asheboro, the bridge was built at a cost of forty dollars by J. J. Welch around 1910. Welch constructed a number of other covered bridges in the area.

Later rebuilt, the Pisgah bridge is the only surviving covered bridge in Randolph County, which once had more of them than any other county in North Carolina. Along with the 1895 Bunker Hill Covered Bridge, near Claremont in Catawba County, it is one of only two left in North Carolina. The Bunker Hill bridge is similar to the Pisgah bridge in form and materials, but it was originally constructed as an open-span bridge and covered in 1900.

Wooden bridges were covered to protect their heavy-timber framing from exposure to the elements, which greatly extended a wooden bridge's life span. The prototypical American covered bridge was built in Philadelphia between 1800 and 1804. Thousands of others were constructed in the United States, but fewer than eight hundred remain.

The Pisgah Covered Bridge is open to the public from dawn to dusk and is located at 6925 Pisgah Covered Bridge Road.

Pisgah Covered Bridge in 1935.

1866 E. W. Gudger, Waynesville Fish Scientist

On August 10, 1866, acclaimed fish biologist Eugene Willis Gudger was born in Waynesville. His ancestors were some of the earliest settlers west of the Blue Ridge Mountains.

Gudger's interest in natural history began as a boy, when a family friend gave him a subscription to *St. Nicholas* magazine and a copy of Jacob Abbott's book *Land and Water*. After attending Emory and Henry College and the University of Nashville, he earned his Ph.D. at Johns Hopkins University.

Gudger first visited the ocean at the age thirty-six when he went to Beaufort to work at the U.S. Bureau of Fisheries laboratory. He quickly fell in love with the sea and devoted his life to studying fish and disseminating his accumulated knowledge. He was considered the foremost authority on several species at the time.

In addition to writing more than three hundred articles, Gudger edited a number of important works, including the *Biography of Fishes*, for the American Museum of Natural History in New York. He served that institution as an associate curator of fish between 1934 and 1938, retiring as honorary associate in ichthyology, a specialty in biology devoted to the study of fish.

Three years before his death, Gudger returned to his hometown. He is buried in Waynesville's Green Hill Cemetery, and his headstone is inscribed "Teacher ~ Ichthyologist."

1942 The Civil Air Patrol and World War II off North Carolina's Coast

On August 10, 1942, pilots from North Carolina's first Civil Air Patrol (CAP) base at Skyco on Roanoke Island began making patrols.

North Carolina's notorious "Torpedo Junction" spurred officials to establish a CAP base near the coast. Aircraft from the base patrolled the area from Norfolk to Ocracoke Inlet. The Navy and Coast Guard also used CAP aircraft to escort convoys along the coast, survey and chart wrecks that might pose risks to navigation, and conduct search and rescue missions.

As the federal and state governments began to see the value in the CAP, a second coastal patrol base was established in Beaufort in 1943. Although critically underfunded, North Carolina's two coastal patrol bases provided vital support for military operations.

While North Carolina's Civil Air Patrol bases were in operation during World War II, only two vessels were torpedoed off of the coast. The civilian airmen assisted military pilots in effectively blockading Torpedo Junction. Service in the CAP was voluntary and did not carry draft deferment. Participating aviators received pay for their time and equipment use when performing official services such as patrol or courier duty.

Today the Civil Air Patrol continues to conduct search and rescue operations and provide disaster relief and emergency services.

1972 Bull Rider Jerome Davis

On August 10, 1972, the young man who would put North Carolina on the bull riding and rodeo map, Jerome Davis, was born in Colorado Springs, Colorado. His father, stationed in Colorado while in the military, brought his family home to their ranch in Archdale, in Guilford County, just six months later.

Davis rode his first bull at age eleven. On his fourth ride he lasted the required eight seconds and committed himself to becoming a competitive bull rider. He won his first event as a freshman in high school, then became the North Carolina State High School Bull Riding Champion in 1990. Two years later Davis won the National Intercollegiate Rodeo Association's Bull Riding Championship. In 1992 he joined the Professional Rodeo Cowboys Association (PRCA), a dream only a few cowboys experience. He had a stellar career on the bull riding circuit, earning a World Championship in 1995, and was elected to the Professional Bull Riders Ring of Honor in 1998.

On March 14, 1998, in Fort Worth, Texas Davis was paralyzed from the chest down after being thrown from a bull. He returned home to Archdale and continues to run the Davis Ranch and his bucking bull and rodeo business.

Civil Air Patrol (CAP) ground personnel relax at Skyco before a patrol. *Left to right:* William E. Crowell (Concord), Benjamin A. Watkins (Hickory), Paul E. Plyler (Albemarle), Woodrow R. Marshall (Rocky Mount), and Melvin R. Daniels Jr. (Wanchese).

AUG 11

1854 Robert B. Glenn of Winston-Salem, Prohibition Governor

On August 11, 1854, Gov. Robert B. Glenn was born in Rockingham County.

After being educated at Davidson College and Richmond Hill Law School, Glenn practiced law in Rockingham and Stokes Counties. His entry into politics came in 1880, when he was elected to a single term in the General Assembly, representing Stokes County.

In 1885 Glenn moved his law practice to Forsyth County and served as U.S. attorney for the western district of North Carolina before returning to politics as a state senator in 1899. While in the General Assembly the second time, he spoke widely on behalf of white supremacy and supported the successful efforts in the legislature to disfranchise black voters.

Glenn ran against the Democratic machine in the 1904 gubernatorial primary for that party and went on to win the general election by a wide margin. He focused his term in office on expanding public education and on increasing funding for hospitals, public health, and care of the insane. He successfully spearheaded a campaign to ban the sale and manufacture of liquor, the "crowning act of my administration," in his words.

After leaving office, Glenn returned to his law practice in Winston-Salem and served on an international boundary dispute commission. He died in 1920.

1875 William A. Graham, Prominent Whig Politician

On August 11, 1875, prominent politician William A. Graham died. He was born in September 1804 in Lincoln County. Graham's father was a Revolutionary War soldier and a pioneer in the region's iron industry.

Attracted to the political arena, Graham aligned himself with the emerging Whig Party. He served in the state legislature from 1833 to 1840 and worked to establish public schools during his tenure as speaker of that body.

He then served for three years in the U.S. Senate before being elected governor in 1844. As governor, Graham pushed the Whig agenda of internal improvements and education. He served briefly as Secretary of the Navy during the early 1850s, ran for vice president in 1852, and returned to Orange County after his unsuccessful bid.

Though he served as a state and Confederate senator during the Civil War, Graham was a vocal opponent of secession. His views frequently conflicted with those of the Confederate government, though he sent five sons to fight for the South. The General Assembly elected Graham to the U. S. Senate in December 1865, but Radical Republicans gained control of Congress and refused to seat Southern delegates.

Graham died in New York while trying to arbitrate a border dispute between Maryland and Virginia.

1909 Distress Signal SOS First Heard at Hatteras, 1909

On August 11, 1909, off the coast of Cape Hatteras, telegraph operator Theodore Haubner called for help from the steamship, S. S. *Arapahoe*. He was momentarily confused because a new telegraph code "SOS" had recently been ratified by the Berlin Radiotelegraphic Conference to replace the old "CQD." Uncertain which signal to send, Haubner sent both. His transmission was the first recorded American use of "SOS" to call for help.

The letters "SOS" themselves do not stand for anything. Their representation as three dots, three dashes, and three dots was distinctive and easy to relay on the telegraph. Just as with "CQD," which meant "calling all stations-distress," the code indicates that radio traffic should cease until the emergency is over, but if possible, those on the receiving end should answer the distress signal.

The disabled S. S. *Arapahoe* was rescued when the signal was heard by the wireless station at Hatteras. Only a few months later, Haubner, the telegraph operator, received an "SOS" from the S. S. *Iroquois*, making him the first American radio operator to both send and receive the distress call.

1913 Keith and Malinda Blalock, Couple in Confederate Service

On August 11, 1913, Keith Blalock died while operating a hand car on a mountain railroad. He was the husband of Malinda Blalock, who was North Carolina's only known female Civil War soldier.

At the beginning of the Civil War, Keith and his wife Malinda lived near Grandfather Mountain in Watauga County. Despite being Unionists, the couple both enlisted in the Twenty-Sixth North Carolina Troops in March 1862. Malinda enlisted under the name Sam. Keith's decision to enlist was made primarily to avoid being drafted by the recently passed Confederate Conscription Act, and Malinda simply did not want her husband going to war without her.

While their regiment was stationed near Kinston, Keith devised a plan to be medically discharged by rubbing his body with poison oak, thus causing a rash. Once he obtained his discharge, his wife disclosed her gender and promptly received a discharge as well.

Upon their return to the mountains, the Blalocks joined Unionist guerrillas operating in and around Grandfather Mountain. Keith was wounded several times fighting Confederate home guard units.

After the war Keith ran for political office in Mitchell County but was defeated. Malinda died from natural causes in 1901. The couple is buried in Avery County.

S. S. *Arapahoe* departing Charleston, South Carolina, circa 1900.

1788 A Taste for Bacon and the Code Duello

On August 12, 1788, Andrew Jackson challenged Col. Waightstill Avery to a duel. The challenge was issued while both lawyers were serving in court in Jonesborough, one of three seats of the Morgan District Superior Court in western North Carolina before the establishment of Tennessee.

According to Avery family lore, the formal, Princeton-educated Avery would often "refer to Bacon," and procure from his saddle bag a copy of Matthew Bacon's *New Abridgement of the Law*, a much consulted legal treatise of that time. The younger Jackson is said to have replaced Bacon's work with an actual piece of bacon that had been wrapped as a volume, one the same size as the book, to avoid detection.

When Avery discovered the switch, he was greatly embarrassed and chided Jackson for his actions, which he declared unsuitable courtroom behavior. Jackson responded with the duel challenge.

After court that day, the men met in a ravine next to the Jonesborough Court House. Jackson fired first and missed. One version of the story says that Avery fired over the head of Jackson; another claims he did not shoot at all, but instead gave Jackson a paternal lecture, and the two left the field as friends.

1881 Showman Cecil B. DeMille, Raised in "Little Washington"

On August 12, 1881, movie producer and director Cecil Blount DeMille was born in Massachusetts, where his family was vacationing for the summer. The DeMille roots, though, were deeply embedded in eastern North Carolina, and Cecil (not yet "C. B.") grew up in Washington along the Pamlico River.

The DeMilles were a show business family. Cecil's father was playwright Henry C. DeMille, a leading figure in New York drama circles, and his niece, Agnes, was a dancer who spent her last years teaching at the North Carolina School of the Arts.

In 1913, C. B. DeMille moved to California and joined Samuel Goldwyn in founding what would become Paramount Pictures. In time DeMille's name became synonymous with spectacle. He produced seventy films including *The Greatest Show on Earth* and *The Ten Commandments*. He also played himself in the classic 1950 film *Sunset Boulevard*. During the production of *Commandments*, he suffered a heart attack after climbing a ladder to the top of the set made to look like Pharaoh Ramses's temple.

DeMille died in 1959 of congestive heart failure. At the time he was negotiating the directing rights to *Ben-Hur*. The Golden Globes Lifetime Achievement Award is named in his honor.

1989 Plott Hound Native to Haywood County

On August 12, 1989, the Plott Hound, a breed developed in North Carolina, was officially adopted as the State Dog.

In the mid-to-late 1800s, people from near and far would travel to Haywood County to get puppies from the Plott family. They would arrive with sacks on the backs of their mules or horses to carry home the prized hunting dogs. The Plotts bred hard-working, tenacious, and loyal dogs that would hunt bears and wild boars with boundless courage. Plott enthusiasts describe the breed as bold and energetic hunting dogs, gentle with people and loyal to their owners.

The dogs, once black, brown or brindle, are now usually brindle—meaning stripes of varying color. They stand twenty to twenty to twenty-five inches at the shoulder, weigh about forty-five to fifty-five pounds, and are strong and fast. The Plott Hound, as the dog is now known, has a distinctive high-pitched bark that is effective in alerting hunters to treed prey.

The Plott family, with roots in Germany, was well established by the early 1800s in the area now known as Plott Valley in Haywood County. It was there that the family refined their dogs to hunt bears in the mountain wilderness.

AUG 12

AUG 13

1587 Manteo, Friend to the Roanoke Colonists

On August 13, 1587, Manteo, an Algonquian Indian, was baptized into the Church of England on Roanoke Island. The baptism was the first in the New World.

A friend to colonists from earlier English attempts to settle on Roanoke Island, Manteo also traveled to England in 1584 and again in 1585. He returned to his home with the members of the 1587 colony, who would later become known as the Lost Colony.

While in England, Manteo met Sir Walter Raleigh and spent time with the scientist Thomas Harriot, with whom he was already acquainted. He worked with Harriot learning English and teaching Harriot the Algonquian language. Raleigh designated Manteo "Lord of Roanoke," and it is possible that his baptism was a requirement of receiving that title.

Manteo proved to be a stalwart friend of the English, helping them navigate the multicultural frontier of the New World. His name lives on today as the name of Dare County's seat.

1914 "Glory" Hancock, World War I Nurse

On August 13, 1914, Madelon Battle Hancock, the most decorated nurse to serve with the Allied Forces in World War I, left for service in Antwerp, Belgium with the first British Hospital Unit.

Hancock grew up in Asheville where her father, Westray Battle, was a prominent physician and outspoken community leader. In 1904 she married Mortimer Hancock, an officer in the British Army and moved with him to England in 1905 after graduating from the Presbyterian Hospital School for Nursing in New York City.

Hancock, who was soon called "Glory" by the troops that she enthusiastically served, went to Belgium with the first detachment of soldiers sent into the war from Britain, and she remained in service with them for the entire war. She was often close to the battle front and survived artillery fire and gassing.

For her skilled nursing of the sick and wounded and her bravery under fire, Hancock received twelve decorations: five each from Great Britain and Belgium and two from France.

Madelon Battle Hancock

1976 Stanley Harris, Booster of Diverse Scouting Initiatives

On August 13, 1976, early Boy Scout leader Stanley Harris died in Greensboro.

Born in Tennessee, Harris was raised in Avery County. He taught school but eventually ended up working for the YMCA, where he took a special interest in introducing boys to the outdoors.

After reading about the Boy Scout movement, which was then getting its start in Great Britain, Harris applied for and received a charter in 1908 for one of the first Boy Scout troops formed in the United States. Two years later he served as one of the charter members in the official founding of the Boy Scouts of America, and seven years after that he joined the Scouts' national organization.

Harris made significant gains in introducing African American boys to scouting. He was made the head of the Interracial Services division of the Boy Scouts and given the task of promoting interracial scouting across the nation. He supported the founding of the first all-black Boy Scout troop in 1916 and during the 1920s helped organize the first all-Native American troop. In 1926 he organized the Scouts' Interracial Service, an initiative to boost racial diversity.

Harris retired from the Scouts in 1947 and moved to Boone, where he remained active in the community.

1998 Banker Ponies Protected Since 1998

On August 13, 1998, Pres. Bill Clinton signed the Shackleford Banks Wild Horses Protection Act.

The act, which amended the 1966 law that created the Cape Hatteras National Seashore, directed the National Park Service to partner with a local non-profit, Foundation for Shackleford Horses, Inc., to manage the herd of wild horses located on the uninhabited nine-mile-long island east of Morehead City between Beaufort Inlet and Cape Lookout.

The banker ponies, as they are often called, are small horses believed to have been descended from Spanish mustangs abandoned in the area about four hundred years ago. Some have also tried to link the horses' ancestry to Ponce de León or the Lost Colony, though their exact lineage is lost to history.

The 1998 act provides for a target range for the herd of between 110 and 130 horses. When the herd exceeds that target, a roundup is held, and excess healthy horses are adopted out to different places around the country.

The seashore, in conjunction with the foundation, is charged with managing so as to preserve the herd's protection and health, as well as those of the natural resources of the seashore.

The Shackleford Banks herd is one of four herds of wild horses up and down the Outer Banks.

Shackleford Banks horses

1880 Confederate General Bryan Grimes, Target of Hired Killer

On August 14, 1880, while returning home from a political convention in Beaufort County, Bryan Grimes was murdered by a hired assassin near Bear Creek, about five miles from his home in Pitt County. The murder was planned to prevent him from testifying in a court case.

Grimes was born in 1828 in Pitt County on his family's plantation, "Grimesland." A successful planter, he served the Confederacy throughout the Civil War. He signed North Carolina's secession ordinance, enlisted soon after, rose to the rank of major general, and served until Lee's surrender at Appomattox.

After the surrender of Confederate troops and the end of the war, Grimes returned home. He worked to rebuild his family's plantation to its former prosperity and again became one of the most successful planters in North Carolina.

Grimes lived in Pitt County with his second wife, Charlotte Emily Bryan, and his children until his death. At that time he was a trustee for the University of North Carolina and well-respected throughout the state.

1945 Couple Immortalized on V-J Day

On August 14, 1945, *Life* magazine photographer Alfred Eisenstaedt captured the spirit of celebration of the United States's victory over Japan in World War II in an iconic photograph of a sailor kissing a nurse in Times Square.

The sailor had been running down the street kissing random women when he was spotted by Eisenstaedt, who snapped a few quick pictures when that sailor grabbed a nurse in white nearby. Because of the chaos in the streets Eisenstaedt did not have time to get the names of the couple.

Many people have claimed to be the sailor or the nurse over the years, but North Carolina native Glenn McDuffie went to some length to prove that he was the kissing sailor. Tired of disputes as to the man's identity, McDuffie asked Lois Gibson, a forensic artist with the Houston Police Department, whether she could make a positive identification.

In 2007 Gibson, who also compared the photo with those of several other kisser-claimants, reported that McDuffie's features were an exact match to those of the sailor in the photograph. He enjoyed several years of celebrity, being invited to fundraisers and veterans' events.

Born in Kannapolis in 1927, McDuffie was fifteen years old when he forged documents to join the Navy. He died in 2014 in Texas.

Photo above taken by Victor Jorgensen, photographer for the Department of the Navy, who was in Times Square near Alfred Eisenstaedt and captured the kiss from a different angle.

AUG 15

1754 U.S. Senator Benjamin Hawkins, Later Emissary to Indians

On August 15, 1754, Benjamin Hawkins, politician and agent for Indian affairs south of the Ohio River, was born in Warren County.

Proficient in French, the young Hawkins was studying at what's now Princeton University when Gen. George Washington recruited him to serve as an interpreter on his field staff. Hawkins then served in the Continental Congress in the years between the Revolutionary War and the adoption of the federal constitution. After its ratification Hawkins became one of North Carolina's first two U.S. Senators.

From an early age Hawkins was interested in the welfare of American Indians. In 1785 he was appointed a commissioner to negotiate with Cherokee and other southern Indians, leading to the Treaty of Hopewell. Soon thereafter he worked with the Choctaw, Chickasaw, and Creek.

In 1796 President Washington appointed Hawkins Principal Temporary Agent for Indian Affairs South of the Ohio River. He chose to live among the Creek Indians in central Georgia. From that point forward, Hawkins's life was dedicated entirely to Indian affairs, though the War of 1812 interrupted his efforts. British emissaries provoked discontent with Creeks and other Indians farther to the west, leaving Hawkins bitterly disappointed with the war and its course.

He died in Crawford County, Georgia in 1816.

1866 Monroe Nathan Work, Chronicler of Black History

On August 15, 1866, Monroe Nathan Work, one of the most distinguished historians of the African American experience, was born in Iredell County.

Both of Work's parents had been enslaved, so with the promise of new horizons outside the South, the family moved to Illinois shortly after he was born. Work attended seminary in Chicago but decided that being a minister wasn't for him and became a sociologist. While teaching in Georgia, he attracted the attention of Booker T. Washington, founder of Tuskegee Institute.

At Tuskegee Work found his calling and life's work. At the height of the Jim Crow era, he dedicated himself to documenting African American life and history and to assisting those seeking social justice.

In 1912 Work began compiling *The Negro Yearbook*, a sort of almanac with information and statistics on the black experience. Among other endeavors he took care to document lynchings, lending credibility to the anti-lynching movement.

His masterwork was his *Bibliography of the Negro in Africa and America*, which appeared in 1928 and included seventeen thousand entries. That year he received the Harmon Foundation Award for Distinguished Achievement.

Work died at his home in Tuskegee in 1945.

1903 Social Work Pioneer Ellen Winston

On August 15, 1903, Ellen Black Winston was born in Bryson City.

Starting out as a teacher and director of guidance for Raleigh high schools, Winston went on to serve as the editor of a series of publications on public relief for the Works Progress Administration. She coauthored three books and wrote hundreds of articles related to social welfare policy and legislation. In 1940 she was appointed head of the Department of Sociology and Economics at Meredith College.

Winston was named commissioner of the N. C. Board of Public Welfare in 1944. In that capacity she served on or advised numerous boards, commissions, and agencies, both state and national. The Welfare Administration, an extension of the Social Security Act, was established in 1963 in the new U. S. Department of Health, Education and Welfare. Winston was appointed the first head of the Administration, directing several national public assistance programs.

Throughout her career Winston was an advocate for professional training for social workers, both black and white. She was also a founding member of the National Association of Social Workers. Although she resigned from her federal post in 1967, she remained active in the social work community until her death.

1920 The "Great Agitator," Golden Frinks

On August 15, 1920, Golden Frinks, a key civil rights activist in North Carolina in the 1960s and 1970s, was born. When he died in 2004, the *News and Observer* took note of the marches he had led and said that he "left footprints all over eastern North Carolina." It was the blessing of Dr. Martin Luther King, Jr. that lent Frinks his distinction. From his base in Edenton Frinks served as North Carolina field secretary of King's Southern Christian Leadership Conference from 1962 until 1977, during the course of which he was jailed eighty-seven times. Clemmenette Bond of Williamston said, "He was *our* Martin Luther King."

The gregarious Frinks was a flamboyant, charismatic speaker and organizer. His initial foray into civil rights took place in Edenton where in 1962 he organized protests at a segregated theater and his home came to be known as "Freedom House." In 1963, for thirty-two days, he led demonstrations in nearby Williamston. In time his activism extended across the state. In 1969 Frinks began a Poor People's March, commencing in Asheville.

Frinks liked the nickname "Great Agitator" and joked that he imagined his role as akin to that of an agitator in a washing machine, part of the mechanism that "got the dirt out."

1973 Jockey's Ridge Patron Saint, Carolista Baum

On August 15, 1973, Carolista Fletcher Baum placed herself in the path of a bulldozer removing sand from Jockey's Ridge and refused to move. The driver cut off the engine and talked with Baum, who, after some time, left the dune unscathed. When the operator left, Baum took the distributor cap so the machine would not start.

Baum had received word of the bulldozer from her three children, who long had climbed the dune for the spectacular views it offered.

Though local groups had talked about protecting the large dune from encroaching development for years, Baum was the driving force that made the idea a reality. She helped form People to Preserve Jockey's Ridge after her dramatic protest, raising money and organizing petition drives to capture the attention of state and local lawmakers. She even drove to Raleigh every day for three weeks to keep the dune in the minds of legislators.

In 1973 the Division of Parks and Recreation issued a report in favor of preserving Jockey's Ridge as a state park, and a year later the dune was declared a National Natural Landmark. When the General Assembly appropriated funds to create the park in 1975, the preservation of the dune was secured for generations to come.

Golden Frinks *(right)* at a protest in Raleigh in 1976.

Carolista Fletcher Baum at Jockey's Ridge.

AUG 16

1883 Diminutive Circus Duo Retired to Salisbury

On August 16, 1883, circus performers John Mertz and Mariah Elizabeth Nail were married on the stage of the Buckingham Theater in Louisville, Kentucky.

According to one story, the justice of the peace asked whether they were old enough to wed because they were so small, with Mariah standing at thirty-six inches and John only about ten inches taller. At the time they married, they were both around thirty years old.

Nail was born in Mocksville in 1852. Her husband Mertz, also known as "Major," was born in Austria or Hungary around 1853. At age twenty-one he joined the circus, where he met Nail. After a long career of touring with several circuses, the pair retired from circus life sometime around 1911 and made their home in Salisbury. Mertz worked there as a store clerk at T. F. Kluttz & Co., among other jobs.

The couple quickly became famous in Salisbury and has continued to live on in the community's memory. Nail passed away at age sixty-nine in 1922. Mertz died in 1938 at age eighty-five. They are buried in Chestnut Hill Cemetery.

John and Mariah Nail Mertz, about 1883.

1918 The Sinking of the *Mirlo*

On August 16, 1918, a German U-boat fired a torpedo at the *Mirlo*, a British tanker hauling gasoline off the North Carolina coast. The torpedo hit the tanker midship, resulting in a giant explosion.

Initially Capt. William R. Williams ordered the ship beached, but when two more explosions broke the tanker in two, he ordered the crew to abandon ship. The men boarded three lifeboats and began heading away from the burning ship. Two of the lifeboats made it to a safe distance from the ship, but the third capsized. Another blast surrounded the men in the water with burning gasoline.

Onshore, Leroy Midgett of the Chicamacomico Lifesaving Station sounded the alarm to Surfboat Crew 1046, and they set out to rescue the distressed crew of the *Mirlo*. It took four attempts for the rescue team to make it past the breakers of the stormy waters, but the men reached the site. As the rescue team approached, a wall of fire blocked the crew's way to the victims, and by the time the team reached them, nine already had died. The rescuers brought the remaining six men to safety.

For the *Mirlo* rescue England and the United States gave the Chicamacomico Lifesavers their highest awards for bravery.

1950 Oconaluftee, Replica Cherokee Village, Approved

On August 16, 1950, the Cherokee Historical Association agreed to build a replica of an eighteenth century Indian village to depict Cherokee daily life and culture before European contact.

The site chosen was forty wooded acres on the slope of Rattlesnake Mountain near the town of Cherokee. Called "Oconaluftee," the recreated village is based on an older Cherokee community known as "Egwanulti," meaning "by the river." Early English explorer William Bartram wrote about the village in his 1775 journals. Gen. Griffith Rutherford's army likely destroyed it during the 1776 campaign against the Cherokee.

The job of creating an accurate replica of the village fell to archaeologists and anthropologists of the Tsali Institute for Cherokee Research. P.A. Willett supervised construction of the village, which features a seven-sided council house, homes, and other circa 1750s structures.

It opened to the public in August 1952, and a botanical garden and nature trail were added in 1954. Today Cherokee guides in authentic attire educate visitors about traditional Cherokee beliefs, government, and family life, while demonstrating ancient crafts, such as pottery, weapon making, and canoe building.

1966 Eno River Guardian, Margaret Nygard

On August 16, 1966, a group led by local activist Margaret Nygard and her husband, Holger, voiced opposition at a Durham City Council meeting to a plan to dam the Eno River. The city had been perusing the plan for more than a year as a means to bolster the local drinking water supply.

Margaret Nygard, a Durham teacher and social worker, and a group of concerned local citizens used the energy generated by that meeting to form the Association for the Preservation of the Eno River Valley, now known as the Eno River Association. The association, in turn, worked with The Nature Conservancy to build a partnership with the area's local governments and the state to formulate a plan to save the natural and cultural resources of the Eno area.

In 1972 the idea for a state park was proposed, and a local farm family donated ninety acres for it. A state conservation board endorsed the park that same year, and the following year Gov. Jim Holshouser officially announced the park's creation.

Thanks to the stewardship of the state and the Eno River Association, Eno River State Park has continued to grow since its inception. Today it encompasses more than four thousand acres along thirty-five miles of the river's course through Orange and Durham Counties.

1816 Samuel Johnston of "Hayes" in Chowan County

On August 17, 1816, Revolutionary-era political leader Samuel Johnston died.

Born in Scotland, Johnston immigrated to North Carolina as an infant. Trained as a lawyer, he represented Chowan County in the colonial assembly until the advent of the American Revolution.

During the Revolution Johnston was a strong leader of the Patriot cause. He was a member of North Carolina's Provincial Council, a delegate to the first four provincial congresses, and worked as treasurer to fund and supply the war effort.

Johnston continued to be active in public life after the war, earning wide respect. When North Carolina's first constitutional convention met in Hillsborough in 1788, Johnston, a leading Federalist, was elected president, even though the majority of delegates were opposed to ratification. He served in the same role in the 1789 convention in Fayetteville.

A relative of royal governor Gabriel Johnston, Johnston served in the state's top job from 1787 to 1789 before being elected one of North Carolina's first U.S. senators in 1789. After serving a single Senate term, he retired from public life briefly until he was chosen for the state legislature, this time representing Martin County.

His last public position was a superior court judgeship between 1800 and 1803, and he died less than two weeks after retiring from that post. He is buried at "Hayes," his Chowan home.

AUG 17

1937 Frank Stick, Lindsay Warren, and Cape Hatteras National Seashore

On August 17, 1937, the U.S. House of Representatives authorized the country's first national seashore at Cape Hatteras.

North Carolina Congressman Lindsay C. Warren sponsored the bill that sought to preserve the distinctive barrier islands of the Outer Banks. Because support for the park waxed and waned over the years, the Cape Hatteras National Seashore was not officially established until 1953. The formal dedication ceremony was held in 1958.

The park was a long-time dream of conservationist and developer Frank Stick, who first came to the area on a fishing excursion in the late 1920s and was impressed with the pristine beaches and seemingly endless opportunities for recreation. He began lobbying for "a coastal park for North Carolina and the nation" soon after moving his family to the Outer Banks in 1929.

Cape Hatteras National Seashore, administered by the National Park Service, now includes more than seventy miles of beach from Nags Head to Ocracoke. Initial plans had called for a much larger park that would include portions of Roanoke and Colington Islands. More than two million people visit the seashore each year to enjoy its beaches, fish, swim, surf, bird watch, or see one of the park's three lighthouses—at Bodie Island, Cape Hatteras, and Ocracoke.

1942 Frank Armstrong of *Twelve O'Clock High!* Fame

On August 17, 1942, Frank Armstrong led a daring daylight bomber attack by the United States. He flew over Axis territory in occupied France and earned the Silver Star, a military honor for valor.

A native of Hamilton, in Martin County, and a graduate of Wake Forest College, Armstrong enlisted in 1928 as a flying cadet. He received and conducted bombardment training and in 1940 witnessed the Nazi blitz bombing of London.

Armstrong's involvement in the war did not end with the 1942 campaigns. In 1943 he led the first U.S. raids over Germany in a B-17 "Flying Fortress," and in 1945 he flew some of the last bombing raids over Japan, targeting oil depots in a B-29. His official military biography states that he "led the first and last heavy bombing raids" of World War II.

In 1948 Beirne Lay Jr., who had served alongside Armstrong on the bombardment team in Europe, collaborated with Sy Bartlett to publish *Twelve O'Clock High!* The authors made clear in the foreword that Col. Frank Savage, the novel's central character, was based on Armstrong. The 1949 film version was nominated for an Academy Award for Best Picture.

Frank A. Armstrong, Jr. sitting in the cockpit of an Air Force jet at Barksdale Air Force Base in Shreveport, Louisiana, mid-1950s.

1587 Virginia Dare, First English Child in the New World

On August 18, 1587, Virginia Dare became the first child born in the Americas to English parents.

She was named in honor of the Virgin Queen of England, Elizabeth I. Her parents, Eleanor and Ananias Dare, were part of the Roanoke Colony, an early attempt by the English to establish a permanent settlement in the New World. Her birth was recorded by her grandfather John White, governor of the colony. White shortly afterward returned to England seeking supplies. It took three years before he could secure passage back to Roanoke Island, and upon his return he found the colonists had vanished.

Virginia Dare thus disappeared from history and entered legend. One of the better-known tales says she was transformed into a white deer by a jealous lover, a Native American witch doctor. Two hunters, one trying to save her and one trying to kill her, shot the white deer with special arrows. The human Virginia was slain, but Virginia as deer lived. White deer are still rumored to inhabit the area.

On August 18, 1937, the state of North Carolina issued a delayed birth certificate to Virginia Dare, partially to promote the newly established outdoor drama *The Lost Colony*.

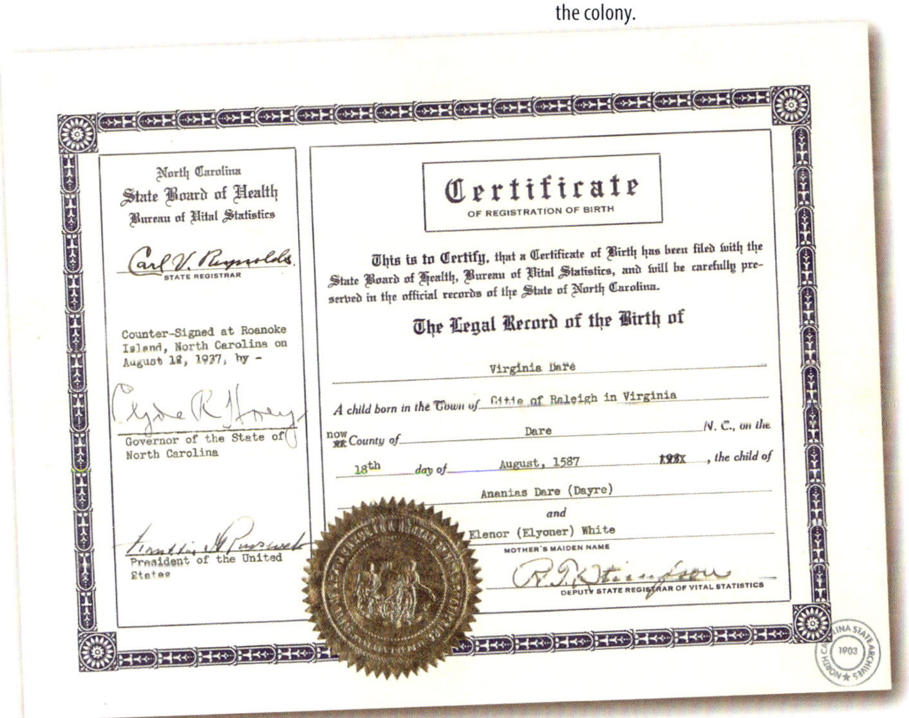
North Carolina
State Board of Health
Bureau of Vital Statistics

Carl V. Reynolds
STATE REGISTRAR

Counter-Signed at Roanoke Island, North Carolina on August 18, 1937, by -

Clyde R. Hoey
Governor of the State of North Carolina

Franklin D. Roosevelt
President of the United States

Certificate
OF REGISTRATION OF BIRTH

This is to Certify, that a Certificate of Birth has been filed with the State Board of Health, Bureau of Vital Statistics, and will be carefully preserved in the official records of the State of North Carolina.

The Legal Record of the Birth of

Virginia Dare

A child born in the Town of Citie of Raleigh in Virginia

now County of Dare N. C., on the

18th day of August, 1587 ~~192X~~, the child of

Ananias Dare (Dayre)

and

Elenor (Elyoner) White
MOTHER'S MAIDEN NAME

R. T. Stinson
DEPUTY STATE REGISTRAR OF VITAL STATISTICS

1590 Origins of the "Lost Colony" Mystery

On August 18, 1590, Englishman John White returned to Roanoke Island to resupply the colony established on the island in 1587, only to find the settlement abandoned. A single word "CROATOAN" was carved on a post in the fort.

In 1587, at the urging of fellow colonists, Governor White had returned to England to gather supplies for the blossoming colony. Before leaving Roanoke Island, White and the colonists agreed that they would carve a message in a tree if they moved. Additionally, a Maltese cross would also be carved if the move was forced. Since White didn't find that distress signal, he was hopeful that the colonists would be found alive. White's granddaughter, Virginia Dare, had been born exactly three years earlier.

After arriving back in England in October 1587, White was prevented from immediately returning to Roanoke Island because of England's war with Spain. His attempt to do so in 1588 ended when pirates stole all his supplies. Finally, he was granted permission to return in early 1590.

White had the misfortune of arriving at Roanoke Island in poor weather and terrible landing conditions, leading to the drowning deaths of seven mariners. The weather forced White to leave without searching adjacent areas for the colony.

1899 Rescue of the Priscilla Crew, 1899

On August 18, 1899, Erasmus Midgett single-handedly rescued the crew of the three-masted cargo ship *Priscilla* after it broke up while being driven ashore by the winds and waves of the San Ciriaco hurricane.

While patrolling on horseback from the Gull Shoal Lifesaving Station near Salvo, Midgett heard cries from the wreck. Around 3:00 a.m. the surfman saw part of the wreckage with several people on it. He knew that there was no time to get help and that he was the only hope for the men.

Getting as close to the wreck as he could, he yelled for the men to jump into the water one at a time. Midgett saved each of the seven men already in the sea by dragging them ashore. Three men were still on the vessel but injured enough that they could not jump. Midgett had to take each of the injured men off and carry him to shore. He thus saved ten members of the crew, including Capt. Benjamin Springsteen of Baltimore. Once all the men were ashore, Midgett got help from the station to transport the wounded to safety.

For his part in the heroic rescue, Midgett received a Gold Lifesaving Medal from then U. S. Secretary of the Treasury Lyman Gage.

A copper version of the Lifesaving Medal awarded to Midgett by the United States Congress.

1945 No Quickie Divorce in 1940s

On August 18, 1945, Caldwell County residents Otis Williams and Lillie Hendrix legally married in the state of North Carolina, ending a five-year battle against bigamy charges.

The saga began in 1940, when Otis, a married storekeeper, and his handyman's wife, Lillie, traveled to Nevada to secure divorces from their respective spouses. After spending the legally required time as "residents" of the state, divorces were granted, and Williams and Hendrix married before returning to North Carolina.

The action infuriated the first Mrs. Williams, who in retaliation brought charges of bigamy against the newlyweds. A Caldwell County court convicted the pair and delivered multiyear prison sentences for each. Subsequent appeals to the Supreme Court resulted in that conviction's overturned, but a dogged state prosecutor continued the crusade.

By that time the spurned Mrs. Williams had died, but her desire to see the couple jailed lived on as county courts upheld the convictions. State courts, however, ultimately decided to take pity on the pair, offering them a reprieve so long as they legally wed in state.

The case made national news, throwing a spotlight on the labyrinth-like nature of divorce law at that time.

1862 The Story Behind Hammocks Beach Earthworks

On August 19, 1862, a Union force commanded by Col. Thomas G. Stevenson of the Twenty-Fourth Massachusetts Volunteer Infantry burned the Confederate fort at Huggins Island near Swansboro. Both the barracks and ammunition magazine collapsed into ashes.

In Fall 1861 North Carolina found its vital defenses at Hatteras Inlet compromised, making the sounds vulnerable to Union naval invasion. Confederate Brig. Gen. Walter Gwynn, in charge of coastal defenses from New Bern to the South Carolina line, strongly recommended construction of a series of small forts to protect critical inlets. Among those was a six-gun battery at Bogue Inlet on Huggins Island.

Construction of the fort was completed in December 1861, and a company of artillery was then stationed at the fort to man the cannons. The company did not remain long at the fort, as they were ordered to join Gen. Lawrence O'B. Branch's brigade at New Bern in March. They took the cannons with them when they marched out of Swansboro.

After the fire only the earthen embankment remained as evidence of the fort's existence. Those earthworks have somehow dodged development and erosion and are now a part of Hammocks Beach State Park.

1933 Black Mountain College, An Experimental School

On August 19, 1933, Black Mountain College was established in Buncombe County by disgruntled faculty from Rollins College in Florida. Unconventional by almost every standard, the college served as an alternative to traditional education and was one of the first schools in the nation to create an educational plan embodying the principles of progressive education. One of the major tenets of the school's plan was to elevate the fine arts to full curricular status.

Owing partly to the imbalance between the arts and sciences, Black Mountain College was never accredited. Despite that fact, many of its graduates enjoyed successful careers in the fine arts, education, and letters. Among the artists who were either students or faculty were architects Buckminster Fuller and Walter Gropius; painters Josef Albers, Willem DeKooning, Robert Motherwell, and Robert Rauschenberg; dancers Merce Cunningham and Paul Taylor; musician John Cage; filmmaker Arthur Penn; and writers Eric Bentley, Robert Creeley, Paul Goodman, Alfred Kazin, Charles Olson, Joel Oppenheimer, and Jonathan Williams.

In 1941 the school moved to a large Internationalist-style building designed by faculty member W. Lawrence Kocher. The school fell into decline following World War II and ceased operation in 1956.

1956 Highland Games at Grandfather Mountain Date Back to 1956

On August 19, 1956, the first Grandfather Mountain Highland Games were held near Linville.

The Grandfather Mountain games were conceived by Agnes MacRae Morton and Donald MacDonald. Already active in several Scottish-affiliated organizations in the U.S., MacDonald was inspired to start games in North Carolina after attending a similar event on a trip to Scotland. Morton heard of a similar gathering in Connecticut and thought that Grandfather Mountain would be the perfect setting to try something comparable in North Carolina. The pair chose the August 1956 date to commemorate the anniversary of an important event in the 1745 Jacobite Rebellion in Scotland, though the games were moved to the second weekend in July two years later.

The Avery County event quickly gained international fame, and its competitions in athletics, bagpiping, drumming, and dancing are recognized worldwide. The games also have the distinction of being the largest "clan gathering" in the world, since they draw so many Scottish family heritage groups.

The tradition of highland games across North Carolina is due to the Tar Heel State's having until well into the 1800s the largest settlement of Highland Scots outside of Scotland.

AUG 19

Buckminster Fuller *(left)* speaking with students at Black Mountain College, summer 1948.

1775 Stage Set for War in Hillsborough, 1775

On August 20, 1775, the Third Provincial Congress, formed to replace the Colonial Assembly dissolved by Royal governor Josiah Martin the previous April, convened in Hillsborough.

Samuel Johnston of Edenton was selected to preside, and the body declared itself the province's temporary government and created the Provincial Council both to conduct business when the Provincial Congress was not in session and to oversee the Committee of Safety.

For the purpose of organizing a militia and arranging representation in the Provincial Council, the congress determined that the six existing judicial districts would become military districts. The districts contained between four and eight counties and were named for the most prominent towns they contained: Edenton, Halifax, Hillsborough, New Bern, Wilmington, and Salisbury.

Each military district was authorized to establish a regiment of minutemen to serve within the boundaries of North Carolina. Furthermore, each of the thirty five counties was asked to raise a company of militia.

The Third Provincial Congress ordered the enlistment of the first two units of Provincial Troops, which were to join the Continental Army later that year.

1917 Terry Sanford, Paratrooper, Governor, University President

On August 20, 1917, future North Carolina governor and U.S. senator Terry Sanford was born in Laurinburg. An Eagle Scout as a youth, Sanford graduated from UNC in 1939 and became an FBI agent before marrying Margaret Rose Knight in July 1942. They later had two children.

During World War II Sanford fought in France as a U.S. Army paratrooper. Returning home a decorated combat veteran, he earned a law degree from Carolina, began a legal career, and soon entered politics.

A Democrat, Sanford served one term as state senator before winning the 1960 gubernatorial race. As governor, he advocated for civil rights and education, led efforts to consolidate the UNC system, and helped create a statewide community college system.

In 1969 Sanford began a sixteen-year stint as Duke University's president. Twice during the 1970s he unsuccessfully sought the Democratic Party's nomination for U.S. President. Then in 1986 he was elected to the U.S. Senate, only to lose his re-election bid in 1992.

During his later years Sanford wrote several books, practiced law, and taught at Duke. He died of cancer in April 1998 at age eighty and was entombed in the crypt of Duke University Chapel.

Terry Sanford files for governor, February 1960.

1953 Long Political Career for Governor Cameron Morrison

On August 20, 1953, the "Good Roads Governor," Cameron Morrison, died.

Born in 1869, Morrison attended school in his native Richmond County. He did not attend college but briefly studied law before opening a practice in Rockingham in 1892. Morrison began his political career as mayor of Rockingham before being elected to the state Senate in 1900. After serving there for one term, Morrison took a twenty-year break from politics before being elected governor in 1921.

A Democrat, Morrison devoted himself to internal improvements. He prompted the legislature to fund the construction of fifty-five hundred miles of hard-surface roads. He also advocated for improvements in higher education and increases in funding to the state's charitable institutions.

Though he was a leader of the "Red Shirts" and promoted white supremacy tactics that included harassment and threats of violence against African American voters earlier in his life, as governor Morrison sought to improve race relations and all but ended lynching in the state.

Following his term as governor, Morrison returned to private life. In 1930 he was appointed to fill an unexpired U.S. Senate term. He served one term in U.S. House in the early 1940s but was defeated in another bid for the Senate in 1944.

Governor Cameron Morrison and his daughter, Angelia, on his inauguration day.

AUG 21

1829 Priestley Mangum and His Innovative Terrace

On August 21, 1829, Priestley Hinton Mangum Jr. was born in Wake County. Educated at Wake Forest College, Mangum would be little known today but for a revolutionary erosion control technique he pioneered in 1881 that became known as the Mangum Terrace.

As a farmer, Mangum faced two significant problems with the lay of his land: first, what to do with the wasted land necessary for ditches to control water runoff; and second, how to incorporate farm machinery that was not adapted for ditched land. His answer, which he engineered with the help of his African American farmhand Tom Jones, was a terracing system comprised of broad ridges with smaller gentle slopes that would control water flow and still permit crop growth and machinery use.

Knowledge of Mangum's system spread by word of mouth in the decade following its development, and soon the Mangum Terrace was being publicized by agricultural periodicals. By 1912 the system had been officially adopted and endorsed by the United States Department of Agriculture, and within another ten years it was utilized in nearly every state in the country.

1831 Nat Turner's Rebellion: Repercussions Felt in N.C.

On August 21, 1831, a slave named Nat Turner led a rebellion against white slave owners in Southampton County, Virginia about twenty miles from the border with North Carolina. Within a day more than fifty people had been killed. The ranks of the rebels swelled to about sixty slaves. The governor called out the militia to end the rebellion, but word of the attacks began to spread across the South.

In North Carolina's northern border counties, panic ensued among the residents. The militia was called out to Hertford, Halifax, and Northampton Counties. Whites in other counties began to arm themselves as well. As rumors and speculation spread that there would be more violence and attacks, many slave owners began to fear that their own slaves were going to rise up against them. As a result, whites began to monitor the behavior of their slaves more closely, and in some cases blacks were arrested and executed. The legislature also passed laws further restricting the rights of slaves and free blacks.

After several weeks on the run, Nat Turner was caught and tried in Virginia, where he was found guilty, sentenced to death, and later that fall hanged.

1918 Cherokee Code Talkers and Allied Success in WWI

On August 21, 1918, British forces began attacking German positions along a ten-mile stretch of the Western Front in northwest France. The assault was part of the World War I action now known as the Somme Offensive.

Attached to the British troops fighting in the region were the 119th and 120th U.S. Infantry Regiments, which both contained a number of Cherokee soldiers from western North Carolina.

In late September and early October, as the offensive continued and preparations were underway to break through the German defensive positions known as the Hindenburg Line, the commanders in the area discovered that German troops were intercepting their telephone communications. The Germans then used those messages to discover the position of Allied forces and attack them.

That's where the Cherokee came in. The signal officers at the time guessed that the Germans wouldn't be able to understand the Cherokee language and directed Cherokee troops to deliver messages by telephone in their native tongue. The tactic proved a success.

The Cherokee "code talkers" were the first known use of Native Americans in the American military to transmit messages under fire, and they continued to serve in this unique capacity for rest of World War I. Their success was part of the inspiration for the better-known use of Navajo code talkers during World War II.

1987 *Dirty Dancing* Filmed at Lake Lure

On August 21, 1987, the blockbuster movie *Dirty Dancing* was released in theaters across the country.

Though set at a resort in the Catskills Mountains of upstate New York, *Dirty Dancing* was shot entirely in Virginia and North Carolina. The filming came to the Southeast almost by accident. When the crew began production in September 1986, they found all the resorts in the New York mountains were closed, so they headed South.

Many of the film's most famous scenes, including the "lake lift" where Patrick Swayze lifts Jennifer Grey in the water and the shots of Grey practicing her moves to the song "Wipe Out" on the stairs on a mountainside, were shot at Lake Lure. The nearby Rumbling Bald Resort's golf course was used for the scene where Grey asks her dad for money, and the Esmeralda Inn was used for interior dance shots.

In 2010 the town of Lake Lure decided to begin celebrating its close association with the smash hit by hosting the *Dirty Dancing* Festival. Now an annual event, the festival draws thousands to Rutherford County each August to commemorate the now classic film and raise money for pancreatic cancer research.

View of a completed Mangum Terrace system in a field near Raleigh, N.C.. The gently sloping land makes necessary only small terrace banks. The rows run across the field in line of greatest level, regardless of the terrace.

1816 North Carolina's "Year Without a Summer," 1816

On August 22, 1816, a heavy frost was recorded in the state.

The unusually early frost was attributed to the Mount Tambora volcano eruption in Indonesia in April of the previous year. The eruption was the most powerful of the nineteenth century and is thought to have caused a number of strange weather phenomena around the world. Mount Tambora is still an active volcano to this day.

The year 1816 is often called "the year without a summer" because of the unusually cold weather during the spring and summer months. The bizarre and destructive weather was the result of massive amounts of volcanic dust being thrown into the upper atmosphere by the eruption.

Much of what we know about the climate of the period comes from *The Records of the Moravians in North Carolina*. Those records indicate a fickle weather pattern of unusual heat in June, an abnormally stormy July, an early August dominated by drought and heat, and the descent of the frost on the 22nd. The frost was followed by more drought, extended periods of rain, then cold, raw weather from late September to the end of the year.

Many crops failed and others had dangerously low yields that threatened the livelihoods and, indeed, the lives of many North Carolinians.

1914 Connie Gay, Country Music Entrepreneur and Starmaker

On August 22, 1914, Country Music Association founder Connie Barriot Gay was born in Lizard Lick in rural Wake County.

After working on his family's tobacco farm as a youth, Gay become an agricultural extension agent. That job led him into radio broadcasting in the 1940s, when he took over the Farm Security Administration's National Farm and Home Hour.

Gay's interest in radio and music grew, and in 1946 he approached the program director of an Arlington, Virginia radio station about starting a country music show called *Town and Country*. Through the show Gay polished the image of what had been known as "hillbilly music," and he is credited with coining the term "country music".

After his radio career ended, Gay went on to be a prime mover and shaker in the growth of the country music industry. Many of the shows he produced sold out to thousands of fans. He teamed up with the *Grand Ole Opry* for several years, planning and promoting shows for radio, the stage, and TV, and in the process discovered Patsy Cline and Jimmy Dean.

After a brief hiatus to address his alcoholism, Gay returned to the public scene to found the Country Music Association and the Country Music Foundation. By 1980 he had earned a spot in the Country Music Hall of Fame.

He died in 1989, leaving a star-studded legacy.

1936 The Nursing Profession and Mary L. Wyche

On August 22, 1936, pioneering nurse Mary L. Wyche died. Wyche was chiefly responsible for establishing nursing as a profession in North Carolina.

Raised in Vance County, she went to work at Rex Hospital in Raleigh and Watts Hospital in Durham shortly after completing her medical training in Philadelphia in 1894. While at Rex in 1901, Wyche organized the Raleigh Nurses' Association. The following year she founded the North Carolina Nurses' Association with fourteen other nurses from around the state. During her six-year tenure as that organization's president, Wyche persuaded the legislature to enact a law concerning the registration of nurses.

Instrumental in the founding of several nursing schools, Wyche retired from active service in 1910 to work on a history of nursing in North Carolina. That history was published two years after her death in 1936. One writer claimed, "What Clara Barton has been to America, Mary Lewis Wyche has been to North Carolina."

1974 By Choice or Coercion

On August 22, 1974, a federal district court judge threw out the suit of Nial Ruth Cox in an action now known as *Cox v. Stanton*.

Cox sought to sue to the state for damages after she was forcibly sterilized under the state's eugenics program at a Plymouth hospital in February 1965. The suit was thrown out in part because she waited too long after the procedure was conducted to file her case. She was represented by a number of attorneys, including Ruth Bader Ginsburg, then co-founder of the Women's Rights Project at the American Civil Liberties Union (ACLU) and the ACLU's general counsel. Cox's attorneys appealed her case to the U.S. Court of Appeals for the Fourth Circuit, which largely upheld the lower court's decision.

Between 1933 and 1977 state action led to the sterilization by choice or coercion of more than seventy-six hundred people through a program authorized by the General Assembly in 1929. Though North Carolina's was only one of many such programs across the country, it was one of the most active.

A movement to compensate those who had been victims of the program began to gain strength in the early 2000s, and in 2013 the General Assembly authorized funds to give each individual victim up to fifty thousand dollars in compensation.

AUG 22

AUG 23

1784 The Lost State of Franklin

On August 23, 1784, the state of Franklin declared its independence from North Carolina. The independence would prove to be short-lived.

Settlers in far western areas had long discussed separating from the Old North State, criticizing the General Assembly for ignoring western interests. Led by John Sevier, the settlers formed their own state. Though they wrote their own state constitution and elected an assembly, western representatives were still sent to North Carolina's General Assembly.

Gov. Alexander Martin was outraged by the separatists and threatened to use force against them. The Confederation Congress, the federal governing body at that time, refused to recognize the new state, which then quickly fell apart. Sevier was elected to the North Carolina Senate in 1789, and the state of Franklin came to an abrupt end. That same year North Carolina ceded some of its western lands to the United States government, and in 1796 those lands became part of the new state of Tennessee.

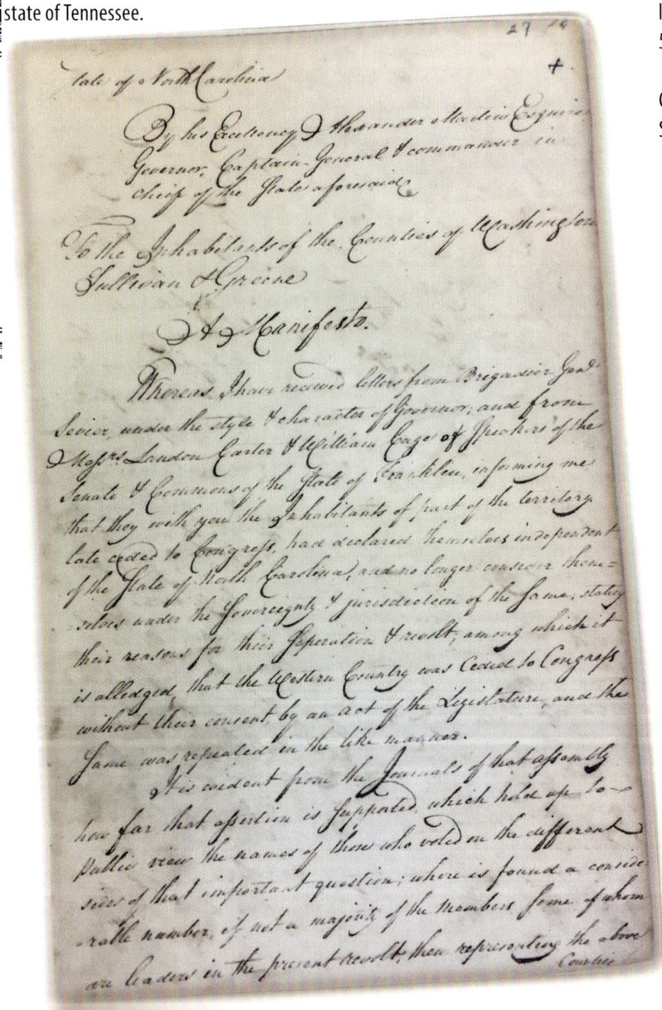
State of North Carolina

By his Excellency Alexander Martin Esquire Governor, Captain General & commander in chief of the State aforesaid

To the Inhabitants of the Counties of Washington Sullivan & Greene

A Manifesto.

Whereas I have received letters from Brigadier Genl. Sevier under the style & character of Governor, and from Messrs. Landon Carter & William Cage as Speakers of the Senate & Commons of the State of Franklin, informing me that they with you the inhabitants of part of the territory late ceded to Congress, had declared themselves independent of the State of North Carolina, and no longer consider themselves under the Sovereignty & jurisdiction of the same, stating their reasons for their Separation & revolt, among which it is alledged that the Western Country was Ceded to Congress without their consent by an act of the Legislature, and the Same was repealed in the like manner.

It is evident from the Journals of that assembly how far that assertion is supported, which hold up to public view the names of those who voted on the different sides of that important question; where is found a considerable number, if not a majority of the members from whom are leaders in the present revolt, then representing the above Counties

Manifesto from citizens of Franklin (*left*).

1934 Duke's Sonny Jurgensen, Key Player for the Washington NFL Team

On August 23, 1934, legendary quarterback Christian Jurgensen, was born in Wilmington. Known to the world as Sonny, the spirited, redheaded Jurgensen is considered one of the all-time best passers in pro football history.

Jurgensen was a multi-talented athlete in Wilmington during the 1940s and 1950s, playing baseball, basketball, football, and tennis. He attended Duke and joined the varsity football squad in 1954 as a defensive back, became the starting quarterback the next year, and led the team to the Orange Bowl.

He then played seven seasons for the Philadelphia Eagles after signing as a fourth-round draft pick in 1957. In 1964 the Eagles traded him to the Washington Redskins, where he spent the rest of his career and helped to change the team's fortunes and image.

Jurgensen achieved legendary status through strength and pinpoint accuracy in passing. Reluctantly forced into retirement in 1975 at age forty-one, he had logged more than 32,000 yards in passing, 255 touchdowns, and an impressive 57% pass completion rate.

In retirement Jurgensen began an enduring sportscasting career, first with CBS and since 1980 for Redskins Radio. He was inducted into the North Carolina Sports Hall of Fame in 1971 and the Pro Football Hall of Fame in 1983.

2005 Alleghany, Ashe, Avery: Top Christmas Tree Producers

On August 23, 2005, the Fraser fir (*Abies fraseri*) was adopted as North Carolina's official state Christmas tree.

The idea came from eighth graders at Spruce Pine's Harris Middle School, who petitioned legislators to bestow the special recognition upon the popular conifer after learning of the economic impact the tree had in the state. The bill was introduced by state representative Philip D. Frye, also of Spruce Pine.

Known as the Cadillac of Christmas trees, fifty million Fraser firs are grown in North Carolina. The tree was named for Scottish botanist John Fraser, who explored the Southern Appalachian mountain region during the late 1700s. The evergreen grows in a cone shape and can reach eighty feet.

Fraser firs represent more than ninety percent of Christmas trees grown in North Carolina. The Tar Heel State's Christmas tree industry is the second largest in the United States, behind Oregon's, and produces twenty percent of all Christmas trees sold in the nation. Trees are raised in more than a dozen western counties, with Alleghany, Ashe, and Avery being the top producers.

North Carolina Fraser firs are known throughout the country and North America. They have been displayed in the White House on twelve occasions, more than any other species of tree.

1814 Dolley Madison and the British Assault on the White House

On August 24, 1814, Dolley Madison rescued several important state documents and a now-famous oil portrait of George Washington from the White House as Washington, D.C. was being burned by invading British forces.

Born Dolley Payne in 1768 in Guilford County, the future First Lady met James Madison through their mutual acquaintance Aaron Burr in Philadelphia in 1794. The couple married less than a year later. While James served as Secretary of State for the widowed Thomas Jefferson, Dolley became the unofficial "first lady," hosting events for politicians and international guests. The 1809 presidential inauguration of her husband, therefore, made for an easy transition to the role of the official First Lady.

When Washington came under siege from the British as part of the War of 1812, President Madison asked his wife to stay behind in the White House and gather important documents so that the building could be abandoned quickly if needed. As the invading force drew near, the First Lady decided to abandon the Pennsylvania Avenue mansion.

Though popular legend tends to tell the story in such a way that Madison herself ripped the portrait out of a frame and hand-carried it and other important documents out of the White House, current historians revisiting the subject argue that household slaves most likely did the heavy lifting under her orders.

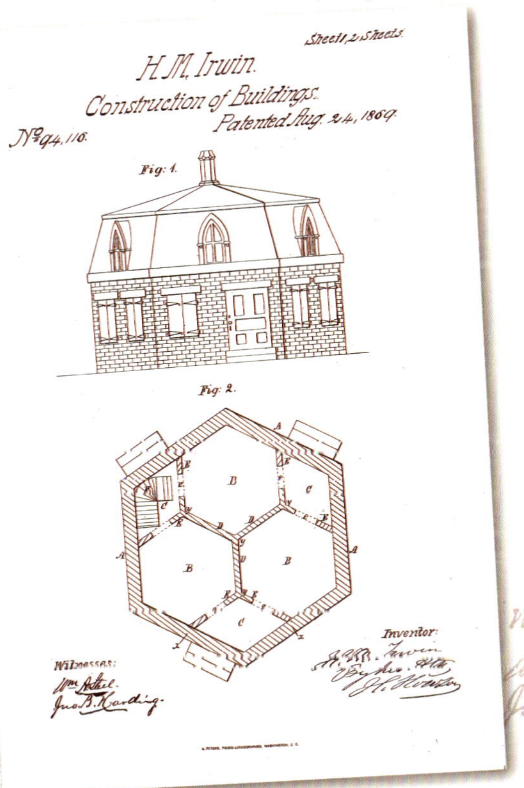

1869 A Hex on Her Houses: Harriet Irwin of Charlotte

On August 24, 1869, Harriet Morrison Irwin became the first woman to patent an architectural design.

She had designed a hexagonal house, planned in such a way that there were no hallways and no four-cornered rooms. Concerned with domestic efficiency, Irwin theorized that her idea utilized space more effectively than a rectangular building and encouraged better airflow. Her ideas received some attention from the press at the time and reportedly inspired at least two houses in Charlotte, though both were later demolished.

Born in Mecklenburg County in 1828 to a prominent clergyman's family, Irwin spent most of her life in and around Charlotte. Aside from her work in architecture, Irwin was an author and social commentator. She wrote primarily nonfiction articles related to history and progress but also one novel concerning her architectural theories, in which the hero lives in a hexagonal house.

She and James Irwin had nine children, five of whom survived infancy. She died in 1897.

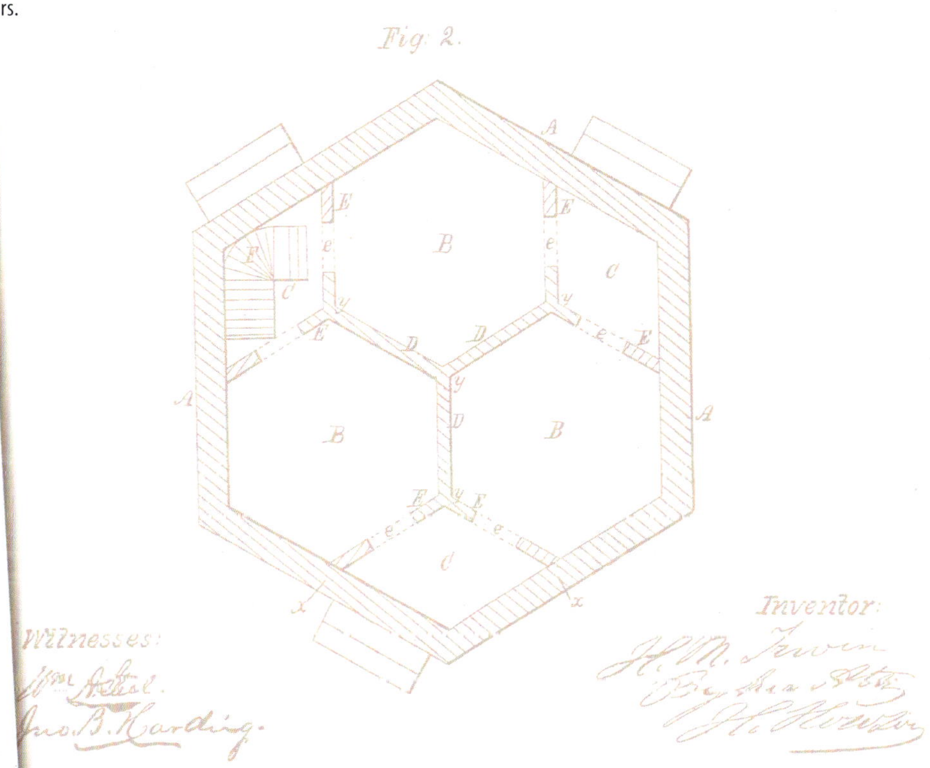

1901 Kenan-Flagler Wedding at Liberty Hall

On August 24, 1901, Mary Lily Kenan, daughter of Capt. William Rand Kenan, married multimillionaire Henry M. Flagler at Liberty Hall in Duplin County. The home of her uncle Thomas Kenan, Liberty Hall, was renovated and lavishly decorated with palms, smilax, and American Beauty and Bridesmaid roses for the ceremony. The wedding was attended by a small group of family and friends.

Much younger than her new husband, Mary Kenan met Flagler through a mutual friend, Pembroke Jones, in Wilmington. As a wedding present for his new wife, Flagler built a fifty-five-thousand-square-foot mansion in Palm Beach, Florida, where the couple lived. That home, Whitehall, is now the Flagler Museum. Liberty Hall in Kenansville is now also a museum.

When Flagler died after falling down some stairs in 1913, Mary Kenan Flagler became one of the wealthiest women in the United States. She did not enjoy it long. In 1917, not long after taking a new husband, she died from an apparent heart attack. The bulk of her fortune was left to her siblings, although a codicil to her will left her new husband five million dollars.

1774 Milestone Move Toward Self-Government, 1774

On August 25, 1774, seventy-one delegates were present at the roll call for North Carolina's First Provincial Congress. It was the first such meeting held in any of the colonies. Though the rebellious Congress was held in New Bern near royal governor Josiah Martin's residence at Tryon Palace, no attempt was made to stop the assembly.

A month earlier William Hooper had convened a meeting of colonists from the Cape Fear region who felt that a Provincial Congress, separate from North Carolina's royal government, was urgently needed. Invitations to send delegates were dispatched and, in response, thirty counties and four towns held elections without delay.

The congress, which lasted only three days, endorsed the proposal that all the colonies hold a Continental Congress. To that end, the group selected William Hooper, Joseph Hewes, and Richard Caswell as delegates to that congress.

Aside from revolutionary topics the delegates also discussed basic rights and responsibilities of government. They were eager to control North Carolina's affairs. The concluding pledge to support the actions of the forthcoming Continental Congress was a testament to their goal of self-government and their preparedness to achieve that goal.

1880 Old Claremont and Education in Hickory

On August 25, 1880, North Carolina granted a charter to Claremont Female College in Hickory. The school, founded by the Evangelical and Reformed Church, started in an old church building. It was modeled after Wellesley College in Massachusetts.

Classes began in September with twenty-one students. Work was completed on a series of college buildings three years later. Following the resignation of Claremont's first president, the school suffered financially until the trustees leased the college to William H. Sanborn, president of nearby Davenport College, who became Claremont's president as well. He resigned the position after four years.

From 1892 to 1907, the college operated with moderate success, attracting students from North Carolina chiefly, but also others from across the South. The trustees, tired of leasing the college to individual presidents, offered the college to the North Carolina Classis of the Reformed Church, that church's governing body in the state. Under the Classis the school was renamed Claremont College.

Claremont operated until 1917, when money troubles caused the school to close indefinitely. Representatives from Horner Military School in Charlotte considered buying the property, but the deal fell through.

Claremont's board of trustees dissolved the charter in 1937. Learning continues at the site as the location for Catawba Valley High School, now operating as Hickory Career & Arts Magnet School.

1962 Little Eva and "The Loco-motion"

On August 25, 1962, Little Eva hit the top of the charts with her recording of "The Loco-Motion." Eva Narcissus Boyd, fresh from her home in Belhaven, can be said to have been in the right place at the right time.

In 1960 Boyd left North Carolina and headed to New York to try to break into the music business. While she sang backup in some studio sessions early on, it was not until "The Loco-Motion" that she got her big break. The seventeen-year-old Boyd worked as a babysitter for songwriters Gerry Goffin and Carole King. The duo wrote the song and asked Boyd to sing on the demo with King doing the backup vocals. While they had intended the song for Dee Dee Sharp, who turned it down, producer Don Kirshner decided that the demo was fine as it was and released it as Little Eva's debut recording.

Little Eva had some modest success with other songs, but none equaled the popularity of "The Loco-Motion." The song has the distinction of being one of the few to reach Number 1 in three different decades with three different artists. Grand Funk Railroad in 1974 and Kylie Minogue in 1987 were the other two.

Boyd died in Kinston in 2003.

Claremont College, Hickory, N.C., circa 1896–1898.

1747 Spaniards Invade Beaufort

On August 26, 1747, Spanish privateers attacked and plundered Beaufort. The attack was the latest in a multi-year period of assaults by the Spanish on the largely undefended coast of North Carolina. It dramatically demonstrated the constant threat the Spanish posed to the small British colony.

Small settlement or not, after three days under siege, the colony's inhabitants fought back and drove the privateers away. From records it is clear that some of the Spanish were taken captive in the skirmish. What was called "the alarm" was in effect until September, when it became clear that the marauders would not be returning.

The next year the Spanish attacked Brunswick and temporarily drove away its inhabitants. As part of an inter-colonial war with the Spanish and French that had roots in Britain's battles with the two countries, the skirmishes ended in 1748 with a treaty that was but a brief respite before the French and Indian War began in 1754.

1902 David Schenck and the Battlefield at Guilford Courthouse

On August 26, 1902, David Schenck, the "father" of Guilford Courthouse National Military Park, died.

Born in 1835 in Lincolnton, Schenck and his family moved to Greensboro for his job as a lawyer for the company that became Southern Railway. He became immersed in local history almost immediately after moving to the area, including a special interest in the Battle of Guilford Courthouse. He traversed the ground with locals, inquiring as to the specific pieces of property associated with the 1781 engagement. He knew that if the battlefield was not protected, it would be lost to encroaching development. In 1886 he recorded in his diary that he had decided to buy the land to, in his words, "redeem the battlefield from oblivion," and the same day he purchased thirty acres of the site to achieve that end.

The following year Schenck organized the Guilford Battle Ground Company. Although he died in 1902, the organization carried on and, through its actions, the battleground was donated to the U.S. Department of the Interior, which organized it as the Guilford Courthouse National Military Park in 1917.

The battlefield was the first from the Revolutionary War to be protected by the federal government. The Guilford Battleground Company, as Schenck's organization is known today, continues to purchase property associated with the site and donate it to the National Park Service.

AUG 26

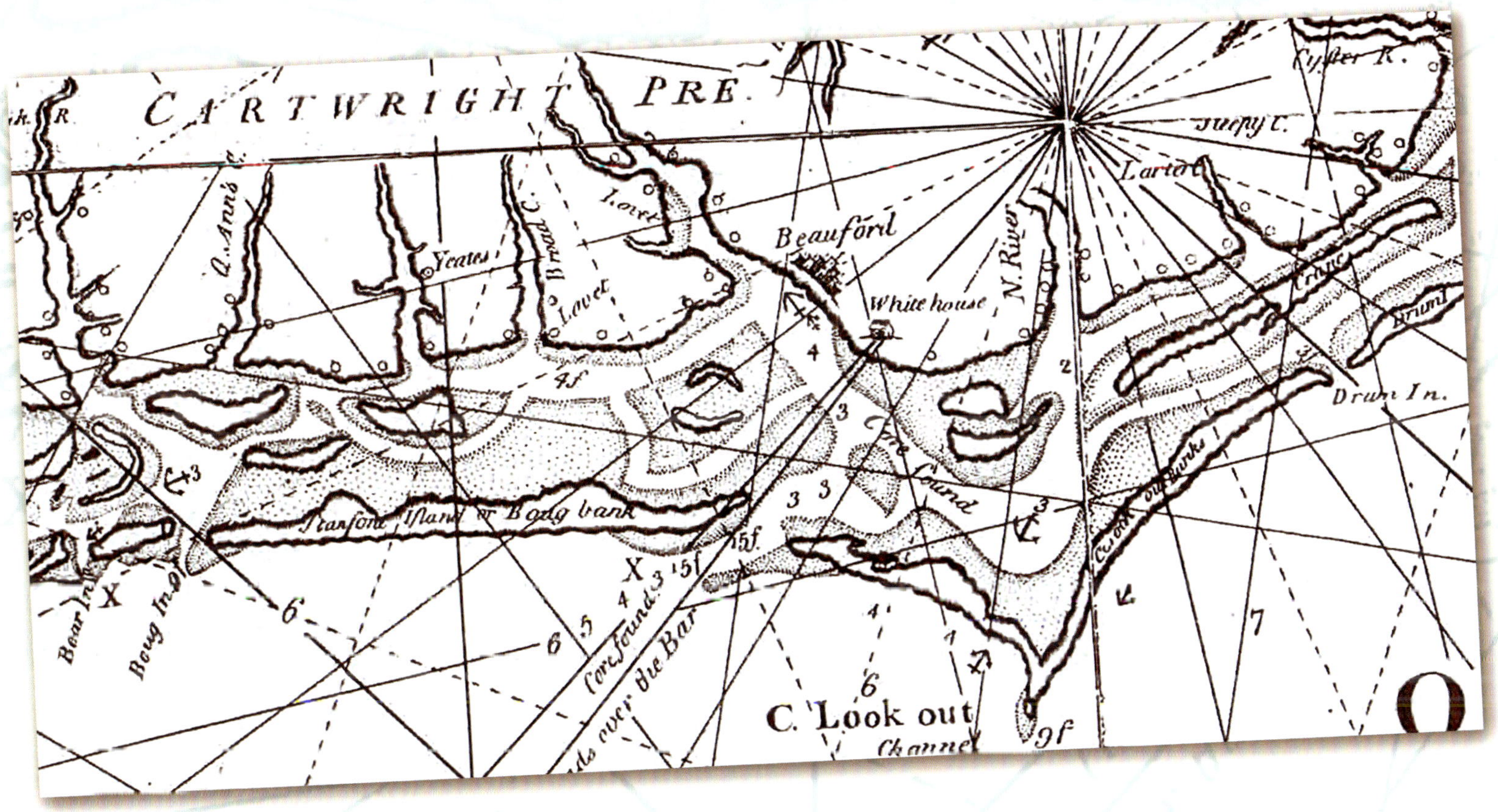

Portion of Wimble's 1738 map of North Carolina, showing Beaufort.

AUG 27

1781 Battle of Elizabethtown Culminated at the Tory Hole

On August 27, 1781, the Revolutionary War Battle of Elizabethtown was fought. Two weeks earlier, Loyalist forces under Col. John Slingsby had captured several Whig—that is Patriot—supporters in what's now Fayetteville. Slingsby brought his prisoners to Elizabethtown in Bladen County.

The day before the battle, a local resident named Sallie Salter entered the Tory camp to sell eggs. Unbeknownst to them, she was a Patriot spy. She reported to Cols. Thomas Robeson Jr. and Thomas Brown, commanders of a band of Bladen County militiamen that had withdrawn to Duplin County. Her information led to a decision to attack Slingsby. This was a considerable gamble, as the Patriot command numbered between sixty and seventy men, while Slingsby's forces totaled three to four hundred.

After a night march the militiamen launched a surprise attack on Slingsby's camp. The resulting confusion was amplified by the successful efforts of the Whigs to make the Tories think that there were far more Patriots present than there actually were.

With Slingsby dead, the Tories retreated to a ravine, afterwards called the "Tory Hole." There they were fired upon until they surrendered. The Patriot victory permanently weakened Tory power in the Cape Fear region.

1891 Tragedy at Bostian Bridge, 1891

On August 27, 1891, one of the worst train wrecks in North Carolina occurred at the Bostian Bridge, two miles west of Statesville.

In the wee hours of the morning, a westbound passenger train jumped the tracks and hurtled off the sixty-foot-high bridge. At the bottom of its fall, seven railroad cars crashed into Third Creek. A few of the passengers walked into Statesville for help. Others crawled out of the wreckage, dazed and confused, and some wandered around. Still others sat on top of the cars until help arrived.

When that help did come in the form of Statesville townspeople, the group began to pull and cut people out of the wreckage. Since the water in the creek was high, some of the injured drowned. By dawn a large crowd of townspeople had arrived and began to move the dead and wounded into town.

The dead were laid out in the Farmers' Tobacco Warehouse. Twenty passengers were killed outright, nine were seriously injured, and about twenty more received minor injuries.

The Bostian Bridge train wreck has been the subject of many ghost-hunting expeditions, as a ghostly specter of the train is said to be seen each year on the anniversary of the tragedy.

1961 Flight of Robert Williams as Racial Tensions Rise in Monroe, 1961

On August 27, 1961, protests in Monroe escalated into a riot, leading to local NAACP leader Robert Williams later being charged with kidnapping and fleeing across state lines.

In late August 1961 a group of Freedom Riders, along with members of other civil rights organizations, traveled to Monroe, where they hoped to assist Williams. He aimed to press charges against a Ku Klux Klansman who had assaulted him the previous year. They planned to carry out peaceful demonstrations.

Despite the group's nonviolent discipline, confrontations escalated. On August 27, as the crowd at the courthouse grew unruly, the police line collapsed, and a white mob attacked some of the activists. The remaining picketers were loaded into cars and taken into custody. Gunfire was heard around Monroe for hours, and a policeman was wounded.

Shortly thereafter, a white couple made a wrong turn onto Williams's street. His supporters forcibly removed the couple from their car and took them to his house, where they were held by armed individuals for a while. They later were released unharmed.

Upon learning of the kidnapping charges against him, Williams escaped with his family to Cuba, where by 1963 he was broadcasting a radio program called Radio Free Dixie.

Bostian Bridge train wreck.

1898 "Brad's Drink" Becomes Pepsi-Cola, 1898

On August 28, 1898, "Pepsi-Cola" got its name.

Beginning in 1893, New Bern pharmacist Caleb Bradham developed and began serving a carbonated drink he called "Brad's Drink." He served the beverage from the soda fountain in his pharmacy at the corner of Pollock and Middle Streets.

As a pharmacist who had undergone some medical training, Bradham believed in the health, energy, and digestive benefits of his sweet and bubbly brew, which originally included the enzyme pepsin and the cola nut. Those ingredients probably resulted in the renaming of the drink, although at some point pepsin was removed from the formula.

After the renaming Bradham managed to purchase the trade name "Pep Cola" from a New Jersey company, and in 1902 he incorporated the Pepsi-Cola Company under North Carolina law. Shortly thereafter he registered a patent for the formula.

From there the business quickly grew. By 1910 the beverage was being bottled at more than three hundred companies in twenty-four states. A combination of factors including fluctuations in sugar prices and supply, imperfect bottling technology, and poor marketing resulted in a failing business after World War I, and Bradham was forced to sell the company.

1942 Laurinburg-Maxton Army Air Base and Glider Warfare

On August 28, 1942, the U.S. Army activated Laurinburg-Maxton Army Air Base in Scotland County. The facility, where glider pilots trained, played a little known role in the Allied victory in World War II.

Germany had pioneered the use of gliders, demonstrating their effectiveness in Holland and on Crete. The individual most responsible for incorporating gliders into the U.S. military was Maj. Gen. William C. Lee, who had initiated the use of airborne forces at Fort Bragg and Camp Mackall.

The Laurinburg-Maxton base housed the First Troop Carrier Command. The forty-six-hundred-acre base contained three sixty-five-hundred-foot long runways that formed a triangle. The triangle's center was 510 acres of Bermuda grass, the landing site for the gliders.

The U.S. Navy and Marine Corps considered the glider concept viable as well and incorporated the craft into their own training exercises. From 1942 to 1945, thousands trained for combat in Scotland County, including troops that took part in the D-Day invasion at Normandy.

At the war's conclusion the base was deactivated. With the advent of helicopters, the military had no further need for the glider program. The Scotland Memorial Hospital was housed on the base's former site from 1946 to 1951, and today the facility houses an industrial park and public airport.

1974 The Real "Norma Rae"

On August 28, 1974, workers at the J. P. Stevens plant in Roanoke Rapids voted to unionize.

The vote to affiliate with the Amalgamated Clothing and Textile Workers Union was the culmination of efforts by Crystal Lee Sutton, who worked for $2.65 per hour folding towels in the plant. It was an important event in North Carolina, which was the least unionized state in the nation at the time.

"Management and others treated me as if I had leprosy," Sutton later recalled. The turning point was when she wrote "UNION" on a scrap of cardboard and stood atop her work station. One by one coworkers cut off their machines, and the plant became quiet. Sutton was fired by J. P. Stevens but later, under court order, was rehired with reinstated back wages. She soon left, however, to become a full-time organizer.

The story of Crystal Sutton and the organizing campaign at J. P. Stevens is depicted in the 1979 film, *Norma Rae*. Sally Field won an Academy Award for Best Actress for her portrayal of Sutton. The real Crystal Sutton, who deposited her papers at Alamance Community College in Burlington, died in 2009.

Laurinburg-Maxton Army Air Base postcard, 1943.

Raleigh Pepsi distributor readies Grape-Ola delivery (*background*).

AUG 29

1879 Influential Black Newspaperman Robert Lee Vann

On August 29, 1879, Robert Lee Vann born was born in Hertford County. Vann attended Waters Training School in Winton, graduating as valedictorian. In 1903 he received a scholarship to Western University of Pennsylvania, where he completed college and law school and served as the first black editor of the student journal.

In 1910 Vann became counsel to the incorporation of the *Pittsburgh Courier* and within a few months became the paper's editor. While continuing his private law practice, he remained the paper's editor, treasurer, and chief counsel until his death. By 1937 the *Courier* was the nation's largest weekly newspaper for African Americans. It became distinguished for its national and international coverage and columns written by black leaders such as W. E. B. DuBois and Marcus Garvey. Vann used the editorial pages to advocate various social and political reforms.

Vann died at his home in Pittsburgh in October 1940 and is buried at Homewood Cemetery in that city. A Liberty ship named after him was launched just three years later in 1943. The former segregated black high school in Ahoskie bore his name; that building later housed a middle school under the same name.

1882 Connie Guion, Pioneering Female Physician

On August 29, 1882, pioneering physician Connie Guion was born on a plantation near Lincolnton.

Educated at Wellesley College and Cornell Medical School, Guion earned her medical degree and interned at New York City's Bellevue Hospital during the flu epidemic of 1918. Her success in a time of crisis there gained her a national reputation in medicine at a time when few women entered the field.

For almost fifty years she was associated with the Cornell medical clinic, where she became a full professor in 1946. Known for working twelve-hour days until her retirement at age eighty-seven, she was described by the *New York Herald Tribune* as the "greatest lady of our time."

At her death in 1971, Dr. Guion was the dean of the nation's women physicians. The first female professor of clinical medicine at an American university, the first female member of the medical board of New York Hospital, and the first living female doctor for whom a major hospital building was named, Guion was a true pioneer for women in the medical field.

She visited her native state often and is buried in Charlotte.

1969 Betty Debnam and the "Mini Page"

On August 29, 1969, the *News and Observer* published the first issue of the "Mini Page."

From its first appearance in the Raleigh newspaper in 1969 to its final publication in 2007, the "Mini Page" engaged children through fun and educational activities. Through the paper, kids could be like adults, reading their own page in the newspaper and learning at the same time.

Created by UNC graduate, *News and Observer* editor, and former elementary school teacher Betty Debnam, the "Mini Page" quickly took off. In 1970 the *Charlotte News* became the first paper outside of Raleigh to publish the section; national syndication followed in 1977. At its peak the "Mini Page" appeared in more than five hundred newspapers weekly.

Debnam was the section's sole staff member for many years, writing and editing all the content and laying the feature out, though she did eventually have two staff members come on board. During her time with the publication, she wrote several "Mini Page" companion books and won numerous awards including the Newspaper Association of America's first Lifetime Achievement Award.

Betty Debnam with the first Mini Page Annual in her home office in 2014.

1794 Andre Michaux Climbed Grandfather Mountain

On August 30, 1794, French explorer and botanist Andre Michaux climbed Grandfather Mountain. Upon reaching the summit, he believed he had climbed the highest peak in North America. Michaux was ultimately proven wrong because Mt. Mitchell rises more than seven hundred feet taller than Grandfather's 5,945 feet.

At the time of the American Revolution, the value of the unexplored regions of the new nation was unknown, especially along the barrier of thickly forested slopes of the Appalachian Mountains. French King Louis XVI appointed Michaux as Royal Botanist and sent him to investigate the plants in America that might be of value.

Michaux's foray to the top of Grandfather was not his last visit to the Tar Heel state. In fact, he frequently returned to North Carolina in search of plants new to science and for the enrichment of French agriculture and forestry. He would describe and name a significant percentage of the vascular plants native to the Carolinas.

1983 Astronaut William Thornton and the Space Shuttle Challenger

On August 30, 1983, Faison native William Thornton barreled into space from Cape Canaveral, Florida aboard the shuttle *Challenger*.

Born in Duplin County, Thornton received bachelors and medical degrees from UNC-Chapel Hill and worked as an electronics engineer before entering the U.S. Air Force. It was during his two-year tour of duty with the Air Force that he became involved in space medicine research and subsequently applied for astronaut training.

After being selected as a scientist-astronaut by NASA in August 1967, Thornton worked on a number of Skylab simulation missions and spent decades doing research work. Two of his primary areas of focus were measuring mass (weight) in space and the reaction of the human body to conditions in space.

Thornton holds more than thirty-five patents that range from military weapons systems to the first real-time EKG computer analysis. Among other things he developed a treadmill for in-flight exercise and designed the first mass-measuring devices for space, which remain in use today.

A veteran of two space flights, Thornton logged over 313 hours in space. After serving as a mission specialist on the shuttle *Challenger* in 1983, he held the same role on *Challenger's* 1985 mission. He retired from NASA in 1994.

1986 A Reunion Without Precedent, at Somerset Place in 1986

On August 30, 1986, "Somerset Homecoming" took place at Somerset Place State Historic Site in Creswell.

The homecoming was the first-ever event of its kind: a reunion of descendants of the enslaved community of a large southern plantation. Organized by Dorothy Spruill Redford, a descendant of the enslaved community and in time the site manager of Somerset Place, the homecoming brought together hundreds of family members from around the country and garnered international attention.

Somerset Place was home to more than 850 slaves when it was active from 1785 until 1865. As a historic site, it was interpreted for years mainly in terms of the wealth of the Collins family, which owned the plantation, and the fact that the operation was among the largest and most economically successful in the state. Redford shifted the site's focus and began telling the stories of all the families who lived there.

Recognizing the enslaved people's contributions to the success of the plantation, Redford was quoted by the *New York Times* during the homecoming as saying, "From this day forward, there will always be a shared recognition. They'll think of the Josiah Collins family, but they'll think of my family too." She described the State Historic Site as "a living monument to ordinary folks—to our toil, our lives, our lineage."

AUG 30

Visitors enjoy the first Somerset homecoming in 1986

AUG 31

1823 Jesse Franklin, Governor from Surry County

On August 31, 1823, former governor Jesse Franklin died at his home in Surry County. He was sixty-three years old.

Born in 1760 in Orange County, Virginia, Franklin moved to North Carolina in 1776. He fought at the Battles of King's Mountain and Guilford Courthouse on the Patriot side and rose to the rank of major.

After the Revolution Franklin served in the state legislature, representing both Wilkes and Surry Counties, before serving a single term in the U.S. House of Representatives and two terms in the Senate. In 1816 Franklin became part of a commission, with David Meriwether and Andrew Jackson, to negotiate settlements with the Cherokee and Chickasaw.

By the time he was elected governor in 1820, Franklin was sixty years old, overweight, and in declining health. Despite his health issues, Franklin carried out his duties conscientiously and with his characteristic simplicity and practicality. He is perhaps best known for reforming the state's penal code and advocating the delineation of the state's borders.

Franklin declined to run for a second term and returned to his Surry County home, where he remained until his death in 1823.

1886 Charleston Earthquake Rattled North Carolina

On August 31, 1886, at 9:50 p.m., the largest earthquake ever recorded on the east coast of the United States destroyed homes and other property in Charleston, South Carolina, leaving as many as 150 dead in that city alone. Registering between 6.6 and 7.3 on the modern Richter scale, the quake cracked chimneys and plaster walls across North Carolina.

The bell in Asheville's city hall tolled as the ground shook. The Reverend Anthony Porter, rector of Holy Communion Episcopal Church in Charleston, was vacationing in Asheville that night. He later recorded what he perceived first as his wife moving furniture, then as carriages arriving in the yard, then as railroad cars approaching, and finally, when a corner of the residence was raised and then slammed to the ground, as an earthquake.

Reports of the quake came in from across the Tar Heel state. The lighthouse keeper at Cape Hatteras felt the rumblings and saw windows broken in the tower. Effects were documented in Elizabethtown, Stovall, Huntersville, Raleigh, Hillsborough, and Waynesville. The Northampton County Courthouse in Jackson had its walls damaged. To this day the large brick chimney outside the Carson House in Marion carries a crack made by the 1886 Charleston earthquake.

1938 Samuel A. Ashe, Confederate Soldier and Historian

On August 31, 1938, historian Samuel A. Ashe died.

A descendant of Gov. Samuel Ashe of Pender County, the historian was born near Wilmington in 1840 and studied at the U.S. Naval Academy. At the outbreak of the Civil War he went to work for the Confederacy as a soldier and engineer. His final assignment of the war was at the Fayetteville arsenal in 1865.

After the war Wilmingtonians elected Ashe to one term in the state House of Representatives. Having moved his law practice to Raleigh while serving in the legislature, he remained in the capital, reviving what became the *News and Observer* in 1881.

As he aged, Ashe's interests moved toward history, and he compiled the still-vital *Biographical History of North Carolina*. He also wrote the two-volume *History of North Carolina*, as well as numerous other historical works.

On what would have been his hundredth birthday, and only three years after his death, Ashe received the rare tribute of a monument on the grounds of the State Capitol when a bronze tablet in his memory was dedicated.

1950 Dorton Arena Architect Matthew Nowicki

On August 31, 1950, architect and designer Matthew Nowicki, best known for engineering the landmark Dorton Arena on the State Fairgrounds, died in a plane crash. He was returning from a trip to India where he was engaged in planning the new Punjab capital city of Chandigarh. He had sketched the arena's preliminary drawings just before his departure.

A Polish immigrant to the U.S., Nowicki and his wife were members of the founding faculty of N.C. State's School of Design. He became involved in the Dorton Arena project after one of his colleagues at State introduced him to North Carolina State Fair Manager J. S. Dorton, who sought to make the fair the most modern in the world.

After his death Nowicki's widow, Siasia, teamed up with Raleigh architect William Dietrick to realize his vision. Upon the arena's completion, its designers were recipients of the first American Institute of Architects Honor Award in 1953, and Dorton Arena was recognized as a National Civil Engineering Landmark. The structure was listed in the National Register of Historic Places in 1973 for its exceptional national significance only twenty-one years after its construction.

Though Nowicki is remembered mainly for his work on Dorton, the project was only one of his masterpieces. Before the Raleigh undertaking, Norwicki was well-known for designing several public structures in Poland, helping to rebuild the greater Warsaw area after World War II, and working on the team that designed the United Nations headquarters in New York.

1781 Opening Volley in North Carolina's Tory War

On September 1, 1781, Tory forces under Col. David Fanning skirmished with the Patriot command of Col. Thomas Wade. The clash is variously known as McPhaul's Mill, Little Raft Swamp, Drowning Creek, and Bettis's Bridge.

McPhaul's Mill was located on Little Raft Swamp near modern Antioch in Hoke County. Fanning arrived at the mill in late August. He received word that Loyalists under Col. Hector McNeill were nearby, pursued by Wade's Patriot force. The two Tory commanders agreed to cooperate to trap Wade. They met at Bettis's Bridge on the morning of September 1. The exact site of the bridge is unknown.

Wade's camp was on a hill between Drowning Creek and Little Raft Swamp. Although badly outnumbered, Fanning decided to attack.

McNeill would block Wade's escape across Bettis's Bridge. Fanning's presence was given away when one of his men accidentally discharged his firearm. Wade's men quickly organized and opened fire. Wade withdrew after a fight of nearly two hours. As McNeill posted only a small force at the bridge, Wade's men were able to escape.

Afterwards Fanning left McNeill and moved to the Deep River, setting the stage for his raid on Hillsborough and capture of Gov. Thomas Burke on September 12, 1781.

1870 Freedom Fighter Abraham Galloway of Southport and Wilmington

On September 1, 1870, African-American activist Abraham Galloway died in Wilmington.

Born in 1837 in what is now the town of Southport, Galloway was the son of a white ship's pilot and a slave. He escaped to the North by ship in 1857 and became active in militant abolitionist circles.

During the Civil War Galloway led black recruitment efforts in the federally occupied northeastern portion of the state to fill the ranks of what would become Gen. Edward Wild's African Brigade. For the volunteers he secured pay equal to that of the Massachusetts regiments, educational opportunities for soldiers' children, and support for their families, most of whom were destitute.

As the war waned, Galloway began shifting his focus to the political struggle for equal treatment and organized the Equal Rights League, which lobbied for rights for freed slaves, including education, protection from violence, and the right to vote.

Galloway and the league organized the state's first freedmen's convention, held in Raleigh in September 1865, to represent the interests of the state's black population as the constitutional convention convened across town.

The apex of Galloway's political career came in 1868 when he was among the first black men to be elected to the state Senate. He would serve there until his death.

HON. ABRAM GALLOWAY.

1896 "Human Spider" Inspired Classic Harold Lloyd Film

On September 1, 1896, Bill Strother, who became nationally acclaimed as the "Human Spider," was born in Wayne County.

Strother acquired his nickname in Kinston in 1915. Frustrated that handbills he ordered to advertise a real estate auction he was organizing did not arrive in time, Strother indicated to a fellow diner at a lunch counter that he'd now have to climb the courthouse walls to advertise the sale. The diner, who happened to be the editor of the *Kinston Free Press*, published a story about the proposed climb, and thousands showed up to watch.

The PR stunt worked, and that day Strother sold a fortune in real estate, while also unknowingly launching his career as the Human Spider. For a while Strother climbed buildings only to advertise real estate sales, but in December 1917 he began climbing just for climbing's sake.

In 1922 silent film star Harold Lloyd saw Strother climb a building in Los Angeles. The chance meeting resulted in movie called *Safety Last!*, in which Lloyd's character climbed a building to win over a girl. Strother played Lloyd's friend "Limpy" Bill in the 1923 release. He continuing climbing buildings across the country before retiring after a fall in 1930.

Strother died in a car accident in 1957.

1898 Carl Schenck and the Cradle of Forestry

On September 1, 1898, Carl Schenck opened the nation's first school of forestry. The school had its roots in 1895, when George Vanderbilt, who had just completed the Biltmore House, hired German-born Schenck to manage and restore his vast woodland properties.

Students who enrolled in Schenck's school used Vanderbilt's forests as a campus, splitting their time between classrooms and fieldwork. Combining theory with practice, they gained experience in the care of nurseries, the transplanting and cultivation of seedlings, timber selection, felling, logging, and sawing.

Schenck had a disagreement with Vanderbilt and left the estate in 1909, establishing the school's winter headquarters in Germany. He struggled to maintain the school as a traveling entity in America, and enrollment dwindled as new forestry schools emerged. Schenck's final class graduated in 1913, and most of the school's alumni (who numbered more than three hundred) became actively employed in the field. In 1914 Vanderbilt's widow sold more than eighty thousand acres of her holdings to the U.S. Forest Service. The acquisition was incorporated into the Pisgah National Forest.

In 1968 the federal government established the Cradle of Forestry on the site of Schenck's school to commemorate the beginning of forestry education and conservation in the United States.

1890 Elon University's Beginnings Date to Nineteenth Century

On September 2, 1890, Elon College opened as a four-year liberal arts college in Alamance County.

Plans for the school had been underway since 1872, when what is now the United Church of Christ decided to open a college. The institution was first called Graham College, but when the trustees were unable to acquire land in that small Alamance County town, a different location for the campus was selected west of Burlington. When the land, filled with old oak trees, was being cleared, the name Elon seemed like a natural fit, since "elon" is the Hebrew word for oak.

The community around the school grew quickly and was incorporated in 1893 as Elon College. The town's streets were given names commemorating important figures in the development of the Christian Church and of the college. In January 1923 the main campus building was destroyed by fire. During the reconstruction, which took about three years, the campus was expanded with five new buildings.

Elon College added graduate degree programs in the 1980s. To reflect the school's diverse programs and growing student body, the college changed its name to Elon University in 2000. With that change the surrounding town changed its name, too, from Elon College to Elon.

Main Building at Elon College, 1901.

1911 Masterful American Artist, Romare Bearden of Charlotte

On September 2, 1911, Romare Bearden, one of the twentieth century's most important African American artists, was born in Charlotte.

Bearden studied at the Art Students League in New York City, Columbia University, and the Sorbonne. For thirty years, he worked on his art at night and on weekends while employed as a social worker in New York City. Bearden's first solo exhibition was in Harlem in 1940. His collages, watercolors, oils, photomontages, and prints depict black culture in a style derived from Cubism. Bearden also was a songwriter and book illustrator, as well as a set designer for the Alvin Ailey American Dance Company.

An advocate for young and emerging talents, Bearden had close associations with distinguished artists, intellectuals, and musicians, including Alvin Ailey, James Baldwin, Duke Ellington, Ralph Ellison, George Grosz, Langston Hughes, Jacob Lawrence, and Joan Miró.

Although his family moved north when he was only four years old, he said of his home state, "Most artists take some place, and like a flower, they sink roots, looking for universal implications. . . .My roots are in North Carolina." Indeed, many of his paintings and collages were drawn from memories of his time in North Carolina.

Throughout his career he received a host of honors, including the Mayor's Award of Honor for Art and Culture in New York City in 1984 and the National Medal of Arts in 1987.

Bearden died in New York City in 1988.

Romare Bearden, 1944.

1952 Mile-High Swinging Bridge Dedicated

On September 2, 1952, gubernatorial candidate William B. Umstead dedicated Grandfather Mountain's Mile-High Swinging Bridge near Linville, and his daughter Merle became the first person to cross it.

Hugh Morton was the man behind the now-famous bridge. In 1947 Morton returned from military service overseas and assumed control of the Linville Improvement Company, which owned Grandfather Mountain. After his grandfather Hugh MacRae died in 1951, the company was dissolved and the next year Morton inherited Grandfather Mountain in the division of land among family. At the time the only road up the mountain led to Cliffside Overlook, where visitors could enjoy the view and a small gift shop. Morton envisioned building a bridge between Grandfather's Convention Table Rock and Linville Peak to improve visitors' access to the best scenic overlooks.

Designed by Greensboro architect Charles Hartmann, Jr., and fabricated by Truitt Manufacturing Company in Greensboro, the 228-foot suspension bridge was reassembled in three weeks at Grandfather Mountain by Craven Steel Erecting Company. The total cost was $15,000.

In 1999, the mostly wooden bridge was rebuilt using galvanized steel at a cost of $300,000.

Former state tourism director Charles J. Parker coined the name "Mile-High Swinging Bridge" at the 1952 dedication. While the bridge's elevation is slightly more than a mile above sea level, it actually hangs only 80 feet above the ground.

And while suspension bridges can swing, especially in high winds, thick cables anchor Grandfather Mountain's bridge to the ground, limiting its movement.

Umstead taking the first steps over Grandfather Mountain's "Mile-High Swinging Bridge" during its dedication in 1952.

1585 North Carolina's Original Tourism Slogan, 1585

On September 3, 1585, Ralph Lane described the Virginia Colony, which included present-day North Carolina, as, "the goodliest soile under the cope of Heaven." Lane, leader of the second group of English voyagers sent to explore the colony, used the phrase in a letter to Richard Hakluyt the elder, an Englishman who promoted New World exploration.

Describing the Virginia Colony as a land of unexplored greatness with many native people living in rudimentary villages, Lane found the climate wholesome and pleasant, stating that no one among his crew fell ill while visiting. He further claimed that the New World had no equal in the known world at the time.

There is debate among historians over whether Lane was giving an accurate description of Virginia or simply trying to increase the likelihood that a permanent English settlement would be established in the colony. Regardless of questions surrounding the description's intent, the phrase "goodliest soile under the cope of heaven" is revered by North Carolinians and seen as an apt accounting of the natural beauty of the state.

1912 Inventor, Businesswoman by Design, Beulah Henry

On September 3, 1912, Beulah Henry, later nicknamed "Lady Edison," received her first patent while living in Charlotte. Her invention, a vacuum ice cream freezer, was followed the next year by improvements to the handbag and parasol.

Although she attended Queens and Elizabeth Colleges in Charlotte, Beulah Louise Henry never had formal training in mechanics or technology. Yet the prolific designer received forty-nine patents and is credited with over a hundred inventions.

Henry was born in Raleigh in 1887. As an adult, she lived in New York City, where she established Henry Umbrella and Parasol Company and later the self-named B. L. Henry Company.

Among her many successful inventions were the double-chain-stitch sewing machine, a duplicating attachment for typewriters, and a duplex sound producer. The designs would spring into her mind fully formed, then she would describe what she saw to draftsmen and mechanics. She once said, "I invent because I cannot help myself."

Henry is one of only a very few American women in the early 1900s who were able to make their livings as inventors.

1960 Fast Food Emporium Opened in Greenville, 1960

On September 3, 1960, Wilbur Hardee opened a drive-in hamburger stand in Greenville, launching what would become Hardee's Food Systems, Inc., the fifth-largest fast-food restaurant chain in the United States.

The former Martin County farm boy and World War II Navy cook initially sold his charcoal-broiled hamburgers and milkshakes for fifteen cents each, mainly to students at nearby East Carolina University. In 1961 Hardee took on two partners and opened a second restaurant in Rocky Mount. By 1963 the business had grown to a five-restaurant franchise.

Hardee lost controlling interest in the operation that same year during a card game with his partners. He later sold his remaining shares for thirty-seven thousand dollars, but his namesake eatery wasn't his only endeavor. During his lifetime he opened eighty-five restaurants throughout the Southeast, including Biscuit Town, Hot Dog City, and Beef and Shake. He also started another hamburger chain called Little Mint that grew to twenty-five locations in the Carolinas.

But it was the Hardee's chain that achieved the greatest success. In 1997 St. Louis-based CKE Restaurants Inc. bought Hardee's, which in 2016 boasted more than two thousand locations worldwide and 1.8 billion dollars in revenue.

1991 Chicken Plant Fire in Hamlet, 1991

On September 3, 1991, a fire swept through the Imperial Food Products plant in Hamlet, killing twenty-five people and injuring fifty-six others in one of the state's deadliest industrial accidents.

The fire started inside the chicken processing plant at about 8:15 a.m., when a hydraulic line ruptured, spraying fluid into gas burners beneath a deep-fat fryer. Blocked and/or locked exit doors prevented workers from escaping the thick smoke and flames. Investigators later found the plant had no sprinkler or fire alarm systems, had never undergone a safety inspection, and had never held fire-safety drills for workers. Outrage over the violations sparked national attention and prompted calls for workplace safety improvements. In 1992 the General Assembly approved a package of workplace safety bills, and the state labor department hired additional inspectors.

In time the Occupational Safety and Health Administration cited Imperial for eighty-three safety violations, resulting in $808,150 in penalties. Plant owner Emmett Roe filed bankruptcy and closed the plant. He accepted a plea agreement on involuntary manslaughter charges and was sentenced to nearly twenty years in prison but was paroled in 1997 after serving four and a half years. Around twenty civil suits were filed against Imperial. Bankruptcy court eventually paid about sixteen million dollars to survivors and victims' families.

First Hardee's franchise restaurant, McDonald Street, Rocky Mount, N.C., early 1980s.

SEP 4

1748 Spaniards Surprised at Brunswick, 1748

On September 4, 1748, sailors from two Spanish ships came ashore and attacked the town of Brunswick. Terrified at the sight of Spanish ships in the Cape Fear River, the residents of the port town gathered as many of their possessions as possible and fled.

A call for help was sounded, and William Dry gathered his company of militia in an attempt to drive the Spanish out. The sixty-seven-man force surprised the Spanish sailors, who were busy looting the town. Unprepared for the encounter, many were killed or captured as they scrambled back to their ships. In the ensuing battle one of the Spanish ships exploded and sank, leading the other ship to disengage and leave the area.

Dry's militiamen and some hired sailors salvaged as many valuables as possible from the sunken privateer, selling the ship's contents and even some Spanish slaves. The proceeds of the sale partially financed the construction of St. Philip's Church at Brunswick and St. James's Church in Wilmington.

The attack had exposed the vulnerability of Brunswick and likely contributed to its eventual abandonment.

1826 John Fulenwider, Lincoln County Ironmaker

On September 4, 1826, early industrialist John Fulenwider died.

Born in Switzerland in 1756, Fulenwider moved to North Carolina with his family and settled in Rowan County. After fighting on the Patriot side at the Battle of Ramsour's Mill, he took up iron manufacturing, along with many others who received land grants of three thousand acres and tax deferrals under the state's 1788 "Act to Encourage the Building of Iron Works."

Fulenwider settled in Lincoln County, finding that it provided all of the essential ingredients for success: iron ore, trees for charcoal, limestone, and falling water. He established two forges around 1795, with the one at High Shoals becoming his most important foundry.

His works produced nails, farm and kitchen implements, bar iron, and wagon wheels, and he developed one of the earliest methods for making pig iron. During the War of 1812, the High Shoals ironworks produced cannon balls for use by the American army. The works operated for more than seventy years, until 1875.

At his death in 1826, Fulenwider left more than twenty thousand acres of land and accumulated wealth to his heirs. He is remembered as part of an important cadre of entrepreneurs who spurred the development of iron manufacturing.

1957 Dorothy Counts Enrolls at Charlotte's Harding High School, 1957

On September 4, 1957, Dorothy Counts enrolled at Harding High School, one of four segregated white schools in Charlotte to receive their first African American students that day. She was accompanied by Reginald Hawkins, a dentist, who would go on to be the first black man in the modern South to seek statewide office when he ran for governor in 1968.

Counts, only fifteen at the time, encountered a mob on the sidewalk. White boys and girls, encouraged by their parents, jeered and spat on her. She endured the harassment stoically and marched proudly into a classroom, where other students hissed, mocked, and threw garbage at her and where the teachers ignored her. Newspaper photographers captured the scene outside and inside the school. The episode embarrassed and shamed many in the city.

After a week Counts's father withdrew her from Harding and moved the family to Philadelphia. She returned to Charlotte for college at Johnson C. Smith University and dedicated her career to work in Queen City nonprofit organizations and as an advocate for child care.

Desegregation of schools in Charlotte was still unresolved twelve years later, when in 1969 Judge Robert McMillan issued a decision mandating busing to achieve integration.

1802 Spaight-Stanly Duel

On September 5, 1802, political rivals John Stanly and Richard Dobbs Spaight, both armed with smooth-bore flintlock pistols, took deliberate aim at each other and fired. It was 5:30 p.m., and the pair were positioned behind the Masonic lodge in New Bern. Approximately three hundred spectators crowded around.

After three rounds of loading and firing, only Stanly's coat had been hit. Bystanders begged the men to stop, but Spaight's supporters urged him on. The gentlemen reloaded and aimed again. On the fourth discharge Spaight fell, struck in his side by a bullet. He died the next day.

The confrontation came after the men exchanged two years of personal attacks through newspapers, handbills, and street corner oratory. Their public bickering reached its climax when Spaight released a flier calling Stanly "a liar and scoundrel," insults which prompted the duel.

Spaight's death outraged his friends and family, who sought to have Stanly tried for murder. Though Gov. Benjamin Williams pardoned Stanly, the General Assembly responded by passing a law that prevented duel participants from holding public office and hit them with a hefty fine. Most duels moved out-of-state as a result.

1891 Asheville's Young Men's Institute, Gift of George Vanderbilt

On September 5, 1891, George W. Vanderbilt II purchased land for the Young Men's Institute in Asheville.

During construction of his lavish home in that city, Vanderbilt decided to establish a community center for his African American workers. The building, constructed in 1892 and 1893, was designed by Richard Sharp Smith, who was also the supervising architect of the Biltmore House.

The Young Men's Institute, or YMI, was the true center of the civic, cultural, and business life of Asheville's black community. It featured a gym, bathing facilities, public library, and classes for children and adults. By 1910 the organization had its own orchestra. Churches, schools, and civic organizations used the venue for gatherings, and a variety of businesses and institutions kept offices in the building.

As the YMI grew, it became less connected with the Vanderbilt family, and in May 1906 it was incorporated, with forty-nine of Asheville's black leaders as board members. During the Great Depression the YMI became part of the YMCA, and that organization closed the building in 1970. After the structure was condemned and threated with demolition, the African American community in Asheville rallied to save it in 1977 and was able to get it placed on the National Register of Historic Places.

The building underwent extensive renovation in the 1980s and remains a vibrant part of the community as the YMI Cultural Center.

1917 Pamlico Pacesetter in School Transportation

On September 5, 1917, the Pamlico County school system inaugurated the first motorized school bus service in North Carolina.

Pamlico, among the most rural counties in the state, sought to make transportation for students faster and easier. Before the widespread use of automobiles, horse-drawn wagons were used to transport students to school, and the state didn't establish that student transportation could come at public expense until 1911.

Pamlico County's first bus was purchased from the Corbitt Company of Henderson and cost $1,379. The bus could seat thirty passengers and was used to transport students in and around Oriental. The introduction of a motorized bus to deliver students from outlying areas to the schoolhouse was considered a logistical triumph. As a result, school districts could move from scattered networks of one-room schoolhouses to modern, centralized schools with more professional staff.

To publicize the innovation, Pamlico's superintendent drove the bus to Raleigh and gave Gov. Thomas Bickett and other politicians a ride around the city. The success of Pamlico's first school bus was quickly followed by similar purchases in other rural counties.

1953 State's On-Campus Nuclear Reactor

On September 5, 1953, a nuclear reactor went online at North Carolina State College (now North Carolina State University) in Raleigh, making it the world's first nuclear research reactor to be designed, built, and operated by an academic institution. Producing thermal rather than electrical watts, the reactor gave nuclear engineering students a hands-on opportunity to learn about nuclear reactor operation.

The roots of N. C. State's nuclear engineering program go back to 1949, when Dean Harold Lampe recruited Dr. Clifford Beck from Oak Ridge National Laboratory to oversee creation of the college's original reactor. The Atomic Energy Commission approved the project in 1950, and Burlington Laboratory was built on campus to house the ten-kilowatt reactor, called R-1.

Corrosion-related fuel leaks soon caused its shutdown, but in 1957 the school upgraded to a more powerful reactor, R-2. Another upgraded model, R-3, went online in 1960 and operated until 1973, when NCSU's one-megawatt PULSTAR reactor was constructed. The university received a federal grant in 2010 to upgrade its PULSTAR to two megawatts of energy, allowing nuclear engineering students to conduct more complex experiments.

The old R-3 reactor was dismantled, and its control panels given to the North Carolina Museum of History in 1984.

"Atomic installation at college" shows three men and a large computer bank and console in the nuclear reactor at N. C. State College, 1958.

1856 Brightleaf Tobacco and the Benefits of Napping

On September 6, 1856, Abisha Slade of Caswell County spoke at an agricultural meeting about "the new process of curing yellow tobacco."

The talk reflected an agricultural breakthrough that had been discovered by one of Slade's slaves by mistake in 1839. The slave, named Stephen, worked as a blacksmith and oversaw the curing process of the tobacco crop on Slade's farm.

One day Stephen fell asleep in the tobacco curing barn, succumbing to the warmth of the curing shed's fire. Waking up he found the fire almost completely out. He retrieved charred logs from his blacksmithing equipment and threw them on the fire, creating sudden, intense heat. The heat cured the tobacco quickly, leaving it with a vivid yellow color.

Stephen's accidental discovery became what is known in the industry as flue-cured tobacco and to consumers as brightleaf tobacco. It was an instant hit with smokers. By 1857 Slade was harvesting twenty thousand pounds annually and making some of the highest profits ever. The sandy, relatively infertile soil of many North Carolina farms was ideal for growing tobacco for such a curing process.

The development of brightleaf tobacco was what ultimately led North Carolina to a dominant position in the tobacco industry.

SEP 6

1958 Art Museum Founding Director William Valentiner

On September 6, 1958, William R. Valentiner, former director of the North Carolina Museum of Art, died in New York after a short illness.

Born in Germany in 1880, Wilhelm Rheinhold Otto Valentiner came to the United States in 1908 as the Curator of Decorative Arts at the Metropolitan Museum of Art in New York. In 1914 he returned to Germany and enlisted as a private in the German Army. There, in 1919, he joined the November Group, an organization of artists with socialist ideals. While in Germany, he advised the Detroit Institute of Arts on its acquisitions, and in 1924, one year after his returning to the U.S., he became the director of that institution. He became an American citizen in 1930. In 1955 he was hired as the founding director of the North Carolina Museum of Art.

During his lifetime Valentiner founded and served as editor of two art journals and as Director General for the "Masterpieces of Art" exhibition for the 1939 World's Fair. He left pieces from his personal art collection to the North Carolina Museum of Art, and the State Archives holds a significant collection of his personal papers.

Valentiner *(left)* with museum guests, 1956.

1846 Two Major Inlets on the Outer Banks Date to 1846

1859 John Merrick of Durham, Founder of North Carolina Mutual

1860 Charles McIver and Female Education as a Public Investment

1881 Georgia Poet Sidney Lanier Died in Polk County

On September 7, 1846, a violent hurricane hit the Outer Banks and opened Hatteras and Oregon Inlets. Families that lived on Hatteras Island later said they had no idea that it was possible for an inlet to form near their homes, but the following morning, "[T]hey saw the sea and sound connected together and the live oaks washing up by the roots and tumbling into the ocean."

Oregon is what's called a dynamic inlet, one prone to natural changes. It has remained open, but between 1846 and 1989, it migrated about two miles south of the original breach. A bridge across Oregon Inlet was completed in 1963. The movement of the inlet and the recent move to replace the bridge continues to cause controversy among citizens, politicians, business leaders, and conservationists.

During the Civil War Hatteras Inlet, thirty miles to the south, was the scene of a federal invasion. Forts Hatteras and Clark were hastily constructed on either side of the inlet in the summer of 1861 and shortly thereafter fell into the hands of federal troops, giving the Union navy an open door into Pamlico and Albemarle Sounds. Today transportation across Hatteras Inlet is sustained by a state-operated ferry.

On September 7, 1859, John Merrick was born into slavery in Sampson County. When he was twelve years old, Merrick and his mother moved to Chapel Hill, where he worked in a brickyard and she was a house servant.

When his mother remarried and moved away, Merrick remained in North Carolina and established himself as a brick mason in Raleigh, working on the construction of Shaw University. Economic fluctuations compelled him to take a second job as a bootblack in a barbershop.

Merrick soon became a barber and advanced through the ranks until he owned five barbershops in Durham by 1892, three for whites and two for blacks. He also helped establish the Royal Knights of King David, a fraternal insurance company.

His experience with the Royal Knights led Merrick to launch what became the North Carolina Mutual Life Insurance Company, later the largest black-owned business in the United States. He was president of Mutual Life until his death in 1919.

During World War II, the Liberty Ship *John Merrick* was launched by the North Carolina Shipbuilding Company in Wilmington.

On September 7, 1860, educator and founding president of UNC-Greensboro Charles Duncan McIver was born in what's now Lee County.

McIver studied at UNC and worked at schools across North Carolina after graduating, developing a strong interest in teacher education. As a leader at what's now the North Carolina Education Association in the late 1880s, he advocated for the improvement of women's education.

After making a number of changes to the way public higher education in the state was organized, in 1891 the legislature approved the establishment of the State Normal and Industrial School for Girls, now UNC-Greensboro. The school was intended to "prepare young women to earn a livelihood in teaching or in business," and when it opened in October 1892, McIver was selected as its president.

McIver stayed in the top job at the Greensboro school until his death in 1906, helping the fledgling institution prosper despite a number of obstacles, including a typhoid fever epidemic in 1899 and the destruction of the main dormitory by fire in 1904.

During his time in Greensboro, McIver remained active in state and regional education circles, serving as president of the Southern Education Association and a University of North Carolina trustee.

On September 7, 1881, Sidney Lanier, widely-acclaimed poet, author, and musician, died at his home in Polk County.

A Georgia native, Lanier spent time in North Carolina during the Civil War when his unit was assigned to help construct Fort Fisher. While there, he wrote some of his earliest poetry. After transferring to the Confederate Signal Corps, Lanier was assigned to a fleet of blockade runners that operated out of the lower Cape Fear River. In 1864 he was captured just off Fort Fisher by the Union Navy. While confined at Point Lookout, Maryland he translated several literary works and reflected on his wartime experiences. His 1867 novel *Tiger-Lilies* was based in part on his Civil War service.

Lanier contracted tuberculosis after his release in 1865 and from then on struggled through intermittent bouts of the disease. He moved to Asheville in 1881, shortly before moving again to Lynn in Polk County. In Lynn he wrote his last poems and succumbed to his illness.

The house Lanier occupied in Lynn still stands, along with a library that bears his name in nearby Tryon. He was immortalized in stone at Duke Chapel in Durham, as one of three "Great Men of the South."

John Merrick, 1917.

Charles Duncan McIver, about 1895.

SEP 8

1663 Colington Island, a Reminder of the Proprietary Era

On September 8, 1663, the first transfer of land under the Lords Proprietors in Carolina took place. The grant was made to Sir John Colleton, himself one of the Lords Proprietors of Carolina.

The piece of land transferred was then called Carlyle or Colleton Island and is now called Colington Island in Dare County. Colleton, a planter who also dabbled in business, finance, and politics, already had large New World holdings in Barbados. Although he had returned to England in 1660, he hoped to expand his West Indies operations into the American colonies.

Colleton's agent, Capt. John Whittie, established a plantation on the property during the winter of 1664 and 1665. At first the island was used primarily for raising cattle and horses, but eventually crops including tobacco, corn, and grapes were planted. Whittie eventually realized a profitable second income by selling oil extracted from whales that washed up on the shore.

Peter Carteret, nephew of one of the proprietors and later governor of the colony, joined Colleton as a partner in the colonial venture. He arrived in the spring of 1665 to take charge of the plantation.

Hurricanes, drought, and floods plagued the settlement, which failed by the 1670s.

1712 Edward Hyde and Turmoil in Early Carolina

On September 8, 1712, Gov. Edward Hyde died of yellow fever at his home on Albemarle Sound.

Born in 1667 in England, Hyde inherited several properties and had ties to royalty. He attended Oxford University but didn't complete a degree. Despite his connections and inheritance, Hyde faced financial ruin and sold much of his property.

In 1708 Hyde petitioned the queen for a governorship in Carolina, specifically the deputy governorship of northern Carolina, which was then available. He received the commission in early 1709 and arrived in Virginia to find a great deal of political upheaval. He remained in Virginia until there was agreement in the colony that Hyde was indeed the commissioned leader.

Hyde assumed his duties as royal governor in 1711 but was in a politically precarious position during the uprising known as Cary's Rebellion. That year the colony also suffered from both a yellow fever epidemic and the outbreak of the Tuscarora War after an attack near Bath.

1896 Jordan Lake's Namesake Served in U.S. Senate

On September 8, 1896, B. Everett Jordan was born in Ramseur. Before being appointed to fill the vacant seat of Sen. Kerr Scott in 1958, he was a successful textile executive who had worked his way up the ladder in one company since the 1920s.

Although several newspapers at the time considered him to have been placed in the Senate as a "seat warmer" for Luther Hodges, who was then governor and popular politically, Jordan was reelected in 1960 and 1966. His work in the Senate focused on Agriculture and Forestry, Public Works, and Senate Rules and Administration Committees. He introduced the tobacco "acreage-poundage" legislation that changed the way tobacco was marketed and valued. He also helped the state to acquire federal funds for water resources and harbor improvements.

Jordan's age and health were key factors in the 1972 Democratic primary race for his Senate seat. He was defeated by Nick Galifianakis, who in turn lost the general election to Republican Jesse Helms.

The Chatham County New Hope Lake project, authorized in 1963, was renamed in honor of Jordan in 1973.

1956 Half-Measure Pearsall Plan Target of Critics

On September 8, 1956, North Carolina voters approved a set of education initiatives known as the Pearsall Plan.

The initiatives had been proposed by an advisory committee on education tasked by Govs. William Umstead and Luther Hodges to respond to the Supreme Court's 1954 *Brown v. Board of Education* decision on school segregation.

The committee concluded that integration "should not be attempted" since there was not enough support for it statewide and recommended that the power of assigning students to schools be moved to the local level. Two other components in the bill allowed residents to call for a referendum on whether their local schools should be integrated and pledged the state to pay private school tuition for students unhappy with their assignment.

Though the plan was opposed by civil rights advocates for blocking court-mandated integration and by ardent segregationists for not doing enough to prevent it, it passed by a wide margin. Most of the components were never invoked, and it was ultimately struck down as unconstitutional by a federal court after a 1966 challenge by renowned civil rights attorney Julius Chambers.

Edward Hyde, oil painting, 1977 (copy of original).

B. Everett Jordan

1820 Heroine of the American Revolution Martha Bell

On September 9, 1820, Martha McFarlane McGee Bell, heroine of the American Revolution, died at her home in Randolph County.

The wife of a Deep River gristmill owner, Bell and her husband were ardent supporters of American independence, and their mill became a gathering place for local patriots during the war. There is also evidence that the Continental Army used the mill to store supplies.

Bell's credit as heroine, though, stems from an incident following the Battle of Guilford Courthouse. British Gen. Charles Cornwallis camped at the Bells' mill for two days, needing to grind corn for his troops and time to rest and treat the wounded. Bell treated the British hospitably and nursed the injured in return for Cornwallis's promise that his troops would do her property no harm. The British left without incident.

When American Gen. "Lighthorse" Harry Lee arrived at the mill shortly after the British departed, he encouraged Bell to visit Cornwallis at his next camp on a ruse related to property damage. Bell acted as a spy for the patriots, noting details as to Cornwallis's troops and supplies.

A monument on the grounds of Guilford Courthouse National Military Park honors Bell.

1961 Our Only Miss America

On September 9, 1961, Maria Beale Fletcher of Asheville became the first—and, so far, only—Miss North Carolina to be crowned Miss America.

Born June 23, 1942, she was the oldest child of Charles Beale Fletcher and Margaret Gatley Fletcher, a nationally touring dance duo. When she reached school age, her parents decided to settle in Asheville, where they founded and operated the Fletcher School of Dance and the Land of the Sky Civic Ballet. Fletcher won her first trophy at age seven for singing and dancing at Asheville's Mountain Youth Jamboree. In 1960 she graduated from A.C. Reynolds High School and headed to New York City to fulfill her dream of being a Radio City Music Hall Rockette. That same year the nineteen-year-old became Miss Asheville. Six months later she claimed the Miss North Carolina title.

At the national pageant in Atlantic City, New Jersey, Fletcher won the preliminary swimsuit competition and, for talent, tap-danced to a recording of herself singing "Somebody Loves Me." With her Miss America scholarship winnings, she earned a degree at Vanderbilt University and became a successful businesswoman, wife, and mother.

2009 The Man Who Destroyed the Recording Industry

On September 9, 2009, Bennie Lydell Glover of Shelby was indicted in Alexandria, Virginia for felony conspiracy to commit copyright infringement.

Two years earlier Glover left work to encounter Cleveland County deputies alongside his truck. As deputies arrested him, the FBI was simultaneously raiding his house.

The popular assumption is that Napster, created in 1999, was chiefly responsible for the plummet in sales of recorded music. But recent accounts make clear that Glover was there first and created the most damage.

Employed at Polygram's CD pressing plant in Kings Mountain, Glover began slipping disks out of the factory as early as 1994. He regularly took movies and video games but found a market for rap CDs, especially artists like Jay Z, Eminem, and in time Kanye West.

He would drop off bags of disks for resale at Shelby barbershops and, via Internet file sharing, found listeners all across the country. Polygram fought back, installing increased security measures, but Glover long evaded the law, sneaking CDs out behind oversize belt buckles past wand-wielding guards.

Glover, who testified against his co-conspirator, pled guilty and served three months in prison. Meanwhile sales of recorded music shrank, with total revenue cut in half between 2000 and 2010.

Maria Beale Fletcher won the Miss North Carolina crown (1961) and Miss America (1962), appeared in an Asheville parade in 1962.

SEP
10

1776 The Rutherford Trace and the Destruction of Nikwasi

On September 10, 1776, during the American Revolution, North Carolina Gen. Griffith Rutherford attacked and burned the Cherokee town of Nikwasi as part of what became known as the "Rutherford Trace." It was part of a united effort by North Carolina, South Carolina, and Virginia to weaken the Cherokee Indians before they could fully ally and coordinate attacks with British troops. The campaign also was retribution for the punishment enacted by the native people against the newly arrived settlers in the west.

Nikwasi covered approximately one hundred acres in what is now Macon County and was a spiritual and ceremonial center for the Cherokee, who inhabited it until 1819, when they were forced off their lands. The present-day town of Franklin was built on it, and a large mound in the commercial district is all that remains of the former Cherokee presence.

The expedition decimated many Cherokee towns in just a few weeks. The destruction of crops, livestock, and food stores effectively ended the military threat of the Cherokee. As refugees, surviving over the winter on wild game, nuts, and fruits, the remaining Cherokee signed peace treaties the following year.

1778 Joshua Lawrence and Schism among North Carolina Baptists

On September 10, 1778, Joshua Lawrence, Baptist minister and one of the founding members of the Primitive Baptist Movement, was born on his family's farm in Edgecombe County.

Lawrence was called to the ministry in 1801, when he was twenty-three. He became pastor of the Falls of the Tar Baptist Church, later founded the Tarboro Baptist Church, and led that church until its division in 1829. Though he was known for his commanding presence in the pulpit and as an eloquent preacher, he didn't have any formal training as a minister.

In 1803 Lawrence became a delegate to the Kehukee Baptist Association and became embroiled in the struggle between missionary and anti-missionary supporters among the North Carolina Baptists. Lawrence believed that it was important to preserve "the Christian religion in its primitive state" and insisted that those in the ministry should not use their positions for material gain.

The author of a number of pamphlets supporting what would later become the Primitive Baptist Movement, Lawrence supported the idea of cutting ties with the missionary Baptist movement, which would later form the Baptist State Convention of North Carolina.

Lawrence continued to preach until his death in 1843.

1934 Road for Charles Kuralt Began, Ended in North Carolina

On September 10, 1934, celebrated CBS journalist, television news anchor, and bestselling author Charles Kuralt was born in Wilmington.

The winner of 12 Emmys and two Peabody Awards, Kuralt showed early promise as a writer. Voted "Most Likely to Succeed" by Charlotte's Central High School class of 1951, the budding writer attended UNC, where he was editor of the *Daily Tar Heel*.

Kuralt's first professional job was with the *Charlotte News*, where he wrote an award winning column called "Charles Kuralt's People." In 1957, at age twenty-three, he became the youngest correspondent ever hired by CBS News.

A decade later, during a period of war and riots, he experimented with a good-news segment on *The CBS Evening News with Walter Cronkite*. Called "On the Road," the feature ran for more than twenty years. During that time Kuralt and his crew wore out six campers in crisscrossing the country's back roads and telling stories about ordinary Americans. He later anchored *CBS Sunday Morning* before retiring in 1994.

Kuralt died in July 1997 at age sixty-two of complications from lupus. At his request, he was buried in the Old Chapel Hill Cemetery on UNC's campus.

1976 Aquariums Date to Bicentennial Year

On September 10, 1976, the facilities now known as the North Carolina Aquariums opened to the public for the first time. Their mission was to promote the awareness, understanding, appreciation, and conservation of the diverse natural and cultural resources of North Carolina's ocean, estuaries, rivers, streams, and other aquatic environments.

Known as the North Carolina Marine Resources Centers until 1986, the aquariums at Manteo, Pine Knoll Shores, and Kure Beach, were originally intended as research facilities than as destinations for visitors. A fifty-three-million-dollar construction program in the early 1990s dramatically expanded the footprint of each facility and offered more opportunities for visitors to interact with nature. Jennette's Pier became part of the state aquarium system in 2011.

Each aquarium and Jennette's Pier highlight the unique aquatic environments found in the region in which it is located and in different locations across the state. Together they welcome more than a million visitors annually and are rated among the best places to visit across the state.

Helping to conserve North Carolina's unique coastal environment and conducting cutting-edge research continue to be central to the aquariums' mission.

Charles Kuralt leaning against the CBS "On the Road" van.

1885 Moses Hopkins, From Slavery to Liberia via Franklinton

On September 11, 1885, Moses A. Hopkins was appointed Minister to Liberia.

Born into slavery in Virginia in 1846, Hopkins worked as a cook in Union camps during the Civil War. In 1866, at age twenty, he learned to read, launching his lifelong interest in education. When he completed his degree in theology in 1877, he was the first African American graduate of Auburn Seminary in New York. Ordained by the Presbyterian Church in 1877, Hopkins moved to Franklinton.

In Franklinton Hopkins founded Mt. Pleasant Presbyterian Church and Albion Academy. He led Albion through its formative years and published a newspaper, *The Freedmen's Friend*, with his wife Carrie. The only known issue is from August 1884.

When Hopkins was appointed Minister to Liberia, he reported to Monrovia within a month. He died there in August 1886. His place of burial is unknown.

1961 A Lift to Winter Tourism, Cataloochee

On September 11, 1961, North Carolina's first ski resort, Cataloochee Ski Slopes, was incorporated. The Haywood County recreation area opened to skiers on December 22.

Tom Alexander, the resort's owner, was a true pioneer, as Cataloochee was not only the first ski resort in the state, but the first south of Virginia. He and wife Judith operated Cataloochee Ranch on top of Fie Top Mountain, which offered horseback riding, fishing, hiking, and lodge and cabin accommodations during the summer months. The plan for an all-season resort was driven in part by Alexander's desire to keep his staff employed year-round.

Because skiing was new to the area, Alexander and his family had to learn by trial and error about such things as creating a functioning tow line. In order to cater to novice southern skiers, Cataloochee's first slopes were not steep and had no turns or moguls. The novelty quickly attracted visitors from across the South and was a boon to local hotel and cottage court owners, who were delighted when their accommodations booked up during the winter months.

North Carolina now boasts six ski resorts in a number of western counties, contributing significantly to winter tourism in the region.

1987 Viaduct an Engineering Marvel

On September 11, 1987, the Linn Cove Viaduct—part of the Blue Ridge Parkway—was completed in Avery County. Internationally recognized as an engineering marvel, the curved bridge spans 1,243 feet and hugs an especially sensitive area of Grandfather Mountain.

Construction began in 1979 and cost about ten million dollars. The S-curve bridge consists of more than 150 precast individual segments joined together on Grandfather Mountain with epoxy glue and tension cables. Each of the segments weighs about fifty tons and is a different shape; only one is square and straight.

To minimize damage to the environment, the bridge served as its own building platform. Workers placed one segment after another, using the bridge as their access road. As a consequence, the viaduct proved that bridges could both achieve their transportation function and preserve the environment at the same time.

Since its opening, the viaduct has received numerous design awards, including a Presidential Design Award in 1984 and the American Consulting Engineers Council Award for Engineering Excellence in 1985. It is operated by the National Park Service as part of the Blue Ridge Parkway.

The Linn Cove Viaduct was the first precast concrete segmental viaduct to be built with the progressive method in the United States.

1781 Thomas Burke, Governor as Prisoner of War

1857 Bounty Off Cape Hatteras in Shipwreck of the Central America

1925 Jurist W. A. Hoke of Lincolnton

1927 Founders Day at UNC-Asheville

SEP 12

On September 12, 1781, Thomas Burke, then only three months into his term as governor, was captured in Hillsborough by Loyalist raiders commanded by Col. David Fanning.

The state at the time was ravaged by war and on the brink of anarchy. The recent departures of both the Continental and British armies left roving bands of Patriot and Loyalist guerrillas in their wake that were subject to no civil or military authority.

Burke, who was in Hillsborough to organize militia activities, was surprised by Fanning and surrendered after a brief fight. Burke was taken to Wilmington, then to South Carolina, paroled, and confined to James Island to await a prisoner exchange.

Fearing that his life was in danger, Burke escaped from his very loose confinement and returned to North Carolina and the governorship, violating both his parole and the code of honor in the eyes of many of his contemporaries. When the embittered Burke convened the General Assembly in April 1782, his rather ambiguous offer to retire from public office was accepted almost without remark. Having served only ten months as governor, two of those as a prisoner, he returned to Hillsborough a ruined and deeply disillusioned man.

On September 12, 1857, the SS *Central America* sank two hundred miles off Cape Hatteras with great loss of life. The side-wheel steamer was bound for New York from Havana when she encountered a hurricane and sprung a leak.

In addition to about five hundred passengers and a crew of one hundred aboard, the *Central America* was carrying mail and more than $1.5 million in gold, including coins minted in San Francisco. Around 145 people aboard the ill-fated ship were rescued by three vessels in the vicinity of the wreck at the time of the sinking, but the rest perished.

The great loss of gold was a contributing factor to the Panic of 1857, a short yet severe economic downturn fueled by a loss of confidence in the banking system. The panic was marked by suspension of gold payments by financial institutions, business failures, factory closings, and a rise in unemployment.

Treasure hunters discovered the wreck of the SS *Central America* in 1988, and salvage of the gold began but was halted by a court order in 1991. In April 2014 Odyssey Marine Exploration resumed recovery of the *Central America's* lost treasure. To date more than 13,500 coins, bars, and ingots have been recovered.

On September 12, 1925, prominent jurist William Alexander Hoke died. Born in Lincolnton in 1851, Hoke attended the Lincolnton Male Academy and later studied law under Chief Justice Richmond Pearson at Richmond Hill. He was admitted to the bar in 1872 and was elected to the North Carolina House of Representatives in 1889.

Hoke's career on the bench began in 1890 when he was elected a judge for the Superior Court. He was elected an associate justice of the North Carolina Supreme Court in 1904 and served continuously until he was appointed chief justice in 1924 upon the death of Walter Clark. He resigned in March 1925 due to failing health.

Hoke regarded his chairing the commission to secure a statue of his friend, former governor Zebulon B. Vance, for the National Statuary Hall in Washington, D.C. as the high point of his life. He delivered the presentation address when the statue was dedicated in 1916. It is said that Hoke was sitting in a chair at Rex Hospital telling his doctor about that day when he died suddenly of heart failure.

On September 12, 1927, eighty-five students enrolled at Buncombe County Junior College, predecessor of UNC-Asheville, for its opening day. At the time, the college was the first in the state to be operated by a county, and tuition was free. It grew into one of the founding institutions of North Carolina's community college system and today is North Carolina's dedicated public liberal arts college.

The college started with initial discussions between A.C. Reynolds, then superintendent of Buncombe County Schools, and T.M. Howerton, L.D. Maney, and D.S. Roberts of the Biltmore School Committee. Its first site was at Biltmore High School, now known as the Historic Biltmore School. Buncombe County Junior College later became Biltmore Junior College and gained its charter under the name Asheville-Biltmore College. The college purchased land for its current location in 1958, with a groundbreaking in 1959, becoming UNC-Asheville a decade later in 1969.

Today, UNC-Asheville celebrates September 12 as Founders Day, a tradition begun in 1997, when the university also dedicated Founders Hall in honor of the pioneering students, staff and faculty of the school and its predecessor institutions that helped build a distinctive educational institution for Asheville and North Carolina. The 2008 celebration included the dedication of A.C. Reynolds Green in honor of the university founder.

The remains of a wood cargo box retrieved from the wreck of the *SS Central America* was filled with freshly minted $20 "Double Eagle" U.S. gold coins struck at the San Francisco Mint in the mid-1850s.

1781 Militia Clash at Lindley's Mill

On September 13, 1781, the largest engagement of North Carolina's "Tory War" took place in present-day Alamance County near Thomas Lindley's mill. In the aftermath of Lord Charles Cornwallis's invasion of North Carolina in the spring of 1781, a prolonged civil conflict erupted in the Piedmont. Whig and Loyalist militias openly attacked each other, as well as neutral parties.

At dawn on September 12, under the cover of a heavy fog, David Fanning's men entered Hillsborough, taking the town by surprise and capturing two hundred prisoners, including much of the General Assembly and Gov. Thomas Burke. Fanning and his men, their prisoners in tow, departed for Wilmington in the afternoon.

Word of the disaster reached Brig. Gen. John Butler of the North Carolina militia that evening. Butler quickly organized men from Orange County to intercept the Tory force. Butler's four hundred men arrived ahead of Fanning at Lindley's Mill. On the morning of September 13, fighting erupted. When it was all over, Fanning had received a serious wound in his arm, forcing him to retire from the field. That night, local Quakers collected the dead and wounded on the field. Local surgeons were called upon to help administer to the wounded.

1938 The Bard of Ottaray, Shepherd Dugger

On September 13, 1938, Shepherd Dugger, chronicler of North Carolina mountain life, died.

In 1881 Dugger, became the first superintendent of Watauga County's public schools. After holding that position for a single four-year term, he opened a hotel at the base of Grandfather Mountain, with partner J. Erwin Callaway. He married Callaway's daughter, Margaret, in 1887. After Margaret's death, Dugger raised two sons and pursued his interests in mining and surveying. He also began to write and publish books and pamphlets related to his beloved mountains, known to the Indians as "Ottaray."

Dugger served as superintendent of roads in Avery County, later calling himself "the Colossus of Roads," and worked as a surveyor and highway engineer for seventeen years, usually traveling the mountain roads by foot, carrying a walking stick. Along the road he gave lectures, read from his works, and stayed in local people's homes.

The writer's most notable books are *The Balsam Groves of the Grandfather Mountain* and *The War Trails of the Blue Ridge*, published in 1892 and 1932, respectively. It's been said of him: "No man knew the Blue Ridge people, lore, habits, and tastes better than Shepherd Dugger. In his day he was the foremost historian of the region and recorder of its traditions."

Dugger is buried in Banner Elk.

1948 Trials and Tribulation: Life in an Iron Lung

On September 13, 1948, eleven-year-old Martha Mason of Lattimore in Cleveland County came down with polio on the very day her parents buried her older brother Gaston, who had succumbed to the disease. They were both victims of a major polio outbreak that year. Martha survived, but became a quadriplegic dependent on an iron lung for the next sixty years.

Mason's condition did not inhibit her spirit or intellectual curiosity. With the help of parents, teachers, and friends she graduated first in her high school class and then *summa cum laude* from Wake Forest in 1960. She wrote newspaper articles with her mother taking dictation, until incapacitating illnesses struck both her parents.

Mason chose to remain at home in an iron lung despite the development of other, less restrictive ventilators, and she was known in Lattimore for her spark and outgoing personality.

In the 1990s the advent of the personal computer and assistive technology broadened her reach and allowed her to realize her dream of writing. Her memoir of her life in the small town, *Breath: A Lifetime in the Rhythm of an Iron Lung*, was published in 2003.

Mason was also the subject of a documentary film, and she appeared in another about the effort to eradicate polio. At her death in 2009, she was believed to be the longest survivor of a life lived in the eight-hundred-pound device.

1952 Village People's Cowboy Hailed from Raleigh

On September 13, 1952, singer Randy Jones of the disco group Village People was born in Raleigh.

Jones grew up in Wake County, graduating from Enloe High School in 1970. After attending the North Carolina School of the Arts and UNC, he began to dance and act professionally in New York City.

The Village People group was the brainchild of record producer Jacques Morali. Jones was cast as the original cowboy in 1977 and remained with the act for three years. The idea of a concept group was not a new one, but the Village People were imbued with such energy, irony, and campy enthusiasm that they were wildly successful. In fact, some form of the group has been performing since the Village People scored their first U.S. hit with "Macho Man" in 1978.

The group racked up a number of big hits in the late 1970s and early 1980s, including "Y.M.C.A.," "In the Navy," "Go West," and "Can't Stop the Music" among others. That period of great creativity was the group's heyday.

Jones lives in Greenwich Village and continues to perform and act.

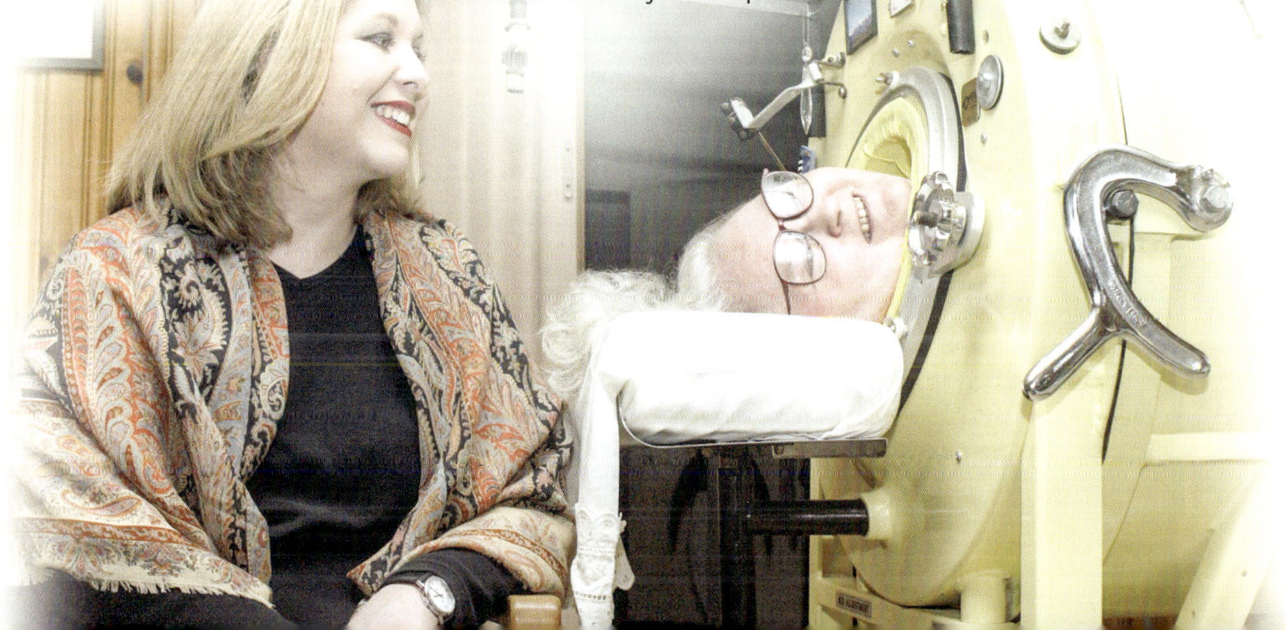

Martha Mason *(left)*, a friend who directed a documentary film about Mary Dalton *(right)*. Photo taken in 2003.

1788 An Independent Man: John Penn's Short Life

On September 14, 1788, John Penn died in Granville County at age forty-seven. With nothing more than a very basic education, Penn rose through legal and political circles to become one of three North Carolinians to sign the Declaration of Independence.

Born in 1741 in Virginia, Penn received instruction in rural schoolhouses. After his father's death, a neighbor offered young Penn use of his library. Through self-instruction Penn acquired knowledge of the law sufficient for admittance to the bar in 1762.

In 1774 Penn and his family settled in what is now Vance County, a center of the colony's growing independence movement. Penn served in the Continental Congress in Philadelphia in 1775 and soon earned the respect of constituents and colleagues. In the summer of 1776, he joined North Carolinians William Hooper and Joseph Hewes in signing the Declaration of Independence.

Later in his career Penn served on North Carolina's Board of War, established by Gov. Abner Nash, and on an advisory council to Gov. Thomas Burke. He retired to his home near Stovall, where he was buried.

In 1894, Penn's remains were transferred to what would become Guilford Courthouse National Military Park in Greensboro.

SEP 14

1862 William Ashe, Railroad Proponent, Handcar Crash Victim

On September 14, 1862, William Ashe, railroad president and commander of the Confederate government's transportation network between New Orleans and Richmond, died after being struck by a train.

Born in 1814 in what is now Pender County, Ashe was a lawyer and rice planter before entering politics. He was elected to the state Senate in 1846 and worked in that chamber to secure appropriations for railroads, particularly for ones that would connect the western part of the state with the port in Wilmington. He was re-elected to the state Senate in 1848 before entering Congress in 1849, where he continued to focus on internal improvements. He became president of the Wilmington and Weldon Railroad in 1854.

An outspoken supporter of secession, Ashe was asked by Pres. Jefferson Davis in 1861 to take control of the Confederate government's rail transportation. When he heard in 1862 that one of his sons had been captured, he commandeered a handcar to make a trip home. As he traveled, an unlighted train struck him during the night.

Ironically, the very thing that Ashe had worked so hard to bring to life took his own.

1934 General Textile Strike of 1934: Violence in Burlington

On September 14, 1934, workers arriving for the morning shift at the E. M. Holt Plaid Mill in Burlington were confronted by aggressive strikers who were determined to completely shut down the mill's operations. The National Guard soon arrived on scene and, using tear gas and bayonets, dispersed the crowd. Five strikers, including a woman, were injured.

That night a bomb made of stolen dynamite exploded outside the Holt Mill. The blast caused roughly a hundred dollars in damages, mostly in broken windowpanes. A second, unexploded bomb was found by authorities the following day under a loom at the Stevens Manufacturing Company.

Authorities labeled the attack a communist plot and rounded up and arrested ten men. Though the violent tactics of the National Guard earlier that morning had galvanized the strikers, support dissolved in the wake of the attempted bombings, and the mill reopened four days later.

Although the case against the alleged perpetrators was weak, four of the arrested accepted plea deals and testified against the other six. Author Paul Green led the League for Southern Labor in public support of the men, who were seen by many as scapegoats. All six defendants were found guilty after a week-long trial.

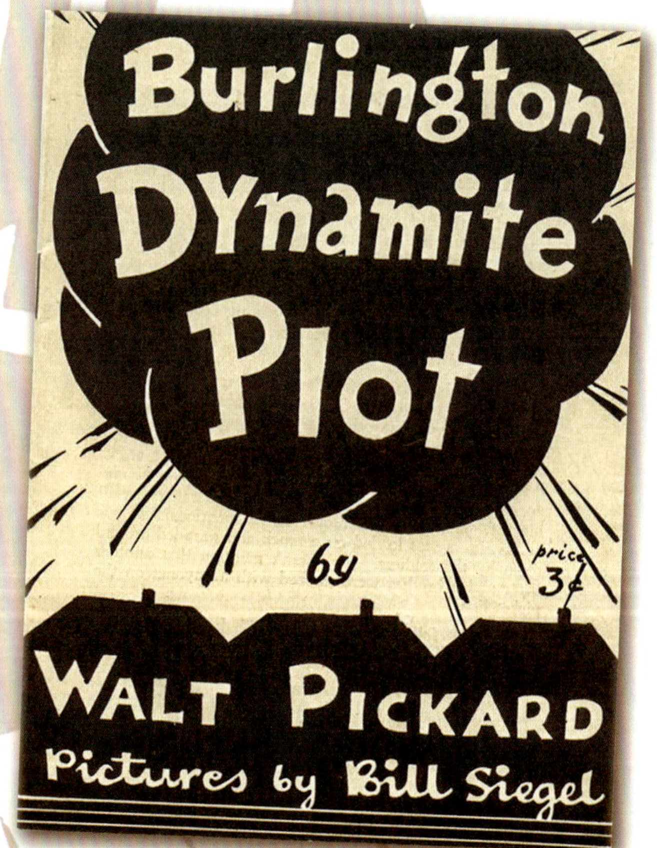

Pamphlet was published and sold as a fundraiser by International Labor Defense, New York, to support the defense of the textile workers on trial, 1935.

1857 Ivanhoe in Warren: Ring Tournaments at Shocco Springs

On September 15, 1857, the resort town of Shocco Springs in Warren County held the first known medieval jousting tournament in North Carolina. It did not involve riders knocking each other off their horses. Instead, participants used lances to spear a three-inch ring off a post.

Such "ring tournaments" became fashionable among the well-to-do in North Carolina in the late 1850s, and after a hiatus during the Civil War, they experienced a revival that lasted until the 1870s. The 1857 contest attracted contestants from as far away as Florida and Texas. Pageantry, costumes, and assumed titles (like the "Knight of the Black Cross") combined with themes of chivalry, honor, and the virtue of womanhood at these festivals. Many times they culminated in the crowning of a "Queen of Love and Beauty."

A newspaper account described the scene: "The Knights were splendidly accoutered, and as they flew past the stand with lances in rest their success was announced by loud cheers mingled with bursts of martial music, which irresistibly carried our thoughts back to the thrilling pages of Ivanhoe. . . ."

1938 Baseball's Gaylord Perry

On September 15, 1938, Major League Baseball pitcher Gaylord Perry was born in Williamston.

Perry grew up helping his tenant farmer family, but his father, who was an athlete and sports fan, gave him time to play sports. Though he played every sport at his high school, Perry was most competitive at baseball.

A right-handed pitcher, Perry drew attention from scouts early and attended Campbell College for two years before turning pro. He signed with the San Francisco Giants and played in their farm system until his big-league debut in 1962.

Quickly developing a reputation for using the "spitball," Perry often appeared to doctor the ball by smearing it with various substances (like petroleum jelly). This might have accounted for the sometimes miraculous spin he could produce.

Regardless of the cause, Perry was a pitching phenomenon. He earned the Cy Young Award, baseball's top honor for pitchers, in both the National and American Leagues, and struck out out 3,534 batters during his plus twenty-year career. Over the course of that career, he played for eight major league teams and won 314 games.

Perry became a member of the North Carolina Sports Hall of Fame in 1973 and was honored with membership in the Baseball Hall of Fame in 1991.

1946 Greensboro Base Vital to World War II Allied Effort

On September 15, 1946, the massive Greensboro Overseas Replacement Depot closed its doors.

The O.R.D., as it was known, originally operated as a training base, but by May 1944, the Air Force had reached its projected capacity, and the facility became the primary point in the eastern U.S. where soldiers were prepared and processed for overseas duty. In February 1945 the O.R.D. took on added duties as a redistribution station, working to place about thirty-one thousand troops in the Far East, as the focus of fighting shifted. In September 1945 the station began processing personnel for separation from duty. Thus, during its period of service, the Greensboro depot provided a wide range of services to the military. More than 330 thousand troops were processed in or out of service or redistributed to another location through the depot.

The base was truly massive. At 652 acres in size, it was the largest base in America located within the boundaries of a city, and as many as forty thousand soldiers were stationed at the Greensboro facility at any given time.

Spread over nearly a thousand buildings, the base included five hundred barracks, fourteen mess halls, fifty-five recreation rooms, four movie theaters, ten post exchanges, five chapels, three libraries, three gyms and a hospital. The base even had its own newspaper and radio station to keep the troops entertained.

SEP 15

Greensboro Overseas Replacement Depot—Last discharge ceremonies at the O.R.D., 1946.

San Francisco Giant Willie Mays *(left)*, ECU Pirate Club member Waightstill "Booger" Scales *(second from left)*, ECU Chancellor Leo Jenkins *(middle)*, his son Jack, and San Francisco Giants Gaylord Perry *(right)*, late 1960s.

1802 Rockfish Storekeeper Destined to be a Founder of California

On September 16, 1802, Thomas Larkin, the first and only U.S. consul to the territory that would become the state of California, was born.

Though not a native North Carolinian, Larkin made his way to the small Duplin County community of Rockfish, where he operated a store, served as justice of the county court, and became the postmaster at age nineteen. After about ten years in the Tar Heel state, he became dissatisfied with life in the South and boarded a ship for Monterey, the capital of Alta California, as it was known under Mexican rule. There he ran a dry goods store and operated flour and saw mills, trading with other Mexican communities and as far away as Hawaii.

In 1843 Larkin was appointed U.S. consul to California. He went on to play an important role in the Mexican War during the presidency of James K. Polk, and covertly worked to encourage secession from Mexico at the request of Secretary of State James Buchanan.

Following the war Larkin moved to San Francisco and represented that city in the 1849 California Constitutional Convention. Benefiting from the economic boom that followed the 1849 gold rush, Larkin continued to engage in land speculation.

He died of typhoid fever in 1858.

SEP 16

1960 From Cotton Field to University: Fayetteville's Methodist

On September 16, 1960, the first class of eighty-eight students was admitted to Methodist College.

About five years earlier, the citizens of Fayetteville offered the Methodist Church a six-hundred-acre tract and two million dollars to establish a school in their town. Fayetteville attorney and future governor Terry Sanford was elected the first chairman of the board of trustees, and L. Stacy Weaver was chosen as the first president.

When it opened, the campus included a grouping of contemporary buildings; the architectural plan, created by Stevens and Wilkinson of Atlanta, earned a national citation for creativity and unity of design.

The school's first major expansion came in 1978, when it began offering two-year associate degrees in addition to four-year bachelor degrees. In 1993 the trustees recommended that the college borrow funds to build additional residence halls over the next five years to accommodate three hundred new residential students. They further recommended that the college undertake a major capital campaign of at least ten million dollars for increasing the endowment and constructing a library addition and two new academic buildings. The school had a record enrollment in 2001 and inaugurated its first graduate program, which trains physicians' assistants.

In 2006 the trustees changed the school's name from Methodist College to Methodist University.

1999 Hurricane Floyd Devastating to Eastern North Carolina

On September 16, 1999, Hurricane Floyd made landfall at Cape Fear as a very strong Category 2 storm.

At its peak in the Atlantic, Floyd was among the largest Category 4 storms on record. Even as it came ashore it was almost twice the size of a normal hurricane. The twelve to twenty inches of rain that fell as a result of Floyd, which arrived only ten days after another hurricane, caused every river in eastern North Carolina to flood.

Among the towns most devastated by Floyd were Rocky Mount, Tarboro, Kinston, and Princeville. The fate of Princeville, a small town founded by freed slaves, tugged especially hard at the heartstrings of many North Carolinians—most of whom had never been there—as the whole town was underwater for days. A Federal Emergency Management Agency (FEMA) official stated that, although he had worked through more than a hundred disasters since 1992, he had never seen flooding as bad as in Princeville.

FEMA declared sixty-six North Carolina counties disaster areas after Floyd.

Damage to Princeville Town Hall was a consequence of Hurricane Floyd in 1999.

1787 Signers in Philadelphia Endorse Federal Constitution

On September 17, 1787, a majority of delegates to the Constitutional Convention in Philadelphia approved the U.S. Constitution, with North Carolina representatives William Blount, Richard Dobbs Spaight, and Hugh Williamson signing on behalf of the state. Despite advocacy for its adoption by Federalists Spaight and Williamson, the North Carolina Convention, first meeting in 1788, declined to ratify the Constitution until the Bill of Rights was proposed in 1789.

Interestingly, Williamson and Blount were not among the delegates originally selected. When the legislature met the previous January, it selected Gov. Richard Caswell, William R. Davie, Willie Jones, Alexander Martin, and Spaight as delegates. Jones, staunchly anti-Federalist, did not accept the appointment, and Caswell was ill and unable to travel. Williamson and Blount were appointed in their stead. Davie and Martin left the convention early, leaving Williamson, Spaight, and Blount remaining as signatories.

Richard Dobbs Spaight, from New Bern, later served as governor, and Hugh Williamson—sometimes referred to as North Carolina's Ben Franklin—was a physician, scientist, scholar, and resident of Chowan County. William Blount, a Bertie County native, was later governor of the territory that is now Tennessee, then U.S. Senator from that state as well.

A plaque in the rotunda of the State Capitol in Raleigh commemorates the three signers.

1862 L. O'B. Branch Rose through Confederate Ranks

On September 17, 1862, Gen. Lawrence O'Bryan Branch was shot and killed by a sharpshooter at the Battle of Sharpsburg.

Born in 1820 in Halifax County, Branch was placed in the care of his uncle, U.S. senator and former North Carolina governor John Branch, following the death of both of his parents. After college at UNC and Princeton, Branch moved to Nashville, Tennessee to work as a newspaper editor and to study law. He opened a law practice in Florida and served as an aide to Gov. Robert R. Reid during the Seminole War. He married on a trip to North Carolina and eventually opened a law practice in Raleigh. In the decade prior to the Civil War, he held a number of prominent positions, including a term in the U.S. House of Representatives.

When North Carolina seceded in 1861, Branch enlisted as a private in the Confederate army but was soon appointed the state's quartermaster general by Gov. John W. Ellis. Branch obtained a commission as colonel of the Thirty-Third North Carolina Infantry and was appointed a brigadier general in January 1862. He commanded his brigade at the Battle of New Bern and led the command at the engagements of Hanover Court House, the Seven Days' Battles, Second Manassas, and Sharpsburg.

1918 Samarcand, 1918–2011: Evolution of a Correctional Institute

On September 17, 1918, Samarcand, the State Home and Industrial School for Girls, was established in Moore County as a correctional institute for young women.

The concept of the school originated through the work of Presbyterian minister A. A. McGeachy, who believed the state needed a protective care center for delinquent juvenile girls, many of whom were homeless or prostitutes.

Intended as the female counterpart to the Stonewall Jackson Training School in Concord, Samarcand offered a school curriculum that focused on Biblical studies, music, science, and math, though the girls received training in weaving, canning, and laundry preparation, too. The girls also worked on the chicken and cattle farm adjacent to the facility.

Discipline at Samarcand could be harsh. Corporal punishment and solitary confinement were often administered, and a 1940 account of the disciplinary ward described mattresses on the floor with no beds and a single washbasin and toilet for nearly thirty girls. In 1974 the school was transferred to what's now the Department of Health and Human Services, remaining a rehabilitation center for delinquent children.

The state closed the facility in 2011. It is now the site of a training academy for corrections and law enforcement officers.

Samarcand industrial school enrollees on the grounds, 1929.

SEP 18

1906 "Cherry Bounce King," Amos Owens

On September 18, 1906, Amos Owens, a notorious moonshiner from Rutherford County, died. Known as the "Cherry Bounce King," Owens was renowned for the delightful mixture of whiskey, honey, and cherries that he made at his "castle" on Cherry Mountain.

Described as a fearless, energetic Irishman, Owens achieved success quickly. People from all over the South visited him to taste his celebrated beverage.

Owens was also an infamous fixture in the local courthouse. Vehemently opposed to taxes on alcohol, he believed that he owed nothing to the government after fulfilling his civic duty as a Confederate soldier. Often arrested for his activities, he was occasionally acquitted for minor crimes but didn't always manage to escape the long reach of the law. He frequently had to pay fines, sometimes spent time in jail, too. At one point he was locked up for an entire year.

Despite the risks that came with it, Owens continued to distill Cherry Bounce, and every summer he hosted lively gatherings at Cherry Mountain to celebrate the cherry harvest. A colorful local figure who embodied the vitality and grit of Tar Heels in the aftermath of the Civil War, Owens didn't stop making moonshine until he was sent to prison in his seventies.

1947 Occoneechee Speedway, NASCAR in Orange County

On September 18, 1947, Bill France Sr. and four other racing entrepreneurs incorporated the Hillsboro Speedway in Orange County, with the aim of bringing auto racing to central North Carolina.

Racing in another form had long been a pastime in the area. The property was previously owned by tobacco magnate Julian Shakespeare Carr, who constructed a horse racing track. That track later became the site of the Occoneechee Speedway.

In the late 1940s France, an auto racing organizer from Daytona Beach, saw the racetrack from the air as he was flying over Orange County. He gathered investors and secured the land. Less than a month later, he and a group of racing promoters formed the National Association for Stock Car Automobile Racing; that is, NASCAR.

The original plan was to build a one-mile oval racetrack with five thousand seats, but, when finished, the Occoneechee Speedway had wooden grandstands that held ten thousand and sloped hillsides that could fit twenty-five thousand more. The track opened in June 1948 with a ten-mile NASCAR race watched by about twenty thousand fans. It closed in 1968, and the site is now on the National Register of Historic Places.

Occoneechee Speedway with a stock car race in progress, c.1955.

1776 Cherokee Defeat by South Carolina Militia, 1776

On September 19, 1776, troops from South Carolina defeated a band of Cherokee Indians in what is now Swain County. The battle took place in a mountain cove known as the "Black Hole" and was coordinated with a larger effort, now known as the Rutherford Campaign, to punish the Indians for raids on white settlers in the area.

The conflict had its roots earlier that month, when Col. Andrew Williamson led two thousand South Carolina militiamen north into Cherokee territory in early September. As they came to the cove, his men marched into an ambush in a gorge. The ensuing battle lasted for nearly two hours. The militiamen were surrounded by Cherokee and forced into a circular formation, leading to the engagement being known in time as the "Ring Fight."

Williamson eventually led a bayonet charge, driving the Cherokees from the field. Relatively few casualties were incurred. The Cherokee left four dead on the field; eleven militiamen were killed and twenty-four wounded.

A week later, Williamson's force united with Griffith Rutherford's men at Hiwassee.

1918 The Spanish Flu Epidemic of 1918

On September 19, 1918, the contagion known as the "Spanish Flu" appeared in the port city of Wilmington. Within a week the hard-struck city reported some four hundred cases of the illness. It was a sign of the devastation yet to be wrought by the pandemic.

At the height of the flu outbreak during the winter of 1918-1919 at least twenty percent of North Carolinians were infected by the disease. The so-called "Spanish Lady" killed nearly fourteen thousand citizens of the state.

A confluence of events created a viral strain of the contagion, and that mutated virus found more victims than normal, due in part to the ongoing world war. Large numbers of people were traveling around the country and the world like never before, and the virus was able to travel by hosts and spread.

The flu outbreak forced a reorganization of the still-budding North Carolina health care system. Home Relief groups formed and only an outpouring of public charity helped to check the spread of the disease. At least seventeen doctors succumbed to the virus while tending to the infected.

Many North Carolina communities suffered during the pandemic, but Wilmington remained the hardest hit by the "Spanish Lady."

1985 *Elizabeth II*, a Legacy of America's Four Hundredth

On September 19, 1985, the *Elizabeth II* made its maiden voyage from Manteo to Ocracoke, Beaufort, New Bern, and back again.

Constructed as part of America's four hundredth anniversary celebration, the sixty-nine-foot, square-rigged sailing ship is meant to be representative of the vessels used to bring the first English colonists to Roanoke Island in the late 1500s. It was named for the original *Elizabeth*, one of the seven ships of Sir Walter Raleigh's second expedition in 1585. That ship was captained by Thomas Cavendish and carried people and supplies to aid England in building a military garrison near what is now Manteo.

Built almost entirely by hand during 1983, the *Elizabeth II* was in the water by early 1984 and was christened by Britain's Princess Anne that summer. A private corporation raised $650,000 to finance the ship's construction, while the General Assembly allocated $1.4 million for the development of other attractions on Roanoke Island.

Though the ship sometimes sails along the North Carolina coast, it is moored at Roanoke Island Festival Park—one of twenty-seven State Historic Sites—for most of the year.

Elizabeth II docked at Manteo in 1995.

SEP 20

1711 Executed by the Tuscarora: John Lawson

On September 20, 1711, explorer and surveyor John Lawson was killed by the Tuscarora.

Lawson and Baron Christoph von Graffenried planned to travel up the Neuse River from New Bern in an attempt to explore the area and discover the river's source. The Tuscarora, angry about incursions into their lands, kidnapping of their women and children, and disrespectful treatment by traders, stopped the expedition and imprisoned the leaders.

Graffenried's account of the incident states that Lawson got into an angry exchange with a Tuscarora leader, which resulted in the seizure and burning of their hats and wigs and a sentence of death for both of them.

The next morning Graffenried reportedly chastised Lawson for antagonizing their captors and spoke with an Indian interpreter.

After several days one of the Indians made a plea on Graffenried's behalf. He was released but kept in a hut, during which time Lawson was executed. It is believed that the Tuscarora thought Graffenried was the governor and that they would incur the wrath of the English if they killed him.

Graffenried later heard of several ways in which Lawson was supposedly executed, but the actual method of death is uncertain.

Lucy Morgan, founder of Penland School of Handicrafts, at the flax wheel with weaving instructor Edward Worst.

1889 Lucy Morgan, Founder of the Penland School

On September 20, 1889, Lucy Calista Morgan was born in Franklin in western North Carolina.

After graduating from what is now Central Michigan University in 1915, Morgan taught school and worked for the Children's Bureau in Illinois. Morgan returned to North Carolina in 1920 to teach at the Appalachian School in Penland. During winter break in 1923, she accompanied a former student to Berea College in Kentucky, where she learned to weave.

Inspired by the Berea community cottage weaving industry, Morgan returned to Penland with a loom and a Craft Revival mission to "...bring about a revival of hand-weaving...[and] provide our neighbor mothers with a means of adding to their generally meager incomes without having to leave their homes...." She had to convince the Episcopal bishop responsible for the Appalachian School to support a weaving program, convince the women of the region to participate, and find a market for their creations. By 1928 the Penland Weavers and Potters was a destination welcoming visitors. Morgan established the Penland School of Crafts in 1929.

Known as "Miss Lucy," she promoted North Carolina crafts to the National Park Service, at the 1933 Chicago World's Fair, at the 1934 International Exhibition of Folk Art in Switzerland, and to visitors from throughout the world. She published a memoir *Gift From the Hills* in 1958, documenting the social value of crafts in strengthening community. Morgan retired to Jackson County in 1962 and continued to visit Penland until her death in 1981.

Her legacy continues as North Carolina communities identify authentic cultural traditions as a resource for arts-based economic development. The Penland School of Crafts has grown to be the premier art craft school in the country.

1920 Food Town (Now Food Lion) Founder Ralph Ketner

On September 20, 1920, grocer, entrepreneur, and philanthropist Ralph Ketner was born in Cabarrus County. Hale and hearty until shortly before his death in 2016, Ketner was known as the longtime television face for the Food Lion grocery store chain.

After college in Indiana and service in World War II, Ketner and two partners opened their first store in Salisbury in 1957. Their primary competitors were Winn-Dixie, Colonial Stores, and A&P. Investors who joined them to raise a total capital of sixty-two thousand dollars in time became millionaires.

What was then Food Town expanded gradually until 1967 when Ketner took his account books and retreated into a Charlotte motel. Three days later he emerged, with the slogan "Lowest Food Prices in North Carolina" and a formula, selling ten grocery categories at cost or below and ensuring all products were cheaper than competitors'. The strategy worked, propelling the chain to expand into Virginia and Tennessee, where the existence of stores with the same name necessitated the change in 1983 to Food Lion.

A Belgian company, Delhaize, acquired majority ownership of Food Lion in 1976. Tom Smith succeeded Ketner as president and commercial spokesman in 1981. The company now has eleven hundred stores and forty-eight thousand employees in eleven southeastern states.

Ketner funded the business school at Catawba College that bears his name.

1958 Martin Luther King's 1958 Surgery Led by North Carolinian

On September 20, 1958, Beaufort County native Dr. John Cordice operated on Martin Luther King Jr. in a Harlem, New York hospital. He is now widely credited with saving Dr. King's life.

Born in the small community of Aurora, east of Greenville, Cordice was raised in Durham. After college and medical school at New York University and work as a doctor alongside the Tuskegee Airmen during World War II, Cordice became a heart surgeon at Harlem Hospital.

On the day in question, King was stabbed by a woman outside a New York department store while autographing copies of a book he was promoting. He was brought to Harlem Hospital, where New York Gov. W. Averell Harriman requested that African American doctors work on him. Cordice, who wasn't even on duty that day, happened to stop by a Brooklyn medical office, where he received a call to come at once and operate on an important person who had been injured. After rushing to the hospital, Cordice and other surgeons used a hammer and chisel to crack King's sternum and remove the blade with which he had been stabbed, thereby saving King's life.

At the time credit for the feat was given to Dr. Aubré de Lambert Maynard, the hospital's chief of surgery, but historians have since concluded that it was Dr. Cordice and Dr. Emil Naclerio, an Italian-American, who truly ensured King's survival.

1752 Federal-Era Power Broker John Gray Blount, of Washington

On September 21, 1752, John Gray Blount was born in Bertie County. He was destined to become one of the wealthiest men in North Carolina, albeit less well-known than his half-brothers William, a Tennessee governor, and Thomas, a member of Congress.

John Gray Blount had business dealings up and down the Atlantic seaboard and extending into the Caribbean, but his base of operation was in Washington in Beaufort County after his 1778 marriage. He made the town his home when it was still known as Forks of the Tar River.

Blount and his partners had substantial shipping interests, owning wharves, flatboats, and seagoing vessels. They also owned sawmills, gristmills, tanneries, and cotton gins, and engaged in agricultural pursuits and the slave trade. Blount was also heavily involved in land speculation, employing agents to buy and sell large tracts in western North Carolina and Tennessee.

Blount represented Beaufort in the state House and state Senate and served in the Constitutional Convention of 1787. He died in 1833 and is buried at St. Peter's Episcopal Church in Washington.

1780 William R. Davie's Victorious Assault at Wauchope Plantation

On September 21, 1780, William R. Davie, in time known as the "Father of the University of North Carolina," led a surprise attack on British troops southeast of Monroe. Cornwallis had marched into North Carolina days earlier after his victory at Camden, South Carolina.

Familiar with the terrain from his boyhood, Davie found the "lawless marauders" on the plantation of James Wauchope at around 2:00 a.m. At sunrise, appearing from the corn that grew right up to the house, Davie and his corps of 150 assaulted the band of three to four hundred Tories, mounted and awaiting their orders to ride. The plan worked, and the enemy fled in confusion, but not before setting fire to the house and other buildings.

By Davie's account, confirmed by reports of Jethro Sumner and William Lee Davidson, sixty Tories were left on the ground, twenty of them dead. No Patriots were killed, and only one was wounded.

The attack, also known as the "Battle of the Waxhaws," was a prelude to the Battles of Charlotte on September 26 and of Kings Mountain on October 7.

1850 Bearded Brinkley Buried at Buladean

On September 21, 1850, Sam Brinkley, who became known in the early twentieth century for one of the world's longest beards, was born near Burnsville in Yancey County.

As an adult Brinkley stood at six feet, two inches, with a beard of five feet, five inches at its peak length. Notoriety came with the remarkable growth of his beard. He began by exhibiting it to the curious, and he went on tour with the Barnum and Bailey Circus. He reportedly earned thousands of dollars by charging people to see his beard, which he kept tucked in a pouch.

Brinkley was a late bloomer when it came to facial hair. According to newspaper accounts, until he was twenty-one, he had no real beard to shave. By twenty-three its growth had reached the astounding rate of a full beard in a week's time. One article reported that the beard was entirely natural, not the result of restorers or invigorators. Another called it "soft and beautiful." For decades Brinkley was known as the world's expert on the cultivation of beards.

He died in 1929 from complications of tonsillitis and is buried at Buladean in Mitchell County, with a striking photo featuring his legendary beard recessed into his tombstone.

Postcard image of S.G. Brinkley, "Longest Bearded Man in the World."

1862 William Gould and His Flight to Freedom

On September 21, 1862, twenty-two fugitive slaves boarded three small sailing boats from the docks on Orange Street in downtown Wilmington and rowed twenty-eight nautical miles to the mouth of the Cape Fear River. The escape was one of the largest ever in the Cape Fear region.

One of the escaped slaves that night was William B. Gould, a twenty-four-year-old plasterer who worked on the Bellamy Mansion. What is known of the daring escape is based on Gould's diary.

The slaves' goal was to reach the Union blockading ships and thus gain freedom. At one point they had to pass directly beneath Fort Caswell, a Confederate stronghold heavily armed to keep Union naval forces out of Wilmington harbor. Escapees aboard all three boats ultimately were picked up by Union ships.

Gould went on to serve aboard two ships in the U.S. Navy. His diary provides unique insight into the Maritime Underground Railroad and the day-to-day life of a former slave fighting to secure freedom for himself.

William B. Gould, c. 1880s.

1711 — Beginnings of the Tuscarora War

On September 22, 1711, the Tuscarora Indians attacked settlers around the Neuse, Trent, and Pamlico Rivers, beginning what would later become known as the Tuscarora War.

The conflict, which erupted between Native Americans and settlers from Switzerland, was fought mostly because of colonial encroachment on Native lands and because of mistreatment of the Indians by colonists. It came after colonists continually ignored treaties signed by their government and the Tuscarora.

After unsuccessfully requesting military aide from Virginia, Gov. Edward Hyde asked South Carolina for help. That colony sent Col. James Moore, who marched his combined force of North and South Carolina militia and allied Indians to Nooheroo-ka in Greene County. He had been informed that the Tuscarora had placed their largest concentration of warriors at a fort there.

The fort fell in March 1713, signaling the end of concerted Indian resistance to colonists. By the end of the Tuscarora War, approximately two hundred whites and a thousand Indians were killed, with an additional thousand Tuscarora sold into slavery and more than three thousand others forced from their homes.

1862 — Lincoln Takes Initial Step to Free Slaves

On September 22, 1862, Pres. Abraham Lincoln issued the Preliminary Emancipation Proclamation, stating his intention to free slaves in states that were rebelling against the Federal government.

Although he had conceived the idea earlier that year, Lincoln heeded the advice of his cabinet and waited for a Union battlefield victory to introduce the proclamation so it would not be viewed as an act of desperation. The Union victory at Antietam gave him the opportunity, and Lincoln seized the moment.

The Federal military governor of North Carolina, Edward Stanly, disapproved of the proclamation. He understood his duty to be to return the state to the Union as it was before the crisis—a Union where slavery was included.

Lincoln offered exclusions and exemptions in the proclamation, including exclusion of any area that had a representative in the Federal legislature. Stanly seized upon this as a possible avenue to forestall the implementation of the proclamation in North Carolina, calling for and holding elections for the statewide office of U.S. Senator. Congress refused to seat the person who won the election, and Stanly resigned rather than implement Lincoln's proclamation.

The final Emancipation Proclamation became active on January 1, 1863, freeing slaves in occupied eastern North Carolina.

1947 — Scholar/Activist John Hope Franklin's Pathbreaking Textbook

On September 22, 1947, John Hope Franklin published *From Slavery to Freedom*, a history of African Americans that traces their origins in Africa, years of slavery, and struggles for freedom.

Still in print with more than three million copies sold, the book has been translated into many languages. It is widely considered the definitive survey text for courses in African American history.

Franklin held teaching appointments at Saint Augustine's and North Carolina Central before capping off his academic career at Duke, where an interdisciplinary and international studies center continues his pioneering work. During his storied career, Franklin served as president of Phi Beta Kappa, the Organization of American Historians, the American Historical Association, and the Southern Historical Association. He was awarded the Presidential Medal of Freedom, the nation's highest civilian honor, in 1995.

Aside from his roles as historian, scholar, civil rights activist, and adviser to presidents, Franklin was known for nurturing more than three hundred orchids in his Durham greenhouse and helping to establish the Durham Literacy Center.

SEP 22

THE TUSCARORA WAR — Main Events

1710
Colonial town of New Bern displaces Tuscarora village of Chattoka

1711
Mid-September — John Lawson is executed near the village of Catechna
September 22 — Tuscarora Indians, in alliance with members of displaced coastal tribes, attack colonists along the Neuse, Pamlico, and Trent Rivers
October 27 — South Carolina resolves to raise troops to fight the Tuscaroras

1712
January 28 — The Barnwell Expedition crosses the Cape Fear River
January 30 — Barnwell's force destroys the Tuscarora village of Narhantes
February 6 — Barnwell reaches the Pamlico River
February 10-26 — Barnwell's force remains idle at Bath
February 27 — Barnwell moves on Fort Hancock at Catechna
April 7 — Siege of Fort Hancock
April 17 — Fort Hancock falls to Barnwell's force
August 8 — South Carolina sends the Moore Expedition to North Carolina
Early December — Moore's force reaches Fort Barnwell, then moves via New Bern and Bath to Albemarle County

1713
January 17 — Moore's force advances from Albemarle County
March 1 — Siege of Fort Neoheroka
March 20-23 — Final attack and capture of Fort Neoheroka

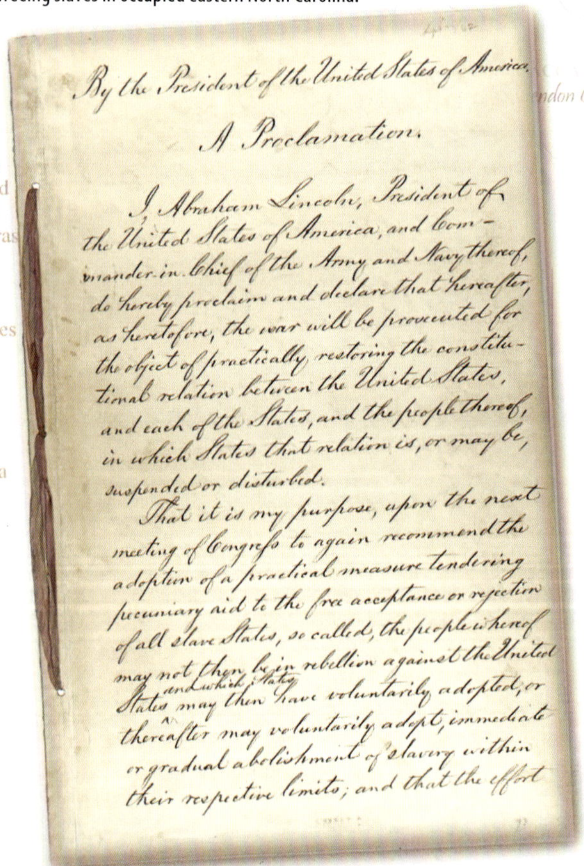
By the President of the United States of America,

A Proclamation.

I, Abraham Lincoln, President of the United States of America, and Commander-in-Chief of the Army and Navy thereof, do hereby proclaim and declare that hereafter, as heretofore, the war will be prosecuted for the object of practically restoring the constitutional relation between the United States, and each of the States, and the people thereof, in which States that relation is, or may be, suspended or disturbed.

That it is my purpose, upon the next meeting of Congress to again recommend the adoption of a practical measure tendering pecuniary aid to the free acceptance or rejection of all slave States, so called, the people whereof may not then be in rebellion against the United States, and which States may then have voluntarily adopted, or thereafter may voluntarily adopt, immediate or gradual abolishment of slavery within their respective limits; and that the effort

Fort Neoheroka

Based on an artist's rendering, from a manuscript housed at the South Carolina Historical Society.

MAPS BY MARK ANDERSON MOORE

1740 James Kenan and the Family Legacy

On September 23, 1740, civic, military, and political leader James Kenan was born.

Kenan began his long career in public service at age twenty-two when he was elected sheriff of Duplin County. After leading local opposition to the British Stamp Act, he served in the colonial assembly and the provincial congress. As a member of the militia in Duplin County, he helped lead a group of volunteers against Scottish Loyalists at the Battle of Moores Creek Bridge in 1776.

Kenan continued his involvement in politics after the Revolutionary War, serving in the state Senate for more than ten terms and as a delegate to the state Constitutional Conventions. Outside of the political arena, Kenan was a member of the original board of trustees for the University of North Carolina, where several buildings are now named for the Kenan family. He was also the first Master of the original Masonic lodge in Duplin County.

Kenan died in 1810 and is buried in Kenansville. His descendants have continued his legacy of philanthropy and public service, making significant contributions to the arts and education in North Carolina.

Liberty Hall, his father's plantation and the site of James Kenan's grave, is now open to the public as a museum.

1930 C. M. Stedman of Fayetteville, Confederate Veteran

On September 23, 1930, Charles M. Stedman, the last Civil War veteran (Union or Confederate) to serve in the U.S. Congress, died.

A native North Carolinian, Stedman was born in Pittsboro in 1841. He graduated from the University of North Carolina in 1861 and enlisted as a private in the First North Carolina "Bethel Regiment." Stedman was promoted to major of the Forty-Fourth North Carolina Infantry. Afterwards he returned to Chatham County to teach. While in Chatham County he studied law and was admitted to the bar in 1865.

His interest in politics began with the 1880 Democratic Convention. He was elected lieutenant governor in 1884 but failed in his bid for the governor's office in 1888. Stedman was a University of North Carolina trustee from 1899 to 1915, the president of the North Carolina Bar Association in 1900, and had a second unsuccessful run for governor in 1904.

First elected as a Democrat to the United States House of Representatives in 1910, he was reelected nine times, serving until his death in 1930. He is buried in Cross Creek Cemetery in Fayetteville.

Congressional cake with 85 candles being presented to Rep. Charles M. Stedman of North Carolina on his 85th birthday by colleagues in the House in 1926.

1933 Medal of Honor Recipient Edwin Anderson of Wilmington

On September 23, 1933, Edwin Anderson, a distinguished U.S. Navy admiral, died in Wilmington.

Born in 1860 near Wilmington, Anderson was educated at the U.S. Naval Academy. His first fifteen years in the Navy included tours of duty in Haiti, Alaska, and the Galapagos Islands; a promotion to lieutenant; and a varied range of duties from protecting the Bering Sea seal trade to aiding a scientific expedition.

During the Spanish-American War, Anderson volunteered to lead two small boats in an attempt to locate and cut Spanish undersea cables and completed the mission under a barrage of Spanish artillery and small arms fire that killed several men. Cited for extreme gallantry, Anderson received an unprecedented five-grade promotion to commander in 1901. After a variety of domestic postings and several foreign tours, Anderson took charge of the battleship USS *New Hampshire* in 1913. His vessel took part in the United States intervention in Vera Cruz, Mexico, and his courage under fire there earned him the Congressional Medal of Honor.

Anderson ended his naval career in charge of the entire Eastern Fleet serving in Asia. He was such a help in delivering emergency medical supplies and food when Japan was devastated by a series of earthquakes in 1923 that the Japanese government sent Anderson gifts each Christmas until his death.

Anderson retired from the Navy in March 1924, returned to Wilmington, and remained there until his death.

1940 Inglis Fletcher and the "Carolina Series"

On September 23, 1940, Inglis Clark Fletcher published *Raleigh's Eden*, the first in her twelve-part series of historical novels chronicling life in colonial and revolutionary North Carolina.

Although not native to North Carolina, Fletcher, through meticulous research and attention to historical detail, introduced millions of readers to the early history of the state. Her books were popular internationally and were translated into eight languages.

A mining engineer's wife, Fletcher traveled extensively with her husband and was first enticed to write during a 1928 stay in Africa. She began researching her genealogy, which led her to the *Colonial Records of North Carolina*, from which she drew inspiration for *Raleigh's Eden*. She fell in love with the history of the Old North State and through the next two decades wrote eleven more volumes of historical fiction.

Fletcher published her second novel, *Men of Albemarle*, in 1942 but did not begin to seriously churn out work until 1944, when she and her husband purchased Bandon Plantation on the Chowan River in Edenton. There she developed the routine of devoting one year to research followed by one year of writing, which led to her publishing ten more books.

1946 UNC-Charlotte's Modest Beginnings

On September 23, 1946, the Charlotte Center opened to offer evening classes to recent World War II veterans.

Established as part of the post-World War II GI Bill, the Charlotte Center got its start in the basement of Central High School. It was the largest of a network of fourteen temporary institutions that officials created across North Carolina to help curb the anticipated overcrowding at traditional colleges and universities.

The state slated the center to close in 1949 as the demand generated by returned soldiers began to dissipate, but local residents led by Charlotte Center director Bonnie Cone fought to keep it open as a two-year institution called Charlotte College to be supported exclusively by local funds and operated by the local school board. It survived, and in 1958 the college was accepted into the North Carolina Community College System. It moved to its current location in 1961 and became a four-year institution in 1964.

Charlotte College became the fourth institution to join the consolidated UNC System the following year, changing its name to UNC- Charlotte. It continued a steady pace of growth throughout the rest of the twentieth century, adding its first graduate degree programs in 1969 and its first doctoral program in 1993.

Today UNC-Charlotte is the fourth-largest institution in the UNC system with an enrollment of more than twenty-six thousand.

1660 First Deed, First House Were Batts's

On September 24, 1660, King Kiscutanewh sold Nathaniel Batts a tract of land in what is now Pasquotank County. The deed, recorded in a Chesapeake, Virginia deed book, included all land southwest of the Pasquotank River from its mount to the head of Begin Creek. Batts was the earliest-known white settler and owner of the earliest-known house within what is now North Carolina. His house, built in 1654 or 1655, is shown on the 1657 Nicholas Comberford map.

Batts was a large property owner in southeastern Virginia and divided his time between his holdings there and the property in what is now northeastern North Carolina. A witness to the deed was another early North Carolina European-settler, George Durant. Batts would also acquire a small island in the nearby Yeopim River that eventually came to be named for him. The northeastern region of the state still has place names that honor Batts and Durant.

The discovery of the 1660 Deed in 1966 made newspaper headlines.

1777 Charlotte's Thomas Polk Saved the Liberty Bell, 1777

On September 24, 1777, Mecklenburg County resident Thomas Polk arrived safely in Allenton, Pennsylvania after escorting the Liberty Bell there from Philadelphia.

Born in Pennsylvania, Polk and his family moved to Anson County before becoming one of the first settlers of Mecklenburg County and promoting the establishment of Charlotte. A prosperous planter, he was active in local and state politics. As the American Revolution began to come into full swing, Polk was appointed colonel of a regiment of North Carolina militia. He fought at Brandywine and spent a harsh winter at Valley Forge.

As invading British forces approached Philadelphia in 1777, Polk was tasked with escorting some important items out of the city to avoid capture. The city's bells—including what was then called the State House Bell and is now known as the Liberty Bell—were included among Polk's precious cargo so they wouldn't be melted down by the British to make cannonballs.

After saving what is now one of our nation's most precious artifacts, Polk continued a successful military career, served on the Council of State, and hosted George Washington during his southern tour. He died at his Charlotte home in 1794.

Liberty Bell, Col. Thomas Polk's Overnight Bivouac, Quakertown, Pennsylvania, September 18, 1777. James R. Mann, 1976.

1780 The Route to Kings Mountain

On September 25, 1780, the "Overmountain Men" met along the Watauga River before heading along the Yellow Mountain Road over the Blue Ridge Mountains.

The Yellow Mountain Road, today part of the Overmountain Victory National Historic Trail, stretches through what is present-day Avery County. In the fall of 1780 an army of backcountry men marched on the road toward the Battle of Kings Mountain. The Appalachian men were called "Overmountain Men" for their having crossed through the backcountry regions of Virginia, Tennessee, North Carolina, and South Carolina on their way to Kings Mountain.

The road begins on the western side of the Blue Ridge Mountains at Sycamore Flats, where groups of militiamen gathered. Taking the Yellow Mountain Road, then the only one that led east, they went through Gap Creek Mountain to the Toe River before heading south to the top of the ridge at Roan High Knob and Big Yellow Mountain. The troops then were paraded on a one-hundred-acre tract of flat land to determine how they were faring on the journey.

The militiamen went on to form a coalition of approximately a thousand troops that fought and defeated the British Army on October 7 at the Battle of Kings Mountain.

1896 Graham Barden, Congressional Education and Labor Chair

On September 25, 1896, long-time eastern North Carolina congressman Graham Barden was born in Sampson County.

After a stint in the Navy and studies at UNC, Barden set up a law practice in New Bern, where he also taught school and coached football. Known for his pleasant disposition, he was often called "Happy" or "Hap." It was that sunny outlook that led him to politics, and he served as a local judge and state legislator before being first elected to Congress in 1935.

While in Congress, Barden had a special interest in education and labor-related issues, chairing the House Committee on Education and Labor from 1949 to 1961 and being key to the passage of the Barden-LaFollette, Taft-Hartley, and Landrum-Griffith Acts, all of which concerned vocational training and labor unions. Though he hardly campaigned during his twelve reelection bids to Congress, Barden fought hard for federal projects in his district, securing a temporary base during World War II and three of North Carolina's four current major military installations.

When he announced his 1961 retirement from Congress, more than a hundred of his colleagues met to try to talk him out of it. He enjoyed a quiet retirement in New Bern and died in 1967.

1974 Doctor Pioneers "Tommy John Surgery," Saves Baseball Careers

On September 25, 1974, Greensboro native Frank Jobe, an orthopedist for the Los Angeles Dodgers, replaced pitcher Tommy John's torn medial collateral ligament in his pitching arm with a tendon from his wrist.

The injury had ended pitching careers since the beginning of baseball, but thanks to Jobe's efforts, John resumed his career after a successful rehabilitation, playing for another fourteen years and amassing 164 victories. The procedure, which has come to be known as the "Tommy John Surgery," has saved the careers of countless pitchers and position players in all levels of baseball ever since.

Jobe, born in 1925, joined the Army at eighteen and served as a supply sergeant in a medical unit with the 101st Airborne during World War II. He was inspired to become a surgeon after witnessing the bravery of army doctors on the battlefield, later recalling, "These guys would be operating in tents with bullets and shrapnel flying around . . . . These guys became my real heroes."

Jobe was honored for his pioneering contributions to baseball during the 2013 Baseball Hall of Fame awards ceremony, seven months before his death. Dodgers president Stan Kasten remembered Jobe as a "medical giant and pioneer" who helped "athletes around the world."

1980 Astrochimp Ham's Retirement Years in Asheboro

On September 25, 1980, Ham, the "Astrochimp," arrived at the North Carolina Zoological Park in Asheboro.

Ham, an acronym for Holloman Aero Med, was born in July 1957 in the French Cameroons in West Africa. He was taken to Holloman Air Force Base in New Mexico when he was about two years old. Space researchers at Holloman began using animals, initially monkeys and mice, in the late 1940s to test whether they could send a living creature into space and return it to Earth alive.

In January 1961 Ham became the first chimpanzee in space aboard the Mercury Redstone rocket on a sub-orbital flight. Following his mission Ham was found to be slightly fatigued and dehydrated but otherwise in good health. His flight heralded the launch of America's first human astronaut, Alan B. Shepard Jr., later that year.

Ham spent many years alone on display at the National Zoo in Washington, D.C. but then was moved to North Carolina, where he could live among other chimpanzees. After his death in 1983, his skeleton was removed for further study, and his other remains were buried at the International Space Hall of Fame in Alamogordo, New Mexico.

Tommy John *(left)* and Frank Jobe *(right)* at the awards presentation during the Hall of Fame Weekend in Cooperstown, 2013. Printed with permission from the Baseball Hall of Fame.

Chimpanzee Ham is greeted by recovery ship commander after his flight on the Mercury Redstone rocket, 1961. NASA photograph.

SEP 26

1780 The Battle of Charlotte

On September 26, 1780, British troops under the command of Lord Charles Cornwallis clashed with Patriot militia led by William R. Davie in Charlotte. The battle was part of Cornwallis's pursuit of the retreating American forces that he had defeated the previous month at Camden, South Carolina.

Attempting to defend what was then only a small hamlet, Davie ordered his men to arrange themselves along a stone wall in front of Charlotte's courthouse and along the flanks of the roads behind several hedges and homes. He intended to ambush the British if they advanced directly into the town center, which they did. The Americans repelled two attacks before being forced to withdraw when British light infantry units turned their flank. Five Americans were killed, six wounded, and an unknown number taken prisoner in the battle. The British suffered forty-four casualties from the skirmish.

Though the battle itself was not decisive, the resistance of the outnumbered Americans symbolized the resolve of the people of the region.

1829 Governor and Congressman Gabriel Holmes, Ally of John C. Calhoun

On September 26, 1829, former governor Gabriel Holmes died suddenly while serving a term in the U.S. House of Representatives.

Born in Duplin County in 1769, Holmes studied law and later practiced in Sampson County. He served in both houses of the General Assembly, was appointed to the Council of State, and served as a trustee of the University of North Carolina before being elected governor in 1821.

Holmes earned the state's top job after a failed attempt to win election to the office the year before and remained governor for three terms before stepping down in 1825 because of a term limit. That same year he was elected to Congress, where he was closely associated with John C. Calhoun.

Throughout his public service Holmes was a strong advocate for higher education, agriculture, and internal improvements. He stressed the need for agricultural courses and progressive techniques in farming, lobbied for state spending on education, and helped improve both land and water transportation.

Holmes died at his home near Clinton and was buried in the family graveyard.

1911 Adelaide Fries and the Moravian Archives

On September 26, 1911, Forsyth County native Adelaide Fries was appointed Archivist of the Southern Province of the Moravian Church.

Born in 1871 from a long line of churchmen, Fries graduated from Salem College with bachelor's and master's degrees. Guided to research primary sources from a very young age by her father, Fries learned to read Old German script so that she could translate the diaries in which she was interested. The culmination of that education came in 1899, when Fries accompanied her father to Germany, where she examined many of the earliest records of the church.

Fries's work as archivist of the Salem church began very unofficially when someone suggested that she find a room somewhere to house all the manuscripts she was collecting. After that, with no official sanction, she began an intense collecting campaign that resulted in the preservation of many valuable papers.

Fries held the official position of archivist for the rest of her life, while pursuing companion interests in genealogy and church history. A popular speaker and author, Fries received honorary doctorates from Wake Forest and UNC.

She died in 1949 and was laid to rest in the Moravian burying ground known as God's Acre.

1934 Longstanding Lions Club Commitment to the Blind

On September 26, 1934, the first annual meeting of the North Carolina State Association for the Blind was held at the Vance Hotel in Statesville, in conjunction with a regional Lions Club conference.

Lions Club International was already committed to civic service on behalf of the visually impaired, and the North Carolina clubs looked for opportunities to carry out the mission. By the 1930s it became clear that the work of the clubs lacked continuity, and the Charlotte Lions Club began to seek ways to improve services for the state's entire blind population.

During the Depression local Associations for the Blind were established in Guilford, Durham, and Mecklenburg Counties. The local associations, together with the Lions Clubs, established the infrastructure for launching a statewide effort to assist North Carolina's blind citizens.

In 1974 the group solidified their connection with the Lions Clubs by becoming the North Carolina Lions Association for the Blind, and it is now known simply as the North Carolina Lions Foundation, Inc.

The original association was successful in focusing public attention on the needs of the state's blind and visually impaired citizens. The modern successor continues the work with projects and programs throughout North Carolina.

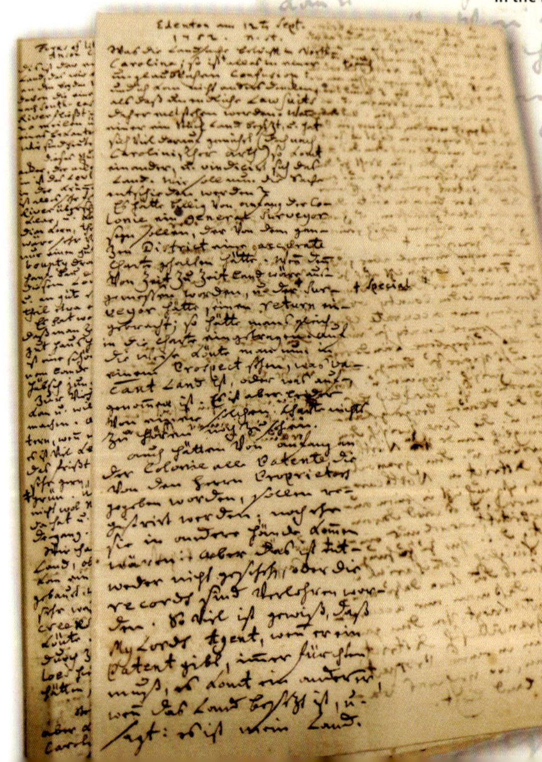

Pages from the 1752 diary documenting Bishop Spangenburg's surveying trip.

Adelaide Fries

1718 A Pirate's Life Was His, Stede Bonnet's

On September 27, 1718, Col. William Rhett captured the so-called "Gentleman Pirate," Stede Bonnet, after a six-hour battle near the headland of the Cape Fear River.

Born into a well-off British family and educated in England, Bonnet advanced in the army to major before leaving the service and moving to Barbados. There he and his wife established a prosperous sugar plantation, the image of wealthy respectability to neighbors, but in 1717, with no apparent explanation, he bought a sloop, named it the *Revenge*, and took up piracy, even though he'd never been a sailor.

Bonnet enjoyed early success as a pirate. He plundered ships up and down the coasts of Virginia and New England, torching all those from Barbados. Nevertheless, his crew, far more seasoned sailors than Bonnet, grew agitated under his command. He suffered his first major setback when he met Blackbeard, who made Bonnet a virtual prisoner and put another man in charge of the *Revenge*.

Blackbeard and Bonnet parted company near Bath, and Bonnet sought clemency from royal Gov. Charles Eden. Eden granted him permission to try to secure a commission as a privateer. While attempting to become a privateer, he discovered that Blackbeard had abandoned the *Revenge*. Bonnet renamed the ship and returned to piracy before being cornered by Rhett.

He was executed several months after his capture.

Engraving of Bonnet from *A General History of the Pyrates* (1724).

1804 Whistler's Mother, North Carolina Native

On September 27, 1804, Anna McNeill Whistler was born in Wilmington. She was made famous in the renowned painting, *Arrangement in Grey and Black: The Artist's Mother*, commonly called *Whistler's Mother*.

Shortly after her birth, Anna McNeill moved with her family to New York. In 1831 she married George Washington Whistler, a close friend of her brother.

After growing up in the U.S. and Russia, attending West Point for a brief time, then moving to Paris to study art, the Whistlers' son, James, began to split his time between Paris and London. He continued to develop his craft, becoming an important figure in contemporary art circles and generating controversy for his greater focus on color and arrangement than on realism.

Anna Whistler moved to London in 1863 to live with her son. He painted her as the figure in *Whistler's Mother* in 1871. The painting was first shown in 1872, extending Whistler's reputation, but it has received mixed reviews throughout much of its history.

Whistler's Mother now hangs in the Musée d'Orsay in Paris and has been rarely exhibited in the United States.

1880 Circus Tragedy in Charlotte, 1880

On September 27, 1880, Chief, a performing elephant, killed his trainer, John King, in Charlotte.

The John Robinson Circus, of which Chief was a part, had arrived in Charlotte that day with two shows planned. Crowds of spectators were camped out near the circus, anticipating the next day's shows. Many of them witnessed the horrifying events of that evening.

Chief, a large male, charged his keeper and smashed the man into a railcar, mangling him to the point that he was dead within minutes. The elephant then charged away from the scene, chased by circus workers who finally caught and lassoed him to an older, female elephant named Mary. Mary appeared to grasp the enormity of the younger elephant's deed and beat him with her trunk as they were returned to the circus grounds.

King was buried in Elmwood Cemetery with the circus band playing and two other circus elephants in attendance. For the grave Confederate veteran Billy Berryhill carved an obelisk monument with an elephant in the shaft.

Chief never worked in the circus again, although he remained with it and marched in the parades until he was exiled to the Cincinnati Zoo. Alas, he did not curb his murderous ways. After killing several other keepers, Chief himself was killed.

1903 Scalded to Death by the Steam: The Wreck of the Old 97

On September 27, 1903, arguably the most famous train wreck in U.S. history, the Wreck of the Old 97, occurred in Danville, Virginia. The mail train was en route to Spencer in Rowan County.

Late leaving and under company orders to get back on schedule, engineer Joseph A. "Steve" Broady had the steam engine rolling at about ninety miles an hour, way too fast for safety. Nine of the nineteen railroad and post office employees on board, including Broady, were killed immediately when the train jumped the Stillhouse Trestle tracks and crashed into a ravine. Three others died later of their injuries, and the other seven were injured but survived.

Three of those who lived, all North Carolinians, believed they survived because they jumped from the train. Spencer was 166 miles away from Monroe, Virginia, the trip's origin, and the route usually required more than four hours. The usual, and safe, speed was about thirty-nine miles an hour.

Shortly after the derailment a ballad, "The Wreck of the Old 97" became popular and has remained a mainstay of bluegrass artists. Various people, most with a close connection to one of the dead from the wreck, have claimed its authorship.

Wreck of the Old 97, taken a few days after the wreck, as the engine has been righted.

1829 David Walker and His *Appeal*, a Transformative Book

On September 28, 1829, North Carolina native David Walker published his *Appeal*.

A free-born African American raised in the Wilmington area, Walker traveled south to Charleston, which had a large free black population, before settling in Boston by 1825. A businessman, Walker also founded the Massachusetts General Colored Association, which actively opposed the colonization of free blacks to Africa. He spoke out publicly against slavery and racism. The *Appeal* carried those efforts into print.

Walker's book argued for the black community to take action against slavery and discrimination. He believed the key was to transform one's self through individual moral improvement by education, temperance, religion, regular work habits, and self-regulation. Through action, Walker contended, blacks could refute racism and claim the rights of citizenship. Walker did not advocate overthrowing the government but rather sought to transform society.

The reaction of North Carolina's white leaders to the *Appeal* was typical of that seen in other Southern states. Unsuccessful in their attempts at restricting the rights of free blacks before its publication, legislators quickly passed a series of limiting acts, including banning similar materials from entering the state, once the book was presented to the assembly.

Walker died in 1830 and is buried in an unmarked grave in Boston.

1938 From the Drifters to "Stand By Me," Ben E. King

On September 28, 1938, soul and R&B singer Ben E. Nelson, better known as Ben E. King, was born in Henderson.

King left North Carolina with his family for Harlem in 1947 and started working in his father's restaurants as a teenager. His remarkable ability to sing both bass and tenor made him appealing to choirs and led him to form a vocal group called the Four Bs with some friends.

In King's early 20s George Treadwell recruited him to sing with the Drifters. While with that group, he recorded such hits as "There Goes My Baby" and "Save the Last Dance for Me." He parted ways with Treadwell after disputes over salary and embarked on a solo career in 1961 with the song "Spanish Harlem." Later that year, he released "Stand by Me," the hit for which he is best known. King's feelings for his soon-to-be-wife Betty inspired the words and his performance, creating a heartfelt classic that remains fresh to this day. Broadcast Music, Inc., dubbed it the fourth most-played song of the twentieth century.

King joined the ranks of the Rock and Roll Hall of Fame in 1988, just one of the many accolades he received during his long career. He died in April 2015.

1959 Creation of Lake Norman Altered the Landscape

On September 28, 1959, Southern Power Company—now Duke Energy—broke ground on the Cowan's Ford Dam on the Catawba River. The dam was the starting point for creating what is now Lake Norman in Catawba, Iredell, Lincoln, and Mecklenburg Counties.

The company's plans for the area actually had their origins in the late 1800s, when the company began buying land around the Catawba River, but it continued to allow people to live on the purchased property for many years. Duke Power began filling the area with water in 1962, but since the Catawba River's flow was not very strong and the dam was not completely finished, it took more than a year to fill the lake. Lake Norman now covers more than thirty-two thousand acres, making it the largest man-made body of water in North Carolina.

In 2012 archivists from Davidson College began a crowdsourcing project to get a firmer grasp of structures and locations that went underwater when the lake waters rose in 1963. One of the most significant of those locations is the original site of the Revolutionary War Battle of Cowan's Ford.

SEP 28

1865 Freedmen's Convention Assembled in Raleigh

On September 29, 1865, five months after the close of the Civil War, the Convention of the Freedmen of North Carolina, a statewide assembly of African Americans, gathered at the African Methodist Episcopal Church in Raleigh. The convention lasted four days with 106 men attending.

Under Pres. Andrew Johnson's Reconstruction plan, the state was required to hold a convention in order to nullify the Ordinance of Secession, abolish slavery, and void the Confederate war debt. Only when this was done would Congress consider North Carolina's bid to rejoin the Union.

That convention was scheduled to take place at the State Capitol on October 2. Since only whites could vote to elect its delegates, the voice of the former slaves would not be heard. The Convention of the Freedmen of North Carolina was timed to draw attention away from the white convention by starting three days earlier. Its purpose was to discuss and make known issues important to the former slaves.

James Walker Hood of New Bern was elected president of the Freedmen's Convention. He stressed that "equal rights before the law" should be the convention's watchwords. The delegates pressed for rights to testify in court, to serve as jurors, to act as counsel, and to vote. The convention closed on October 3.

1918 "Old Hickory" Division Breaks Hindenburg Line

On September 29, 1918, the Thirtieth Infantry Division broke the Hindenburg Line, an important segment of the German defensive network on the Western Front during World War I. The action was part of a series of Allied assaults known as the Hundred Days Offensive, which led to the Armistice of November 1918.

The Thirtieth Division was organized from National Guard regiments from North Carolina, South Carolina, and Tennessee, supplemented by volunteers and draftees from around the United States. It was nicknamed the "Old Hickory Division" because of the historic ties that all three states had to Andrew Jackson.

The Division was assigned to the Second Corps of the American Expeditionary Force, which in turn was detached and operated under the control of the British. During the attack on the Hindenburg Line, the Division was part of the British Fourth Army.

The 119th and 120th Infantry Regiments, originally North Carolina National Guard units, led the assault. The Germans opened fire and inflicted heavy casualties. The attack of the 119th made little progress, but the 120th captured the village of Bellicourt after heavy fighting, breaking the Hindenburg Line.

Later in the afternoon the Australian Corps took over the assault and further exploited the initial breakthrough.

1995 John Hope Franklin, From Greenwood to the White House

On September 29, 1995, Pres. Bill Clinton awarded the Presidential Medal of Freedom, the nation's highest civilian honor, to John Hope Franklin of Durham.

A pioneering historian who focused on the social and economic conditions of African Americans, Franklin, a native Oklahoman, was educated at Fisk and Harvard before moving to North Carolina in 1939 to teach at St. Augustine's and North Carolina Central. He taught elsewhere and returned in 1982 to join the history faculty at Duke, where he remained until his death in 2009.

Not just a historian, Franklin helped shape American history. His research formed the historical basis for the groundbreaking NAACP brief that led to the Supreme Court's dismantling of school segregation in the 1954 *Brown v. Board of Education* decision, and in 1965 Franklin joined a cadre of academics who supported Dr. Martin Luther King Jr. on the Selma to Montgomery civil rights march.

During the course of his long career, Franklin wrote more than fifteen books and received honorary degrees from almost a hundred institutions. His 1947 book *From Slavery to Freedom* is still widely regarded as the best single-volume history of African Americans and has sold more than three million copies.

Freedmen's Convention historical marker.

John Hope Franklin about 1997.

SEP 30

1922 Home of the Airborne and Special Forces, Fort Bragg

On September 30, 1922, Camp Bragg, the U.S. War Department's World War I-era field artillery training facility near Fayetteville, was re-designated Fort Bragg and made a permanent Army post.

A 1918 commission led by Gen. William J. Snow chose the 251-square-mile site in southeastern North Carolina for a military training complex because of its varied terrain, adequate water supply, mild climate, and available rail facilities. Named for Confederate Gen. Braxton Bragg and built by civilian laborers, the camp was initially intended to host six brigades of soldiers, though postwar demobilization and budget cuts pared it down to two brigades.

During World War II both the 82nd and 101st Airborne Divisions moved to Fort Bragg, and thousands of artillerymen trained there, as did the Ninth and Tenth Infantry Divisions and the famed Second Armored Division. In 1952 Fort Bragg became headquarters for the U.S. Army Special Operations Command.

Since 2000 the fort's soldiers have participated in combat and humanitarian operations around the world. They continue to serve a vital role in the war on terror.

Today Fort Bragg supports fifty-seven thousand military personnel, eleven thousand civilian employees, and twenty-three thousand family members, making it one of the largest military complexes in the world.

1956 St. John's at Colonial Williamsboro in Vance County

On September 30, 1956, St. John's Episcopal Church in Williamsboro was reconsecrated by the Right Reverend Edwin A. Penick, Bishop of the Diocese of North Carolina, following the building's careful restoration. The Anglican church building constructed in 1773 is one of only three intact colonial-era churches remaining in North Carolina and the only one of frame construction.

The simple but well-crafted rectangular gable-front building rests on a Flemish-bond brick foundation, is sheathed in molded weatherboards, and features a modillion cornice and tall sixteen-pane-over-sixteen-pane double-hung sash windows that illuminate the bright interior characteristic of an Anglican auditory church. The interior has an arched ceiling, the original gallery with turned posts, and boxed pews.

Master carpenter John Lynch built the church according to specifications drawn up in 1771, but it took two years of sporadic effort to complete. The small town of Williamsboro sprang up around the building at the heart of the wealthy plantation community in what would become northern Vance County. It originally was named Nutbush Church and was consecrated as St. John's in 1825.

1970 Fairgrounds Hosted Last NASCAR Race on Dirt Track

On September 30, 1970, the last NASCAR race on a dirt track was held in Raleigh at the State Fairgrounds. Richard Petty took the day's top prize in what was billed as the Home State 200.

Dirt-track racing appeared in the South just before World War I. When the N.C. State Fair moved to its present site in 1928, the increasingly popular sport came with it. As a premier venue with access to fairgoers from across the state, the speedway boosted the racing phenomenon.

The half-mile track has only seen three NASCAR events in its history. The first, held in 1955, was called due to rain while Junior Johnson was leading. The next was fourteen years later in 1969; James Hylton won. The last was the 1970 event, though the grandstand remains and sections of the old track are used each October.

Safety concerns were the main reason more modern, paved tracks replaced their dirt counterparts. The remains of some of the old ones still dot the Carolinas, with saplings poking through the stands and undergrowth overtaking sites where stock car racing had its start.

Fort Bragg in 1938.

1706 First Town Lots Recorded in Bath

On October 1, 1706, the first town lots in Bath were recorded and acknowledged in court. The lots belonged to Christopher Gale, the first chief justice of the colony.

Bath, incorporated in 1705, is North Carolina's oldest town. In 1707 the town included a gristmill and the colony's first shipyard. Other North Carolina firsts in Bath include the public library, St. Thomas's Church, and the post road.

In the eighteenth century, Bath was a thriving town of vital importance to the fledgling colony. It became the colony's first port in 1716. An official document called it, "the most proper place within the said Province for ships to take in masts, pitch, Tar, Turpentine and other Naval Stores for the use of his Majesty's Fleet." Bath was home to colonial governors Robert Daniel, Thomas Cary, Charles Eden, and Matthew Rowan.

When the Beaufort County seat was moved to Washington in 1785, twelve miles away, Bath lost much of its trade and status, becoming the quiet, rural town that it is today. Historic Bath is one of twenty-seven North Carolina State Historic Sites.

1864 Rose Greenhow, Confederate Spy, Drowning Victim

On October 1, 1864, Rose O'Neal Greenhow died while trying to run the blockade into the port of Wilmington.

The Washington, D.C. socialite and spy had been in Europe trying to win support for the Confederacy from England and France. While she found a great deal of sympathy there, neither nation would officially sanction the Southern government.

Greenhow, who had been imprisoned in 1861 by the Federal government for spying, was on her way home to Richmond in 1864 on board the blockade runner *Condor* when it was pursued by a blockader. Although the *Condor* was within the protective reach of the guns at Fort Fisher, Greenhow did not know that and was afraid of recapture by Federal authorities, so she insisted on being put into a small boat to make for shore. She was the only woman aboard and the only person who drowned when the small boat capsized.

At the time of her death, twenty-five hundred dollars in gold was found in her clothes, which she received from the sale of a book published in London about her imprisonment. Greenhow's body was carried first to Fort Fisher, then to Wilmington, where a full military funeral was conducted. She is buried at Oakdale Cemetery.

Rose O'Neal Greenhow with her youngest daughter and namesake, "Little" Rose, at the Old Capitol Prison, Washington, D.C., 1862.

1918 Pasteurization Initiative in Tarboro, 1918

On October 1, 1918, the Tarboro Town Council passed an ordinance making it illegal for unpasteurized milk or cream to be sold within the town limits.

The ordinance also established a municipal milk plant—the first of its kind in the nation—where local producers could bring their milk to be pasteurized, processed, and sold. The local law resulted from an epidemic of typhoid fever, dysentery, and colitis that had claimed several lives. Outbreaks like these were more common in small towns than big cities because many rural places lacked access to large commercial dairies using refrigeration and pasteurization to ensure that milk was safe to drink.

First housed in the town's water plant with deliveries done by horse-drawn carriage, the Tarboro plant's product became popular because of its low prices. By 1924 it operated in a separate building with delivery by trucks.

Tarboro's milk plant became an international model, and officials from across the county and around the world came to learn from the small Edgecombe County town's example.

The plant closed its doors in 1965.

OCT 2

1866 Just Stepped Out, Robert Patton of Burke County

On October 2, 1866, seventeen-year-old Robert Logan Patton filled a pillow case with bread, sweet potatoes, and his belongings and ran away from his Burke County home.

Patton's mother encouraged her young son to attend winter school sessions, where he learned vocabulary, mathematics, and geography, sparking in Patton a deep appreciation for education. Following a short stint in the state's Home Guard in the spring of 1865, he daydreamed of attending Wake Forest College. His father, though, expected him to remain home, help run the farm, and support the family.

When his father woke him two hours before sunrise to bring in wood for the fires on that October day in 1866, Patton simply threw his bag over his shoulder and slipped away into the darkness with only five cents to his name. Over the course of the next ten years, Patton received a teaching certificate, attended Phillips Exeter Academy, and graduated from Amherst College.

The college graduate then returned to Burke County, gathered the firewood for which he had been sent so many years earlier, and brought it into the house. Patton stayed in Burke and dedicated his entire life to teaching.

1894 State School for the Deaf Opened in Morganton

On October 2, 1894, the North Carolina School for the Deaf opened with 104 students and eight teachers. The first superintendent was Edward McKee Goodwin, who served in that position until his death in 1937.

A state-supported school for the deaf and blind was first proposed in 1816, but no provision was made for such an institution until the 1840s when Gov. John Motley Morehead took up the cause. In 1844 the legislature appropriated five thousand dollars for the school, and the following year the Governor Morehead School was established in Raleigh to teach the deaf, dumb, and blind. By 1890 a movement was afoot to create a separate school for the deaf to alleviate overcrowding at the Raleigh campus.

Morganton civic leaders organized by Samuel McDowell Tate sought the new school, offering the state five thousand dollars and a hundred acres on "Spa Hill," a picturesque hilltop setting on the outskirts of town. Construction began in 1891. The monumental Main Building was the first to be erected and still dominates the campus.

Today the North Carolina School for the Deaf campus in Morganton has a large campus and students in kindergarten through twelfth grade. An eastern campus opened in Wilson in 1964.

1961 The Battleship North Carolina Arrives in Wilmington

On October 2, 1961, the battleship USS *North Carolina* came to Wilmington. The mighty ship opened to the public just a couple of weeks later.

At the time of her commissioning on April 9, 1941, she was considered the world's greatest sea weapon. During World War II, the *North Carolina* participated in every major naval offensive in the Pacific area of operations and earned fifteen battle stars.

The battleship survived many close calls and near misses, with one hit when a Japanese torpedo slammed into the battleship's hull on September 15, 1942. A quick response on the part of the crew allowed the mighty ship to keep up with the fleet. By war's end the battleship had lost only ten men in action and had sixty-seven wounded. After serving as a training vessel for midshipmen, the *North Carolina* was decommissioned in 1947.

In 1958 the announcement of her impending scrapping led to a statewide campaign by citizens of North Carolina to save the ship and bring her back to her home state. The campaign included a special effort among North Carolina's schoolchildren, and of the 1.1 million children in school at the time, seven hundred thousand gave at least a dime.

The battleship remains in Wilmington today, standing sentinel in the Cape Fear River.

1981 Harry Golden of the Carolina Israelite, One of a Kind

On October 2, 1981, journalist and humorist Harry Golden died. He achieved wide fame as publisher of the *Carolina Israelite*, which he issued between 1944 and 1968 from Charlotte to an international audience.

Golden's trademark was to use humor and satire to oppose Southern racial and political practices. Martin Luther King Jr. called him one of "our white brothers who have grasped the meaning of this social revolution and committed themselves to it."

He first came to national attention in 1956 after he testified before the Pearsall Commission that white Southerners did not seem to mind standing with African Americans: "It is only when the Negro 'sets' that the fur begins to fly." Thus, he suggested, public schools could be painlessly integrated by providing desks but no seats. He went on to suggest sixteen more plans that mocked Southern racial mores.

Wide circulation of his "Vertical Negro Plan" generated interest in his writing, and in 1958 a compilation of his columns, *Only in America*, became a bestseller. He advised Robert Kennedy in his 1964 and 1968 campaigns for the U. S. Senate and the Democratic presidential nomination.

In 1979 Golden received the North Carolina Award for Literature. He is buried in Hebrew Cemetery in Charlotte.

1900 Famed Writer Thomas Wolfe is Born in Asheville

On October 3, 1900, Thomas Wolfe, the famed writer from Asheville, was born. Wolfe attended public schools there for seven years while living in his mother's boardinghouse with the rest of his family.

Growing up in Asheville formed the basis for his thinly-veiled autobiographical novel *Look Homeward, Angel*, which was published in 1929. Asheville residents easily recognized themselves in the text, and Wolfe received letters from irate readers who felt wrongly portrayed in the book. It was 1937 before he would return to his childhood home, having published many short stories and a second novel, *Of Time and the River*, in the meantime. Although he planned to spend the summer writing in a rented cabin, Wolfe worked little, being constantly disturbed by visitors and undergoing family strife. He began to ponder the many implications of the phrase "You can't go home again," which became the title of a novel that would be published in 1940, two years after his death.

His mother's former boardinghouse, known as the "Old Kentucky Home," made famous as "Dixieland" in his first novel, is now a State Historic Site.

Thomas Wolfe

1960 Andy Griffith Show Debuts

On October 3, 1960, the first episode of *The Andy Griffith Show* aired on CBS Television.

The program starred Mount Airy native Andy Griffith and focused on life in the fictional community of Mayberry, North Carolina, said to be have been modeled after Griffith's hometown. Already a Broadway, radio, and film actor, Griffith landed the role of Mayberry Sheriff Andy Taylor in an episode of *The Danny Thomas Show*, wherein the sheriff arrested Thomas's character for running a stop sign.

Eight months after the *Danny Thomas* episode aired featuring Sheriff Taylor, *The Andy Griffith Show* debuted. Filmed at Desilu Studios in California, the wholesome half-hour show featured the small-town antics of the widowed Sheriff Taylor, his bumbling deputy Barney Fife (Don Knotts), son Opie (Ron Howard), spinster housekeeper Aunt Bee (Frances Bavier), and other colorful Mayberry characters. Unlike most comedic sitcom stars, Griffith played the straight man. Neither Griffith nor the show won awards during its eight seasons, but co-stars Knotts and Bavier received a combined total of six Emmys.

When *The Andy Griffith Show* ended in 1968, it was the number-one ranked show on television. Its 249 episodes still appear in syndication.

Andy Griffith

1777 Francis Nash Mortally Wounded at the Battle of Germantown

On October 4, 1777, Francis Nash, brigadier general of the North Carolina Continental Troops under Gen. George Washington in the American Revolution, was mortally wounded by a cannonball at the Battle of Germantown, near Philadelphia.

Born in Virginia in 1742, Nash moved to North Carolina before 1763. He lived in Hillsborough with his brother, Abner, who would later serve as governor of North Carolina. Francis Nash worked as a lawyer and merchant, was clerk of court, and served as an assemblyman before the Revolutionary War began. He was a lieutenant colonel and colonel of the First North Carolina Regiment of Continental Troops before being promoted to brigadier general of the North Carolina Continental Troops.

Pvt. Hugh McDonald described Nash's fateful injury, "We lost our General, Frank Nash, who was killed by the cannon ball which struck his horse behind his right thigh, and passing through, cut off his right thigh." In army orders on the day of Nash's funeral, Washington urged all officers to "attend and pay their respect to a brave man who died in defense of his country."

Nash County is named in his honor.

OCT 4

1856 Benjamin Hedrick, Chapel Hill Heretic

On October 4, 1856, Benjamin Hedrick, a professor of chemistry at the University of North Carolina, published his "Defence" in the *North Carolina Standard*, a Raleigh newspaper. The letter was his response to the newspaper's campaign against him after he announced his support for the presidential candidacy of Republican John C. Fremont in August of that year.

The crux of the issue was slavery. Though not a militant abolitionist, Hedrick did not support the expansion of slavery and advocated Fremont's election because he shared Fremont's views on the matter. Fremont was an ardent abolitionist.

The *Standard* did not simply call for Hedrick to be dismissed from the university. It stated, "No man who is avowedly for John C. Fremont for President ought to be allowed to breathe the air or tread the soil of North Carolina."

Hedrick's colleagues advised that he not respond to the *Standard's* attacks, but he ignored them and published the defense of his position. University students burned him in effigy, the trustees fired him, and the faculty issued a statement assuring the people of the state that the faculty had no more "Black Republicans," white southerners' epithet for whites who sympathized with the hated party. Hedrick left his native state soon after and lived the rest of his life in New York and Washington, D.C.

1986 Wry Television Journalist David Brinkley a Wilmingtonian

On October 4, 1986, Graham native Rachel Oliver-Cobbin became the first North Carolinian to be crowned Miss Black America.

Oliver-Cobbin first stepped on the pageant scene while a student at Cummings High School, winning the title of Miss Cummings High in 1983. That victory influenced Oliver-Cobbin, a talented singer, to pursue opportunities in entertainment, leading her to enter the Miss Black Massachusetts pageant while attending Emerson College in Boston. She claimed that title in June 1986 and moved on to the national pageant in Hampton, Virginia in October.

In addition to the national crown, Oliver-Cobbin took home a two thousand dollar award and a fur coat. After winning the competition, she embarked on a speaking tour of high schools, warning students of the dangers of drugs and encouraging them to pursue their dreams.

In the 1990s Oliver-Cobbin joined the R & B band Atlantic Starr as a lead vocalist, recording five albums with the group. Today the accomplished singer and UNC-Greensboro graduate can be found in her home county of Alamance, where she continues to mentor young men and women.

1997 Lemur Jovian, Star of Zoboomafoo

On October 4, 1997, Jovian, the lemur that many television watchers came to know as Zoboomafoo, was introduced to the custom-made sound stage at the Duke Lemur Center.

Jovian was a *Coquerel's sifaka*, a species of lemur native to Madagascar. He was selected to appear in the educational wildlife show, *Zoboomafoo*, produced by Chris and Martin Kratt. The latter was a graduate of Duke University and had volunteered at the Lemur Center while in school.

The award-winning children's show starred Jovian as *Zoboomafoo* and included a puppet lookalike for scenes in which *Zoboomafoo* talked. For the program a sound stage was attached to the animal-care building where Jovian lived with his parents while the live portions of the show were being filmed.

Zoboomafoo ended production in 2001. Jovian enjoyed his retirement in a natural habitat enclosure at the Lemur Center. He died November 10, 2014 at age twenty.

The Duke Lemur Center, formerly the Duke University Primate Center, was established to explore the genetic foundations of primate behavior. Today researchers investigate a wide variety of subject matter, including behavior, physiology, paleontology, and conservation biology.

Jovian, relaxing at the Duke Lemur Center.

1751 James Iredell, U.S. Supreme Court Justice

On October 5, 1751, James Iredell was born. Few people have had more influence on the modern American judicial system than this lawyer, judge, and writer. Originally a representative of the Crown, he challenged the colonial court system and was instrumental in the creation of its American successor.

Iredell emigrated from England to Edenton in 1768. As he practiced law and worked as a customs comptroller, his personal convictions clashed with professional interests. Finding fault with colonial courts, he expressed his dissent through a number of insightful essays. Among his finest works were his criticisms of British rule in America. Iredell realized that British laws were not always feasible on American soil, and having reached that conclusion, he joined the revolutionaries.

After the Revolutionary War Iredell found himself at the center of judicial reform. In 1777 he was appointed to the superior court, and he later served the state as attorney general. Iredell was among the most influential Federalists, who were advocates of a strong federal government. When North Carolina ratified the federal constitution in 1789, George Washington appointed Iredell as one of the first federal Supreme Court judges.

Iredell County is named in his honor.

1909 East Carolina Set Up to Educate Teachers

On October 5, 1909, the East Carolina Teachers Training School opened its doors with the mission of providing young men and women the training they needed to be able to teach in the public schools of North Carolina.

The school was established in Greenville in 1907 at the urgent persuasion of former governor and Greenville resident Thomas Jordan Jarvis. There were seven other eastern North Carolina communities vying for the institution including Edenton, Washington, Kinston, New Bern, Tarboro, Rocky Mount, and Elizabeth City.

When the school opened in October 1909, there were eleven faculty members to teach the 104 women and nineteen men enrolled in a two-year training program. In 1911 sixteen members of the first class graduated, all of them women. The first man to graduate, Henry Oglesby, did not do so until 1932.

The school began offering four-year degrees in 1921. When it offered its first master's degree in 1929, it also began to diversify its curriculum. The institution was renamed East Carolina University in 1967 and was incorporated into the UNC system five years later.

Today East Carolina University is the third largest school in the UNC system, with an outstanding reputation in the fields of teacher training, music, art, and medicine.

1946 Popcorn Sutton, Moonshiner and Colorful Character

On October 5, 1946, Marvin "Popcorn" Sutton, notorious moonshiner and cultural icon, was born in Maggie Valley.

Sutton, a gritty, spirited fellow, first learned how to concoct illegal alcohol from his father, whose Scots-Irish ancestors had been avid distillers in keeping with their cultural tradition. Sutton carried on the family legacy in Cocke County, Tennessee, where he became famous not only for his liquor but for his role in moonshine culture.

Sutton published an autobiography entitled *Me and My Likker* in 1999 and continued to spread his love for moonshine when he starred in the documentary *This is the Last Drum of Likker I'll Ever Make* in 2002. Through the book and the documentary Sutton conveyed the immense amount of work he put into distilling liquor. Not only was he witty and wild, he was also truly passionate about his trade.

Ultimately, Sutton's notoriety attracted the attention of the law. In 2009 he was convicted of illegal distilling and possession of firearms. Rather than spending the required eighteen months in jail, he chose suicide. Despite his untimely end, Sutton's lively spirits and cultural pride proved him a true mountain man.

Moonshiner Popcorn Sutton in one of his still houses, March 2007.

1947 James E. Shepard, Founder of North Carolina Central University

On October 6, 1947, James Edward Shepard, founder of North Carolina Central University, died in Durham.

The eldest of twelve children, Shepard was born in Raleigh in 1875. After graduating from Shaw University with a pharmacy degree in 1894, he married Annie Day Robinson, granddaughter of the renowned antebellum furniture maker Thomas Day.

In 1898 Shepard became one of the first seven investors in the North Carolina Mutual Life Insurance Company in Durham. The company eventually became the largest black-owned business in the South. In 1907 he helped incorporate the Mechanics and Farmers Bank, another successful black-owned institution in Durham.

Apart from his businesses, Shepard was very active in politics and education. He served as a clerk in the Register of Deeds Office in Durham County and as Raleigh's deputy collector for the Internal Revenue Service. In 1910 he opened what eventually become N.C. Central University. The school became a public institution and the first publicly-supported liberal arts college for blacks in the country in 1923. Shepard served as the college's president until his death in 1947.

1963 Fire Destroys Bandon, Home of Inglis Fletcher

On October 6, 1963, Bandon, the beloved plantation home of author Inglis Fletcher, burned.

Fletcher, the author of the *Carolina Series*, twelve historical novels set in eastern North Carolina during the colonial and revolutionary periods, purchased the early nineteenth century property with her husband in 1944. The mansion and several outbuildings were situated on just over sixty acres north of Edenton on the shores of the Chowan River.

The house had been unoccupied for eighteen years and was in a state of disrepair when the Fletchers bought it. A schoolhouse on the grounds dated to the 1750s, while the plantation house itself was completed around 1800. At the time of the fire, Fletcher and her grandson were watching television on Bandon's second floor. The blaze was discovered by neighbors, who spotted flames coming from the roof. The fire was believed to have started in the attic. Although the mansion was fully engulfed by the time firefighters arrived, neighbors had moved much of the antique furniture on the first floor out onto the lawn.

Fletcher sold the land the following year, and the schoolhouse was moved to Edenton.

James E. Shepard, ca. 1925.

1967 Duke Grads Nation's First Physician Assistants

On October 6, 1967, three students graduated from Duke's Physician Assistant (PA) Program and became the first PAs in the country.

When Dr. Eugene A. Stead Jr., then chairman of Duke's Department of Medicine, established the PA Program in 1965, it was the first of its kind in the nation. A two-year course that trained students to practice medicine and provide health care services under a doctor's supervision, the program aimed to address the problem of physician shortage, particularly in rural areas throughout North Carolina.

While the initial recruitment targeted ex-military corpsmen who possessed some medical experience, Duke's PA program soon attracted a wide range of applicants, including women and people of color seeking new career opportunities in medicine.

Today there are nearly a hundred thousand PAs practicing across the United States. The success of the profession during the second half of the twentieth century is due in part to the early efforts of PA leaders, graduates, and students in North Carolina. They worked to have the profession legally recognized and accredited, founded the American Academy of Physician Assistants, the official organization for the profession, and were instrumental in the development of certification and continuing-education guidelines.

1974 Governor Luther Hodges Dies

On October 6, 1974, former North Carolina governor Luther Hartwell Hodges died. After a career in business, he made industrial development the hallmark of his administration and was instrumental in the establishment of the Research Triangle Park.

The "Businessman Governor" was born in 1898 to a tenant farmer. He served as a second lieutenant in World War I and graduated from UNC in 1919. He returned home to Spray (now Eden) to take a position as secretary to the general manager of the Marshall Field and Company mills. Hodges remained with Marshall Field, retiring in 1950 as a vice president.

In 1952 Hodges launched a successful bid for lieutenant governor. When Gov. William B. Umstead died in 1954, Hodges became governor; he was reelected in 1956. His greatest success was the Research Triangle, the business park founded in 1956, which he called the "heart and hope of North Carolina's industrial future."

Shortly after Hodges's term as governor ended, Pres. John F. Kennedy selected him as Secretary of Commerce. He served in that post until December 1964. For the rest of his life, his energies were directed largely to the Research Triangle Foundation, on which he served as board chairman from 1965 to 1972.

Governor Luther Hodges at dedication of restored Old Jail, Halifax, April 12, 1955.

1780 Patriot Forces Defeat British at Kings Mountain

On October 7, 1780, Patriot forces defeated the British in the Battle of Kings Mountain, the beginning of the end of British control in the South.

Patriots had created an atmosphere of Tory persecution in western North Carolina, and in September 1780 British Maj. Patrick Ferguson decided to subdue the rebellious region. He warned mountain residents that if the insurrection continued, he personally would "lay waste their country with fire and sword."

Patriot volunteers accepted Ferguson's challenge. Roused by the threats, many of those who gathered against Ferguson did so only to protect their communities. Joseph Winston and Benjamin Cleveland raised militias in Surry and Wilkes Counties, then marched to Burke County, where they met Maj. Joseph McDowell's volunteers. Militia groups came from surrounding states—those from Tennessee were known as the "Overmountain Men."

When Patriot forces arrived at the foot of Kings Mountain, they found Tories camped at the top, prepared to repel any attack. Surrounding the base of the mountain, columns of men engaged the Tory line, and eventually the lofty position caused Loyalists to fire over the heads of those Patriots who raced up the incline to overrun the first defensive line. Major Ferguson was killed, and the Loyalist militia was overwhelmed. The battlefield is now a National Military Park in South Carolina.

1799 Half-Ton Pickup a Challenge for Pallbearers

On October 7, 1799, Mills Darden, a true giant among men in his time, was born in Northampton County.

In his lifetime, and for some hundred years afterward, Darden was considered the world's largest man. By today's standards he is neither the heaviest nor the tallest, but he is the heaviest tall man and the tallest heavy man. At the time of his death, Darden was seven feet, six inches tall and weighed a little more than a thousand pounds.

Though a native North Carolinian, Darden moved to Tennessee when he as a young adult. Self-conscious about his appearance, the giant posed for no portraits. In 1839 a tailor who made a coat for Darden had three two-hundred-plus-pound men button themselves inside the coat and parade about the court square in Lexington, Tennessee. Another source reported trousers with a seventy-six-inch waist and a hat sized 8½ and about twenty-eight inches around the crown.

Remarkably, Darden worked as a farmer for much of his life. When the work became too strenuous for a man of his stature, he opened a tavern, where his moderate fame was an advantage. Married twice, he had numerous children. Upon his death in 1857, it took seventeen men to place Darden in his eight-foot-long coffin.

Death of Major Ferguson at King's Mountain. Engraving depicting the death of British Major Patrick Ferguson at the Battle of Kings Mountain, October 7, 1780.

OCT 8

1826 Matt Ransom, Confederate General and U.S. Senator

On October 8, 1826, Matt Whitaker Ransom, Confederate general, U.S. senator and minister to Mexico, was born in Warren County.

After graduating from the University of North Carolina, Ransom studied law. He married and moved to Northampton County in 1853, where he practiced. Serving in the legislature at the outbreak of the Civil War, Ransom enlisted as a private in the Confederate Army, joining the Thirty-Fifth North Carolina Regiment, which he eventually would command. He was wounded three times during the war and was eventually promoted to brigadier general.

After the war Ransom became a strong supporter of reconciliation between the regions. He was elected to the U.S. Senate in 1872 and represented North Carolina there until 1895. A strong supporter of Pres. Grover Cleveland, he was posted to Mexico as the "Minister Plenipotentiary and Envoy Extraordinary," serving in that role until 1897, when he returned to Northampton County and retired from public service.

He died in October 1904. A bust of Ransom, commissioned by the North Carolina Historical Commission, was placed in the rotunda of the State Capitol in 1911.

1912 Millie McKoy, Conjoined Twin, Died

On October 8, 1912, Millie McKoy, one of the conjoined twins known as Millie-Christine died. Christine, who could not be separated from her sister, died the following day.

The twins were born into slavery near Whiteville, in Columbus County, in 1851. During their lifetime physicians took great interest in their physiology and, after much study, determined that they shared portions of their pelvis and spinal cord. The twins were intelligent, and although they were two separate personalities, they considered themselves one person.

Railroad lines even issued letters to conductors, instructing them to require only one ticket for the "dual woman." Exhibited initially as a curiosity, the twins eventually learned to sing and dance. Exceptionally talented singers, Mille-Christine was often billed as the "Carolina Nightingale."

The twins were prosperous after emancipation and were able to purchase the property on which they were born. They built a ten-room house there, where they lived between tours. Appearing around the world, the duo even performed for Britain's Queen Victoria at one point.

Buried near their home, their original lead grave marker read, "A soul with two thoughts. Two hearts that beat as one."

Millie-Christine McKoy, ca. 1866.

1915 Warren Grove School, North Carolina's first Rosenwald School

On October 8, 1915, the Warren Grove School, North Carolina's first Rosenwald School, was completed. During the 1914–1915 academic year, North Carolina received funding for its first Rosenwald schools, although the Rosenwald Fund's school building program did not begin until the nonprofit was incorporated in 1917. Using Tuskegee's architectural plans for school houses as a model, the Warren Grove School in Chowan County, a two-teacher floorplan, was built for a total cost of $1,622. The black community had contributed $486, the white community and the school system furnished $836, and Julius Rosenwald himself had contributed $300, the maximum amount initially allocated for any schoolhouse.

Sears and Roebuck president Rosenwald and Booker T. Washington established the fund to provide grants to African American communities to improve education. By 1928 one in every five rural schools in the South was a Rosenwald school; the schools housed one-third of the region's rural black schoolchildren and teachers. At the program's conclusion in 1932, it had produced 4,977 schools, 217 teacher's homes, and 163 shop buildings that served 663,625 students in 15 states. Financial aid from the Rosenwald Fund often subsidized only fifteen to twenty percent of a building's total cost. To cover the balance, monies from local and state education departments, as well as white communities (a requirement of aid from the fund) were used. In North Carolina the fund assisted with 817 projects in ninety-three counties.

Warren Grove School, 1980s.

1973 Archie Ijames, Associate of Jim Jones of the Peoples Temple

On October 8, 1973, the board of directors of the California-based Peoples Temple passed a resolution establishing a "Branch Church and Agricultural Mission" in Guyana. The settlement would come to be known as Jonestown, and church assistant pastor Archie Ijames was one of six authorized to help establish the mission.

Born in Davie County in 1913, Ijames first met Peoples Temple founder Jim Jones at an event in Indianapolis. Originally skeptical about joining Jones's church, Ijames was persuaded by Jones's ostensible humility and honesty and by the Peoples Temple's commitment to transcend racial divides. Ijames's family was embraced by Jones's church, and Ijames eventually rose to become Jones's associate pastor. After first staying behind to tend the Indianapolis Peoples Temple congregation, Ijames eventually followed to Jones to California.

Ijames accompanied Jones on a December 1973 scouting trip to Guyana, and after faking a health scare, Jones convinced Ijames to stay in Guyana and make all the final arrangements for the Temple's new mission. Soon after Jones's arrival back in the U.S., tensions began to rise between Jones and Ijames, primarily because Jones was driving a wedge between Ijames and his family. After reuniting with his wife, Ijames and she left Guyana, attempting to take forty-five thousand dollars of the Temple's money with them. They ultimately gave back the money and returned to the United States.

Despite the difficulties and the fact that Jones had at one point ordered a hit on him, Ijames stayed committed to the Peoples Temple and its principles of integration and communalism. He remained with group at its San Francisco location, and received much media attention there after the mass suicide in Guyana in March 1978.

1837 Maritime Disaster Off Ocracoke in 1837

On October 9, 1837, the steamship *Home* ran into a powerful hurricane that became known as the "Racer's Storm." The ship was en route from New York to Charleston and was operating with a damaged boiler.

Steamships, built for speed and comfort, were not designed for rough ocean travel, so the choppy surf was treacherous for the *Home*. Hoping to wait out the storm, Capt. Carlton White grounded the struggling vessel about a hundred yards offshore near Ocracoke Village, but the surf tore the vessel apart.

Although there were 135 people aboard, there were only three lifeboats (one of which was destroyed in the wreck) and a mere two life preservers. The two men who secured the life preservers lived, but seventy passengers and twenty-five crew members were lost.

It was not until 1852 that Congress enacted legislation that required ships to carry an adequate number of life preservers.

1866 W. W. Kitchin, North Carolina-Style Progressive Politician

On October 9, 1866, future governor William Walton Kitchin was born near Scotland Neck. Educated in local schools and at Wake Forest, he studied law and in 1888 opened a practice in Roxboro.

A Democrat, Kitchin entered politics at a time when his party's fortunes were at a low point. He was the sole Democrat elected to either house of the Congress from North Carolina in the fall 1896 election.

After twelve years in Congress, Kitchen was elected governor in 1908. While he held the state's top job, he worked to increase expenditures for education, public health, care for the mentally handicapped, and drainage of swamp lands.

In line with the national efforts to break up trusts and regulate business, Kitchin backed legislation to strengthen antitrust laws, require better sanitation, and set a ten-hour workday in factories. He also advocated prohibiting work by children under age thirteen and licensing foreign corporations doing business in the state. During his term thirteen hundred miles of roads were constructed. He served as governor for four years, then returned to practicing law.

In 1919 a stroke forced Kitchin into retirement, and he returned to Halifax County. He died in 1924.

W. W. Kitchin and family, c. 1906. *Pictured from left to right*: Anne Maria Kitchin, W. W. Kitchin, Sue Arrington Kitchin, Clement Kitchin (seated), Elizabeth Kitchin, Musette (Sue) Satterfield Kitchin, Musette Kitchin (on her mother's lap).

OCT 10

1902 Opening of Palmer Memorial Institute

On October 10, 1902, the Palmer Memorial Institute, a preparatory school for African-Americans, opened in Sedalia. Founded by scholar Dr. Charlotte Hawkins Brown, the school was dedicated to providing educational opportunities for blacks in rural North Carolina.

In its early years the school's curriculum focused on the industrial and domestic sciences and included grades ranging from elementary to high school. Once the first public school for African American students opened in Sedalia, Palmer closed its elementary program and evolved into a college preparatory school. To compensate for the loss of local students to the public school, it began recruiting top students from out-of-state. In addition to providing a stellar academic curriculum, PMI also emphasized the importance of proper etiquette and training in the arts.

The school, which educated more than two thousand students during its history, was forced to close its doors in 1971. In 1987, after much campaigning by Dr. Brown's family, friends, and former students, the state of North Carolina bought the campus and created the Charlotte Hawkins Brown Memorial State Historic Site.

1917 Jazz Giant Thelonious Monk of Rocky Mount

On October 10, 1917, Thelonious Monk was born in Rocky Mount. Though Monk lived most of his life in Manhattan, his North Carolina roots ran deep.

Monk's style was original and unorthodox, incorporating elements of stride piano and gospel to create a "rhythmic virtuosity," striking dissonant notes and playing skewed melodies. He collaborated with Charlie Parker, John Coltrane, and many other noted jazz musicians of the time. Along with Dizzy Gillespie, another of his collaborators, Monk is credited as an architect of bebop. The third composition he copyrighted, and his first as sole composer, was also his best-known, "'Round Midnight."

Personally, Monk had a reputation as the ultimate hipster, with his goatee, skullcap, and bamboo-rimmed sunglasses. He often left his keyboard to dance while onstage and at random moments on the street or in public spaces would twirl for several minutes. Viewed by some as temperamental and eccentric, he is described by his biographer Robin Kelley as essentially rebellious. Kelley documented that Monk suffered from bipolar disorder most of his adult life.

In 1972 Monk withdrew from public appearances and was hospitalized intermittently until his death. Among his last extended stands was a week at the Frog and Nightgown in Raleigh's Cameron Village in 1970. A park in his hometown has carried his name since 2000.

1934 R. D. W. Connor Appointed First Archivist of the United States

On October 10, 1934, Franklin D. Roosevelt appointed R. D. W. Connor as the first Archivist of the United States.

Born in Wilson in 1878, Connor attended college at UNC, where he was editor-in-chief of the newspaper, literary magazine, and yearbook during his senior year. After college, he taught in public schools across eastern North Carolina and worked with the N.C. Department of Public Instruction, promoting public education through speeches and articles while also serving in a voluntary capacity as secretary to the newly formed North Carolina Historical Commission, a post to which he was appointed in 1903.

In 1906 Connor accepted a salaried position as Secretary of the Historical Commission. His stalwart leadership and investigative mind guided the agency, now the Office of Archives and History, through its early years. Early in his tenure with the state, Connor wrote, "No people who are indifferent to their past need hope to make their future great."

When Roosevelt appointed Connor to the national post, he again found himself having to build an archival program from the ground up. Connor successfully educated Washington bureaucrats on the need for proper records management and justified the urgency for protecting records of archival quality. He remained as Archivist of the United States until 1941.

Palmer Memorial Institute Class of 1948.

1896 African American Surfmen and Daring Rescue of the E. S. Newman

On October 11, 1896, the Pea Island Lifesavers, led by Richard Etheridge, made their most dramatic rescue, that of the survivors of the schooner *E. S. Newman*.

The United States Lifesaving Service (USLS) established eighteen stations along the Outer Banks in the late 1870s and early 1880s. Black veterans of the United States Colored Troops found work in the stations not only as cooks and stewards but also as lifesavers, known as surfmen.

In 1879 a ship wrecked near Pea Island and received no assistance. When the survivors reached shore, they found the surfmen of the Pea Island station fast asleep. An inquiry by the Lifesaving Service found the members of the all-white crew grossly negligent; they were fired.

In their place the senior inspector suggested the appointment of a local African American veteran, Richard Etheridge, as the new station keeper. A former army sergeant, he proved exceptional at his job. Etheridge hired a crew composed mainly of veterans with whom he had served. Until its closing in 1947, Pea Island remained the only all-black facility in the USLS.

1918 World War I Medal of Honor Recipient Robert Blackwell

On October 11, 1918, Person County native Robert Lester Blackwell was killed when he attempted to deliver a message asking for help for his unit near St. Souflet, France.

Blackwell's unit had been cut off from the remainder of the force engaged in battle and was exposed to artillery and machine gun fire. The platoon commander ordered that a messenger be sent back for help; that man was promptly killed, as was the second man sent behind him. Blackwell volunteered for the task and also lost his life. He was posthumously awarded the Congressional Medal of Honor. The citation commended Blackwell for his "conspicuous gallantry and intrepidity above and beyond the call of duty."

Blackwell's father received the award in a ceremony in the State Capitol. Gov. Thomas Bickett spoke, noting that no medal could compensate for Blackwell's death. The family subsequently donated the medal to what is now the North Carolina Museum of History.

Blackwell was one of two North Carolinians to receive the Congressional Medal in World War I, the other being Samuel I. Parker. Blackwell also received the Cross of War from both the Portuguese and Italian governments.

1947 Herschel Johnson Advocated Partition of Palestine, 1947

On October 11, 1947, as the newly created United Nations debated the partition of Palestine and the creation of the state of Israel, North Carolinian Herschel Johnson was at the center of the deliberations.

The plain-spoken career Foreign Service officer understood that no plan could satisfy both Arabs and Jews, but "if we are to effect through the United Nations a solution to this problem, it cannot be done without the use of the knife." The plan, with the support of the Soviet Union, passed the Assembly by a 33–17 vote.

Born in Atlanta in 1894, Johnson moved to Charlotte with his family when he was six. He attended UNC and Harvard before joining the State Department in 1920. He served in junior roles in American embassies in Switzerland, Bulgaria, Honduras, Mexico, and Great Britain, where he acted as ambassador after the death of Robert W. Bingham and the departure of Joseph P. Kennedy.

In 1946 Johnson became acting U.S. representative to the U.N. He followed his service in New York with the ambassadorship to Brazil. A lifelong bachelor, he died in 1966 and is buried in Charlotte's Elmwood Cemetery.

Pea Island Lifesavers. The caption on the back of the photo reads "All Black Crew, Pea Island Life Saving Sta., Hatteras Island, N.C."

OCT 12

1793 Old East, UNC-Chapel Hill Landmark

On October 12, 1793, Grand Master Mason and future North Carolina governor William R. Davie helped lay the cornerstone of Old East, the nation's oldest state university building, now a dormitory at UNC-Chapel Hill.

The brick building housed the university's first student, Hinton James, in 1795, and later the future eleventh U.S. president, James K. Polk. Over the years Old East has also held classrooms and offices. It was home to the university library from 1853 through 1869.

Set at the crest of McCorkle Place, the structure originally stood two stories tall but had a third floor added in 1824 to mirror Old West, another dormitory constructed opposite it. The "north towers" added to both buildings in 1848 became the library and debating chambers for the university's two literary societies. Old East was home to the Philanthropic Society (the "Phi"), which took in students from eastern North Carolina, while Old West housed the Dialectic Society (the "Di"), which claimed students from the western half of the state.

Condemned as unsafe in 1922, Old East was extensively remodeled in that year and again between 1991 and 1993, when air conditioning and elevators were added. It became a National Historic Landmark in 1966.

1858 Thalian Hall Opens in Wilmington

On October 12, 1858, Thalian Hall in Wilmington opened with a gala celebration. Long a cultural and political center of Wilmington, Thalian Hall's origins lie in the Thalian Association, a theatrical company organized in 1788 that took its name from Thalia, the Greek muse of comedy.

When the previous theater facility began to garner negative attention from traveling troupes, Wilmington's town fathers decided to construct a new facility, which would serve as a theater, library, and city civic center. Over the years, it has been referred to as Thalian Hall, the Wilmington Opera House, and the Wilmington Academy of Music. Thalian Hall survived the Great Depression, receiving a fifty-thousand-dollar Works Progress Administration grant for renovations and performances. After the Second World War a new series of renovations took place, followed in 1973 by a period of rebuilding after a catastrophic fire. The most recent restoration occurred in 1990.

Today Thalian Hall continues to serve Wilmington in the capacity originally intended in 1858—hosting theatrical events and housing city offices.

1923 Monument Dedicated 1923 at Bennett Place Symbolizes Unity

On October 12, 1923, the Unity Monument was dedicated at Bennett Place in Durham, memorializing the end of the Civil War and reunification of the country.

Sponsored by the Samuel Tate Morgan family and the state of North Carolina, the monument is composed of two Corinthian columns symbolizing the Union and the Confederacy topped by a beam bearing the word "Unity." The inscription on a stone at the monument's base details the surrender of Confederate troops by Gen. Joseph E. Johnston to Gen. William T. Sherman in 1865 at the farmhouse owned by James and Nancy Bennitt.

Sherman and Johnston met at the Bennitt farm three times during the month of April 1865 to negotiate the war's largest surrender of Confederate troops. Their first meeting came just two days after Lincoln's assassination. Although Lee's April 9 surrender to Grant at Appomattox Court House is often considered the end of the Civil War, Johnston's April 26 surrender of the armies of the Carolinas, Georgia, and Florida to Sherman is more correctly viewed as the close of the conflict.

Following the surrender, the two generals became friends. Johnston even served as a pallbearer at Sherman's funeral in 1891.

1961 Anvil or Hammer: John F. Kennedy at Kenan Stadium, 1961

On October 12, 1961, Pres. John F. Kennedy, ten months into his thousand days in office, spoke to a crowd of thirty thousand at Kenan Stadium in Chapel Hill.

The occasion was University Day, the annual observance of the founding of the University of North Carolina in 1793. His remarks echoed his inaugural address: "I ask you to give to the service of our country the critical faculties which society has developed in you here. I ask you to decide whether you will be, as Goethe put it, an anvil or a hammer."

Two days before the event, UNC Pres. Bill Friday learned that only ten thousand people were expected to attend. He called principals in a wide radius encouraging them to offer their students a rare chance to see a president. A capacity audience turned out.

Joining Kennedy and Friday on the platform were Gov. Terry Sanford and federal Commerce Secretary Luther Hodges, a former North Carolina governor himself. As the ceremony concluded, a child approached the President, asking for an autograph. Kennedy borrowed a fountain pen from Friday, then absentmindedly pocketed it.

A bystander who observed the theft later wrote the White House, and Kennedy returned the pen to Friday with a humorous note of apology.

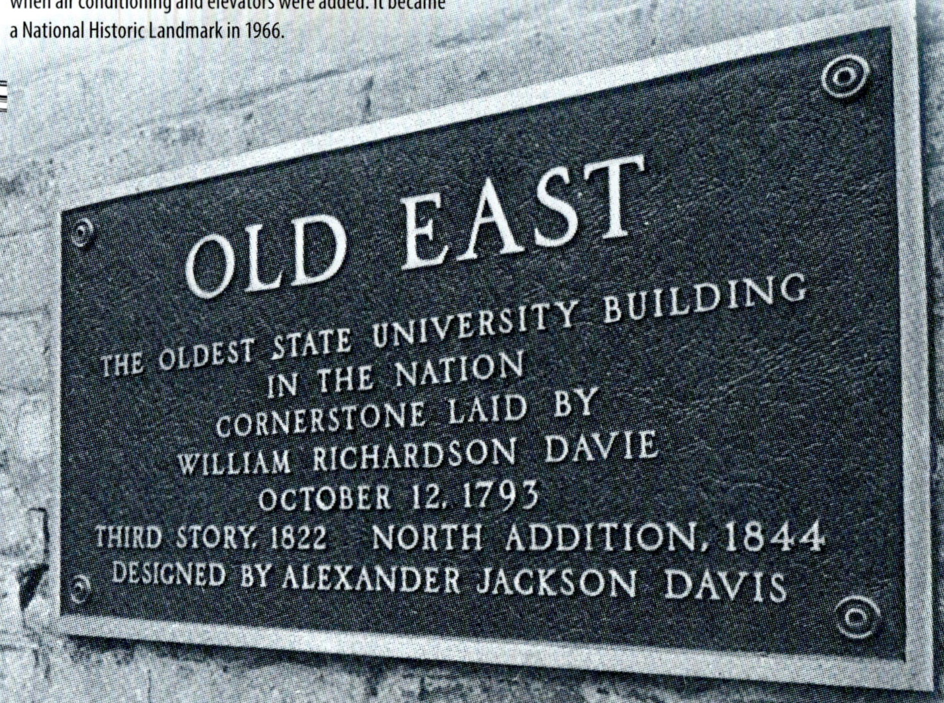

Old East – building (*background*) and plaque (*left*)

1845 "General" Julian Carr and Tobacco in Durham

On October 13, 1845, tobacco magnate Julian S. Carr was born in Chapel Hill.

After serving in the Confederate cavalry and returning to a hometown largely in decline, Carr pursued business interests in nearby Durham. In 1870 he joined two partners there in the manufacture of Bull Durham Smoking Tobacco. Owing to Carr's marketing skills, the brand and its hometown became internationally famous. Tobacco was only the first of his successful businesses, which also included banking and textiles.

Carr's interests extended well beyond business. A generous philanthropist, he supported the education of a number of individuals, provided the funds for a dormitory at UNC, and helped establish Trinity College, the forerunner to Duke. As a politician, he was less successful; he failed in runs for the governorship and the U.S. Senate, mostly because he refused to play hardball.

Despite his political failings, Carr was one of the most popular North Carolinians of his era. He was often called General Carr, and following the death of his wife Nannie in 1915, he was courted heavily. He often signed notes to female admirers as "Your Sweetheart General."

1938 Gospel Music's First Lady, Shirley Caesar of Durham

On October 13, 1938, Shirley Caesar, an award-winning gospel singer and preacher was born in Durham. Her beginnings were humble. She and her eleven siblings lost their father when they were young. She immersed herself in church, family life, and singing, which she began at age ten.

When Caesar was nineteen years old, she met Albertina Walker, a famous gospel singer, who was impressed with her raw talent and invited her to join her group, The Caravans. Performing across the United States, Caesar saw the racial adversity prevalent in America during the late 1950s and early 1960s. After eight years with the group, she opted for a solo career, giving her the opportunity to preach and to effect change.

Her many accolades include eleven Grammy, fifteen Dove, and thirteen Stellar Awards. Having released more than twenty albums and a dozen singles, Shirley Caesar is commonly known as the "First Lady of Gospel Music."

She continues to be active in the Triangle community, preaching at Mount Calvary Word of Faith Church in Raleigh, operating her Outreach Ministries in Durham for more than forty years, and inspiring many through her talent and selflessness.

1982 Jim Thorpe's Olympic Medals Reinstated

On October 13, 1982, Jim Thorpe's medals from the 1912 Olympics were reinstated.

The famed athlete, who lived from 1888 until 1953, was born in a cabin on an Indian reservation in Oklahoma and was educated at Indian boarding schools nearby. In 1904 he enrolled at the U. S. Indian Industrial School in Carlisle, Pennsylvania. While at Carlisle, Thorpe was coached by Glenn "Pop" Warner, who added him to the track team. Recognizing his talent as an athlete, Warner suggested that Thorpe train for the 1912 Olympic Games.

In 1909 Thorpe played semi-professional baseball in North Carolina for the Rocky Mount Railroaders and the Fayetteville Highlanders.

At the 1912 Olympics in Stockholm, Sweden, Thorpe won gold medals in the two newly-created multi-events, the pentathlon and the decathlon. Sweden's King Gustav V called him "the greatest athlete in the world." A year later, after word spread that Thorpe had played semipro baseball, he lost his amateur status and was forced to return his Olympic medals.

In 1982, nearly thirty years after Thorpe's death, the International Olympic Committee unanimously restored his Olympic medals.

Jim Thorpe at the 1912 Olympics.

OCT 14

1886 University President, U.S. Senator Frank Porter Graham

On October 14, 1886, Frank Porter Graham was born in Fayetteville.

Graham became a history instructor at UNC in 1914 but left to serve in the Marines during World War I. He was elevated to the rank of first lieutenant before returning to Chapel Hill as an assistant professor. He secured a full professorship in 1927 and three years later became president of the university. When the University of North Carolina, North Carolina State College, and the North Carolina College for Women merged in 1932, Graham became the first president of the Consolidated University of North Carolina.

In 1949 Graham resigned from the UNC system to accept an appointment to fill the U.S. Senate seat vacated by J. Melville Broughton's death. Graham's 1950 Democratic senate primary race against Willis Smith has become legendary for the mudslinging and posturing. He lost the primary but maintained a commitment to public service. He became the United Nations mediator and representative to India and Pakistan in 1951 and served as an assistant secretary general of the United Nations before retiring in 1967.

Graham then returned to Chapel Hill, where he died in 1972. The 1968 student union building at Chapel Hill bears his name.

1927 Charles Lindbergh Lands in Greensboro

On October 14, 1927, Charles Lindbergh landed at Lindley Field in Greensboro to celebrate its opening.

Greensboro businessmen in the 1920s touted their city as the site for a major airport, Greensboro being the mid-point between northern cities and those in the Deep South. Leaders from Greensboro, High Point, and Winston-Salem worked to establish an airfield on property purchased by Guilford County and Greensboro from Paul C. Lindley in 1927. Drawing visitors to the opening ceremony for Lindley Field was national hero Lindbergh in his famous airplane, *Spirit of St. Louis*.

Lindbergh had completed the first nonstop solo flight from New York to Paris in May 1927. Drawing on his success, he flew throughout the United States to encourage air flight. He visited Lindley Field as part of a three-month tour that took him to forty-eight states and eighty-two cities, racking up 147 speeches and 1,290 miles of parade routes.

As a result of Lindbergh's tour, interest in the uses of flight, particularly the use of air mail, exploded. His Greensboro visit, one of only two in North Carolina during the tour, highlighted the potential prominence of the city as an aviation center.

1965 Randall Jarrell, "War Poet"

On October 14, 1965, poet Randall Jarrell was struck and killed by a car while walking at dusk along the side of NC 54 Bypass in Chapel Hill. At the time he was staying in the hospital there, recovering from a suicide attempt and being treated with antidepressants. He left behind nine volumes of poetry, four books of literary criticism, four children's books, five anthologies, a novel, and a reputation as a brilliant, if troubled writer.

Born in 1914 in Nashville, Tennessee, Jarrell attended Vanderbilt University, where he captained the tennis team and studied under Robert Penn Warren. Hoping to become a pilot, Jarrell entered the Army Air Force in 1942. He failed to qualify and served as a celestial navigation instructor for the remainder of the war. From that experience came Jarrell's best known poem, "The Death of the Ball Turret Gunner," ending with the line "When I died they washed me out of the turret with a hose."

In the fall of 1947 Jarrell began teaching at what is now UNC-Greensboro, where he would live and work for the remainder of his life.

OCT 15

1810 Alfred Moore, Soldier and Supreme Court Justice

On October 15, 1810, Alfred Moore, Revolutionary War officer and associate justice of the United States Supreme Court, died. Born in 1755 in New Hanover County, Moore was descended from the early settlers of the Cape Fear region and was the grandson of the founder of Brunswick Town.

During the Revolutionary War Moore was commissioned as a captain in the First North Carolina Continental Regiment. He saw action at Brunswick Town, Moores Creek Bridge, and Charleston before resigning and returning home to manage the family estates. At the war's conclusion Moore began a lengthy career in public service, first as a state senator from Brunswick County, then as state attorney general. He resigned that position in 1791 to return to the state assembly a year later. In 1795 he ran for a United States Senate seat but lost.

In October 1799, upon the death of Justice James Iredell, Pres. John Adams appointed Moore an associate justice of the United States Supreme Court. Moore retired from the Supreme Court in 1804 due to ill health. He is buried in the graveyard of St. Phillips Church in Brunswick Town. Moore County is named in his honor.

1951 Wake Forest Sets Up New Campus, 1951

On October 15, 1951, Pres. Harry S. Truman spoke at the groundbreaking ceremony for the Winston-Salem campus of Wake Forest College (since 1967, Wake Forest University). The president spoke for twenty minutes, covering the history of the college and praising the people who made the move possible. A scale model of the planned campus was available for attendees to examine.

The move was several years in making. College trustees and the Baptist State Convention had agreed to move the school to the Forsyth County site during the previous decade, after the Z. Smith Reynolds Foundation promised to fund the college in perpetuity if it moved. Charles and Mary Babcock, the daughter of R. J. Reynolds, donated 350 acres near Reynolda House for the campus.

The school's roots, though, go back much further. The Baptist State Convention launched Wake Forest Institute in 1834 with an enrollment of sixteen on the site of a Wake County plantation. Designed to teach Baptist ministers and laymen, the school required students to spend half their day performing manual labor on the plantation.

In 1838 the school was renamed Wake Forest College, and the provision for manual labor was abandoned in favor of rigorous academic training. The village in Wake County that developed around the college became known as Wake Forest.

1954 Hurricane Hazel Makes Landfall

On October 15, 1954, Hurricane Hazel made landfall at Long Beach. The storm's arrival in North Carolina occurred on a full-moon high tide, maximizing the impact of the storm surge on the barrier beaches of Sunset Beach, Ocean Isle, Holden Beach, Long Beach, Carolina Beach, Wrightsville Beach, and Topsail Island.

Devastation was widespread but nowhere was the impact more severe than on Long Beach (present-day Oak Island), where a seventeen-foot storm surge swept away 352 of the 357 structures on the island. The dramatic surge was, and remains, singular in North Carolina's recorded history.

Hazel was the only Category Four hurricane of the twentieth century to strike North Carolina. Its winds topped 140 miles per hour. After landfall it tracked inland, and battering winds cut a wide swath northward toward Raleigh. High winds toppled trees, ripped roofs, and tore down signs and power lines across the state. Hazel was responsible for ninety-five deaths in the U.S., including nineteen in North Carolina. It remains the standard by which other North Carolina hurricanes are measured.

Large oceanfront buildings are reduced to rubble in the aftermath of Hurricane Hazel in Atlantic Beach *(background photo)*.

Three men are in the distance survey the destruction and debris scattered over the landscape in Southport after Hurricane Hazel (*right*).

1928 Five and Dime Roots of North Carolina Museum of Art

On October 16, 1928, Robert Phifer, an art collector and native North Carolinian, died. He bequeathed seventy-five paintings and over a million dollars to the North Carolina Art Society. The next year the first in a series of temporary art exhibition spaces opened in the Agriculture Building in Raleigh.

In 1947 Robert Lee Humber of Greenville lobbied the General Assembly for a bill to provide one million dollars to purchase more works of art for the state. The money was needed to match an equal amount from an anonymous donor, later identified as department store owner Samuel H. Kress. The bill passed, and the appropriation made North Carolina the first state to inaugurate an art collection with public funds.

The initial legislative appropriation was used to purchase 139 European and American paintings and sculptures. The Kress Foundation matched the appropriation with a gift of seventy works of art, primarily from the Italian Renaissance.

The North Carolina Museum of Art moved to its present location in 1983. Through the 1990s and into the new millennium, the museum experienced unprecedented growth in its art collection—both in quality and diversity. In addition to exhibit rotations, the museum offers educational programs for students, teachers, and visitors. The year 2010 saw the completion of a state-of-the-art new home for its permanent collection. That building has itself been called "a work of art."

1961 Dorton Arena Dedicated in 1961

On October 16, 1961, the Livestock Judging Pavilion at the North Carolina State Fair was dedicated and renamed the J. S. Dorton Arena, honoring the memory of "Doc" Dorton, longtime fairgrounds manager who had died earlier that year.

Internationally recognized for its revolutionary architectural design, the pavilion opened in 1952. Its soaring, criss-crossed parabolic arched roof amazed fairgoers right from the start. The innovative creation was the work of Matthew Nowicki, a Polish architect who was then head of of the architecture department at what is now N.C. State's School of Design.

Nowicki had sketched the building's preliminary drawings in 1950, before his departure for India, where he was engaged in planning the new Punjab capital city of Chandigarh. Returning to the United States, he was killed in a plane crash in Egypt, and Raleigh architect William Dietrick carried out the construction of Nowicki's visionary work. Recipient of the first American Institute of Architects Honor Award in 1953, and recognized as a National Civil Engineering Landmark, the arena was listed in the National Register of Historic Places in 1973 for its exceptional national significance only twenty-one years after its construction.

1976 Rick Dees' 1976 Novelty Hit, "Disco Duck"

On October 16, 1976, Rick Dees's "Disco Duck" hit Number One on the Billboard charts. At the time of the novelty hit, Dees was working as a disk jockey at a radio station in Memphis, Tennessee.

Rigdon Dees III was born in Florida but was raised in Greensboro. He attended Grimsley High School and graduated from UNC-Chapel Hill with a degree in radio, television, and motion pictures. Dees went on to work at several radio stations across the South. He wrote and recorded "Disco Duck" as a parody of the glut of disco songs popular in the late 1970s. It was perfect timing for the song, which ended up being his only hit recording.

Dees went on to become one of the most famous DJs in the country, hosting long-running shows such as *The Weekly Top 40*. He also has acted in television shows and movies, and has done voiceovers for movies, including Disney's *The Hunchback of Notre Dame*.

His many accolades include membership in both the National Association of Broadcasters and the National Radio Halls of Fame and a star on the Hollywood Walk of Fame.

J.S. Dorton in front of Dorton Arena in 1951.

1859 Lewis Leary, John Brown Accomplice, from Fayetteville

On October 17, 1859, Lewis Leary was fatally wounded during John Brown's raid on the arsenal at Harpers Ferry.

Originally from Fayetteville, Leary was a free mulatto who came from a family of saddle-makers. He moved to Oberlin, Ohio in search of economic opportunity and because the town was considered to be among the most racially progressive in America. Once there, he gravitated toward the growing abolitionist movement and joined the Anti-Slavery Society.

In 1859 John Brown, a vehement anti-slavery advocate, was looking for men to spark a slave insurrection on the East Coast. Leary joined him enthusiastically. Brown's men, though, lacked the resources needed to mobilize local slaves, who had not been properly notified of the insurgency.

Local militia held off the raiders until Robert E. Lee's Marines formally intervened. Brown's men were unable to stockpile the weaponry or to escape. While attempting to flee, Leary was wounded and died several hours later.

Though the raid failed, Leary's death was not in vain. Brown's raid threatened the South by proving that a slave insurrection was possible, and the seizure was lauded in the North. The episode marked the obvious division between North and South, which would shortly culminate in the Civil War.

1862 Contract to Build Confederate Ironclad CSS Neuse

On October 17, 1862, the contract was signed to build the Confederate ironclad gunboat CSS *Neuse*.

The vessel was needed to bolster southern naval defenses and to prevent Union occupation of the state's sounds and estuaries. The *Neuse* was one of twenty-four ironclad warships completed by the Confederacy. It was completed in April 1864 and began patrolling the Neuse River that spring. Within weeks the *Neuse* became stuck on a sandbar one-half mile below Kinston, and it remained there nearly a month.

In March 1865 Union forces advanced on Kinston, and the CSS *Neuse* became threatened with capture. Capt. Joseph H. Price ordered his men to scuttle the ship. Shortly after the war, salvage operations removed most of the machinery and armor from the wreck site in the river.

The vessel was raised in the spring of 1963 and placed on display at what was then Governor Caswell Park in Kinston. It is now at the CSS *Neuse* Civil War Interpretive Center in downtown Kinston. The new facility is enclosed and climate controlled, with exhibits telling the stories of the Neuse and eastern North Carolina during the Civil War.

2003 "Choo Choo" Justice Barreled Down the Football Field

On October 17, 2003, football star Charlie "Choo Choo" Justice died at his home in Cherryville at age seventy-nine.

A native of Asheville, Justice acquired his nickname in the Navy, into which he was drafted in 1943. Seeing him dodge tacklers for the Bainbridge Naval Training Center team, an officer remarked, "He looks like a runaway train. We ought to call him 'Choo Choo.'"

After the war Justice played for UNC, though many other colleges vied for his talents. From 1946 to 1949, while he played for the Tar Heels, the team had a record of 39–9–2, went to three bowl games, and even achieved a Number One ranking in the AP Top 10. Justice was named National Player of the Year in 1948, was runner-up for the Heisman Trophy in 1948 and 1949, and remains in the record books at UNC for a number of achievements.

Justice played for the Washington Redskins in the National Football League in 1950 and again between 1952 and 1954, then retired to work in the oil business and later in the insurance industry. He was inducted into the North Carolina Sports Hall of Fame in 1963.

OCT 17

Transporting the CSS *Neuse* to downtown Kinston in 2012.

OCT
18

1853 Antebellum Roots for North Carolina State Fair

On October 18, 1853, the first North Carolina State Fair opened in Raleigh just south of downtown. At the initial fair, as with those that followed, all manner of plants, animals, and handicrafts were entered for review. Cash prizes were awarded for first and second place entries.

In preparation for the first fair, citizens were encouraged to invite fairgoers into their homes, as it was anticipated that public facilities would not be adequate to accommodate everyone. Indeed, on its busiest day four thousand people attended the first State Fair. During that first year and for many years following, the Raleigh and Gaston Railroad transported all of the presentation materials at no charge and offered attendees a half-price trip to Raleigh.

The Civil War and its aftermath interfered with fair operations from 1861 to 1868. The fair was re-opened in 1869 by the Agricultural Society and remained at the same location until 1872. In 1873, through assistance by the City of Raleigh, the Agricultural Society purchased a fifty-five-acre tract on Hillsborough Street and moved the fair to that location.

In 1928 the fair moved to its present location on Blue Ridge Road, where every October brings the sweet smell of cotton candy, the roar of the midway, and the chance to take home a prize for agricultural products.

1867 African American Baptists in North Carolina Organized, 1867

On October 18, 1867, the first meeting of the General Baptist Convention opened at the First African Baptist Church of Goldsboro.

After the Civil War African Americans withdrew from Baptist churches across the state and established their own association, the General Baptist Convention, as the black counterpart to the Baptist State Convention. The withdrawal stemmed from strong white opposition to social equality and the desire of both races for separate churches.

In September 1867 a group of ministers called for an assembly. Each black Baptist church was asked to send its minister and two delegates. The planned assembly was held at the same time as the annual meeting of the white convention, from which it received advice and five hundred dollars in financial support. Known for a time as the General Association for Colored Baptists, the group has been called the General Baptist State Convention since 1947.

Though the creation of the organization came at a time marked by poverty, discouragement, and bitter struggle, by 1882 the group represented eight hundred churches and ninety-five thousand members. Today the convention represents over a half-million members.

The First African Baptist Church of Goldsboro still owns the tract where the original meeting took place.

1929 Thomas Wolfe and "The Old Kentucky Home"

On October 18, 1929, Charles Scribner's Sons published *Look Homeward, Angel*, the best-known novel by Asheville author Thomas Wolfe.

Inspired by a marble angel outside his father's monument shop on Pack Square, Wolfe wrote his first and largely autobiographical novel about the fictional Gant family, wherein the father is a volatile stonecutter and the mother a business-minded boardinghouse operator.

Wolfe was only six when his own mother, Julia Westall Wolfe, left her husband and older children and bought "The Old Kentucky Home," a rambling Victorian boardinghouse in downtown Asheville, to which she brought young Tom. With his family divided, Tom felt lost amongst his mother's tenants and resentful of the changes the tourists were wreaking on his hometown.

Always aware of the life and people around him, Wolfe later turned his observations into a novel in which his mother's boardinghouse became "Dixieland," and Asheville, the fictional town of "Altamont." Although names were changed, Asheville residents still recognized Wolfe's characters as themselves and were scandalized. Only in 1937, a year before he died, did Wolfe return home to visit. He was, however, buried in Asheville's Riverside Cemetery. His mother's boardinghouse is now the Thomas Wolfe Memorial, one of twenty-seven State Historic Sites.

Photos of the N.C. State Fair, October, 1955.

1781 Road to Yorktown via the North Carolina Piedmont

On October 19, 1781, Lord Cornwallis surrendered more than eight thousand troops to a combined Franco-American force at Yorktown.

The surrender came on the heels of much fighting in North Carolina. From January to March 1781, Cornwallis's army pursued troops, including some local militia, under Daniel Morgan around the state. He continued chasing Morgan's successor, Nathanael Greene, in what became known as the "Race to the Dan."

The campaign included several skirmishes, namely Cowan's Ford, Bruce's Crossroads, Clapp's Mill, and Weitzell's Mill. It culminated in the Battle of Guilford Courthouse, the largest engagement fought in North Carolina during the Revolution. Although he defeated the Americans, Cornwallis lost more than a quarter of his army, so many men that he had to retreat to British-held Wilmington. Charles Fox, a British Parliamentarian, reportedly exclaimed upon learning of Cornwallis's losses, "Another such victory will ruin us."

After Guilford, as Cornwallis's army marched for Virginia and Greene headed into South Carolina, North Carolina became a battleground for an ongoing civil war between local Patriots and Tories. Loyalist David Fanning terrorized the region and in September captured Gov. Thomas Burke and other lawmakers in a raid on Hillsborough. Fanning left North Carolina for the relative safety of the British forces at Charleston after the surrender at Yorktown.

1874 R. J. Reynolds Tobacco Empire Takes Shape

On October 19, 1874, R. J. Reynolds purchased his first lot, next to rail lines in Winston, from the Moravian Church.

Born into a prosperous Virginia tobacco family, Reynolds started what he called the "Little Red Factory" in 1874 with just seventy-five hundred dollars and some college and business school under his belt. A year later the factory and its twelve workers had produced 150,000 pounds of southern flat-plug chewing tobacco.

By the time of Reynolds's death in 1918, the company had grown to a workforce of ten thousand spread across 121 buildings in Winston-Salem. The diversified tobacco manufacturing business included chewing and pipe tobacco and the legendary Camel cigarette. Other popular Reynolds brands included Winston, Salem, Vantage, and Doral.

Outside of the business arena, both Reynolds and his wife Katherine became known for their progressive politics, philanthropy, and efforts to improve conditions for their workers.

1948 Truman Joins His Predecessors in Raleigh, 1948

On October 19, 1948, Pres. Harry S. Truman visited Raleigh and delivered the main address at the unveiling of the "Presidents North Carolina Gave the Nation" monument on Union Square, which surrounds the State Capitol, one of North Carolina's twenty-seven State Historic Sites.

The work honors the three presidents born in North Carolina: Andrew Jackson of Union County, seventh president of the United States (1829–1837); James Knox Polk of Mecklenburg County, eleventh president of the United States (1845–1849); and Andrew Johnson of Wake County, seventeenth president of the United States (1865–1869). Interestingly, while North Carolina claims all three presidents as native sons, all were elected while residents of Tennessee.

The North Carolina State Capitol, completed in 1840, is one of the finest and best preserved examples of a major civic building in the Greek Revival architectural style. The previous Capitol building was destroyed by a fire in 1831.

The Capitol housed all of North Carolina's state government until 1888. The Supreme Court and State Library moved into a separate building in 1888, and the General Assembly moved into the State Legislative Building in 1963. Today the governor, lieutenant governor, and their immediate staffs occupy offices on the first floor of the Capitol.

R. J. Reynolds (*above*).

Charles Keck's statue honoring three North Carolina-born U.S. presidents: James K. Polk, Andrew Jackson, and Andrew Johnson, outside the State Capitol in Raleigh, North Carolina (*left*).

1862 Annie Carter Lee, From Virginia to North Carolina and Back

1864 Stephen Ramseur, Casualty of Shenandoah Campaign

1898 N.C. Mutual and Provident Association Organized

1942 Race Relations Milestone Meeting at NCCU, 1942

OCT 20

On October 20, 1862, Annie Carter Lee, daughter of Robert E. Lee, died in Warren County. She had been taken ill with typhoid fever while visiting the Jones Springs resort there.

Lee sent both Annie and her sister Agnes to North Carolina in June 1862, when Union troops occupied their home in Arlington, Virginia. When Annie died, it was not possible to take her body back to Arlington, which was then behind enemy lines. The owner of the Jones Springs Hotel offered to have her body buried in his family cemetery, and the Lees accepted.

Zearell Crowder, a Confederate soldier, created the eleven-foot tall obelisk that marks her grave to this day. It was dedicated in a ceremony in 1866. The Lee family and the citizens of Warren County paid for the monument, and Robert E. Lee visited the grave in 1870.

In 1994 descendants of the Lee family had Annie's body removed from the Warren County grave and interred with the rest of the family at Washington and Lee Chapel in Virginia.

The obelisk remains in the Jones Family Cemetery located on Annie Lee Road.

North Carolina Postcard: "Monument of Anne Carter Lee, Daughter of Gen. Robert E. Lee, Warren County."

On October 20, 1864, Confederate Maj. Gen. Stephen Dodson Ramseur died from wounds received the previous day.

Born in 1837 in Lincolnton, he attended Davidson College, where he studied mathematics briefly before entering the United States Military Academy at West Point in 1856. There he became close friends with several future Union generals, including George Armstrong Custer.

After graduation Ramseur served with the Third United States Artillery, stationed in Washington, D.C. He never reported to his new command after a promotion in February 1861. Instead, he resigned his commission and offered his services to the Confederacy.

After briefly serving with an artillery unit, Ramseur was appointed colonel of the Forty-Ninth North Carolina, a regiment he led with distinction at Malvern Hill, where he was severely wounded. Promoted to brigadier general and assigned a brigade in the Second Corps of the Army of Northern Virginia, he led his brigade at Chancellorsville, Gettysburg, the Wilderness, Spotsylvania, and Cold Harbor. In the fall of 1864, Ramseur led his division in the Shenandoah Campaign. On October 19, 1864, he was mortally wounded at Cedar Creek, Virginia. Taken prisoner, he died the next day at Union headquarters, surrounded by many of his former friends and West Point classmates, including General George A. Custer.

On October 20, 1898, John Merrick and six fellow investors met in the office of Dr. Aaron Moore to organize the North Carolina Mutual and Provident Association.

Among the group of African American leaders were educators James E. Shepard and Edward A. Johnson. The company was incorporated in February 1899 and opened for business two months later. Merrick, who served as president, is generally acknowledged as the founder. Dr. Moore, who succeeded him as president in 1919, is called the co-founder, but Moore acknowledged in 1920 that it was Merrick who took the initiative in the organization. Along with C. C. Spaulding, Moore's cousin, they formed the "Triumvirate" that led North Carolina Mutual Life Insurance Company (the name was changed in 1919) for over fifty years.

The company spawned allied businesses, among them Mechanics and Farmers Bank, a hosiery mill, a real estate company, a drugstore, and several publications. The firm helped earn Durham its national reputation as "Black Wall Street" and the "Capital of the Black Middle Class." When famed African American leader W. E. B. Du Bois visited Durham in 1912, he observed an unparalleled level of black entrepreneurship, with North Carolina Mutual in the vanguard of the enterprise.

On October 20, 1942, fifty-seven African American professionals from across the South convened the Southern Conference on Race Relations in Durham at what is now North Carolina Central University. Chiefly responsible for the gathering was Gordon B. Hancock, a nationally-syndicated columnist and professor at Virginia Union University in Richmond.

The group, made up of ministers, physicians, educators, businessmen, labor officials, and social workers, was mostly male, with only five women in attendance. P. B. Young of the *Norfolk Journal and Guide* lent his paper's support. Delegates divided themselves into seven committees to look at political and civil rights, industry and labor, service organizations, education, agriculture, military service, and social welfare.

Benjamin Mays, president of Morehouse College in Atlanta, called for the group to draft a conference statement. The product was the "Durham Manifesto," a call for a middle ground on civil rights, rejecting unequivocal denunciation of segregation and calling on the nation to address issues of racial discrimination. Louis T. Austin, editor of the *Carolina Times* in Durham, was largely unsupportive of the effort.

The group in time laid the groundwork for the creation of the biracial Southern Regional Council.

North Carolina Mutual and Provident Association first home office, 1906 (*background*).

1851 Courtroom Slaying in Morganton, 1851

On October 21, 1851, Burke County legislator William Waightstill Avery called the life's work of Samuel Fleming of Yancey County, his rival in the General Assembly, a "fraud."

The argument started over a court case in which Fleming was battling over the estate of his deceased wife with her family. Avery, then a prominent attorney and political figure, was representing Fleming's wife's family.

Fleming was so outraged over Avery's comments that he left the courthouse and bought a cowhide whip, with which he scourged Avery. Avery was unarmed and a much smaller man than Fleming. The confrontation ended with Avery too weak to fight back but came to a head again several weeks later when the two men crossed paths in a different courtroom.

As the pair entered the courthouse in Morganton, Fleming was hurling insults at Avery, who did not fight back; not, that is, until they actually entered the courtroom. While Fleming was finishing his business with the court clerk, Avery shot and killed him, not five feet from the presiding judge.

Avery immediately surrendered himself to local authorities, and his trial began days later. A week after the incident, the jury in his case found him "not guilty by reason of emotional insanity."

1866 Tom Dula: Poor Boy Was Bound to Die

On October 21, 1866, Tom Dula was convicted of the murder of Laura Foster. It was daybreak when the jury returned the verdict in the Iredell County Courthouse, where the trial had been moved from Wilkes County. The jury had not received their orders from the judge until about midnight the night before. It deliberated during the night. The defense moved for an arrest of judgment, which was overruled, and the judge pronounced his sentence: that Thomas Dula be hanged by the neck until dead on November 9, 1866. Former governor Zebulon B. Vance represented Dula pro bono.

Speculation abounded as to why Vance took the case, one of the few he ever lost before a jury. Regardless of his motives, he gave a spirited defense and succeeded in twice taking the case to the North Carolina Supreme Court. The crowds of spectators and reporters that appeared in the courtroom were as likely there to see the charismatic Vance as they were to hear the sensational testimony. Ultimately, the High Court upheld the conviction, and Dula was hanged for the crime in May 1868.

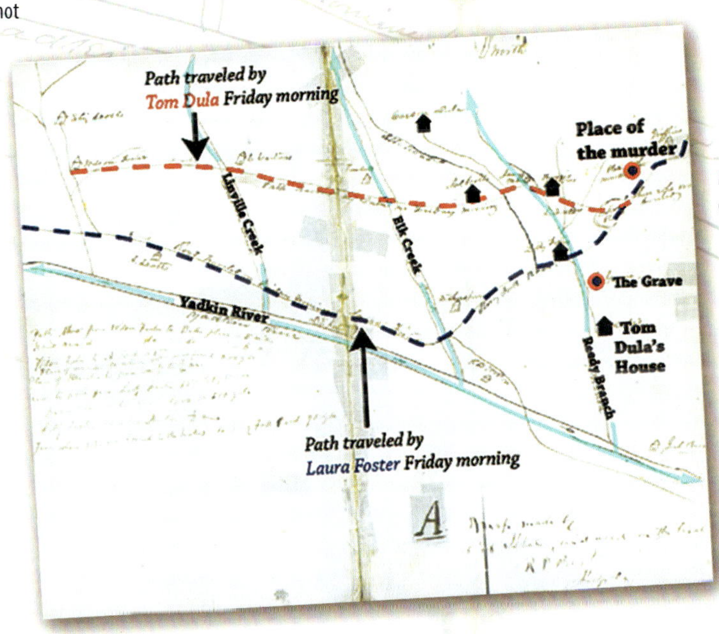

Map with an overlay illustrating Laura Foster's and Tom Dula's routes the day of Foster's murder.

The original map drawn by Col. Isabel in the trial of Tom Dula, used as "exhibit A" [Jan 1867] (*background*).

1993 Madonna and Child in a Landscape Selected for a USPS Stamp

On October 21, 1993, *Madonna and Child in a Landscape*, a work by the Italian Renaissance painter Cima de Conegiano that is part of the North Carolina Museum of Art's permanent collection, was selected as the U.S. Postal Service's Christmas Stamp.

The Museum's collection of Italian paintings ranks among the finest in the country. Since its initial acquisition in 1947 of 139 works of European and American art, purchased with a one million dollar appropriation of state funds, the North Carolina Museum of Art has grown to be one of the nation's finest museums. Housed in a state-of-the-art building completed in 2010, its major holdings include European painting from the Renaissance to the nineteenth century, Egyptian art, sculpture and vase paintings from ancient Greece and Rome, American art of the eighteenth through twentieth centuries, and international contemporary art. Other strengths include African, ancient American, pre-Columbian, and Oceanic art, and Jewish ceremonial objects.

1780 Washington Makes Greene Commander of Southern Army

On October 22, 1780, Gen. George Washington ordered Maj. Gen. Nathanael Greene to assume command of the southern army. Greene took command in Charlotte, Dec. 3, 1780.

Born in 1742, Greene was raised in a Quaker household that denounced warfare. He nevertheless developed a keen interest in military history and tactics as a young man and was expelled from his Quaker meeting in 1773 for having attended a military parade. Subsequently joining the local militia, he took an active role in early efforts towards American independence. At the outbreak of war, Greene moved swiftly through the American ranks and was promoted to brigadier general in 1775 during the Siege of Boston.

The next year, at age thirty-four, he became the youngest officer promoted to major general in the Continental Army. Greene was one of Washington's closest confidants and most respected commanders throughout the war. As commander of the Southern Army, he performed remarkably and proved himself a genius of strategy and logistics. His command of American forces led directly to the British defeat at Yorktown in 1781 and, therefore, ultimately to American independence.

Greensboro and Greene County are both named in his honor.

Nathanael Greene portrait, 1785.

1931 C. A. Penn and the Lucky Strike Brand

On October 22, 1931, Charles Ashby Penn, developer of Lucky Strike cigarettes, died.

Penn was born in Virginia in 1868 but moved with his family to Reidsville in 1874. In Rockingham County his father established the F. R. Penn Tobacco Company, processing chewing and smoking tobacco. Charles joined the company after graduating from high school.

In 1911 the Penn Tobacco Company was purchased by the American Tobacco Company, the conglomerate run by James B. Duke. Penn prospered under his new employer, becoming a director of the company in 1913 and vice president for manufacturing in 1916.

Though the Lucky Strike brand originated with a company that American Tobacco had acquired in 1905, Penn perfected the cigarette's blend and manufacturing process. He also invented the slogan that became synonymous with the brand: "It's Toasted."

Soon Lucky Strike became America's best-selling cigarette. Penn enlarged his father's old tobacco factory in Reidsville to produce Lucky Strikes, quickly making the Rockingham County town among the nation's top tobacco production centers; it adopted the nickname "Lucky City." Penn's family was also involved in the community. His brother constructed an English manor house known as Chinqua Penn, and he himself established Reidsville's first library.

Upon Penn's 1931 death, he was celebrated as the "first citizen" of Reidsville. At that time forty billion Lucky Strike cigarettes were being sold annually.

1932 Artist Elliott Daingerfield of Fayetteville and Blowing Rock

On October 22, 1932, painter Elliott Daingerfield died at age seventy-three in New York and was buried in Cross Creek Cemetery in Fayetteville, where he was raised.

Daingerfield left for New York when he turned twenty-one to apprentice at the National Academy of Design. He joined the Holbein Studios in 1884, where he was influenced by the naturalist Barbizon School technique and by artist George Inness.

Recuperating from diphtheria in Blowing Rock in 1886, Daingerfield began painting the surrounding mountains and built three homes, one of which, "Westglow," today operates as a spa and is open to the public.

Daingerfield returned to the northeast and taught composition at the Philadelphia School of Design and the Art Students League in New York City. He received the National Academy of Design's Clark Prize for the best figure composition in 1902 and later traveled in the southwest under commission by the Santa Fe Railroad Company, painting the Grand Canyon in 1911.

His work is noted for capturing the light and mood of various scenes and is now featured in some of the leading museums of the South and the nation, including the N.C. Museum of Art in Raleigh, the High Museum of Art in Atlanta, and the Smithsonian American Museum Art in Washington, D.C.

1711 Baron von Graffenreid and the Swiss Colony of New Bern

On October 23, 1711, Baron Christoph von Graffenreid, founder of the Swiss colony of New Bern, penned a lengthy description of his capture by the Tuscarora Indians.

In mid-September of that year, Graffenreid and John Lawson led a surveying expedition up the Neuse River. Lawson was the Surveyor General of the colony and well-known to the Indians. When the Indians discovered the party both in their territory and unannounced to their leader, King Hancock, they captured the men and took them to the Tuscarora village of Catechna, near present-day Grifton.

The Indians were angry over encroachment on their lands, and they believed the surveying party was out to take more. Graffenreid was spared, but Lawson was executed. Held at the village for several weeks, Graffenreid bargained for the safety of the New Bern colony. Nevertheless, the Tuscarora, in alliance with other aggravated tribes, attacked settlements on the Pamlico, Neuse, and Trent Rivers, and in the Core Sound region, in what would become known as the Tuscarora War.

After his release from the Tuscarora, Graffenreid wrote his account of the ordeal in order to explain Lawson's fate and to clarify the promises that he made to the Indians during his capture.

1896 Introduction of Rural Free Delivery, 1896

On October 23, 1896, the first rural free delivery (RFD) mail service in North Carolina was established in the small community of China Grove, near Salisbury in Rowan County.

Postal service via RFD included the delivery of all postal items, free of charge, to citizens at their homes, eliminating the need to visit the local post office. Initially only two citizens were willing to accept the service. Local skepticism about the mail delivery stemmed from concerns about theft and reliability. Postmaster J. C. Deaton, with two assistants, canvassed the area around China Grove, pleading for local residents to try the system. The new routes covered approximately eighteen miles in Rowan County and were slowly expanded as citizens began to trust the RFD system. Although development was slow, today's postal system derives from the scheme first tested out in North Carolina.

Mail service began in North Carolina in the 1730s as the colonial government extended postal routes through the Carolinas to Charleston. By the 1780s there were only four post offices in North Carolina. By 1851 the number of post offices had increased to nearly eight hundred.

OCT 23

US Mail carrier with horse and buggy, most likely at Blount's Creek, Beaufort County, ca. 1915.

1823 Bennehan and Cameron Interests Merged at Stagville

On October 24, 1823, Richard Bennehan purchased more than four hundred acres known as Horton Grove from William Horton. The land became part of Bennehan's vast holdings across what are now Granville, Durham, Orange, and Wake Counties.

The plot then included only the modest Horton home, but by 1860 it had incorporated several two-story, four-room timber-frame slave quarters, some smaller tobacco barns, and the Great Barn, which was the center of the extensive Stagville plantation.

Most of Horton Grove's structures were built by Paul Cameron, Bennehan's grandson. Family records reveal that the unique design of the slave cabins was a deliberate attempt on Cameron's part to provide a healthier living environment for his slaves.

Stagville was one of the largest pre-Civil War plantations in the upper South. By 1860 the Bennehan-Cameron family owned nearly thirty thousand acres, several businesses and almost nine hundred slaves, and Stagville, a plantation of several thousand acres on its own, was at the center of the enormous estate.

Horton Grove was added to the National Register of Historic Places in 1978, and today Historic Stagville is one of twenty-seven State Historic Sites.

Horton Grove slave dwellings.

1911 Wrights Experiment with Gliders, 1911

On October 24, 1911, Orville Wright set a world soaring record of nine minutes and forty-five seconds of unpowered flight on the Outer Banks.

Famous for the first powered flight in a heavier-than-air craft with his brother Wilbur in 1903, Orville Wright returned to Kitty Hawk after nearly eight years to conduct more experiments with flight. This time he was accompanied by one of his other brothers, Lorin; his nephew, Horace; and a friend who also served as the pilot during the experiments.

The 1911 attempts differed from the more famous 1903 ones in that they were with a non-powered glider. Since the Wrights had already shown that powered flight was possible, these tests were more focused on safety and were designed to try out new equipment. That new equipment ultimately had to stay under wraps because newspaper reporters came out to watch the experiments every day they were conducted.

Between October 16 and 26, Wright made nearly one hundred glides. Most of them were made into winds of thirty-five miles per hour or faster. The record-breaking, nearly ten-minute glide was into fifty-miles-per-hour wind and did not reach the 120-foot distance that the powered flight had made earlier. That record would stand internationally until 1921.

Side view of glider flying as a kite near the ground, Wilbur (*left*) and Orville (*right*) at Kitty Hawk, 1901.

OCT 25

1774 Women of Edenton Resolve to Forego English Tea, 1774

On October 25, 1774, women in Edenton resolved to stop buying English tea and cloth in protest against taxation without representation. The event became known as the Edenton Tea Party. The women, some of whom likely gathered at a home in Edenton, drew up resolves, which were signed by fifty-one local ladies.

In January of 1775 a British newspaper reported that "many ladies of this Province [North Carolina] have determined to give a memorable proof of their patriotism," resolving not to drink tea or use British cloth any longer. The step was a momentous one for colonists, because drinking tea was an English tradition that defined social gatherings. To suspend the custom, a part of everyday life, showed just how disgusted they were with the English government. Like the Boston Tea Party, the Edenton Tea Party was a bold demonstration of patriotism and belief in individual rights.

Penelope Barker, wife of the treasurer of the Province of North Carolina, is believed to have organized the protest.

1969 Durham's Malcolm X Liberation University

On October 25, 1969, Malcolm X Liberation University opened in Durham.

Founded by black activist Howard Fuller and named for the recently slain civil rights leader, Malcolm X, the school was established in response to protests by students at Duke University over the lack of an African American studies program there. The school was first housed in what was once a hosiery mill on Pettigrew Street.

In its first year the university had twelve students and forty teachers. The curriculum expressly focused on meeting the needs of black students to further the cause of the black liberation movement. In a two-year program students took courses on the history of Africa, slavery, and colonialism, then received technical training to prepare for careers that focused on civil rights.

The school struggled financially despite some strong initial support from the Episcopal Church. It moved to Greensboro in 1970, leaving a small presence in Durham, and closed its doors in 1973. Fuller later attributed the school's failure to an overemphasis on Africa as an important factor in the lives of American blacks.

1988 Cue Sport Champion Luther "Wimpy" Lassiter

On October 25, 1988, professional pool player Luther Lassiter died while practicing the sport he loved at his Elizabeth City home.

Born in Pasquotank County in 1918, Lassiter took an interest in pool at an early age, and the owner of a local pool hall in Elizabeth City let him practice there for free in exchange for cleaning the place after closing. He dropped out of school at sixteen to pursue billiards full-time.

He gained the nickname "Wimpy" thanks to his insatiable appetite for hot dogs and soda, much like the character who ate hamburgers in Popeye cartoons.

After making money from pool mostly by challenging others to matches for money throughout the 1940s (that is, "hustling"), Lassiter began to play the sport professionally in the early 1950s. He won his first championship title in 1962 and had more than twenty major titles to his name overall. Though he retired from pool in 1975, he continued to play in some smaller tournaments.

In 1983 Lassiter became the first, and so far only, person to be inducted into the N.C. Sports Hall of Fame for billiards. He was inducted into the Billiard Congress of America Hall of Fame that same year.

Lassiter is still considered by many to be the finest nine-ball player of all time.

Howard Fuller (*facing out*), founder of Malcolm X Liberation University, talks with a student outside of Malcolm X Liberation University in Durham, ca. 1969.

1858 James H. Young, African American Leader in 1890s

1895 Illegal Forward Pass, 1895, Set Up College Football Rule Change

1951 Carl Durham, Champion of Pharmaceutical Reform

OCT 26

On October 26, 1858, James H. Young was born into slavery near Henderson. Thanks in large measure to his father's emphasis on education, Young was hired to work in the office of Col. J. J. Young, an internal revenue collector. While working in that office, he became involved with the Republican Party.

An industrious worker, Young was selected for multiple government patronage positions. As owner and editor of the *Raleigh Gazette*, the principal voice of black politics in North Carolina in the 1890s, Young became involved in the movement to merge the Republicans and Populists and became a central figure in the resulting Fusion movement. He was elected to the state legislature from Wake County in 1894 and 1896.

A lifelong advocate for equality and reform, Young succeeded in getting the Raleigh city charter amended to better represent the African American community and played a pivotal role in the election of Gov. Daniel L. Russell. The Republican governor appointed Young colonel of a black regiment during the Spanish American War.

After the white supremacy campaign of 1898, Young and other prominent black politicians were prevented from participating in state politics. He spent the remaining years of his life working as a federal revenue collector and running private businesses. He died in 1921.

On October 26, 1895, UNC fullback Joel Whitaker threw the first forward pass in football to his teammate George Stephens.

The history-making throw happened in Atlanta, where the Tar Heels were playing the University of Georgia Bulldogs. Whitaker was punting from the Carolina end zone and, to avoid the Georgia players charging him, tossed the ball forward. As luck would have it, Stephens was the one to catch the toss. It probably looked to many in the audience like the ball was knocked out of Whitaker's hands and the whole situation was an accident.

After catching the pass, Stephens sprinted seventy yards down the field, scoring a touchdown and stunning his opponents. Such a pass was then illegal, but despite Georgia coach Glenn Warner's best efforts to get the play thrown out, the touchdown stood since the referee hadn't seen the pass.

Legendary athlete and coach John Heisman happened to be in the stands that day. After he saw the fateful throw, he spent years lobbying the predecessor organization to the NCAA to change the rules. That didn't happen until 1906, when the forward pass was legalized as part of an overhaul of college football's rules.

On October 26, 1951, Pres. Harry S. Truman signed into law the Durham-Humphrey Amendment to the 1938 Food, Drugs and Cosmetic Act. Cosponsored by North Carolina native Rep. Carl T. Durham and future vice president Hubert Humphrey Jr., the amendment sought to regulate the distribution of medication.

Before its passage drug manufacturers decided for themselves whether their drugs could be sold with or without the supervision of medical professionals. The lack of standardization allowed consumers to easily purchase almost any drug over the counter, exposing them to great harm.

To correct this problem, the Durham-Humphrey Amendments established two official classes of drugs (over-the-counter and prescription), defined classification criteria, and appointed the Food and Drug Administration as the governing body for the classification process. The system remains in place to this day.

During the course of his twenty-two-year congressional career, Durham, who hailed from Orange County and was a pharmacist by profession, served on the Joint Committee on Atomic Energy, the House Armed Services Committee, the International Atomic Energy Agency, and as a delegate to the 1954 Atoms for Peace Conference in Geneva.

James H. Young (*left*)

"The Only Druggist in Congress," Rep. Carl T. Durham of North Carolina (*right*).

1864 The Ironclad Albemarle and the Battle of Plymouth

On October 27, 1864, the Confederate ram CSS *Albemarle* was sunk. The *Albemarle* was commissioned and launched in April 1864, departing directly for Union-occupied Plymouth. Since the iron plating was not yet complete, forges were installed on the deck, and craftsmen worked on the ship as it floated down the Roanoke River.

The *Albemarle* easily bypassed Fort Gray, slipping further downstream toward Plymouth. Two Union steamers, the *Miami* and the *Southfield*, were targets of the next naval action. The *Albemarle* rammed the *Southfield*, which sank. The *Miami's* commander was killed when a shell that he fired at the *Albemarle* ricocheted back to the *Miami*, so close were the two vessels. The *Miami* fled downstream. The *Albemarle* was liberated to steam to Plymouth and pound the city's Union defenses, providing significant support to Gen. Robert F. Hoke's troops who recaptured Plymouth on April 20.

Though the *Albemarle* fought in only one other engagement, the boat, moored at Plymouth, remained a threat to Union forces. Lt. William B. Cushing was dispatched to North Carolina with orders to destroy the *Albemarle*. On October 27, 1864, Cushing torpedoed the vessel from a small launch in the river, clearing the way for Union forces to recapture Plymouth and subsequently the entire Sound region.

1901 George Watts Hill, Tar Heel in Cloak

On October 27, 1901, George Watts Hill was born to a prosperous family in Durham. He would inherit wealth, commanding a fortune earned in banking, and over time would demonstrate an abiding sense of devotion to his country.

The gathering storms of war in 1939 roused alarm in Hill and led to his involvement in the secret war against Hitler. In the face of neutrality advocates, he signed onto "A Summons to Speak Out" and enlisted the support of three dozen Tar Heel businessmen, educators, and journalists on behalf of intervention in Europe. In March 1942 he joined what soon became known as the Office of Strategic Services (OSS).

Hill's administrative experience made him invaluable to the OSS's chief, "Wild Bill" Donovan, who placed him in charge of the camouflage unit and of devices central to the work of spies, such as disguises, fake uniforms and passports, and listening equipment. After the war Hill returned to banking but also played roles in health care reform, desegregation, and, as a UNC trustee, the overturn of the Speaker Ban.

He died in 1993, the year that UNC named its alumni center for him.

1961 Salvage of the CSS Neuse from the Muck

On October 27, 1961, Henry Casey, Lemuel Houston, and Thomas Carlyle began serious efforts to salvage the remains of the ironclad CSS *Neuse* from the Neuse River in Kinston. The first stages of recovery proceeded easily, since the river level was low and the weather was ideal, but ultimately the project would take much longer than anticipated.

Local interest was strong and many people came to the site to observe the work of the trio and their fellow volunteers. Donations were collected from spectators, and anyone willing to work was given a shovel. During the next two years financial support continued to pour in from various local and state agencies.

The ship began to suffer damage from high water, exposure to the air, and vandalism, making the need to finish the job more urgent. In May 1963 D. C. Murray, a house mover, contracted to remove the vessel from the river, and within a few months Gov. Terry Sanford allocated ten thousand dollars to relocate and preserve the ship's remains.

The recovery process was completed in 1964, when the vessel was relocated to Caswell Memorial Park, where a State Historic Site was established. Today, the remnants of the ship are housed in a museum in downtown Kinston.

OCT 27

CUSHINGS DARING AND SUCCESSFUL EXPLOIT

Depiction of the attack on CSS *Albemarle* by a torpedo launch commanded by Lieutenant William B. Cushing, USN, at Plymouth, North Carolina, October 27, 1864.

OCT 28

1798 Anti-Slavery Leader Levi Coffin

On October 28, 1798, Levi Coffin, anti-slavery leader and reputed "conductor" on the Underground Railroad, was born in the Guilford County Quaker community of New Garden.

He joined the Quakers of New Garden in 1818 and soon after began a Sunday school in the schoolhouse adjoining the meeting house. As an opponent to slavery, he joined Guilford County's first manumission society. Together with his cousin Vestal Coffin, he began a school for slaves, teaching them about Christianity and hosting Bible reading on Sunday afternoons. Slave owners opposed this and forbade their slaves to attend. Within a few years Coffin moved to Newport, Indiana.

Newport, now known as Fountain City, was on one route of the Underground Railroad through which slaves escaping to freedom passed. Coffin and his wife Catherine joined the movement and made their house a "station" to shelter runaways and provide safe passage into Canada. During the twenty years they lived in Newport, the Coffins helped about two thousand slaves escape to safety. One of those was "Eliza," the slave depicted by Harriet Beecher Stowe in *Uncle Tom's Cabin*. Every one of the slaves who passed through the Coffin house reached freedom.

1854 State's Longest Plank Road Reaches Salem

On October 28, 1854, the Fayetteville and Western Plank Road was completed. Stretching from Fayetteville nearly 150 miles west to Forsyth County, it was the longest plank road in the state.

Plank roads were wooden highways, which were easier to navigate than rough, rutted, and often muddy dirt roads. Tolls were collected along the route to pay for their maintenance.

The plank road movement began in North Carolina in the late 1840s in response to arguments from many that the state's existing road system was the worst in the country. Enthusiasm for such projects grew, and by 1860 nearly five hundred miles of plank roads had been laid in North Carolina.

They failed to flourish for a variety of reasons. First, building these roads was slow, difficult work. One crew could be expected to lay only about forty miles in a year. Also, railroads were faster, and the public cheated the toll system by avoiding tollbooths. The Civil War ultimately destroyed much of the infrastructure.

Though decidedly a failure, the plank road movement was an important step by the state toward improving transportation infrastructure for economic growth.

Fayetteville and Western Plank Road. John A. Shore holding a piece of the plank road in Bethania, 1959. Shore owned the general store that is shown in the background.

1936 Famed Musician Charlie Daniels

On October 28, 1936, musician Charlie Daniels was born in Wilmington.

Daniels developed an interest in music early in life and was strongly influenced by a number of styles. He honed his skills on guitar, mandolin, and fiddle in North Carolina, learning to play his first chords from his friend Russell Palmer. After graduating from Goldston High School in 1955, he formed a rock and roll band with Palmer, playing a Saturday show on a Sanford radio station.

Moving back to Wilmington, Daniels began playing with an R&B group, The Rockets. Their recording of "Jaguar" was picked up for national distribution by Epic in 1957. Throughout the 1960s Daniels gained more national attention, co-writng a song performed by Elvis Presley and playing with Bob Dylan.

In 1970 he formed the Charlie Daniels Band, which gained fame for playing its acclaimed melding of rock, country, blues, bluegrass, and gospel. The band's hits include "Uneasy Rider," "Long Haired Country Boy," "The South's Gonna Do it Again" and "The Devil Went Down to Georgia."

Daniels's many musical accolades include membership in the Grand Ole Opry, induction into the N.C. Music Hall of Fame, and several Grammy, Country Music Association and Gospel Music Association awards.

1958 Guinean President Visited Triangle, 1958

On October 28, 1958, Pres. Sékou Touré of Guinea visited the Triangle on a two-week tour of the United States.

Touré specifically asked the State Department to show him the South as part of his official visit, and North Carolina was selected as Touré's only stop in the region after hotels in downtown Atlanta indicated they would not serve the African party.

Though he was in the Triangle for just under twenty-four hours, Touré made the most of the time in the area, attending a dinner hosted by Gov. Luther Hodges at the Morehead Planetarium in Chapel Hill, having lunch with Duke University officials, and visiting what's now N.C. Central University. He and his party also toured the North Carolina Mutual Life Insurance Company, then the world's largest black-owned business, and were the first black guests to stay at the Carolina Inn.

Over the objections of some of their staffers, Governor Hodges and First Lady Martha Hodges put an emphasis on warmly receiving Touré. The couple met him and his group at the airport on their arrival from Washington, D.C. and put the governor's official vehicles at their disposal. The meal Hodges hosted in Chapel Hill is also cited by at least one source as likely the first integrated official dinner in the South since Reconstruction.

After leaving North Carolina Touré made stops in Chicago and Los Angeles before returning to Africa.

1618 Execution of Sir Walter Ralegh, 1618

On October 29, 1618, Sir Walter Ralegh was beheaded on a charge of treason in London. The former court favorite of Elizabeth I of England had fallen far from his once-respected status.

Born sometime around 1554, Ralegh was, before leading efforts to colonize the New World, a true Renaissance man, serving as a courtier, soldier, poet, historian, and member of Parliament.

His first foray into colonization began in in 1584, when he received a royal patent for colonizing the region between Florida and Nova Scotia. An exploratory voyage to Roanoke Island led to the establishment of a colony in 1585, but it was abandoned due to supply problems. In another ill-fated expedition the crew left the colonists at Roanoke Island, and when a relief expedition arrived in 1590, the colonists were missing—the now-famous Lost Colony.

In 1603 Ralegh was implicated in a plot against James I and imprisoned for more than ten years. In 1617 he led an expedition into Spanish-controlled Guyana in search of a legendary golden city. The enterprise failed, and the diplomatic crisis that expedition caused led to the restoration of Ralegh's treason charges and his execution.

North Carolina's capital city of Raleigh stands as a reminder of his important role in the origins of the state.

1901 Buffalo Bill's Wild West Show Train Disaster

On October 29, 1901, early in the morning, "Buffalo Bill" Cody's Wild West Show met with disaster in Davidson County.

An engineer on a freight train misread a telegraph message reporting that Cody's train was in two sections and returned his train to the track after the first section of Cody's had passed. The freight train and the second section of the Wild West train collided, with engineers and firemen jumping just moments before impact.

The wooden cars of both trains were obliterated, and dead and severely wounded animals were strewn around the accident site just outside of Linwood. An eyewitness reported that "the two engines seemed to have tried to devour each other." The accident was devastating for the show's horses; about a hundred were killed or had to be put down. Cody's favorite saddle horse, "Old Pap," perished in the collision. Cody sat down and wept upon surveying the destruction. Annie Oakley, the show's headliner, suffered temporary paralysis. The wreck was cleared from the tracks by the afternoon of the accident, and regular rail traffic resumed the same day.

Today the local museum has artifacts from the show, and residents are said to own livestock descended from animals that survived.

1929 The Stock Market Crash

On October 29, 1929, the stock market crashed earning the day the epithet "Black Tuesday." It was the beginning of the Great Depression, but hard times had hit North Carolina's farmers well before the 1930s and its Great Depression.

In the 1920s North Carolina was still very much a rural state. Half of the total population lived on working farms. Agriculture was the largest industry. But farmers' incomes had declined steadily.

The scale and severity of the Great Depression demanded more assistance than farmers could provide on their own. Gov. O. Max Gardner (1929–1933) pledged to improve agricultural and rural life. He introduced the "Live-at-Home" program, which encouraged Tar Heels to grow more food crops for their families and livestock and fewer cash crops for sale.

Home demonstration agents working under the direction of North Carolina State College (now North Carolina State University) assisted the program by showing women across the state how to can and preserve food. Agricultural extension agents in every county taught farmers the benefits of crop rotation, deeper plowing, better seed selection, crop diversity, and correct use of fertilizer. The amount of land devoted to cotton soon fell by 536,000 acres, and corn production increased by ten million bushels.

Buffalo Bill Cody, otherwise known as W.F. Cody, demonstrating his exceptional marksmanship skills on horseback, 1907.

1629 Originally Carolana, for King Charles I

On October 30, 1629, England's King Charles I granted much of what is North and South Carolina to his attorney general, Sir Robert Heath. The land was referred to as Carolana, meaning the "land of Charles."

The goal of grants like these was to settle and claim parts of the New World for England without costing the government very much money or effort. Basically, the crown would grant control of lands to individuals with the expectation that they would do the hard work and develop what they were given.

Apparently, one of the motivations behind the grant to Heath was interest in establishing a colony for a group of French Protestants. Although the group received permission to settle in the colony in 1630, they were ultimately unable to reach Carolana and were left stranded in Virginia. The English Civil War, which began in 1642, ended attempts at colonizing Carolana.

The Carolana grant is important because it was the first time that the land south of Virginia was envisioned as a separate settlement and because it is the original source for the name "Carolina."

OCT 30

King Charles I of England, 1636.

1855 Death of Edward Dudley of Wilmington, Governor

On October 30, 1855, Edward Dudley, North Carolina's first governor elected by a vote of the people, died.

Born in Onslow County in 1789, Dudley served in both houses of the state legislature, was colonel of the Onslow County militia during the War of 1812, and filled a vacant seat in Congress before winning the state's first gubernatorial election in 1836. Before that time governors were elected by the members of the General Assembly. In the 1836 election, after advocating for the development of the Whig Party as an alternative to then-dominant Democrats, Dudley was perfectly positioned for his win over Richard Dobbs Spaight Jr.

Dudley's administration initiated a period of progress. The completion of several railroads, the beginnings of the public school system, and the opening of several colleges were all highlights of his tenure. After his term in office, Dudley returned to leading the Wilmington and Raleigh Railroad, which he had helped organize shortly before his election.

He retired to his home on the Cape Fear River, where he died in 1855. Dudley is buried in Wilmington.

1918 Bishop J. W. Hood of the AME Zion Church

On October 30, 1918, James Walker Hood died.

A missionary in the African Methodist Episcopal Zion Church, Hood was sent in 1863 to North Carolina, where he served black congregations in New Bern and Beaufort. He established a North Carolina Conference of the AME Zion Church in 1864, became a church bishop in 1872, then moved to Fayetteville, his home for the rest of his life.

As part of his role in the church, Hood helped to establish Zion Wesley Institute, now Livingstone College, as a school to train black students for the ministry and to become good citizens of their state as teachers and artisans. He presided over the school's board of trustees for over thirty years.

Besides his role in the church, Hood also became involved in politics as a vocal and successful advocate for the rights of blacks. In 1865 he presided over the statewide freedmen's convention and later participated in the 1868 state constitutional convention and the national Republican convention of 1872. He also held several government positions, including assistant state superintendent of public instruction, magistrate, and assistant superintendent of the North Carolina Freedmen's Bureau.

Bishop James Walker Hood (ca. 1891–1894).

1754 Arthur Dobbs and His Mixed Success as Royal Governor

On October 31, 1754, Arthur Dobbs, the newly minted governor of North Carolina, arrived in the colony.

He had previously been a very successful politician in Ireland, serving as a member of the Irish Parliament and as the engineer and surveyor general of the country. Dobbs had been interested in the American colonies as a whole since the 1730s and during the 1750s was responsible for the immigration of about five hundred Protestant families from the northern part of Ireland to North Carolina.

For the first few years of his tenure, Dobbs was a successful governor. He promoted unity, industry, military strength, and loyalty to the Crown. Always trying to avoid the ongoing conflict between northern and southern factions, he attempted to establish the capital near a centrally-located town that is now Kinston. He finally settled on moving to Brunswick in 1758, where he built a home and encouraged the building of St. Philip's Church. Within four years, however, turmoil once more broke out, and Dobbs was forced to dissolve the colonial assembly in 1759.

By 1764, with factionalism rampant, Dobbs asked for and received a leave of absence. He died in March 1765 without having left the colony. He is buried at St. Philip's Church.

1765 Stamp Act Protest in the Port City, 1765

On October 31, 1765, angry Wilmingtonians held a mock funeral for Liberty the day before the Stamp Act was to go into effect.

The Stamp Act levied taxes on most forms of paper in the colonies, including newspapers, letters, pamphlets, and wills. While Parliament intended to defray costs incurred from stationing British troops in the colonies at critical sites such as Boston, the imposition of the tax drove many colonies to the brink of rebellion.

Distressed about the impending tax, concerned citizens of Wilmington assembled and placed an effigy of Liberty in a casket and carried the casket in a mock funeral procession to the churchyard, where they planned to bury it. Just before committing the casket to the earth, a member of the group checked liberty's vital signs, and detecting a pulse, the colonist rose up and proclaimed "LIBERTY had still an Existence in the Colony!"

Other similar acts of defiance in North Carolina and elsewhere took their toll on British resolve. Within a few months the colonies learned that Parliament had repealed the Stamp Act.

1886 Commodore Council Invents BC Powder in Durham

On October 31, 1886, Commodore Council, inventor of the famous BC headache powder, was born in Chatham County. He and his family moved to Durham, where he later made his living as a pharmacist after being educated at Duke and UNC.

Though to "take a powder" meant to leave the scene and thereby shirk responsibility in most of the country during the 1940s, in North Carolina the expression meant something entirely different. Headache powders, usually mixtures of aspirin and caffeine, proved to be remarkably popular in the Tar Heel State, where Goody's and Stanback Powders also had their roots. Mill workers especially benefited from the quick-acting powders, since they could be taken on the factory floor, keeping them at work and productive.

Council, who was known to many as "Conny," invented BC Powder in 1906 while working at Germain Bernard's Durham drugstore. The two men chose the name by combining the first letters of their surnames. They hired their first salesman in 1917, just in time for soldiers to carry BC Powders out of the South and around the world during World War I.

Council died in 1960 and is buried in Durham's Maplewood Cemetery. BC Powder is still available at drugstores today.

OCT 31

Arthur Dobbs, Esq., Captain General, Governor in Chief and Vice Admiral of the Provence of North Carolina.

Five Points Drug Co., ca. 1926. The flat-iron building at the corner of Main and Chapel Hill Streets housed a drug store and other businesses where BC Headache Powder was invented by Germain Bernard and Commodore Council.

1838 Cherokee Indian Tsali Captured

On November 1, 1838, a Cherokee Indian known as Tsali was captured.

Tsali, also known as "Charley," was among those who refused to leave North Carolina after a group of Cherokee leaders signed a treaty ceding their tribal lands to the United States. He, his family, and a few friends had gone into hiding in the spring. From here the story diverges into what is in the oral histories and what is in the written records. Cherokee oral tradition tells of Tsali's group being captured and harassed by federal troops. By this account he decided to fake an injury and, with the others, ambush the soldiers in order to escape. In the ensuing skirmish one soldier was killed and two others wounded, one mortally. The Cherokee group escaped and hid until learning that if the men responsible would give themselves up, all the other Indians in hiding could remain in North Carolina. The legend maintains that Tsali agreed to be executed so that the others could stay. Among the Cherokee he has become a legendary hero, depicted in the outdoor drama *Unto These Hills*.

NOV 1

At the time the legend flourished, few of the government records related to the event were available for research. What those documents reveal differs from the oral tradition. On November 1, 1838, U. S. soldiers found and captured Tsali's group. While being marched to the command base, some of the Cherokee attacked the soldiers and escaped. Oconaluftee Citizen Indians, a group of Cherokee who were exempt from the removal, and a few other fugitive Cherokee offered help with the understanding that anyone who helped to find Tsali's band would be allowed to stay in North Carolina.

A former neighbor of Tsali's known as Euchella (Utsala) led about sixty men in search of Tsali. On November 24 Col. William S. Foster, who was ordered to find Tsali, wrote to his commander, Gen. Winfield Scott that the mission was a success—that, of the twelve Indians who had been in the original group, all but Tsali had been recaptured, and the three men most culpable in the attack "were punished yesterday by the Cherokees themselves in the presence of the 4th Regt. of Infantry." Foster had made clear in other communications that he did not believe that Tsali was one of the murderers. His conviction is explicit in his dismissing the search party and leaving the area. The next day, though, Euchella and another Indian caught Tsali and executed him. Foster issued a proclamation in support of Euchella and his men and sent Scott a petition signed by residents in favor of the Indians' wishes to stay.

Euchella and his men were given permission to remain in North Carolina with the Oconaluftee Citizen Indians. Eventually these groups would be recognized as the Eastern Band of Cherokee Indians.

Tsali's story began to take shape with its embellished twist in 1849, and he has since become a folk legend. The significant difference in the two stories, of course, is that documents indicate that Tsali never surrendered and thus never made the noble sacrifice for which he is idolized. Regardless, the events were tragic and the outcome heartbreaking, and the saga is now immortalized in Cherokee lore.

1859 Cape Lookout Light Lit

On November 1, 1859, the Cape Lookout Lighthouse was lit for the first time.

Begun in 1857, the lighthouse took two years to construct, replacing a previous light built around 1812. The present tower, rising 208 feet, became the model for all subsequent lighthouse construction along the Outer Banks, especially the Cape Hatteras, Bodie Island, and Currituck Lighthouses.

Built to alert sailors of the dangerous shoals on the southern tip of Core Banks, an area known since the late sixteenth century as the "horrible headland," the light could be seen from up to nineteen miles out at sea. Until the completion of the Cape Hatteras Lighthouse in 1870, the Cape Lookout light was the tallest such structure south of New Jersey.

In 1873 the Light House Board assigned the familiar diamond pattern to Cape Lookout's light, and the small community around the lighthouse took the name "Diamond City" around 1885 as a result. Though the community prospered for a brief time, largely due to the success of the whaling industry, it was abandoned after a strong hurricane in August 1899 nearly destroyed it.

Today the Cape Lookout Lighthouse is one of the main attractions on the Cape Lookout National Seashore, administered by the National Park Service.

1947 "Copperhead Cuddlers" in Durham, 1947

On November 1, 1947, Durham police raided the Zion Tabernacle Church on Peabody Street and confiscated a copperhead snake being handled in a church service.

While no arrests were made that night, pending examination of the snake to determine whether it was venomous, during the next several days individuals, including Rev. Colonel Hartman Bunn, were reminded of a city ordinance banning the handling of poisonous reptiles. An expert at what's now the N.C. Museum of Natural Sciences verified that the snake was a copperhead.

Bunn and other members of the church continued to handle snakes at ceremonies on subsequent nights, vowing to take their fight to the Supreme Court. After he was arrested, Bunn pleaded not guilty in recorder's court before a standing-room-only crowd and asked for a continuance.

On November 19, Bunn and his snake tender, Benjamin Ralph Massey, were found guilty and fined. Both appealed to Superior Court. As he left the courthouse, this phase of the "Copperhead Cuddlers" case finished, Bunn made an impassioned speech on the steps in which he compared the police who confiscated his snakes to Hitler's SS Elite Guard.

Snake handlers from the Zion Tabernacle Church in Durham, 1949.

1795 President James K. Polk and Manifest Destiny

On November 2, 1795, James Knox Polk, the eleventh president of the United States, was born on a farm just south of what is today Charlotte. Polk moved to Tennessee in 1806 but returned to his home state to attend the University of North Carolina.

His first election was to the Tennessee state legislature in 1823. He then became a member of the U.S. Congress, and in 1837 he was elected governor of Tennessee. Polk narrowly won election to the presidency over Henry Clay in 1844, making him at age forty-nine the youngest president to that date.

Polk entered the presidency with a clear plan of action; foremost among his goals was westward expansion. Seen by contemporaries as conscientious and attentive to the needs of the country, in his presidential campaign, he promised not to run for a second term. True to his word, he did not.

While Polk's original North Carolina home is long gone, a cabin accurate to the period is open to the public at the President James K. Polk State Historic Site in Pineville.

1984 Velma Barfield, Serial Killer

On November 2, 1984, Velma Barfield, from Cumberland County, became the first woman in the nation executed by lethal injection. She was convicted of first-degree murder for the arsenic poisoning of her boyfriend, Stuart Taylor, in 1978.

After her arrest and the subsequent investigation, authorities discovered a pattern of mysterious deaths around Barfield. She eventually confessed to three other murders, including that of her mother. In her confession she claimed that she poisoned the others to hide the fact that she had stolen money from each to support her addiction to tranquilizers and painkillers. She argued that she intended only to make them sick so as to give her time to restore the funds she had taken. Interestingly, her two husbands also died under unusual circumstances. Though it was believed she had a hand in those deaths as well, Barfield denied accusations to that effect.

For six years Barfield's attorneys filed appeals to overturn her conviction, but all failed. They argued that due to her excessive drug use, she did not realize what she was doing would result in the death of her victims. Their goal was to get her off death row and have her sentence reduced to life in prison.

2007 LaGrange Country Boy to Harlem Gangster

On November 2, 2007, *American Gangster*, a film starring Denzel Washington based on the life of North Carolina native Frank Lucas, was released to wide acclaim.

Born near LaGrange in 1930, Lucas saw his older cousin lynched by the Ku Klux Klan in 1936 for looking at a white woman walking down the street. He credited that moment with launching him into a life of crime.

Already a criminal at age sixteen, in 1946 Lucas moved to Harlem, which he'd been told was the "promised land" for African Americans. His crime spree in New York began with thievery but soon descended into murder and drugs. In the 1960s and 1970s Lucas "owned" his neighborhood in Harlem, buoyed by his fearlessness and by the locals' addiction to his particular brand of heroin. A rather flamboyant gangster, his signature was a fifty-thousand-dollar chinchilla coat with a matching ten-thousand-dollar hat.

Lucas brought five brothers into the family "business." Calling them the "Country Boys," he said that city boys were not reliable and that he could trust only good old country folks. First arrested in 1975, Lucas never served more than a few years behind bars, trading information for time.

Although many details in the movie are disputed, it conveys the likable nature of the country boy, Frank Lucas.

1835 Mount Mitchell Declared Highest Peak in Eastern U.S.

On November 3, 1835, Elisha Mitchell, a professor at the University of North Carolina, announced that a peak in the Black Mountains of North Carolina was the highest in the eastern United States.

The news aroused considerable interest. He estimated the mountain's height at 6,672 feet, only twelve feet short of the present official height of 6,684 feet. A "controversy of major proportions" ensued in the 1850s between Mitchell and U.S. Rep. (and later Sen.) Thomas L. Clingman, who called into question the accuracy of Mitchell's earlier observations and measurements.

On June 27, 1857, Mitchell slipped and fell to his death in a deep pool at the bottom of a sixty-foot waterfall while exploring the Black Mountain range in an effort to prove his claim. Initially interred in a cemetery in Asheville, Mitchell's remains were moved in 1858 to the top of the mountain, which was named in his memory at that time.

Mount Mitchell became North Carolina's first state park in 1915. The modern observation tower at the summit is adjacent to Elisha Mitchell's gravesite.

1936 Thad Eure, N.C. Secretary of State for Over a Half-Century

On November 3, 1936, Thad Eure was elected to his first term as North Carolina's Secretary of State. Eure would go on to hold the post for thirteen terms, serving in the job for a total of fifty-three years.

Born in Gates County in 1899, Eure served as mayor of Winton and a member of the General Assembly before he decided to run for Secretary of State in 1931 at the behest of Gov. O. Max Gardner.

Eure, like other secretaries of state, was responsible for chartering corporations and publishing the *North Carolina Manual*, a biannual guide to government, among other duties. He was known for being available to new legislators for advice and maintained a literal open-door policy; never closing his door to the public.

Though Eure was famous for asking voters to "give a young man a chance" during his first campaign, he sometimes referred to himself as "the oldest rat in the Democratic barn" by the end of his career. In 1987 Pres. Ronald Reagan recognized Eure for holding public office longer than any official in United States history.

Thad Eure died in 1993.

1949 Palmer Graduate Cast as Lionel Jefferson

On November 3, 1949, television actor and writer Michael Evans was born in Salisbury.

Evans attended school at the elite Palmer Memorial Institute in Sedalia until his family moved to Los Angeles. In California he finished high school and began to study acting.

Before finishing his training, Evans landed the part of Lionel Jefferson on Norman Lear's hit 1970s TV show *All in the Family*. Evans's Lionel was a liberal, rational, and clever counterpart to his irritable father, George Jefferson, and his neighbor, the boisterous bigot Archie Bunker. So entertaining were the Jeffersons that in 1975 the family premiered in its own series, in which they moved out of the Bunker's neighborhood into a "deluxe apartment in the sky."

Only months into the production of *The Jeffersons*, Evans created *Good Times* with his writing partner, Eric Monte. The show, a spinoff from *Maude*, another Lear production, was one of the first sitcoms to feature a primarily African American cast. The demands of writing *Good Times* led Evans to abandon his role as Lionel Jefferson for a few years. While involved with the Lear television productions, he also appeared in several TV movies.

Michael Evans died of throat cancer in 2006.

1979 Klan-Nazi Shooting Left Five Dead in Greensboro

On November 3, 1979, the "Death to the Klan" March took place in Greensboro. The march resulted in a shootout between members of the Communist Workers Party (CWP), the Ku Klux Klan, and a neo-Nazi group.

Only four city police officers were assigned to the demonstration in hopes that the low profile would avoid trouble. An unusual stipulation of the parade permit was that CWP members would not carry weapons. The Klan had been informed of the march and planned an armed confrontation, but the CWP was not warned of this.

Demonstrators gathered at Morningside Homes, where the march was slated to start, singing protest songs and making picket signs. Local media filmed them. Unknown to anyone else, some of the CWP workers had weapons in their vehicles. Klansmen and Nazis drove past the assembling demonstrators. The heckling turned to a physical confrontation and escalated to shooting.

Five CWP workers, often using a media van for cover, were killed in eighty-one seconds of shooting. Only one vehicle from the ten-vehicle caravan of Klan members and neo-Nazis was apprehended, though numerous CWP members on the scene were arrested. The next day fourteen Klansmen and Nazis were charged with first-degree murder, felony riot, and conspiracy.

NOV 4

1782 John Branch, Governor of North Carolina and Florida

On November 4, 1782, John Branch, future governor of North Carolina, was born in Halifax.

During the period Branch was raised in Halifax, the town was the center of North Carolina's political life. In fact, another prominent politician of the era, John Eaton, was born just a few years after Branch in the same area. Both men would go on to serve in Andrew Jackson's cabinet and as governors of Florida.

Branch was remarkably progressive for his day. As North Carolina's governor for three years beginning in 1817, he endorsed much of the reform agenda of Archibald D. Murphey, a leading progressive advocate, who is known as North Carolina's "father of education." Among other things, Branch took steps to promote public education, initiate internal improvements, and liberalize the penal code.

Initially an ally of Jackson, Branch came in time to be identified with John C. Calhoun and nullification. Branch's opposition to Jackson contributed significantly to the rise of the Whig Party in North Carolina. At the 1835 state constitutional convention Branch even argued for the removal of religious qualifications for office and against the disfranchisement of free blacks.

Branch later moved with his family to Florida and in 1843 was appointed governor of that territory. It was during his term in office that Florida became a state. He died in 1863 and is buried in Halifax County.

Photo of Richard Gatling *(left)*.

1862 Richard Gatling Patented the Gatling Gun

On November 4, 1862, Richard Jordan Gatling patented his six-barrel repeating gun known as the Gatling Gun.

Gatling was born in Hertford County in 1818. His first invention was a screw propeller for a boat, but he lost the patent to another inventor. He then patented a rice-seed planter, which he converted to a wheat planter after moving to the Midwest. There he earned a medical degree and practiced as a physician.

At the onset of the Civil War, Gatling was distressed by the number of troops dying from disease. He believed that if he could invent a gun that fired more efficiently, the armies would then need fewer soldiers. With that in mind, Gatling invented the gun that bore his name—the first Gatling gun was capable of firing two hundred rounds per minute. He continued to improve upon the gun, patenting a new model in 1865.

Before selling his patent rights to the Colt Firearms Company in 1870, he created a gun capable of firing twelve hundred rounds per minute. Needless to say, the humanitarian benefits that inspired Gatling to invent such a weapon were never realized.

1950 Charles Frazier and the Crafting of Cold Mountain

On November 4, 1950, Charles Frazier was born in Asheville.

Growing up, Frazier has admitted, he was "a great reader of junk." When he was introduced by a friend to some of the better works of American literature, he was hooked. After earning his Ph.D., he traveled widely and co-wrote a Sierra Club travel guide to the Andes region.

In 1986 Frazier returned to his home state, taking a teaching position at North Carolina State University. During that time he researched all aspects of mountain culture, folklore, and natural history. He knew that he wanted to write a novel but was unsure of the precise subject. He had a moment of clarity when his father recounted the story of a great uncle, a Confederate soldier who deserted, leaving his hospital to return to his home at Cold Mountain.

Quitting his teaching job to stay home with his daughter, Frazier spent most of his time writing. The resulting book, based loosely on the family legend and more firmly rooted in the wider Appalachian milieu, was on the bestseller list for sixty-one weeks and won the Sir Walter Raleigh and National Book Awards for fiction in 1997. *Cold Mountain* was adapted for a film, released in 2003 to wide acclaim.

The patent of Gatling Gun from the U. S. Patent Office *(background)*.

1988 Hornets Establish NBA in Charlotte, 1988

On November 4, 1988, the original Charlotte Hornets franchise played their first game, a 113-93 loss to the Cleveland Cavaliers.

That first game was a formal affair, with men in tuxedos and women in evening gowns, and when the new team hit the court, they were wearing a new style of uniform in teal and purple, making a fashion statement that swept the nation. The creation of internationally-known clothing designer and Chapel Hill native Alexander Julian, the uniforms were also distinctive for their use of pinstripes—a first for a National Basketball Association team.

In 1985 the NBA set plans to expand by four teams by the 1988-1989 season. Kannapolis entrepreneur George Shinn sought to bring one of those teams to Charlotte, assembling a group of prominent local businessmen to rally behind the effort and pointing out that the Charlotte Coliseum, then under construction, would be one of the league's largest arenas.

Though the Hornets finished their inaugural season with a record of twenty wins and sixty-two losses, they were a runaway hit and led the NBA in attendance, a feat they would achieve seven more times in Charlotte. Perhaps one of the highlights of that first season came just before Christmas, when the Hornets beat Michael Jordan and the Chicago Bulls 103–101 at the buzzer in Jordan's first return to North Carolina as a professional.

Longtime league executive Carl Scheer was the team's first manager, and veteran college and pro coach Dick Harter was the first head coach. Notable players from the first season include ex-Pistons guard Kelly Tripucka, sharpshooting rookie Rex Chapman, and floor general Muggsy Bogues, the shortest player in NBA history at 5'3."

The team owned by Shinn relocated to New Orleans in 2002, and the NBA established the Charlotte Bobcats in 2004. After the New Orleans team rebranded as the Pelicans, the Hornets name returned to Charlotte in 2014.

NOV 5

1820 Governor and UNC Founder William Davie Died

On November 5, 1820, soldier, politician, and founder of the University of North Carolina William R. Davie died at age sixty-four.

Davie graduated from the College of New Jersey (later Princeton) in 1776 and moved to Salisbury, to study law. Davie had a brief military career in 1779–1780 but was wounded. Later he organized cavalry along with mounted infantry and embarked on a campaign of partisan attacks in the Carolina backcountry.

Around 1786 Davie built the house in Halifax that still bears his name. He would represent Halifax in the General Assembly off and on for the next ten years. Davie was selected one of North Carolina's five delegates to the Confederation Congress of 1787, and he campaigned for the Constitution's ratification. At the 1789 state convention in Fayetteville that ratified the Constitution, Davie introduced a bill to charter a state university. As founder, he guided the university through its formative years.

Elected governor of North Carolina in 1798, Davie went on to represent the United States in treaty negotiations, eventually retiring to his plantation in South Carolina, where he died.

1827 Congressional Rivals Shoot It Out

On November 5, 1827, Congressman Samuel Price Carson shot Robert Brank Vance, his predecessor in the House and uncle of Civil War-era governor Zebulon Vance.

Early that morning the two engaged in a duel just south of the North Carolina-South Carolina border and the present-day Tuxedo community in Henderson County. Dueling adhered closely to an accepted body of rules, by which gentlemen walked ten paces, turned, and fired upon one another.

Vance, who died the next day, was born in Buncombe County and elected to Congress in 1823. Carson was born in Pleasant Gardens near Marion. He was elected to Congress in 1825, forcing Vance into an unwanted early retirement. Vance ran for election again in 1827. It was a bitter campaign, during which Vance accused Carson's father of turning Tory during the Revolutionary War and called Carson a coward in his hometown. Carson held his temper until after the election, which he won. He then challenged Vance to the duel.

Vance was buried in his family cemetery on Reems Creek. Carson moved to Texas and was appointed Secretary of State there in September 1836. He died two years later.

1922 Tuberculosis Vaccine Perfected in Asheville

On November 5, 1922, medical pioneer Karl von Ruck died in Asheville. Born in Turkey in 1849 and raised in Germany, he immigrated to the United States shortly after receiving his medical degree.

Von Ruck, who studied and treated tuberculosis and related lung and throat diseases, settled in Asheville because the climate was therapeutic for people with such problems. There he opened a research laboratory and sanitarium before focusing his efforts on creating a vaccine for tuberculosis. He produced such a vaccine in 1912 in the hopes of preventing children from contracting the disease. The vaccine was found to both prevent and treat TB. Von Ruck was instrumental in establishing Asheville as the primary area for tuberculosis treatment in the United States.

He continued his medical research and treatment of patients until only weeks before his death in 1922. Karl von Ruck is buried in Asheville's Riverside Cemetery.

1957 Two Troopers Murdered, 1957

On November 5, 1957, North Carolina State Trooper Wister Lee Reece was shot and killed near Ellerbe, and less than half an hour later Trooper James Thomas Brown was murdered near Sanford. The crimes would grip the nation.

Reece's murder came after a traffic stop. Witnesses described the car that was stopped as a black Oldsmobile with Pennsylvania license plates. During the next few weeks a nationwide manhunt, the largest ever in North Carolina's history, ensued. An Oldsmobile was found abandoned in Chattanooga and fingerprints recovered.

About ten days after the shooting, the FBI honed in on New Yorker Frank Wetzel as a person of interest and several days later found him jailed in California. His fingerprints matched those inside the Oldsmobile, though a witness, who said he was a hitchhiker in the assailant's car at the time of Reece's shooting, gave a description of the gunman that didn't match Wetzel.

Wetzel, who had escaped from a New York mental institution, had been on his way to break his brother out of prison in Mississippi, where the younger man was on death row. He was convicted of both murders in 1958 at separate trials, and he remained in prison until his death in 2012 at age ninety. Wetzel maintained his innocence until his death, pointing to that facts that Brown was shot nearly 50 miles away from Reece and the murders were committed roughly twenty minutes apart.

Karl Von Ruck's Winyah Sanitarium, Asheville, N. C..

1755 Dobbs Taps Waddell as Indian Negotiator, 1755

On November 6, 1755, Capt. Hugh Waddell was named North Carolina's commissioner in treaty negotiations with the Catawba and Cherokee.

At the beginning of the French and Indian War, it was imperative that England's colonies solidify their alliances with neighboring native tribes. North Carolina was particularly concerned with relations between the Cherokee and the Catawba. The two tribes had been enemies for generations, yet both were allies of England, and both had grievances with colonial settlers.

Informed that Gov. Robert Dinwiddie of Virginia was sending commissioners to negotiate alliances, North Carolina Gov. Arthur Dobbs decided to add a delegation from North Carolina. He appointed the senior military officer in the western part of the colony, Waddell.

Waddell was to, "Joyn with the Virginia Commissioners And Treat with the Cherokees and Catawbas," which he did for "above a month" in February and March 1756. Dobbs was certain that the efforts would ensure continued support of the English cause by the Cherokee and Catawba.

The Cherokee ultimately remained loyal to the British, and the Catawba did not, though by the outbreak of the American Revolution most of Catawba were in South Carolina. American troops clashed with the Cherokee during the Rutherford Expedition of 1776, with the Patriot troops destroying most of their towns and crops.

1860 Rector Adam Empie of Wilmington's St. James Episcopal Church

On November 6, 1860, clergyman and educator Adam Empie died.

Born in New York in 1785, Empie attended Union College before being ordained an Episcopal minister. He traveled to North Carolina in 1811 after being appointed rector of St. James's Church in Wilmington. There he instituted a number of new programs and enlarged the congregation exponentially.

In 1814 Empie left Wilmington to become a professor and the first chaplain at the U.S. Military Academy at West Point. He returned to North Carolina a few years later, worked at the same parish, and helped to organize the Episcopal Church in North Carolina, before becoming president of the College of William and Mary in 1827. The Williamsburg, Virginia school grew and prospered during his nearly ten-year tenure.

Empie returned to Wilmington in 1853 due to poor health but continued working with Episcopal schools in Raleigh and Richmond. He died in 1860 and is buried in Oakdale Cemetery.

1865 A Civil War Surrender Six Months After Appomattox

On November 6, 1865, the CSS *Shenandoah* lowered the Confederate flag, and James I. Waddell surrendered command of the vessel to British authorities in Liverpool. The surrender came a full six months after Robert E. Lee's surrender at Appomattox. In that time Waddell, a native of Pittsboro, had led his men on the only circumnavigation of the world by a Confederate ship.

The *Shenandoah* was a Confederate raider, and as such, its objective was to destroy Union merchant ships. It captured thirty-eight Union vessels and took more than a thousand prisoners of war while it was in commission. The crew did not know about Lee's surrender until June 1865 because of slow communication. The *Shenandoah* captured twenty-five vessels between May 27 and June 28.

Waddell received official word of the Confederate defeat while approaching San Francisco in August 1865. Directing his ship southward to avoid retribution for what the Union considered acts of piracy, he rounded Cape Horn during Fall 1865 and sailed for England, where he surrendered in Liverpool.

1973 Honor for State's Cherished Capitol Building

On November 6, 1973, the State Capitol became a National Historic Landmark. The designation by the U.S. Secretary of the Interior is reserved for nationally significant historic places that possess exceptional value or quality in illustrating or interpreting American history. There are fewer than twenty-five hundred of them across the country.

The Capitol that stands today was not the first in Raleigh. That first building was completed in 1794 and burned in 1831. The cornerstone of the present State Capitol was laid at the site of the former State House in 1833. The exterior walls are built of gneiss, a type of granite that was quarried in southeastern Raleigh and hauled to the site on the horse-drawn Experimental Railroad, the state's first railway.

Completed in 1840, the Capitol is one of the finest and best-preserved examples of a major civic building in the Greek Revival style of architecture. It housed all of North Carolina's state government until 1888, when the Supreme Court Building (now the Labor Building) was completed across Edenton Street. The General Assembly left the Capitol and moved into the State Legislative Building in 1963.

NOV 6

CSS *Shenandoah*. Nineteenth century photographic reproduction of an artwork depicting the ship under sail.

NOV 7

1918 Billy Graham Born in Charlotte

On November 7, 1918, Billy Graham was born in Charlotte. A worldwide symbol of evangelism, he has preached to millions of people. Hundreds of millions more, in every corner of the globe, have heard his message through television, radio, print, and film.

Ordained by the Southern Baptist Convention in 1940, Graham studied Scripture at Florida Bible Institute and graduated from Wheaton College in Illinois in 1943. It was during a tent crusade in downtown Los Angeles in 1949 that Graham and his evangelistic team were launched into worldwide prominence. Originally scheduled for three weeks, the meetings drew overflow crowds each night for more than two months. Subsequent crusades, both in the United States and overseas, witnessed similar enthusiasm.

In 1950 Graham founded the Billy Graham Evangelistic Association. The organization, now headquartered in Charlotte, is also home to the Billy Graham Library. The Billy Graham Training Center is located in Asheville.

Often listed by the Gallup organization as one of the "Ten Most Admired Men in the World," Graham prayed with twelve U.S. presidents since Harry Truman. He died on Feb. 21, 2018, at his home in Montreat.

1944 Water Impoundment Began at Fontana Dam

On November 7, 1944, water impoundment began at Fontana Dam in western North Carolina.

At 480 feet Fontana is the highest dam east of the Rocky Mountains. Like other TVA projects, it was constructed for flood regulation, regional power, and economic development. Electricity generated by the dam was also used to power Oak Ridge, Tennessee, where research on development of the atomic bomb was underway.

Several communities were covered under the resulting 10,600-acre Fontana Lake. Forty cemeteries and 2,043 known graves were relocated. At the peak of construction more than six thousand workers worked shifts around the clock. In 1947 the workers' village was converted into the present-day resort community of Fontana Village.

The concrete dam, which is 376 feet wide at its base, and the accompanying six-story glass-walled powerhouse at its foot cost about $74,681,000; that's about $969,883,116 in today's dollars. Every five years the lake's waters are drawn down for dam inspection, and during those periods the remnants of earlier times can be seen.

1950 Ponder Brothers, Madison Powerbrokers

On November 7, 1950, Elymas Yates "E. Y." Ponder was elected sheriff of mountainous Madison County, defeating Republican incumbent Hubert Davis by thirty-one votes.

Davis disputed the outcome and, supported by his deputies, refused to relinquish the office. Ponder brought suit in superior court, and Davis was ordered to vacate his office in early January 1951. Davis appealed the case to the state Supreme Court, which ultimately decided in Ponder's favor. A genial man who never wore a uniform and rarely carried a gun or drove a marked patrol car, Ponder remained "the law" in Madison County until 1986.

Ponder's younger brother, Zeno, was appointed chairman of the county elections board in 1950. An army veteran with a wispy mustache and wily manner, he promptly remade Madison, a long-time Republican stronghold, into a Democratic machine. Nearly every election over the next forty years was fraught with charges of voting law violations and, occasionally, violence.

Zeno Ponder ran for public office only once. In 1964 he sought a state senate seat. When the results of the primary election were tabulated, they showed that Ponder had won more votes in some precincts than there were registered voters. Though the election was overturned, the Ponders remained powerful into the mid-1980s.

1954 William B. Umstead, Governor for 22 Months

On November 7, 1954, attorney, teacher, congressman, and North Carolina governor William B. Umstead died of heart failure.

Born on a Durham County farm in 1895, Umstead served as a lieutenant in the Eighty-First "Wildcat" Division during World War I before being elected to Congress. During his three terms in the House of Representatives and a single term in the Senate, Umstead focused mostly on rural issues, including soil conservation and rural electrification.

Elected governor in 1952, Umstead suffered a heart attack just two days after his 1953 inauguration and spent most of his term as governor confined to his bed, forcing him to run meetings and conduct other state business in the Executive Mansion.

A political moderate, Umstead advocated for fair parole for prisoners, bonds for school construction, and better conditions in mental institutions during his time in the state's top job. He also oversaw school desegregation after the Supreme Court's Brown decision, creating a biracial panel to study the process and make recommendations to the General Assembly to ensure it was rolled out as smoothly as possible.

Umstead was the first North Carolina governor to die in office in more than fifty years. He is buried in the Mount Tabor Church Cemetery north of Durham.

Billy Graham, 1966.

Appalachian Trail and Fontana Dam, North Carolina.

1789 Military-Political Leader Richard Caswell

On November 8, 1789, Richard Caswell, the first governor of the independent state of North Carolina, suffered a stroke that led to his death.

Before becoming governor, Caswell served as a member of the colonial assembly for twenty-one years. In 1771 he led part of Gov. William Tryon's army in its defeat of the Regulators at the Battle of Alamance. With the approach of the Revolution, Caswell was made a commander of militia and led his brigade in the decisive victory over Loyalist forces at Moores Creek Bridge.

When the Fifth Provincial Congress convened at Halifax late in 1776, Caswell served as its presiding officer and as chairman of the committee to draft the state's constitution. He was then elected governor to the first of three successive one-year terms allowable under that constitution.

When his third term expired in April 1780, Caswell was pressed into duty as commander of the state militia. He was elected to the state Senate in 1780 and served there for the next four years.

Caswell returned to the governorship in November 1784 and was reelected to that post in both of the next two years. After reaching the three-consecutive term limit, Caswell was elected to the state Senate in 1789.

Caswell died in Fayetteville after suffering a stroke in the Senate chamber. He is buried near Kinston.

1950 Photographer Ignatius Brock of Asheville

On November 8, 1950, internationally-renowned photographer and painter Ignatius Brock died at age eight-three.

Born in Jones County in 1866, Brock got his start in photography as an apprentice at the Gerock Studio in New Bern. He moved to New York to study art at the Cooper Union Institute, then returned to North Carolina and opened his first studio in Asheville.

Though at first he mostly painted landscapes and used photographs simply as sketch notes for future paintings, Brock turned to photography as his primary art form because of his considerable skill with a camera. His focus in photography was on portraits and landscapes, and his fame quickly began to grow as he won several international photographic competitions and had his work featured in many of the prominent magazines of the time. Brock was also interested in the technical aspects of photography and invented a blue light bulb for use in darkroom processing.

Throughout his career Brock maintained studios in Asheville for both painting and photography. His thousands of works in both media provide a fascinating glimpse into the history of western North Carolina during the first half of the twentieth century.

1965 Medal of Honor Recipient Lawrence Joel

On November 8, 1965, Specialist/Sergeant First Class Lawrence Joel of Winston-Salem, a Korean War veteran, began a routine patrol near Bien Hoa, Vietnam. Joel and his unit, the First Battalion of the 503rd Airborne Infantry, were ambushed by a Viet Cong battalion that outnumbered them six to one. Wounded twice by machine gun fire, Joel, who was a medic, bandaged his wounds, self-administered a shot of morphine, and continued to tend to his unit's many wounded paratroopers.

The fighting continued for nearly twenty-four hours, and during that time Joel put his life at risk to save the wounded in his company and another unit. After the battle he spent three months in Saigon and Tokyo hospitals before returning to the United States.

In March 1967 Joel received the Congressional Medal of Honor from Pres. Lyndon B. Johnson. He was the first medical aid man ever to receive the award, the first living African American to receive the award since the Spanish American War, the first enlisted man to receive the award from President Johnson, and the first soldier from Winston-Salem to be so honored.

A career soldier, Lawrence Joel retired from the service in 1973 and died in 1984. He is buried in Arlington National Cemetery.

Lawrence Joel at a parade in his honor, Winston-Salem, 1967.

NOV 9

1861 Alexander H. Stephens Visited Wilmington Arms Factory

On November 9, 1861, Confederate vice president Alexander H. Stephens visited the Wilmington Arms Factory and "made a spirited address" while holding a sword and lance. He promised to carry the weapons to other parts of the Confederacy to show others what "the Old North State was doing."

Louis Froelich and a partner opened the factory that month, offering swords, bayonets, lances, and bowie knives. They soon renamed the company C.S.A. Arms Factory.

By the summer of 1862, Froelich was sole owner of the factory. A yellow fever epidemic that July killed most of his workers, and a fire the following February destroyed the main building. Shortly afterward Froelich moved his remaining operations to Kenansville. Three months later a Federal expedition burned the factory to the ground.

Froelich rebounded, and by November 1863 the factory was again operational. Today, Froelich swords, of which only a few dozen are known to remain, are some of the rarest and most valuable Confederate artifacts.

1882 Medical Pioneer S. S. Satchwell

On November 9, 1882, Solomon S. Satchwell, physician and founding member of the Medical Society of North Carolina, died in Burgaw.

During the 1850s Satchwell became one of the preeminent physicians in the state. In 1852 he reported to the Medical Society on his malaria research, determining that the disease was the most frequent killer of people in the South. He recognized the correlation between bodies of stagnant water and the disease but did not surmise that the disease was transmitted by mosquitoes.

From 1854 to 1856, Satchwell served as the Society's secretary and later president, and in 1858 he was one of the main proponents for the publication of the *Medical Journal of North Carolina*. The following year he successfully lobbied the state legislature for the authorization of a state board of medical examiners. Throughout his career he worked diligently to improve the status of the medical profession in North Carolina.

During the Civil War Satchwell served as the head surgeon at the Confederate hospital at Wilson. After the war he opened a private practice in Pender County and remained working in the medical field until his death. He is buried in Oakdale Cemetery in Wilmington.

1973 Floyd McKissick and Soul City

On November 9, 1973, civil rights activist Floyd McKissick broke ground on Soul City in rural Warren County.

The Soul City project sought to improve the economic prospects of underprivileged African Americans by providing them with affordable housing and creating an alternative to urban slums. Warren County was chosen for the project because it was one of the poorest areas in the state.

McKissick, the driving force behind the project, was the first African American man to go to law school at the University of North Carolina and thought that economic power was the first step to political freedom. The project received several million dollars in support from the state and federal governments, as well as from private donors.

The first facility constructed at Soul City was an impressive water system and factory called SoulTech I. But the whole project was largely derailed by a 1975 exposé in the *News & Observer* that charged McKissick with corruption. Even though the accusations were later discredited, the controversy that surrounded the article led to the project's being audited and caused it to lose support from the business community. It fell into a slump and effectively ended when the U.S. Department of Housing and Urban Development withdrew its support in 1979.

Floyd B. McKissick (*left*) and Kimp Talley (*right*) stand in front of huge 20 ft. steel and concrete sculpture at the entrance to Soul City at the intersection of U.S. Highway 1 and Soul City Blvd.

1979 Aviator Louise Thaden and the Ninety-Nines

On November 9, 1979, early aviation pioneer Louise Thaden, died of a heart attack in High Point.

One of the first women to make flying her business, Thaden flew her first solo flight and received her pilot's license in 1927. By 1928 she set the woman's altitude record at 20,260 feet, and the next year she claimed the woman's endurance record after flying for twenty-two hours, three minutes, and twenty-eight seconds. That same year she was the first woman to win the National Air Races. She also teamed up with Amelia Earhart and Ruth Nichols in 1929 to found Ninety-Nines, a group intented to provide inspiration and fellowship to female pilots.

Thaden continued to set records until retiring in 1938 to spend more time with her family. That year she published her autobiography, *High, Wide and Frightened*, about her time in the early days of aviation.

One of the great women of the Golden Age of Aviation, Thaden was born in Arkansas in 1905. She and her husband Herbert moved to High Point in 1956 and established Thaden Engineering, a company for developmental engineering in plastics. She remained active in local aviation until her death.

NOV 10

1739 James Murray and the Argyll Colony

On November 10, 1739, Wilmington merchant James Murray wrote his friend Henry McCulloh about the promising prospect for settlement by Scots in the upper Cape Fear region. Murray himself had been in America for only four years and wished to see his fellow Scots populate the backcountry.

The lands that Murray promoted became the Argyll Colony. That name is best known today for a knitted sock pattern but originates from a county in western Scotland. In 1740 five leaders of the colony petitioned the Assembly for an exemption from taxes in order that their numbers might flourish.

The new immigrants became the vanguard for a wave of settlers, and by the 1770s Highland Scots comprised about a third of the population of the Cape Fear region. The lower Cape Fear area became known as the "Valley of the Scots."

Murray was an ally of colonial governor Gabriel Johnston, also a Scot. Murray kept his home at "Point Repose" north of Wilmington and grew rice and indigo on his land. Among North Carolina's leading Loyalists, he went into exile in Nova Scotia after the Revolutionary War and died there in 1781.

1898 Wilmington Coup

On November 10, 1898, the year's white supremacy campaign culminated with a coup in Wilmington, marking the onset of the Jim Crow era of segregation in the state. Though traditionally termed a "race riot," many have called the event a massacre.

In the days preceding the November election, a local citizen named Alfred Moore Waddell called for the removal of the Republicans and Populists then in power in Wilmington. He proposed in a speech that the white residents, if necessary, "choke the Cape Fear with carcasses." Adding to Wilmington's trouble were Alex Manly's writings in the *Daily Record*, a local black-owned newspaper.

Tensions came to a head on November 10, when Waddell led about five hundred white men to the *Daily Record* office. In expectation of violence, Manly, along with many other black citizens, had already fled the city. The mob broke into the building, a fire broke out, and the top floor of the building was consumed. The crowd swelled to nearly two thousand as it moved across town, spreading violence. There were an untold number of African Americans who were killed.

1903 Drexel and the Furniture Maker That Took Its Name

On November 10, 1903, Drexel Furniture was founded by six partners in the small Burke County town of Drexel. One of the partners, Samuel Huffman, managed the business until his death in 1935. His son Robert then took control of the operation.

Robert Huffman transformed Drexel from a small enterprise manufacturing mostly low-cost pieces to one of the leading producers of traditional and modern furniture in the country. Throughout the 1950s the company acquired a number of its competitors, and in the 1960s it secured several lucrative contracts with the U.S. State Department and many schools and hospitals. Those deals literally took the brand around the world.

In the late 1960s, 1970s, and 1980s the company changed hands a number of times, eventually becoming part of the massive Masco Corporation, which sells various home improvement and construction products.

Today Drexel is a division of Furniture Brands International, which owns a number of other North Carolina furniture companies, including Broyhill, Hickory Chair, and Thomasville.

1945 Just Happy to Be Here: Donna Fargo

On November 10, 1945, Yvonne Vaughan, better known by her later stage name Donna Fargo, was born in Mount Airy.

After growing up in North Carolina, Vaughan moved to California, where she finished college and began teaching English by day and singing in Los Angeles clubs by night. She met Dan Silver, who agreed to be her manager, and her singing career soon took off.

In 1966 the couple, who would eventually marry, moved to Phoenix. There she adopted the name Donna Fargo and began recording. Although she had not achieved wide commercial success, Fargo was named the Academy of Country Music's "Top New Female Vocalist" in 1969.

Fargo, who wrote her own songs, signed with Dot Records in 1972 and released "The Happiest Girl in the Whole USA," which topped the county music chart and peaked at Number 11 on the Billboard Hot 100 pop chart. Her follow-up song, "Funny Face," performed even better. Both qualified as gold records. The next year Fargo logged more country music hits, won a Grammy Award, and was named "Top Female Vocalist" by the Academy of Country Music. Her songs have been recorded by a variety of artists.

In 2015 a section of highway in Mount Airy was named in her honor, billed as "the Happiest Road in the Whole USA."

Alex Manly historical marker.

Donna Fargo, 1978.

NOV 11

1949 Long-Delayed Dedication of NCSU Belltower, 1949

On November 11, 1949, the Belltower, a prominent landmark on the campus of North Carolina State University, was dedicated. Gov. Gregg Cherry was one of the many dignitaries in attendance.

Conceived as a memorial to those alumni who died in service to the country during World War I, the Belltower is a symbol of the university and a gathering point for the campus community. The cornerstone was laid in 1921, with sections added in 1924, 1925, and 1926.

Despite the Great Depression and World War II, construction continued through the 1930s and 1940s. The Depression-era federal Works Progress Administration program supplied the funds to complete construction of the stone tower in 1937. The class of 1938 donated a clock, and the class of 1939 added flood lighting. Subsequent alterations included the addition of chimes, a shrine room, and a memorial plaque. That plaque listed thirty-five alumni as having died, but one name of an alumnus was included erroneously, as thirty-four had actually been killed. That name was altered but left on the plaque to represent the unknown soldiers from NSCU and elsewhere.

Students and alumni are currently raising money to add real bells to the tower.

1976 Jesse Helms and Viewpoint

On November 11, 1976, WRAL-TV broadcast the last segment of *Viewpoint*, a nightly series of political editorials, which ran on the station for nearly sixteen years.

One of the first televised outlets for punditry in North Carolina, *Viewpoint* was a springboard for the growing conservative movement. For Jesse Helms it became a podium to spread his politically conservative views on topics such as integration and national defense, as the world around him was changing drastically.

Nearly three thousand *Viewpoint* segments aired on Raleigh's CBS affiliate every weekday after the evening news broadcast and again the next morning. It was also syndicated to the Tobacco Network, which then included more than sixty radio stations statewide.

Viewpoint helped usher in political change across the state. In 1970 Helms announced on one broadcast that he would be changing his party affiliation from Democratic to Republican, boosting the political shift in North Carolina's electorate.

The final *Viewpoint* aired four years after Helms left television to campaign for a U.S. Senate seat in 1972.

Belltower at North Carolina State University.

1836 P. T. Barnum Begins to Organize Circus

On November 12, 1836, Phineas Taylor "P. T." Barnum arrived in Rocky Mount after leaving Aaron Turner's Traveling Circus, for which he managed the sideshow acts and took tickets. Barnum convinced some of the Turner acts to join his own traveling circus.

Their first stop was in Rocky Mount Falls (now Rocky Mount). Arriving on a Saturday evening, Barnum spent the night at the Stage Coach Inn. In his autobiography he wrote that the next morning he accompanied the landlord to the Baptist church.

Before entering the church Barnum noticed a grove with a stand and benches. Desiring to speak to the congregation, Barnum was permitted by the preacher to speak for a half an hour after the service. Approximately three hundred people stayed to listen to Barnum preach. While he was not yet known as the "Greatest Showman on Earth," it is reported that the crowd was certainly pleased with his performance.

1903 Four Claims about North Carolinians and the Civil War

On November 12, 1903, the North Carolina Literary and Historical Association appointed a committee to settle scores remaining from the Civil War.

The following spring the association received the committee's report, boasting "First at Bethel, Farthest at Gettysburg, Farthest at Chickamauga, and Last at Appomattox." These claims had been emblazoned upon the Confederate monument erected at the Capitol in 1895 and stamped upon the covers of the regimental histories collected in 1901, popularly known as *Clark's Regiments*.

Just as Gov. Charles B. Aycock sought to redeem the state from a legacy of ignorance, the members of the association sought to raise the cultural awareness of citizens. Early leaders made it their task to "correct printed misrepresentations about the state." J. Bryan Grimes, who took office as Secretary of State when Aycock was governor, persuaded the Literary and Historical Association to answer perceived slights upon the state.

North Carolinians were particularly irked by and contentious about competing claims made by Virginians. A ninety-page publication on the topic, with documentation and first-hand accounts, appeared in 1907 under the auspices of the North Carolina Historical Commission.

P. T. Barnum (ca. 1860–1864) carte de visite.

1867 "Girl's Work" Her Life's Work, Jane McKimmon

On November 13, 1867, Jane McKimmon, leader of North Carolina's home demonstration movement, was born.

State-sponsored home demonstration work began in North Carolina in 1911. McKimmon, who was known for keeping a neat garden on Raleigh's Blount Street, was hired to "take charge of the 'girl's canning work.'"

McKimmon expanded the size and scope of the program, expanding its enrollment from 416 women in fourteen counties to seventy-five thousand women in all of North Carolina's hundred counties by 1941. Her work, by one estimation, "led rural women and girls to a fuller, more comfortable, and efficient life."

McKimmon was the first woman in the nation to receive the Distinguished Ruby Award of Epsilon Sigma Phi, the honorary extension fraternity. In 1966 she was elected to the North Carolina Agricultural Hall of Fame, which is located in the Agriculture Building in downtown Raleigh. The continuing education center at North Carolina State University, built in 1975, is named in her honor.

1989 Eastern North Carolina Artist Francis Speight

On November 13, 1989, award-winning artist Francis Speight died at age ninety-three in his Greenville home.

Speight grew up on a Bertie County plantation before enrolling in college at Wake Forest. While there he took art lessons at Meredith College. After briefly serving in the Army during World War I, Speight studied and taught at the Pennsylvania Academy of Fine Arts, where he would remain for more than forty years.

Speight focused on painting rural and suburban landscapes, and though some of his work was inspired by his adopted Pennsylvania, he continued to depict the landscapes of his native eastern North Carolina as well.

In 1961 Speight moved back to North Carolina, where he taught as an artist-in-residence at East Carolina College (now East Carolina University) until his retirement in 1976.

Speight's work remains on display in public and private art collections across the country. He was the first North Carolina artist to be honored with an exhibition of his works in the newly opened N.C. Museum of Art in Raleigh. His many accolades include the North Carolina Award and memberships in the National Academy of Design and the American Institute of Arts and Letters.

1997 Gambling Comes to Cherokee

On November 13, 1997, Harrah's Cherokee Casino, the first casino in North Carolina, opened in Cherokee on the reservation of the Eastern Band of Cherokee Indians (EBCI). Owned by the EBCI and operated by Caesars Entertainment Corporation, the casino complex recently expanded and now offers live table games, slot machines, and traditional video gaming machines, as well as a spa. Its amenities also include a twenty-one-story hotel, a conference center, an events center, and several restaurants.

When Harrah's Cherokee first opened, it offered only video poker. In August 2012 the U.S. Department of the Interior approved an amended agreement between North Carolina and the EBCI allowing live dealers. That agreement earmarked the state's share of gaming revenues for public education, while most of the remaining money was to be distributed annually among tribal members.

Because of the new jobs and local economic upswing created by Harrah's Cherokee, the Eastern Band has been able to make major improvements in healthcare, housing, education, and public safety on its reservation. In September 2015 tribal officials opened Harrah's Cherokee Valley River Casino & Hotel in Murphy.

Jane S. McKimmon (*third from left*), head agent of the North Carolina Home Demonstration Program at a canning demonstration.

1892 Senator and Jurist A.S. Merrimon

On November 14, 1892, U.S. Senator and Chief Justice of North Carolina A.S. Merrimon died. Born in 1830 in Transylvania County, Merrimon studied law alongside Zebulon B. Vance in Asheville. Before the Civil War he held a variety of public offices in Asheville, serving as a solicitor for Buncombe County and in the legislature in 1860 and 1861.

Though an opponent of secession, Merrimon enlisted in the Confederate Army at the outset of the Civil War. Soon after, he was appointed solicitor for the Eighth Confederate Congressional district. For the remainder of the war, he used that position to try to quell violence in the western part of the state between pro-Confederate and Unionist factions.

A prominent lawyer throughout the late 1860s and early 1870s, Merrimon ran unsuccessfully for governor in 1872 but was elected to the U.S. Senate the following year. While in the Senate he spoke against a civil rights bill and attacked Republicans and their causes in general. He returned to private practice after one term until Gov. Thomas J. Jarvis appointed him to the state supreme court. He was elevated to chief justice six years later.

Merrimon is buried in Oakwood Cemetery in Raleigh.

1937 Mystery of the Dare Stones

On November 14, 1937, a team of Emory University professors revealed the transcription of a message carved on a rock discovered by Louis Hammond in Chowan County earlier that year. The text of their transcription reads:

Side 1	Side 2
Ananias Dare &	*Father Soone After You*
Virginia Went Hence	*Goe for England Wee Cam*
Unto Heaven 1591	*Hither / Onlie Misarie & Warre*
Anye Englishman Shew	*Tow Yeere / Above Halfe Deade ere Tow*
John White Govr Via.	*Yeere More From Sickenes Beine Foure & Twentie /*
	Salvage with Message of Shipp Unto Us / Smal
	Space of Time they Affrite of Revenge Rann
	Al Awaye / Wee Bleeve it Nott You / Soone After
	Ye Salvages Faine Spirits Angrie / Suddaine
	Murther Al Save Seaven / Mine Childe /
	Ananais to Slaine wth Much Misarie /
	Burie Al Neere Foure Myles Easte This River
	Uppon Small Hil / Names Writ Al Ther
	On Rocke / Putt This Ther Alsoe / Salvage
	Shew This Unto You & Hither Wee
	Promise You to Give Greate
	Plentie Presents
	EWD

The message on what came to be known as the "Dare Stone" appeared to be Eleanor White Dare's recounting from almost 350 years earlier of the fate of the Lost Colony. The Dare Stone's authenticity is still debated, but the most recent study of the stone done by David LaVere at UNC-Wilmington leaned toward confirming its veracity.

Not long after Hammond turned the stone over to scholars, he disappeared. Later efforts to find him or to locate information about him proved fruitless. Since a number of events related to the Lost Colony, including the debut of a new outdoor drama by Paul Green, were underway to commemorate the 350th anniversary of the English attempt to establish a permanent colony in the New World at that time, some believed the stone to be a promotional stunt.

Complicating the authenticity questions were a number of other "Dare Stone" discoveries in scattered locations. These came to light after the public offer of a reward for such stones. All but the original are universally deemed forgeries.

1953 Andy Griffith's "What It Was, Was Football"

On November 14, 1953, Chapel Hill-based Colonial Records label released Andy Griffith's monologue "What It Was, Was Football." Colonial was owned by newspaper publisher Orville B. Campbell, who had heard Griffith perform the comedy bit at a luncheon earlier that year.

The narrator of the story is a young man who happens upon a football game—something he had never experienced before. His retelling of the game includes this description of the football: "It was that both bunches full of them wanted this funny looking little pumpkin to play with. They did. And I know, friends, that they couldn't eat it because they kicked it the whole evening and it never busted."

"What it Was, Was Football" helped launch Griffith's career, which ultimately took him from North Carolina to Broadway. He went on to star in movies and television shows and to become a Grammy Award-winning singer. The release was also one of Colonial's most successful, and one of the best selling comedy records of all time.

After many years in front of the camera, Griffith returned to North Carolina and settled in Manteo, where he remained until his death in July 2012.

The original Dare Stone. Side 1 (*above*) and Side 2 (*below*).

NOV 15

1846 Peter Stuart Ney Confesses to be Napoleon's Confidante

On November 15, 1846, Peter Stuart Ney, a teacher in Rowan County, is said to have made a deathbed confession that he was, in fact, Napoleon Bonaparte's most trusted commander, Marshal Michel Ney. Marshal Ney was rumored to have escaped execution in 1815 and fled to America.

The story of Peter Stuart Ney first appeared in 1856 in a widely distributed article written by one of Ney's students. The teacher is said to have denied the rumors except when intoxicated but made a full confession on his deathbed: "I will not die with a lie on my lips, I am Marshal Ney of France." Later, researcher William Henry Hoyt amassed conclusive evidence that the true Marshal Ney did not escape the firing squad. He also found an 1820 application for citizenship filed by Peter Stuart Ney in South Carolina and a record of his baptism in Scotland.

Despite this counterevidence the American Ney's grave at Third Creek Presbyterian Church in the town of Cleveland reads: "In memory of Peter Stuart Ney/ A native of France and soldier of the French Revolution under Napoleon Bonaparte/ Who departed this life November 15th, 1846/ Aged 77 years."

1921 Movie Silent About Fate of Colonists

On November 15, 1921, Gov. Cameron Morrison and a host of other state dignitaries gathered in Raleigh for the debut of a silent movie about the Lost Colony entitled *The Earliest English Expeditions and Attempted Settlements in the Territory of What Is Now the United States, 1584–1591*. Conceived as an educational tool, the film was produced on the Outer Banks and starred Dare County residents as Indians and English settlers.

Mabel Evans Jones, then the superintendent of the Dare County Schools, came up with the idea for the film and was featured in it as Eleanor White Dare, the mother of the first documented English child born in the New World, Virginia Dare. Dr. William Horton of Raleigh portrayed John White, Eleanor's father. The clergyman who baptized Virginia in the film was the Rev. R. B. Drane, the long-time rector of St. Paul's Episcopal Church in Edenton.

The forty-six-minute, five-reel movie toured the state. It was the first silent movie produced in North Carolina, and at the height of its popularity it was part of North Carolina's official history curriculum for public schools.

Paul Green's 1937 outdoor drama *The Lost Colony* was inspired in part by Jones's film. For several decades the film was lost, but in 2011 a copy was discovered and digitized.

1933 Charlotte Heist Foiled, 1933

On November 15, 1933, noted criminal Roger "The Terrible" Touhy orchestrated a mail truck robbery in the heart of Charlotte.

At the time of the robbery, Touhy was battling mobster Al Capone for control of illicit alcohol sales in Chicago. While awaiting trial for kidnapping, Touhy sent four men in his gang south to "raise" money for his defense. Although Charlotte had no connection to organized crime at the time, it was a burgeoning hub of the financial industry.

The theft took place in broad daylight. Members of Touhy's gang ambushed the truck by driving out in front of it from an alleyway as it made its way down Third Street. The gang members got out of their car and moved toward the mail truck. At least one of the group brandished a machine gun as the others disarmed the driver. Two of Touhy's gang easily clipped the lock on the truck with wire cutters, threw out the mail clerk they found inside, and within two minutes, stole about one hundred thousand dollars in cash and bank notes.

Charlotte detective Frank Littlejohn conducted an extraordinary investigation, and within two weeks of the heist, three suspects were in jail, and the fourth was dead in an apparent mob knockoff.

1958 Fear Runs Rampant in Henderson, 1958–1959

On November 15, 1958, the Textile Workers Union of America called a strike at the Harriet-Henderson Mills in Henderson. The union had targeted cotton mills across the state since 1946 as part of "Operation Dixie." By 1958 more than a thousand local workers had enrolled in the union, accounting for one in seven of all union members in the state.

A wave of violence swept across Henderson in 1959 after negotiations between the mill owner and the union broke down. Windows were shot out at mill headquarters. Strikers pulled a truck driver from his cab. Organizer Boyd Payton was injured when rocks were thrown at his car. Dynamite blasts damaged a strikebreaker's house and a boiler room. Gov. Luther Hodges assigned 150 Highway Patrolmen and several National Guard units to the scene.

Payton and seven others were indicted, convicted, and sentenced to six to ten years in prison. The judge declared, "Fear has run rampant in Henderson and Vance County. It must end right here." The company returned to a full work force but organizers did not formally call off the strike until June 1961. In that year Gov. Terry Sanford shortened the sentences of and later granted clemency to Payton and others.

The Harriet-Henderson Mills picket line, 1959.

1764 Federal Comptroller John Steele of Salisbury

On November 16, 1764, early political leader John Steele was born in Salisbury.

After being educated near Statesville, Steele pursued several business ventures. His first political post was as tax assessor for the Salisbury area. He held several local offices in Rowan County and was sent to negotiate relations with Native American tribes before being elected to represent the area in the General Assembly in 1787.

Steele took part in both of North Carolina's two federal constitutional conventions and served in Congress during its first two sessions. A staunch Federalist, he was an ally of Alexander Hamilton. After losing a vote in the General Assembly in a bid to become a U.S. senator, he returned to the state legislature and became active in the state militia.

Pres. George Washington appointed Steele Comptroller of the Treasury in July 1796, a high-ranking job roughly equivalent to the Treasury Department's general counsel today, and he remained in that post into the Jefferson administration.

Returning to North Carolina, Steele devoted his attention to managing his plantations and local politics in Rowan County. Before his death in 1815, Steele served in the General Assembly several more times, helped settle border disputes with both South Carolina and Georgia, and was a trustee of UNC.

1765 Stamp Master's Hand Forced, 1765

On November 16, 1765, North Carolina's stamp master, William Houston, resigned his post amid demonstrations against the Stamp Act. The Stamp Act of 1765, the first direct tax placed on the American colonies by Great Britain, was intended to raise revenue to defray Britain's national debt. The measure met with great disdain throughout the colonies.

Houston, a Duplin County physician and early Irish immigrant, was selected as the stamp distributor in 1765 after Parliament passed the Act. His appointment led to public demonstrations and Houston's being hanged in effigy in Wilmington, New Bern, and Cross Creek throughout October 1765.

Upon arriving in Wilmington the following month to take his post, Houston was confronted by several hundred protestors. He publicly declared that he did not want to be responsible for government actions with which the public disagreed, but the unsatisfied crowd forced him to the county courthouse anyway, where he penned his resignation.

After the resignation Houston evidently regained a level of respect. The following year he became clerk of the Committee of Public Claims at New Bern, and later he was appointed a justice of the peace for Duplin County.

1933 Blue Ridge Parkway Project Approved

On November 16, 1933, the Blue Ridge Parkway project received approval. The Blue Ridge Parkway, part of the National Park Service system, extends 469 miles through the Southern Appalachians, linking Shenandoah National Park in northern Virginia with Great Smoky Mountains National Park in North Carolina and Tennessee.

In 1934 Department of the Interior Secretary Harold Ickes chose the final route through western North Carolina, rejecting one that would have gone through eastern Tennessee. His decision came after intensive lobbying from both states.

In September 1935 work began on a section extending southward from the North Carolina-Virginia line. Workers were secured from the unemployment rolls of Alleghany County, as provided for in the Parkway legislation's relief provisions. The final section of the highway, including the Linn Cove Viaduct, was completed around Grandfather Mountain in 1987.

Designed for leisurely travel, the road is free of commercial development. From the outset attention has been given to preserving the natural beauty of the area and providing the traveler with uncluttered vistas. Each year more than twenty-two million people travel the parkway. It has become an economic driver for western North Carolina.

1951 Federal Writers Project Director Edwin Björkman

On November 16, 1951, renowned writer, journalist, and literary critic Edwin A. Björkman died in Asheville.

Born and raised in Sweden, Björkman worked as a clerk, journalist, and actor before coming to the United States in 1891. Upon arrival he briefly stopped in Chicago, then joined a Scandinavian colony in Minnesota, writing for newspapers to support himself. He later wrote for several papers in New York, served in the short-lived League of Nations' news bureau, and taught Scandinavian drama at Yale before moving to Waynesville in 1925.

In North Carolina Björkman worked as the literary editor of the *Asheville Times* and during the Depression directed the North Carolina Federal Writers Project of the Works Progress Administration. While working with that project, he led the effort that produced *North Carolina: A Guide to the Old North State*.

Throughout his career Björkman was a prolific writer, producing no less than ten original novels and translating countless plays and other works into English from European languages. He married four times before dying at age eighty-five and is buried in Asheville's Riverside Cemetery.

"Tunnel in the Craggy Mountains, Blue Ridge Parkway, North Carolina."

1753 Moravian Men from Pennsylvania Arrived in Forsyth County

On November 17, 1753, fifteen Moravian men from Pennsylvania arrived in present-day Forsyth County on the land they called Wachovia. Bethabara, which means "House of Passage," was the first community built in Wachovia.

In 1752, Moravians traveled south on the Great Wagon Road in search of a large tract of available land suitable for farming. They selected a one-hundred-thousand-acre tract of land in the Piedmont region of North Carolina.

By the end of 1756, the settlers had built a church, gristmill, saw mill, tannery, pottery, distillery, and other crafts shops. In 1766 the Moravians began building a town called Salem in the center of the Wachovia Tract. By 1772 most essential buildings had been built and industries transferred to the new town.

As Bethabara dwindled from a central town to farmland, it came to be called Old Town. Today visitors can visit Historic Bethabara Park to get a glimpse of what this early community looked like.

NOV 17

1862 Respected Pastel Artist Drew Upon Civil War Experience

On November 17, 1862, nineteen-year-old James Wells Champney drafted a collection of small images titled *First impressions of North Carolina, sketched in cars on the [way] to newbern.*

The son of a painter-illustrator, Champney apprenticed in Boston to become a master wood engraver, but the outbreak of war interrupted his artistic training. He volunteered for the Forty-Fifth Massachusetts Regiment and deployed to North Carolina in November 1862 as part of the reinforcements for the Union occupational forces then at New Bern.

Like many artists-turned-soldiers, Champney used his artistic abilities to document his wartime experiences, depicting military installations, soldiers, African Americans, civilians, and other scenes in and around New Bern. When he left the service after falling ill with malaria in July 1863, Champney had filled two sketchbooks, which are now held by the Outer Banks History Center.

After the war Champney moved to Europe to study under renowned artist Pierre Édouard Frère. He returned to the United States an expert in pastels and established a studio in New York City, where he worked for the remainder of his life. He died unexpectedly at age fifty-nine after falling down an elevator shaft.

1908 An Advocate for Cities: The N.C. League of Municipalities

On November 17, 1908, local officials from across North Carolina met in Charlotte to discuss their experiences in city and town management. Gov. Robert Glenn joined them, as did the mayors of Boston, Houston, and Roanoke, Virginia.

Gathered in the five-hundred-seat auditorium of the Charlotte Academy of Music, those present voted to form the Carolina Municipal Association, for the "advancement of good civic management in all municipalities." Twenty-two North Carolina cities enrolled as founding members of the group. The association has met annually since, and it changed its name to the North Carolina League of Municipalities (NCLM) in 1934. Today the Raleigh-based League represents over 530 Tar Heel cities and towns.

The organization's accomplishments include advocacy that has led to zoning regulations and group insurance for municipal employees. In 1951 the NCLM led an effort to provide for a percentage of state gasoline tax revenues to be passed to local governments for road development and improvement. More recently it advocated successfully for the local option sales tax and for the return of historic preservation tax credits.

1949 Cameron Village Trend-Setter for Raleigh and the South

On November 17, 1949, Cameron Village, one of the first shopping centers in the Southeast, opened in Raleigh. It was part of a larger, 158-acre planned development that also included single-family homes and several apartment buildings.

Some of the first shops to open in Cameron Village were Colonial Stores, the Village Restaurant, Roses 5-10-25¢, and PHR Cradle Shops. More than sixty-five stores—including a dry cleaner, shoe repair shop, butcher, beauty shop, two barber shops, and a movie theater— and 112 professional offices were open at the complex within two years.

Cameron Village was enormously popular during the 1950s and 1960s, luring business away from downtown Raleigh, but it faced increasing competition from larger malls like Crabtree Valley in the late 1960s and early 1970s. In the 1970s "The Underground," a below-ground area with popular restaurants and nightclubs, was completed, though it was short-lived, with most establishments there closing during the 1980s.

The complex underwent major renovations in the 1990s and 2000s and remains a popular Raleigh shopping destination to this day.

Depiction of Fort Mason by James Wells Champney, 1863.

1781 British Forces Leave Wilmington and N.C., 1781

On November 18, 1781, British forces under Maj. James Craig evacuated Wilmington. Previously the town was threatened by the Loyalist campaign that culminated in the Battle of Moores Creek Bridge in 1776 and was afterwards briefly blockaded by a British fleet.

Major Craig captured Wilmington, North Carolina's major seaport, in January 1781. With fewer than three hundred men available for duty, he could do nothing to expand British control of the area. He received little support from local Loyalists, due to the small size of his command. In April Craig was briefly joined by the main British force in North Carolina under Lt. Gen. Charles Cornwallis, who had withdrawn eastward to be resupplied after the Battle of Guilford Courthouse.

Following Cornwallis's departure for Virginia, Craig was left to hold Wilmington. In October Gen. Griffith Rutherford of the North Carolina Militia launched a campaign to recapture the town for the Patriot side. Defeating Loyalist forces in a series of small clashes, the Militia gradually closed in. Outnumbered, Craig had no choice but to evacuate the town by sea.

His departure marked the end of a British presence in the state, although some Loyalist activity continued.

1799 Name of James Glasgow Expunged from the Map

On November 18, 1799, Glasgow County, in eastern North Carolina, was renamed Greene County.

In 1791 Dobbs County was split. Half became Lenoir County, named for Revolutionary War general William Lenoir, and half became Glasgow County, for North Carolina's first Secretary of State, James Glasgow.

Among other duties, Glasgow oversaw the military grant program that awarded land to soldiers who served in the Continental Line during the American Revolution. Warrants for land were easily forged, which led to Glasgow's downfall. In 1797 future president Andrew Jackson wrote a letter to the governor exposing the ongoing land frauds. Charges became official, and Glasgow was brought to trial. The jury handed down five indictments; Glasgow pled not guilty.

After ten days in court, Glasgow was found guilty of three charges: issuing a fraudulent warrant, issuing a duplicate warrant with two separate grants on it, and issuing a grant without proper evidence of the assignment. The residents of Glasgow County did not want to be identified with a criminal, and the county was renamed Greene, for Revolutionary War hero Nathanael Greene.

While Glasgow's name disappeared from the map, his misconduct left a lasting mark in North Carolina's history. The court that tried Glasgow ultimately became the North Carolina Supreme Court.

1879 Jim Crow-Era Fair for African Americans

On November 18, 1879, the first North Carolina Colored State Fair opened in Raleigh. Born out of the desire by men of the Colored Industrial Association of North Carolina to showcase the progress made by African Americans after Emancipation, the fair was based on the successful model of the State Fair held by the State Agricultural Society since the 1850s.

Usually held in November, the fair combined agricultural and industrial displays with contests for exhibitors. Parades and speeches featuring politicians and other prominent people took place throughout the days of the fair. One of the founders of the association was Charles N. Hunter, a former slave and prominent black educator in Raleigh. He remained the fair's guiding force until it ceased.

Held on the original grounds of the Agricultural Society's fair, the Negro State Fair was similar in format but on a smaller scale. It quickly became a social occasion for African Americans and received a small legislative appropriation for a time. Hunter fought to keep the fair viable, though it was never a large moneymaker, and by 1931 the state's racial politics had dealt it a fatal blow.

1915 Confederate Women's Home Opens in Fayetteville

On November 18, 1915, the Confederate Women's Home opened in Fayetteville.

Mrs. Hunter G. Smith proposed establishment of a home in North Carolina for Confederate widows and daughters some years earlier during the 1908 convention of the North Carolina Division of the United Daughters of the Confederacy (UDC). In 1913 the legislature granted ten thousand dollars for building purposes and five thousand dollars per year for maintenance. The UDC accepted responsibility for the home's operation. To live in the home, a woman had to be sixty-five or older; a wife, daughter, or widow of a Confederate veteran; and in need. She also had to sign her property and pension over to the state.

Originally the home was scheduled to close in 1950, but it twice received ten-year reprieves. By 1981 only seven women lived in the house, and it was not practical to keep it open. Today sixty-five women are buried in a cemetery on the grounds. Its counterpart institution for Civil War veterans, the Confederate Soldiers Home, operated in Raleigh from 1891 to 1938.

Illustration depicting a scene from the first North Carolina Colored State Fair, 1879.

NOV 19

1850 *Raleigh Register*, North Carolina's First Daily Paper

On November 19, 1850, the *Raleigh Register* became North Carolina's first newspaper to be published daily.

The Register traces its roots to 1799 when it was founded by English immigrant Joseph Gales, who had already successfully published several newspapers in England. Gales ran the paper until his retirement in 1833. Under his leadership it was one of the major publications in the state and was widely regarded as the leading political voice for the National Republican Party, also called the Anti-Jacksonian Party.

Gales started publishing the paper semiweekly only when the General Assembly was in session, but eventually settled upon weekly publication. He brought his son Weston in as a partner, and Weston would eventually go on to be the paper's publisher.

It became a daily under Seaton Gales, grandson of the founder, who enlarged the paper's operation and added a telegraph service. His efforts, though, soon proved unsuccessful, and by January 1851 the Register had stopped publishing each day. Gales tried to revive paper by retrofitting its offices with the latest technology, but it was sold at public auction by 1856.

1863 The Emancipator and the Animator: Lincoln at Gettysburg

On November 19, 1863, at Gettysburg, Pres. Abraham Lincoln paid tribute to the men who gave the "last full measure of devotion" on that hallowed ground four months earlier.

In the course of the battle between July 1 and 3, over seven thousand men were killed, and it's estimated that North Carolinians represent one in four of the battle's overall Confederate casualties. The day's losses were recorded by photographer Timothy Sullivan. The Gettysburg Address was less well documented, the primary record being stereographs by Alexander Gardner. Images from both events have been digitized and made available by the Library of Congress.

In 2013 UNC-Asheville professor Chris Oakley, a former Disney animator and screenwriter, worked with several students to create the "Virtual Lincoln Project." The project's objective was to recreate the Gettysburg Address in 3-D animation. In the course of that work, Oakley discovered what he believes to be an image of Lincoln in a crowd scene.

A different image of Lincoln, sans top hat, on the dais alongside his Secretary of State, William Seward, had long been believed to be the only shot of the president at Gettysburg. Others contend that a top-hatted, bearded man on horseback is Lincoln. Oakley's discovery drew wide press attention and renewed interest during the Civil War sesquicentennial.

1958 Kingston Trio Tops the Charts with "Tom Dooley"

On November 19, 1958, the Kingston Trio's version of the folk song "Tom Dooley" hit Number One on the music charts. The song is based on the true story of Tom Dula, hanged in Statesville in 1868 for the murder of Laura Foster.

The case drew wide attention, including a series of reports that appeared in the *New York Herald*. Dula was buried in a family cemetery near Elkville. Many in the community to this day defend him, arguing that he took the fall for a woman named Ann Melton. North Carolina guitarist Doc Watson's grandmother claimed to have heard Melton's deathbed confession that she, not Tom Dula, killed Laura Foster.

While Watson sang the traditional folk ballad "Tom Dula," the best-known version of the song is the Kingston Trio's. Members of the group visited Dula's grave on a concert swing through the state.

Professor Chris Oakley.

1858 Cherokee Warrior Junaluska Died

On November 20, 1858, distinguished Cherokee warrior Junaluska died. Little is known of his early life.

Although he was not chief, Junaluska spoke for the tribe in 1811, when he refused the Shawnee request for the Cherokee to join in fighting against the influx of settlers. As further indication of his loyalty to the United States, he recruited a hundred warriors to join the government's war against the Creek Indians in 1813. It is an account from this conflict that credits him with saving Andrew Jackson's life at Horseshoe Bend, Alabama.

Junaluska returned to his farm in North Carolina and lived a quiet life until Pres. Andrew Jackson called for the removal of the Cherokee to Oklahoma in 1838. He survived the Trail of Tears but later walked home to North Carolina.

In 1847 the North Carolina General Assembly granted Junaluska citizenship, 337 acres of land, and one hundred dollars in recognition of his military service. The land was at Cheoah, near what is now the town of Robbinsville, and was, ironically, part of his property before the Cherokee removal.

A photo believed to be Junaluska, taken shortly before his death.

1932 Asheville Monument to German Prisoners of War

On November 20, 1932, more than five thousand people gathered at Riverside Cemetery in Asheville to dedicate a monument to eighteen German prisoners of war buried there.

The POWs were sailors captured during World War I. They were transferred from their initial holding location on Ellis Island to a detention center in Hot Springs in Madison County. More than twenty-three hundred German POWs eventually would be housed at Hot Springs. While there, the prisoners endured a typhoid epidemic that resulted in the deaths of the eighteen men buried at Riverside Cemetery. The Madison County camp has become known for the Bavarian village that the homesick internees built there.

The monument was dedicated by the Kiffin Rockwell Post of the American Legion. The German ambassador to the United States and several other high-ranking German officials attended.

Riverside Cemetery, located along the French Broad River, dates to 1885 and is open to the public. It is maintained by the City and Asheville and encompasses eighty-seven acres.

Photo of Junaluska marker.

NOV 21

1757 Creating the Town of Halifax

On November 21, 1757, the town of Halifax was established by the colonial legislature, which was meeting in New Bern. The act called for the establishment of a town on the lands of James Leslie on the Roanoke River. The new town was named Halifax, in honor of George Montagu, the second Earl of Halifax.

The site for the town is just south of the Virginia border and at the intersection of major north-south and east-west roads, with falls and rapids just upriver. The positioning made Halifax the head of river navigation, and quickly made it a trading center and river port for goods moving between the backcountry, the plantations and Virginia.

The original plan called for 120 half-acre lots to be laid out on a grid on a four-acre market area. The buyer of each lot was required to build a house of certain size within three years. Within a year, the town and its area prospered enough that a new county, Halifax, was created with the village as its county seat.

Today the Historic Halifax State Historic Site encompasses many of the original town lots.

1789 North Carolina Becomes the Twelfth State

On November 21, 1789, the General Assembly, meeting in Fayetteville, ratified the United States Constitution, making North Carolina the twelfth state of the Union.

The process was not easy, considering that in 1788, the General Assembly actually declined to ratify the United States Constitution, suggesting many amendments and calling for a Bill of Rights. On November 16, 1789, a second convention met to take up the matter again. The Constitution, with the addition of the Bill of Rights, was ratified five days into the convention.

In 1778 Fayetteville built a large brick structure, called the State House by its builders, to house the General Assembly in the event the town was chosen as the new state capital, but the Convention of 1788 in Hillsborough chose Raleigh over Fayetteville. Despite this the General Assembly did meet in Fayetteville several times before moving permanently to Raleigh in 1793.

The State House where North Carolina became a state remained standing until 1831, when it was destroyed by a fire that devastated much of Fayetteville.

1894 Warren Wilson College Established

On November 21, 1894, the Asheville Farm School, the primary forerunner of Warren Wilson College, was established as a mission school by the Women's Board of Home Missions of the Presbyterian Church. The site selected was a 420-acre farm in the Swannanoa Valley about ten miles east of Asheville.

By combining farm work with education, the school aimed to provide new opportunities for young men in the mountains. In 1942 the school merged with the Dorland-Bell School, a Presbyterian institution for young women in Hot Springs. Junior college classes were added and the new school was named for Warren H. Wilson, a leader in Presbyterian rural mission work.

In 1966 Warren Wilson became an accredited, four-year, liberal arts college offering the bachelor of arts degree. The school is no longer associated with the Presbyterian Church's national missions, but true to its origins, Warren Wilson requires that every student, in addition to classwork, contribute three hours of labor each day to the college in return for room and board.

1901 The Mystery of Beautiful Nell Cropsey

On November 21, 1901, Nell Cropsey disappeared from the front porch of her family home near the Elizabeth City waterfront. The Cropsey family had moved to Elizabeth City from New Jersey in 1898.

The case grabbed national media attention, making newspaper headlines up and down the East Coast. The night Cropsey disappeared she had broken up with her boyfriend of three years, Jim Wilcox. After spending the evening together in the parlor with her sister Ollie and Wilcox, the couple stepped onto the front porch and into legend. Wilcox maintained that he left Nell there on the porch after she broke up with him. She never returned to the house and was found in the Pasquotank River thirty-seven days later.

Wilcox was arrested and tried. The case, built on circumstantial evidence, was a sensation in its own right. Protesters and mobs interrupted until the judge declared a mistrial and ordered a new trial in a nearby county. Wilcox was eventually convicted but in 1920 received a pardon from Gov. Thomas Bickett. Fourteen years later Wilcox took his own life.

Nell Cropsey's death remains a mystery, at least for some.

Asheville Farm School, 1890s.

1718 Blackbeard's Death: Off With His Head

On November 22, 1718, the infamous pirate Blackbeard was killed.

The "Golden Age of Piracy" flourished briefly along the North Carolina coast in the early eighteenth century. Foremost among the pirates was Edward Teach, aka "Blackbeard." He lived briefly in the town of Bath during the summer of 1718.

Teach is reported to have been a privateer during Queen Anne's War (1701–1714) and turned to piracy afterward. In 1717 Blackbeard and his fellow pirates captured the French slaveship *La Concorde* in the eastern Caribbean. With his new ship, renamed *Queen Anne's Revenge*, Blackbeard cruised the Caribbean taking prizes. In May 1718 the pirates arrived off Charleston, South Carolina. In perhaps the most brazen act of his piratical career, Blackbeard blockaded the port for nearly a week.

Soon after, Blackbeard's fleet attempted to enter Old Topsail Inlet (now Beaufort Inlet). The vessels grounded on the ocean floor and were abandoned.

Six months later, at Ocracoke Inlet, Blackbeard encountered ships sent by the governor of Virginia, led by Lt. Robert Maynard. In a desperate battle Blackbeard and several of his crew were killed. Maynard returned to Virginia with the surviving pirates and a grim trophy, Blackbeard's severed head.

1790 Elizabeth Steele, Nathanael Greene, and a Legendary Encounter

On November 22, 1790, Elizabeth Maxwell Steele, a legendary patriot during the American Revolution, died at her home in Salisbury.

Twice widowed, Steele was the only woman operating a tavern in Rowan County before the war. She was self-sufficient, wealthy, and well-connected, and during the Revolution she used her means to become what she called a "great politician." But Steele wasn't a politician in the modern sense of the word. Rather, she looked out for her family's and her community's interests by seeking and sharing information about the war.

Legend has it that in February 1781 Steele overheard Gen. Nathanael Greene in her tavern complaining of being "fatigued, hungry, and penniless." The story goes that she gave Greene two satchels of money and that the relieved general then took a portrait of King George III off the wall and wrote on the back, "O George, Hide thy face and mourn." He then hung the picture up backwards.

The portrait survives with those words chalked on the reverse. There is no way to authenticate the story, but it is known that Greene was in the vicinity at the time. Irrespective of the legend, Steele was an exceptional woman who was vital to local discourse during the Revolution.

NOV 22

Blackbeard the pirate, engraving published in Charles Johnson, *A General History of the Lives and Adventures of the Most Famous Highwaymen, Murderers, Street-Robbers, & c.*, 1736.

NOV 23

1881 "Aunt Abby" House, Confederacy's "Angel of Mercy"

On November 23, 1881, Abby House, known as "Aunt Abby," died.

She was born around 1796 and raised near Franklinton. Little is known of her life before the Civil War. Described as being stooped, grim-looking, and often smoking a corncob pipe, House carried one or two canes at all times, reputedly both to help her walk and to help her make points—and occasionally to whack those who didn't get her point the first time.

Honoring her promise to nurse, and bring home to bury if necessary, her eight nephews during the Civil War, House traveled rails and walked roads to care for the boys. She saw that her services were needed by more than just her kinfolk, and she began to help other Confederate soldiers in need. She frequently worked in close proximity to battles.

Described by Gov. Zebulon Vance as "the ubiquitous, indefatigable and inevitable Mrs. House," she often paid visits to leaders of the Confederacy, including Jefferson Davis. In 1877 she took an honored place on the platform at Vance's inauguration.

As House grew feeble, former Confederate soldiers showed her their appreciation by building her a small cottage in Raleigh. William Woods Holden and Governor Vance, among others, were frequent visitors.

1902 Walter Reed Died

On November 23, 1902, Walter Reed, head of the U.S. Yellow Fever Commission in Cuba, died. During his time in Cuba, he had conclusively demonstrated that mosquitoes transmitted the deadly disease. Reed called Hertford County home for much of his life before medical school.

He graduated from medical school at the University of Virginia at seventeen and continued his education at Bellevue Hospital Medical College in Manhattan. He joined the U.S. Army Medical Corps in 1875, eventually becoming curator of the Army Medical Museum in Washington, D.C. and a professor at the army medical school.

By the outbreak of the Spanish-American War, Reed was considered a pioneer in the field of bacteriology. His interest in the cause of yellow fever was timely, as epidemics broke out in camps in Cuba and elsewhere. In 1900 Reed led the fourth U. S. Army Yellow Fever Commission.

Reed was buried in Arlington National Cemetery. An army hospital completed in 1909 in Washington, D.C. was named in his honor. The museum of which he was curator is now the National Museum of Health and Medicine.

Walter Reed, in Washington D.C. at the age of 31.

1925 John C. Campbell Folk School Based on Danish Model

On November 23, 1925, Olive Dame Campbell and Marguerite Butler incorporated the John C. Campbell Folk School in Brasstown. They named it after Campbell's late husband.

An educator, social worker, and early chronicler of Appalachian life, John C. Campbell became interested in western North Carolina as a youth working for his father's railroad company. When a charitable organization funded his desire to study social and economic conditions in the mountains, he and his new bride settled in Asheville in 1913. Both believed efforts to improve mountaineers' lives should be tied to education and the preservation of the region's traditional folk heritage.

The idea of establishing a folk school intrigued Mr. Campbell, but he died in 1919 before seeing it realized. Mrs. Campbell later visited folk schools in Denmark and decided to model her husband's namesake school after them, offering non-competitive adult classes in traditional music and dance, crafts, agriculture, and nature studies.

Area residents donated the needed land, labor, and building materials, and classes began in December 1927 with Campbell serving as the school's first director. She died in 1954, but the school, now listed on the National Register of Historic Places, remains a destination for artists and tourists alike.

1963 Raleigh Connection to JFK Assassination a Mystery

On November 23, 1963, as the clock neared midnight in Raleigh, an attempt was allegedly made at the Dallas County jail in Texas on behalf of Lee Harvey Oswald to contact one or two phone numbers in the 919 area code. It was the day after Oswald was arrested for the assassination of John F. Kennedy.

What has come to be dubbed the "Raleigh Call" went unrecorded in the Warren Commission investigation. Later in the 1960s one of the Dallas County switchboard operators on duty that night shared a story about the call with authorities. The operator reported that she had been asked to call two numbers in Raleigh, although without success, and then threw away the memo slip from the fruitless calls. Apparently, she later recreated a slip, as a souvenir, that included two phone numbers, along with the name "John Hurt."

Little has come of the story, and mysteries surrounding the call have contributed to assassination conspiracy theories. In July 1980 both the *Spectator* and the *News and Observer* printed articles attempting to expose details about the call, its related personalities, and the chain of events, but the "Raleigh Call" and any Oswald connection to Raleigh remain an unsolved mystery.

John C. Campbell Folk School.

1970 Alford Plea Tied to Forsyth Case

On November 23, 1970, the U.S. Supreme Court decided the *North Carolina v. Alford* case. The court ruled that a defendant could plead guilty to a crime while still maintaining his innocence. This type of plea is now commonly called an Alford Plea, after the defendant in the proceedings.

The litigation began in Forsyth County. Henry Alford was indicted for first-degree murder in 1963. Though he maintained his innocence, Alford ultimately pleaded guilty to second-degree murder on the advice of his attorney, who told that him that since the prosecutor had fairly substantial evidence against him, he would probably be convicted and might get the death penalty.

Alford appealed to a federal court, saying that he was coerced into pleading guilty. That court found his appeal convincing and overturned his plea, but the state ultimately appealed that decision to a circuit court and then to the U.S. Supreme Court.

The Supreme Court upheld Alford's plea, saying that a court can accept a guilty plea as long as the defendant is adequately represented, "intelligently" chooses to enter into the deal, and there is strong evidence of actual guilt.

Today forty-seven states, including North Carolina, continue to accept Alford Pleas.

1877 Wreck of the USS Huron on the Outer Banks, 1877

On November 24, 1877, the USS *Huron* ran aground near Nags Head, en route for Havana from New York. Cmdr. George P. Ryan chose to sail close to shore rather than have to travel against the Gulf Stream or take the time to maneuver a route beyond the current.

During the night rough seas and dense fog hindered the officers' ability to navigate the treacherous coastline. The *Huron* came too close to the shore and ran aground around 1:30 A.M. Although the closest lifesaving station was only two miles away, it was closed until December. Some of the sailors braved the strong currents and cold temperatures. Thirty-six made it to the shore, and ninety-eight died.

Two months later another eighty-five men died when a second ship, the *Metropolis*, ran aground north of the *Huron* wreck. The two disasters prompted Congress to fund additional lifesaving stations and to increase their months of operation.

Today the wreck of the USS *Huron* is on the National Register of Historic Places. In 1991 the North Carolina Department of Cultural Resources designated the wreck site as North Carolina's first Historic Shipwreck Preserve.

2003 North Carolinian Perished Aboard the Titanic

On November 24, 2003, Gov. Mike Easley proclaimed "Oscar Scott Woody Day." The day honored a Roxboro native who died in the sinking of the RMS *Titanic*, postal clerk Oscar Scott Woody. Interest in Woody was spurred by a 1999 exhibit at the Smithsonian National Postal Museum on the five clerks aboard the ill-fated vessel.

The *Titanic* sank on Woody's forty-first birthday. He was one of five postal clerks aboard the vessel, all of whom perished in the line of duty. After the ship struck an iceberg, they opened the registered mail cage of the ship's post office below decks and attempted to drag about two hundred sacks of registered mail upstairs to the decks, in the hopes that it could be saved.

A 1912 article in Raleigh's *News and Observer* said, "More than one North Carolinian today, when it was learned that the dead mail clerk hailed from 'down home,' expressed their satisfaction that North Carolina courage had not been found wanting in that fearful test . . ." and noted that he "died like a North Carolinian."

Wreck of the USS *Huron* near Ocracoke Inlet, 1881.

NOV 24

1780 Planning North Carolina's Revolutionary War Defense

On November 25, 1780, senior officers of the Southern Department of the Continental Army met at Camp New Providence, near Charlotte, to develop a strategy to respond to Gen. Charles Cornwallis's impending invasion of North Carolina.

Decisions made at the meeting led to the Battle of Cowpens, perhaps the most complete American victory of the Revolutionary War. Between October and December 1780 the Americans took the opportunity provided by Cornwallis's retreat into South Carolina to regroup their army at the winter encampment.

The number of men at Camp New Providence ranged from thirteen hundred to twenty-six hundred and consisted of both militia and Continental forces. Most of the major historical players in the Southern Campaign, including Gens. Horatio Gates, William Smallwood, and Daniel Morgan, as well as lesser-known but equally important figures such as Otho Holland Williams, John Eager Howard, and Thaddeus Kosciuszko were stationed there.

1784 Josiah Collins Acquires Somerset Place Assemblage

On November 25, 1784, Josiah Collins, a wealthy merchant and shipper from Edenton, entered into a verbal partnership with Dr. Samuel Dickinson and Nathaniel Allen to acquire a large body of land "surrounding and bordering upon" Lake Phelps.

The partnership, known as the Lake Company, agreed to cut a canal from the Scuppernong River to Lake Phelps to drain the land and farm rice and other staples on it. Collins eventually bought his two partners' shares and renamed the property Somerset Place, after the county in England where he was born.

Somerset Place remained in the Collins family for three generations, and by 1865 it was one of the upper South's largest plantations. Over its life dozens of white employees, two free black employees, and more than 850 enslaved people lived and worked on the land. By the outbreak of the Civil War, the complex featured more than fifty buildings, including a hospital and an Episcopal chapel.

Somerset Place became a State Historic Site in 1969. In the 1980s under the leadership of site manager Dorothy Spruill Redford, it set a national example for interpreting the stories of the enslaved community.

1864 A Riot at Salisbury Prison

On November 25, 1864, a riot between Union prisoners of war and their Confederate guards broke out at the Confederate military prison at Salisbury.

Salisbury Prison, a former cotton mill, was initially established to house Union POWs waiting to be exchanged. With the end of prisoner exchanges and the inability of the Confederate army to transport detainees to other camps, Salisbury became the main POW camp for the Virginia Theater in September 1864, and its prison population swelled. The influx of prisoners caused conditions to deteriorate, and food rations to be reduced.

Prisoners organized an attack after having gone a reported forty-eight hours without food. A mob of inmates overpowered guards during a shift change. Many of the guards threw down their weapons and fled. Prisoners armed themselves with the discarded weapons, but they lacked additional ammunition.

Outside guards turned cannons on them, firing grape and canister shot, and Confederate troops at a nearby train station ran over to assist in quelling the riot. A prisoner wrote in his diary of the event, "It lasted but a few moments, nevertheless, in that short time eighty-one were killed and as many wounded."

Somerset Place.

1744 Alexander Mebane, Patriot and UNC Trustee

On November 26, 1744, Alexander Mebane was born at Hawfields in Orange County.

An ardent Patriot, Mebane played an active role in the Revolutionary War. In December 1776 he served as a delegate to the Provincial Congress in Halifax and the following year became sheriff of Orange County, a post he held until 1780. Mebane also served as an officer in the Orange County militia.

At the war's conclusion Mebane was elected as an Orange County representative to the General Assembly and served as brigadier general of the Hillsborough District militia. He also served as auditor of the Hillsborough Constitutional Convention of 1788 and the Fayetteville Convention of 1789. An Anti-Federalist, Mebane voted against ratification unless a bill of rights was included.

That same year Mebane joined the first board of trustees of the University of North Carolina. In 1792 he served on the committee that chose New Hope Chapel Hill, an area named for a church building located there, as the site for the new school. He even helped lay the cornerstone of Old East, the first building erected on campus. In 1793 Mebane was elected to Congress.

The Alamance County town of Mebane is named in his honor.

1787 Judicial Milestone Set in New Bern, 1787

On November 26, 1787, *Bayard v. Singleton*, a landmark North Carolina court case that set a precedent for the exercise of judicial review, was decided in New Bern. That year Elizabeth Cornell Bayard filed suit to reclaim lands and property of her father, Samuel Cornell, which had been confiscated at the close of the American Revolution because of Cornell's loyalist sympathies.

Bayard's attorneys argued that the 1785 confiscation acts passed by the state violated a provision set forth in the state's 1776 constitution that guaranteed anyone a trial by jury in a case involving the potential of loss of property. The case was heard by the forerunner to the North Carolina Supreme Court.

Although it appeared clear that the confiscation acts did indeed violate the state constitution, there was no precedent in the 1780s for a court to refuse to enforce a legislative act. The court ultimately took the case and reluctantly agreed that they could not enforce an act that violated the state constitution, sending the case to trial.

While the court decided against Bayard—stating that her father was not a citizen and therefore could not have owned land in the first place—the *Bayard v. Singleton* case set the precedent for judicial review within the American legal system.

1827 Alfred Moore Scales, Confederate Veteran and Governor

On November 26, 1827, future governor Alfred Scales was born in Reidsville.

He studied law at UNC and privately under William Battle, before winning election as the equivalent of today's Rockingham County district attorney. He quickly moved up the political ladder, serving in the General Assembly in the early 1850s before being elected to Congress later that decade.

Scales joined the Confederate Army a month before secession and continued his service until the surrender at Appomattox. After the war Scales was reelected to the General Assembly and the U.S. House.

It wasn't until 1884 that the Democratic Party nominated Scales for governor. He won the state's top job over Republican Tyre York, making him the forty-fifth governor of North Carolina. Like many other governors of the era, Scales focused his efforts on education and internal improvements such as railroads and highways. One of the highlights of his tenure was the establishment of the school that later became North Carolina State University.

After stepping down as governor, Scales left public life and moved to Greensboro, where he continued to practice law and got involved in banking. He died in 1892.

Alfred Moore Scales

NOV 27

1802 John Baptista Ashe, (Almost) Governor

On November 27, 1802, John Baptista Ashe, who had just been elected governor, died before being able to take office.

Born near Wilmington in 1748, Ashe's early career was marked by military service in both the War of Regulation and American Revolution. After independence he was elected to the General Assembly from Halifax and quickly became popular in legislative circles. He was unanimously chosen speaker in 1786.

Ashe's first foray onto the national scene came in 1785, when he was nominated as a delegate to the Continental Congress but failed to win election to the post. Despite that setback he was elected to Congress the next year and also took an active role in North Carolina's 1789 Constitutional Convention.

After North Carolina ratified the federal Constitution, Ashe was elected to the First and Second Congresses, where he voted on a number of important issues, including the site of the new nation's capital and excise taxes on liquor.

When a committee of the legislature arrived at Ashe's Halifax home in 1802 to tell him of his election to the governorship, they found him ill. He died several days later.

1864 Braxton Bragg Takes Command

On November 27, 1864, Gen. Braxton Bragg was given command of the Department of North Carolina of the Confederate States Army.

Braxton Bragg (1817–1876), Gov. Thomas Bragg (1810–1872), and Congressman John Bragg (1806–1878), brothers, were among the six sons of Thomas and Margaret Bragg. They grew up in Warrenton and attended the Warrenton Male Academy.

Braxton Bragg attended West Point, where he graduated fifth in his class. He served with distinction in the Mexican War and returned to Warren County in 1848. He retired to Louisiana in 1856 but returned to the military at the onset of the Civil War. He rose through the ranks, eventually becoming commander of the Army of Tennessee. Returning to North Carolina by the end of the war, he surrendered at Durham Station in April 1865, a result of negotiations between Gen. William Tecumseh Sherman and Gen. Joseph E. Johnston at Bennett Place.

Fort Bragg in Fayetteville is named for him.

1962 Martin Luther King, Jr. Reveals His Dream in Rocky Mount

On November 27, 1962, Martin Luther King, Jr. delivered a speech in Rocky Mount. Before a crowd of nearly two thousand in the gymnasium at Booker T. Washington High School, King used a number of expressions that made their way into his landmark "I Have a Dream" address at the Lincoln Memorial, which was part of the March on Washington in August 1963.

Near the close of his Rocky Mount speech, King built toward these lines: "I have a dream that one day right here in Rocky Mount, the sons of former slaves and the sons of former slave owners will meet at the table of brotherhood, knowing that one God brought man to the face of the Earth. I have a dream tonight that one day my little daughter and my two sons will grow up in a world not conscious of the color of their skin, but only conscious of the fact that they are members of the human race. . . ."

Clayborne Carson, editor of the King Papers, notes that while this was not his first use of the "I have a dream" phrase, it "appears to be an important new rhetorical formulation." By the spring and summer of 1963 the words were among the most frequent of King's refrains.

1981 Mel Tomlinson, Master of Ballet and Modern Dance

On November 27, 1981, Mel Tomlinson made his debut as the only African American member of the New York City Ballet.

Born in Raleigh in January 1954, Tomlinson became interested in dance after participating in gymnastics in high school. He received a B.F.A. from what's now the University of North Carolina School of the Arts (UNCSA) after studying there for only two years. After graduation Tomlinson began touring the country with the Agnes de Mille Heritage Theatre, which was founded at the school.

In 1974 Tomlinson switched his focus from modern dance to ballet and joined the Dance Theater of Harlem, where he quickly rose to the position of soloist and performed in *Manifestations*, *Swan Lake*, and *Scheherazade*. He took leave for a time to join Alvin Ailey's American Dance Theater, which produced mostly modern pieces.

Tomlinson became a soloist with the New York City Ballet shortly after joining the company, and he remained there until 1987, when he returned to his home state and joined the faculty at UNCSA. Since leaving UNCSA, Tomlinson has taught at or performed with the Boston Ballet's CITYDANCE program, the Boston Conservatory of Music, Harvard University, UNC-Charlotte and what's now the Charlotte Ballet.

Dr. Martin Luther King, Jr., about 1966, speaking at a program in his honor, at North Carolina Central College in Durham.

1814 Johnston Blakeley, Hero of the War of 1812

On November 28, 1814, Congress promoted Johnston Blakely to the rank of captain for his stellar performance in the ongoing war with Great Britain.

Born in Ireland but raised in Wilmington, Blakeley joined the navy as a young man and had a great deal of experience when the War of 1812 was declared. Shortly after the war's outbreak he was ordered to Massachusetts to oversee construction of a new sloop, the *Wasp*.

Blakeley left port aboard the *Wasp* in May 1814 and captured his first prize the following month. By the end of June, he had captured and burned four more enemy vessels.

Blakely's crowning achievement came on June 28 when the *Wasp* defeated the British sloop-of-war HMS *Reindeer* during a brutal exchange of cannon fire and multiple attempts by the British sailors to board the *Wasp*. Damaged in the fight, it sailed to France to offload prisoners and seek repairs. Blakely and his crew captured two more prizes on route.

As news of Blakeley's success filtered back to the United States in October and November, he became a hero. It's unclear whether he ever learned of his promotion as the *Wasp* disappeared while returning to the United States from Europe.

1861 John Blue, Inventor of Agricultural Tools

On November 28, 1861, inventor John Blue was born in what is now Scotland County.

Raised on a cotton farm, Blue had an interest from a young age in inventing tools to make life easier. Before he left the family farm to start a life of his own, he often tinkered in his father's blacksmith shop. Despite the crude tools available to him there, he was able to invent the first cotton-stalk cutter.

Blue struck out on his own in 1883 and continued to invent agricultural tools on the side, including an iron cotton planter and a fertilizer spreader. After a few years he founded a business on his farm with his father. The business grew steadily into a factory that made a variety of agricultural tools in addition to repairing them. The factory eventually got so large that Blue added a foundry to supply his own iron.

Over the course of his career, Blue continued to invent new products and secure patents for them. His son, John Jr., took over the business after his father's death, and though it shifted its operations to Alabama after a major fire, the company continues to operate to this day as CDS-John Blue.

1948 The State's First Poet Laureate

On November 28, 1948, Arthur Talmage Abernethy was appointed Poet Laureate, just before the end of Gov. R. Gregg Cherry's term of office.

Abernethy's term was to expire with the end of Cherry's term. He was therefore officially Poet Laureate for only a few weeks, from November 28, 1948 through January 5, 1949. Nonetheless, because Gov. Kerr Scott did not appoint a successor, Abernethy remained the designated Poet Laureate until August 1953, when Gov. William Umstead appointed James Larkin Pearson to the post.

Abernethy's career included time as a professor and a journalist, and he also served as a magistrate and justice of the peace, frequently filing his annual reports in verse. He also found time to write more than fifty books and thousands of poems. The books covered history, southern folklore, and evangelical subjects. Surprisingly, history records that none of his poetry was published in book form.

Johnston Blakely.

1906 Samuel Spencer Casualty of Rail Crash

On November 29, 1906, Samuel Spencer, president of the Southern Railway Company, died in a violent collision on his own railroad.

A Confederate veteran and influential businessman, Spencer accompanied guests to Wake County to hunt quail. His private car and several others became detached from the engine due to a faulty connection and came to a dead stop on the track about fourteen miles south of Lynchburg, Virginia. As Spencer and his guests slept, the Washington and Southwestern's Vestibule Limited smashed into their car at forty mph, splintering it into "matchwood."

The heap of wood and metal then caught fire, burning many of the bodies almost beyond recognition. Spencer and his guests were especially vulnerable since his private car was the last on the train and the first to be hit. African American passengers also suffered greatly since their car was struck next and the engine split it nearly in two. Eight people died and ten were injured. Adding to the tragedy was the alleged looting of the injured and the shattered rail cars by passengers from the Washington and Southwestern train.

Many well-known businessmen of the time attended Spencer's funeral, including his good friend J. P. Morgan.

1931 Tragic Pairing of Tobacco Heir and Torch Singer

On November 29, 1931, Zachary Smith Reynolds married Broadway actress Libby Holman. The young tobacco heir had just spent the better part of a year following the starlet and torch singer around the world until she finally agreed to marry him.

The young couple wed in secret in the parlor of a Monroe, Michigan justice of the peace. It took place just a few days after Reynolds's first wife, textile heiress Ann Cannon Reynolds, was granted a divorce from him in Reno, Nevada on grounds of cruelty.

The marriage between Reynolds, age twenty, and Holman, age twenty-five, was a tumultuous one between two very complex individuals. The couple kept their marriage a secret until May 1932, when they claimed to have just been married in Honolulu.

The union wouldn't last long, either. Reynolds died of a gunshot wound to the head shortly after an argument at a 1932 party at the couple's Winston-Salem estate turned violent. While Holman was indicted for murder, the case never went to trial. The charges were dropped, and the death ruled a suicide.

1942 SS James Iredell Launched

On November 29, 1942, the SS *James Iredell*, a Liberty Ship constructed by the North Carolina Shipbuilding Company, was launched.

Along the Tar Heel coast maritime industries mobilized with the coming of World War II. Mine sweepers were built at New Bern and submarine chasers at Elizabeth City; naval repair stations operated at Morehead City and Southport. By far the largest construction effort of the war, the building of 243 Liberty Ships and other cargo vessels, took place at a shipyard on the Cape Fear River three miles south of downtown Wilmington. Workers there could complete a ship, from the laying of the keel to the launch, in twenty-five days.

Initially the yard built only Liberty Ships, cargo vessels 440 feet in length. Called "ugly ducklings," the Liberty Ships were the workhorses of the war. Vessels built at Wilmington were named for prominent historical figures, many of whom were from North Carolina. James Iredell, for instance, was one of the first U.S. Supreme Court Justices.

The SS *James Iredell* was scuttled as a breakwater off Omaha Beach as part of the U.S. invasion of German-occupied France on June 8, 1944.

1978 Isolated Portsmouth, Once Booming Trade Center

On November 29, 1978, the village of Portsmouth in Carteret County was added to the list of the National Register of Historic Places.

The Portsmouth Village Historic District boasts 250 acres of ocean views and quaint town buildings. Located between the North Core Banks and Ocracoke Inlet in a secluded portion of a tract now protected as part of the Cape Lookout National Seashore, Portsmouth Island saw its last permanent residents in 1971.

Among the largest settlements south of Virginia by 1760, Portsmouth became a booming village for shipping and trade. Some estimate that by 1852 more than two-thirds of North Carolina's imported goods passed through Portsmouth Island. By 1860 almost seven hundred people called Portsmouth home. During the Civil War Union troops targeted the village, prompting some residents to leave the island permanently.

With the increasing use of railroads for transport of goods, the shipping industry in Portsmouth suffered, causing the town to become a small fishing village. Though no permanent residents live on Portsmouth today, the unassuming island supports graceful scenic views and a variety of plant and wildlife.

Visitors can also explore a number of buildings in the historic Portsmouth village, including the town church, the post office and general store, and residential homes.

Portsmouth Village Historic District.

NOV 29

1853 Convicted Murderer Assaults Prosecutor, 1853

On November 30, 1853, Hyde County resident and Baptist preacher George Washington Carawan shot the prosecutor who secured his murder conviction and then turned the gun on himself.

Only an hour before the shooting, a jury found Carawan guilty of the murder of schoolteacher Clement H. Lassiter. Carawan accused Lassiter of having an affair with his wife and shot down the unsuspecting man in November 1852. Carawan forced one of his slaves to assist him in burying the body on a corner of his property before fleeing to Tennessee for a year. When he attempted to return home, Carawan's slave spotted him and promptly alerted neighbors of his master's return.

A citizens' arrest quickly landed Carawan in jail, and the subsequent trial resulted in a guilty verdict. The judge had just dismissed the jury when Carawan drew a pistol from his shirt, took deliberate aim at prosecutor Edward Warren, and fired. The shot struck Warren just above his heart but did not kill him. Carawan, wrestling with his own attorneys, then turned the gun on himself and ended his own life.

The trial and dramatic end of the murderous preacher gained national attention and riveted newspaper readers throughout the country.

1952 Charles George, Medal of Honor Recipient

On November 30, 1952, Charles George died at age twenty near Songnae-dong, Korea. PFC George, a member of the Forty-Fifth Infantry Division, had sustained injuries the night before when he threw himself on a grenade to shield his comrades. With enemy forces near, George suffered from his wounds in silence to protect his company.

Born in 1932 within the Qualla Boundary, the North Carolina home of the Eastern Band of Cherokee, George was given the Cherokee name "Tsali," which translates to English as Charles or Charlie. He grew up in Birdtown in Swain County before enlisting in the U.S. Army during the Korean War.

For his bravery during the last hours of his life, George was awarded the Congressional Medal of Honor posthumously in 1954. His parents, who spoke no English and had never ventured beyond the North Carolina mountains, traveled to Washington, D.C. to receive the medal.

In 2002 the Veterans Administration Medical Center in Asheville was renamed in his memory.

1956 Heavyweight Champion Floyd Patterson of Cleveland County

On November 30, 1956, Cleveland County native Floyd Patterson, only twenty-one years old at the time, became the youngest undisputed heavyweight boxing champion in history after knocking out Archie Moore in the fifth round of a title match.

Born in the small town of Waco in January 1935, Patterson left North Carolina for New York City with his family at a young age. He got his start in boxing training under the legendary manager Constantine "Cus" D'Amato and began fighting on the amateur circuit in 1950. He was selected for the 1952 Summer Olympics in Helsinki and earned a middleweight gold medal while he was there.

Patterson successfully defended his title four times but lost it to Swedish boxer Ingemar Johansson in June 1959. He won the title back from Johansson in June 1960, becoming the first heavyweight to regain the championship. Patterson retained the title in a third match with Johannson in March 1961 but lost it for what would be the last time in September 1962.

On retiring from the sport in 1972, Patterson had a record of fifty-five wins, eight losses, and one tie. He was inducted into the United States Olympic Committee Hall of Fame in 1987 and the International Boxing Hall of Fame in 1991.

Statue of Charles George created by Hendersonville sculptor James Killian Pratt, a U.S. Navy veteran who was also a patient at Charles George VA Medical Center. The statue is on the medical center campus. An identical statue stands in Asheville.

Floyd Patterson in New York, 1962.

1566 The Spanish Explore the Interior

On December 1, 1566, Spanish Capt. Juan Pardo left Santa Elena (in present-day South Carolina) with 125 men to explore the region and claim the land for Spain while pacifying local Indians. He also hoped to find an overland route from Santa Elena to the Spanish silver mines in northern Mexico.

In January 1567 Pardo and his company arrived at Joara, a large native town in the upper Catawba Valley near the eastern edge of the Appalachian Mountains. At Joara he built Fort San Juan and manned it with thirty soldiers. Although previous expeditions to the interior had made seasonal encampments or had temporarily occupied native towns, Pardo explicitly built Fort San Juan to expand Spanish holdings. In so doing he founded the earliest European settlement in the interior of what is now the United States. Although relations between the two groups were good initially, by May 1568 news reached Santa Elena that Indians had attacked all of Pardo's forts and that all were destroyed.

In Morganton, where significant Spanish ceramics and hardware have been recovered, archaeologists have identified a compound of five burned buildings. It is believed that the Spanish artifacts and burned buildings represent the material remains of Fort San Juan.

DEC 1

1875 A Brick Beacon, the Currituck Beach Lighthouse

On December 1, 1875, the Currituck Beach Lighthouse was lit for the first time.

Built in response to the many wrecks in the forty miles of "dark space" of coastline without lighthouses at the time, the idea for the structure was conceived in 1872. Construction began in 1873, and when completed, the 162-foot lighthouse was left unpainted to distinguish its exterior from other lighthouses along the coast. The last of the major brick lighthouses built on the Outer Banks, the building exhibited unique craftsmanship and a red-brick design that draws visitors to this day.

A keeper's house was added in 1876, and for years those who lived there tended to the original source of the tower's light: an oil-lamp with five wicks, the largest of which was four inches in diameter. After the building was electrified and automated in 1939, the need for keepers diminished. By the 1970s the lighthouse, especially the keeper's quarters, had fallen into disrepair.

Working in concert with the state, a local preservation group began to restore the Currituck Beach Light in 1980. Work was largely completed in 2011.

The Sand Island Light off Alabama's Gulf Coast was built using the plans from Currituck, though it is slightly smaller and has a less powerful beacon.

1890 Self-Declared Indian Chief Sylvester Long

On December 1, 1890, Sylvester Long, who would live most of his life as a self-described Indian chief named Buffalo Child Long Lance, was born in Winston. Though his parents claimed mixed Indian ancestry, neither had proof of their lineage since they both had been born into slavery. The family was, in the standards of the then-segregated South, labeled "colored."

Long ran away with a circus twice in his youth. The second time he joined the Wild West Show, where he met a Cherokee Indian who taught him words and phrases of the tribe's native language. Long used his knowledge of the Cherokee language to trick admissions officers at the Carlisle Indian Residential School in Pennsylvania. He later attended a military school where he began to use the name Sylvester Long Lance and his classmates dubbed him "Chief."

Long served in the Canadian military during World War I, and by the time he returned from service, he styled himself a Plains Indian, first Blackfoot and later Blood. A noted journalist, author, and actor, he was one of the most famous Indians in North America in the 1920s. He even designed a running shoe based on moccasins.

1922 Massive Fire Sweeps Across New Bern, 1922

On December 1, 1922, the Rowland Lumber Company in New Bern caught fire. While firefighters were still battling the Rowland blaze, a second fire started in a residence on Kilmarnock Street. It was reported that the flames "spread out like a giant fan" until they reached the Neuse River. Altogether about one thousand homes, businesses, and churches burned that day. Fire crews from Kinston and Washington, along with men from the Coast Guard Cutter *Pamlico*, assisted the firefighters of New Bern. About three thousand people, or a quarter of the population of New Bern at the time, were left homeless—and of those, the majority of the families were African American.

Soldiers from Fort Bragg shipped eight freight cars of tents, cots, and other supplies that were used by the Red Cross to set up a temporary tent city for the victims. Clothing and money were collected from people in nearby towns and even from the naval base in Norfolk, Virginia. One of the positive effects of the fire was the construction of a hospital for African Americans, Good Shepherd Hospital.

Studio portrait of Chief Buffalo Child Long Lance, Regina, Saskatchewan, ca. 1908.

1793 Diplomat John Gustavus Adolphus Williamson

On December 2, 1793, John Gustavus Adolphus Williamson, the first American diplomatic representative to Venezuela, was born in Person County.

In 1826 Williamson was appointed Consul of the United States to the Republic of Colombia. He remained there until 1832 when he returned to the United States and married. He stayed in the United States for a while but then returned to Colombia alone. While back in the United States to visit his wife, he learned that the government was going to recognize the Republic of Venezuela (newly separated from Colombia). Well acquainted with the language and the area, Williamson was selected to be the first American diplomat to Venezuela in 1835.

While in Caracas, Williamson faithfully kept a diary. The surviving manuscript is an important personal narrative of Venezuela's formative years and a vivid account of current world events, as the author recorded his thoughts after reading newspapers received by mail.

Williamson died in 1840 and is buried in the English Cemetery in Caracas. An edited and annotated version of his diary is in the State Archives of North Carolina; the original is housed at Louisiana State University.

1903 The Bassett Affair: Test Case for Free Speech

On December 2, 1903, the trustees of Trinity College, the predecessor institution of Duke University, voted not to accept the resignation of history professor John Spencer Bassett, opting instead to issue a strong statement on the necessity of free speech.

Bassett attempted to resign from Trinity because of a controversy that stemmed from an article he wrote for the October 1903 issue of the *South Atlantic Quarterly*. In its pages Bassett, Tarboro-born and nationally heralded as a scholar, praised Booker T. Washington as "all in all the greatest man, save General Lee, born in the South in a hundred years."

Such praise for a black man was unusual and, in the poisonous racial atmosphere of the times, led to calls for Bassett's resignation. Josephus Daniels of the *News and Observer* led the attack. Neither the praise for Robert E. Lee nor the fact that Trinity was a private institution made any difference to Bassett's critics.

Notwithstanding the backing from Trinity, Bassett left North Carolina three years later for a better job at Smith College in Massachusetts. In doing so, he reasoned that he "could not write history and direct public sentiment" at the same time.

The episode, now commonly referred to as the Bassett Affair, remains a landmark in the history of academic freedom.

1924 New Roundhouse at Spencer, 1924

On December 2, 1924, the Bob Julian Roundhouse at the Spencer Shops Southern Railway Repair Facility opened. The structure replaced a smaller fifteen-stall roundhouse that had been built in 1896. The new building was more than twice the size, with thirty-seven work bays for repairing and servicing Southern Railway's growing number of locomotives. Southern officials announced the project in February 1924, and construction began almost immediately. In addition to the roundhouse, a new turntable was built to accommodate the increased number of stalls.

Remarkably, the old structures were demolished and the new ones erected in only ten months. The new 120,000 square-foot roundhouse and the hundred-foot turntable cost approximately five hundred thousand dollars. Railroad officials named the new facility for the roundhouse supervisor, Bob Julian.

The Bob Julian Roundhouse is now a part of the North Carolina Transportation Museum at Historic Spencer Shops. Visitors can see restored locomotives, passenger cars, a mail car, and a World War II hospital car in the refurbished roundhouse. They can take a ride on the still-functioning turntable and learn more about the roundhouse's history, as well as the entire facility that made up the once-thriving Spencer Shops.

Bob Julian Roundhouse at Historic Spencer Shops.

1679 Bewitched from the Start

On December 3, 1679, a North Carolina law was passed directing local juries to investigate "felonies, witchcraft, enchantments, sorceries, and magick arts, among other crimes."

Throughout history witchcraft was often blamed for bad luck, illnesses, crop failures, and infidelity. Unlike the infamous witch trials in Salem, Massachusetts, many cases in North Carolina were dropped, not prosecuted. In most of the cases that were brought to trial, the accused were found innocent. Those accused of witchcraft often successfully countersued their accusers.

As early as 1768, royal governor William Tryon issued commissions to the Justices of the peace to hear cases involving charges of enchantment, sorceries, and art magick, and as late as 1951 a law was written and passed by the General Assembly against witchcraft in North Carolina. A case was considered in Morganton against a potential witch as late as 1976. The law was finally repealed in 2004.

DEC 3

1820 Omar Ibn Said Joins the Presbyterian Church

On December 3, 1820, Omar Ibn Said, one of the best documented practicing Muslim slaves in America, joined the First Presbyterian Church in Fayetteville.

Omar is believed to have arrived in Charleston in 1807, shortly before the foreign slave trade was terminated. He fled from his cruel master, running for about a month before arriving in Fayetteville in 1810. There he was jailed and advertised as a fugitive slave. During his imprisonment he used coals from the fireplace to write on his cell walls in Arabic.

Omar eventually was purchased by James Owen of Bladen County. He lived with some degree of privilege at the Owen plantation. He actively practiced his Islamic faith for many years, and Owen procured a copy of the Qu'ran in English for him in order to facilitate his learning English. As he learned English, the Owens hoped that he might convert to Christianity. To that end Owen procured a Bible in Arabic for Omar in 1819. The 1811 Bible is now owned by Davidson College.

Omar Ibn Said, ca. 1850.

1968 Beach Music Classic "Girl Watcher"

On December 3, 1968, the O'Kaysions, a pop music group, earned a gold record for their hit, "Girl Watcher."

Originally from Wilson, the blue-eyed soul group is generally known as a beach music band. With Donnie Weaver as the lead singer, the band first formed as the Kays in 1959, but it wasn't until 1968 that they scored their biggest hit with "Girl Watcher." The song remained in the Top 10 for nine weeks.

"Girl Watcher" was recorded at Pitt Sound Studio in Greenville on a local label but was released nationally by ABC Records. The song's catchy tune and lyrics have made it ripe for parody, and in 1987 it was reworked as "I'm a Wheel Watcher" to promote the TV game show *Wheel of Fortune*.

Incarnations of the band still perform, but the original members have reunited only once to be inducted into the Carolina Beach Music Awards Hall of Fame in 2003. Wayne Pittman, the group's guitarist, is the only original member still playing. He also serves as the band's manager.

1837 Mint Sets Up Shop in Charlotte, 1837

On December 4, 1837, a branch of the United States Mint opened in Charlotte.

The 1799 discovery of a seventeen-pound nugget by John Reed in Cabarrus County secured North Carolina's place as the epicenter of the nation's first gold fever epidemic. Since miners in North Carolina supplied almost all of the gold sent to the U. S. Mint in Philadelphia, Charlotte residents were determined to attract a branch office. The U.S. Mint agreed, and construction began in 1835. It was completed two years later on West Trade Street.

Before the Civil War the Charlotte mint processed more than five million dollars of gold currency in $1, $2.50, and $5 denominations. During the war the building was converted into a Confederate hospital and command center, but it reopened as a U.S. Assay Office in 1868. It tested precious metals and minerals for public quality assurance until 1913.

The building remained vacant until the expansion of a post office threatened it. A group of citizens then relocated the structure to the exclusive Eastover area. In 1936 the mint underwent extensive renovations. It opened as part of the Mint Museum of Art in June of that year, a century after its original dedication.

Front of Charlotte Mint, ca. 1930.

1865 North Carolina Approves the 13th Amendment

On December 4, 1865, the North Carolina General Assembly approved the Thirteenth Amendment to the U.S. Constitution, which abolished slavery.

In order for a state to be readmitted to the Union following the Civil War, Pres. Andrew Johnson required states to approve the amendment. Ten days following North Carolina's vote, the requisite three-quarters of the states had approved its ratification, and it thus became law.

The legislature's 1865 action came almost three years after the Emancipation Proclamation, which outlawed slavery in the southern states. Following passage of the Thirteenth Amendment, the freedmen's convention met a few blocks northwest of the North Carolina State Capitol. The assembly was the first effort by the state's African Americans to press for full political rights.

In December 2010 officials of the North Carolina Office of Archives and History and others met to dedicate and unveil four plaques commemorating the extension of civic and voting rights. In addition to one focusing on the Thirteenth Amendment, the others so remembered were the Fourteenth Amendment (granting rights to all citizens), the Fifteenth Amendment (extending voting rights to new citizens) and the Nineteenth Amendment (extending voting rights to women).

1994 Pioneer Dunker, Tar Heel Charlotte Smith

On December 4, 1994, Charlotte Smith, then a member of the UNC Tar Heels women's basketball team, became the second collegiate women's player ever to dunk. The first dunk had come nearly ten years earlier, when West Virginia University player Georgeann Wells accomplished the feat in a game against the University of Charleston.

A native of Shelby, Smith had a stellar career with the Tar Heels. She was the ACC Rookie of Year in 1992 and ESPN's National Player of Year in 1995. By the time she left UNC-Chapel Hill, she had scored nearly twenty-one hundred points, grabbed twelve hundred rebounds, and became one of only two women's basketball players at UNC to have her jersey retired.

Smith entered the 1996 pro women's basketball draft and was picked by the Colorado Xplosion in the third round. She was traded to the San Jose Lasers shortly thereafter and moved to the Charlotte Sting in 1999 and the Washington Mystics in 2005. She was briefly on the Indiana Fever in 2006 before retiring from pro ball.

Smith's time coaching women's basketball overlapped with her time playing professionally. She is now the head women's basketball coach at Elon University.

Charlotte Smith at UNC-Chapel Hill

DEC 5

1770 Upper House of Assembly Meets at Tryon Palace

On December 5, 1770, the Upper House of Assembly first met in the Council Chamber of the newly-constructed "Government House" in New Bern. Later that evening, Gov. William Tryon hosted a grand ball, complete with fireworks. The newly built Government House was not celebrated by all North Carolina citizens, however. In fact, many people, upset over the taxes imposed to build the structure, began to call the Government House "Tryon's Palace."

Tryon Palace served as the backdrop for North Carolina's transformation from colony to statehood. In May 1775 then royal governor Josiah Martin fled the palace as patriot forces approached New Bern. When North Carolina became an independent state, the first four governors resided in Tryon Palace until Raleigh became the new capital in 1794.

After a fire destroyed all but the kitchen and stable offices in 1798, most of the original land was utilized in highway and housing developments. In the 1940s public interest and private donations convinced the state to consider the feasibility of bringing Tryon Palace back to life. The palace, reconstructed according to the original design, opened as a public museum in 1959. Now a State Historic Site, Tryon Palace stands as a reminder of North Carolina's rich historical legacy.

1854 Oakdale, Wilmington's Antebellum Cemetery

On December 5, 1854, the first lots of Oakdale Cemetery in Wilmington were sold.

Oakdale, Wilmington's first municipal burial ground, is one of the most beautiful and scenic graveyards in the Old North State. It remains the city's largest cemetery and is noted for the abundance of prominent Wilmingtonians and other North Carolinians who are buried there.

The cemetery's roots can be traced to early 1852, when several prominent citizens of Wilmington met to discuss establishing a new burial ground. A site was selected on a neck of land northeast of the town limits on the east bank of Burnt Mill Creek, and an initial tract of sixty-five acres was purchased for eleven hundred dollars.

Many who died before the cemetery was established were later re-interred at Oakdale. A large area of unmarked graves reveals the mass burial ground where victims of the 1862 yellow fever epidemic were interred.

Civil War-era burials are numerous, including a mass grave marked with a large monument for hundreds of Confederate soldiers killed in battle at Fort Fisher in 1865. Oakdale is also the resting place of Rose O'Neal Greenhow, a Confederate spy who drowned in the surf off Fort Fisher in 1864.

1902 Fred Olds and the Hall of History

On December 5, 1902, the Hall of History, the predecessor of the North Carolina Museum of History, opened in a small room inside the old Agriculture Building in downtown Raleigh. "Curiosities" collected from across the state by former newspaperman Frederick Augustus Olds and historical artifacts from the State Museum (now the North Carolina Museum of Natural Sciences) filled the Hall's walls and exhibit cases, constituting the core of its collection.

Olds became the fledgling museum's first director. During his thirty-two-year tenure, he visited all of the state's hundred counties, amassing nearly thirty thousand historically significant objects and the stories connected with them.

In 1965, after moves to two other locations, the Hall of History was renamed the North Carolina Museum of History. Three years after that it moved into a new building on East Jones Street, sharing space with what is now the North Carolina Office of Archives and History and the State Library.

The museum finally received a home of its own in 1994, when its current building opened on East Edenton Street. Today the four-story facility has a large staff, 150,000 objects in its collection, and is the flagship of six other museums in the state history museums division.

1962 Landmark Civil Rights Health Care Case

On December 5, 1962, a U.S. district court dismissed a suit against two Greensboro hospitals challenging "separate but equal" treatment in private, non-profit hospitals. The case was ultimately overturned on appeal.

The suit, now known as *Simkins v. Cone*, was brought by African American medical professionals and their patients against the Moses H. Cone Memorial and Wesley Long Community Hospitals. Their objective was to gain admission privileges for the medical professionals and their patients.

The plaintiffs argued that even though the hospitals were private institutions, their "separate but equal treatment" was unconstitutional because the institutions received state and federal funding under a 1946 federal law and various federal regulations. The district court held that because the hospitals were not agencies of the state, the suit should not go forward. The U.S. Court of Appeals for the Fourth Circuit found that the institutions were connected to the government and that discriminatory treatment violated the Constitution.

Since the U.S. Supreme Court declined to review the case, the decision was legally binding only in Maryland, Virginia, West Virginia, and the Carolinas, but the ruling helped turn the tide toward hospital desegregation across the South. It was the first time a federal court prohibited racial discrimination by a private entity.

School group visiting the Hall of History, about 1940.

1809 First Jewish Legislator and Religious Liberty

On December 6, 1809, Jacob Henry, North Carolina's first Jewish legislator, delivered a rousing speech about religious liberty to the General Assembly.

Henry represented Carteret County in 1808 and 1809, a time when people were bound constitutionally to affirm the "truth of the Protestant religion" before holding any public office. He served his first term without incident, but in 1809 a newly-elected representative took issue with Henry's religious affiliation and introduced a resolution to remove him from office.

The legislators decided to take up the resolution the next day, giving Henry time to prepare his defense. Without specifically mentioning Judaism he addressed "natural and inalienable rights" and equalized religious sects with phrases such as "the ruler of the universe."

Ultimately, Henry was allowed to retain his seat. His inspiring and eloquent speech to the 1809 General Assembly has been published and quoted frequently ever since and is considered a touchstone of religious rights and tolerance.

Visitors to Beaufort can see the Federal-era house that he built at 229 Front Street, where it still stands. Henry lived there with his wife, Esther Whitehurst, whom he married in 1801.

1955 Gyrocopter Took Flight in Kitty Hawk, 1955

On December 6, 1955, Russian immigrant Dr. Igor Bensen made the world's first gyrocopter flight in Kitty Hawk.

After working for General Electric, Bensen created his own company, Bensen Aircraft Corporation, to mass produce personal flying machines near Raleigh-Durham Airport. The Bensen Gyro-Copter was designed to be built by the purchaser in a garage with ordinary hand tools. It was relatively inexpensive, with kits priced at less than two thousand dollars. The finished product could be converted from a gyrocopter to an automobile by locking the rotary blades in place.

The most famous of Bensen's gyrocopters was the *Spirit of Kitty Hawk*, in which he duplicated the first flight of the Wright Brothers on its sixtieth anniversary in 1963. During the next few years the craft set more national and world records than any other civilian rotary aircraft in the world. Law enforcement agencies and crop dusters continue to use gyrocopters in their work. A highly modified Bensen Gyro-Copter appeared in 1967's James Bond film, *You Only Live Twice*, complete with non-standard smokescreens and rocket launchers.

The Bensen Aircraft Corporation closed in 1989.

1968 London Years of Sweet Baby James

On December 6, 1968, James Taylor released his first and self-titled album, *James Taylor*.

Produced by Paul McCartney for Apple Records, the album featured "Carolina in My Mind," one of the Taylor's most recognized songs. He recorded the album between July and October 1968 at Trident Studios in London. The Beatles were recording *The White Album* during the same time in the same studios, and McCartney and George Harrison were both featured on versions of "Carolina in My Mind."

Although born in Boston, Taylor moved to Chapel Hill in 1951, when he was three, and he was strongly influenced by the landscape of the area. The product of a musical family, Taylor began to show a strong talent of his own early on. He played in various bands in the early 1960s, but by the end of the decade he moved to London to concentrate on a solo career after being plagued by a combination of depression and drugs.

When *James Taylor* was released, the artist, having fallen back into drugs, was unable to promote it. Critics were complimentary and positive, but Taylor's hospitalization hampered its success.

Though released as a single, "Carolina in My Mind" reached only No. 118 on the charts. Taylor wouldn't receive wide recognition until the release of his second album, *Sweet Baby James*, in 1970.

Fifty Gyrocopters pose for a group portrait during a typical Fly-In of the Popular Rotorcraft Association, ca. 1970s.

DEC 7

1939 A Preservation Milestone for North Carolina

On December 7, 1939, the North Carolina Society for the Preservation of Antiquities, predecessor to what's now Preservation North Carolina, met for the first time in the ballroom of the Carolina Hotel in Raleigh.

Col. Joseph Hyde Pratt, a geologist and veteran of the Thirtieth "Old Hickory" Division that broke the Hindenburg Line during World War I, presided. Janie Gosney was secretary-treasurer. The December general meeting followed an October 20 organizational meeting in the State Capitol.

The inclusion of a broad range of civic-minded citizens from across the state propelled the group. The keynote speaker was Gertrude Carraway of New Bern, who called for the restoration of Tryon Palace. Others addressed the need for similar work in Bath and for collaborative efforts between historians and archaeologists. Projects endorsed at that first session included the identification of a plantation house, a covered bridge, a waterwheel mill, and multiple battlefields for restoration projects.

Within two years the organization had chapters in Raleigh, Greensboro, Goldsboro, and Asheville. The death of Colonel Pratt in 1942 and the onset of World War II slowed the group's progress, but its sound footing ensured its success.

1941 A North Carolina Pearl Harbor Story

On December 7, 1941, Japanese planes staged a surprise attack on U.S. military forces at Pearl Harbor. It is the day that, in the words of Pres. Franklin D. Roosevelt, will "live in infamy," and it is the day that led the U.S. to enter World War II.

Roosevelt had ordered American forces to deploy at Oahu, Hawaii in hopes of deterring further Japanese expansion. War minister Hideki Tojo took power in Tokyo in October and set in motion the events of December 7. In two waves 350 Japanese planes took part in the assault resulting in the deaths of 2,403 Americans.

Harley Jolley, a veteran of the Civilian Conservation Corps, taught history at Mars Hill College after the war. Enrolled in the Army Air Force and stationed at Hickam Air Field, he was asleep when the attack commenced at 7:55 a.m. His bunkmate, hearing the commotion, suggested that "the damn Navy is at it again." The truth of the matter soon became painfully obvious. Jolley rushed to a guard position at the perimeter of the field and judged that he was "very fortunate" to have avoided injury. He served in the military for the entire war, mostly in France and Belgium.

1946 Minibikes and the Wrestling Mat: The McCrary Twins

On December 7, 1946, Billy and Benny McCrary, the world's largest twins, were born in Hendersonville.

After contracting measles at age four, the twins' weights quickly ballooned. By age ten they each weighed two hundred pounds, and by sixteen each tipped the scales at more than six hundred pounds. Billy and Benny would top out at 814 and 784 pounds, respectively, according to the *Guinness Book of World Records*. Their enormous size has since been attributed, at least in part, to pituitary gland damage caused by the early bout of measles they both experienced.

To stem the boys' growth, their parents bought a farm, believing perhaps the boys would burn up calories while working. But they had wanderlust and quickly quit high school to move to Texas and brand cattle. In a promotion with Honda Motorcycles and Holiday Inn, the McCrarys rode motorcycles from East to West Coasts. They entertained on the *Tonight Show* and at Myrtle Beach, big men atop tiny minibikes. They went on to become professional wrestlers under the name of the McGuire Twins, training in Mexico and appearing across the U.S. and Japan.

Billy died in 1979 during a minibike stunt at Niagara Falls. Benny took other wrestling partners, among them Andre the Giant, before entering a semi-retirement devoted to golf and evangelism. He died in 2001. Their fame continues to grow. They have been immortalized in animation on *The Simpsons* and *Family Guy*.

1970 Archaeological Work at Future Jordan Lake

On December 7, 1970, the groundbreaking for what would become Jordan Lake took place. The lake was full about twelve years later. Its namesake was U.S. Sen. B. Everett Jordan.

Today many North Carolinians enjoy the water, beaches, trails, and woodlands at Jordan Lake State Recreation Area, but it was not always a recreational space. After a devastating tropical storm in 1945, the government began to look at methods of flood control for the Cape Fear River Basin. In 1962 the Army Corps of Engineers submitted a plan that recommended building three reservoirs. Ultimately, only the construction of Jordan Lake was realized.

As a regulatory requirement, a thorough archaeological investigation had to be conducted. That cultural resources management project was conducted in 1978 and 1979 by a Michigan company, led by principal investigator Steve Claggett, who ultimately would return to North Carolina to become state archaeologist.

The project's archaeological surveys determined that there were about 350 sites in the area; extensive excavations focused on two. Archaeologists verified that Indians had inhabited the vicinity as far back as the Early Archaic Period—or about ten thousand years ago. To this day the work stands as one of the largest salvage archaeology programs carried out in the state.

Archaeology work, 1979, at site of the future Jordan Lake.

1827 James Iredell Jr. Became Governor

On December 8, 1827, James Iredell Jr. became governor.

He was born in Edenton in 1788 to parents of the highest social and political standing. His father, James Iredell Sr., was a prominent Federalist leader and an associate justice of the United States Supreme Court. His mother, the former Hannah Johnston, was the sister of Gov. Samuel Johnston of Edenton and niece of royal governor Gabriel Johnston.

The younger Iredell was educated at Edenton Academy and the College of New Jersey (now Princeton University). Returning to North Carolina, he studied law and was admitted to the bar in 1809. During the War of 1812, he commanded a company of volunteers in the defense of Norfolk, and in 1815 he was commissioned a brigadier general in the North Carolina militia. He later served in the state legislature before being elected governor.

After his gubernatorial term Iredell established a law practice in Raleigh and served as a commissioner to revise the state's laws. He also reported cases for the North Carolina Supreme Court, administered a law school, and published an authoritative three-volume digest of court cases in the state.

James Iredell Jr.

1840 S. B. Alexander, Advocate for Agriculture

On December 8, 1840, Sydenham Benoni Alexander, Confederate officer, legislator, and agriculturalist, was born in Mecklenburg County.

Though Alexander graduated from the University of North Carolina in 1860, the Civil War intervened before he could begin his professional life. He enlisted in the First North Carolina Volunteers in April 1861, saw action, and was promoted through the ranks to captain before he joined the staff of Gen. Robert Hoke as an inspector-general.

After the war Alexander became a successful farmer. He was appointed the master of the Grange in North Carolina in 1877. Two years later he was elected as a Democrat to the state Senate, where he would go on to serve several terms.

As his involvement in state politics deepened, Alexander was central to the formation of the college that would become North Carolina State University. He was appointed commissioner of the state board of agriculture, president of the North Carolina State Fair, and president of the North Carolina Railroad. He also became the first president of the North Carolina Farmers' Alliance.

Alexander was elected to the U.S. House of Representatives for two successive terms. In 1901 he returned to the North Carolina Senate, where he helped to appropriate two hundred thousand dollars for public schools.

1908 Entrepreneur and Philanthropist Moses Cone

On December 8, 1908, pioneering textile entrepreneur Moses Cone died at age fifty-one. He was buried in Blowing Rock on his thirty-six-hundred-acre country estate, now part of the Blue Ridge Parkway.

The eldest son of immigrants from Bavaria, Moses and his brother Ceasar began contracting with southern mill owners to market their textiles in 1891. They opened their own mill in Greensboro in 1895 and by 1902 were operating White Oak Mill, the largest denim manufacturer in the world at the time.

Moses Cone was a conservationist and philanthropist. The Cone mill villages provided a social support network for their workers, and Cone hired the farmers from whom he bought his Blowing Rock land to continue to work there. He brought in whitetail deer, several varieties of apples, white pine, and hemlock, and developed three lakes stocked with bass and trout.

Cone also advocated for education. He gave four dollars to the schools of Blowing Rock for every dollar raised by its citizens and contributed to the start of Appalachian State University, serving on its original board. His widow Bertha sustained the estate until it was left to the Moses H. Cone Memorial Hospital in Greensboro upon her death in 1947.

DEC 9

1861 Confederate Prison at Salisbury Opened, 1861

On December 9, 1861, the Confederate prison at Salisbury took in its first Union prisoners.

Early in the war the Confederacy purchased an old cotton mill in southeast Salisbury for fifteen thousand dollars and converted the structure into a place of confinement. Many of the incarcerated spent their time writing, whittling, or playing baseball. These constituted some of the first baseball games played in the South. One prisoner noted that early life within the prison was "more endurable than any other part of Rebeldom."

In time, though, the Salisbury prison surpassed its capacity. In the autumn of 1864, it contained almost seven thousand prisoners, far more than the facility was designed to accommodate. Statewide supply shortages and rampant disease led to a surge in death rates, forcing guards to prepare mass graves for deceased inmates and casualties from nearby hospitals.

Near the close of the war, conditions at the prison convinced leaders to conduct prisoner exchanges, the most notable of which took place in February 1865. In April of that year, Gen. George Stoneman's Union troops set fire to the prison, which had been abandoned and converted into a supply depot. Only the garrison house of the original prison camp survived.

"Bird's-eye View of Confederate Prison Taken in 1864.

1868 Body Politic of the Eastern Band of Cherokee Indians

On December 9, 1868, at a Grand Council held at Cheowa (modern day Robbinsville), the body politic of the Eastern Band of Cherokee Indians (EBCI) was created.

Nimrod Jarrett Smith, who served as Clerk of Council during these critical early gatherings, was deeply involved in Cherokee politics. At age twenty-five Smith enlisted with William Holland Thomas's Sixty-Ninth North Carolina Volunteer Infantry, also known as "Thomas's Legion," and rose by 1865 to the rank of First Sergeant of Company B. After the Civil War the Cherokee sought to solidify not only their land holdings, but also their very existence in the state.

On December 1, 1870, the new Cherokee government was ratified at another Grand Council in which Flying Squirrel was elected as the first Principal Chief of the Eastern Band of Cherokee Indians. Smith would later hold that title from 1880 to 1891.

Nimrod Jarrett Smith pictured in *Eastern Band of Cherokees of North Carolina*.

1921 Marshal Ferdinand Foch in Monroe, 1921

On December 9, 1921, Ferdinand Foch, formerly the commander-in-chief of all Allied armies in World War I, gave a speech at the Union County Courthouse praising America's role in the conflict. He was joined by Gov. Cameron Morrison and former governor Thomas Bickett.

A month earlier Foch, who was on a speaking tour of the United States, helped Vice Pres. Calvin Coolidge break ground on the Liberty Memorial in Kansas City. The memorial honors the fallen soldiers of World War I from Kansas and Missouri and now houses the National World War I Museum.

Already in his early sixties at the outbreak of World War I, Foch was a career military man in the French army and a veteran of the Franco-Prussian War. By 1914 he was commander of a French corps, and in four years he rose to command all Allied armies, including those of America and Britain. Angered by what he perceived as lenient punishments and restrictions on Germany at the Treaty of Versailles, Foch reportedly exclaimed, "This is not a peace. It is an armistice for twenty years!"

Foch returned to Europe in 1922 and died nine years later. He is interred in Paris at the building known as "Les Invalides" next to Napoleon Bonaparte's tomb.

1958 Roots of the John Birch Society

On December 9, 1958, in Indianapolis Chowan County native Robert Welch founded the John Birch Society, which was named for a Georgia missionary who was killed by Chinese Communists just after the close of World War II. Welch got the society started with a seventeen-hour speech to a group of eleven businessmen from across the country.

A devout Baptist and fervent opponent of communism, Welch came from a prosperous farming family. After graduating from high school at age twelve and completing a degree at UNC, Welch founded a candy business in Massachusetts. He became very successful in that industry and began to turn his attention to writing books and fighting what he perceived as a coziness with Communists inside the federal government.

After accusing Pres. Dwight Eisenhower of being a dedicated Communist and claiming that Communists controlled sixty to eighty percent of the United States, Welch and his organization began to garner widespread media coverage. The John Birch Society's members were known for being secretive and devoted to the anti-Communist cause.

After peaking in the mid-1960s with around a hundred thousand members, a staff of more than 250, and an annual budget of eight million dollars, the organization began a steady decline in lockstep with the diminishing threat posed by communism.

Welch retired in 1983 after a stroke and died in 1985.

1718 Until He Be Dead: The End of Stede Bonnet

On December 10, 1718, Stede Bonnet, the "Gentleman Pirate," was hanged in South Carolina.

An unlikely buccaneer, Bonnet was born in 1688 in Barbados, orphaned at a young age and inherited a sizable plantation. By 1715 he was married and held the rank of major in the Barbadian militia. In 1717 he gave up his life among the island's planter elite, deserting his family to become a pirate.

Instead of capturing a vessel, Bonnet launched his pirating career in the way in which he was accustomed to doing business—he purchased and armed a ship and hired a crew. Bonnet was known to have been in league with Blackbeard on occasion, including during the siege of Charleston's harbor. Despite his pardon by Gov. Charles Eden, Bonnet returned to piracy, establishing a base near modern-day Southport.

South Carolina, responding to the piratical threat to the colony, sent a ship north in search of pirates. A fierce battle took place in September 1718, the largest and bloodiest of the pirate conflicts in the colony's waters. Members of the captured crew were executed in Charleston, effectively ending the "Golden Age of Piracy" in the Carolinas.

1775 Oldest Grave in Salisbury's Old English Cemetery

On December 10, 1775, Daniel Little died and was laid to rest on land that became the Old English Cemetery in Salisbury. He was the first of many to be buried on the property, eventually donated to the city by Thomas Frohock and located downtown near the courthouse.

Little was one of the Rowan County's earliest settlers. He immigrated to the American colonies from Germany, first settling in Pennsylvania before coming to North Carolina around 1753.

Fluent in both German and English, Little quickly became one of the leaders of the county and by 1756 was constable. The inscription on his gravestone reads: HERE LYS THE BODY OF CAPT DANL LITTLE LATE OF SALISBURY WHO DIED DECEMBR THE 10TH 1775 AGED 44 YEARS. A stone later placed on the grave includes the words, "First Grave."

Two theories exist as to how the Old English Cemetery got its name. The first stems from a belief that the site includes unmarked graves of several British soldiers. The British army under Cornwallis occupied Salisbury in February of 1781. Another theory holds that it is called the English cemetery in order to distinguish it from the Lutheran/German cemetery on the eastern side of town.

1825 William Miller, Governor During War of 1812

On December 10, 1825, former North Carolina governor William Miller died in Key West, Florida.

Born around 1783 in Warren County, Miller worked as a private lawyer, the state's attorney general, and a member of the General Assembly before first being elected governor in 1814. He went on to serve three terms in the post and was the first to occupy the newly completed Governor's Palace at the south end of Raleigh's Fayetteville Street.

Active on the national political stage, Miller supported the military policies of Pres. James Madison during the concluding weeks of the War of 1812 by ordering out additional militia forces for potential service on the southern frontier.

In North Carolina Miller lent his support to the early efforts to establish a system of public education, helped improve trade and transportation, and sought to reform the penal code and judicial system. One of his appointees to the bench was instrumental in the organization of the North Carolina Supreme Court.

In 1825 Pres. John Quincy Adams appointed Miller a diplomatic agent to Guatemala. He died of yellow fever en route to assume his new post and was probably buried at sea.

Engraving of Stede Bonnet in Charles Johnson's *A General History of the Pyrates*, ca. 1725.

1789 The General Assembly Chartered UNC

On December 11, 1789, the General Assembly passed a bill chartering a state-supported university. The idea was not new. North Carolina's Constitution of 1776 directed the establishment of "one or more universities" to be supported by state funds so that education could be provided to citizens at an affordable rate.

Due to the Revolutionary War and the financial burdens that the state incurred as a result, the legislature was reluctant to approve a bill for a university. It was largely through the efforts of William R. Davie of Halifax that the University of North Carolina was chartered by the legislature in 1789.

A site in rural Orange County was selected for the university in late 1792. A group of Orange County farmers previously had donated funds and a parcel of 1,290 acres of land atop New Hope Chapel Hill, an area named for the Church of England chapel that stood there.

The University's first building, now known as Old East, served as both dormitory and classroom. It opened on January 15, 1795, and the first student, Hinton James, arrived from New Hanover County on February 12.

DEC 11

1790 Modern Novelist Discovered Farquard Campbell

On December 11, 1790, a state Senate resolution declared that Farquard Campbell's actions during the Revolutionary War were justifiable.

Campbell's early life remains a mystery, but it is known that he emigrated from Scotland by the 1750s. He rose to prominence in Cumberland County, first as a justice of the peace, then as a surveyor and a representative in the legislature. Campbellton, which later became Fayetteville, was named in his honor.

After the Battle of Moores Creek Bridge, Campbell was found guilty of aiding the British and was imprisoned for about two years. He reestablished himself politically and was thus forgiven.

The name Farquard Campbell might sound familiar to readers of Diana Gabaldon's *Outlander* series of books. Much of the fourth book, *Drums of Autumn*, takes place in eighteenth century North Carolina, and in that volume Campbell appears as a fairly significant character—a local justice of the peace and loyal friend of Jamie Fraser's aunt, Jocasta Innes. He is described in the novel as "the usual justice in this district."

Gabaldon paid considerable attention to the veracity of her portrayal of North Carolina in the 1700s, writing about a great many real and thinly-veiled characters from the state's history.

1924 The Duke Endowment: Enriching the Carolinas

On December 11, 1924, James B. Duke established the Duke Endowment with an initial gift of forty million dollars. The Endowment received an additional sixty-seven million dollars at Duke's death the following year.

Philanthropy was nothing new to the Duke Family. Washington Duke, James's father, and Benjamin, his brother, were both noted for their philanthropic work, which was supported with the proceeds from their tobacco and electric power businesses. The Endowment initially supported colleges, universities, hospitals, and orphanages in North and South Carolina, and the Methodist church in North Carolina.

Two especially noteworthy early programs of the Endowment were the construction of dozens of community hospitals in North Carolina, which established a national model for rural health care, and a "Summer Preacher Program" designed to offer Duke Divinity School students opportunities to serve and train in rural churches.

Today the Endowment is among the world's largest foundations. It continues to focus on helping people and strengthening communities in North Carolina and South Carolina by nurturing children, promoting health, educating minds, and enriching spirits. Since its inception the Endowment has awarded more than three billion dollars in grants, including nearly $1.5 billion to Duke University.

Farquard Campbell was one of the founders of Old Bluff Presbyterian Church in Wade, seen here in 2003.

James B. Duke with his daughter, Doris, in 1919.

1906 George Ladshaw, Accidental Hero to Kayakers

On December 12, 1906, George Ladshaw submitted a survey of the Green River basin in Henderson and Polk Counties, proposing dams and hydroelectric power plants along the waterway.

Recommendations in his report on the "Available Power and Cost of Development" would have destroyed the riverbed and natural flow of the Green River, which today is legendary among kayakers for its exciting slides and drops. Other parts of the river are popular for tubing, canoeing, and kayaking for beginners.

The most treacherous section of the Green, called the Narrows, consists of a series of Class V rapids with names such as "Go Left and Die," "Gorilla," and "Sunshine" that challenge even the most seasoned kayakers. Since 1996 Saluda has been home to "The Green Race," a world-class kayak race on the Narrows, attracting participants and thrill-seekers from around the globe.

Devotees of the Green River rapids have become aware of the so-called Ladshaw Plan, possibly because of an archival collection of documents related to speculation in lands digitized by UNC-Asheville. Today kayakers celebrate the great near-miss of having never known the precipitous rapids of the Green River by recognizing December 12 as Ladshaw Day.

1957 Food Lion Rooted in Salisbury

On December 12, 1957, the first Food Town—now known as Food Lion—opened in Salisbury. The chain began when brothers Ralph and Clifford Ketner teamed up with family friend Wilson Smith to leave Winn-Dixie and try their own hands in the grocery business.

The chain remained relatively small until 1968, when younger brother Ralph started what's now known within the company as "The Great Change." Ketner cut prices dramatically, selling many items at or below their wholesale cost, and marketed the brand with the "everyday low prices" concept that other chains like Wal-Mart were beginning to embrace at the time. Food Town grew dramatically during the 1960s and 1970s, increasing its sales fifty-fold and adding nearly one hundred stores during those two decades alone.

The brand changed its name from Food Town to Food Lion in 1983, after discovering another chain had the same name. The lion concept came from the Belgium-based Delhaize Group, which acquired the company in the 1970s.

Today Food Lion operates more than thirteen hundred stores with seventy-three thousand employees in eleven states throughout the South and Mid-Atlantic region.

1989 A House Fire That Benefitted Historic Preservation

On December 12, 1989, the circa 1751 Palmer-Marsh House at Historic Bath caught fire, but what might have been a tragedy turned out to be a win for preservationists.

The fire stripped off fifteen layers of exterior paint. The site took the opportunity to conduct an analysis, called chromo-chronology, of the historic paint on both the interior and exterior of the building. The analysis determined that the entire exterior of the house – siding, shutters, and doors – was originally painted Spanish brown. Spanish brown, or red ochre as it is sometimes called, is part of a large family of natural earth pigments whose color is produced from iron oxide (rust) or the mineral hematite. It was a very stable and inexpensive paint and the most commonly used color throughout the colonies during the eighteenth century.

Although the color may not appeal to modern aesthetics, the faithful re-creation of the original exterior paint scheme furthers efforts to achieve the most historically accurate interpretation of the state's historic buildings. Now a National Historic Landmark, the home reflects a more authentic visual picture. It reopened to the public in June 1993 and remains an important attraction at Historic Bath.

Palmer-Marsh House, ca. 2016.

1915 Soybean Oil Developed in Elizabeth City

On December 13, 1915, the Elizabeth City Oil and Fertilizer Company repurposed equipment to generate the nation's first commercially-processed soybean oil. The modified machine was originally designed to produce cottonseed oil and cotton by-products.

Originally from China, soybeans first came to America as ballast in sailing ships. Around 1870, farmers in northeastern North Carolina began growing them as livestock food and fertilizer. After boll weevils, a type of beetle, infested the South's cotton crops in the early 1900s, an increasing number of Tar Heel farmers turned to soybean production.

By 1915 the state had become the nation's top soybean producer. World War I sparked an interest in soybean oil for industrial products, and with cottonseed mills looking for ways to stay in business, soybean processing seemed to be a sensible solution. After the experiment in Elizabeth City proved successful, other cottonseed mills in North Carolina also began crushing soybeans.

Today North Carolina ranks seventeenth nationally in soybean production. Protein-rich soybeans have a multitude of uses. They are processed and used in both human and livestock food as nutritional enhancements. And soybean oil, while also found in foods, is an important ingredient in industrial products such as plastics, lubricants, and biofuels.

DEC 13

1951 Dressmaker Madame Hancock of Winston-Salem

On December 13, 1951, North Carolina dressmaker Molly McCoy Hancock died.

Born in 1863, McCoy grew up in Rockingham County with her five siblings. Her mother owned one of the first sewing machines in the area and wove her own cloth. Hancock learned how to be a seamstress by watching her mother work. She found the work so engaging that she ended up designing and making dresses for her sisters and classmates.

Eventually Hancock's passion took her to New York to study fashion. Later, she opened a sewing room in Reidsville in 1884, the same year she married Thomas Hancock. They had one child, a boy named for his father.

The couple moved to Winston-Salem, where she operated a custom dressmaking shop that she ran for sixty years, often traveling to New York to obtain fabrics and see the latest Parisian designs. By World War II Hancock employed forty seamstresses, who used her patterns to make wedding gowns, trousseaux, day and evening wear, smallclothes, christening gowns, and even shrouds.

Most knew her best as "Madame Hancock," a nickname coined by her husband. It was a title she earned for being considered a couturiere, a rare designation for an American, and an even rarer one for a North Carolinian.

1986 Ella Baker and the Student Nonviolent Coordinating Committee (SNCC)

On December 13, 1986, Ella Baker, civil rights leader and organizer of the Student Nonviolent Coordinating Committee (SNCC), died. Called "the mother of the civil rights movement" by at least one scholar, Baker culminated a life dedicated to civil rights work by organizing the meeting to establish SNCC at her alma mater, Shaw University, in April 1960.

Baker graduated from Shaw in 1927, moved to New York, and joined the Young Negroes Cooperative League in 1930 with the aim of developing black economic power through collective planning. In 1940 she began working for the National Association for the Advancement of Colored People (NAACP) as field secretary and eventually rose to director of branches.

Baker joined with Martin Luther King Jr. and others in 1957 to organize the Southern Christian Leadership Conference (SCLC); she was the only woman present. After the sit-ins in Greensboro, she organized the meeting at Shaw that established SNCC. She advocated that the nascent organization be student-directed and not under the umbrella of the SCLC. The members of SNCC were the "shock troops" of the civil rights movement, called "probably the most courageous and the most selfless" of the activists of the 1960s by John Hope Franklin.

Ella Baker, ca. 1940's.

1786 General Robert Howe, Revolutionary War Commander

On December 14, 1786, Robert Howe, a Continental army general, died on his way to Fayetteville to serve in the House of Commons.

Howe was born in 1732 in New Hanover County. He inherited a considerable fortune and owned several large plantations in the region. When Brunswick County formed, Howe was elected to the colonial assembly, a post he held for six terms. He also served as a militia officer and commanded Fort Johnston from 1769 to 1773.

During the War of the Regulation, Howe commanded the artillery at the Battle of Alamance. At the outbreak of the American Revolution, Howe served as a member of Tryon's Wilmington Committee of Safety and led the local militia that took control of Fort Johnston. In 1775 Howe was appointed colonel of the Second North Carolina Continental regiment. He was promoted to brigadier general in 1776. While he was serving in South Carolina, Howe's plantations were burned by British troops.

Howe was ultimately appointed commander of the Southern Department and was promoted to major general on October 20, 1777. He was the highest-ranking officer from North Carolina to serve in the American Revolution.

Gen. Robert Howe.

1862 First Battle of Kinston, 1862

On December 14, 1862, Union forces under the command of Gen. John G. Foster launched their second attack on Confederate Gen. Nathan G. "Shanks" Evans at the First Battle of Kinston.

Foster's men had approached Kinston the day before and came upon the Confederate defensive forces. After a heated exchange of fire, Evans withdrew to earthworks along Southwest Creek near the Neuse River and prepared for Foster's second attack. Evans positioned about two thousand North Carolina and South Carolina troops in a semicircle. Supported by heavy artillery fire, the Union troops broke through the Confederate left flank. Evans ordered a retreat to Kinston, which was eventually abandoned by the Confederate troops as they retreated towards Goldsboro.

The target of Foster's Raid, as it came to be known, was the Wilmington and Weldon Railroad bridge at Goldsboro, a prime strategic transit point in eastern North Carolina. Along the way Foster's men also attacked the construction site of the ironclad CSS *Neuse* at what is now Seven Springs. Foster's actions had minimal impact, and the Confederate forces in the area returned to business as usual upon the Union troops' return to New Bern.

Gen. John G. Foster.

1804 "Walton War" Between Georgia and North Carolina

On December 15, 1804, Buncombe County constable John Havner was killed, beginning what became known as the "Walton War."

Today it seems unlikely that a tract of land in Transylvania County would have been claimed as part of the State of Georgia, but that was the case in 1803, when Georgia laid claim to the territory and named it Walton County. Gov. James Turner of North Carolina actively defended the state's claim, leading to confusion for the eight hundred or so residents of the region.

The dispute was submitted to Congress, where a committee initially accepted Georgia's claim. Meanwhile lawlessness prevailed in the area. It was difficult for Buncombe County to assert authority over Georgians. Events came to a head late in 1804 when Waltonians killed the constable. The Buncombe County militia marched into Walton County, taking ten Walton officials prisoner.

On June 15, 1807, officials of the two states met at the Buncombe County Courthouse and set out to fix the boundary. They discovered that North Carolina's claim was accurate. The Georgia commissioners were "astonished and mortified." They relinquished claim to the territory the same year, and amnesty was granted to those responsible for the violence, but confusion reigned for some time.

1836 Emeline Pigott, Confederate Spy

On December 15, 1836, Confederate spy Emeline Jamison Pigott was born in Carteret County. Living on a farm on Calico Creek, near what is now Morehead City, she witnessed many of the hardships the Civil War brought on, when Confederate and, later, Union soldiers were encamped nearby.

Involved in the Confederate cause early in the war, Pigott became active in nursing as well as gathering supplies for the Confederacy after the death of Pvt. Montford Stokes MacRae at Gettysburg. Piggott had fallen in love with MacRae several years earlier. She organized fishermen to get information that she passed along to her contacts. She also distracted Union soldiers, enabling her brother to carry food to Confederates nearby, and she served as a courier, carrying in specially-made pockets under her hoop skirt food, medicine, and mail to designated locations for pickup.

Arrested on suspicion of spying, Pigott was imprisoned and taken to court repeatedly but was never brought to trial. While in prison, an attempt was made on her life, but even after her release she continued to aid the Confederacy, remaining true to the cause until her death in 1919.

1862 Foster's Raid, Part Two

On December 15, 1862, Federal and Confederate forces clashed at what's today known as Seven Springs but was then called Whitehall.

Part of Union general John G. Foster's raid from New Bern to Goldsboro in late 1862, a Federal contingent of three companies of cavalry and several pieces of artillery entered Whitehall hoping to capture or destroy the railroad bridge. They found the bridge burned by the Confederates to protect the ironclad CSS *Neuse*, which was being built on the other side of the river, where several regiments of Confederate troops under Brig. Gen. B. H. Robertson were stationed.

When the battle ended the next day, the dense woods along the bank had been cut down for a quarter of a mile back from the river by Federal artillery fire, and the construction materials for the *Neuse* were damaged or destroyed.

Federal causalities were heavy because Foster placed troops in exposed locations along the river bank, while the Confederate casualties were low since geographical restrictions on the river at the site of the conflict allowed only one regiment at a time to engage Union troops.

In recent years questions have arisen about the Whitehall battle, with speculation that many of the Union casualties were the result of friendly fire and that body counts were purposefully under-reported by the Federal government.

Emeline Pigott, ca. 1865.

1859 John A. Copeland Jr., Participant in John Brown's Raid

On December 16, 1859, John A. Copeland Jr. was executed for his participation in John Brown's raid on the United States Arsenal at Harpers Ferry, Virginia.

Copeland, a free mulatto, was born in Raleigh in 1834. In 1843 his family moved to Oberlin, Ohio and became involved with the abolitionist movement. In 1858 Copeland assisted in the rescue of a man who was arrested for being a fugitive slave and was arrested for his actions but never tried.

Remaining an ardent abolitionist, Copeland and another North Carolinian, Lewis Leary, joined with John Brown in Ohio in September 1859. When Brown attempted to cause a slave revolt by taking the arsenal in October 1859, Copeland, Leary, and another man were assigned the task of taking the Hall's Rifle Works at the arsenal. When surrounded, the three raiders attempted to flee across the Shenandoah River. Only Copeland survived, but he surrendered and was put on trial for murder and slave insurrection.

Upon his conviction Copeland was sentenced to death at the gallows in Charleston, Virginia. At his death Copeland reportedly said, "If I am dying for freedom, I could not die for a better cause – I had rather die than be a slave."

1870 The Light at Cape Hatteras

On December 16, 1870, the specially-designed Fresnel lens of the Cape Hatteras Lighthouse was lit to mark Diamond Shoals.

In 1794 Congress authorized the original ninety-foot sandstone tower, completed in 1802. By the 1850s complaints were voiced about the inadequacy of its light, and in 1861, during the Civil War, it was damaged by Union shelling. After the war top priority was given to constructing a new lighthouse. Upon completion the lighthouse, measuring 180 feet from the foundation to the light and 208 feet from the bottom to the top of the roof, was the world's tallest. It remains the tallest brick lighthouse in this country.

In 1935 shoreline erosion threatened the lighthouse, and it was abandoned. In its place a skeleton tower was built to the northwest above Buxton Woods. The Civilian Conservation Corps (CCC) helped stabilize the area, and on January 23, 1950, the 1870 tower was reactivated. In 2000 the National Park Service, working with a private contractor, moved the lighthouse one-half mile west to save it from the Atlantic Ocean. The lighthouse is open to the public on a seasonal basis.

1959 Three Sheets to the Wind: On Flight They're Dubious

On December 16, 1959, the Man Will Never Fly Memorial Society was formed in Kitty Hawk.

With a motto of "Birds Fly—Men Drink," the society continues to party each year from the afternoon of December 16 until 10:45 a. m. on December 17, the time at which the Wright brothers "allegedly" took their first flight. Society members are "dedicated to the principle that two Wrights made a wrong at Kitty Hawk."

Each year the society gives two anti-aviation awards to those who have done the most to deter the advance of aviation, the Orville Proxmire Award and the Aviation Hall of Infamy Award. The last four presidents of the United States, Chuck Yeager, and Snoopy are among the winners of the two awards.

According to members of the society, many of whom are pilots, the awards program serves to separate the cocktail hour from the serious drinking that follows. While the society does not oppose flight in winged creatures, it draws its line in the sand at flying machines. Its mission statement quotes a Dayton, Ohio newspaper editor as saying, "Man will never fly. And if he does, he will never come from Dayton."

The Cape Hatteras Lighthouse, painted with black and white spirals for recognition during the day, is the tallest brick light tower in the United States.

DEC 17

1776 Declaration of Rights: Milestone at Halifax, 1776

On December 17, 1776, the Fifth Provincial Congress at Halifax issued the North Carolina Declaration of Rights. Consisting of twenty-five articles, the document outlined the basic rights of citizens of the new state and became part of the state constitution, which was issued the following day.

The Declaration of Rights was the work of a twenty-eight-man committee chaired by the president of the congress, Richard Caswell, and it was modeled on English legal and political traditions. The first provision emphasized that all political power comes from and is vested in the people. Other articles guaranteed free and frequent elections; prohibited excessive bail, fines, and punishments; enshrined the right to a fair and speedy trial by jury; protected freedom of the press, assembly, and worship; ensured taxation by public consent only; established the right to bear arms in state defense; placed the military under civil control; and barred the creation of laws with retroactive penalties. Notably, at the time these rights applied to free people only, not to slaves.

In an ironic twist, the citizens of the state did not vote on either the Declaration of Rights or the new constitution. Instead, they went into effect on the authority of the Fifth Provincial Congress.

1894 John White, Vance's Envoy to England

On December 17, 1894, John White, who during the Civil War purchased supplies for North Carolina in England, died of a stroke.

Born in Scotland in 1814, White emigrated to Warrenton in 1828 to join his brother who was already living there. By the outbreak of the Civil War, he had become a prominent merchant.

A year into the war, Gov. Zebulon Vance commissioned White to secure military provisions in England. He secured contracts with the firm of Alexander Collie and Company for shipping supplies to North Carolina in exchange for bonds on cotton that would be shipped using blockader runners. A percentage of the supplies went to the Confederate government, while the rest went exclusively for the support of North Carolina's troops.

White returned to North Carolina in early 1864 but was later reappointed for a similar mission. Arriving in London near the end of the year, he was unable to reestablish contact with the North Carolina government before the end of the war and returned home in the summer of 1865.

Robert E. Lee and his daughter Agnes stayed with the Whites during the former general's visit to the state in April 1870.

1903 First Powered Flight

On December 17, 1903, Orville and Wilbur Wright made their first successful powered flight in a heavier-than-air craft.

Their story began in Dayton, Ohio, where the brothers owned and operated a bicycle store. Seasonal slumps in sales forced them to expand, and they decided to try designing a self-propelled aircraft. After six years of studying the principles of flight, the Wright brothers developed several prototypes, some being gliders and others self-propelled, and began looking for proving grounds along the East Coast.

Their search ultimately led them to Dare County's Kill Devil Hills, where strong winds provided lift and sandy grounds increased chances of a safe landing. After months of setbacks and unsuccessful attempts, at 10:53 on the morning of December 17, the Wright Flyer, under its own power, defied gravity for twelve seconds, clearing a distance of one hundred feet.

Twenty-nine years later, in 1932, the federal government erected a monument at Kill Devil Hills, where the historic flight took place. Orville Wright was the guest of honor at the ceremony.

First powered, controlled, sustained flight at Kill Devil Hills, N.C. Orville Wright at the controls of the machine, lying prone on the lower wing. Wilbur Wright, running alongside to balance the machine, just released his hold on the forward upright of the right wing.

Form No. 168.

THE WESTERN UNION TELEGRAPH COMPANY.

INCORPORATED

23,000 OFFICES IN AMERICA. CABLE SERVICE TO ALL THE WORLD.

This Company TRANSMITS and DELIVERS messages only on conditions limiting its liability, which have been assented to by the sender of the following message. Errors can be guarded against only by repeating a message back to the sending station for comparison, and the Company will not hold itself liable for errors or delays in transmission or delivery of Unrepeated Messages, beyond the amount of tolls paid thereon, nor in any case where the claim is not presented in writing within sixty days after the message is filed with the Company for transmission.

This is an UNREPEATED MESSAGE, and is delivered by request of the sender, under the conditions named above.

ROBERT C. CLOWRY, President and General Manager.

170

RECEIVED at

176 C KA CS 33 Paid. Via Norfolk Va

Kitty Hawk N C Dec 17

Bishop M Wright

7 Hawthorne St

success four flights thursday morning all against twenty one mile wind started from Level with engine power alone average speed through air thirty one miles longest 57 seconds inform Press home Christmas .

Orevelle Wright 525P

1742 John Wright Stanly of New Bern, Debtor to Financier

On December 18, 1742, John Wright Stanly was born.

As a young man living in Jamaica, Stanly partnered with shipping merchants to export cargo from the Caribbean to the American colonies. One partnership proved disastrous; a Philadelphia merchant accused Stanly of owing him money, and Stanly was sent to debtor's prison there in 1768.

Eventually able to clear his name, Stanly left Philadelphia for South Carolina in 1772. While en route to Charleston, a shipboard friendship with a North Carolina resident and a storm off Cape Hatteras led Stanly to New Bern, where he discovered a town full of opportunity.

In New Bern Stanly became a successful ship owner and merchant. He was also a privateer for the Patriot cause during the Revolution, loaning Gen. Nathanael Greene substantial sums for his North Carolina campaign. After the war Stanly invested in his adopted town's future, becoming the New Bern Academy's first president. He died in 1789 of yellow fever.

Today his handsome late Georgian-style residence is part of Tryon Palace Historic Sites and Gardens.

1767 "Cherokee Clay" and Wedgwood Pottery

On December 18, 1767, an agent of England's Wedgwood Potteries finished extracting several tons of fine white clay from the mountains of North Carolina.

By the 1740s people in England and in the American colonies knew of the valuable white clay deposits in the Cherokee region of the North Carolina mountains. A British patent was filed around 1744 "for the production of porcelain from an earthy mixture, produced by the Cherokee Nation in America."

With increasing interest in creating porcelain in England and the colonies, Josiah Wedgwood launched efforts to secure what was called Cherokee Clay. He hired an agent, Thomas Griffiths, to travel to America to conduct the business. Griffiths went to the settlement of Ayoree in the Cherokee Middle Towns (Iotla in present Macon County) to negotiate an arrangement for the purchase of five to six tons of Cherokee Clay. The clay was carried down the mountains by pack horses. Griffiths delivered the Cherokee Clay to Josiah Wedgwood in April 1768.

Because of the expenses incurred Wedgwood never pursued additional shipments of the clay. His supply lasted fifteen years. In 1783 he wrote that Cherokee Clay was the basis of his newly manufactured biscuit porcelain.

The light blue, green, navy and white decorated pieces are known as Jasper Ware. The black figural lion is known as Black Basalt.

1777 William Polk at Valley Forge

On December 19, 1777, the Continental Army, including the North Carolina Brigade, entered winter encampment at Valley Forge, Pennsylvania.

Among the North Carolinians was nineteen-year-old Maj. William Polk. He had been shot through the mouth while shouting orders at Germantown in October—the ball knocked out teeth and shattered his jaw. So Polk was recuperating for much of the harsh winter at Valley Forge. He served with distinction in the Continental Line, having seen action at some of the Revolution's fiercest battles including Brandywine, Camden, Cowan's Ford, Cowpens, and Eutaw Springs. After the Guilford Courthouse battle he was promoted from major to lieutenant colonel and henceforth known as "Colonel Polk."

With the establishment of the State Bank in 1810, Polk was elected its first president, serving in that position from 1810 to 1819. In 1821 he spoke at the dedication of the Canova statue at the State Capitol. Four years later he welcomed Lafayette, with whom he had fought at Brandywine, to Raleigh and breakfasted with him at his North Street home.

At his death Polk was the last surviving field officer of the North Carolina Line.

DEC 19

1929 Depression-Era Gubernatorial Imperative: "Live at Home"

On December 19, 1929, Gov. O. Max Gardner sponsored a "Live at Home" dinner. The purpose of the special meal, the signature event of Live at Home Week, was to "emphasize North Carolina products and industries."

Only North Carolina grown and processed products, donated by companies and farmers in the state, were served. Celery came from Graham, flour from Shelby, and a three-pound lemon from a Pollocksville farm was used to make lemon pies. Klondike Farm in Elkin provided Guernsey milk in capped bottles packed in ice. The 350 guests for the event represented the North Carolina Press Association and Council of State.

The purpose of Governor Gardner's Live at Home Program was to promote the agricultural self-sufficiency of the state. His partners in the endeavor were N.C. State University, the N.C. Department of Agriculture, and the N.C. Cooperative Extension.

The dinner was a resounding success, as it encouraged many newspaper editors to publish Extension materials and promote the program. The program itself was successful enough that farmers came closer to satisfying the state's food needs in 1929 than in any other year since World War I.

Frame from a 1941 exhibit about Live at Home farming.

1820 Bewitched in Tennessee

On December 20, 1820, Tennessee farmer and Edgecombe County native John Bell died at his home in Robertson County, Tennessee. Decades later Bell's demise was attributed to the "Bell Witch," a poltergeist that allegedly tormented the family between 1817 and 1821.

There are no contemporary sources for the legend. The earliest known mention was published in an 1886 history of Tennessee. The first full treatment was written in 1894 by newspaper publisher Martin Van Buren Ingram, supposedly based on a reminiscence in the diary of an adult son of Bell, who was a child at the time of the purported events. The original copy of the diary has never surfaced. All subsequent accounts derive from or elaborate on Ingram's book.

According to Ingram an invisible entity with a female persona physically and verbally harassed members of the Bell family, especially John and his daughter Betty. The witch supposedly poisoned Bell with a mysterious potion. Various theories for the witch's origin and motives rely on Ingram's "evidence" and often contradict the historical record.

The Bell Witch story partially inspired the film *The Blair Witch Project*. A number of recent films and television shows have been made about the Bell Witch legend itself.

1820 Washington Duke Born

On December 20, 1820, Washington Duke, patriarch of the Duke tobacco empire, was born on a farm in Orange County.

In 1852 Duke built a two-story frame house for his family on a three-hundred-acre farm on the outskirts of what is now Durham. The house was the birthplace of Duke's only daughter, Mary Elizabeth, and his sons James Buchanan Duke and Benjamin Newton Duke. The family forever changed industry, education, and philanthropy in North Carolina.

After the Civil War Washington Duke and his sons began to process brightleaf tobacco into a form for smoking. They labeled the product "Pro Bono Publico" (For Public Good). Union soldiers who had smoked the brightleaf tobacco while in the South began ordering the Duke tobacco.

In 1884 the Duke family acquired the Bonsack cigarette-processing machine, allowing W. Duke, Sons and Company to become one of the leading cigarette producers in the country. In 1890 the elder son, James, arranged for the Duke company to merge with four competitors and become the American Tobacco Company. The Duke family accumulated great wealth, much of which they used for worthy projects, including transforming Trinity College into Duke University.

1900 Fire at Buies Creek, 1900

On December 20, 1900, a fire at Buies Creek Academy consumed every wooden campus building except a large tabernacle.

The academy was the forerunner of Campbell University. It was founded as a Baptist institution of higher learning in 1887 by James Archibald Campbell. In its first year the academy had an enrollment of only twenty-seven. By 1898 the academy had three buildings and more than sixty students.

Campus legend holds that the origin of the university's rather unusual mascot, the Fighting Camel, can be traced to the fire. When local entrepreneur Zachary Taylor Kivett found Campbell moping after the blaze, he asked, "Why are you in bed? I thought Campbells had humps on them." Kivett pledged on the spot to build a new brick building, which was completed in 1903 and was named for him. It is the oldest building on the present campus.

In 1926 the school became a junior college, and its name was changed to Campbell College in honor of its founder. Thirty-five years later the school was promoted to a senior college and in 1979 received its university status. Three years before officially becoming a university, the college opened Campbell School of Law.

1942 New River to Camp Lejeune

On December 20, 1942, Marine Barracks New River was renamed Camp Lejeune in honor of the thirteenth Commandant and Commanding General of the Second Army Division in World War I, Maj. Gen. John A. Lejeune.

The Camp Lejeune story began in 1940. World War II had been raging in Europe for more than a year, and military planners were preparing forces for America's eminent entry into the fight. An East Coast amphibious training facility was needed, and 110,000 acres were purchased in North Carolina. Close to ports at Wilmington and Morehead City, Lejeune was a logistical gem. When planners added in the remote pine forests and miles of beach, the value of Camp Lejeune as a home training base for Marines was unbeatable. Congress authorized more than fourteen million dollars for construction of the base in April 1941, and in May the base's first commander was appointed.

Camp Lejeune's value to the Corps in World War II was evident through the contributions of Marines trained or based there. Billed as the "Home of Expeditionary Forces in Readiness," Camp Lejeune is the largest Marine base on the East Coast.

U.S. Marines at Camp Lejeune leap from towers, 1943.

War dogs at Camp Lejeune, 1943.

1756 Fort Dobbs Gets an Inspection

1918 Editor Walter Hines Page, Ambassador to Great Britain

2000 Harper House in Hickory an Architectural Gem

DEC 21

On December 21, 1756, Commissioners Richard Caswell and Francis Brown inspected the recently completed Fort Dobbs. Their report to the colony's assembly described "a good and Substantial Building" that was fifty-three feet by forty feet, with oak pillars supporting the structure, which rose almost twenty-five feet. Soldiers were able to simultaneously fire up to one hundred muskets from the walls of the fort, making Fort Dobbs an imposing headquarters on the Carolina frontier.

Western expansion in North Carolina forced England to protect colonists in the wilderness. To that end the provincial assembly appropriated one thousand pounds in March 1756 for the construction of a defensive fortress. Gov. Arthur Dobbs chose a location in present-day Iredell County and charged Col. Hugh Waddell and his frontier company of fifty men with protecting against the encroaching French both the fort and the colonists' trading rights with Indians. It was the only permanent provincial frontier fort in the colony of North Carolina.

Fort Dobbs, now one of North Carolina's State Historic Sites, is the only one dedicated to the French and Indian War (1754–1763), the North American chapter of the broader Seven Years War between England and France.

On December 21, 1918, journalist and diplomat Walter Hines Page died in Pinehurst.

Born in 1855 in what's now Cary, Page was drawn to journalism and in 1883 founded the *State Chronicle* newspaper in Raleigh with financial backing from his father, Frank Page, who by then had moved to Moore County, where he prospered in the lumber industry. Active in the educational realm, the younger Page was among the founders of the Watauga Club, an organization that advocated for the economic and social betterment of North Carolina and helped found what's now North Carolina State University.

In 1885 Page turned the *Chronicle* over to Josephus Daniels and moved to New York, shifting from daily journalism to the editorship of *The Atlantic Monthly*. In 1899 he established a publishing firm with Frank Doubleday. An articulate public speaker, Page was a popular orator, who primarily focused on education, politics, and the new South.

Outspoken in his promotion of Woodrow Wilson for president in 1912, Page was tapped to serve as the twenty-eighth president's ambassador to Great Britain. After the outbreak of World War I, he was a strong supporter of the Allied side and frequently encouraged the Wilson administration to intercede.

Due to failing health, Page returned to North Carolina in the fall of 1918. He was buried at Old Bethesda Cemetery in Aberdeen.

On December 21, 2000, descendants of the Harper family arranged for the acquisition of the 1887 Queen Anne-style Shuler-Harper House in Hickory by the Catawba County Historical Association in order to ensure its future preservation and to serve as a museum and cultural center for the community. Following a successful fundraising effort, the house was fully restored. The restoration highlighted its picturesque and highly decorative exterior design and exquisite interior finishes.

The house was built for local banker David Webster Shuler and would ultimately be used by six other families, including three generations of the Harper family. Owner of the Harper Motor Company, Finley Gwyn Harper Sr. purchased the house in 1923, and through the years family members valued and preserved the residence's impressive architectural design.

The Shuler-Harper House stands out as one of the state's finest Queen Anne-style houses with its fanciful exterior walls, round corner tower, multi-gabled roofline, and inviting wraparound porches. The interior features latticework archways, richly hand-worked mantels, paneled wainscoting, stained glass, parquet floors, and an ornate staircase.

"Fort Dobbs, 1756"; painting by Robert Steele.

The Shuler-Harper House photo by Bill Garrett.

1789 — Six Western Counties Ceded

On December 22, 1789, North Carolina formally ceded six western counties to the Continental Congress, leading to the eventual establishment of the new state of Tennessee.

Settlement of the western frontiers of North Carolina and Virginia first began in the late 1700s. The North Carolina legislature authorized the creation of six new counties in the region between 1779 and 1784 as population there grew and expressed a desire for self-governance.

In 1784 a new state was organized and named after Benjamin Franklin. The new state was never formally admitted to the union, and the state's five-year history was largely marked by strained relations with local Native Americans, North Carolina leaders, and the Continental Congress.

The Franklin legislature met for the last time in 1788. The western lands were folded back into the jurisdiction of North Carolina the following year, only to be ceded to the Continental Congress shortly thereafter. Ultimately, Tennessee was admitted to the union in 1796.

1859 — An Arrest Over Anti-Slavery Materials

On December 22, 1859, the sheriff of Guilford County arrested Daniel Worth for circulating literature that denounced slavery.

Born near Greensboro in 1795, Worth was likely educated in a school led by Levi Coffin, the reputed "conductor" of the Underground Railroad. Like many other Quakers in the region, Worth moved to the Midwest, settling in Indiana in 1823. He returned to North Carolina as a missionary in 1857 and preached across the Piedmont, distributing antislavery materials at public gatherings. Newspapers denounced him and called for his arrest.

Worth's offense was punishable by one year in prison and, at the discretion of the court, a whipping. He was tried and convicted in the spring of 1860 in Asheboro. He also lost upon appeal in Greensboro. Released on a three-thousand-dollar bond, he jumped bail and made his way to New York, where in May he denounced North Carolina as a "den of slavery."

He made the rounds in abolitionist circles, including a stop at Henry Ward Beecher's church, where the famed minister, brother of Harriet Beecher Stowe, proclaimed himself unworthy to unfasten Worth's shoes. Worth soon returned to Indiana, where he died in 1862.

1965 — Ruth Cannon, Preservationist

On December 22, 1965, Ruth Cannon died, bringing an end to a life of extraordinary dedication to preservation and to North Carolina history.

Born Ruth Coltrane into a banker's family in Cabarrus County, she married Charles Cannon, longtime president of Cannon Mills Company in Kannapolis. A history major at Greensboro College, she was a stalwart member of heritage groups, including the Colonial Dames and the Daughters of the American Revolution.

Cannon's true mark came about independently of those organizations. In 1939 she was among the founders of the North Carolina Society for the Preservation of Antiquities, a group that continues to exist today under the name Preservation North Carolina. That same year she headed the book committee for the Garden Clubs of North Carolina and began an initiative that resulted in the pioneering publication, *Old Homes and Gardens of North Carolina*. She presented a copy to Gov. Clyde Hoey late in 1939.

Cannon was instrumental in organizing the restoration of Tryon Palace and Historic Bath, and she helped to found the Elizabethan Gardens in Manteo. The Cannon Cup, which she established and is named for her husband, has been given each year since 1948 for distinguished work in historical research, preservation, and restoration.

Ruth Cannon helped establish The Elizabethan Gardens, in Manteo.

DEC 23

1794 Bald Head Island Lighthouse Lit

On December 23, 1794, the Bald Head Island Lighthouse was lit for the first time. The lighthouse, planning for which began in 1783, was the first one authorized in North Carolina (the second was Ocracoke for which plans began a year later). In 1789 Benjamin Smith, who recently had acquired the island, promised the state ten acres for use as a site for a lighthouse.

Congress appropriated funds for the lighthouse in 1792. The state legislature levied a tax to help fund the beacon. Around 1812 the lighthouse was damaged beyond repair due to the effects of soil erosion. Congress appropriated fifteen thousand dollars for a replacement. Daniel Way accepted the contract in July 1816 and finished the new lighthouse the following year. Use of "Old Baldy," as it is known, was discontinued in 1835.

The oldest lighthouse on the North Carolina coast, it was placed on the National Register of Historic Places in 1975. "Old Baldy" is distinctive for its eight-sided design. Modern restoration efforts have returned the lighthouse to its nineteenth century appearance. A reproduction of the 1850s keeper's cottage stands alongside the sentinel.

1848 Dorothea Dix Hospital Authorized

On December 23, 1848, the General Assembly approved the construction of an "Insane Hospital of North Carolina."

The approval was the result of intense lobbying by Dorothea Dix, noted advocate for the mentally ill.

A 182-acre site was chosen in southwest Raleigh, and in 1853 Dr. Edmund Strudwick of Hillsborough became the first physician and superintendent of the facility. Construction was not completed until 1856. The building's first two wings accommodated 274 patients. The hospital was renamed "Dix Hill" after Dorothea Dix's grandfather, Dr. Elijah Dix, because Dix refused to accept the honor.

The first patient arrived at Dix Hill in February 1856 and was diagnosed with "suicidal mania." By the beginning of the Civil War in 1861, Dix Hill had 193 patients on the premises. In April 1865 Union troops camped on the grounds.

By the early 1900s the public had begun to accept mental illness as a disease and pressured the state legislature to increase the capacity of all hospitals within the state. As a result, two branch facilities were opened in Morganton and Goldsboro. In August 2012 the hospital, by then called Dorothea Dix Hospital, moved its last patients to Central Regional Hospital in Granville County.

1929 Inventor and Ax Man John Council of Bladen County

On December 23, 1929, inventor and machinist John P. Council died.

A native of Bladen County, Council showed an interest in all things mechanical from an early age. He translated that interest into the Council Tool Company in 1884 after trying his hand at several other enterprises and studying the turpentine industry in Georgia.

The company steadily grew, moving from a small blacksmith shop near his home to Lake Waccamaw in 1902, where a local railroad line established a stop specifically to transport his goods. Council tirelessly worked to improve his product, trying out a variety of materials, but continued to focus on tools specific to the turpentine industry. His company also stood out for its focus on employing only local people and making them profit participants in the business.

By 1910 Council Tool controlled ninety percent of the trade in turpentine-specific tools. To this day it is owned by the Council family and focuses on the manufacture of tools for forestry and fighting fires.

In 2008 an ax made by Council Tools was featured on the History Channel's *Modern Marvels* episode about the history of the ax.

1992 Sedaris's Elf Tale Instant Hit for NPR

On December 23, 1992, David Sedaris made his debut on *Morning Edition* on National Public Radio, reading his now-famous essay "The Santaland Diaries." *Morning Edition* received an unprecedented number of requests for tapes of the day's program.

Billed as an "autobiographical confession of a penniless, gay, would-be soap opera writer" the eight-minute comic monologue recounts Sedaris's time working as Crumpet the Elf at Macy's Department Store at Herald Square in New York City. Rich with acerbic wit and cynicism and read in "the blasé tone of someone reading a train schedule," the "Diaries" launched his career as a writer and humorist.

Sedaris was discovered in Chicago, where he moved from North Carolina at age twenty-seven. Ira Glass, then working at WBEZ, heard him reading excerpts of his diaries to audiences and invited him to appear on Glass's artsy radio show, *The Wild Room*.

"The Santaland Diaries" was later published in the collections *Barrel Fever* (1994) and *Holidays on Ice* (1997). The essay, now a holiday classic, is read every December 23rd on "Morning Edition."

Sedaris won the Thurber Prize for American Humor in 2001 and continues to write essays for publication and for his devoted NPR audience.

Dorothea Dix Hospital Staff (*left to right*): Dr. George L. Kirby, Mrs. Whitaker, W. R. Crawford, Dr. Faison, and Dr. McGeachey, 1896.

Bald Head Island lighthouse, 1970.

1902 R. A. Fessenden and the Beginnings of Radio

On December 24, 1902, Reginald Fessenden, who had previously engaged in experiments on the Outer Banks, made the first intentional wireless radio broadcast, playing his violin and reading a passage from the Bible.

Fessenden came to North Carolina in 1900 under the auspices of the United States Weather Bureau to conduct experiments in wireless telegraphy on Roanoke Island. His two years' work attracted considerable publicity. While in North Carolina, he transmitted the first varying musical notes. The 1902 transmissions were said to have been "very loud and plain" and as easy to understand as hearing sounds over an ordinary telephone. Relayed from Buxton, the broadcasts were received forty-eight miles north on Roanoke Island. The experiment's station at Buxton no longer stands, but the foundations for a tower used by Fessenden do remain.

A prolific inventor, Fessenden patented more than five hundred ideas, mostly in the field of radio. He is recognized as the originator of the continuous wave principle in wireless transmission.

Fessenden died in 1932. The inventor's papers, an enormous and varied collection spanning much of his working life, are housed in the State Archives of North Carolina.

1937 Mary Van Landingham, Remembered for Humility Quip

On December 24, 1937, writer and cultural leader Mary Van Landingham died in Charlotte.

Born in Charlotte in 1852 to a family with deep roots in the area, Van Landingham made a name for herself by becoming active in several civic and cultural organizations, including the Daughters of the American Revolution, North Carolina Society of the Colonial Dames, and North Carolina Folklore Society. The first woman to be invited to speak to the North Carolina Literary and Historical Association and the Mecklenburg Historical Society, she is perhaps best remembered for a speech she gave to the latter group in March 1900.

During that speech she attributed North Carolina's relatively unimpressive literary output to the fact that the state was a "Vale of Humility between Two Mountains of Conceit," those "mountains of conceit" being the states of Virginia and South Carolina. Van Landingham's comments were widely reported in the press and became part of the popular lexicon used to describe North Carolina's cultural scene.

Though an outspoken commentator on North Carolina arts and culture, Van Landingham was a fairly successful writer in her own right. Throughout her life she wrote newspaper articles on current events and historical topics, and in 1922, she published a book of essays, articles, and speeches.

1960 "Aunt Samantha" Bumgarner, Traditional Musician

On December 24, 1960, fiddle and banjo player and old-time ballad singer Sarah Samantha Biddix Bumgarner died.

Born in Tennessee in 1878, Bumgarner grew up in Dillsboro in Jackson County. Her father was the well-known fiddle player Has Biddix, and when he was not around, Samantha used his fiddle to teach herself how to play. She also taught herself how to play the banjo.

Bumgarner and Eva Smathers Davis from Sylva made history when they recorded a number of songs for Columbia Records in 1924, including "Shout Lou," "Fly Around My Pretty Lil' Miss," and "Cindy in the Meadow." They are credited as the first women to record country music.

Known as "Aunt Samantha," Bumgarner played at banjo competitions in the Appalachian region. For more than thirty years, she performed at Bascom Lamar Lunsford's annual Mountain Dance and Folk Festival in Asheville. This kept her in the public eye, and she gained a loyal following. Her career bridged the traditional Appalachian music ways with the rise of modern country music.

In 1939 Bumgarner was among a select group of mountain musicians who played at the White House for Franklin and Eleanor Roosevelt and King George VI and Queen Elizabeth of England.

Fessenden's wireless station at Cape Hatteras.

Samantha Bumgarner, 1937.

DEC 25

1812 State Library of North Carolina is Founded

On December 25, 1812, the North Carolina General Assembly enacted the law that created what is now the State Library of North Carolina, to be administered by the Secretary of State. The law called for the collection and safekeeping of books, documents, laws, acts, and journals for the use of General Assembly members, state agency heads, and Supreme Court justices.

In 1831 most of the collection was destroyed in the State Capitol fire. The new State Library, which included a copy of John Lawson's *New Voyage to Carolina* donated by former president James Madison, moved into the new State Capitol in 1840 and had a fulltime librarian by 1843.

In time it became a lending library for the entire state and participated in national and international book exchanges to enlarge the collection. State Librarian Carrie Broughton was the first female head of a state agency in North Carolina. She expanded the collection, including the genealogy section, which is now recognized as one of the richest in the Southeast.

Still vital after two hundred years, the State Library is the official repository for North Carolina government publications; provides information about North Carolina history, culture and demographics; and is a nationally recognized leader in digital initiatives.

1929 Alton Stewart and "Man's Conquest of the Air"

On December 25, 1929, Alton Stewart, who popularized flying in North Carolina, died in a plane crash. Stewart had been at the helm of a flight that originated in Raleigh and stopped in Angier to pick up passengers. As he approached the fairgrounds in Dunn, he made a steep climb before plunging into the ground.

Stewart's interest in flying came from his time at Camp Bragg's Pope Field during World War I. After the war, he began flying regularly and beginning in 1924 worked with Curtiss-Wright Flying Service in Raleigh. He often gave public exhibitions and became one of the best-known pilots in the state. He helped plan airfields in Goldsboro, Marion, Rocky Mount, Gastonia, and elsewhere across North Carolina.

Stewart enjoyed exposing average folks to the miracle of flight. For as little as three dollars, he offered cockpit seats to passengers so they could have the thrill of racing through the clouds. Press accounts of the period give him considerable credit for popularizing aviation in the state.

Ben Dixon McNeill of the *News and Observer* flew with Stewart and documented his exploits. The newspaper paid tribute to Stewart's life with an editorial page drawing captioned, "He died in man's conquest of the air."

1929 Lawson Family Tragedy

On December 25, 1929, Charlie Lawson murdered his wife and six of their seven children before killing himself in Stokes County.

The tragedy occurred on their farm, just days after Lawson had taken the whole family into town, bought them new clothes, and had them sit for a studio portrait. The eerie photograph, an unusual expense for a poor family of that era, indicates that he likely considered the crime for some time before carrying it out. His motive remains a mystery.

Lawson sent his sixteen-year-old son off on an errand before going to the tobacco barn, where he shot and bludgeoned his two middle daughters, Carrie and Maybell. He then went to the house and killed the remaining members of his family, including four-month-old Mary Lou. He positioned the bodies by putting rocks under their heads and crossing their arms. Afterwards he hid out in the woods, apparently pacing around a tree while neighbors and police gathered at the house. All there heard the gunshot when Lawson took his own life.

The sole survivor of the tragedy, James Arthur Lawson, later married and had children before dying in an automobile accident in 1945.

The murders inspired a number of songs and stories, including a 1956 folk ballad recorded by the Stanley Brothers.

1944 Flying Ace George Preddy, Christmas Casualty

On December 25, 1944, Greensboro native George E. Preddy Jr., the top P-51 Mustang ace during World War II, was shot down by friendly ground fire.

Preddy was a barnstormer pilot before the war. He tried three times to become a naval pilot but was rejected because of health problems. The Army Air Corps accepted Preddy, placing him on a waiting list for a cadet class. In 1940 he joined the National Guard, and he received his wings in December 1941.

In July 1942 Preddy was involved in a midair collision during training. Following a three-month recovery, he returned to the United States and was eventually assigned to the 487th Fighter Squadron, which was sent to Great Britain. He shot down his first plane in December 1943.

In April 1944 his squadron received the P-51D Mustang, and Preddy became the 487th's temporary commander. He downed six planes on a single day in August of the same year, earning a Distinguished Service Cross, the nation's second highest award, in the process.

Preddy was shot down during the Battle of the Bulge while flying in his plane, the *Cripes A'Mighty*, in pursuit of a German plane. He is buried at the Lorraine American Cemetery in France

Alton Stewart plane crash, ca. 1929.

George Preddy after a mission in which it was claimed that he destroyed four German fighters.

1919 Confederate General, Postbellum Politician William R. Cox

On December 26, 1919, Civil War soldier, planter, and politician William Ruffin Cox died in Richmond, Virginia.

Born in Scotland Neck in 1832, Cox was raised and educated in Nashville, Tennessee. In 1857 he returned to North Carolina, where he owned a large plantation in Edgecombe County and established a law practice in Raleigh.

During the Civil War Cox was successively major, lieutenant colonel, and colonel of the Second Regiment North Carolina State Troops. In 1864 he was promoted to temporary brigadier general. Cox's Brigade was credited in postwar North Carolina lore as having fired the last shots by a unit of the Army of Northern Virginia at Appomattox.

After the war Cox became active in politics. As chairman of the State Democratic Executive Committee in the mid-1870s, he played a major role in the downfall of Reconstruction in North Carolina. He was subsequently appointed a Superior Court judge. From 1881 to 1887, Cox represented several Piedmont counties in Congress, where he was a supporter of civil service reform. From 1893 until 1900, Cox was secretary for the United States Senate. He was also a prominent speaker and writer on Confederate topics.

Cox is buried in Raleigh's Oakwood Cemetery.

1959 Burnham Colburn of Asheville and Mineralogy

On December 26, 1959, businessman and amateur geologist Burnham Colburn died in Asheville.

A native of Michigan, Colburn after arriving in North Carolina, helped to organize the Biltmore Estate Company, which sought to help local youths achieve independence by teaching them traditional crafts to sell for the economic benefit of the region. Before the end of his career, he was also heavily involved in North Carolina's banking industry.

Colburn was a man of many hobbies. A meticulous genealogist, he was a descendant of Mayflower settler Myles Standish and an active member of the Society of Mayflower Descendants. He was also interested in archaeology, helping to found the North Carolina Archaeological Society, but he is best remembered today for his lifelong interest in geology.

Geology was actually what brought Colburn to North Carolina, since he wanted to be closer to the rich mineral deposits found in the mountains. He was instrumental in founding the Southern Appalachian Mineral Society (SAMS), and it was that organization that inherited most of Colburn's vast personal collection of minerals upon his death.

In 1960 SAMS combined Coburn's collection with those of several other members to open the Colburn Earth Science Museum. The museum continues to operate in downtown Asheville to this day.

1985 Junior Johnson Pardoned by Ronald Reagan

On December 26, 1985, Robert Glen "Junior" Johnson received a full and unconditional pardon from Pres. Ronald Reagan for his 1956 conviction in federal court for moonshining.

Young Johnson was caught firing up his father's still and became entangled in a barbed wire fence while trying to escape. The conviction put Johnson on a forced eleven-month, three-day hiatus from his other career as a rising NASCAR star.

Johnson, like many early NASCAR drivers, got his first high-speed driving experience in a souped-up automobile loaded with illegal liquor. He was a natural as a driver and always made it a point of pride that the revenuers never caught him on the highway. He parlayed his experience on the back roads of North Carolina into one of the most successful careers in NASCAR history.

When Johnson retired as a driver in 1966, he became one of the most successful crew chiefs and owners in the sport's history. He was also a thriving and respected businessman in Wilkes County, having made lucrative investments in real estate, livestock, and meat processing.

Junior Johnson was in the first group of five inductees into the NASCAR Hall of Fame in 2010.

Junior Johnson with his car at the North Carolina Museum of History, 2006.

DEC 27

1752 Survey for a Moravian Settlement Began

On December 27, 1752, the survey for a Moravian settlement began in what is now Clemmons. Bishop August Spangenberg led the frontier expedition that selected the land that became known as the Wachovia tract.

The original survey contained only about seventy-three thousand acres, so five additional parcels were surveyed, bringing the total to 98,985 acres. Spangenberg judged the tract to be about fifty percent good land, twenty-five percent medium, and twenty-five percent poor. He was enthusiastic about the numerous springs and creeks and the promise of potential sites for mills. He was satisfied that they had identified "the best land yet vacant" in the colony.

A settlement in North Carolina offered Moravians the prospect of serving their neighbors, establishing "a town where the Moravian ideals of Christian living might be practically realized," and teaching Indians about the Gospel.

Spangenberg selected the name Wachau for the settlement in honor of Moravian leader Count Nicholas Ludwig von Zinzendorf, whose ancestral estate in Austria bore the name. In North Carolina the Latin form of the name, Wachovia, prevailed.

Today the original Wachovia tract encompasses much of the city of Winston-Salem. Old Salem Museums and Gardens preserves and interprets the colonial town of Salem.

1857 Henry Plummer Cheatham, Advocate for Equality

On December 27, 1857, Republican congressman, educator, and conservative and diplomatic advocate for racial equality Henry Plummer Cheatham was born into slavery near Henderson.

Cheatham graduated from Shaw University in 1882 after being educated at a common school for blacks in Granville County and went on to help found the North Carolina Orphanage for the Colored Race at Oxford. He then returned to Shaw for graduate school and served briefly as principal of the State Normal School in Plymouth, before moving into a nearly twenty-year career in government and politics in the late 1880s.

Despite increasing Jim Crow legislation and disfranchisement of blacks in the 1880s, Cheatham defeated white candidate Furnifold Simmons in 1888 to be elected to the U.S. House of Representatives, becoming the only black member of Congress from 1889 to 1893. After failing to win re-election in 1894, he was appointed by Pres. William McKinley as Recorder of Deeds for the District of Columbia in 1897 and served there until 1901.

He then returned to North Carolina to finish out his career, serving as a director of the orphanage in Oxford until his death in 1935. He also served as a delegate to the Republican State Convention of 1892 and the Republican National Conventions of 1892 and 1900.

1927 Bath to Broadway: Edna Ferber and "Show Boat"

On December 27, 1927, the musical *Show Boat* premiered on Broadway at the Ziegfeld Theatre in New York City. Composer Jerome Kern and lyricist Oscar Hammerstein II adapted Edna Ferber's 1926 novel to the stage.

Show Boat was the first dramatic musical on Broadway, featuring a strong plot and incorporating lyrics into the staging. Its classic songs like "Ole' Man River,' "Can't Help Lovin' Dat Man," and "After the Ball" were further popularized by soprano and Winston-Salem native Kathryn Grayson in the 1951 film adaptation.

Ferber's story about the interconnected lives surrounding a river showboat was based on the four days she spent on the James Adams Floating Theatre in Bath. Already a Pulitzer Prize-winning writer, Ferber visited Beaufort County to research river theater and while on her trip met performers Charles Hunter and Beulah Adams, who were fans of her work and had staged her stories.

Ferber took a second trip to North Carolina in April 1925 to meet a showboat in Bath. She lived, played, worked, rehearsed, and ate with the theater company on the huge boat, gathering inspiration and stories from Charles Hunter and her observations of the audiences. The novel and musical dramatize timeless themes of racial injustice, tragic romance, gambling, and small town values.

James Adams Floating Theatre in Edenton, 1925.

1700 John Lawson Began His Expedition

On December 28, 1700, explorer John Lawson set out from Charleston on a journey through the backcountry of Carolina. He was accompanied by a party of five Englishmen and various Indian guides.

In late January 1701 the Lawson expedition crossed into what is now North Carolina in the vicinity of present-day Charlotte. The party met a number of Indian tribes, including the "Esaws," Sugaree, and Catawba, and the explorers resumed their journey along the Trading Path, a route that stretched north and eastward through the interior of the province.

In February, while most of his party decided to travel straight to Virginia, Lawson and a companion continued their trek through Carolina. The route eastward led them to Occaneechi Town, near present-day Hillsborough. At Occaneechi Lawson met an Indian named Enoe Will, who agreed to guide the explorer to the English settlements along the coast, and on February 23, 1701, the explorers reached the English settlements near present-day Washington. The expedition lasted fifty-nine days and covered about 550 miles through the forbidding Carolina backcountry. Lawson, with a keen eye for detail, recorded his observations and in 1709 published *A New Voyage to Carolina*.

1878 Apples to Oregon: The Journey of Henderson Luelling

On December 28, 1878, "Father of the Pacific Fruit Industry" Henderson Luelling died in Oakland, California.

Born in Randolph County in 1809, Luelling was a Quaker active in the Underground Railroad before he risked his life to take fruit trees to the West Coast via the deep-rutted Oregon Trail.

Also known as the "Johnny Appleseed of the West," Luelling moved to Salem, Iowa in 1837, where he and others established the Abolition Friends Monthly Meeting and where a trapdoor in his house led to a haven for fugitive slaves.

In 1847 Luelling, traveling by ox-team, left Iowa in a seven-wagon caravan with his wife, eight children, and seven hundred grafted fruit trees, primarily apples, but also pears, cherries, and peaches. Half of the stock of trees, buried in a compost of soil and charcoal, died en route, as did two of his oxen.

With the assistance of Indian guides, Luelling arrived in the Willamette Valley, drawn there by the writings of John C. Fremont and the accounts of Lewis and Clark. He established a nursery, sold thousands of trees in Oregon and California, and brought several new varieties of fruits to the market.

His brother Seth, who accompanied him, introduced the Bing cherry.

1976 Lindsay Warren, Congressman and Government Watchdog

On December 28, 1976, legislator and U.S. comptroller general Lindsay Warren died.

A Washington, North Carolina native, Warren became involved in Democratic politics at a young age, serving as chair of the Beaufort County Democratic Party before being elected to the state Senate in 1917. In Raleigh Warren was closely associated with O. Max Gardner's political machine.

First elected to Congress in 1924, Warren served in that body until 1940. On Capitol Hill he was known for his work in agriculture, conservation, and government reform. Two of his signature accomplishments were securing legislative approval for the Cape Hatteras National Seashore and the Wright Brothers Memorial.

Warren left Congress after being appointed comptroller general of the United States, and head of the U.S. General Accountability Office (GAO). Before retiring to the Outer Banks in 1954, he transformed the GAO from an agency in crisis to the strong government watchdog it remains today.

Returning to North Carolina didn't mean the end of political involvement for Warren, though. Nearly fifty years after first serving in Raleigh, he was elected to a single term in the General Assembly in 1961. He died in 1976 and is buried in Beaufort County.

Lindsay Warren in his Washington office, April 1938.

1808 Andrew Johnson, Tailor's Apprentice Path to White House

On December 29, 1808, Andrew Johnson, the seventeenth president of the United States, was born in Raleigh.

The history of Johnson's early life is anecdotal at best, as the poverty his family endured inevitably meant that there are few written records of their lives. In early adolescence Johnson apprenticed under local tailor James J. Selby, where along with skills of the trade, he learned basic reading and writing competencies.

Johnson moved to Greeneville, Tennessee in 1826 and prospered as a tailor and later as a politician. Styling himself an advocate for the common man, Johnson was elected to the Tennessee legislature for several years. He represented the First District of Tennessee in Congress for five consecutive terms, then served two terms as governor of Tennessee. He went on to be elected a United States senator.

Abraham Lincoln appointed Johnson military governor of Tennessee in 1862. Johnson was named Lincoln's running mate for the successful 1864 re-election campaign, and Lincoln's assassination raised Johnson to the Presidency on April 15, 1865.

The small loft in which Johnson was supposedly born was situated near Casso's Inn, a half-block from the State Capitol in Raleigh. It since has been reconstructed and relocated to Mordecai Historic Park.

1835 Treaty of New Echota and the Trail of Tears

On December 29, 1835, U.S. government officials and about five hundred Cherokee Indians claiming to represent their sixteen-thousand-member tribe met at New Echota, Georgia, and signed a treaty that led to the forced removal of the Cherokee from their southeastern homelands to Indian Territory west of the Mississippi River.

The Treaty of New Echota gave the Cherokee five million dollars and land in present-day Oklahoma in exchange for their seven million acres of ancestral land. Though the majority of Cherokee opposed the treaty and Principal Chief John Ross wrote a letter to Congress protesting it, the U.S. Senate ratified the document in March 1836.

Aware of the lack of support for the treaty among the Cherokee, Pres. Martin Van Buren proposed a two-year extension to allow the Cherokee time to move. Still, by May 1838 only two thousand Cherokee had moved voluntarily.

That spring the federal government sent seven thousand soldiers under Gen. Winfield Scott to evict the remaining Cherokee. They built six forts in North Carolina to hold captured Indians until their forced westward journey could begin.

The twelve-hundred-mile trek, begun in October 1838, lasted six months. Along the way an estimated ten to twenty-five percent of the tribe died of disease, starvation, and exhaustion. Today their route is known as the Trail of Tears.

DEC 29

1833 Rail Line Linked Wilmington and Weldon

On December 30, 1833, the North Carolina General Assembly approved the charter for the Wilmington and Raleigh Railroad Company.

Though there was an initial lack of financial support for the project from Raleigh citizens, the founders of the Wilmington and Raleigh hoped to capitalize on the plentiful industry and agriculture of the Roanoke River Valley and points north. In 1836 the Wilmington and Raleigh incorporated the Halifax and Weldon Railroad into their company, making Weldon the new terminus of the line.

The Wilmington and Weldon Railroad opened in May 1840 as the longest railroad in the world at the time. It provided essential transportation and communication during the Civil War, becoming known as the "lifeline of the Confederacy." The line moved goods and supplies from the single open Confederate port of Wilmington to Robert E. Lee's army in Virginia. The fall of Wilmington and subsequent closing of the port to the Wilmington and Weldon Railroad were major factors leading to Lee's surrender at Appomattox.

Colorized print of an aerial photograph of the Vick Chemical Company tract and buildings, 1933.

1854 Lunsford Richardson, Inventor of VapoRub and Junk Mail

On December 30, 1854, Lunsford Richardson, inventor of Vicks VapoRub, was born in Johnston County.

After graduating from Davidson College with a degree in Latin in 1875, Richardson began to work with his brother-in-law, Dr. Joshua Vick, at Vick's drug-manufacturing company in Selma. There he used his Latin skills to learn the names of chemicals used as drugs and became a pharmacist.

In 1890 Richardson moved to his wife's hometown of Greensboro, where he bought W.C. Porter's drugstore with a partner. The drugstore was largely unremarkable, except for the fact that the famous writer O. Henry worked there as a teenager.

While running the pharmacy in Greensboro, Richardson continued to work on developing new remedies with Vick's company. He went on to patent twenty-one medicines, including Vick's Magic Croup Salve in 1894. Renamed Vicks VapoRub in 1911, that remedy is still sold today. The salve in the blue jar is made of menthol, camphor, oil of eucalyptus, and several other oils, blended in a base of petroleum jelly.

Richardson didn't limit his innovations to the medicine cabinet. Credited with being one of the first to market to post office box holders without personalizing the materials, he is widely to considered to have invented "junk mail."

A trustee of the Palmer Memorial Institute in Sedalia and a champion of race relations, Richardson died in 1919, the victim of the Spanish flu outbreak that widely increased the demand for his product.

Vicks advertising stand

1873 Judge John Kerr, Longtime Congressman

On December 30, 1873, John H. Kerr was born in Yanceyville.

Educated at what is now Wake Forest University, Kerr began practicing law in Warrenton in 1895. After serving as town attorney and as mayor, he was elected judge of the Superior Court in 1916. Judge Kerr, as he was known thereafter, served on the bench until 1923.

That year Kerr was elected to the U.S. House of Representatives, where he would go on to serve fifteen terms, until 1952. He was the third generation of his family to be named John Kerr and the third generation to be elected to Congress.

In the House Kerr was active on the agriculture, appropriation, and public building committees. The Kerr-Smith Tobacco Act of 1934, which he co-sponsored, evolved into a program of price supports and allotments for tobacco farmers that would have a lasting legacy.

Kerr is best remembered for seeking and receiving Congressional support in the 1940s for a flood control project on the Roanoke River. The lake created by the hundred-million-dollar dam at Buggs Island, Virginia was dedicated in October 1952 as the John H. Kerr Dam and Reservoir. Kerr had been defeated for re-nomination a few months earlier. He died in Warrenton in 1958 and was buried in the Fairview Cemetery.

DEC 31

1862 The USS *Monitor* Sank

On December 31, 1862, the ironclad USS *Monitor*, sank during a storm off the coast of Cape Hatteras. Four officers and twelve crewmen were lost.

A technological marvel in its day, the vessel was designed and built by John Ericsson, a Swedish inventor. In developing the ship, Ericsson obtained 240 patents for equipment, including forty-five related just to its turret. Rather than a standard-hulled ship, the Monitor was a large raft-like boat with a large revolving turret that supported two eleven-inch smoothbore guns. It weighed 987 tons.

The first engagement between ironclad ships occurred on March 9, 1862, when the *Monitor* and the CSS *Virginia* (formerly the *Merrimack*) met at Hampton Roads, Virginia. After a four-hour battle, the Virginia retreated, giving the *Monitor* the tactical victory.

The *Monitor* was found in 1973, bottom up and in about 240 feet of water. The North Carolina Office of State Archaeology participated in the identification of the wreck. The wreck site, sixteen miles off the coast of Cape Hatteras, became the first National Marine Sanctuary in 1975. In 2001, the *Monitor's* thirty-ton steam engine was recovered, and the turret was raised from the ocean floor the following year.

The USS *Monitor* in the James River, Virginia, July 9, 1862.

1900 Selma Burke, Renowned for FDR Portrait on the Dime

On December 31, 1900, sculptor Selma Burke was born in Mooresville.

Fascinated by African ritual objects and other sculptural pieces, Burke made sculpture by shaping white clay from her parents' farm as a child. After being educated at what is now Winston-Salem State University and trained as a nurse at St. Agnes Hospital Nursing School in Raleigh, Burke moved to New York City to work as a private nurse.

Inspired by the Harlem Renaissance movement emerging around her, Burke began to focus on art. In 1938 she studied with Aristide Maillol and Henri Matisse in Europe after earning both Rosenwald and Boehler Foundation Fellowships. After completing an M.F.A. at Columbia University in 1941, Burke began to teach art, first at the Harlem Community Art Center and later at schools she founded in New York and Pittsburgh.

Burke's most famous work, a portrait of Pres. Franklin D. Roosevelt that now graces the dime, came about from a competition to sculpt the president for the Recorder of Deeds Office in Washington, D.C. After feeling that she couldn't capture the likeness of Roosevelt from photographs, Burke wrote the White House and, to her surprise, was granted a sitting with the president.

Eleanor Roosevelt later visited Burke's studio to view the finished plaque. Though the likeness on the dime is officially credited to U.S. Mint Chief Engraver John Sinnock, scholars believe that Sinnock borrowed Burke's original design.

Burke's last monumental work, a statue of Martin Luther King Jr. that graces Marshall Park in Charlotte, was completed in 1980. She died in New Hope, Pennsylvania in 1995.

1906 "The Fire is Spreading": Landmark Revival in Dunn

On December 31, 1906, preacher Gaston Barnabas Cashwell, an adherent of the Holiness movement, opened a revival in a tobacco warehouse in the Harnett County town of Dunn.

He had just returned from the Azusa Street Mission in Los Angeles, where a similar revival he led had roused the faithful. There and again in Dunn people in search of salvation assembled. A church leader later wrote that charismatic churchgoers traveled to Dunn and "were soon happy in the experience, speaking in tongues, singing in tongues, writing in tongues, shouting, leaping, dancing, and praising God."

Cashwell wrote to the organizer of the California revival that people "from all over the country" attended the Dunn revival and that "many have come from South Carolina and Georgia and have received their Pentecost and gone back . . . the fire is spreading."

Cashwell became the informal leader of the Pentecostal movement in the Southeast, and the Dunn revival has been hailed for it place in Holiness history. Several movements adopted his Azusa Street message. His revival in Dunn challenged the region's Holiness churches to redefine their theological doctrines, uniting many of them in Pentecostalism.

Selma Burke with her bust of Booker T. Washington, 1935.

1990 New Year's and the Lowly Opossum

On December 31, 1990, Brasstown residents began their tradition of the "Possum Drop" when Clay Logan dropped a ceramic possum from the roof of his convenience store.

The tradition began because local inhabitants call the Clay County village the "Opossum Capital of the World." While this claim may be difficult to prove, the town has become known internationally from news coverage of its offbeat approach to ringing in the New Year.

The first event was small, but it quickly became a community affair with the use of live specimens of North Carolina's official State Marsupial. Today the bash is billed as a family event, with music and a Miss Possum drag queen contest.

In recent years use of living creatures has come under criticism from animal rights activists, resulting in the drop of a roadkill possum one year and of a box covered with possum pictures in 2013. Controversy surrounding the event has involved lawsuits by the activist group People for the Ethical Treatment of Animals and the passage of a 2013 state law allowing for lawful capture and release of the creature, presumably to support possum drop activities. After an additional legal challenge by PETA, the 2014 General Assembly passed H.B. 1131 allowing opossum trapping only in Clay County each year from December 26 to 31.

Use of a live possum for the annual event continues to be argued in North Carolina's courts.

IMAGE CREDITS

KEY

LOC	Library of Congress
NARA	National Archives and Records Administration
OSA	North Carolina Office of State Archaeology
NARA	National Archives and Records Administration
NCDCR	North Carolina Department of Natural and Cultural Resources
NCHPO	North Carolina Historic Preservation Office
NCMOH	North Carolina Museum of History
NCSHS	North Carolina State Historic Sites
RBNCOAH	Research Branch, North Carolina Office of Archives and History
SANC	Iconographic Collection, State Archives of North Carolina
SLNC	State Library of North Carolina

JANUARY

1 Reprinted with permission of the *News and Observer*, N&O Collection, SANC.
2 Mt. Olive Pickle Company.
3 (Marker) RBNCOAH; (Branch) SANC.
4 LOC.
5 (Pearson and Stafford) SANC.
6 SANC.
7 (Marker) RBNCOAH; (McKee) McKee family.
8 SANC.
9 NCMOH.
10 RBNCOAH.
11 LOC.
12 Davidson College Archives.
13 Prezell R. Robinson Library, St. Augustine's University Archives.
14 LOC.
15 LOC.
16 NCSHS.
17 LOC.
18 SANC.
19 North Carolina Postcards, North Carolina Photographic Archives, UNC-Chapel Hill.
20 (both images) LOC.
21 SANC.
22 SANC.
23 (Hanna leg) RBNCOAH; (patent) United States Patent and Trademark Office.
24 United States Air Force.
25 (Eller) ca. 1966. (©1966 Sports Films & Talents, Inc., Minneapolis, Minn., NCMOH); (Gardner) SANC.
26 Wilson County Public Library.
27 (Cheerwine building) NCHPO; (Andre the Giant) Rankin Museum of American Heritage.
28 NASA.
29 (White) SANC; (entrance to Nantahala National Forest) SANC.
30 (Holden) SANC; (Knapp) Ducks Unlimited.
31 (*Metropolis*) SANC; (American Tobacco Company) SANC.

FEBRUARY

1 Dell Upton.
2 *Frank Leslie's Illustrated Newspaper*, February 27, 1864, p. 356.
3 Reprinted with permission of the *News and Observer*, N&O Collection, SANC.
4 SANC.
5 (Thomas) SANC; (marker) RBNCOAH.
6 NCSHS.
7 LOC.
8 (both Boyce images) SANC.
9 Photograph by Hugh Morton, courtesy of the University of North Carolina at Chapel Hill.
10 (Price) "Sketch Book of Livingstone College and East Tennessee Industrial School" 1903; (Lumbee homecoming parade) Elmer W. Hunt Collection, Mary Livermore Library, Special Collections, UNC-Pembroke.
11 (Jacobs portrait and advertisement) SANC; (Oakley) LOC.
12 (James historical marker) RBNCOAH; (Ransom) SANC.
13 (both images) Marine Corps Archives and Special Collections.
14 Linda Fox, NCDNCR.
15 Fort Macon State Park.
16 *Harper's Weekly*, March 30, 1872; (Lincoln Memorial) LOC.
17 SANC.
18 Martha Blakeney Hodges Special Collections and University Archives, UNC-Greensboro.
19 NCSHS.
20 (Princeville historical marker) RBNCOAH; (airplane) RuthAS, Creative Commons.
21 Roland Godefroy, WikiMedia Commons.
22 SANC.
23 (Fuller) SANC; (patent) U.S. Patent Office.
24 Daily Reflector Image Collection, Joyner Library, East Carolina University.
25 (Revels) LOC; excerpt from F. P. Venable, "'Fall of Blood' in Chatham County," *Journal of the Elisha Mitchell Scientific Society* (1884).
26 (Kraft Paper marker) RBNCOAH.
27 (Moores Creek Bridge) Moore's Creek National Battlefield; (Cooper) LOC.
28 Mark Brown, North Carolina Transportation Museum, NCSHS.
29 Chick Jacobs, *Fayetteville Observer*.

MARCH

1 (furniture) NCMOH; (Day residence and workshop) Historic American Buildings Survey.
2 SANC.
3 (Mount Mitchell) Brian Stansberry, courtesy of Wikicommons; (P. W. Horne with students), Elizabeth City State University Archives, G. R. Little Library.
4 (Keckley) Moorland-Spingarn Research Center, Manuscript Division, Howard University; (Lincoln) Still Picture Records Section, Special Media Archives Services Division, National Archives and Records Administration.
5 North Carolina Collection Photographic Archives, Wilson Library, UNC-Chapel Hill.
6 *Frank Leslie's Illustrated Newspaper*, April 2, 1864.
7 SANC.
8 Jim Willard, NCSHS.
9 (North Carolina A.&T. College band) SANC; (Aptheker) Jock Lauterer Photographic Collection, North Carolina Collection Photographic Archives, Wilson Library, UNC-Chapel Hill.
10 SANC.
11 SANC.
12 SANC.
13 North Carolina Collection, University of North Carolina Library at Chapel Hill.
14 (Williamson) SANC; (nature photos) Alligator River National Wildlife Refuge.
15 (dogwood trees) SANC; (conservator and weapon) Underwater Archaeology Branch, Office of State Archaeology, North Carolina Office of Archives and History.
16 (background) H. H. Brimley, "Whale Fishing in North Carolina," *Bulletin of the North Carolina Department of Agriculture*, 14 (April 1894); (fishermen with shad boat) SANC.
17 Forsyth County Public Library Photograph Collection, Winston-Salem.
18 SANC.
19 *Frank Leslie's Illustrated Newspaper*, April 22, 1865.
20 (marker) RBNCOAH; (Blalocks) public domain.
21 H. H. Brimley Papers, SANC.
22 SANC.
23 (Fort Macon) *Frank Leslie's Illustrated Newspaper*, May 17, 1862; (Spencer Shops) NCSHS.
24 (Carolina Charter) SANC; (King) Miriam and Ira D. Wallach Division of Art, Print Collection, New York Public Library.
25 (Spaight) SANC; (Cosell) Publicity photo for *Monday Night Football*.
26 Forsyth County Public Library Photograph Collection, Winston-Salem.
27 SANC.
28 (Körner's Folly) LOC; (Erlanger Mills) SANC.
29 Hugh Morton Collection, North Carolina Collection Photographic Archives, Wilson Library, UNC- Chapel Hill.
30 SANC.
31 Rowell Bosse North Carolina Room, Transylvania County Library.

APRIL

1 (all images) SANC.
2 WikiMedia Commons.
3 Thomas Built Buses.
4 (Brimley and Valvano) SANC.
5 (Pope Field) Durwood Barbour Collection of North Carolina Postcards, North Carolina Collection Photographic Archives, Wilson Library, UNC-Chapel Hill; (Hunt) SANC.
6 (aerial view of Camp Greene) SANC; (Wootten photo by H. H. Brimley) SANC.
7 (Lumina) Durwood Barbour Collection of North Carolina Postcards, North Carolina Collection Photographic Archives, Wilson Library, UNC-Chapel Hill; (surfing at Wrightsville Beach) Cape Fear Surfing Archive, UNC-Wilmington.
8 NCSHS.
9 Reed Gold Mine, NCSHS.
10 North Carolina Collection Photographic Archives, Wilson Library, UNC-Chapel Hill.
11 (Holt) SANC; (Arts Council) N. C. Arts Council.
12 (Halifax Resolves plaque) NCSHS; (Salisbury prison lithograph) Durwood Barbour Collection of North Carolina Postcards, North Carolina Collection Photographic Archives, Wilson Library, UNC-Chapel Hill.
13 *World Telegram & Sun* photo by Ed Ford, LOC.
14 Graveyard of the Atlantic Museum.
15 North Carolina Collection, Wilson Special Collections Library, UNC-Chapel Hill.
16 U.S. Geological Survey Historical Library.
17 NARA.
18 (King) LOC; (Rodgers historical marker) RBNCOAH.
19 *Annual Report of the North Carolina Agricultural Experiment Station* (1896).
20 *U.S. News & World Report Magazine* Photograph Collection, LOC.
21 (both images) NASA.
22 SANC.
23 (Ervin) LOC; (Reynolds Building) Durwood Barbour Collection of North Carolina Postcards, North Carolina Collection Photographic Archives, Wilson Library, UNC-Chapel Hill.
24 (marker) RBNCOAH; (Polk) NCMOH.
25 (Endor Iron Furnace) Photograph by Anthony O. James, SANC; (Lemon) NARA.
26 Montford Point marines using field telephone and two-way field radio, 1943, LOC; (The Unity Monument at Bennett Place) NCSHS.
27 (background) John Carter Brown Library, Brown University; (Slaughter) SANC.
28 (Grave of Cancetto Farmica and receipt for payment of funeral expenses) Beacham McDougald; (Valvano) reprinted with permission of the *News and Observer*, N&O Collection, SANC.
29 (Chimney Rock Hill Climb) Russ Roland Collection; (White House meeting) Gerald R. Ford Presidential Library and Museum.
30 *Frank Leslie's Illustrated Newspaper*, May 16, 1863.

MAY

1 SANC.
2 (marker) RBNCOAH; (Wray) Photograph by Eric Frommer.
3 (marker) RBNCOAH; (duel lithograph) LOC.
4 (Travis) EMR, Wiki Commons; (Green) SANC.
5 *The Photographic History of the Civil War: The Navies*, VI (1911).

6 SANC.
7 (background) Liberty Hall Restoration, Kenansville; (Johnson) reprinted with permission of the *News and Observer*, News and Observer Collection, SANC.
8 Reprinted with permission of the *News and Observer*, News and Observer Collection, SANC.
9 (USCGC *Icarus*) U.S. Navy; (Italian POWs) U. S. Army Signal Corps.
10 (Busbee) Jugtown Pottery; (planetarium interior) reprinted with permission of the *News and Observer*, News and Observer Collection, SANC.
11 (Bagley statue) SANC; (deputized white citizens) reprinted with permission of the *News and Observer*, News and Observer Collection, SANC.
12 (both images) SANC.
13 (Vance) SANC; (Shell station) photograph by David Bjorgen, courtesy of Creative Commons.
14 North Carolina Symphony.
15 Photo by Albert Barden, SANC.
16 SANC.
17 (Leonard) photograph by Mark Mathosian, Flickr; (Cramer engraving) Mint Museum Archives.
18 (both images) courtesy of Steven Wilson, Save the Speedway.
19 (Fort Hamby marker) RBNCOAH; (Presley) LOC.
20 (both images) NCMOH.
21 Conservation and Development Department, Travel and Tourism, SANC.
22 (camp scene) SANC; (pier) North Carolina Postcard Collection, North Carolina Collection Photographic Archives, Wilson Library, UNC-Chapel Hill.
23 (Mabley) James Kriegsmann, WikiMedia Commons; (Vietnam Veterans Memorial) Donald Lee Pardue, Creative Commons.
24 (ruins St. Philips Church) Albert Barden, SANC; (St. Philips Church, NCHPO; (Vollmer) SLNC.
25 (marker) RBNCOAH; (rustic cross grave marker) Louis T. Moore Collection, courtesy of Susan Taylor Block and the New Hanover County Public Library.
26 SANC.
27 (U.S. Navy B-1 Band) courtesy of Alex Albright; (Coal Glen mine) H. H. Brimley Collection, SANC.
28 (background) *Popular Science Monthly*, volume 57; (solar eclipse) County Photograph Collection, North Carolina Collection Photographic Archives, Wilson Library, UNC-Chapel Hill.
29 SANC.
30 (both images) SANC.
31 (marker) RBNCOAH; (Lytch) SANC; (Rudolph mugshot) Cherokee County Sheriff's Office.

JUNE

1 Photo provided by Dan Moury, NCMOH.
2 Duke University Archives.
3 (Lumina) Durwood Barbour Collection of North Carolina Postcards, North Carolina Collection Photographic Archives, Wilson Library, UNC-Chapel Hill; (newspaper) *Greensboro News & Record*.
4 Bayard Morgan Wootten Photographic Collection #P0011, North Carolina Collection, Wilson Library, UNC-Chapel Hill.
5 (marker) RBNCOAH; (Porter) Miriam and Ira D. Wallach Division of Art, Prints and Photographs, Photography Collection, New York Public Library.
6 (marker) RBNCOAH; (Lunsford) Lomax Collection, LOC.
7 (both images) Moravian Archives.
8 (Taylor) MIT Museum; (Taylor marker) RBNCOAH; (Dodd) International News photo, Creative Commons.
9 TW Garner Food Company.
10 (Johnson driving) photo by Louis Van Oeyen, Prints and Photographs Division, LOC; (portrait) Richard Kyle Fox, *The Life and Battles of Jack Johnson* (1909).
11 SANC.
12 SANC.
13 Traditional Voices, Burnsville.
14 Charles Ellms, *The Tragedy of the Seas* (1848).
15 (background) SANC; (costumed characters) Land of Oz.
16 Tryon Palace Historic Sites and Gardens.
17 (Rains) LOC; (actors and background) Flat Rock Playhouse.
18 SANC.
19 Photo by Charles Clark, SANC.
20 SANC.
21 (both images) SANC.
22 Photo by H. Reid, Norfolk, Va., SANC.
23 Virginia Williams and the Civil Rights Heritage Project, Durham County Public Library.
24 Photograph by Eddie Belk, NCHPO.
25 Courtesy of Joe Elliot.
26 (Helper) SANC; (bar code) RBNCOAH.
27 NCMOH.
28 North Carolina Postcard Collection, North Carolina Collection Photographic Archives, Wilson Library, UNC-Chapel Hill.
29 (Macon) drawing by Katie Price; (Moonlight Graham) North Carolina Collection, Wilson Library, UNC-Chapel Hill.
30 (Burns) SANC; (broadside) Capus Waynick Papers, J. Y. Joyner Library, East Carolina University.

JULY

1 (Bushyhead), Institute of Outdoor Theatre Collection, J. Y. Joyner Library, East Carolina University; (Murray) North Carolina Collection, University of North Carolina at Chapel Hill.
2 (*Hope of Liberty* title page and Prohibition poster) LOC; (marker) RBNCOAH.
3 SANC.
4 Institute of Outdoor Theatre Collection, J. Y. Joyner Library, East Carolina University.
5 (Vance) SANC; (Coe) North Carolina Collection Photographic Archives, Wilson Library, UNC-Chapel Hill.
6 (background) LOC; (advertisement) Rowell Bosse North Carolina Room, Transylvania County Library; (Love) North Carolina Collection Photographic Archives, Wilson Library, UNC-Chapel Hill.
7 *Frank Forester's Horse and Horsemanship of the United States* (1857).
8 Sydney B. Flower, *The Goat-Gland Transplantation* (1921).
9 Conservation and Development Travel and Tourism photo files, SANC.
10 Hugh Morton Collection at the North Carolina Collection, Wilson Library, UNC-Chapel Hill.
11 LOC.
12 Bill Garrett, NCHPO.
13 (early power trucks) Duke Energy Archives; (Krispy Kreme) LOC.
14 Southern Railway Company, *The Floods of July*, 1916, (1917).
15 (both images) photos by Steven M. Falk, courtesy of the Ernie Barnes Family Trust.
16 (marker) RMNCOAH; (Gill) SANC.
17 (Love Valley concert attendees) Ed Buzzell; (Coltrane) John Brinkman, National Archives of the Netherlands, Fotocollectie Anefo, public domain.
18 (marker) RBNCOAH; (Parker) public domain.
19 (Saunooke) Hugh Morton Collection of Photographs and Films, North Carolina Collection Photographic Archives, Wilson Library, UNC-Chapel Hill; (Hamilton) photograph by Cliff1066, Flickr.
20 Tabitha Marie DeVisconti Papers, J. Y. Joyner Library, East Carolina University.
21 Duke University Archives.
22 (background and portrait) National Park Service.
23 (Hyman) NARA; (Kyser) reprinted with permission of the *News and Observer*, N&O Collection, SANC.
24 (Royall) Edwin W. Pauley Papers, Harry S. Truman Library and Museum; (background) LOC; (Haid) Samuel A. Ashe, *Biographical History of North Carolina from Colonial Times to the Present* (1905).
25 *An Impartial History of the war in America* (1780), LOC.
26 Duke University Archives.
27 NARA.
28 Capus Waynick Papers, J. Y. Joyner Library, East Carolina University.
29 (both images) NCSHS.
30 SANC.
31 SANC.

AUGUST

1 Family of Leonard Herring.
2 Group poses with confiscated illegal liquor outside Johnson County Courthouse, 1951: (*left to right*), Roy D. Hinton, jailor; J. T. Smith; Hugh Lamb; unidentified; Barney Henry, sheriff; Alvin Narron; _____ Massengill; Ernie Beasley; and unidentified. Flowers is not in this photograph. SANC.
3 (marker) RBNCOAH; (Lady Olga) public domain.
4 Reprinted with permission of the *News and Observer*, N&O Collection, SANC.
5 Hunter Library, Western Carolina University.
6 Photo courtesy 352nd Fighter Group Association Archive.
7 Baseball Hall of Fame.
8 Reynolda House Museum of American Art Archives.
9 SANC.
10 Dare County Regional Airport, Manteo.
11 LOC.
12 Courtesy of Bob Plott.
13 (Hancock) North Carolina Collection, Pack Memorial Public Library, Asheville; (horses) Cape Lookout National Seashore, National Park Service.
14 (Grimes) Portrait Collection, North Carolina Collection Photographic Archives, Wilson Library, UNC-Chapel Hill; (kiss photo) Department of Defense, Department of the Navy, Naval Photographic Center, NARA.
15 (Frinks) reprinted with permission of the *News and Observer*, N&O Collection, SANC; (Baum) Outer Banks History Center.
16 (Mertzes) Davie County Public Library; (marker) RBNCOAH.
17 Frank Armstrong Collection, J. Y. Joyner Library, East Carolina University.
18 (promotional birth certificate) SANC; (medal) NCMOH.
19 Black Mountain College Papers, Western Regional Archives, SANC.
20 (Sanford) reprinted with permission of the *News and Observer*, N&O Collection, SANC; (Morrisons) NCMOH.
21 J. S. Cates, *The Mangum Terrace in Its Relation to Efficient Farm Management* (1912).
22 RBNCOAH.
23 (both images) SANC.
24 U.S. Patent Office.
25 *Biennial Report of the Superintendent of Public Instruction of North Carolina*, 1896–1898.
26 SANC.
27 SANC.
28 (Pepsi images) LOC; Laurinburg-Maxton Army Air Base postcard, United States Army Air Force.
29 Photo courtesy of Michael Hobbs, UNC-Chapel Hill School of Education.
30 NCSHS.
31 William Henry Deitrick Papers, SANC.

SEPTEMBER

1 (Galloway) William Still, *Underground Railroad* (1872); (marker) RBNCOAH.
2 (Elon) Elon University Archives; (Bearden) photograph by Carl Van Vechten, LOC; (bridge) courtesy of the Grandfather Mountain Stewardship Foundation.
3 SANC.
4 Reprinted with permission from the *Charlotte Observer*.
5 Reprinted with permission of the *News and Observer*, N&O Collection, SANC.
6 (tobacco) Durwood Rogers and Duke Homestead State Historic Site; (Valentiner) reprinted with permission of the *News and Observer*, N&O Collection, SANC.
7 (Merrick) photograph originally published in a biographical sketch, 1920, by Robert McAnts Andrews; (McIver) Martha Blakeney Hodges Special Collections and University Archives, UNC-Greensboro.
8 (Hyde) NCMOH; (Jordan) SANC.
9 SANC.
10 SANC.
11 Photo by David Haas for the Historic American Buildings Survey/Historic American Engineering Record/Historic American Landscapes Survey, LOC.
12 Photo courtesy of Donn Pearlman.
13 Photo courtesy of Mary M. Dalton.
14 North Carolina Collection, Wilson Library, UNC-Chapel Hill.
15 (soldiers) Greensboro Historical Museum; (Perry and others) University Archives, East Carolina University.
16 SANC.
17 SANC.
18 SANC.
19 Bill Garrett, NCHPO.
20 SANC.
21 (Brinkley) SANC; (Gould) William B. Gould IV.
22 (background) Joe A. Mobley, *The Way We Lived in North Carolina*; (proclamation) NARA.
23 LOC.
24 Painting reproduced courtesy of James R. Mann.
25 (Jobe and John) Baseball Hall of Fame; (Ham) NASA.
26 (diary entry and Fries) Moravian Archives.
27 (Bonnet) *A General History of the Pyrates* (1724); (Wreck of the Old 97) public domain.
28 Duke Energy Archives.
29 (marker) RBNCOAH; (Franklin) North Carolina Collection Photographic Archives, Wilson Library, UNC-Chapel Hill.
30 Fort Bragg Cultural Resource Management Program.

OCTOBER

1 (Greenhow) LOC.
2 Naval History and Heritage Command.
3 (Wolfe) SANC; (Griffith), Bill Garrett, NCHPO.
4 David Haring, Duke Lemur Center.
5 Neal Hutcheson.
6 (Shepard) James E. Shepard Memorial Library Archives, Records and History Center, North Carolina Central University; (Hodges) SANC.
7 Anne S.K. Brown Military Collection, Brown University Library.
8 (McKoy) LOC; (Warren Grove School) NCHPO.

9 SANC.
10 SANC.
11 Durwood Barbour Collection of North Carolina Postcards, North Carolina Collection Photographic Archives, Wilson Library, UNC-Chapel Hill.
12 SANC.
13 Public domain.
14 Greensboro Historical Museum.
15 (both images) SANC.
16 SANC.
17 NCSHS.
18 Reprinted with permission of the *News and Observer*, N&O Collection, SANC.
19 (President's statue) photo by Carol M. Highsmith, LOC; (Reynolds) *A Biographical History of North Carolina: From Colonial Times to the Present* (1905).
20 (North Carolina Mutual office) SANC; (Lee monument) North Carolina Postcards, North Carolina Collection Photographic Archives, Wilson Library, UNC-Chapel Hill.
21 SANC.
22 National Portrait Gallery, Smithsonian Institution.
23 SANC.
24 (Horton Grove) Bill Garrett, NCHPO; (Wrights) LOC.
25 Photograph by Bill Boyarsky courtesy of the North Carolina Collection, Durham County Public Library.
26 (Young) "The Military and Historical Portrait Group of the Officers of the Third North Carolina U.S.V. Infantry in the War with Spain" (1899); (Durham) Harris & Ewing, photographer, LOC.
27 U.S. Naval History and Heritage Command.
28 Photograph Collection, Forsyth County Public Library, Winston-Salem.
29 LOC.
30 (King Charles I) Anthony van Dyck, Royal Collection, Windsor Castle; (Hood) C.M. Bell Studio Collection, LOC.
31 (Dobbs) Miriam and Ira D. Wallach Division of Art, Prints and Photographs, Print Collection, New York Public Library; (Five Points Drug Company), Durham Historic Photographic Archives, North Carolina Collection, Durham County Public Library.

NOVEMBER

1 Reprinted with permission of the *News and Observer*, N&O Collection, SANC.
2 LOC.
3 (background) SANC; (flyer) Greensboro Historical Museum.
4 (background) U. S. Patent Office; (Gatling) Brady-Handy Photograph Collection, LOC.
5 Durwood Barbour Collection of North Carolina Postcards, North Carolina Collection Photographic Archives, Wilson Library, UNC-Chapel Hill.
6 U.S. Naval History and Heritage Command Photograph.
7 (Fontana Dam) Carol M. Highsmith Archive, LOC; (Graham) LOC.
8 Forsyth County Public Library Photograph Collection, Winston-Salem.
9 Photograph from the Program Records Relating to Soul City, 1974–1979 in Department of Housing and Urban Development Record Group, National Archives.
10 (marker) RBNCOAH; (Fargo) Gene Pugh.
11 SANC.
12 Charles D. Fredricks & Co., "Specialité," 587 Broadway, New York, LOC.
13 SANC.
14 Brenau University, Gainesville, Georgia.
15 Courtesy of Gill Clopton and Henderson Police Department.
16 North Carolina Postcard Collection, North Carolina Collection Photographic Archives, Wilson Library, UNC-Chapel Hill.
17 James Wells Champney Sketchbook, Outer Banks History Center, Manteo.
18 SANC.
19 (Oakley) Luke Bukoski for UNC-Asheville; (Gettysburg photos) Alexander Gardner, LOC.
20 (Junaluska) SANC; (marker) RBNCOAH.
21 Warren Wilson College.
22 Engraving published in Charles Johnson in *A General History of the Lives and Adventures of the Most Famous Highwaymen, Murderers, Street-Robbers, &c*, (1736).
23 (Reed) Wellcome Collection; (woodcarvers) SANC.
24 U.S. Naval History and Heritage Command.
25 NCSHS.
26 (marker) RBNCOAH; (Scales) Brady-Handy Photograph Collection, LOC.
27 SANC.
28 Portrait Collection, North Carolina Collection Photographic Archives, Wilson Library, UNC-Chapel Hill.
29 Bill Garrett, NCHPO.
30 (statue) courtesy of Armenthis Lester, Charles George VA Medical Center; (Patterson) Franklin D. Roosevelt Library Public Domain Photographs, NARA.

DECEMBER

1 Copyright *Atlanta Journal-Constitution*, courtesy of Georgia State University.
2 Mark Brown, North Carolina Transportation Museum.
3 Randolph Linsly Simpson African-American Collection, James Weldon Johnson Memorial Collection, Yale Collection of American Literature, Beinecke Rare Book and Manuscript Library, Yale University.
4 (street scene) Mint Museum Archives; (Smith) NCMOH.
5 SANC.
6 Durwood Barbour Collection of North Carolina Postcards, North Carolina Collection Photographic Archives, Wilson Library, UNC-Chapel Hill.
7 OSA.
8 (Iredell Jr.) SANC; (Cone) Greensboro Historical Museum.
9 (Salisbury Prison) Durwood Barbour Collection of North Carolina Postcards, North Carolina Collection Photographic Archives, Wilson Library, UNC-Chapel Hill; (Smith) Henry B. Carrington, *Eastern Band of Cherokees of North Carolina* (1892).
10 LOC.
11 (church) photograph by Gerry Dincher; (Dukes) David M. Rubenstein Rare Book and Manuscript Library, Duke University.
12 Jim Willard, NCSHS.
13 (marker) RBNCOAH; (booklet) Shaw University.
14 (Howe) Benson J. Lossing, *The Pictorial Field-Book of the Revolution* (1852); (Foster) Brady-Handy Photograph Collection, LOC.
15 SANC.
16 LOC.
17 (both images) LOC.
18 Executive Mansion Collection, NCMOH; photo by Matt Waehner, SANC.
19 Farm Security Administration, Office of War Information Photograph Collection, LOC.
20 (Marines jumping) Still Pictures Branch, NARA; (dogs) Marine Corps University Research Archives, Quantico, Virginia.
21 Fort Dobbs State Historic Site; Bill Garrett, NCHPO.
22 Photo by Captain Tucker, WikiCommons.
23 (Dix Hospital staff) SANC; (Bald Head Island lighthouse) SANC.
24 (Fessenden images) SANC; (Bumgarner) Ben Shahn, photographer, LOC.
25 (Stewart plane crash) SANC; (Preddy and plane) 352nd Fighter Group Association Archive.
26 NCMOH.
27 SANC.
28 Harris & Ewing, photographer, LOC.
29 (Johnson) Alexander Gardner, photographer, LOC; (Ross) LOC.
30 (both images) Greensboro Historical Museum.
31 (*Monitor*) U.S. Naval History and Heritage Command Photograph; (Burke) Pinchos Horn, photographer, Archives of American Art, Smithsonian Institution.

INDEX

C

D

E

F

G

H

I

J

N

O

P

Q

R

S

T

U

V

W

X

Y

Z